THE BEST PLAYS OF 1995–1996

THE OTIS GUERNSEY
BURNS MANTLE
THEATER YEARBOOK

THE BEST PLAYS OF
1995–1996

EDITED BY OTIS L. GUERNSEY JR.
AND JEFFREY SWEET

Illustrated with photographs and
with drawings by HIRSCHFELD

LIMELIGHT EDITIONS

EDITOR'S NOTE

FOR THE 77th time, a *Best Plays* team has worked its unique magic (requiring a bit more application than the mere waving of a wand) and produced this most comprehensive, accurate and in places sparkling account of one year in the living New York and cross-country theater. From Melvyn B. Zerman, whose Limelight Editions logo proclaims our publishing identity, to the apprentice press agent who phoned in that last-minute factual detail, we're proud of our team and its coordinated 1995–96 result in this volume. It would be impossible to compile a complete list of *Best Plays* contributors, but if we were to try we'd have to start with at least 60 journalists, publicists and theater people in the New York area and another 50 in the theater-loving towns and cities from coast to coast. Many of their names appear in the program listings; many do not. *Best Plays* readers enjoy the fruits of their efforts, as do those of us who have bylines in this yearbook, and we're most grateful to all of them for making it possible for us to collect and use the wealth of information contained herein.

Much of the credit for *Best Plays* accuracy belongs to Jonathan Dodd, who has overseen the 31 volumes edited by the undersigned, from the Dodd, Mead years onward; and the editor's meticulous wife, who also labors mightily in the oversight process. The sparkle is provided by Associate Editor Jeffrey Sweet in his incomparably informed account of the season on and off Broadway; by Mel Gussow in his review of the off-off-Broadway season's highlights; by the regional theater critics (Christopher Rawson, Michael Grossberg, Marianne Evett) who reviewed the American Theater Critics Association's selections of this year's outstanding plays in cross-country production; graphically by Al Hirschfeld in his drawings of the season's most striking theater personalities; and, of course, in the excerpts from the Best Plays themselves, which illustrate in literary form the peaks of that great mountain range of dramatic achievement by our playwrights which has distinguished every one of the 77 seasons this yearbook series has documented.

The comprehensive abundance and detail of our factual content stands greatly to the credit of Assistant Editor Camille Dee who compiles the off-off-Broadway section and edits the regional theater coverage. We have Rue E. Canvin to thank for the necrology, the publications listing and other details; Jeffrey A. Finn for our section on major New York cast replacements; and Sally Dixon Wiener and David Lefkowitz (a new member of our team, editor and publisher of *This Month on Stage*) for a Best Play synopsis apiece. And among the many others to whom this book is particularly indebted are Michael Kuchwara (New York Drama Critics Circle voting), William Schelble (Tony Awards), Thomas T. Foose (historical advisories), Henry Hewes (former *Best Plays* editor, supervising the Hall of Fame listing), Ralph Newman of the Drama Book Shop, David A. Rosenberg (Connecticut Critics Circle Awards), Paul Faberson (Joseph Jefferson Awards), Don Shirley (Los Angeles Critics Awards), Caldwell Titcomb (Boston Theater Awards), as well as the more than 100 previously mentioned theater people who respond untiringly to our inquiries.

Our coverage of the outstanding scenery and costume designs of 1995–96 includes examples of their original drawings graciously contributed by Marina Draghici (*The Shriker*), Roger Kirk (*The King and I*) and Paul Tazewell (*Bring in 'da Noise Bring in 'da Funk*) at our request. We appreciate the assistance of David Leopold of the Margo Feiden Galleries in setting up the section of Hirschfeld drawings, and we are grateful for the photographs generously provided by the production offices and illustrating the "look" of the theater year onstage in New York and across the country, the work of Chris Bennion, Michael Brosilow, Barry Burns, Co-Motion/Irish Rep, Susan Cook, David Cooper, Michal Daniel, Robert DiScalfani, T. Charles Erickson, Ric Evans, Matthew Gilson, Leo Haug, Martha Holmes, Ken Howard, Sherman M. Howe Jr., Susan Johann, Suzanne Karp Krebs, Liz Lauren, Joan Marcus, Dan Rest, Carol Rosegg, Jon Simon, Diane Sobolewski, Richard Termine, Jay Thompson, Martine Voyeux and Jessica White.

Much has been made of the importance of musical and straight-play revivals and screen-to-stage retreads in making the New York theater season of 1995–96 a resounding success with the theatergoing public. Well, it was our gifted, dedicated dramatists who created those good old scripts and scores in the first place, just as it was our dramatists who created the shining new works in the Best Plays section of our 77th consecutive theater yearbook. And it will be our dramatists whose new and revived creations will enhance the next 77 seasons. We have our dramatists to thank most of all for the power to light up every theater year, be it with the incandescent inventions of this very minute, or the glowing achievements of the past.

OTIS L. GUERNSEY Jr.
Editor

September 1, 1996

CONTENTS

Drawings by HIRSCHFELD

THE SEASON
ON AND OFF
BROADWAY

Bring in 'da Noise Bring in 'da Funk

Above, Savion Glover, Vincent Bingham, Jimmy Tate and Baakari Wilder and *below right*, Ann Duquesnay in the Glover-George C. Wolfe-Reg E. Gaines-Duquesnay-Zane Mark-Daryl Waters show subtitled A Rap/Tap Discourse on the Staying Power of the Beat and described by Jeffrey Sweet as "the season's peak accomplishment on the musical stage"; *below*, a quote from the Gaines verses which accompany some of the action

Rhythmic Time Traveler

Do ya know da reason why
Bangin beats on big pots while burnin up greens
Foolin massa inta thinkin he barn be clean. . . . .
Bent back snappin tabacka on crusty grey knees
Or sneaks in missey redroom wit a bunch a maddog fleas
Beat be a big fat grin front a tight lipped cuss
Makin ends meet when dare ain't never enough
Zig zaggin pigtails upside sessey's nappy head
Hearin ancestors spirits laffin do dey bones
Be stone cold dead
Beat be da beats all bent down and torn
Cries delilah makes when her baby bein born
Beats be da beats singin rhythm to our feet
Makes a dad soul right happy
Be da way dat we speak

BROADWAY AND OFF BROADWAY
By Jeffrey Sweet

AS THE voters and panelists for the various awards surveyed the 1995–96 season, they had the unusual sensation that, in contrast to too many seasons in the recent past, there was actually serious competition in most categories, and plenty of it.

There were several significant new plays. There were a few new musicals of consequence (which is to say more than usual). There was a string of stirring revivals. And stage after stage was lit with extraordinary performances.

The gods of the season smiled particularly brightly on mature women. Leading ladies above the age of 40 commonly complain of the paucity of work. Not this year. Several actresses reaffirmed the staying power of their celebrity in starring performances: Carol Burnett in *Moon Over Buffalo,* Julie Andrews in *Victor/Victoria* and Zoe Caldwell in *Master Class* were three of Broadway's hottest draws. (Indeed, in the cases of Burnett and Andrews, they proved their power by drawing in spite of indifferent material.) Other notable and established women who brightened New York stages included Uta Hagen in *Mrs. Klein,* Ellen Burstyn in *Sacrilege,* Mary Louise Wilson in *Full Gallop,* Rosemary Harris, Elaine Stritch and Mary Beth Hurt in *A Delicate Balance,* Phyllis Newman in *The Food Chain,* Blythe Danner in *Moonlight,* Judith Ivey in *A Fair Country,* Eileen Heckart in *Northeast Local,* Rita Moreno in *The Size of the World,* Olympia Dukakis in *The Hope Zone,* Penny Fuller and Mia Dillon in *New England,* Laura Esterman in *Curtains,* Jayne Atkinson in *The Skriker,* Donna McKechnie in *State Fair,* and, of course, Carol Channing, who returned in *Hello, Dolly!,* playing the role she originated before many in the audience were old enough to vote (or, for that matter, fingerpaint). In addition, Betty Buckley made a considerable splash when she recreated her acclaimed London performance as Norma Desmond, replacing Glenn Close in *Sunset Boulevard.*

A number of veteran playwrights brought new works to New York as well. Such established figures as Brian Friel, Athol Fugard, Arthur Laurents, August Wilson, A.R. Gurney, Terrence McNally, Caryl Churchill, Lanford Wilson, Donald Margulies and Harold Pinter were represented by local premieres (Friel, Fugard and Laurents serving as their own directors). Stephen Sondheim, in collaboration with George Furth, also offered a new work, though not in his accustomed role as composer-lyricist. A thriller called *Getting Away With Murder,* it foundered, but he was

3

The 1995–96 Season on Broadway

PLAYS (6)

Moon Over Buffalo
Sacrilege
MASTER CLASS
Getting Away With
  Murder
SEVEN GUITARS
The Apple Doesn't Fall

FOREIGN PLAY
IN ENGLISH (1)

Racing Demon

MUSICALS (5)

Chronicle of a Death
  Foretold
Victor/Victoria
State Fair
Big
RENT
  (transfer)

REVUES (3)

Swinging on a Star
Riverdance
Bring in 'da Noise, etc.
  (transfer)

SOLO SHOWS (5)

Buttons on Broadway
Patti LuPone on Broadway
Danny Gans on Broadway
Love Thy Neighbor
Jack

SPECIALTIES (2)

Radio City Music Hall:
  Christmas Spectacular
  Spring Spectacular

REVIVALS (22)

Roundabout:
  The Play's the Thing
  Company
  The Father
  The Night of the Iguana
Circle in the Square:
  Garden District
  Holiday
  Bus Stop
  Tartuffe: Born Again
Hello, Dolly!
The Tempest
  (transfer)
Cinderella
National Actors Theater:
  The School for Scandal
  Inherit the Wind
  A Christmas Carol
  (return engagement)

Fool Moon
Paul Robeson
A Midsummer Night's
  Dream
The King and I
A Funny Thing Happened,
  etc.
A Delicate Balance
Buried Child
An Ideal Husband

Categorized above are all the new productions listed in the Plays Produced on Broadway section of this volume.
Plays listed in CAPITAL LETTERS have been designated Best Plays of 1995–96.
Plays listed in *italics* were still running on June 1, 1996.

(or should have been) consoled by sparkling revivals of *Company* and *A Funny Thing Happened on the Way to the Forum.*

The trend of solo performance pieces continued. Many of these performers either recounted comeback-and-coping stories from personal experience (a crippling accident, overweight, showbiz humiliation) or offered insight into a cultural perspective (Jewish, Cuban, gay).

As usual, much of what appeared on the various New York stages originated elsewhere. Among the regional companies represented by productions in New York, either on or off Broadway, were the Philadelphia Theater Company and the Mark Taper Forum (*Master Class*), Steppenwolf (*Picasso at the Lapin Agile* and *Buried Child*), the Old Globe (*Overtime* and *Getting Away With Murder* under the title *The Doctor Is Out*), Trinity Rep (*The Hope Zone* and *Northeast Local*), Actors Theater of Louisville (*Below the Belt*), the Woolly Mammoth Theater Company (*The Food Chain*), Great Lakes Theater Festival (original producer of *The School for Scandal* revival), Yale Rep (*The Size of the World*), the Goodman (original producer of *The Night of the Iguana* revival), Bay Street Theater (*By the Sea by the Sea by the Beautiful Sea*) and Seattle Rep (*A Fair Country*). Foreign managements originating work that arrived on these shores included the Gate Theater of Dublin (*Molly Sweeney* and *Moonlight*), the Market Theater of Johannesburg (*Valley Song,* which arrived via Princeton's McCarter Theater); and Britain's Royal National Theater (*Mrs. Klein*), Royal Shakespeare Company (*A Midsummer Night's Dream* and *New England*), Traverse Theater (*Moscow Stations*), Hempstead Theater Club (*Curtains*) and Royal Court (*The Skriker*).

Though Broadway is commonly thought of as a commercial entity, quite a few of the offerings under its umbrella this season were produced by non-profit organizations. Five companies—the Roundabout, Lincoln Center, the National Actors Theater, Circle in the Square and the New York Shakespeare Festival—offered two or more shows that appeared in the Broadway listings. Both of the Festival's Broadway offerings, *The Tempest* and the tap spectacular *Bring in 'da Noise Bring in 'da Funk,* were staged by the company's artistic director, George C. Wolfe.

A number of other directors had multiple credits this year: Scott Elliott (*Curtains* and *The Monogamist*), Gloria Muzio (*Below the Belt* and *The Play's The Thing*), Robert Falls (*The Night of the Iguana* and *The Food Chain*), Mark Wing-Davey (*The Skriker* and *Troilus and Cressida*), David Warren (*The Amazing Metrano* and *Holiday*), Nicholas Martin (*Overtime* and *Full Gallop*), Graciela Daniele (*Dancing on Her Knees* and *Chronicle of a Death Foretold*), Gerald Gutierrez (*Northeast Local* and *A Delicate Balance*) and Leonard Foglia (*Master Class, Lonely Planet* and *By the Sea by the Sea by the Beautiful Sea*).

Among design teams, some dazzled and some quietly and understatedly offered support that was just right. The musicals tended toward dazzlement (*The King and I, Bring in 'da Noise Bring in 'da Funk, Chronicle of a Death Foretold*), although one would be hard put to find more startling images than the sets and costumes Marina Draghici supplied for Caryl Churchill's epic of malevolent spirits, *The Skriker.* Less overwhelming, but wonderfully judged, were the disquieting homes that

THE KING AND I—This production of the Richard Rodgers-Oscar Hammerstein II musical is a show of many bests in the *Best Plays* 1995–96 citations: best revival, best costumes (*above*, samples of Roger Kirk's designs), best leading performances by Donna Murphy as Anna and Lou Diamond Phillips as the King (*pictured below*), as well as best direction (by Christopher Renshaw), scenery (by Brian Thomson) and lighting (by Nigel Levings)

hosted the unhappy families of *A Delicate Balance* (set by John Lee Beatty, lighting by Pat Collins) and *Buried Child* (set by Robert Brill, lighting by Kevin Rigdon).

As pleased as the editors of this volume are to compliment the talented artists and craftspeople who help realize the authors' intentions, our primary charge is to congratulate the authors with Best Play citations. To quote Otis L. Guernsey Jr. in past volumes, "The choice is made without any regard whatever to the play's type— musical, comedy or drama—or origin on or off Broadway, or popularity at the box office or lack of same. We don't take the scripts of bygone eras into consideration for Best Play citation in this one, whatever their technical status as American or New York 'premieres' which didn't have a previous production of record. We draw the line between adaptations and revivals, the former eligible for Best Play selection but the latter not, on a case-by-case basis." The choices of Best Plays primarily reflect the editors' taste, though prizewinners that receive wide critical support from others are also included.

Our choices for the Best Plays of 1995–96 are listed below in the order in which they opened in New York (a plus + sign with the performance number signifies that the play was still running on June 1, 1996).

Mrs. Klein
(Off B'way 257+ perfs.)

Master Class
(B'way 219+ perfs.)

New England
(Off B'way 54 perfs.)

Valley Song
(Off B'way 68+ perfs.)

Molly Sweeney
(Off B'way 145 perfs.)

Rent
(Off B'way 56 perfs.)
(B'way 36+ perfs.)

A Fair Country
(Off B'way 119+ perfs.)

Seven Guitars
(B'way 72+ perfs.)

The Skriker
(Off B'way 17 perfs.)

Curtains
(Off B'way 13+ perfs.)

MOON OVER BUFFALO—Randy Graff, Dennis Ryan,
Philip Bosco and Carol Burnett in the comedy by Ken Ludwig

New Plays

Though Michael McGarty's set is concretely persuasive as the stage of a recital hall, Terrence McNally's *Master Class,* a play about legendary diva Maria Callas's attempt to teach three singers in front of an audience, is not journalism. Reportedly, the real master classes Callas gave (some of which McNally observed) were quiet, intense sessions and featured detailed and considered critiques of the students. McNally's version is certainly not quiet, and the criticism he has Callas give is not particularly detailed or considered (if it were, it might lull theatergoers to sleep), but you could hardly ask for more intensity. As the three singers step forward, they trigger in Callas floods of enthusiasm, sarcasm and memories.

Truth to tell, McNally's Callas is a teacher to whom no self-respecting pupil would care to be subjected. Though she is full of insights about opera and the importance of art, this is offset by the humiliation she heedlessly heaps on the students she jokingly refers to as her victims. Whether or not McNally so intended, the Callas he presents here seems to be taking revenge on the students for their ability to do what she can herself no longer do—sing.

But then, as I say, this is not journalism. McNally is using the form of the master class as a conceit through which to draw a vivid and complex portrait of the legendary singer. On the one hand, she convincingly represents herself as a humble servant of the composer; on the other hand, seldom has the stage hosted a character of such grand and casual arrogance. We admire Callas's perfectionism, her commitment to artistry and her history of great performances, but few of us would want to trade places with her. She seems to be a prisoner in her skin, a monster caught in a legend of her own construction—simultaneously playing the role to the hilt and resenting the way it makes others view her.

Do I go too far in seeing in this play McNally's comment on the current position of the arts in American society? McNally certainly has particular cause to be sensitive to the frequently abrasive relationship that exists between the arts and the society they reflect and from which they spring. (A production of his Best Play, *Lips Together, Teeth Apart* caused a cultural civil war in a small town in the South. Local politicians voted to end public funding for arts projects in that area.) Viewed from this perspective, Callas represents both the inspirational and disruptive aspects of culture. The task of the true artist is not merely to be decorative, but frequently to challenge, question, disturb. The ambivalence McNally's Callas excites—alternately beguiling and appalling us—echoes the ambivalence many feel when confronted by performances and images that upset the equilibrium. As McNally's Callas speaks of what she believes she and her colleagues contribute to the world, I get the feeling it is McNally himself attempting to speak through his fabulous monster to a public that is not crying out with sufficient vigor in protest against the cuts in the N.E.A. and other culture programs.

Leonard Foglia directed the polished and impassioned production. Karen Kay Cody and Jay Hunter Morris made fine foils as the first two students, and Audra McDonald was formidable as a student who protests Callas's destructive behavior. Center stage, Zoe Caldwell gave one of those performances that theatergoers press to their hearts—extravagant, vulnerable, terrifying, human.

Master Class was but one of a series of plays inspired by historic figures. Set in 1934 London, Nicholas Wright's *Mrs. Klein* concerns the psychologist Melanie Klein, her daughter Melitta and Klein's new assistant, Paula. As the play begins, Klein has recently received news that her only son Hans has died under mysterious circumstances in Hungary. The exploration of those circumstances and the assigning of responsibility for them provide much of the humor of the evening.

The 1995–96 Season Off Broadway

PLAYS (29)

MTC:
The Radical Mystique
NEW ENGLAND
Overtime
By the Sea, etc.
Circle Repertory:
Lonely Planet
Riff Raff
The Hope Zone
The Size of the World
Second Stage:
Crumbs From the Table of Joy
Oblivion Postponed
Dark Rapture
The Food Chain
Young Playwrights
Picasso at the Lapin Agile
Lincoln Center:
Northeast Local
A FAIR COUNTRY
Playwrights Horizons:
The Monogamist
Black Ink
Arts & Leisure

American Place:
Spoonbread and Strawberry Wine
The Slow Drag
Public Theater:
Wasp and Other Plays
Dancing on Her Knees
Venus
The Chang Fragments
Nixon's Nixon
Below the Belt
The Shattering
The Boar's Carcass

FOREIGN PLAYS IN ENGLISH (6)

Roundabout:
Moonlight
MOLLY SWEENEY
MRS. KLEIN
VALLEY SONG
THE SKRIKER
CURTAINS

MUSICALS (10)

john & jen
Zombies From the Beyond
Pendragon
Splendora
Jam on the Groove
RENT
Floyd Collins
Take It Easy
Cowgirls
Zombie Prom

FOREIGN-LANGUAGE PLAYS (4)

Brooklyn Academy:
Madame de Sade
In the Loneliness of the Cottonfields
Don Juan
The Inconstant Lovers

SOLO SHOWS (13)

The Springhill Singing Disaster
Too Jewish?
Moscow Stations
Full Gallop
Dick Gregory Live
Rendez-vous With Marlene
The Amazing Metrano
Nude Nude Totally Nude
A Line Around the Block
Spoke Man
Bein' With Behan
Tovah: Out of Her Mind
Papa

REVUES (4)

Pets
We'll Meet Again
Bring in 'da Noise, etc.
Forbidden Hollywood

REVIVALS (10)

Twelve Dreams
Shakespeare Marathon:
The Tempest
Troilus and Cressida
King Lear
Dangerous Corner
The Threepenny Opera
Nunsense
Blue Window
The Green Bird
I Do! I Do!

SPECIALTIES (7)

Grandma Sylvia's Funeral
Pomp Duck and Circumstance
R&H Rediscovered:
I Married an Angel
America's Sweetheart
Encores!:
One Touch of Venus
Du Barry Was a Lady
Chicago

Categorized above are all the new productions listed in the Plays Produced Off Broadway section of this volume.
Plays listed in CAPITAL LETTERS have been designated Best Plays of 1995–96.
Plays listed in *italics* were still running June 1, 1996.

Yes, I said humor. I seem to be in the minority, but I think the play is a comedy. A comedy rooted in pain, yes, but a comedy nevertheless. Indeed, there are times it verges on farce, but, instead of people abruptly slamming in and out of doors at breakneck speed, the three characters abruptly slam in and out of their various roles. Mrs. Klein is simultaneously a leading light in London's psychoanalytic establishment, a stern employer, and a grieving mother. Melitta is simultaneously her mother's daughter, a grieving sister and an analyst owing allegiance to a different branch of theory than that of her mother. Paula is simultaneously an employee, a potential surrogate daughter and (yes) an analyst, too. These three spend the evening shifting from one to another of these and other positions—sometimes locking into analytic poses to dissect each other, sometimes invoking their personal roles to manipulate each other.

The transitions between roles are often so swift as to induce whiplash. For instance, in a key passage late in the play, Paula leads Klein through a line of inquiry that reveals what is likely the truth about Hans's death, triggering a wrenching outburst of emotion from her employer. Barely a minute later, the two trade places and Paula is on the couch and Klein is analyzing. That they can swap status with the speed it would take to exchange hats and not, for all their intelligence, recognize that they are doing so strikes me as wonderfully, subtly funny.

To pull this off, you need three actresses capable of embracing absurd behavior with high seriousness. Amy Wright and Laila Robins played Paula and Melitta like a pair of terriers on the opposite sides of a piece of liver. In her first stage role in too many years, Uta Hagen displayed an emotional dexterity that was virtuosic, storms of tears swept away by biting sarcasm in turn supplanted by detached wisdom. In common with Caldwell, Hagen persuaded you that you were in the presence of a great if monumentally difficult woman.

To compound the ironies of the evening, there was a Pirandello-esque subtext to the production itself. For years at HB Studios, which she co-founded with her late husband Herbert Berghoff, Uta Hagen has maintained a reputation as one of America's best-respected acting teachers. Wright studied with her there, and both she and Robins also teach there, as does the director, William Carden. (So, for that matter, some years ago, did I.) In fact, this production of *Mrs. Klein* began its life at HB Studios. The stage was thick with metaphor!

Probably the least-known historical figure onstage this year is Sartje Baartman, a/k/a the Venus Hottentot, a black woman who, in the early 1800s, left South Africa to be exhibited in a London freak show by virtue of her large rear end. (Reportedly, this aspect of her anatomy inspired the bustle.) Suzan-Lori Parks's play *Venus* is interested both in the way this woman was exploited and the degree to which she was complicit in her exploitation. Unfortunately, after introducing her protagonist and announcing her thematic concerns, Parks confuses repetition with development. In the production at the Public Theater, matters weren't helped by Richard Foreman's direction and stage design. Instead of applying himself to the task of discovering what imagery would best serve the world Parks created, Foreman imposed on it his own trademarks—a constantly lit red light bulb, taut lines of string extending over the audience's heads, etc. Somehow, in the title role Adina Porter managed not to be overwhelmed by all the stylistic folderol, implying there might be more to the story of Sartje Baartman than Parks and Foreman chose to show us.

Continuing the parade of historical figures, Richard Nixon and Henry Kissinger are put through their paces in Russell Lees's *Nixon's Nixon*. Lees sets his play as Nixon is contemplating resignation under fire during the Watergate scandal. Kissinger is urging him to take the plunge. He is also urging Nixon to advise Gerald Ford, the president-to-be, to retain him in his position of Secretary of State so that he will be able to finish what he characterizes to the self-pitying Nixon as "our work." During the course of the action, Nixon switches between cajoling Kissinger to offer him some shred of comfort and compelling him to re-enact with him highlights of his presidency. Much of the play is undeniably funny, but, after decades of satire from Second City, the Committee and *Saturday Night Live,* not to mention Phillip Roth, Jules Feiffer and Mort Sahl, there is precious little that hasn't already been said about Nixon, and said more succinctly. (It was quite a season for Nixons—the Nixon-Kissinger relationship was the subject of a TV movie, Oliver Stone wrote and directed a nearly incoherent and interminable feature on the late President's life and career, and, as I mention elsewhere, the late President popped up again as a figure in the revue *Forbidden Hollywood.*)

Steve Martin pressed Einstein and the century's dominant painter into stage service in his *Picasso at the Lapin Agile.* One night in 1904, in a modest Paris bar called the Lapin Agile, young Picasso and Einstein encounter each other and, after a little bantering, recognize that, despite their devotion to different disciplines, they are part of the elect whose visions will transform the new century. And that's pretty much it in terms of what happens in the play.

If the play is short on much of a story in which to invest one's sympathies, it is long on playfulness. Martin is new to playwriting, and he has a good deal of fun mocking theater's conventions. The fourth wall is violated so frequently it might as well have a revolving door (at one juncture a character borrows a program from the audience in order to prove a point), and the actors turn downstage with soliloquies not so much because they have something urgent to say as because Martin figures, as long as they're being paid, they might as well do a little work. Such a whimsical mode is hard to maintain for a full evening, especially when there is no plot to speak of, and Martin does not quite sustain the intermissionless 90 minutes. But much of the piece is as charming as he wants it to be. In the New York premiere, Mark Nelson made a bemused and ingratiating Einstein, a man capable of thinking big thoughts without being consumed by self-importance.

Martin met with less success with *WASP and Other Plays,* a disappointing bill of one-acts at the Public Theater. Another bill of one-acts, *By the Sea by the Sea by the Beautiful Sea,* consists of pieces for two women and one man on a stretch of beach in the morning, the afternoon and at night by Joe Pintauro, Lanford Wilson and Terrence McNally. Pintauro's contribution, concerning a woman, her brother and the brother's wife waiting for the day to dispose of a dead parent's ashes, suffers from too many lines beginning, "I feel—". When characters explain themselves endlessly, the author runs the risk of reducing an audience to passivity. Terrence McNally's piece, about a married man cheerfully and guiltlessly flirting with two women, has high spirits but swings from one amusing line to another without communicating much of an underlying sense of purpose. The most substantial of the three is Lanford Wilson's piece, in which a man whose sexual morality is less than scrupulous discovers an area in which he must stand on principle. In production, the evening was best appreciated as a celebration of the resourcefulness and versatility of three fine performers—Lee Brock, Timothy Carhart and Mary Beth Fisher.

Earnestness in today's dramatists seems to be deeply suspect. Disdain, ambivalence and regret appear to be the prevailing colors of much contemporary playwriting. Perhaps the lack of heroism we see in public life makes us suspicious of the attempt to portray heroes in contemporary drama. (Heroism in the classics and period plays is easier to take. The image of yesterday as a simpler time when people took courageous moral stands is as wired into our belief systems as is the conviction, from years of movies, that the past is sepia colored.) So along comes an imperfect but very earnest play like Sacrilege, and many of today's critics get deeply uncomfortable.

The leading character is Sister Grace, a nun who annoys the Vatican by pressing for priesthood for women. Grace is drawn as spunky and idealistic, with a quick, cheerful wit and a disarming directness. The play tells how these qualities lead both to her helping a con man from the street find his calling as a priest and to her being removed from her position in the church by agents of the Vatican so that she can no longer follow her own calling.

Diane Shaffer, the playwright, wrote a well-structured problem play in which the various perspectives of the issue are articulated in an entertaining and credible manner. Where the play falls short is in conveying the emotional and spiritual hold the church has on Sister Grace and her need to be attached to it, flawed though she may view it. When Shaffer has Grace talk about the pain her expulsion has caused her, it sounds like talk. Shaffer has not established sufficiently the passionate connection between Grace and the institution that both inspires and subjugates her. No, Sacrilege does not achieve all that it attempts, but I think it deserved better than the condescending dismissal it received. There was ample evidence from the audience around me that the intellectual and emotional issues were communicating.

Though her voice seemed strained at the performance I attended, Ellen Burstyn played Sister Grace with good humor and a bracing forthrightness. As the cardinal who is her chief antagonist and sometime friend, Herb Foster found the dichotomy between his position in the church and his personal sympathies. Don Scardino directed with his usual tasteful understatement.

Like the Catholic church of Sacrilege, the Church of England in David Hare's Racing Demon is an institution born of an earlier society and culture, created to address needs of an earlier age. In these plays, both churches, in order to maintain authority, resist evolution urged by contemporary realities. In Hare's play, too, a principled central figure comes to grief challenging inflexible orthodoxy.

The key difference is that while Sister Grace is constantly a-bubble with her enthusiasms, Lionel, the priest of *Racing Demon,* is exhausted spiritually and emotionally. He doubts that performing the sacraments does much good for the poor people who are his constituents and so concentrates on being of as much secular value as he can, acting as a social worker with a collar. For the most part, the best he seems to be able to do is listen with genuine concern.

Ironically, it is the enthusiast in Hare's play, the Rev. Tony Ferris newly arrived in Lionel's parish, who is the play's antagonist. He's full of enthusiasm, yes, but for a rigid and unflinching theology that, Hare implies, is likely to do more harm than good. The immediate product of Ferris's agitation is to help a piggy bishop drive Lionel out of the church. And fundamentalist attitudes similar to those of Ferris lead to the resignation of another of the parish's principled team, Harry Henderson, because he is about to be exposed as a homosexual.

My problem with the play is that Hare seems to be so conscientious about addressing the various problems facing the Church of England today I could almost hear the sound of his pencil marking off a checklist. "Gay priests? Did that one. Women in the church? Yup, got that. Class warfare among the clergy? Check." The speeches and scenes are always scrupulously written, but the fastidiousness with which Hare addresses his agenda is at the price of the illusion of life being lived on the stage. He seems to have written every scene with an implied topic heading, as if he would prefer to have written a collection of essays.

As was true in his problematic *The Secret Rapture,* Hare finds it difficult to write about a virtuous central character without allowing that figure to succumb to passivity. Josef Sommer did subtle and affecting work as Lionel, but Brian Murray and George N. Martin, playing characters conceived with more energy (respectively, Henderson and a hissable conservative ogre), made more vivid impressions.

(This raises an interesting craft question—how do you write about exhausted goodness without making its embodiment suffer from dramatic enervation? I don't have an answer, but there are clues in the way Chekhov wrote the doctor in *Uncle Vanya.*)

For years, the playwright Richard Nelson (not to be confused with the lighting designer of the same name) has had a problem similar to Hare's, appearing to be more interested in placing ideas onstage than creating worlds peopled by characters with independent lives. The good news is, his Best Play *New England* represents a breakthrough. Though *New England* is "about something," his themes and ironies aren't trumpeted as self-consciously as in some of his past work. With this script, Nelson has acquired a new and welcome light-handedness.

The suicide of a dispirited community college music teacher brings together in his Connecticut house his middle-aged mistress and various members of the family he has left behind. With the exception of the French wife of one of his children, all of them are English expatriates (hence the double meaning of the title). Beyond the catalytic tragedy, what they have in common is disdain for the country in which they have chosen to live. Much of the humor of the play lies in the spectacle of these

RACING DEMON—Josef Sommer, John C. Vennema and George N. Martin
in the play by David Hare

articulate ninnies passionately criticizing a society that is oblivious to their disapproval.

Along the way, Nelson deals with the spiritual nausea caused by cultural dislocation. None of these people has any sense of where to find home in the States. Nor, for that matter, if they were to return to the England of today, would they be likely to recognize *it* as home. Nelson's characters have nostalgia for a country of the mind, a country that is now as much a fiction as the England P.G. Wodehouse wrote about for decades after he left it.

What is particularly impressive is that Nelson has expressed these ideas via a genuinely amusing sex comedy. A writer who has aspired to Shavian models, Nelson here offers work that would do credit to Alan Ayckbourn, particularly in showing how would-be high-mindedness can be undercut by twinges of the carnal. The pretensions of most of the characters are deflated when their private natures are inadvertently revealed. In his *Some Americans Abroad*, Nelson did something similar but was unable to give us much reason to care. Here, despite their hypocritical posing, Nelson musters affection for his characters.

In the Manhattan Theater Club production, the script had the blessing of a well-matched ensemble of actors under the direction of Howard Davies. Especially good were Larry Bryggman as both the deceased and his cheerfully cynical half-brother, Penny Fuller as the mistress who keeps learning how much she didn't know about the man with whom she shared her bed, and Mia Dillon as a compulsive control-freak.

Jon Robin Baitz's Best Play *A Fair Country* also deals with a family displaced from their home, but to more disturbing effect. The Englishness of Nelson's characters makes them figures of fun. The Americanness of the family about whom Baitz writes contributes to their tragedy. The father, Harry Burgess, acts as a cultural attaché, bringing artists to South Africa in the belief that the humanistic values that are embodied in their art will serve the American image abroad and encourage reform in the repressive society where he is stationed. (It is no accident that some of the play is set during the Carter administration when much was made of this country's moral mission in the world.) In exchange for getting the posting away from the tensions of South Africa that he believes are hastening the emotional disintegration of his wife, Patrice, Harry allows himself to be manipulated into passing along to his superiors the names of South African friends his elder son Alec, a radical journalist, has been cultivating. The friends are decimated, and Harry's knowledge of his responsibility destroys him and the family in whose interests he thought he was acting.

The debt Baitz owes both Arthur Miller's *All My Sons* and Eugene O'Neill's *Long Day's Journey Into Night* is evident. As in the Miller, a father is torn between what he sees as his personal and professional obligations. As in the O'Neill, the interweave of responsibility between two sons and their parents for their shared tragedy is not subject to simplistic parsing. Though there are occasional passages that sound as if they began as notebook jottings for which Baitz hoped to find mouthpieces, the play is the most assured work yet by this talented writer. Under the direction of Daniel Sullivan (who also directed Baitz's *Substance of Fire*), it was given a clear and bracing production at Lincoln Center's Mitzi Newhouse Theater. Laurence Luckinbill was touching in his essential decency as Harry. Ferocious, funny, pathetic and unstable, Patrice offered Judith Ivey one of the richest roles of her career.

Arthur Laurents's black comedy *The Radical Mystique* also investigates the U.S. government's complicity in the unravelling of a family. At the end of the Sixties, an FBI agent tries to pressure a liberal and socially prominent household into cancelling a party in support of a radical cause. By the play's end, what the agent has revealed to the family and their friends about their own secrets and impulses has taken its toll. Though crackling with Laurents's characteristic intelligence, the play feels too schematic and the characters miss achieving the dimensions of human beings.

Richard Dresser's *Below the Belt* concerns three Americans abroad, a "checking" team trapped in a corporate manufacturing installation in an unnamed country. (The product they are checking remains as anonymous as the country.) At its best, their constant jockeying for useless dominance on this barren terrain plays like paranoid variations on Abbott and Costello's "Who's on First" routine, but the verbal gambits ultimately become repetitious and the play runs out of steam well before the end of the second act. Judd Hirsch, Robert Sean Leonard and Jude Ciccolella batted about Dresser's tautologies and defective syllogisms with assurance under Gloria Muzio's direction.

Christopher Kyle's *The Monogamist* concerns a poet named Dennis Jensen who, shortly after publishing a volume celebrating monogamy, discovers that his wife is not as convinced of its virtues. This sends him into a tailspin out of which he never emerges and sets up encounters with dismaying representatives of the younger generation whose values (or lack of same) further disorient him. Kyle has a talent for the satiric line, but the many good lines don't add up to a convincing play. Trying to portray confusion and shallowness, the play itself succumbs to them with an almost ceaseless flow of easy shots at the avant garde and literary pretentions. (Satirizing the literary set is a recurrent theme at Playwrights Horizons, which this season also produced Steve Tesich's disappointing portrait of a drama critic's decline, *Arts & Leisure.*) I had problems, too, with director Scott Elliott's production, which piled on such devices as using rock songs for commentary and interpolating video clips meant to convey something or other about talk shows and celebrity. These devices have been worked to death in recent seasons; it's time for a moratorium on them.

Happily, later in the season Elliott reconfirmed his reputation as a young director of great gifts with his staging of English playwright Stephen Bill's Best Play *Curtains.* On her 86th birthday, Ida yearns to be relieved of a life that has become as painful to her as to those relatives who have ostensibly gathered to celebrate it. At the end of the first act, after Ida has failed in an attempt at suicide, one of her three daughters, Katherine, fulfills what she understands to be her mother's intention by smothering her with a pillow. In the second act, Katherine and her family try to sort out their feelings as, offstage, a doctor examines the body and considers whether or not to report the death as natural.

Though some of the second act involves a debate on euthanasia and assisted suicide, this is not so much an issue play as a portrait of the dynamics of a family under stress. As Bill constantly shifts the configuration of the players on the stage, the effect is almost kaleidoscopic—new aspects of the characters are revealed whenever anyone enters or exits, ironies and contradictions bloom, and the stress of the tragic creates the necessity for humorous release. The various voices in the script (originally presented in England in 1987 at the Hempstead Theater Club) were subtly blended by director Elliott. In a strong cast, two performers were particularly fine—David Cale as Douglas, Ida's acerbic son-in-law, and Laura Esterman as Katherine, here doing work every bit the equal of the work that won her multiple awards as the lead in *Marvin's Room* (in which she also played a woman dealing with an infirm parent). After its initial run under an off-off-Broadway agreement, *Curtains* moved to a well-deserved commercial extension.

Trish Vradenburg's Broadway comedy-drama, *The Apple Doesn't Fall . . .,* also concerning a daughter's relationship to a deteriorating mother, was a victim of its own glibness, though the author didn't deserve the merciless pasting she received from critics too palpably eager to drop-kick a work written by someone with a background in television.

I find myself admiring Nicky Silver's *The Food Chain* more than liking it. In three scenes, Silver describes a circle of whining obsessives. What are they obsessive about? Eating, not eating, loneliness, sex, appearance. The title suggests the author's Darwinian approach to comedy. Everyone in the play consumes or is consumed by; they are defined to the audience and to themselves *by* their consumption. I suppose this is Silver's satiric point (augmenting the slogan from the Sixties, "You are what you eat" with "and what you're eaten by"), and he certainly generates a generous number of laughs out of his variations on this theme within the course of the piece's single act. But I find the play off-putting in ways I don't think the author intended. He seems to invite the audience to enjoy with him his characters' misery. Silver offers scant sympathy for any of them, and implies disdain for anyone who would waste serious concern for them. Maybe it's not hip of me, but I can't muster much appetite for mocking people in pain. Few of the people around me had such compunctions; the audience laughed gleefully and constantly. Robert Falls directed a production that seemed completely to fulfill the intentions of the script, getting a particularly fine and subtle performance out of Phyllis Newman as a Jewish mother who volunteers on a crisis hotline but has little to offer her compulsive, over-eating, suicidal son.

Now that I think of it, one would have to look long and hard among the season's plays to find much good news about the American family or the prospects of a marriage staying together. Of the plays I've already discussed, *A Fair Country, Below the Belt, The Monogamist, Arts & Leisure* and *WASP* feature domestic failures. Add to this gloomy list Kevin Heelan's *The Hope Zone* (a former alcoholic fails to rescue her daughter from her demons), Tom Donaghy's *Northeast Local* (a working-class marriage fails), Han Ong's *The Chang Fragments* (a Chinese-American hangs himself in a flophouse leaving the wife and children he deserted to pick up the emotional pieces), and Charles Evered's *The Size of the World* (an aging couple fail to transform a disturbed boarder into a substitute for their alienated son). All of these plays gave their casts opportunities to shine in individual scenes (I was particularly impressed with the versatile Rita Moreno's child-like Vivian Merkle in Evered's play), but none of these quite came together as satisfying evenings. *The Hope Zone* and *The Size of the World* were both Circle Rep offerings, as were Laurence Fishburne's *Riff Raff* (which he directed and in which he also starred to mixed response) and Steven Dietz's subtle but attenuated *Lonely Planet,* in which the attempt of a gay man named Jody to isolate himself from the AIDS crisis by hiding in his map store is challenged by his friend Carl's insistence on filling the shop with chairs belonging to dead friends.

Because one of my scripts was in direct competition with August Wilson's new play for a writing award, the senior editor of this volume has suggested I not flirt with the appearance of conflict of interest by offering a review of Wilson's *Seven Guitars.* (I am, however, on record in previous volumes as being one of Mr. Wilson's admirers, and I consider it a great compliment to have been nominated in his company.) At rise, a group of black men and women mourn a blues singer named Floyd (Schoolboy) Barton who has recently been killed. In flashback, Wilson offers a group portrait of the mourners, their corner of 1948 Pittsburgh and the circumstances leading up to the killing. The production was under the direction of Wilson's usual collaborator, Lloyd Richards. (A review of this play by Michael Grossberg appears in The Season Around the United States section of this volume.)

More killing—a *whole lot* more killing (the entire company is ultimately dispatched)—filled the two acts of Stephen Sondheim and George Furth's comedy-thriller, *Getting Away With Murder.* (This represents Sondheim's first attempt at a stage piece without song, though he has non-musical TV and film credits.) Members of a therapy group discover that their doctor has been murdered prior to their arrival. In the first act, they try to figure out which of them delivered the fatal blow. Just before the act break, the guilty party is revealed (to the audience only), and the second act is concerned with the murderer's strategies to avoid detection. Underneath the mechanics, Sondheim and Furth seem to intend a satiric commentary on how the city encourages the flourishing of the seven deadly sins, but the script cannot manage sufficient gleeful black humor necessary to keep the conceit afloat.

I am in the minority among the press, but I had a fine time at A.R. Gurney's *Overtime,* a frolicsome sequel to Shakespeare's *Merchant of Venice* in which the action magically shifts to the 20th century and Verona clearly is somewhere on the American East Coast. The play is set during Portia's party in the wake of her victory over Shylock. The words "party" and Gurney immediately call to mind *The Perfect Party* and *Later Life.* As in both of those Best Plays, Gurney uses the party as a metaphor for cultural diversity in a free society. More an extended sketch than a fully realized work, *Overtime* isn't in the same league as the earlier two plays, but its cheerful and optimistic spirit are wonderfully welcome at a time when so much of what calls itself comedy makes you want to slit your wrists in despair for humanity.

Taking place in 1953, *Moon Over Buffalo* is the third of Ken Ludwig's three scripts set against America's showbiz past. This time, the leading figures are a husband-and-wife acting team named Charlotte and George Hay playing *Cyrano* and *Private Lives* in rep as they do personal battle and try to advance their faltering careers. Ludwig is less than a scrupulous craftsman here. If you're going to write a period piece, you should make some attempt to get the details of the period right, especially when getting them wrong is liable to jar. (I don't want to drift into the arcane, but the Frank Capra movie that provides the excuse for much of the play has nothing to do with the kind of films Capra made.) The piece is also filled with anachronisms. (Was the phrase "out of the closet" common parlance in the early Fifties?) But the script in general seems to suffer from a lackadaisical attitude on the part of the writer.

Ludwig was very lucky to have Carol Burnett to play the female lead. So was the audience. Burnett hasn't been on Broadway since the musical *Fade Out—Fade In* countless moons over Buffalo ago, and it was a treat to see her on a stage again, even in less than top-drawer goods. Much of the fun of the evening was in watching the pleasure she was getting in giving pleasure. Many of her laughs came from her reactions to the goings-on around her, and, as her errant husband, Philip Bosco gave her plenty to which to react.

The last time playwright Caryl Churchill collaborated with director Mark Wing-Davey, the result was the Best Play *Mad Forest*, a prophetic portrait of Rumania in transition, one scene of which featured a dialogue between a vampire and a dog. Their newest collaboration, again a Best Play, continues their exploration of the interaction of the supernatural and contemporary life. *The Skriker* posits that swarms of malign fairies and other spirits make it their business to haunt and bedevil contemporary Londoners. In particular, Churchill is concerned with how the friendship of two young women is affected by the constant intrusion of the title creature, a malevolent shapeshifter who pops up in a variety of guises to tempt and taunt them and look with unhealthy appetite on the illegitimate daughter one of the women has during the course of the play.

I can't honestly tell you that I understand all the action of this play. What the Skriker wants, aside from the pleasure of disruption, is not clear. But there are flashes of theatrical brilliance here. Churchill mirrors the title figure's shapeshifting with the constant transformation of the language. The Skriker's lines are a dizzying and disorienting outpouring of puns and allusions. In Churchill's world, language itself is not to be trusted—it is constantly turning against itself, against fixed and concrete meaning. Jayne Atkinson played the many faces of the Skriker with mordant humor and authority. Mark Wing-Davey surrounded her with a gallery of supporting spirits that constantly prowled the stage. And what a stage! Designed by Marina Draghici, it was filled with surprises—a skyline made of milk cartons, an underworld buffet of repulsive entrees set for ghouls, a magic fountain, a talking sofa. The disquieting mood was artfully supported by John Gromada's intricately scored sound and Judith Weir's music. If much of *The Skriker* resists coherent analysis, its production at the Public was one of the season's most exciting events. (Less successful was another of the Public's offerings featuring otherworldly characters, Nilo Cruz's *Dancing on Her Knees*, in which spirits of a dead dancing team visit a drag queen under the supervision of a pair of angels.)

Several writers of Best Plays of previous seasons—Donald Margulies, David Ives, David Mamet and Catherine Butterfield—introduced works new to New York on the city's off-off-Broadway stages. Primary Stages presented Margulies's *The Model Apartment*, which concerns an aging Jewish couple trying to escape memories of the Holocaust and their obese and unhinged daughter named Debby, who follows them to what they hoped was to be a peaceful retirement in Florida. The play, which won Margulies his second Obie, derives its considerable power from the recognition that Debby is equivalent to the Holocaust—a nightmare that cannot be evaded or domesticated by sentiment. Primary Stages also presented David Ives's *Ancient History*, the story of how and why a relationship that should work doesn't. Under the title *No One Will Be Immune*, the Ensemble Studio Theater presented a collection of five one-acts by David Mamet scrupulously directed by the company's artistic director, Curt Dempster. The pieces themselves were of varying impact; some were little jewels, others felt like technical exercises from his copybook. Three of them

THE FOOD CHAIN—Hope Davis, Tom Mc-Gowan and Patrick Fabian in Nicky Silver's play

served to showcase David Rasche's range—smug and silly as a clergyman in *A Sermon,* long on theory but short on action in *Sunday Afternoon,* and terrified in the piece that lent its title to the evening. The central characters of Catherine Butterfield's *Where the Truth Lies* are a couple that seem to be happily married who offer shelter to the wife's sister on the run from what may or may not be an abusive husband. In trying to fathom the true dynamics of the sister's marriage, the couple examines previously unexplored and disturbing fault lines in their own. This provocative premise wasn't fulfilled in the script that reached production, though. In her eagerness to articulate her themes, Butterfield has succumbed to writing a series of earnest clichés along the line of, "Why have you never said this before?" "Maybe I was afraid to look honestly at my life before. Maybe I was afraid of what I would find." Butterfield's Best Play *Joined at the Head,* which sparkled with original imagery, established that she is more than capable of doing better.

Harold Pinter long ago achieved the rare status of being a writer whose name not only conjures up a body of work but a specific theatrical territory. He has been less than prolific as a playwright in recent years, so the American premiere of a new work from him is news. I wish I could say that the play itself, *Moonlight,* had impressed me more.

On one side of the stage, Andy, a civil servant with a mocking tongue, lies dying as his wife, Bel, sits by his bed. On the other side, his sons Jake and Fred joke around and refuse to visit their father. On a platform above them, Bridget, whom one infers is a daughter who died young, looks down on the family she left behind and wishes them peace. There is also the odd visit from Maria and Ralph, friends and possibly past lovers of Andy and Bel. I say "possibly" because it's not easy to tell whether the carnal memories Andy and Bel crank up about Maria and Ralph are real or the product of verbal gamesmanship.

Verbal gamesmanship dominates in this work. Andy and Bel are cheerfully, almost lovingly abusive of each other in their dialogues, and the boys spend most of their time drinking and parodying the social nattering of the middle class they seem determined to escape. But Pinter has played precisely these verbal games so many times and more successfully before that here they feel threadbare. The style seems to be shaping the content rather than serving it. I kept wanting him to put aside the garnish and bring on the meat. But mostly what he serves up here is garnish.

There are a few lovely moments: Andy, drinking a forbidden drink and recalling the daughter he lost, Bel trying to penetrate her sons' jokes about a Chinese laundry in the hope of affecting a reconciliation. These moments made me long for the play that I sense is buried under the reflexive facetiousness.

Karel Reisz directed a cast of notables for the Roundabout production. Most successful were Blythe Danner as Bel, delicately revealing the grief under the apparent self-possession, and Liev Schreiber (looking a bit like the younger Pinter) as Jake, the embittered older son. Jason Robards's very strengths as a master of colloquial phrasing (so useful in taking the starch out of some of O'Neill's more awkward writing) seem at war with the stylization required for Pinter. His inability to muster (or lack of interest in attempting) a convincing British accent didn't help make one believe that he inhabited the same world as the others in the cast.

Robards was much more effective in his other performance at the Roundabout this season as Mr. Rice, the surgeon who gets a chance to repair a career ruined by alcoholism and despair when the title character of Brian Friel's Best Play *Molly Sweeney* becomes his patient. Molly has been blind since early childhood, but it hasn't kept her from building a fulfilling life as a physiotherapist or from embracing a circle of friends. Nor does it keep her from marrying. It is her marriage to the enthusiastic Frank that brings her to Rice. Frank has a history of throwing himself body and soul into projects, and curing Molly's blindness becomes his latest. Once it is determined that Rice can perform an operation that will restore her sight, Frank sets Molly's course.

Friel is writing here of the damage that can be caused by heedless good intentions. Both Rice and Frank hope to enrich their self-esteem in their gift to Molly without giving much thought of the consequences. The operation is indeed a success in the sense that she emerges from it with the ability to see. But its success is the cause of her destruction. Being able to see the world profoundly changes her relationship to it. Ultimately she is unable to adapt and withdraws into catatonia.

Several critics compared *Molly Sweeney* to Friel's *Faith Healer.* As in the earlier play, the three characters never play scenes together. But, in *Faith Healer,* the three monologues were given in isolation. In *Molly Sweeney,* the monologues are intercut, and Friel reaps the dramatic rewards of the juxtaposition of the three very different voices. Friel wrote the play for Catherine Byrne, and under his direction she brought an intensity and musicality to the part. Robards was immensely touching as a man groping for a second life. Cast in the play's most flamboyant part, Alfred Molina, in his American stage debut, was extraordinary as Frank, ludicrous and vulnerable in his manic optimism.

Like Pinter and Friel, Athol Fugard is a world-renowned dramatist facing the twilight of his career, and like Pinter's play, Fugard's Best Play *Valley Song* deals with the approach of the last season of life. However, whereas Pinter's protagonist never achieves resolution with the younger generation his sons represent, the two aging men in Fugard's work ultimately make sweet and satisfying peace with Veronica, the young woman who speaks for youth.

Abraam Jonkers is an aging Coloured tenant farmer in the beautiful, semi-desert area of South Africa called the Karoo. During the play, Abraam (also called Oupa or grandfather) finds his comfortable way of life threatened by two developments. For one thing, the land on which he and his family have farmed for generations is being purchased by a white man, and he is unsure whether he will be expelled by the new landlord. (Since the new landlord is called "The Author" and represents Fugard himself, the audience has little fear that this will happen, of course.) For another, Veronica, the teenage granddaughter he has raised since her mother died, has discovered her passion for singing, and she is determined to leave the Karoo and try to strike out on her own as an artist in the larger world.

It's a small story, but implicit in the tale are the larger changes that have occurred in South Africa since the end of apartheid. Though The Author and Oupa are of different races and different economic situations, they share familiarity with the past and are reluctant and a little fearful of the new world. They also are both anxious for and envious of Veronica's youth and hope. Ultimately, the old men find comradeship in the land they love and are able to give their blessings to Veronica. The blessings differ—Oupa's is the blessing of blood family, The Author's is the blessing of the artistic family.

The construction of the piece is amiably awkward; Fugard's considerable reputation does not rest on his technical felicity, and he has his usual trouble with exposition. But the impression this piece makes is of unpretentious, honest folk art, like a piece of wood picked up in the Karoo and carved with patience by its author. The stolidity can sometimes try the patience, but offsetting it is the vibrant portrait of Veronica. She is idealized youth, almost too glowing and virtuous to be true. As writer, director and co-star, Fugard was lucky to play opposite LisaGay Hamilton, her quicksilver charm and skipping rhythms in beguiling contrast to Fugard's four-square, steady pace. Though from different times, races and worlds, Hamilton reminded me of nobody so much as the young Audrey Hepburn, radiating ingenuous delight. In a season in which so much necessarily sorrowful news was delivered, she was especially precious.

Here's where we list the *Best Plays* choices for the outstanding straight play achievements of 1995–96 in New York, on and off Broadway. In the acting categories, clear distinction among "starring," "featured" or "supporting" players can't be made on the basis of official billing, which is as much a matter of contracts as of esthetics. Here in these volumes we divide acting into "primary" or "secondary" roles, a primary role being one which might some day cause a star to inspire a revival in order to appear in that character. All others, be they as vivid as Mercutio, are classed as secondary. Furthermore, our list of individual standouts makes room for more than a single choice when appropriate (most particularly appropriate in this season of splendid performances by leading women). We believe that no useful purpose is served by forcing ourselves into an arbitrary selection of a single best when we come upon multiple examples of equal distinction.

PLAYS

BEST PLAY: *A Fair Country* by Jon Robin Baitz; *Mrs. Klein* by Nicholas Wright

BEST REVIVAL: *A Delicate Balance* by Edward Albee

BEST ACTOR IN A PRIMARY ROLE: George Grizzard as Tobias in *A Delicate Balance;* Alfred Molina as Frank Sweeney in *Molly Sweeney;* George C. Scott as Henry Drummond in *Inherit the Wind*

BEST ACTRESS IN A PRIMARY ROLE: Zoe Caldwell as Maria Callas in *Master Class;* Uta Hagen as Mrs. Melanie Klein in *Mrs. Klein;* LisaGay Hamilton as Veronica Jonkers in *Valley Song;* Rosemary Harris as Agnes in *A Delicate Balance;* Elaine Stritch as Claire in *A Delicate Balance*

BEST ACTOR IN A SECONDARY ROLE: Brian Murray as Harry Henderson in *Racing Demon;* Ruben Santiago-Hudson as Canewell in *Seven Guitars*

BEST ACTRESS IN A SECONDARY ROLE: Viola Davis as Vera in *Seven Guitars;* Laura Esterman as Katherine in *Curtains;* Allison Janney as Boo in *Blue Window;* Laila Robins as Melitta Klein in *Mrs. Klein*

BEST DIRECTOR: Scott Elliott for *Curtains;* Gerald Gutierrez for *A Delicate Balance*

BEST SCENERY: John Lee Beatty for *A Delicate Balance;* Robert Brill for *Buried Child;* Marina Draghici for *The Skriker*

BEST COSTUMES: Marina Draghici for *The Skriker*

BEST LIGHTING: Kevin Rigdon for *Buried Child*

CITATION FOR SOUND DESIGN: John Gromada for *The Skriker*

CITATION FOR SOLO PERFORMANCE: Marga Gomez for writing and performance in *A Line Around the Block*

VICTOR/VICTORIA—Julie Andrews in the title role of the Blake Edwards-Henry Mancini-Leslie Bricusse musical, a performance cited among the year's best by Tony nominators and *Best Plays*

New Musicals and Revues

In 1964, George Roy Hill directed a nimble and knowing comedy about adolescence from a Nunnally Johnson script called *The World of Henry Orient* (based on a novel by Johnson's daughter Nora). It resurfaced some years later as a musical called *Henry, Sweet Henry.* Under Hill's direction, with a script, again, by Johnson, it proved to be a flat and disappointing affair. A couple of seasons back, Neil Simon attempted to transform his engaging film comedy, *The Goodbye Girl,* into a musical of the same name. It, too, proved to be a disappointment.

This season again, a movie maker of proven gifts, Blake Edwards, transformed one of his most successful pictures, *Victor/Victoria,* into a musical for the stage. This time, the attempt reteamed not only the original screenwriter-director, but also the original composer and lyricist—Henry Mancini and Leslie Bricusse—and, most importantly, the original star, Edwards's wife Julie Andrews. And again, the result is discouraging.

Does this mean that no film makers can successfully guide their own work to musical adaptation? No. Just that, if one has, I'm not aware of it.

Set in the Paris of the Thirties, *Victor/Victoria* certainly has musical theater possibilities. It tells of Victoria Grant, a down-on-her-luck English singer who is persuaded by a gay friend named Toddy to pretend to be a female impersonator named Victor. Playing a man playing a woman, Victoria becomes a major cabaret star. A visiting Chicago gangster named King Marchan catches her/his act and finds himself drawn to the performer, not being quite sure of the gender of the object of his obsession. The premise offers the promise of a comic meditation on sexuality and gender roles; Lord knows successful musicals have been built on flimsier conceits than this.

Unfortunately, it's as if a solid blueprint for a building had been turned over to contractors not up to the job. The structure of a workable book is here, but line-by-line most of the dialogue is flat-footed, obvious and repetitious. It seems that a joke based on the juxtaposition of the words "king" and "queen" is attempted every few minutes. More seriously, the attraction between Victoria and King has to be taken on faith. As written, one simply has no idea why Victoria would find the smug and bullying gangster so instantly appealing.

The score, too, is a letdown. Henry Mancini, who for decades wrote some of the movies' most enchanting and sophisticated melodies, composed the bulk of the music. Sadly, it is not up to his own high standards. Frank Wildhorn, the composer brought in to augment the score after Mancini's death in 1994, contributed nothing better. Most distressing is the bulk of the work by veteran lyricist Leslie Bricusse. The lyrics are almost always a frontal assault on ideas that have already been articulated in preceding scenes, rendering the songs dramatically irrelevant. In addition to embracing unrewarding ideas for numbers, Bricusse has frequently executed these ideas in a slapdash manner, particularly the songs "Chicago, Illinois," "Louis Says," and "Paris Makes Me Horny." Bricusse seems not to have figured out a way to depict vulgarity without writing vulgarly.

Here and there are hints of the show *Victor/Victoria* could have been. An extended balletic routine in which most of the principals narrowly miss discovering each other in a pair of adjoining hotel suites is a jewel, and there is a beguiling little duet called "You & Me" in which Victor and Toddy celebrate their friendship. If only the rest of the show had lived up to these passages.

Among the show's good news, Robin Wagner's scenery and Willa Kim's costuming had the assured panache of classic Broadway designing. And, most happily, the cast was strong. Rachel York, as the stereotypical blonde moll with a propensity for malapropisms, played the mostly wan material she was assigned with such guts and commitment that she deserves a medal. Tony Roberts brought all of his considerable experience as a comic performer to bear on the part of Toddy, his wryness transforming many a clumsy line into something approaching the sound of wit.

Of course, the raison d'etre of this enterprise was Julie Andrews. A couple of years ago, matched with much better material in the Sondheim revue *Putting It Together,* she reaffirmed her ability to make a direct connection with an audience's heart. Even though the promise of *Victor/Victoria* was unfulfilled, Ms. Andrews was still able to make magic enough to offer patrons ample reason to be grateful.

Yet another movie was the basis of *Big,* which, like *Victor/Victoria,* features a central character with a secret identity. Based on the popular film directed by Penny Marshall and written by Gary Ross and Anne Spielberg, the show tells the story of a young teenage boy named Josh who gets his wish to be "big" and is moved into an adult's body while retaining his teenage mind. He ends up working at a toy company, getting his first taste of the politics of the work place and romance, then ultimately returning with relief to the arms of his mother and the natural cycle of growth and development.

For much of the first act, *Big* seems securely on track. The awkwardness and frustrations of puberty are evoked in a tuneful series of songs and exuberant dances featuring young Josh and the other kids of his New Jersey suburb. His transportation into an adult body via a carnival booth contraption and his initial confusion are also well-handled.

But the show loses its footing when Josh enters the adult world. The corporate in-fighting at the toy company is a mild echo of *How to Succeed in Business Without Really Trying* (complete with a back-stabbing Bud Frump-like character named Paul). More seriously, Josh's relationship with a fellow executive named Susan doesn't register. The joke in the film was that she fell in love with what she projected onto him, misinterpreting his naivete as self-possession and a lack of pretension. We simultaneously understood scenes from both his and her perspectives. This has been lost in the transition to the stage. In John Weidman's book, her attraction to him seems to be necessary to move the story forward rather than the result of the inter-action of their personalities. The fact that she persuades herself that she has fallen in love with someone she so thoroughly misreads makes her appear dumb or self-delusional. Her song that he is "One Special Man" reads like an effort on the part of the writers to persuade the audience to believe what they haven't been able to dramatize. I have a theory that when the adjective count soars, it's a pretty good indication that a lyricist is in trouble. In too many of *Big*'s songs, the usually adroit lyricist Richard Maltby Jr. seems to be trapped into having characters earnestly explain the obvious. Too often, the audience is ahead of the characters.

Every now and then, though, the show delivers. Especially poignant is "I Want to Know," a song for the interior voice of Young Josh as his older alter ego is being introduced to sex. And, as the tale moves into the home stretch (and, not-so-coincidentally, away from the office scenes), the story begins to accumulate emotional power, bringing the hoped-for lump-in-the-throat ending.

The most consistent pleasures of the evening were offered by David Shire's energetic and tuneful music and the performances by Daniel Jenkins and Patrick Levis as older and younger Josh, Barbara Walsh as his mother and Brett Tabisel as his smart-ass best friend.

State Fair also came to Broadway via Hollywood. Twice filmed with Rodgers and Hammerstein songs, this tale of an Iowa family's mild adventures escorting Father's boar and Mother's mincemeat to statewide competitions, and the flirtations their son and daughter have with more "sophisticated" types, isn't long on story. The score, some of it culled from the films and others from other Rodgers and Hammerstein projects (including some cut-outs), doesn't represent the team at its strongest, although "It Might As Well Be Spring" (for which they won an Oscar for best song) is a classic. The strongest moments in the show belonged to Scott Wise as a wise-cracking reporter, pushing his hat forward and dancing with an athletic grace that recalled the late Gene Kelly. I don't think the show deserved the nearly universally savage reviews it received; its homespun qualities brought heartfelt cheers from the audience surrounding me. I might not have felt like joining in, but I can't pretend that something wasn't connecting for most of those people.

The choices characters make are largely what define them. Early in *Floyd Collins,* the title character finds himself trapped in the Kentucky cave he has been exploring. Being unable to free himself, he has no option but to await what we know from history (the show is based on a true story) will be a sad fate. Lacking a choice, he certainly has the audience's sympathy, but he is not in a position to drive the show dramatically.

Billy Wilder, Lesser Samuels and Walter Newman engaged similar material in their script for Wilder's acerbic film, *Ace in the Hole.* Their solution was to focus on an unscrupulous reporter covering the story of the trapped victim. (In order to prolong the story and the notoriety it is bringing him, the reporter uses his influence to prolong the rescue operation, and, in so doing, dooms the victim and himself.) I'm not suggesting that collaborators Tina Landau and Adam Guettel should have adapted the Wilder film (though they could have done worse; Wilder scripts have been turned into the musicals *Promises, Promises, Sugar, Sunset Boulevard* and *Silk Stockings*), but I wish they had found *some* character to drive the action. Their failure to do so is reflected in the fact that an unusually large percentage of the lyrics are written in the past tense.

Though *Floyd Collins* is dramatically unfulfilling, it is an occasion for celebration nonetheless. Adam Guettel is the real thing—a musical theater composer of enormous talent (which may be genetic—his grandfather was Richard Rodgers and his mother is Mary Rodgers Guettel). A passage early in the score in which Floyd yodels in counterpoint with his echo is wonderfully inventive. (Musical yodeling runs in the family, too. Remember "The Lonely Goatherd"?) Guettel's score was beautifully served by orchestrator Bruce Coughlin, who wrote intricate and sophisticated arrangements in an American folk vein for a small ensemble featuring a fiddle, guitar, harmonica, percussion and keyboard. The production also benefitted from the tour de force lighting design of Scott Zielinski. *Floyd Collins* did not succeed, but it is a work that promises much for the future.

Bring in 'da Noise Bring in 'da Funk is a theatrical essay on the relationship between history and art that is rousing and thoughtful rather than preachy and self-important. Director George C. Wolfe and choreographer-star Savion Glover collaborated seamlessly to show how the roots and evolution of tap mirror much of the black experience in America. From section to section, the focus shifts. Sometimes the view is general—describing, for instance, black flight from the South to cities such as Chicago and the influence of urban rhythms on what had begun as a rural art. Sometimes the view is specific—such as Glover's dazzling extended solo in which his search for his own style serves as a metaphor for a search for identity. The sequences are augmented by a series of impressionistic poems/lyrics by Reg E. Gaines. Downtown, Gaines himself was less than effective performing this material. When the show moved to a well-deserved run on Broadway, Jeffrey Wright, a Tony-winner for his work in *Angels in America,* took over, bringing polished performance skills to the frequently sparkling words.

In addition to Wright, Glover was surrounded by an extraordinary company of performers—dancers, musicians and singer Ann Duquesnay (whose versatility could teach Caryl Churchill's shapeshifter a thing or two). If Wolfe has shown a weakness in the past as a director, it has been an over-dependence on flashy scenic elements. In this production, however, the sets by Riccardo Hernandez, lighting by Jules Fisher and Peggy Eisenhauer, projections by Batwin + Robin and costuming by Paul Tazewell enhanced rather than gilded the lily. *Bring in 'da Noise Bring in 'da Funk* was the season's peak accomplishment on the New York musical stage.

The similarly-titled *Jam on the Groove* didn't have the socio-political aspirations of *'da Noise,* but its program of hip-hop dancing served up a series of jaw-dropping combinations only the terminally jaded could fail to cheer.

Dance was also the central element in *Chronicle of a Death Foretold,* Graciela Daniele's attempt to stage Gabriel Garcia Marquez's novel. Set in a small Latin American town, the story tells of a young man who is marked for death when a young woman claims that he has dishonored her. No secret is made of her two brothers' vow of revenge, but somehow the young man never finds out from anybody in the community about the danger he is in, despite the fact nobody (including the brothers) really wants him to die. The tale means to illuminate the degree to which the townspeople are imprisoned by their rigid machismo ethic. But the show never makes it clear whether the woman's accusation is true; so, when she finally meets what was staged as a fairy-tale-like happy ending, we haven't sufficient information to know what to feel about her happiness. In addition, the piece lacks narrative coherence; characters are hard to keep straight, the scrambled chronology makes it difficult to figure out who did what when.

Despite the frustration I felt in watching this confusion, I was riveted by the performance I saw. The sets by Christopher Barreca, the costumes by Toni-Leslie James and the lighting of Jules Fisher and Beverly Emmons combined to make a world of nearly hypnotic vividness and intensity. Daniele's choreography was muscular and dramatic and supported by a throbbing and melodic score by Bob Telson. This is the latest of Daniele's experiments in dance-dominated theater pieces. She has missed more often than she has hit, but I never come away from one of her pieces without learning something new that the stage can do.

Revues focussing on the accomplishments of single writers—particularly single writers whose careers were not devoted to writing material designed to be performed in a dramatic context—tend to wear out their welcome with me. Such was the case with *Swinging on a Star,* an evening of numbers with lyrics by Johnny Burke. Burke certainly contributed the words to a large number of standards, and a lot of the songs brought smiles of recognition, but they were not designed to serve theatrical purposes. Michael Leeds, the show's director and writer, and choreographer Kathleen Marshall attempted to provide scenarios to support the songs, but mostly the results felt strained. The talented cast worked cheerfully and with great energy, but the effect was of an overlong TV special.

BIG—Daniel Jenkins and John Cypher (*in center*) and company in the John Weidman-David Shire-Richard Maltby Jr. musical based on the 1988 motion picture

Some years back, Gerard Alessandrini opened a genuinely clever little show mocking aspects of the theater called *Forbidden Broadway.* It became something of a cottage industry, spawning a series of subsequent editions and playing in many venues miles from the scene it satirized. This season, Alessandrini introduced *Forbidden Hollywood,* his assault on the movie world. The results, alas, fell considerably short of the earlier show. Though there were some amusing moments (Sharon Stone singing of her habit of doffing clothes in films to the theme song of TV's *Rawhide,* and Richard and Pat Nixon singing their version of *Gigi*'s "I Remember it Well"), too many of the songs made easy fun of targets not worth the gunpowder or bravely satirized the dead and infirm. What, for instance, was the satiric point of the sequence in which Marlene Dietrich sang "Falling Apart Again" as her arm fell off? The cast outshone its material, coming up with a series of well-observed impersonations of celebrities past and present, with the help of a parade of witty costumes by Alvin Colt.

Cowgirls is something between a revue and a musical. Such plot as there is hangs on the idea that a classical string trio has been booked accidentally into a country music venue. The venue will fold unless the trio succeeds in transforming itself into a credible country band. I was more impressed by the charm and versatility of the all-female cast of six (most of whom could play a variety of instruments as well as sing, move and act) than I was by the material. Other talented performers were shown to less advantage in *Zombie Prom,* a blatant and unrewarding attempt to put *Grease* and *Little Shop of Horrors* into a mixmaster.

Manhattan's 57th Street has recently seen the opening of a series of theme restaurants—eating establishments such as Planet Hollywood where the attraction is less the quality of the entrees than the opportunity to sit in close proximity to a prop Sylvester Stallone. With so many restaurants indulging in the theatrical, it's not surprising that someone would think of making theater more, uh, restaurantical? The result was *Pomp Duck and Circumstance,* a revue played under a red tent made up of circus acts and comedy often only inches away from patrons eating a gourmet meal. (I make no claim to being a food critic, but I would have happily indulged in seconds had they been available.)

The show itself featured elegantly staged feats of balance, timing and nerve by performers who wouldn't be out of place in the Cirque du Soleil alternating with slapstick intervals centering on a cast of cartoony figures—a temperamental chef, an obnoxious food critic, an amply endowed and underdressed chanteuse, a head waiter better suited to the military, etc. The mix was beguiling, and I expect it will make lots of people happy when it moves to its scheduled home in Las Vegas.

Even before it opened, the rock musical *Rent* was the stuff of theatrical legend. The night after its dress rehearsal, composer-librettist Jonathan Larson died of an aortic aneurysm at age 35. Since *Rent*'s subject is young talent facing early death, audiences couldn't help watching the show with the awareness of irony at cruel work. The irony was underscored by the show winning the 1996 Pulitzer Prize for drama (as well as the Critics and Tony Awards).

As much as I admire elements of *Rent* (and as much respect as I have for members of the jury), I cannot agree that it merited the Pulitzer over *A Fair Country, Seven Guitars, Master Class* and *New England.* An update of *La Boheme,* instead of Parisian garrets *Rent* is set in the East Village of the Nineties. Mimi in *Boheme* is a shy, tubercular seamstress, poor but with a pure soul. In Larson's version, Mimi dances in an S&M bar, snorts coke and seems not to much care which man is her sexual partner of a given evening. Her only claims to our sympathy are that she looks hot in skin-tight pants, and she's doomed to die of AIDS. Indeed, she and the show's two male leads (one of whom is also HIV positive) are not particularly engaging characters—almost constantly angry and depressed with a plentitude of easy disdain for the so-called normal world. (In contrast to the heterosexual characters, the show's gays are all good-hearted and wise.)

The strongest aspect of the show is its music, a river of melody and rhythm that justifiably reminds many of Galt MacDermot's work in *Hair.* But *Rent* resembles *Hair* in its weaknesses, too. In both, the lyrics are wildly erratic, sometimes achieving poetry, sometimes settling for little more than rhymed lists. By the time it reached Broadway, *Hair*'s book made little narrative sense; though *Rent* makes frequent reference to the material from which it was drawn, much of its book is made up of scenes that serve little dramatic purpose.

But criticizing *Rent* is almost as beside the point as was criticizing *Hair*. *Hair* was an irrefutable fact, one of the defining moments of the theatrical culture of the Sixties. Despite its flaws, *Rent* is one of the defining moments of the Nineties. Performed with fervor by a gifted cast of newcomers, it speaks to the fear and the defiance of its generation with a directness and energy that no other musical of recent memory approaches.

Here's where we list the *Best Plays* choices for the musical, revue and special-attraction bests of 1995–96.

MUSICALS, REVUES AND SPECIAL ATTRACTIONS

BEST MUSICAL: *Bring in 'da Noise Bring in 'da Funk*

BEST MUSIC: Adam Guettel for *Floyd Collins*; Jonathan Larson for *Rent*

BEST STRUCTURE AND TEXT: Reg E. Gaines, Savion Glover and George C. Wolfe for *Bring in 'da Noise Bring in 'da Funk*

BEST REVIVAL: *The King and I* by Richard Rodgers and Oscar Hammerstein II

BEST ACTOR IN A PRIMARY ROLE: Lou Diamond Phillips as The King of Siam in *The King and I*

BEST ACTRESS IN A PRIMARY ROLE: Julie Andrews as Victoria Grant in *Victor/Victoria*; Donna Murphy as Anna Leonowens in *The King and I*

BEST ACTOR IN A SECONDARY ROLE: Mark Linn-Baker as Hysterium in *A Funny Thing Happened on the Way to the Forum*; Tony Roberts as Carroll Todd in *Victor/Victoria*

BEST ACTRESS IN A SECONDARY ROLE: Veanne Cox as Amy in *Company*; Ann Duquesnay in *Bring in 'da Noise Bring in 'da Funk*

BEST DIRECTOR: Christopher Renshaw for *The King and I*; George C. Wolfe for *Bring in 'da Noise Bring in 'da Funk*

BEST CHOREOGRAPHY: Savion Glover for *Bring in 'da Noise Bring in 'da Funk*

BEST ORCHESTRATION: Bruce Coughlin for *Floyd Collins*

BEST SCENERY: Riccardo Hernandez for *Bring in 'da Noise Bring in 'da Funk*; Brian Thomson for *The King and I*

BEST LIGHTING: Jules Fisher and Beverly Emmons for *Chronicle of a Death Foretold*; Jules Fisher and Peggy Eisenhauer for *Bring in da Noise Bring in da Funk*; Nigel Levings for *The King and I*; Scott Zielinski for *Floyd Collins*

BEST COSTUMES: Roger Kirk for *The King and I*; Paul Tazewell for *Bring in da Noise Bring in da Funk*

SPECIAL CITATION: Ensemble of *Bring in 'da Noise Bring in 'da Funk*

A LINE AROUND THE BLOCK—Marga
Gomez, author and star of her solo show at the
Joseph Papp Public Theater

Solo Performances and Special Attractions

At a luncheon for the American Theater Critics Association, Rob Becker, the
talented monologist starring in *Defending the Caveman,* commented that he and his
fellow solo performers represent a conservative movement in the theater. As he
understood it, for years actors played in one until some Greek guy came up with
the innovation of having a couple of characters talk to each other onstage.

Becker phrased these comments jokingly, but there is more than a little truth to
what he said. Belt-tightening triggers conservative impulses, and in a year when
economic pressures put new notches into the belt, the result was a constant stream
of solo performances on all levels of production.

Many of these were autobiographical in nature. *The Amazing Metrano,* starring
Art Metrano in a piece fashioned by him and co-author Cynthia Lee, told of how a
fall from a ladder left him fighting paralysis. Mixing amiably cornball jokes with the

confessional, Metrano traced the course not only of his physical healing but the parallel healing of what he described as having been a life in shaky shape. Metrano's style was to invoke the shtick of the stand-up comic in order to approach his more serious matter. In contrast, Colin Martin, in his *Virgins and Other Myths* offered OOB, drew on all of his skills as a conservatory-trained actor to tell the harrowing story of his journey from being a youngster confronting his gayness through teenage exploration and confusion, sexual addiction and hustling to what he represents as being a healthier life today.

The Public Theater featured two gifted women in solo shows in repertory. Marga Gomez lovingly told the story of her father, comic Willy Chevalier, in *A Line Around the Block*. In the process she made vivid the alternate world of Spanish-speaking variety that flourished in New York, a world invisible to the Anglos. At the piece's end, Gomez portrayed her father in several minutes drawn from his act, a passage that was both a tribute to his raffish style and a display of his child's considerable gifts. Andrea Martin's *Nude Nude Totally Nude* featured many of the characters Martin developed as a performer at Toronto's Second City and on television in the *SCTV* series. Interwoven with these old friends were musings on the challenges she faces as a single, middle-aged mother trying to make sense out of her show business career and her newly-explored Armenian roots. Similar to Gomez's show, the high point of Martin's presentation was the invocation of a parent, a stunningly precise portrait of her mother that speaks volumes of Martin's largely untapped abilities as a dramatic actress.

The Public didn't have a monopoly on shows dealing with women and show business. Playwrights Horizons presented *The Springhill Singing Disaster* featuring Karen Traut in the chronicle of how her childhood obsession with the folk music movement led her to a performing career. Traut struck comic gold dealing with her adolescent attempts at seriousness, dressing in somber black and singing songs of the struggle of working folk while growing up comfortable and indulged in a suburb of Boston.

Patti LuPone returned to Broadway with yet another show business chronicle. With the assistance of a backup chorus, she plowed through a high-energy set of songs from shows with which she has been associated—*Evita, The Robber Bridegroom, Les Misérables* and, of course, *Sunset Boulevard,* giving a taste of the Norma Desmond New York never got to see. In *Buttons on Broadway,* Red Buttons floated through a couple of hours of wispy comic material and nostalgic anecdotes almost entirely on undeniable charm. Charm was also a big part of Avi Hoffman's engaging ramble through song and story called *Too Jewish. Danny Gans on Broadway* featured a Las Vegas-style entertainer whose genuine talent for impressions doesn't seem to extend to choosing decent material to support them. Tovah Feldshuh and Jackie Mason also were well received in their solo efforts.

A few performers chose to go solo playing someone other than themselves. Mary Louise Wilson brought editor-curator Diana Vreeland to life in *Full Gallop,* which she co-authored with Mark Hampton. Wilson tossed off epigrams about fashion, high society and celebrity with great verve and spirit. The show was warmly received by the bulk of the critics.

And, finally, three solo shows featured three accounts of men who were on the losing end of the bottle. *Moscow Stations,* based on a semi-autobiographic novel by the late Venedikt Yerofeev, featured Tom Courtenay as a Russian whose alcoholism is intended to echo the general despair of contemporary Russia. Courtenay is always worth watching, but two hours of bemused philosophical inebriation was one hour too many. Len Cariou, undertaking Ernest Hemingway in *Papa,* regaled us with boastful tales while he put away drink after drink. Working from a script by John deGroot, Cariou didn't shy away from revealing the author's darker angels. As he got drunker, the pain and fear that would ultimately drive Hemingway to suicide were brought into sharp focus. As for Nicol Williamson, his John Barrymore in *Jack* (which he co-authored with director Leslie Megahey) had little to do with Barrymore's style or way with language, but the eccentric energy he brought to the stage made for a riveting performance. How I would like to see him take on Walter Burns in *The Front Page!*

Cited by *Best Plays* among the year's best performances are *(left)* Elaine Stritch as Claire and Rosemary Harris as Agnes and *(above)* George Grizzard as Tobias (also a Tony winner) in the revival of Edward Albee's play

Revivals

I didn't see the first production of James Lapine's *Twelve Dreams* at the Public Theater, so I cannot compare it to the version Lapine mounted this season at Lincoln Center. The story tells of a young girl named Emma who gives her father (an analyst) a book she has made describing 12 of her dreams—dreams apparently foretelling her death. The piece was elegantly designed, filled with arresting imagery and sustaining a mysterious and unsettling mood, but I had no idea what I was supposed to take away from it. Oh, I read the material relating the play to Jungian theory with interest, but I was left with annoying questions on a basic story level: Why does Emma die? Because she dreams the dreams? Or does she dream the dreams because, on some level, she knows she's going to die? Which brings back the question of what is killing her. (I'm tempted to believe that she dies of atmosphere.)

As for the dreams themselves, they are enacted onstage, but if there hadn't been a guide to them printed in the program, I would have had no idea what these enactments represented. I'm always leery of plays that require information not presented onstage in order to be understood.

So, by most conventional criteria, *Twelve Dreams* was unsatisfying. And yet, there were frequent flashes of great beauty. *Crazy for You* star Harry Groener showed new dimensions of his talent as the sober and repressed father, and Donna Murphy offered another of her vivid performances as a beautiful and not entirely sympathetic patient with a secret. As much as I was confused by it, I felt richer for having seen it.

It's easy to see why Craig Lucas's *Blue Window* has been a favorite of actors in scene study classes. It has juicy monologues and nicely-observed scenes dense with subtext, and it's steeped in understated pathos. The action is in three stages—the preparations for a party, the party itself and the party's aftermath. These stages offer the opportunity to watch an ensemble of youngish people, mostly connected with the arts, wearing both their private and party faces. Written early in Lucas's career, this script shows the promise he would later fulfill with *Prelude to a Kiss* and the original version of the musical *Three Postcards.* If it feels more like a collection of character sketches given a context than a play, it still offered the opportunity to watch a group of gifted actors do subtle and affecting work under the direction of Joe Montello. I was particularly taken by Allison Janney as Boo, the lesbian family therapist who finds herself unable to stop talking.

Tennessee Williams was represented by two Broadway productions this season. The first, *Garden District* at the Circle in the Square Uptown, was a program of two one-act plays set in New Orleans, *Something Unspoken* and *Suddenly Last Summer.* The former is a slender two-hander between a grande dame and her assistant in which the unspoken something (the older lady's carnal interest in the younger) is hinted at without much development. Directed by Theodore Mann, even with the considerable talents of Myra Carter and Pamela Payton-Wright it couldn't command much interest. Under Harold Scott's direction, *Suddenly Last Summer* featured another pair of actresses, Elizabeth Ashley as Mrs. Venable and Jordan Baker as Catherine Holly, the young lady she hopes to have lobotomized so as to keep the world at large from learning the secrets of her would-be poet son Sebastian and the grisly way he met his death. I have never been able to quite take this play seriously. I picture Williams writing it with chuckles of glee at the sensation his story of cannibalism would stir. Indeed, the piece bubbles with hysteria. (The overripe atmosphere is underlined by his decision to set the action in a heated indoor garden.) The bill was not generally received well by the press, but the audience I saw it with was vocal in its enthusiasm for the way Baker handled the revelation of Catharine's tale.

The image of a travelling poet platonically accompanied by a woman recurs in Williams's other revived play, the superior *The Night of the Iguana* at the Roundabout. In this case, the poet is the elderly Nonno accompanied by his spinster granddaughter, Hannah. On the night in question, they find themselves in a shabby Mexican resort hotel run by lusty Maxine. Maxine's husband has died recently, and she's hoping to have his place in her bed taken by Shannon, a bedraggled tour guide and lapsed minister who has chosen this evening to stop in and flirt with having a break-down. Robert Falls (who last season staged an admirable *The Rose Tattoo* at Circle in the Square) directed Cherry Jones, William Petersen and Marsha Mason as Hannah, Shannon and Maxine in three nicely-balanced performances. Jones managed to make achingly human what may be the most purely good character in modern American theater. (Incidentally, correspondence between Williams and Katharine Hepburn made public this season reveals that the dramatist wrote the part for and to some degree based it on Hepburn, who had recently had an unhappy experience playing Mrs. Venable in the film version of *Suddenly Last Summer.* Unwilling to sign a contract to play the show on Broadway for more than six months, she saw the role she loved go to Margaret Leighton.) In contrast to Richard Burton's famous film portrayal of Shannon as a tortured Olympian, Petersen played him as someone who is still subject to and baffled by adolescent impulses; the choice worked well. Marsha Mason completed the trio with a Maxine whose good-hearted bawdiness did much to dispel the cute-as-a-button image she was plagued with in so many movie roles. (Point of trivia: some years back in Los Angeles, Mason excelled in the title role in *The Heiress,* the same role in which Cherry Jones won a Tony last season.) To sum up: this was the Roundabout doing what the Roundabout does best—offering a solid revival of an American classic.

During the Fifties, Williams and his friend William Inge were two of the most visible and popular American playwrights. They drew on the same acting and directing pool and dealt with many of the same issues. Williams, a Southerner, specialized in lush verbal arias. Inge, a product of the Midwest, reflected that region's characteristic tendency toward terseness and understatement. The Roundabout served Inge well a couple of seasons ago with *Picnic.* This year, the Circle in the Square's co-artistic director, Josephine Abady, undertook *Bus Stop* with less success.

Part of the problem was that *Bus Stop* has aged less gracefully than *Picnic.* Inge clearly meant his audience to have some sympathy for the alcoholic, poetry-spouting Dr. Lyman (more poetry!) and his habit of laying hands on underage women. With our increased awareness of sexual misconduct by teachers and priests and other authority figures entrusted with the keeping of youth, today we're less likely to view such behavior as a weakness to be forgiven so easily. (Williams's work, too, is filled with such figures—Shannon gets in trouble with a teenage charge in the tour he's leading, and Blanche has a habit of bedding her students.) Inge gave the eager cowboy Bo the overgrown adolescence characteristic of so many of Williams's men (Shannon, Stanley, Brick, Big Daddy, Mangiacavallo, the Gentleman Caller), but without the complexity his colleague was able to muster. Where Inge excelled was in his more mature supporting characters, and it's no surprise that Larry Pine and Kelly Bishop, as an aging cowboy and waitress, were the most interesting figures on the stage. Billy Crudup as Bo and Mary-Louise Parker as Cherie, the reluctant and charmingly dim object of his attentions, did well as Inge's not very credible youngsters.

Circle in the Square's other revival of an American play, David Warren's staging of Philip Barry's *Holiday,* seemed to be out of tune with its audience. Even played by the gifted Laura Linney, it was hard to be sympathetic with the character of Linda Seton who, blessed by wealth, spends most of her time making cracks about the hollowness of other people's lives without doing much constructive herself.

Holiday is set in 1928, only three years after the trial that was the basis of Jerome Lawrence and Robert E. Lee's play *Inherit the Wind.* In 1925, a Tennessee school-teacher named John Scopes was tried for violating that state's law against teaching the theory of evolution in the public schools. Clarence Darrow was among the lawyers who joined the defense team, and former presidential candidate and populist William Jennings Bryan seized on the opportunity to return to the public eye as a sort of guest star for the prosecution. In their script, Lawrence and Lee virtually announced that they were granting themselves a license to reshape and fictionalize a bit by renaming Scopes, Darrow and Bryan; here they are called Bertram Cates, Henry Drummond and Matthew Harrison Brady. The dramatists made Cates a pariah in the town; Scopes had in fact been recruited by liberal elements in his community to teach evolution precisely *to* trigger a test case. They also gave Cates a girl friend (conveniently the daughter of the local fire-breathing minister), timed Brady's death more elegantly than history timed Bryan's, and made Drummond the sole defense lawyer (in fact, Darrow was teamed with another famous attorney, Dudley Field Malone). Borrowing from Darrow's famous tactic of putting Bryan on the stand to testify on religion, in *Inherit the Wind,* Drummond, too, puts Brady on the stand to reveal the logical contradictions and cracks in fundamentalist beliefs. Lawrence and Lee rewrote the encounter to make Brady's humiliation more pronounced than it was in real life, but then (similar to McNally) they were after drama, not journalism.

John Tillinger didn't succumb to the temptation to gussie up the material with ostentatious directorial flourishes. His staging was a meat-and-potatoes accounting of a play that still has much to say. (While the cast was rehearsing, the New York *Times* ran a chilling article on fundamentalists' current campaign against so-called secular humanism in the nation's schools.) The supporting cast was solid, with Anthony Heald doing the expected fine work as a cynical, blank-verse-reciting Hornbeck (read H.L. Menken) and Tom Aldredge whipping up a storm as a hellfire preacher. I would have preferred more edge from Charles Durning as Brady, but his final scene, in which the old politician realizes his supporters have turned away from him, was very affecting.

Of course, the centerpiece of any production of this play has to be Drummond, and the Drummond here was George C. Scott. Scott's health was palpably rocky, but rather than use his infirmity as an excuse for laziness, he charted a remarkably rigorous performance in defiance of it. His Drummond was not the easy-going font of avuncular wisdom that others have played, but a man who was in a constant battle not only with the attitudes that surrounded him but with his own impulses to react with impatience and sarcasm. Scott's Drummond was an ironist, laughing at jokes he never bothered to tell because he doubted that anybody within the sound of his voice would understand them. When, at the end, he confronted Hornbeck's cynicism, it was as if he were facing down his own dark angels. It was a valiant performance by a master actor who refused to allow the betrayals of his body to keep him from doing first-rate work. (The other National Actors Theater production this season was a bland *School for Scandal* somewhat redeemed by Simon Jones's scoundrel.)

Sam Shepard reportedly rewrote a substantial amount of his Pulitzer Prize-winning play *Buried Child* for its Broadway revival by the Steppenwolf Theater Company. This impressed the Tony Awards people sufficiently to nominate it, not in the revival category, but as a new play. Shepard tells of a young man named Vince who brings his girl friend for a visit to his family's farm in central Illinois in 1978. The family is a pretty appalling group. Seated on a ratty sofa in front of a flickering TV, Vince's grandfather Dodge flails around in an alcoholic stupor while Dodge's wife, Halie, is setting her sights on a local minister. One of their children, Bradley, accidentally cut one of his own legs off some years before. A bubbling cauldron of violence, he can only be kept in check by the confiscation of his prosthesis. And Vince's father, Tilden, seems to be in a perpetual daze as he hauls in the sudden and surprising vegetation from what for years has been a blighted garden.

Much is implied of the relationship between the vegetation and the buried child of the title—a baby to which Halie gave birth and whom, it is revealed, Dodge killed. (One critic claimed that the child was the product of an incestuous encounter between Tilden and his mother. If so, this bit of information got past both me and my companion during the performance.) But Shepard offers no suggestion as to why, after all these barren years, the garden has started to flourish at this particular time. I believe that the action of a play has to happen now because it could not happen before or later. But in *Buried Child,* much of what happens seems to be occurring now because the curtain is up.

If I have reservations about the overall architecture of *Buried Child,* I still admire much of it, particularly the bleakly funny dialogue between Dodge and the offstage Halie at the top of the play and the enormous fun Shepard has with the unconventional use of props. (Tilden burying his sleeping father under a blanket of corn husks was one of the most striking images of the season.) Much of the production, too, was admirable, from the outsized house designed by Robert Brill to the wonderfully creepy lighting by Kevin Rigdon. James Gammon and Lois Smith were exuberantly grotesque as Dodge and Halie, and Terry Kinney was moving as an anguished Tilden. Though at times I feared for the strain on much of the company's vocal chords, the staging by Gary Sinise was a feast of bravura gestures and bleak slapstick.

When *A Delicate Balance* won the 1966 Pulitzer Prize for drama, it was widely assumed that the honor was awarded as an apology by the administrators to Edward Albee for refusing to cite *Who's Afraid of Virginia Woolf?* a few years before. Viewed today, the play towers above several of the intervening Pulitzer winners.

In their late middle age, Agnes and Tobias have a passionless marriage and share their home with Agnes's alcoholic sister Claire. The three maintain the delicacy of their balance with the ritual of the extended cocktail hour and sporadic bursts of literate rancor and gamesmanship. This unquiet equilibrium is disturbed by two events—the return to the house of their daughter in the wake of the latest in a series of failed marriages, and the arrival of their best friends, Harry and Edna, who announce that they are moving in permanently to seek refuge from the unnamed terror that suddenly seized them in their own home. These turns of events set into motion a dramatic debate on the competing bonds and obligations of family and friends. Agnes and Tobias are leading lives in which the search for love has given way to responsibilities dictated by the roles in which they have been cast. Albee seems to be expressing his grudging admiration for those who take their unwanted duties seriously, keeping the parade going in an orderly manner in spite of their suspicion that it is heading for a void.

Years after she sang of "the dinosaurs surviving the crunch" in the original production of *Company,* Elaine Stritch was again playing such a dinosaur in *A Delicate Balance,* but here with a control and specificity that took the breath away. (Of course, she was aided by the fact that onstage an alcoholic truth-teller usually has license to say the outrageous, and Albee is a master at writing the outrageous.) George Grizzard was deceptively easygoing as Tobias but frightening in his intensity and vulnerability when euphemisms failed, and Rosemary Harris was an exemplary and uncompromising Agnes. This was one of the most compelling offerings of the season.

Frank Langella gave the tour de force performance he intended in the Roundabout production of Strindberg's *The Father,* but it was as if he used up all of the oxygen on the stage. The rest of the cast, most of whom have distinguished themselves in other productions, got little chance to make much of an impression, so what was supposed to be a battle to the death played as if a giant were being overwhelmed by fleas. (Our historian Thomas T. Foose provides this footnote to the play itself: "The first Strindberg play in English in New York was *The Father.* It opened April 9, 1912 at the Berkeley Lyceum and ran 31 performances. Warner Oland—the same actor who some years later played both Fu Manchu and Charlie Chan—wrote the English adaptation for this 1912 staging and played the Captain.")

The Roundabout also presented P.G. Wodehouse's adaptation of Molnar's *The Play's the Thing* under the direction of Gloria Muzio. The production was pretty badly worked over by the daily press, but, by the time I caught up with it a few weeks into the run, it was a trim and efficient showcase for the comic talents of Peter Frechette, Paul Benedict, J. Smith-Cameron and Keith Reddin.

The punning title *Tartuffe: Born Again* refers not only to the fact that Fredya Thomas's script is an adaptation of the Molière play but also to the title character being played as a contemporary Southern evangelist on a cable TV station. Thomas follows Molière's structure closely but tosses in a stream of references to current political figures and issues. (At the end, Orgon and family aren't saved by intervention from the king but by a benevolent FBI agent.) The conceit of the updating is obvious and reductive, but enough Molière is still there that, with the aid of a strong cast under the direction of David Saint, the evening proved to be the best of Circle in the Square's offerings this season. John Glover revelled in the demagogic aspects of Tartuffe, and Haviland Morris, Alison Fraser, Kevin Dewey, Jane Krakowski and

Richard Bekins each had delicious comic turns as members of the household trying to free David Schramm's sweetly credulous Orgon from the parasite's spell.

How instructive it was to see Peter Hall's revival of Oscar Wilde's *An Ideal Husband* within weeks of Emily Mann's splendid revival (at the McCarter Theater) of Henrik Ibsen's *A Doll's House.* Both deal with reputations at risk because of the threatened revelation of documents detailing past indiscretions. And both are about marriages in which the parties have idealized each other to such a degree that disillusion is inevitable. The differences between the two plays are as telling as the similarities. Once she has seen her husband fall from his pedestal and she has her epiphany about the real nature of her marriage, Ibsen's Nora packs her bags and is out the door. (I happen to believe that her responsibility not to damage her children by so abruptly abandoning them should have counted for more. But that would have made for less vivid theater.) In *An Ideal Husband,* Wilde seems to be saying that the inevitable by-product of a too-rigid moral code is hypocrisy. Principles are important, but, when dealing with all-too-fallible human beings, the ability to compromise and forgive may make the difference between a successful life and lonely rectitude.

Peter Hall's production brought these themes to life, assisted in no small part by Carl Toms's immaculately conceived set designs which contrasted the idealized forms of paintings, sculpture and architecture with the flawed human beings they dwarfed. In a strong cast, Martin Shaw (fitted out with a pronounced paunch) attracted the most attention as Lord Goring. Wilde gave the bulk of the play's brightest lines to Goring, and Shaw and Hall have obviously decided to play him as Wilde's alter ego. This is fine for the wit, but, coming across gay (as Wilde was), it short circuits the passages concerning Goring's own romantic dealings. Though Goring is insistent about honesty between spouses, in this interpretation, when he courts and wins the hand of a young woman at the end of the play, one can't help believing that he is engaging in behavior as dishonest as anything he spent the rest of the play condemning. This has the disconcerting effect of suggesting that the figure who is supposed to represent the play's ethical compass is himself a hypocrite.

Declan Donnellan, who directed the admirable Cheek by Jowl staging of *As You Like It* at the Brooklyn Academy of Music last season, returned to the OOB phase of that venue, the New Wave Festival, with that company in a production of *The Duchess of Malfi.* There was no lack of Donnellan's characteristically bold staging choices, but he didn't tell the story clearly enough, so the effects were largely for naught. This season's Brooklyn Academy of Music mainstage schedule included visits of revival productions by Ingmar Bergman and the Comédie Française, the latter including Marivaux' *La Double Inconstance* (The Inconstant Lovers). Our Mr. Foose notes that "This was the first major production in New York of this play. Earlier offerings in 1980–81 by Meat and Potatoes and in 1984–85 by the Neighborhood Group are barely worth mention," adding that the Guthrie Theater in Minneapolis did it in 1987 and the McCarter Theater in Princeton in 1994, and it has been staged in England.

When you're committed to producing all of Shakespeare (as is the New York

INHERIT THE WIND—George C. Scott as Henry Drummond and Garret Dillahunt as Bertram Cates, lawyer and defendant, in the National Actors Theater revival of the play by Jerome Lawrence and Robert E. Lee

Shakespeare Festival's Marathon), you end up having to cope with some problematic works. *Troilus and Cressida* is among the dramatist's most challenging. The play rambles back and forth between various figures on both sides of the Trojan War. Sometimes Shakespeare misplaces his title characters for so long that when they reappear you have to remind yourself that the play is supposed to be about them. A play this disorganized needs a concept that imposes some order for it to have a hope of coherence. Instead, director Mark Wing-Davey made the play even less coherent with a dizzying mixture of design and performance styles, tossing out imagery from the Comédie Française to Vietnam. Despite the muddle, Stephen Spinella managed to make a strong impression as Pandarus, but the gifted Elizabeth Marvel as Cressida seemed to be dazed by the chaos around her.

Marvel did much better later in the season subtly charting the deterioration of Regan in Adrian Hall's production of *King Lear*. F. Murray Abraham, in the title role, had a moving encounter with Thomas Hill's Gloucester in a late scene, but the production was more a compendium of directorial impulses than a unified whole. (One sequence, in which Lear hallucinated Goneril and Regan drifting around wearing nothing but transparent shifts, was a particular head-scratcher.)

The best Shakespeare offered by the Festival this season, *The Tempest* represented the Shakespearean directing debut of its artistic director George C. Wolfe. Confession: I've never much cared for this play. Prospero announces his objective to seek, through magic, restitution for the injuries done him, and he does so without much hindrance. (Caliban's conspiracy with the clowns to overthrow the master he loathes never poses a serious threat.) That this is believed to be Shakespeare's last composition lends the play biographical interest (it is commonly assumed that Prospero putting down his magic staff was Shakespeare's way of commenting on his retirement), but I find it lacking in dramatic tension. Wisely, Patrick Stewart chose to play Prospero's chief conflict as being not with any other character on the stage but within himself, having to cope with the warring drives of revenge and reconciliation. Stewart had the power to make the struggle riveting, and he shared the stage with the engagingly spunky Miranda of Carrie Preston. Enhanced by music and imagery from Mardi Gras, *The Tempest* was a big party and moved successfully to a second life on Broadway.

Broadway's other Shakespeare was Adrian Noble's rambunctious *A Midsummer Night's Dream*, courtesy of the Royal Shakespeare Company. In collaboration with set designer Anthony Ward and lighting designer Chris Parry, Noble created a forest out of pulsing golden light bulbs suspended from cables, large umbrellas that brought principals in from the flies, and doors that appeared according to their own whims. Among a strong company, I particularly enjoyed Desmond Barrit as Bottom (he surely will play Falstaff soon), Emily Raymond aquiver with confusion and sincerity as Helena, and Alex Jennings, who adroitly managed to play both Theseus and Oberon with a constantly shifting balance of autocracy and sensitivity.

The most interesting aspect of *I Do! I Do!* is archeological. Based on Jan de Hartog's play *The Fourposter,* this musical with words by Tom Jones and music by Harvey Schmidt is a chronicle of five decades of a marriage that begins in 1898. Given the jaundiced view so many contemporary pieces have about marriage, there is something refreshing about one that views it as a grand, fulfilling, life-long adventure. Unfortunately, the writing is extremely generic and unspecific, and the issues that are raised are dispatched with cuteness rather than rigor. The evening's chief appeal was the chance to share the company of stars Karen Ziemba (who was a memorable Lizzie in the New York City Opera's production of Schmidt and Jones's much better musical, *110 in the Shade*) and David Garrison. I can only hope that they will soon be offered more interesting and challenging assignments. *I Do! I Do!* was originally produced on Broadway in the Sixties by David Merrick, directed by Gower Champion. Another Merrick-Champion success from those years, *Hello, Dolly!,* fared better in a revival featuring the original Dolly, Carol Channing. Both show and star were warmly welcomed. The production, which had toured around the country, subsequently left for international dates.

Stephen Sondheim saw two of his early efforts as composer-lyricist offered in new productions. Director Jerry Zaks and star Nathan Lane, who teamed up for the memorable revival of *Guys and Dolls* some seasons ago, reunited for *A Funny Thing Happened on the Way to the Forum,* reaffirming the show's claim to being among the funniest of musicals. Lane's performance as Pseudolus, the slave who will go to almost any length to achieve freedom, was a conscientious compendium of classic shtick. My hunch was that, as the show settled into a long run, Lane, one of our most gifted clowns, as well as being an accomplished actor, would find opportunities to break out and play a bit more with the material than he did on the night I saw him. Lewis J. Stadlen (who himself would make a fine Pseudolus) was a delightfully randy dirty old man, and Ernie Sabella was engagingly reprehensible as the pimp next door. I was particularly taken with Mark Linn-Baker's Hysterium, his button eyes constantly alight with panic.

Sondheim's score for *Forum* contains gems such as the opening "Comedy Tonight" and "Everybody Ought to Have a Maid," but it was with *Company* that he established himself as the pre-eminent musical theater writer of his time. (His time has lasted many years; *Company* was originally produced in 1971, and Sondheim's most recent musical, 1994's *Passion,* displayed him still at the peak of his powers.) Scott Ellis's revival of *Company* (which, like *A Funny Thing,* featured new orchestrations by the master, Jonathan Tunick) offered the treat of revisiting a score featuring nothing *but* gems, many of the lyrics including phrases that have entered the language—"Sorry—Grateful," "The Ladies Who Lunch," etc.

The only disappointment? "Smart remarks do not a person make," comments one character. Though the structure of George Furth's book—part revue, part internal emotional inventory—is still impressive, too much of the script is made up of smart remarks that do not people make. Some of the characters seem to exist only for the situation in which they find themselves, e.g. the couple that decides to divorce but continues to live together. Given the thinness of some of the characters, it is fortunate that the production was cast with some of the most personable performers in New York, including Kate Burton, Diana Canova, Charlotte d'Amboise, John Hillner, Jane Krakowski, Timothy Landfield, La Chanze, Debra Monk, and Robert Westenberg (who have God knows how many Tony nominations and awards among them). Where the script was lacking, their charm, talent and energy made up the difference. The part of Amy, featuring the neurotic tour de force, "Getting Married Today," has always been the launching pad for a comedienne to take flight, and, frantic and vulnerable, Veanne Cox made the most of her opportunity. Boyd Gaines (who also has a couple of Tonys to his credit) opened the run as Bobby, the eternal bachelor about whom the show revolves; I saw his excellent standby James Clow.

The King and I was especially well served by the revival directed by Christopher Renshaw. Though the show features elements familiar from previous productions (nobody would dare put on "The Small House of Uncle Thomas" without the Jerome Robbins choreography), there was much new here. The scenery, lighting and costumes by, respectively, Brian Thomson, Nigel Levings and Roger Kirk overwhelmed the eye with exotic colors and shapes. Donna Murphy's Anna was as impressive as everyone expected it to be, especially striking in her tenacity and fire. As the other title character, Lou Diamond Phillips proved to be one of the happiest surprises of the season. With the possible exception of Stanley Kowalski and Brando, no part has been so identified with its interpreter as the King and Yul Brynner. Phillips tempered authority with insecurity, implying that his King had grown up used to so much power that he never had the opportunity to entirely mature. The boyishness of a nearly absolute monarch in contest with a woman whose only strength is her complete confidence in her rectitude made for a series of bracing confrontations and gave the show a resonance that had added irony for an audience that grew up with Vietnam. (Though Anna is English, there is little doubt that she was conceived as a character representing the same kind of liberal missionary fervor that fueled America's misguided adventures in southeast Asia.)

NEW RODGERS & HAMMERSTEIN MUSICAL?—A production number in this season's stage version of the famous R & H movie musical *State Fair*

Offstage

At the end of the season, the accountants of the League of American Theaters and Producers confirmed the general perception that this had been a strong season. According to their figures, the 1995–96 total for Broadway was $436,107,774, up 7.3 percent from $406,306,661 in 1994–95. The news from the road was better—$810 million, a 15.3 percent gain on the previous season's $694,577,296. This brought the combined Broadway and road box office to almost $1.24 billion, a 12.4 percent improvement on last year.

Part of this improvement was owing to the number of offerings. This season, the League counted 38 new Broadway productions, as opposed to last year's 29. There was also a modest but noticeable increase in the number of tickets bought. And yes, part of the rise came from some ticket prices creeping upwards. Our *Best Plays* count—slightly different in standards than the League—was 44 shows against 35 last season.

Still, there was a strong sense that the good news wasn't only economic. In the final weeks of the season, show after show—a large number of them revivals—

opened to enthusiastic reviews. This followed the now-expected pattern—in the fall, activity is relatively sluggish, and then, in the spring, a barrage of major projects booms into town, opening as closely as possible to the cut-off date for Tony and other award considerations. (The most successful of off-Broadway's commercial entries were *Mrs. Klein* and *Picasso at the Lapin Agile.* Otherwise, most of the action off Broadway was under the auspices of non-profit managements.)

Despite Broadway's booming spring, there is a strong sense that things could be a lot better. This sense has been given expression by the Broadway Working Initiatives Group, an organization made up of several factions that have long battled each other—producers, theater owners, artists and technicians. By joining with the city to put up $100,000 to hire Bain & Co., a Boston consulting firm, this season they offered hope of a new spirit of cooperation. Bain's assignment: to study Broadway's workings and recommend what might be done to attract new audiences and revitalize production—especially the production of new plays. Once upon a time, almost every new American play of consequence premiered within shouting distance of Times Square. For many with fond memories of those years, Broadway won't truly be Broadway again unless, as a matter of course, straight plays of substance once more premiere next door to productions of musicals and revivals. Among plans being given serious consideration is the establishment of a Theater Trust that would provide financial support to producers undertaking the risky business of offering new works on the city's larger stages.

There are those, though, who insist that Broadway's character and purpose have changed irrevocably and that a wish for a return to the good old days of Jed Harris, Helen Hayes and George Abbott is equivalent to campaigning for a return to the elegance of the Victrola. Rather than getting mired in nostalgia, observers such as *Newsday*'s Linda Winer believe Broadway should embrace its evolved identity as the showcase for works hearty enough to make their ways there; the development of new pieces should be left where they now regularly originate, on the non-profit stages—both in New York and regionally. (It hasn't escaped the notice of the theater community that the winners of the last three Pulitzer Prizes—*Three Tall Women, Young Man From Atlanta* and *Rent*—began off off Broadway.) Operating on relatively low budgets, non-profits such as the Vineyard, Primary Stages, New York Theater Workshop and the New Group (as well as such established off-Broadway institutions as Manhattan Theater Club and Playwrights Horizons) are in a better position to take risks on new talent and material and to encourage experimentation and research. Perhaps the money proposed for the Trust might be better distributed to help seed the work of these companies.

Certainly such money is badly needed in the face of the withdrawal of public funding for the arts. The assault on the National Endowment for the Arts continued this year. The Republican-dominated House and Senate voted a 39 percent cut in the N.E.A.'s budget, resulting in the elimination of many programs and the withdrawal of support for many small theaters. Indeed, some House Republicans went on record about their hopes to ultimately close down the N.E.A. entirely (though there were signs at the end of the season that more moderate voices were beginning to make themselves heard). New York's Governor Pataki, too, made cuts, removing about 15 percent of the state's support of the theater.

The cuts are not only distressing in themselves, but also because their loss lessens the amount likely to be realized from charitable sources. Bill Luers, president of the Metropolitan Museum of Art, was quoted in the *Times* as saying, "What has to be recognized is that we think there's a five- or six-to-one match from the private sector for every dollar from the federal government. That's a huge amount of money." Luers observed that grants from government agencies to arts institutions act as endorsements of those institutions, making fund-raising from other sources easier. The loss of such endorsements means a consequent and proportionate loss of funds from other likely funders.

Financial concerns at Circle Rep led that company, under the leadership of artistic director Austin Pendleton and executive director Milan Stitt, to give up its lease on Circle in the Square Downtown, the first time that company has not had a performing space to call home. The company hopes to produce a three-play season next year but at this writing doesn't know where. It also hopes to present new works in a 75-seat second stage at Circle Rep's offices.

In the meantime, there are signs of revitalization midtown. On 42nd Street between Seventh and Eighth, where feline imagery in storefronts used to commonly refer to slang for female genitalia, a large mural of Dr. Seuss's friendly Cat in the Hat now dominates. Echoing this transformation, the street itself is being made over from a synonym for porn, drugs, prostitution and general sleaze to a showplace suitable for the entire family. The first of the 42d Street theaters to be reborn was the 499-seat New Victory (nee the Victory), which opened its doors on December 11, 1995 after a $11.4 million renovation. Dedicated to providing entertainment for children with their families, in its first season it presented new works by Julie Taymor, Bill Irwin and Jay Harnick's long-running Theaterworks company, plus a revival of the Goldoni classic *The Green Bird* in the Albert Bermel-Ted Emory translation, with original music by Elliot Goldenthal. The New Victory also initiated a schedule of daytime school performances, workshops and apprenticeships. With "New" in its name, it now claims to be the oldest theater in New York. Our historian Thomas T. Foose informs us, "It opened September 27, 1900 with James A. Herne's *Sag Harbor,* in which appeared James, Julie and Crystal Herne, plus Lionel Barrymore. It was originally called the Republic Theater and was built by Oscar Hammerstein."

Other stages on the block are scheduled to return to life within the coming months. The New Amsterdam Theater, acquired by the Disney company, is under reconstruction expected to cost $35 million. When completed in 1997, the building will contain offices for Disney Theatrical Productions and a stage that will serve as the launching pad for their future legit ventures. (Apparently the success of the live version of *Beauty and the Beast* at the Palace Theater has awakened the company to the millions to be mined by reconceiving old Disney movies into stage shows and developing new stage works for the traditional Disney audience.) Down the street, Garth Drabinsky, the Toronto-based producer of *Kiss of the Spider Woman* and

Show Boat, has acquired the buildings that housed the Lyric and Apollo. He plans to spend a reported $22.5 million constructing a new 1,839-seat theater in this shell to serve as the New York home for his projects. It, too, is scheduled to open in 1997.

The League of American Theaters and Producers hired Jed Bernstein to replace retiring Harvey Sabinson as its new executive director. Bernstein is the first person to come to the job from outside the theater, and he was offered his three-year contract largely because of his background as an advertising executive. The idea, apparently, is to bring contemporary marketing strategies to bear on promoting the idea of Broadway.

Speaking of retirements, Kitty Carlisle Hart, who personified New York State's efforts on the part of the arts, also stepped down this year amidst unanimous praise for her enthusiasm and the tireless job she did as chair of the New York State Council on the Arts. She was succeeded by Earle I. Mack, a real estate executive with close ties to Governor Pataki and an interest in developing new ways to market New York culture. Another transition: after four years, Don Scardino stepped down from his job as artistic director of Playwrights Horizons; he will maintain a title as a director-in-residence. The new artistic director is former artistic associate and literary manager Tim Sanford.

Stars' offstage ailments, injuries and dilemmas took their toll on several productions this year. *Busker's Alley,* a $5 million musical that was scheduled to open on Broadway, closed out of town when top-billed Tommy Tune broke his foot. Vocal problems forced Boyd Gaines, *Company*'s leading man, to forego a number of performances of the show. Julie Andrews was out of *Victor/Victoria* for several performances and ended up cancelling her scheduled vacation to help make up for the production's loss of revenue during her absence. And *Master Class*'s Zoe Caldwell was forced to cancel a show in mid-performance as a result of a disagreement with a serving of seafood.

George C. Scott's battle with illness during rehearsals and previews of *Inherit the Wind* raised the question of whether he would be in shape to open in the show at all. Producer Tony Randall stepped in to substitute in the role of Henry Drummond several times, and the scheduled opening date was postponed. Scott was able to gather enough strength to begin performing regularly, the show finally opened, and his performance was received with some of the best reviews of his career and a nomination for the Tony Award. By the time the nomination had been announced, however, Scott had left town, citing a medical problem that needed immediate attention in California, though there was some speculation that a much-publicized lawsuit brought against him by a woman whom he employed may have also provided some motivation. The show, which had extended its run in the wake of its enthusiastic reception, closed early. One could only feel for Randall. He had worked tirelessly to raise the money to realize his dream of reviving *Inherit the Wind* and to raise the public estimation of his National Actors Theater, only to see circumstances outside his control cripple what should have been an unalloyed triumph. (At the season's end, Randall insisted that *Inherit the Wind* would return with a rested and healthy Scott in the fall.)

Another non-profit theater saw the scheduled transfer to a commercial booking of one of its biggest successes cancelled. The Scott Ellis-directed production of *Company* was supposed to complete its run at the Roundabout and reopen shortly after at the Brooks Atkinson Theater. But the show's commercial producer, John Hart, reportedly concerned about Boyd Gaines's illness resurfacing, wanted to replace the star, and Ellis and the rest of the show's team refused. Hart pulled the plug, and the air was full of recriminations, including some heated comments about Mr. Hart by the show's composer-lyricist. *Variety* quoted Sondheim as saying, "My guess is that he couldn't raise the necessary money. The real lesson of this is that there are no producers any more. There are dilettantes like John Hart, and there are theater owners."

At a time when the amount of TV coverage of theater in New York is diminishing, there was some good news—Channel 1, New York's local cable all-news station, broadcast the entirety of the Drama Desk Awards live from the New Victory Theater. The camera work was slapdash and the sound was less than dependable, but Tony Randall was a droll host, and the winners—not limited to the 40-second acceptance speeches mandated at the Tony Awards—had room to breathe and project something of the sparkle the evening was meant to celebrate. The funkiness of the proceedings was ingratiating. Rather than the frantic race against time that is the subtext of the Tonys ("if we don't finish by 11 o'clock, CBS will be pissed at us"), the Drama Desk shambled along at its own pace. The event wasn't staged for TV as are the Tony Awards. It was an event that TV happened to attend. The Tony broadcast had more technical shine. More of the spirit of the theater and a sense of the theater community suffused the Drama Desk telecast.

As for the 50th annual Tony Awards, they were at the center of so much controversy this season that the battles around them made the front pages of all the New York dailies. The nominating committee, exercising the independent judgment for which it was appointed, was seen as complicit in a sinister plot to snub big-budget shows that were still running, in favor of some that had closed early. Specifically, *Big* and *Victor/Victoria* were passed over in the "best musical" category for *Chronicle of a Death Foretold* and *Swinging on a Star.* There were some other omissions that raised eyebrows—the lack of recognition to Patrick Stewart for *The Tempest,* Cherry Jones for *The Night of the Iguana,* Frank Langella for *The Father* and Brian Murray for *Racing Demon.* Tempers flared, particularly those of producers who felt their shows weren't sufficiently appreciated. Mobs began to heat tar and pluck feathers. That stalwart supporter of the stage, the New York *Post,* ran a cartoon subtly characterizing the nominators as boobs and incompetents. Rude cracks questioning the legitimacy of their parentage piled up in the areas devoted to showbiz discussion on the internet.

The "best musical" nominations raised an immediate problem: under the rules, Tony voters are only supposed to vote in categories in which they have seen all nominees. By some estimates, only 100 of the eligible 700-odd voters had actually seen *Chronicle;* so, going strictly according to Hoyle, only those 100 were qualified

Two examples of Paul Tazewell's outstanding costume designs, Tony-nominated and cited by *Best Plays*, for *Bring in 'da Noise Bring in 'da Funk*

to vote for best musical. At this writing, it was probable that public airing of this year's problems would result in a reform of the Tony rules.

In association with his fellow *State Fair* producers, David Merrick, at 84 still game for a fight, filed suit when the nominators specified that only four of the 15 Rodgers and Hammerstein songs for the show were deemed eligible for consideration for the award for "best score." (The others were declared ineligible because this stage production was not the vehicle of their introduction.) Merrick reportedly considered distributing cotton to Tony voters so that they could block out the charms of "It Might As Well be Spring." When the day in court arrived, Judge Sheila Abdus Salaam of the state Supreme Court denied the *State Fair* producers' request for an injunction to stop the voting in the original score category. In the meantime, of course, *State Fair* had been mentioned in the newspapers on a daily basis.

The biggest stink—and what a lovely and theatrical stink it was!—came from Julie Andrews. Angry that the only nomination *Victor/Victoria* had received was for her performance, the star stepped forward at the end of a curtain call and announced that she was going to show solidarity with her "egregiously overlooked" colleagues by refusing her nomination. The ballots went out with her name on them anyway, but Andrews did not participate in the Tony ceremonies or broadcast. Some applauded her stand on principle, some saw it as a stroke of publicity genius. I gather it was good for morale backstage, but I think her action gave encouragement to those who would seek to undermine the committee's independence and the integrity of the award. Her friend Carol Burnett attended the ceremony (she was nominated for best actress) but expressed her solidarity with Andrews by refusing to participate in the telecast.

As it happens, the Tony producers began the broadcast with a cheerful wink at Andrews by running video of her in a short scene with Richard Burton from *Camelot*. Tony host Nathan Lane made a number of good jokes about the various controversies to an audience primed to appreciate them (referring obliquely to the fact that he hadn't been nominated the year before for *Love! Valour! Compassion!,* he commented that he'd been a poster child for the "egregiously overlooked"). Absent stars Julie Andrews and George C. Scott didn't win; Donna Murphy and George Grizzard did. Lane and Zoe Caldwell also picked up their expected awards. *Rent* won for best musical and its composer-librettist, Jonathan Larson, won posthumously for both score and book. Terrence McNally won his second Tony in a row for best play; unlike last year, TV audiences got to hear his acceptance speech. The other substantial winners were the revivals of *The King and I* and *A Delicate Balance.*

At season's end, one could almost hear a large and satisfied sigh. Despite all that threatened it, the theater had its best season in years. The triumphant shook each other's hands, those who stumbled rose and dusted themselves off; and, after a pause, most turned their sights to next season.

A GRAPHIC GLANCE

1995–96
Drawings
By Hirschfeld

Patrick Stewart as Prospero in *The Tempest*

Frank Langella as The Captain in *The Father*

Honoring the 10th anniversary of the
Marquis Theater within the Marriott
Hotel on Times Square, this Hirschfeld vision remembers (*left*) Jim Dale
and Maryann Plunkett in *Me and My
Girl*, which opened there August 10,
1986, and this season's popular musical attraction (*right*), Julie Andrews in *Victor/Victoria*

Robert Whitehead and his wife Zoe Caldwell, co-producer and star of *Master Class*

THE COMPANY OF *COMPANY*—*At top, in an arc*, Timothy Landfield, Patricia Ben Peterson and Danny Burstein; *second row, in an arc*, Jane Krakowski, Debra Monk, Jonathan Dokuchitz, John Hillner, Veanne Cox and Diana Canova; *front row*, Kate Burton, Boyd Gaines, La Chanze, Charlotte d'Amboise and Robert Westenberg

Michael Lombard (*top left*), Charles Durning, George C. Scott, Garret Dillahunt, Anthony Heald (*top right*) and Kate Forbes in *Inherit the Wind*

Left, on opposite page, Red Buttons in his solo show *Buttons on Broadway; above,* Dennis Ryan, James Valentine, Carol Burnett, Andy Taylor and Kate Miller (*on sofa*), Jane Connell, Philip Bosco and Randy Graff in *Moon Over Buffalo*

Backed up by their ensemble in *Big* are Patrick Levis, Daniel Jenkins, Crista Moore, Jon Cypher, Brett Tabisel (*foreground*) and Barbara Walsh

Playwrights

Below, Arthur Miller at 80; *on opposite page*, Steve Martin, author of this season's *Picasso at the Lapin Agile* and *WASP and Other Plays*

Taye Diggs (*at top*), Daphne Rubin-Vega, Gwen Stewart (*at bottom*), Adam Pascal, Wilson Jermaine Heredia, Anthony Rapp, Idina Menzel (*at bottom*) and Jesse L. Martin in the Pulitzer, Tony and Critics Award-winning musical *Rent*

Below, Jodi Long, Kandis Chappell, Christine Ebersole, Josh Mostel (*seated*), Frankie R. Faison, Terrence Mann and John Rubinstein in the Stephen Sondheim-George Furth comedy thriller *Getting Away With Murder*

Left, on opposite page, a Hirschfeld tribute to Carol Channing, who returned to Broadway this season in the *Hello, Dolly!* role she created in 1964. The artist's homage extends to David Merrick, producer of the original *Dolly*, as a ringmaster (*bottom right*) through whose hoop are jumping three famous former Dollys: Miss Channing, Pearl Bailey and Ethel Merman

Mary Beth Hurt, John Carter, Rose-mary Harris, Elizabeth Wilson, George Grizzard and Elaine Stritch in Edward Albee's *A Delicate Balance*

Julie Andrews, Rachel York (*at top*), Tony Roberts and Michael
Nouri with members of the company in the musical *Victor/Victoria*

Left, on opposite page, John Glover in
the title role of *Tartuffe: Born Again*

Nathan Lane, Mark Linn-Baker, Ernie Sabella, Lewis J. Stadlen and
Courtesans in *A Funny Thing Happened on the Way to the Forum*

David Shiner and Bill Irwin in *Fool Moon*

Below, Everett Quinton, artistic director of the Ridiculous Theatrical Company and performer in its productions including this season's *Call Me Sarah Bernhardt*—of which he is also the author—seen at the makeup table

Below, Herb Foster, Ellen Burstyn and Giancarlo Esposito in *Sacrilege*

Right, on opposite page, Lou Diamond Phillips and Donna Murphy as The King and Anna in *The King and I*

STARS IN THE 1995–96 FIRMAMENT—Together on this imagined stage are some of the leading ladies who graced the New York theater so conspicuously this season: Carol Burnett in *Moon Over Buffalo*, Carol Channing in *Hello, Dolly!*, Julie Andrews in *Victor/Victoria*, Zoe Caldwell in *Master Class*, Elizabeth Ashley in *Suddenly Last Summer* and Uta Hagen in *Mrs. Klein*

THE TEN
BEST PLAYS

Here are the details of 1995–96's Best Plays—synopses, biographical sketches of authors and other material. By permission of the playwrights, their representatives, publishers, and others who own the exclusive rights to publish these scripts in full, most of our continuities include substantial quotations from crucial/pivotal scenes in order to provide a permanent reference to style and quality as well as theme, structure and story line.

In the case of such quotations, scenes and lines of dialogue, stage directions and descriptions appear *exactly* as in the stage version or published script unless (in a very few instances, for technical reasons) an abridgement is indicated by five dots (. . . . .). The appearance of three dots (. . .) is the script's own punctuation to denote the timing of a spoken line.

Best Play Citation

○○○
○○○
○○○
○○○
○○○
○○○ MRS. KLEIN

A Play in Two Acts

BY NICHOLAS WRIGHT

Cast and credits appear on page 321

NICHOLAS WRIGHT was born in Cape Town, South Africa on July 5, 1940. He attended Rondebosch Boys' High School, trained as an actor and migrated to London where he joined the Royal Court Theater as casting director in 1967. He became assistant director in 1968 and was placed in charge of its experimental Theater Upstairs in 1969. From 1975 to 1977 he served as the Royal Court's co-artistic director (with Robert Kidd). The Royal National Theater has been his home base since 1984 (Wright was its literary manager until 1989 and is now an associate director). It was the National which produced his Mrs. Klein *(concerning a real-life child psychoanalyst who was at the height of her reputation and powers in 1934, the time of the play), moving later to the West End and productions around the world, notably this one off Broadway October 24 for Wright's first Best Play citation and indeed his first American production of* Best Plays *record.*

In addition to his many directing credits, Wright is the author of several plays produced in London: Treetops, One Fine Day, The Gorky Brigade, The Crimes of Vautrin, The Custom of the Country *and* Desert Air. *He expressed his personal views in* 99 Plays *(a book about playwriting from Aeschylus to the present) and* The Art of the Theater, *a series of articles published in the* Independent. *Wright's directorial and screen play credits are numerous. He is married and lives in London.*

Time: Spring of 1934
Place: London

ACT I

SYNOPSIS: In her sitting room Mrs. Klein, 52, dressed in black, is sitting at her desk at right, sorting through papers, some of which conjure up memories which cause her to weep. The room is furnished with a sofa at center, various files and cupboards along the walls, lighted by a tall window at left and entered up left through the ground floor hall of this town house.

A colleague in her early 30s, Paula, has come to be of whatever assistance Mrs. Klein happens to need, and has brought her a seed cake. Soon the two of them are seated on the sofa, drinking coffee, while the older woman probes her own feelings.

MRS. KLEIN: . . . . . Chiefly what I feel is numbness. Here inside. As though some vital part of me has been removed. The tears don't help. All they do is make a thorough nuisance of themselves. And then they stop and leave me feeling exactly as I did before. Remote. Closed up. And dead. You'll have some cake?

PAULA: Yes, thank you.

MRS. KLEIN: So: my work goes on. I read, I write, I entertain a few old friends. I see my patients. Clear a space. I'm on my own today. My cleaning woman has a family crisis in Southend. Or so she says. The truth is that she needs a break from my unnatural calm. And so do I. But there we are, I may not like it but I'm stuck with it. I don't know why. I don't have insight into my emotions, not just now. Some other time. So: eat.

Mrs. Klein had given Paula a poem to read, written by Mrs. Klein's son when he was only 15, a love poem to an idealized mother. "I doubt she ever existed. Not in life," Mrs. Klein remarks, but to her son she was real, she was *"the mother."*

Laboriously, Mrs. Klein explains to Paula all the arrangements she has made for going away on a trip. She hands over the house keys to Paula, provides her with money for expenses and describes the editing she wants Paula to do on the proofs of a German-language edition of one of her books (she is Melanie Klein, the famous child psychoanalyst).

At her desk, she picks up a problematical letter which has arrived: "Marked 'To await return.' It comes from Dr. Schmideberg. I don't like it. I don't even like the envelope. It looks as though it's about to burst with hostile matter. This is what professional enemies are like. They're vampires. They're dependent. They want love. And so they nag and pester. Should I read it? Should I leave it? Should I burn it? If I burn it, can I blame the post? I'll—. No, I can't decide." She puts the letter down.

Mrs. Klein expects Paula to have the proofs ready for the first post to Vienna on Wednesday. Mrs. Klein won't be here—she is off to attend a funeral—but she trusts Paula to do the job properly, she has observed her work at the Institute.

MRS. KLEIN: . . . . . I liked your comments after Edward Glover read his paper on suggestion. At that scientific meeting. You were very acute. You shut him up for weeks, that's no mean tribute. When was it now? At Christmas. Yes, the seminar-room was full of shopping bags. That *was* you?

PAULA: It was.

MRS. KLEIN: I knew it. Tell me, who is worse, in your professional estimation, Glover or Schmideberg? No. I mustn't compromise you. Glover's not a dunce exactly, but he's too dogmatic. Like some mid-Victorian, mutton-chop-whiskered tyrant of the breakfast table, ghastly. (*Laughs, then stops.*) Dr. Schmideberg needs help. (*Pause.*) The heck with it.

She goes to the drinks cabinet and pours two sherries.
So we've never met? I felt I knew you.

PAULA: We've been introduced. But never—

MRS. KLEIN: Never sat and talked. It's very pleasant.

They chat about Paula's background: she has been married to a doctor, not an analyst; he is based in Zurich; they are both Jewish refugees from Germany, and Paula's mother and brothers still live there; and Paula and her husband, who was the more political of the two, are now divorced. The political situation, Mrs. Klein observes, "won't get better. I can't stop it. You can't. Can your husband? In these terrible times we live in? And it doesn't interest me to try. That's not my style."

Paula has a 9-year-old daughter living with Catholic friends in Berlin until Paula can find a proper place for her to live here in London—not Bethnal Green, "a slum," where Paula now lives and practices. Mrs. Klein decides to give Paula her son Hans's poem.

Paula wonders why, with so many English friends, Mrs. Klein didn't ask someone she knows to help while she's away. The latter explains that she was on holiday last week when she received a phone call from her sister-in-law, Mrs. Vago, in Budapest. Her son Hans had met with a climbing accident. At this time, when Mrs. Klein is going to Budapest, she doesn't trust her English friends to provide the proper form of sympathy: "Not with this. Not now. They don't feel homelike. I want my home around me. I want the good things close and safe. I want to hear the German language."

Mrs. Klein gives Paula Mrs. Vago's Budapest phone number and a box of Hans's letters to store for safekeeping. Paula helps her get her travelling things together, as the doorbell rings, signalling the arrival of the taxi. Attending to last-minute details, Mrs. Klein locks the liquor cabinet, hides the keys in the bookcase and Dr. Schmideberg's letter in a file drawer. Mrs. Klein departs. Paula settles down to work on the proofs.

After the passage of some hours, the front door is heard opening and closing, and Melitta—in her early 30s, Mrs. Klein's daughter—enters. Melitta and Paula are previously and well acquainted, but Melitta is surprised to find Paula here (Paula explains that she had written Mrs. Klein a letter and was asked to call on her) and surprised to find that Mrs. Klein left on her trip only today—she'd been supposed to go earlier in the week. Melitta is nervous, impulsive, inquiring about the work Paula is doing, curious about a footnote about her work in the proofs (apparently Melitta is also an analyst), noticing that one of the books in the bookcase has been moved out of place (where Mrs. Klein hid the keys), tidying up here and there, finding that the liquor cabinet is locked and finally settling on the subject of her mother.

MELITTA: . . . . . How did she seem?

PAULA (*tidies up her papers for an orderly start next day*): Her dreams have stopped, I don't know if she told you. And she cries from time to time, but the tears don't help. She's still denying the loss. Is this what you want to know, I don't—

MELITTA: Go on.

PAULA: She's trying to reinstate the lost loved object: keeping Hans's letters in a place of safety. Tearing other papers up, because she sees them perhaps as hostile. She has periods of elation. And of deep depression. She's in mourning.

MELITTA: Did she mention me?

PAULA: She said you had the car.

MELITTA: What else?

PAULA: I don't remember.

MELITTA: You're a liar.

PAULA: That may be. I can't discuss it, not at this time of night. I'm sorry, Melitta.

While Paula goes to put on her hat and coat, Melitta tries the file drawers and finds them locked too. Paula returns, eyes tired from reading proof, on her way home via the Underground. Melitta asks her to stay a while, after which she'll drive Paula home in the car. Melitta complains that everything in the house is locked up, and Paula agrees, "She's locked the cellar door, she's locked the rooms upstairs. It's symbolic. The house is her."

Melitta phones Mrs. Klein's cleaning-woman (revealing in the process of identifying herself on the phone that *she* is the "Dr. Schmideberg" mentioned previously) to ask where the keys are hidden. She is infuriated by the information that the cleaning-woman is away for the weekend.

MELITTA (*rings off*): Damn that woman. Damn her. God rot her to hell. Vile crone. I've begged my mother a thousand times to sack her. But she won't. She can't. She sees the cleaning-woman as her mother. Wouldn't you say?

PAULA: It crossed my mind, Melitta, but I didn't like to call attention to it. Can we go now?

MELITTA: Did she get my letter?

PAULA: Yes.

MELITTA: And did she read it?

PAULA: Not while I was there. She said you'd marked it to await return. No, let's be frank. She felt attacked by it. She's feeling persecuted at the moment, or she'd know you wouldn't hurt her at a time like—But she feared you might. So she was hostile to the letter and to you. But not you, her daughter. No. To Dr. Schmideberg. She only spoke of you as Dr. Schmideberg. The daughter's good, she loves her, but the doctor's bad, it's casebook stuff. It won't last. She'll read your letter soon. In fact, she probably took it with her.

MELITTA: Jesus Christ.

PAULA: What now?

MELITTA: I'm feeling sick.

PAULA: Do you want a glass of water?

MELITTA: No.

PAULA: Try putting your head between your knees.

MELITTA: I need a drink.

PAULA: Let's see what we can do.

    Goes to the drinks cabinet. Examines it. Takes out the top drawer.

I thought so.

    Reaches down inside.

One can always find a way in somehow, as my professor would say.

Paula takes out a bottle of whisky and pours two drinks. They discuss anxiety dreams, their analysts and their mother transferences. Melitta suspects that Paula is "burrowing in" with Mrs. Klein.

PAULA: I have a mother of my own. I don't need yours. If that's the undercurrent. Why do you think I'd want to hurt you? Why? You're like a sister to me. You've been kind and good and generous to me. Nobody else from home has helped me. Not till now. Until your mother, true. Who seems neurotically attached to me for some strange reason. Or some obvious reason. I can't help it. And I'm under no illusions. And I don't care tuppence for your boring little Oedipal tangles. I have other problems, thank you. I've a daughter in Berlin, I have consulting-rooms in Bethnal Green.

MELITTA: Who put you there?

PAULA: Not her.

MELITTA: They all did. At the Institute. Committee level. Refugees not wanted. Not in Hampstead. Too much healthy competition. That's why they've dumped you all in these extraordinary places. And she's right behind it.

PAULA: You don't surprise me. Analysts are only human. If you threaten our professional livelihoods you'll get some very primitive responses. That was grubby of you.

MELITTA: Did she tell you how he died?

PAULA: She said a climbing accident.
MELITTA: He killed himself.

Melitta has deduced from details acquired from her Aunt Jolan Vago over the phone that her brother Hans took his own life. Melitta's letter to her mother informs her of this. If Mrs. Klein read it, she knows; if not, not. The letter, Melitta adds, was "Very detailed. Very convincing. Very persecutorily sadistic," and if Mrs. Klein had read it, Paula observes, it would have been "horrible." Melitta agrees and has come here to try to retrieve it. Giggling under the influence of a couple of drinks, they imagine Mrs. Klein on her journey reading a magazine, perhaps, then—if she had taken it with her—turning to the letter, opening it.

MELITTA: And then she reads—she reads—
PAULA: "You cow, you murderess—"
MELITTA: No no no—it's worse than that—
PAULA: "Bitch, you killed him—!"
          They slowly stop giggling. Then one of them starts giggling again, and
          both collapse with laughter but this time with a sense of guilt. They stop.
          Pause. They share a handkerchief, wipe their eyes.
Maybe she won't believe it.
MELITTA: She's not stupid.
PAULA: No.
MELITTA: It'll kill her.
PAULA: Yes, it very likely will.
MELITTA: Except she could have left it here. It could be in this room.

Paula remembers that Melitta noticed that a book had been moved, puts two and two together and finds the keys where Mrs. Klein had hidden them. Just as Melitta has opened the top file drawer and pulled it all the way out, Mrs. Klein comes into the room. She has obviously decided not to go on the trip after all. She sends Paula to get her bags and pay the taxi driver and greets Melitta warmly, urging her to stay the night in her old room. Melitta asks at once, "Did you get my letter?" Mrs. Klein avoids answering for the moment but alludes to Paula's presence, "She found the keys, I notice. And the whisky. Make me a cup of tea. I need to make a note of something, personal, not unpleasant. Turn the heating on."

Melitta goes, and Mrs. Klein opens her notebook, turns on music, wipes tears from her eyes. There is an interlude during which she makes notes. Paula comes in but is sent off by Mrs. Klein's comment, "I'm working." The interlude ends when Melitta enters with the tea tray.

Paula has been sitting in the hall but is now invited to join the others in the living room. Mrs. Klein explains that she was dozing on a bench in Dover station and began to dream: "I saw a mother and her son. The son had either died or was about to die. The mother was dressed in black, her collar was white. I didn't feel sad to see them. I felt slightly hostile. So: I woke. And saw the boat-train about to leave

Laila Robins as Dr. Schmideberg (Melitta), Uta Hagen as Mrs. Klein and
Amy Wright as Paula in a scene from *Mrs. Klein* by Nicholas Wright

for London, so I took it," returning home instead of taking the boat to Europe as
planned.

Mrs. Klein sends Paula on an errand and confides to Melitta that it occurred to
her she might meet her former husband at the funeral, and that was one reason she
didn't go on to Budapest. As Paula returns, Mrs. Klein and Melitta are discussing
Mrs. Klein's dream and conclude that Mrs. Klein's denial of her son's death is weak-
ening.

Once again Mrs. Klein sends Paula out of the room—this time to take a bath—
and mother and daughter soon return to the subject of the letter. Mrs. Klein hasn't
read it, she admits, and permits Melitta to take it back, out of the bottom desk
drawer. Mrs. Klein had originally felt hostility to the letter because she assumed it
would be an attack on her paper on criminality. Melitta admits that she *will* probably
attack her mother's criminality paper in their professional publication.

MRS. KLEIN (*suddenly angry*): Why do you do this? (*Pause.*) What I write, I've
learned and proved in twenty years of clinical practice. And you've seen the results.

MELITTA: I have. You're a great clinician. But Mother, you can't write rubbish and expect me not to say it's rubbish.

MRS. KLEIN: No I don't, because I know you see the so-called rubbish, "dreck" you called it once, the *poisonous faeces,* aimed at you in person. I can see it, everyone else can see it. It's an embarrassment. Why exhibit your sores in public, darling?

MELITTA: Sores?

MRS. KLEIN: Yes sores, emotional sores. If I fought back you'd see some dreck all right. I could finish your career. Only I won't attack my daughter.

MELITTA *(suddenly angry, shouts):* No, you get your lttle toadies to attack your daughter.

MRS. KLEIN: I don't write papers for my fellow thinkers.

MELITTA: You'll do anything to win. You'll pack committees, you'll fiddle agendas, you'll steal other people's patients.

MRS. KLEIN: When did I steal a patient? Whose damn patient?

MELITTA: Mine last month.

MRS. KLEIN: He begged for refuge. You'd confused him. You're a bad clinician.

MELITTA: Why?

MRS. KLEIN: You want the truth? Good, fine. You reassure your patients. When they cry, you hug them. And you say their clouds have silver linings and you give them tips on life. What can they learn from that about themselves? All they learn is that you're nice to them, which as a matter of fact you aren't, you're bloody destructive. Take that patient. All his life, like everyone else, like you, like me, like all the world, he has projected his infant experiences on to the people around him. But it's only now, with me, he starts to see them. Now, in that powerful, terrifying thing we call the transference. Because, unlike his wife or child or you, I am detached. So the *screen,* as it were, is blank. And he projects and sees, *on me,* those images from his cradle. You obscured that screen with your emotions. You felt pity. And you felt protective. Rubbish. Dreck, dreck, dreck. If you want to be an analyst of any worth you have to trust your patients with the truth. However harsh. They're strong. They'll take it.

> *Melitta gives her her letter.*

What is it?

MELITTA: It's the truth about Hans.

> *Goes out. Curtain.*

ACT II

Some time later, Mrs. Klein and Paula are seated on the sofa while Melitta is upstairs having her bath. The letter is still unopened and unread. Mrs. Klein, sensing that one of the major depressions in her life is coming on, tears up the letter, throws the pieces in the waste basket and discusses the dream she just recently experienced at Dover.

PAULA: Your mother and son.

MRS. KLEIN: *This* mother and son. And the associations ran as follows: picnic, father, sibling envy, Battle of Waterloo. That's hopeless. Battle of—(*Pause.*) Homework. I think I'm getting somewhere. Brother's homework. (*Pause.*) There is a nasty woman comes to mind who brought her equally nasty som to help my brother with his homework. I was twelve. It seems to me that mother and son was them.

PAULA: Why dream about them now?

MRS. KLEIN: Because I never forgot that evening. It was horrible, frightful. Everybody was upset. My mother was in tears, my brother rushed into his room and slammed the door, I could have killed them both.

PAULA: For being upset?

MRS. KLEIN: Because they—No, not *them.* This woman and—(*She registers the misunderstanding.*) I *thought* it was—(*Ponders the implication.*) I'm feeling worse now. Like the ceiling's getting lower . . . . .

Paula is telling Mrs. Klein that she also has a dream about a lowering ceiling, when Melitta enters garbed in a dressing gown and carrying bedclothes to make up the couch for Paula. Mrs. Klein admits that maybe she didn't really mean to go to Budapest but would have done so if Melitta had dragged her. She also claims she opened Melitta's letter, but doesn't want to discuss it right now.

MELITTA: We'll talk about it over breakfast.

MRS. KLEIN: Maybe.

PAULA: If she doesn't want to read it then, she shouldn't have to.

MELITTA: If she—

MRS. KLEIN: *That* was tactless.

MELITTA: But she said she had. She said—

MRS. KLEIN: If I may clarify? I opened it and Paula told me not to read it, so I tore it up. Omnipotence. I'm doing a lot of it. I was interpreting my dream just now, and Paula led me to an obvious breakthrough, and I wouldn't listen.

MELITTA: Tore it up?

MRS. KLEIN: I wouldn't listen! Something's being resisted.

MELITTA: Yes it is!

MRS. KLEIN: But what?

MELITTA: I'll tell you.

MRS. KLEIN: Good, you tell me. Well?

PAULA: I'll go upstairs.

MRS. KLEIN: I want you here.

MELITTA: Why can't we talk about it just we two?

MRS. KLEIN: Because there's no such thing as just we two. There's always a third. At least a third. The mother. Perhaps the father, perhaps a rival sibling. Always the room fills up. Start with two, why not with three? Either way we'll end up throwing a party. Good, let's start.

Melitta begins to reconstruct what happened to her brother Hans from the time
he left his boarding-house last Friday. She is soon diverted, however, to her childhood past, complaining that her mother didn't pay enough attention to her, left her
in the care of her grandmother, even missed her birthday.

MRS. KLEIN: Oh, so now we're to get to the momentous crisis. I missed your
birthday, and you're scarred for life.
MELITTA: I am. Not just—
MRS. KLEIN: And maybe the cat jumped on your cradle so now you can't drink
milk. Melitta, that is popular psychiatry, it's rubbish, it's for chambermaids. So you
had a bad experience, rise above it. Take it to your analyst, she's good, I like her.
Where'd we got to. Yes: he left the boarding-house and—let me tell you something.
I would walk you to the square. And find a bench. When you were five or six, a
difficult age, and Hans was three. I'd buy you ice creams, and I'd introduce you to
the pigeons. And I'd watch the fountain. And I'd sit and wait to go back home where
Mother would have staked her claim to Jewish motherhood by cooking a five-course
dinner. And I'd feel despair. That this was it. My life. My waste of life. So I escaped.
And don't think you've got cause to feel resentful. You've a doctorship, a fine career,
and if you choose to throw it away that's your decision. Now: he travelled to the
mountains. How?

Hans bought a one-way ticket on the bus, Melitta declares—no return ticket was
found on his body, he wasn't coming back (but his last letter to her was cheerful
enough, Mrs. Klein interjects). Hans took nothing with him to read or eat. He bought
breakfast and left all the change he had as a tip for the waiter—and there were no
banknotes in his wallet. He was wearing ordinary shoes, not climbing boots, and his
body was found at the foot of a cliff which is considered a beauty spot, with a
telescope at the top for viewing.

The lack of a book is significant, in Melitta's opinion, because Hans always had
a book with him except during a period when Mrs. Klein stopped him from reading
because books were "symptomatic of his hero-worship for his father"; stopped his
music lessons after she called violin-playing "a repressed masturbation fantasy";
broke up two of Hans's affairs, one homosexual and one heterosexual. Mrs. Klein
analyzed both of her children intensively—they were her first patients, and she wrote
them both up.

MELITTA: . . . . . How does it go? "She has so far (she is now fifteen) shown only
an average intelligence." That was me. That's what she wrote about me.
MRS. KLEIN (to Paula): It seemed important to remain detached.
MELITTA: But Mother . . .
        Pause.
MRS. KLEIN: Yes, I know.
PAULA: She was your daughter.
MRS. KLEIN: Yes.

Pause.

MELITTA: I'd lie there trying to think up what to say to her. Trying to think of something so banal, so ordinary that she couldn't interpret it. My history lesson. "What's history about?" she'd ask me. In her clinical voice. My mother in her clinical voice, imagine. I'd say: "Oh, history lessons, that's what people did in ancient times, battles and so on." She'd say: "What happened in ancient times is you, the infant, seeing your father and me having sexual intercourse. *That's* the battle." It sounds absurd. It wasn't. That was the worst of it: she's so damn good. I felt that slotting into place, the snap, the "Yes, that's right." And I'd be stuck with a horrible truth about myself I couldn't deal with. I wanted to protect her from it, but she wouldn't let me. Kept on sucking it out. My poison. Kept returning it. She used to light her cigarette, her special way, the match pushed forward so the sparks shot into my lap. That was my hatred flying back. The carved brown cabinet stood there waiting my command to fall and crush her. Or the mat to trip her up. She spilled the ashtray. Muck on the varnished floor. My vengeful shit. All that was good, destroyed. My mother destroyed. My fault. My guilt.

MRS. KLEIN: I did good work.

MELITTA: And the results?

MRS. KLEIN: You're not so bad. It's Dr. Schmideberg I'm not too fond of.

MELITTA: I'm Dr. Schmideberg. Can't you understand?

MRS. KLEIN: I'm Melanie Klein.

Continuing on the subject of Hans, Melitta tells how her brother met a pastor he knew on the train station platform: "He hoped the pastor wouldn't be shocked by something he might hear about him. He said he was sure what he was doing was right." Then Hans went and caught the bus instead of the train.

Mrs. Klein considers the possibility that Hans left a sort of message for her by selecting a site that looked across the valley toward Rosenberg, a mountain symbolic of the breast—the mother's breast upon which the child projects both his warmest good feelings and his strongest hatreds. Melitta begins to weep when Mrs. Klein advises her that it is her duty to lead her neurotic patients through "that primitive jungle" where the infant suddenly sees its mother as a whole person, both good and bad: "This is the dawn of guilt. It leads to fathomless depression. It is out of that depression he must climb in order to become a healthy adult." Mrs. Klein finishes by asserting that the wicked and the loving mother are one and the same, and if you hurt one you also hurt the other. Melitta, in tears, contradicts her.

MELITTA: It isn't true. There are bad mothers. Mothers who are totally bad. You're one. We never felt you loved us. You were interested in us, that's all. But we loved you. He loved you terribly, terribly. And you could never accept his love for what it was. You always changed it. Made it yours. Everything had to be yours. Whatever we did, whatever we had, whatever we wanted. You'd make us think it wasn't really happening, or we didn't like it. Or you'd choose it for us. Anything. A dress in a shop, a train set, my degree.

Laila Robins and Uta Hagen as daughter and mother in *Mrs. Klein*

MRS. KLEIN: I chose your husband?

MELITTA: I was compensating.

MRS. KLEIN: Quite.

MELITTA: I was neurotically dependent on you.

MRS. KLEIN: So you made a break for freedom.

MELITTA: Yes, I bloody well did.

MRS. KLEIN: What's interesting is that you chose a man my age. A mother-substitute. And what a disaster he turned out to be. A drunk, a fool. You fled from bondage into bondage. And you always will as long as you are crippled by your unresolved ambivalence towards me. So, resolve it. I can't. Nobody can but you. It's your job. Do it.

   Pause.

The alternative is suicide. Either actual, as in Hans's case. Or else, symbolic, which is how you're going at present. And I can't lose any more children. Help me, darling. Forget the Institute. Forget the rows, the meetings. That's for weekdays. Tonight you are in my house. We're mother and daughter. And I'm saying, Melitta, Melchen, dearest, sweetheart, what must we do to have a sensible, adult, mother-and-daughter friendship?

MELITTA: You don't want one.

Try her, Mrs. Klein challenges. Free-associate. Tell her mother what Melitta thinks she needs in order to be free. First, Melitta planned to attend a concert next week with her husband and means to go through with it even though her mother has returned (that's O.K. with Mrs. Klein). Then there are six teaspoons she'd like to have (also O.K.). Then Melitta wants to buy out Mrs. Klein's share of the car they own together (still O.K., and Melitta writes a check then and there). Then Melitta states her plan to remain in London, practicing, and asks her mother to cease trying to influence her to move to New York. Mrs. Klein's response is, "As your mother I'm delighted. As your colleague I must warn you, I shall give no quarter. If your activities are inconsistent with your membership of the Society, I shall say so, so will others, you'll be forced to resign. You'll have to become some kind of therapist nonsense, thumping cushions with your patients. This may sound harsh, but it's the truth. Let's have things open and honest between us. As I know you want."

Finally, Melitta has decided to change her analyst without consulting her mother. Her new analyst, she informs Mrs. Klein, is Edward Glover, Mrs. Klein's arch-rival and severest critic. Mrs. Klein surprises even herself by reacting with uncontrollable anger to this news, hurling the contents of her glass at Melitta, then trying to make Melitta eat scraps of the torn-up letter.

Paula pulls Mrs. Klein away and separates mother and daughter until Mrs. Klein calms down. The three are then able to manage a discussion of the various relationships: Glover has a backward daughter and sees Melitta as "the brilliant child he's always wanted"; Melitta sees Glover as "the father you betrayed"; Glover sees Mrs. Klein as "the wanton mother casting aside the wonderful father Freud"; to Paula, Melitta represents "my dead sister" and she may also be a stand-in for Paula herself, "the unloved daughter."

Mrs. Klein believes that her dream suggests that she loved Hans but also had mixed feelings about him.

MELITTA: And you wished to harm him.

MRS. KLEIN: Wished it on some primitive level.

MELITTA: Primitive but effective.

MRS. KLEIN: So you think I killed him.

MELITTA: He killed you. He killed that you in him.

MRS. KLEIN: And why?

MELITTA: To punish it.

MRS. KLEIN: No, this I can't go along with. He wished to save the me he loved from his sadistic onslaughts. So he killed them. And in doing so, killed himself. Now don't look blank, Melitta. Just because you never tried it. When did you save me from your sadistic onslaughts?

MELITTA: Mother, that's why I'm here. Hans died because he couldn't bring himself to hate you.

MRS. KLEIN: What about you, you can?

MELITTA: I can. I do.

MRS. KLEIN: Although there must be some ambivalence.
MELITTA: No. Not now.

To illustrate her feelings, Melitta takes her door key off her keyring and tries to hand it to her mother, but Mrs. Klein ignores it and heads upstairs for bed with her sleeping potion. Paula confides to Melitta that she intends to go on with Mrs. Klein, "I need her in all kinds of ways."

Melitta goes upstairs to get dressed. Paula picks up the phone and dials the Budapest number Mrs. Klein had left with her previously. While she's waiting for the call to be completed, Melitta returns, on her way out. She is going to leave her door key as a sign that she now intends to try to get along without her mother: "I'll write a book. And leave my husband. Have a child and go to China. In that order. But if not: I'll grovel down from Hampstead Garden Suburb in the morning at about eleven." But in the meantime, her pride will not permit her to retrieve the key, and she exits.

Paula finally is connected to Hans's Aunt Jolan Vago in Budapest. Paula identifies herself as calling on Mrs. Klein's behalf to say she won't be coming to the funeral. Paula suggests that there's something Mrs. Vago hasn't told them about Hans. Paula listens and seems satisfied at what she hears, then rings off, lies down on the couch and closes her eyes.

Music bridges the time to some hours later with daylight showing in the crack of the curtains. Mrs. Klein comes in, wakes Paula, draws the curtains to let the sun into the room, searches for and finds her paper on criminality and asks Paula to stay on through the day and share a prayer or perhaps a glass of sherry.

Mrs. Klein reminds herself that she'd better tell the Budapest people she's not coming and learns that Paula has already notified them. Paula explains that the tone of one of Hans's letters to his mother reminded her of her relationship with her own mother, filling letters to her with trivia to avoid the real facts of her life. Paula sensed that Hans was "hiding something. So I moved the material round and found a different interpretation," which her phone call to Budapest then confirmed. Hans had fallen in love with an older woman.

PAULA: In her thirties. She's a singer. Jolan likes her. She lives in Budapest. She has a husband there and children. Two: a boy and a girl.
MRS. KLEIN: Surprise me. And?
PAULA: I understood it all. It's simple. Hans was meeting her at the station. They planned to spend the Easter holiday together. He was waiting on the platform, and he saw the pastor. He felt nervous. So he lied: he said that he was going to Budapest, to see Aunt Jolan, knowing the pastor knew her. He asked him to forgive him. But he wasn't ashamed: he knew that what he was doing was right. The train came in. They took the bus. She put the tickets in her handbag. He didn't bring a book or climbing boots. Why should he? They breakfasted together, and he left an enormous tip; he wanted to impress her.
MRS. KLEIN: Why the mountains?

PAULA: They'd booked a room in the tourist hotel. He left his money there. She took it to Budapest and gave it back to Mrs. Vago. She said he'd gone for a walk. While she was getting dressed. Mid-afternoon. She waited. Then she went to find him, and she—That was the first she knew. It seems he'd tried to find a path that isn't there now. And the ground had fallen away. That's all. That's all.

Pause.

MRS. KLEIN: What's so interesting is that I feel intense resentment. Not of you, so much, you meant well. But this *woman,* who the hell was she, what's her name?

PAULA: I don't know.

MRS. KLEIN: A singer?

PAULA: Yes.

MRS. KLEIN: Opera? Cabaret?

PAULA: Mrs. Vago didn't tell me.

MRS. KLEIN: Had they—? Yes, that afternoon you say. *(Pause.)* I cannot adjust to this. I can't accept it. *(Angry.)* What the hell are you trying to tell me, that he died by chance?

Pause. Paula shocked and upset.

He never mentioned her. Not once, not once. Who are her parents?

PAULA: I didn't ask. Where she comes from, where they met. It's nothing to do with—*(Suddenly angry, shouts.)* Don't you see? It's nothing to do with you, you stupid bloody woman. He was free.

MRS. KLEIN: No, no. The facts remain the same—*(Pause. She crumples.)* Oh God, I've lost him. *(She starts to cry. Cries for a long time. After a bit she holds her hand out.)* Come.

Paula holds her hand. After a bit Mrs. Klein stops crying.

Real tears. So my denial is *greatly* weakened. Yes, I'm starting to recover. *(Pause.)* I said the facts remained the same. Well, *certain* facts. My guilt remains. So does my wish to make amends. Now my appointment book is somewhere.

She finds it. Opens it.

This is what you want?

PAULA: It is.

MRS. KLEIN: Because you must be sure.

PAULA: I'm sure.

MRS. KLEIN *(looks through her appointment book):* Where are we? *(Looks upwards.)* And the ceiling's moving upwards. I feel open. Easier. Tears, you know, are very much equated with excreta in the unconscious mind. Through tears the mourner eases tension, casts bad objects into the outside world. You know my fees?

PAULA: I do.

MRS. KLEIN: They're what's expected. You must decide to place that value on my time. And yours.

PAULA: I'll manage.

MRS. KLEIN: I can offer you Mondays, Wednesdays, Fridays, Saturdays. At eleven a.m. Now must I put these in my book, you tell me.

PAULA: Eleven o'clock is fine.

Mrs. Klein writes times in her book.

In fact, we're late.

MRS. KLEIN: I beg your pardon?

PAULA: It's Saturday now. And look at the clock. We've lost five minutes.

Paula persuades Mrs. Klein to start the sessions at once. The next one will be in the consulting room upstairs but this one can be staged less formally, right here. Paula settles herself on the couch, while Mrs. Klein pulls up a chair and *"waits with a singular expression of alertness: her professional manner. Different from the way she's looked at any previous point in the play."*

PAULA: I'm worried about the doorbell.

MRS. KLEIN: You worry that if it rings I might abandon you.

PAULA: I know you won't. You told me yesterday. You said the world must wait. *(Pause.)* I know this isn't helpful, but I can't help thinking as an analyst. You feel guilty about your children.

MRS. KLEIN: Mm. Hm.

PAULA: You see the harm you've done.

MRS. KLEIN: Go on.

PAULA: You want to pay them reparation. But for one of them it's too late.

MRS. KLEIN: Mm. Hm.

PAULA: You want to pay Melitta reparation. *(Pause.)* You're doing so now. *(Pause.)* I terribly want you to reply to that.

MRS. KLEIN: You were afraid I'd left you.

PAULA: No. I felt content.

MRS. KLEIN: You felt—

The doorbell rings. Mrs. Klein does not react to it.

You feel perhaps that you've replaced Melitta as my daughter.

Doorbell.

PAULA: I have.

Doorbell.

MRS. KLEIN: Mm. Hm.

PAULA: I feel—

MRS. KLEIN: I'm listening.

Doorbell. Curtain.

Tony Award

○○○
○○○
○○○
○○○
○○○
○○○ # MASTER CLASS

A Play in Two Acts

BY TERRENCE McNALLY

Cast and credits appear on page 284

TERRENCE McNALLY was born in St. Petersburg, Fla., November 3, 1939 and grew up in Corpus Christi, Texas. He received his B.A. in English at Columbia where in his senior year he wrote the varsity show. After graduation he was awarded the Harry Evans Travelling Fellowship in creative writing. He made his professional stage debut with The Lady of the Camellias, *an adaptation of the Dumas story produced on Broadway in 1963. His first original full-length play,* And Things That Go Bump in the Night, *was produced on Broadway in 1965 following a production at the Tyrone Guthrie Theater in Minneapolis.*

McNally's short play Tour *was produced off Broadway in 1968 as part of the Collision Course program. In the next season, 1968–69, his one-acters were produced all over town;* Cuba Si! *off Broadway in the ANTA Matinee series;* Noon *on the Broadway program* Morning, Noon and Night; Sweet Eros *and* Witness *off Broadway that fall, and in early winter* Next *with Elaine May's* Adaptation *on an off-Broadway bill that was named a Best Play of its season.*

McNally's second Best Play, Where Has Tommy Flowers Gone?, *had its world premiere at the Yale Repertory Theater before opening on Broadway in 1971. His third,* Bad Habits, *was produced OOB in 1973 by New York Theater Strategy, directed then and in its off-Broadway and Broadway phases in the 1973–74 season by Robert Drivas. His fourth,* The Ritz, *played the Yale Repertory Theater as* The Tubs *before opening on Broadway January 20, 1975 for a run of 400 performances. His fifth,* It's Only a Play, *was produced in a pre-Broadway tryout under the title* Broadway, Broadway *in 1978 and OOB under the new title by Manhattan Punch Line in 1982. It finally arrived in the full bloom of an off-Broadway production—and Best Play designation—January 12, 1986, for 17 performances at Manhattan Theater Club, which also produced his sixth Best Play,* Lips Together, Teeth Apart, *June 25, 1991 for 406 performances, a Lortel Award winner.*

McNally's seventh Best Play, the book for the musical Kiss of the Spider Woman *with a John Kander-Fred Ebb score, took a circuitous route to Broadway acclaim. After a 1990 tryout in the short-lived New Musicals Program at SUNY Purchase, N.Y. and a Toronto production, it went on to an award-winning London staging in 1992 before reaching Broadway May 3, 1993, just in time to win that season's Critics best-musical award and the Tonys for book, score and show—and remained for 906 performances. His eighth Best Play,* A Perfect Ganesh, *was put on by Manhattan Theater Club June 27, 1994 for 124 performances. McNally's ninth Best Play,* Love! Valour! Compassion! *was produced by MTC November 1, 1994 for 72 performances, then moved to Broadway February 14 for an additional 249 performances and received the Tony for best play and the Critics Award for best American play.*

With Master Class, *McNally joins the half-dozen illustrious playwrights whose Best Play citations have moved into double digits (Maxwell Anderson 19, George S. Kaufman 18, Neil Simon 15, Eugene O'Neill 12, Moss Hart 11, Philip Barry 10).* Master Class, *his tenth Best Play, opened on Broadway November 5 and won the best-play Tony.*

Other notable McNally presentations in one of the most active and successful playwriting careers in his generation have included Whiskey *(1973, OOB); the book for the John Kander-Fred Ebb musical* The Rink *(1984, Broadway);* The Lisbon Traviata *(1985, OOB; 1989, off Broadway at MTC);* Frankie and Johnny in the Clair de Lune *(1987, off Broadway at MTC for 533 performances); sketch material for MTC's musical revue* Urban Blight, *1988; in 1989,* Preclude and Liebestod *and* Hope *OOB and* Up in Saratoga *in regional theater at the Old Globe in San Diego; and in 1990, a revival at MTC of his* Bad Habits. *McNally adapted his own* The Ritz *and* Frankie and Johnny *for the movies and is the author of a number of TV plays, including the 1991 Emmy Award-winning* Andre's Mother. *He has been the recipient of Obies, Hull-Warriner Awards (for* Bad Habits *and* The Lisbon Traviata*); fellowships from CBS, Rockefeller and two from the Guggenheim Foundation; and a citation from the American Academy of Arts and Letters. He lives in Manhattan and has served as vice president of the Dramatists Guild, the organization of playwrights, composers, lyricists and musical book writers, since 1981.*

To illustrate in these pages the depth of the McNally work as well as its narrative breadth, we represent Master Class *here not with a detailed synopsis but with a single section almost in its entirety—events leading to the end of Act I—framed in the central character's opening and closing comments to the audience.*

ACT I

SYNOPSIS: Maria Callas enters a classroom where an Accompanist is seated at the piano. She will be teaching a master class in singing before a roomful of students, and there is a chair where she can sit when not pacing to and fro, acting out her comments.

The house lights are still up when Maria walks forward and addresses the audience as though it were the student audience of her class.

MARIA: No applause. We're here to work. You're not in a theater. This is a classroom. No folderol. This is a master class. Singing is serious business. We're going to roll up our sleeves and work. I appreciate your welcome but enough is enough. *Basta. Fini.* Eh? So. How is everyone? Can you hear me? I don't believe in microphones. Singing is first of all about projection. So is speech. People are forgetting how to listen. They want everything blasted at them. Listening takes concentration. If you can't hear me, it's your fault. You're not concentrating. I don't get any louder than this. So come down closer or leave. No takers? What? You're all scared of me? Eh? Is that it? I don't bite. I promise you. I bark, I bark quite a bit actually, but I don't bite. I don't know what you're expecting. What did they tell you? I hope you're not expecting me to sing. Well, we shall see what we shall see. *Alora,* so, let's begin. Where is the first student? Who is the first student? Are they here? When I was a student, I never missed a lesson. Never. Not once. I was never late for one either. In fact, I was usually early. I never wanted to leave the conservatory. I lived, ate and slept music. Music is a discipline. Too many of you are looking for the easy way out. Short cuts. No. If you want to have a career, as I did, and I'm not boasting now, I am not one to boast, you must be willing to subjugate yourself ... is that a word? ... subjugate yourself to the music. Always the music. You are its servant. You are here to serve the composer. The composer is God. In Athens, and this was during the war, I often went to bed hungry, but I walked to the conservatory and back every day, six days a week, and sometimes my feet were bleeding because I had no proper shoes. I don't tell you this to melodramatize. Oh no. I tell you to show you who I am. Discipline. Courage. Here. Right here. From the guts.

These lights. Who is in charge of these lights? Is someone in charge of these lights? May we have the lights in the auditorium off, please? This is really terrible. We can't work under these conditions. I'm not going to ask a student to come out here until these lights are taken care of. This is what I was talking about. Attention must be paid to every detail. The lights. Your wig. The amount of stage dust. A career in the theater demands total concentration. One hundred percent detail. You think I'm joking? I'm not joking. You wait, you'll see. If you're ever so lucky to sing in one of the great theaters. I mean La Scala. I mean Covent Garden. I mean L'Opera. I mean Vienna. I mean the Metropolitan. You think it's easy? A great career? Hah! That's all I have to say to you. Hah! Is this my chair? I don't see a cushion. I asked for a cushion. Thank you.

The house lights are turned off. Maria gets acquainted with her accompanist, Manny. Then Sophie De Palma, a soprano dressed in fluffy pink and lacking what Maria has described as "a look" to make her interesting, presents herself and her singing for Maria's criticism and the edification of the "student audience." Before she sings a note, Sophie is subjected to Maria's comments about her appearance and style, interpolated with reminiscences of Maria's own great career. There are interruptions when a stagehand brings Maria the requested cushion, and then a footstool. Finally Maria urges Sophie to sing but stops her with more advice after she has sung only one word, "Oh." When Sophie is allowed to sing, interruptedly, Maria urges her to emphasize her consonants and keep in mind the meaning of the words she is singing.

SOPRANO: This is hard.

MARIA: Of course it's hard. That's why it's so important we do it right. "This is hard." Where am I? I thought I was somewhere where people were serious. This is not a film studio where anyone can get up there and act. I hate that word. Act. No! Feel. Be. That's what we're doing here. "This is hard." I'll tell you what's hard. What's hard is listening to you make a mockery of this work of art. "Mockery" is too strong a word. So is "travesty." I'm not getting any juice from you, Sophie. I want juice. I want passion. I want you.

SOPRANO: I'm not that sort of singer.

MARIA: Well try. Just once in your life, try.

SOPRANO: I'm not that sort of person either.

MARIA: What sort of person are you then?

SOPRANO: I just want to sing.

MARIA: Am I stopping you?

SOPRANO: No. You're.

MARIA: We don't have to finish this if you're unhappy.

SOPRANO: I don't know what you're talking about.

MARIA: Yes you do. You just don't want to do it. Everyone understood what I was talking about when I was singing. They simply didn't want to listen. Too difficult. Too painful. Too controversial. At my final performance at La Scala in *Pirata* in the Mad Scene when I came to the words *"il palco funesto"*—"the fatal scaffold"—I pointed to the general manager in his box, the same man who had said my services in his theater were no longer necessary, and hurled the words right at him. I don't know what came over me, I was possessed, like a Fury, and I went right to the stage apron, just meters from where he was sitting, and I sang *"il palco funesto."* The audience gasped. Ghiringhelli reeled from the force of it. They say it was the greatest ovation in the history of La Scala. He ordered them to ring down the fire curtain to stop my applause. Why deal with someone like me when you can have Tebaldi or Sutherland or Sills? I don't blame them. I did but I don't now. They said they didn't like my sound. That wasn't it. They didn't like my soul. Too. What? Too. Something. You have a lovely voice, you know. A charming sound.

SOPRANO: Thank you.

MARIA: Much lovelier than mine ever was. And no one ever accused me or my voice of charm. That was my sister. She was the charming one. The pretty one. The one the boys. Wanted. Anyway. *En tout cas.* All that got her wherever she is, I don't know, we don't speak, and got me where I am, sometimes I think the whole world knows where that is, or was, and which is right now up here with you talking to you about your voice, your sound. Who you are. Who are you? Sophie De Palma, you've told us your name but who are you? Tears will get you nowhere, darling. Not in the theater, not in real life. Certainly not with me. No one cares how many nights I cried myself to sleep. I sang *Norma* better than anyone had in years and I interpolated a high F at the end of the first act. That's all people cared about. When you're fat and ugly (and I'm not saying that you are either of those things) you had better have a couple of high F's you can interpolate into your life. No one cares about your damp pillow. Why should I? Did you care about mine? Did anyone? But that's another story. I can cry all I want now (don't worry, I won't. Tears come hard when you're me) but you can't, Sophie De Palma. You've got to sing for your supper. Sing for your salvation. Shall we try again?

> *Soprano nods. Maria gives her a tissue and glances at her watch.*

Did you know one of my baptismal Greek Orthodox names was Sophie?

SOPRANO: No.

MARIA: Cecilia Sophia Anna Maria Kalogeropoulou. December Two, Nineteen . . . But that was in another life. *Allora. Cominciamo. Ricominciamo.* Again.

SOPRANO: Again? I haven't. Once. I'm sorry.

MARIA: Remember to use the words. From "*Gran Dio.*"

SOPRANO *(sings):* "*Gran Dio . . .*"

MARIA: What are you doing?

SOPRANO: I'm sorry?

MARIA: What does it say in the score?

SOPRANO: I begin on the C above middle C and . . .

MARIA: I'm not talking about notes. There's a direction from the composer.

SOPRANO: There is?

> *Soprano goes to piano and looks at the music Accompanist is playing from.*

MARIA: This is what I've been talking about the entire time. This lack of detail. This sense of "nothing matters."

SOPRANO: You mean, "*inginocchiandosi*"?

> *She has difficulty with the word.*

MARIA: I mean "*inginocchiandosi.*"

> *She doesn't.*

SOPRANO: Is it important?

MARIA: It's life and death, like everything we do here.

SOPRANO: I don't know what it means.

MARIA: We can see that.

SOPRANO: It's a reflexive verb, I know that much. It means I do something to myself.

Zoe Caldwell as Maria Callas in Terrence McNally's *Master Class*

MARIA: Don't tempt me to tell you what that might be. Kneel.
SOPRANO: Kneel?
MARIA: It means "kneel." *Cosi!*
    She drops to her knees and opens her arms wide.
"*Gran Dio!*" This is how we speak to God. On our knees, *a terra,* our arms open to
Him. "*Non mirar il mio pianto.*" Do not heed these tears I shed. "*Io gliel perdono.*"
I forgive him them. The orchestra is sounding like an organ here. A church organ.
What is Bellini up to? "*Quanto infelice io sono, felice ei sia.*" Let him be as happy
as I am unhappy. "*Questa d'un cor che more e l'ultima preghiera.*" This is the last

prayer of a heart that is dying. That explains the organ. It's all in the music. *"Ah, si!"* She says it again. She has to. *"Questa d'un cor che more e l'ultima preghiera."*

SOPRANO: I see what you mean now.

MARIA: What do you do now? What does the score say?

SOPRANO *(haltingly):* *"Guardandosi la mano—"*

MARIA *(impatiently):* *"Guardandosi la mano come cercando l'anello."* She's looking for the ring that isn't there, Sophie. *(She looks at her left hand for the ring.)* *"L'anello mio."*

SOPRANO: My ring!

MARIA: *"L'anello."*

SOPRANO: The ring.

MARIA: *"Ei me l'ha tolto."*

SOPRANO: He took it from me.

MARIA: *"Ma non puo rapirmi l'immagin sua . . ."*

SOPRANO: But he cannot from me take image his. His image.

MARIA: *"Sculta ella e qui . . ."*

SOPRANO: Sculptured it is here.

MARIA: Here! *". . . qui . . . nel . . . petto."*

SOPRANO: In my heart. Amina takes Elvino's faded flowers from her bosom.

   Accompanist begins playing the introduction to the aria proper.

MARIA: Just listen to the music and think about what the words mean. It's all there, Sophie. These composers knew the human heart. All we have to do is listen.

Maria voices a passage from the opera, demonstrating its cadences and emphases.

MARIA: . . . . . Something like that, Sophie, eh? You see what I mean now?

SOPRANO: I think so. Thank you.

MARIA: You think you can do that?

SOPRANO: I'll. Yes.

MARIA: Did you mark your score? Those phrases I pointed out?

SOPRANO: No.

MARIA: Why not?

SOPRANO: I don't have a pencil.

MARIA: Then how do you expect to remember what you've learned? Five, maybe ten years from now, you'll be singing this role in some little theater somewhere, and you'll be saying to yourself, "What did she tell me? What did she say?" . . . . . All right. Let's hear it again. With a broken heart this time.

   I hate to say it, but you should wear longer skirts or slacks. During daytime it's all right. But you must remember, I'm sorry I'm bringing this up, but the public that looks at you from down there sees a little more of you than you might want. Eh? It's no use now. You should have thought of it before. Forgive me, eh? No laughing. This is a serious matter. Maestro.

   Accompanist begins to play again.

I want you to imagine you are Amina. I want you to be great. This is opera, Sophie.

You're not in a drug store buying a pill. You're alone on a great stage. Make us feel what you feel. Show us *that* truth.

> *Soprano begins the recitative again as lights fade on Soprano and Accompanist and come up strong on Maria, who is hearing her performance of the same music. So are we.*

How quickly it all comes back. The great nights.

> *She listens.*

Ma. Luchino, perche? Why do you have me wearing jewels? I am supposed to be a poor Swiss village girl. "You are not a village girl. You are Maria Callas playing a village girl." *Ah, capisco, capisco!* I understood.

> *She listens.*

This was a terrifying moment. The beginning. In the utter, utter silence, my voice filling the void of that vast, darkened auditorium. I felt so alone, so unprotected. *Coraggio.* It's begun.

> *She listens.*

What were they expecting?

> *She listens.*

Ari always said, They're not coming to hear you, no one comes to hear Callas any more. They've come to look at you. You're not a singer. You're a freak. I'm a freak. We're both freaks. They've come to see us. You're a *monstre sacree* now. We are both *monstres sacrees.* And we are fucking.

I don't like that word, Ari.

Fuck you, you don't like that word.

This phrase. Lovely. And I did it well.

Did you hear what I said? Before you were just a singer. A canary who sang for her supper. A fat, ugly canary. And now you are a beautiful woman who fucks Aristotle Onassis.

Ari.

This is how I talk. This is how I have always talked. This is who I am. I'm coarse. I'm crude. I'm vulgar. Unlike some people, I remember from whence I came.

I remember. I remember too well.

They listen to you sing this boring shit music and clap and yell *Brava! Brava La Divina!* but what they all want to know is what we do in bed. The two Greeks. The two sweaty, piggy, beneath-them Greeks. The richest-man-in-the-world Greek and the most-famous-singer-in-the-world Greek. Together we rule the world. I have people by the balls and I squeeze. I squeeze very hard and without pity. I have you by the balls, Cecilia Sophia Anna Maria Kalogeropoulou. Everyone is for sale and I bought you.

This part. "She sang Amina's great lament in a voice suffused with tears."

You give me class. I give you my big thick uncircumcised Greek dick, and you give me class. I give you my wealth, and you give me respect where I never had any. I give you safety from your terror of the theater, you don't have to go there anymore. I give you everything you want and need but love. I'm lucky. I don't need love. I have class now.

"He" laughs.

Everyone needs love, Ari. I'm proud. I'm very proud, but when it comes to this, to love, to you, to us, I am not.

I don't give love to anyone but my children. Have a child of mine and I will love him. Yes?

Yes, Ari.

Hey, canary, chin up. Look at me. You don't need love either. You have theirs. The snobs and the fags. They adore you. The snobs all want to take you to dinner at Lutece, and the fags all want to be you. Frankly, I'm not threatened. You hate it when I call you canary, don't you? It's affectionate. Can't you hear the affection in canary?

I was good tonight. I was very good.

Why don't you give all this up? It's *caca, skata* anyway. Eh? You know it, I know it. You live on the boat. You can go anywhere you want, stay as long as you want, buy anything you want, within reason. Always within reason. I hate a woman who tries to bleed a man dry. Of course she would have to be some woman to bleed this motherfucker dry. Do you know how much I'm worth? Do you have any idea of just how much money I have? I breathe money, I sweat money, I shit money.

I don't have to sing anymore? I won't if you don't want me.

Okay, so you don't sing anymore. You don't retire, you stop. There's a difference. Retiring is depressing. Stopping is class. They beg you. You're adamant. No means no, you tell them. I bet you didn't know I had that word in me, did you? Adamant. It means unshakable or immovable, especially in opposition. Hard. Like diamonds. That's us, baby.

That's us, Ari. A matched pair.

But when I want you to sing, you sing. You sing only for me. I have you under the most fucking exclusive contract anybody ever had. And when I ask you to sing, you know what you're going to sing for me, baby? None of that opera *skata*. That song I taught you about the whore from Piraeus who took it five different ways at the same time. I had to tell you what four of those ways were.

I don't like that song, Ari.

Where have you been all your life, canary? Don't they fuck in the opera house?

I don't like that song.

Sing it anyway.

> *The aria proper has ended. We hear the audience applaud.*

I never heard their applause here. I was too deep in a dream. Like Amina, I'd been sleepwalking. But there I was on the stage of La Scala. I was beautifully dressed, heavy with diamonds, real diamonds, my hair in a tight chignon bound with real white roses flown to Milan the day of the performance from the south of France. "The ghost of Maria Taglioni," one critic wrote. I was beautiful at last.

> *The music continues directly into the cabaletta conclusion of the scene and opera itself. We hear Maria's voice singing "Ah, non giunge."*

I keep thinking of a pretty, slim blonde girl back at the conservatory in Athens. Mme. De Hidalgo gave her the part of Amina at the student recital. I was so heartbroken but I wanted to scratch her face with my nails at the same time, too. I was cast as a nun in *Suor Angelica* instead. But I want to sing Amina in *Sonnambula,* Mme. De Hidalgo. With your voice and figure you're better off as a nun, my child. Look at me now, Mme. De Hidalgo. Listen to me now. Sometimes I think every performance I sing is for that pretty, slim, blonde girl taking all those bows at the Conservatory. Whatever happened to her with her freshly laundered blouses and bags full of oranges? My sister was another slim pretty blonde. They're not up here, either one of them. I'm up here. The fat ugly greasy one with the thick glasses and bad skin is up here and she's dressed by Piero Tosi and she's wearing so many diamonds she can scarcely move her arms and she is the absolute center of the universe right now.

I know they're all out there in the dark. My enemies. My mother. My sister. The other singers. Smiling. Waiting for me to fail. The daredevil stuff is coming up. The hullabaloo. I'm not afraid. I welcome it. Reckless. You bet, I'm reckless! Someone said I'd rather sing like Callas for one year than like anyone else for twenty! Now the embellishments. The second time around. Never do it the same way twice. Flick your voice here. Lighten it. Shade it. Trill. Astonish.

> *She listens. Slowly the rear of the stage will become the magnificent interior of La Scala.*

Now the genius part of this production. Visconti has the house lights in the auditorium begin to come up while I'm still singing. Slowly, slowly. We're both waking up from a dream, the audience and me. The effect is unheard of. There's never been a night like this in the history of La Scala. The theater is garlanded with fresh roses hung from the boxes. The audience is magnificently dressed. It's the biggest *prima* of the season. There's Tebaldi. There's Lollobrigida. Magnani. The Rainiers. They're all here. And here I am. Dead center-stage at the greatest theater in Europe singing roulades in full voice. Hurling notes like thunderbolts. Daring anyone to challenge me. They can all see me but now I can see them. We are in the same room together at last. I have everyone where I want them. They're not smiling now. With each phrase, I come closer to the footlights. The auditorium grows brighter and brighter my voice goes higher and higher. People have stopped breathing. My revenge, my triumph are complete. The applause is washing over me. I only have one note left to sing. Ah, yes, it's over. I've won again!

> *Maria stands listening to the ovation. It is tremendous. When it fades to silence, the lights have faded back to the level of the master class. Both the Soprano and the Accompanist are waiting anxiously for her appraisal.*

That was better.

SOPRANO: Thank you.

MARIA: Much better.

SOPRANO: Thank you.

MARIA: We'll take a break now.

> *Maria goes to her chair, takes up her purse and leaves the stage.*

SOPRANO *(to Maria):* Thank you. (*To Accompanist.*) Thank you. I thought she was going to critique me. I guess she liked me. (*To Accompanist.*) Now how do I get offstage? They should teach us that. They should teach us a lot of things they don't.

ACCOMPANIST: Your score.

SOPRANO: Thank you.

> *He returns her score and they go off. The stage is bare except for the piano and Maria's chair. The house lights are fully up now. End of Act I.*

ACT II

After a delayed entrance and a few comments on aspects of her profession and popularity, Maria receives the next student, another soprano, Sharon Graham, who has come to the class dressed to the nines in an evening gown and prepared to sing the Lady Macbeth aria in the Letter Scene. Maria rebukes Sharon for being over-dressed and sends her out so that she can return, making a dramatic entrance in her role. But when the Accompanist plays the music for the entrance, there is no Sharon. She has apparently walked out on the class.

The next student is a tenor, Anthony Candolino, with a BA in music and an MFA in voice. He admits right up front that he wants singing to make him rich and famous. Maria finds that the tenor knows less than he should about the role he's prepared to sing and tries to dismiss him, but he refuses to go: he's come to sing, and he's going to sing, and he expects Maria to coach him on how to become an artist as well as a singer. Maria advises him on technique and feeling as he performs an aria from *Tosca,* and she sends him off with praise.

It's time for the next student, and the second soprano, Sharon, has decided to come back and try again. She performs her entrance as Lady Macbeth and begins to sing but is stopped. Questioned by Maria, Sharon reveals that she knows what the words she is singing mean, but she has never read them in the Shakespearean original. Maria proceeds to show Sharon how to make Lady Macbeth's entrance carrying a fateful letter more effectively dramatic. During this demonstration, "*Ma-*

Zoe Caldwell and Audra McDonald as teacher and pupil in *Master Class*

ria begins to sing the first lines of Lady Macbeth's recitative. What comes out is a cracked and broken thing. A voice in ruins. It is a terrible moment."

Sharon sings her Lady Macbeth aria, with Maria coaching her after almost every line of the text. She sends Sharon off again to re-enter with the letter and do the scene over, with Maria promising not to interrupt her this time. Sharon makes her entrance again and begins the aria. Maria starts to speak the words Sharon is singing; then, after a light change, it is Maria's voice at La Scala we are hearing in the same aria. Again, Maria imagines she is talking to others, first to a suitor whom she rejects, then to Ari, announcing that she is pregnant. Ari is displeased to hear this, so Maria ends her pregnancy. She is losing her voice and finally is fired by La Scala. But Ari is all she wants now, and her dream ends with her begging him to marry her.

Sharon's Lady Macbeth aria ends. Maria observes that Sharon should in future seek roles less demanding than Lady Macbeth, "more appropriate for your limitations."

SHARON: I wish I'd never done this. I don't like you. You can't sing any more, and you're envious of anyone younger who can. You just want us to sing like you, recklessly, and lose our voices in ten years like you did. Well, I won't do it. I don't want to. I don't want to sing like you. I hate people like you. You want to make the world dangerous for everyone just because it was for you.

She leaves. There is an awkward silence.

MARIA: So. *Po po po.* I think we should stop there. Miss Graham thought I wanted her to sing like Maria Callas. No one can sing like Maria Callas. Only Cecilia Sophia Anna Maria Kalogeropoulou could sing like Maria Callas. I'm very upset. I'm hurt. As strange as it may seem to some of you, I have feelings, too. Anyway. That's another story. Et cetera, et cetera, eh? Maybe this whole business of teaching is a mistake. Thank you, Manny. That will be all.

Accompanist exits.

If I have seemed harsh, it is because I have been harsh with myself. I'm not good with words, but I have tried to reach you. To communicate something of what I feel about what we do as artists, as musicians and as human beings. The sun will not fall down from the sky if there are no more *Traviatas.* The world can and will go on without us, but I have to think that we have made this world a better place. That we have left it richer, wiser than had we not chosen the way of art. The older I get, the less I know, but I am certain that what we do matters. If I didn't believe that. You must know what you want to do in life, you must decide, for we cannot do everything. Do not think singing is an easy career. It is a lifetime's work; it does not stop here. Whether I continue singing or not doesn't matter. Besides, it's all there in the recordings. What matters is that you use whatever you have learned wisely. Think of the expression of the words, of good diction, and of your own deep feelings. The only thanks I ask is that you sing properly and honestly. If you do this, I will feel repaid. Well, that's that.

She gathers her things and goes. Blackout. Curtain.

Best Play Citation

○ ○ ○
○ ○ ○
○ ○ ○
○ ○ ○
○ ○ ○
○ ○ ○ # NEW ENGLAND

A Full-Length Play in One Act

BY RICHARD NELSON

Cast and credits appear on pages 317–318

RICHARD (JOHN) NELSON, playwright (as distinguished from another Richard Nelson, lighting designer), was born in Chicago on October 17, 1950, graduated from Hamilton College in 1972 and has pursued a long and fruitful career in New York and regional theater. He has served as literary manager of the Brooklyn Academy of Music Theater Company (1979–81), as associate director of Chicago's Goodman Theater (1980–83) and as dramaturge of Minneapolis's Tyrone Guthrie Theater (1981–82). Meanwhile, he was writing plays. His first New York production was Conjuring an Event *at American Place March 10, 1978, two years after its first production in cross-country theater. According to the* Best Plays *record, there have followed an adaptation of Dario Fo's* Accidental Death of an Anarchist *on Broadway (1984) and of Beaumarchais's* The Marriage of Figaro *on Broadway (1985);* Principia Scriptoriae *at Manhattan Theater Club (1986); the one-acter* The Return of Pinocchio *off Broadway (1986); the book of the Broadway musical* Chess *(1988);* Some Americans Abroad *at both Lincoln Center theaters (1990) and* Two Shakespearean Actors *at the Vivian Beaumont (1992, Tony-nominated for best play);* Misha's Party *co-written with Alexander Gelman, OOB in a Reading Room Reading (1993);* Life Sentences *OOB at Second Stage (1993), and* New England *which was commissioned and pro-*

117

duced in London by the Royal Shakespeare Company and then was produced here by Manhattan Theater Company on November 7, its author's first Best Play.

Nelson's long list of stage works produced in regional theater and abroad includes Columbus and the Discovery of Japan, The Vienna Notes, Jungle Coup, Conjuring an Event, Bal, Rip Van Winkle or The Works, An American Comedy, Between East and West, Roots in Water, *an adaptation of Strindberg's* The Father *(produced by Roundabout on Broadway this season) and translations of* Three Sisters, Il Campiello, Don Juan *and* Jungle of Cities—*plus a new play,* The General from America, *scheduled for production this year. Nelson is also the author of the screen play for* Ethan Frome *and has written extensively for radio and TV, both in the U.S. and for the BBC.*

Nelson has received Thomas J. Watson, NEA Creative Writing, Guggenheim and NEA Playwriting Fellowships and has been awarded grants from the Office of Advanced Drama Research, the Rockefeller Foundation and the Lila Wallace Fund. He is married, with two daughters and lives in New York State.

Time: Over a weekend

Place: A farmhouse in western Connecticut, just across the border from New York State

Scene 1

SYNOPSIS: Harry Baker, in his 60s, a professor of music at the local community college, is joined in his study by his girl friend, Alice Berry, 54, who has come to see how he's feeling. Harry has been suffering from a headache and is obviously in low spirits. He is barely able to take it in that Alice's ex-husband's brother, Tom Berry, has arrived for the weekend, as expected. Tom, in his 40s, enters the study and is introduced to Harry. After Tom and Alice leave the study, Harry turns on the CD player for a violin rendition of Debussy's "The Girl with the Flaxen Hair," opens his desk drawer, takes out a revolver and cocks it. He then takes off his glasses and notices that they are dirty.

> *With a handkerchief, Harry begins to clean them, then realizes what he is doing, laughs to himself and stops. He puts down the glasses, picks up the gun and puts the barrel to his head. Alice enters from the hallway.*

ALICE: Tom's so happy to be—(*She sees what Harry is doing. Screams:*) Nooooooo!!!!!!!!!!!

> *Harry pulls the trigger. Gunshot. And he is dead.*

Scene 2

Much later that same evening, Tom is in the kitchen getting himself a snack of milk and cereal. A feature of this room is "*a large rustic wooden table which has been used both for eating and as a sort of desk. Piles of papers, bills, catalogues, etc.; a phone, whose cord extends to the wall, making a kind of obstacle for anyone going around the table. There is a transistor radio on the table.*" Alice enters, drink in hand, announcing that Elizabeth Baker, the late Harry's middle child, will arrive momentarily. Also converging on the homestead are Alfred Baker (Harry's brother), Paul Baker (Harry's son) with his wife Sophie and Gemma Baker (Harry's oldest). They are all English expatriates, living in America, except Sophie, who is French.

Alice has been cleaning up the study and is reminded of happier times by photos of herself and Harry in Bermuda last month. She apologizes to Tom for not being able to treat him as a house guest should be treated but persuades him to stay on for the weekend and help her face Harry's family, including Elizabeth, who's "going to walk into here and start telling us all what to do."

Elizabeth Baker, 37, enters, meets Tom, reacts crisply to the situation, requests a soft drink and insists on going out to fetch her own luggage.

> *Alice sees that Tom has been looking at the album and looks over his shoulder.*

ALICE *(pointing to a photo):* Harry bought that bathing suit for me in Hamilton. That was so unlike him. He was scared to buy me anything. Afraid, he said, I'd just take it back. *(She smiles.)* It took me about two days to get the nerve to wear it in public. Finally—I did. *(Short pause.)* After your brother—
> *Tom looks at her.*
I'd convinced myself I'd never meet another man. You see other women my age, and . . . You see yourself in their shoes. I expected nothing. Then I met Harry.
> *Elizabeth enters with her bag. Pause. For a moment no one knows what to say.*
(Finally.) Here's your seltzer.

ELIZABETH *(as she drinks):* I had lunch with Dick Riley last week. Your name came up, Alice. He said you were the best managing editor they'd ever had.
> *Finishes drinking.*
What a shame it was when you left. *(Beat.)* So—know that even after a couple of years, you're still missed.

ALICE *(to Tom):* I was cheap. I didn't know any better. That's all he means. *(Turns to Elizabeth.)* The man at the funeral home—he's not bad. He's not what you'd expect.

ELIZABETH: Good.
> *Beat.*

ALICE: Gemma and Alfred have made it as far as Denver. They have to wait till morning for the next flight. They called.

ELIZABETH: Good. *(Beat.)* I mean good that they called, not that they have to wait—

ALICE: I understood. And Paul and Sophie—they'll get a flight in the morning as well. *(Turns to Tom.)* From L.A.

TOM *(to Elizabeth):* I was amazed when she told me everyone lives in the States . . . . . That's rare, isn't it?

Instead of answering him, Elizabeth turns to Alice and reviews the sleeping arrangements for the family members converging on this house. They will rely on Chinese takeout to solve the cooking problem.

ALICE: . . . . . Harry loves their dumplings. *(She stops. Corrects.)* He loved them. *(Short pause. Alice tries not to cry; she turns to Elizabeth.)* He did it in front of me. I think that's what I can't forgive him for. *(Beat.)* But I don't think he meant to hurt me.
ELIZABETH: No—
ALICE: Because, he loved me.
    She takes Elizabeth's hand.
Your father was a very—tired man.
ELIZABETH: I know. And he'd been tired for years—long before he'd met you, Alice.
ALICE *(looks up at her):* Thank you.
    Beat.
ELIZABETH: This isn't a surprise.

Alice and Elizabeth agree that Harry was "a refined and cultured man" with "impeccable taste." They exit to make the sleeping arrangements.

Scene 3

In early evening of the next day, the members of Harry's family have all arrived. In the kitchen, Paul (Harry's son, 32) and his sister Gemma (the older daughter, 39) are discussing their trips while Alice and Tom prepare the table for a Chinese dinner. The phone rings, and Alice answers it: "Yes. At eleven. Here in the garden. Yes, Harry would have liked that."

Harry's twin brother Alfred will be down in a moment, so the group prepares to sit down to dinner. But Paul points out that his wife Sophie is still napping.

PAUL: I just think she might feel—I don't know—to come down and find us all eating dinner . . .
    Beat.
ELIZABETH: Couldn't you wake her up, Paul? I wouldn't want people waiting to eat because of me.
GEMMA: The food'll get cold.
PAUL: She didn't sleep at all last night. Or on the plane.
    Beat.
ELIZABETH: We can reheat it for her later, then.
ALICE: Maybe she's reading, I'll go and see if—*(Starts to go.)*

PAUL: Let her sleep! Please. I want her to get some sleep.

Beat.

GEMMA: So we're to—what? The food's here. This makes no sense.

PAUL: I told her we wouldn't be eating for a while. That's what Alice told me—

ALICE: Because I thought there'd be a wait—

TOM: There wasn't any wait at the restaurant.

ALICE: On a Saturday night?! That's incredible. It's such a popular place.

Short pause.

GEMMA: So what are we going to—?

ELIZABETH *(over this):* What if we don't sit down? What if we—say, put out the food and whenever anyone wants to—buffet-style. So no one's missing anything. How's that, Paul? We can keep reheating it, so it's always ready.

GEMMA: Sophie can't get upset about that.

PAUL: It wasn't because she'd get upset—

GEMMA: I mean, it sounds fair.

PAUL *(continuing):* She's not the one upset, I am. I told her—she doesn't care. Why should she care? Whatever we want to do is fine with—

ELIZABETH: Fine! Then we'll need some plates.

ALICE: I'll get them.

PAUL: How would you feel if you walked in on—and there was your husband surrounded by his sisters, having dinner, and you'd been told—

ELIZABETH: We understand, Paul. Forget it.

They discuss arrangements: Alice plans to have Harry cremated and his ashes scattered in the garden. Gemma was angry at her father when she heard the news about his suicide (she had warned him she'd hate him if he did any such thing). Elizabeth was shocked and wonders if anyone else was, but there are no replies.

Alice comes in with the plates and Tom with a bottle of wine. Alice immediately lights a cigarette—she wasn't permitted to smoke in here while Harry was alive, but she plans to do her own thing now. *"Alfred, Harry's twin brother enters. Tom sees him and nearly cries out in shock—irrationally thinking that this is Harry's ghost."* When things settle down, Alfred reports that Sophie is up and in the bathroom. Paul suggests they can now set the table for a sit-down meal, as Alfred examines the food.

ALFRED: It smells good. Harry always loved food.

TOM: Did he?

ALFRED: Loved it. Talked about nothing else.

ALICE: That's not true, Alfred. He rarely—

ALFRED: Who cares? Now we can say anything we want about the bastard.

Short pause, Alfred stands at the table; and suddenly he nearly collapses. Everyone hurries to him, to grab him. As they do, they shout, "What's wrong? Sit down! Get him some water! Are you all right?, etc."

ALICE *(with a glass of seltzer):* Here, drink this.

Alfred drinks. He holds up his hands—to show that he will be fine. He drinks some more.

ALFRED *(finally):* You said—in the study? Down the hall. (*Beat.*) That's where it was? *(Alice nods.)* I just looked in. I didn't see anything. Have you been cleaning, Alice? *(Beat.)* Get someone in. Do yourself a favor. *(He sips, then:)* I threw up—in the study. I couldn't get anything to clean it up with. Sophie was in the bathroom.

    Beat.

GEMMA: We'll clean it up, Uncle Alfred.

Paul comes in with his wife Sophie, 41, French, a U.S. resident for a number of years. Sophie wonders why they're not eating in the dining room. Paul immediately reacts to this by offering to help move, and the others follow his lead, even though Elizabeth opts for remaining here in the kitchen.

On the phone, Alice tells a caller that flowers would be appreciated instead of a gift to charity, because Harry had no favorite charity that they know of. After she puts down the phone she asks, "Why are we moving? Why can't we stay where we are?" but follows the others off.

Scene 4

A short time later, in the kitchen, Elizabeth has obviously won her point, because all are sitting around the table eating their Chinese meal, which has turned out to be less than appetizing. Tom asks Paul what kind of work he does in L.A., and Paul responds that he's a "reader," i.e.: he reads movie scripts and advises on their development. Alfred calls the movies "rubbish," getting a reaction from Paul.

PAUL: . . . . . I'm learning what people want!

ALFRED *(yelling back):* They don't know what people want!

PAUL: And in England they do? (*Beat.*) In London today there aren't three people who know how to make a successful movie. That's my opinion.

    Short pause. No one knows what to say.

SOPHIE: And if Paul hadn't moved to L.A., we never would have met.

    Short pause, as Paul's family bite their tongues.

ELIZABETH: Uncle Alfred, you're here. I wouldn't criticize.

ALFRED: They pay me twice what I got at Hull. Full stop. *I* didn't come for the culture.

TOM *(to Alice, referring to Alfred):* What does he do—?

ALICE: He teaches English. *(Short pause. To everyone:)* Tom *teaches*—acting.

    Everyone politely nods or mumbles, "Oh, really."

(To Paul:) So he's in the performing arts as well.

TOM: Not in L.A. In New York.

PAUL: For theater?

TOM: Some.

PAUL: I'd of thought you couldn't make a living from the theater—

TOM: Students of mine—they do television, films, plays. I mostly do accents. *(Beat.)* For Americans trying to be—*(Shrugs.)* English? As well as the other way around.

ELIZABETH: There's a lot of need for—?

TOM: I survive. *(Beat.)* I do the best I can. It's a living. *(To Paul.)* I like Los Angeles too.

GEMMA: For me—New Mexico is paradise. Isn't it, Uncle Alfred? I sit on my porch, brush in hand and paint and before me . . . I don't even have to put on shoes! Before me is a landscape that is not only the most extraordinary I've ever seen, but it also *changes.* Totally, completely remakes itself, I don't know, five hundred times a day! Because of the light, the clouds, even the density of the air. I don't mean just shadows, I mean one minute it's yellow and the next it's blue! *(She smiles and shakes her head.)* It's so different from England. Or the Alps or Provence where everything's fixed. Some mornings what gets me out of bed is the thought that if I weren't out there to paint it all, it'd be lost for good.

Alice mentions that New England is also beautiful, though she hasn't seen as much of it as she'd like. She came to visit Harry for a weekend about two years ago, then began coming often and staying longer, finally quitting her job and settling in. But most of what she's seen is between here and New York City. Tom and Elizabeth live in New York, he on the West Side, she on the East.

Sophie feels the need for a lie-down and orders Paul to come with her and help her find "an aspirin or something." In her absence, Elizabeth comments that "Sophie's no more French than I am," having lived in West Hollywood from age 8 on. Sophie's accent, Elizabeth believes, is put on in order to please her husband.

Tom notes that they are living all over the United States and wonders if that is unusual. Harry came over here 20 years ago, planning to stay only for one semester but staying on and on. One by one the others, of school age, followed him to America—all except their mother, Harry's wife, who remained in England and died only two months ago (Harry went over for the funeral). Paul returns, reporting that Sophie is fine. The others put him in the conversational picture.

ALFRED: We were telling Tom how Harry came to the States.

PAUL: You've told him that Mother just threw him out?

ALICE: Did she?

PAUL: She'd had enough of him. She used to say that marrying Father was like buying a boat; your happiest times are when you get it, and when you get rid of it. *(He laughs, no one else does.)*

ALICE: What exactly had your father done for your mother to throw him out?
    Beat.

ELIZABETH *(after checking with her siblings):* She never said. I don't think we ever asked.

GEMMA: There's a lot we don't know. Why didn't they ever divorce—*(Gemma is about to continue a list.)*

ALICE *(interrupting):* Harry was still married to your mother?

GEMMA: Didn't you know that?

Tom changes the subject, speaking to Paul about Sophie (who is just tired, not sick), to whom Paul has been married less than a year. Alice goes to get another bottle of wine—"I know where Harry's best stuff is hidden"—and in her absence, Elizabeth wonders if it means anything that Harry never told Alice he was married. Alfred reports that Harry once told him his relationship with Alice was "comfortable."

They discuss the cremation idea and, on the whole, are against it. They decide to tell Alice they want their father buried and the service in the garden tomorrow to be a memorial.

Alfred remarks to Tom that in the case of twins there's always a good one and a bad one, and he intimates that in their case Harry was the bad one: "He wasn't very nice to me." Harry had suggested that Alfred wouldn't be able to make it in America. But Alfred managed to land a more important teaching position than Harry.

The phone has rung and was answered elsewhere while they are talking. Alice comes in with the wine, commenting, "That was the funeral home—we can pick up the ashes any time now." She doesn't notice that this strikes the others dumb. She turns her attention to the pages of a photo album. Tom breaks the embarrassed silence by asking Paul, "Read any good film scripts lately?," causing Alfred to choke with laughter. Paul answers Tom's question with a statement: "The funny thing about living in America as a foreigner is the way you see other foreigners act. They love to criticize. Everything's—what? Rubbish? Some things are and some things aren't. That's how I see things, but . . . I had a friend from London visiting. To him, everything was either stupid or plastic or barbaric. Then you couldn't get him out of the damn sun. At night you couldn't get him away from the damn TV. *(He sips his water.)* But I know why this is. I've thought about this a lot. It's all so—threatening. It's too much for some people to handle. The size of everything. The importance of everything. So they're actually being defensive. They're scared."

Paul has also been thinking about movie scripts, he says, finally answering Tom's question, and he believes that if the margins on the 22,000,000 pages of the 10,000 scripts in circulation on any given day were reduced by just three spaces, 200 trees would be saved. And now it's Alice who changes the subject.

ALICE: I did know—about Harry being married.

Short pause. She goes back to looking at the album

ALFRED *(looks at Alice; then):* He talked to me about you, Alice. Harry. *(She looks up.)* He said the nicest things. He told me how much he loved you. This new "gal" he called you. He said—you were everything to him.

She nods and goes back to the album.

ELIZABETH *(to Paul):* There are so many Brits in publishing here. I have friends—Americans who say the only way to advance is to go first to England—or fake a British accent. *(She laughs.)*

GEMMA *(to Tom):* Work for you! *(Laughter.)*

TOM *(over this):* So that's why they take my classes!

More laughter. Short pause.

GEMMA: All of my English friends—such as they are in New Mexico—make fun. It's an easy place to make fun. On the one hand, I suppose Paul is right—they're scared. We are. But on the other, you can't help yourself—there's so much that's crazy.

ELIZABETH: Father used to make fun—lest we forget.

PAUL: Father was scared too.

GEMMA: He didn't make fun, he hated. The last time I called him—he just started ranting.

PAUL: About?

GEMMA: He hated this country and everything it tries to be. Or doesn't try to be.

PAUL: He loved looking down his nose—

ELIZABETH: I never took him seriously when he talked like that. It was just talk. I laughed at him, Paul.

PAUL: You encouraged him.

ELIZABETH: He made me laugh, as I've just said. And he wasn't scared, Paul— he was angry.

PAUL *(erupts):* If the man wasn't scared, then why the hell are we here?!! And he hated, all right! But the only thing he really hated was himself!! *(Beat.)* Isn't that now obvious?

Pause.

ALICE *(holding up the album):* You all might be interested in this. The photos go back years. You're all in here.

ELIZABETH: Pass it around.

ALICE: In a minute, when I'm done.

She continues to look through the album as she lights a cigarette.

ALFRED: I'm all in favor of keeping your sense of humor about things. Sometimes I think it's the only thing of any value that we have left. And if Americans wish to make fools of themselves in front of us—day after day after day after day—what are we supposed to do, cover our eyes? Well, I don't. *(Shrugs.)* So shoot me, Paul.

Gemma asks the others if they've heard Paul doing his American accent, and soon they are all clamoring for Paul to perform. At this moment Sophie enters in nightgown and robe to find out what the noise is all about, is annoyed to see that it is the result of having some fun from which she's excluded and exits after telling Paul she'll wait up for him.

Paul does a one-line American imitation in a Brando-Pacino style, much to the others' enjoyment. Sophie returns. She had promised to call her 9-year-old daughter, Claire (who is devoted to Paul), at 7 o'clock her time. It's too early to do so yet, and to go to bed (as Elizabeth remarks somewhat regretfully).

T. Scott Cunningham and Margaret Whitton as Paul
and Sophie in *New England* by Richard Nelson

Scene 5

In the kitchen an hour or so later, Sophie is talking to Claire on the phone while
Tom tells Paul a story about a prep school production of *The Importance of Being
Earnest,* illustrating an aspect of eccentric American behavior. Paul has a story, too:
"I'm in line at the grocery store. I obviously must have said something, because this
fellow behind me, hearing the accent I suppose, says *(American),* 'What the fuck is
going on with that Queen of yours? Why she letting 'em push her around! If I was
Queen, I wouldn't let nobody push me around! That lady needs some balls!'
(Smiles.) They say whatever comes into their heads, I swear."

Paul talks to Claire on the phone while Sophie goes to fetch a book to read to
her, as she always does at night. Gemma finds out that Tom was married to an
English girl who went home to England after their divorce, taking their children,
boys now 6 and 9 years old. Tom tells a story about a student who told him, "I want

to try some of that British bullshit acting, you know—with the funny voice." And he tells another story about a female acting student who thought nothing of playing Iago ("My last drama teacher said there were no male or female parts any more—only people parts") but balked at playing Othello because "only a black man can play a black man."

TOM: They don't see themselves. They don't question themselves.

PAUL: And the things you can't say. Sometimes I think a decent English comic would be in prison in a wink in this country.

GEMMA *(entering from the sink):* I thought you loved America?

PAUL: You can love something and still find fault with it.

SOPHIE *(enters with the book):* I'd put it in your bag for some reason. *(She notices the phone on the table.)*

PAUL: We had a nice talk.

> *Sophie picks up the phone and begins to read from* Charlie and the Choc-olate Factory *to her daughter.*

TOM: If they weren't so thin-skinned. Sometimes you just want to scream: "RELAX!"

> *Noise outside.*

GEMMA: They're back from their walk.

TOM: Anyway, why did you let me go on like that? It must have been very boring, you should have stopped me.

> *Alfred, Alice and Elizabeth enter from their walk; Alice and Alfred wear Wellingtons.*

ALICE: What a beautiful night. You should have come with us, Gemma.

PAUL: You've been gone for ages. Where was there to walk? I thought Father only had half an acre.

ELIZABETH: We walked through other people's. They don't have fences.

> *She looks to Gemma who picks up more plates.*

GEMMA: I've been picking up.

ELIZABETH: You shouldn't have to do it all.

GEMMA: I was hoping I wouldn't have to.

SOPHIE *(to everyone):* Would you mind—? Please. Sh-sh.

> *She continues to read on the phone.*

PAUL: Sophie, I don't think you can ask everyone . . . it's the kitchen—

SOPHIE: Fine! I'm sorry I'm in the way.

PAUL: No one said—

SOPHIE: I'll go upstairs. If it isn't a big bother, could someone hang up the receiver when I get to the phone upstairs?

> *She goes, carrying her book.*

ELIZABETH: Is that the same call she was making—?

Alfred goes for another bottle of wine. Elizabeth goes to look for some stomach medicine, and the others help with the cleaning up. Paul defends Sophie's recent behavior, "Sometimes she says things without thinking. Who doesn't?" On the walk, Alfred has suggested Alice go to bed with him, and her feeling about it is, "Maybe by tomorrow night . . . . . I don't give a shit." Tom urges Alice to think carefully about this, and she finally tells him, "I'm not going to bed with him. It's nice being asked, though."

Alfred returns with the wine and Elizabeth with the medicine. Elizabeth wonders who's going to pay for Sophie's phone call, angering Paul, who stalks off to talk to Sophie about it.

They discuss tomorrow's ceremony. Paul has hinted he wants to sing something; Alice was going to read a poem; Tom suggests they make a list of the things each of them wants to do. But the conference is interrupted by an attack of stomach pain suffered by Elizabeth, followed by the entrance of an angry Paul.

PAUL: I'll pay for the goddamn call!!! What do you want—a check Cash?!!! Whatever you want!! Just get off my back!! She's trying to talk to her daughter!! Is that so bad?! Can't you leave her alone?!! She's up there crying now. She thinks you hate her! I can't stand it any more!! Grow up!!!
    He suddenly becomes aware that Sophie is behind him. She has been crying.
SOPHIE: Paul, your sisters meant well. You shouldn't talk to them like that. *(Beat.)* Apologize. *(Beat.)* You heard me. Apologize.
    Beat.
PAUL: I'm sorry.
SOPHIE *(tries to smile):* I'm going to bed now—everyone. Goodnight. *(Everyone except Paul says "Goodnight" or "Goodnight, Sophie." Sophie turns to go, then turns back.)* Paul, stay up as late as you want. And visit. *(She leaves.)*

Alfred has found a jigsaw puzzle of the Grand Canyon and is working on it. Gemma takes Elizabeth up to bed, promising to come back and help with the washing-up. Paul tells her he'll do it—"It's my job at home"—and goes to the sink, while Tom sits with Alfred and Alice. She tells them about a beautiful student of Harry's, a favorite who will probably attend the ceremony tomorrow. To avoid any misunderstanding, Harry explained to Alice his special attention to her was because she was "the best violin student I've ever had in America." Harry loved teaching, and this student, he said, was fulfilling his teaching talent to its utmost. Alice felt ashamed of her misgivings about this relationship.

ALICE: Then one day I happened by his office door. It was opened a crack. There's also a little window. And there she was with him. She had her violin. I saw her put it under her chin. Raise her bow. And I don't know what I was prepared for, Alfred, but—she was the worst violinist I have ever heard. *(She smiles without looking up.)* I mean, it was painful. *(Beat.)* He screwed around all the time. Though after hearing the girl play I realized there was some suffering on his part as well. It wasn't all . . . *(Shrugs.)* Maybe even more suffering than pleasure. *(She smiles.)* We can hope.

> *Short pause. She reaches over and takes Alfred's drink and takes a sip.*

So—a few months ago Harry was in England? At his—wife's funeral? What did she die of? Do we know?

> *Beat.*

ALFRED: Her liver. She was a drinker.

> *Alice takes another sip of Alfred's drink.*

ALICE: It was a nice walk. Harry never wanted to take a walk with me after supper. Except—when we were courting. For that one week—he would.

> *She looks at Alfred. He looks up. They look into each other's eyes. Tom turns away and tries to be invisible.*

Scene 6

At 1 a.m., Tom and Paul are still in the kitchen, working on the puzzle. There's a banging/pounding noise upstairs which has been going on for an hour or so and which the men (and Gemma, who emerges from the sink area in nightgown and robe, having made herself a cup of tea) assume is the consummation of the Alfred-Alice relationship which had begun to evidence itself earlier in the evening. Paul is the only one who feels that this is actually offensive.

Alfred once told Paul a story about a student who stood up in a class about Shelley and said, "What the hell does any of this have to do with my life? Why do I even have to listen to you? You worthless Englishman!! Don't you know you are nothing now? That you count for nothing in this world! This is our world! Get it?! So why don't you just shut up and listen!!" In this country, Alfred says, "The students grade the teachers," so he had to just sit and take it.

Elizabeth enters in her robe, complaining about the noise upstairs, which now seems to have stopped. Commenting on the difficulties of sleeping tonight, Gemma remarks that the light was on in Sophie's room when she came down (Paul feels he ought to go up to her but remains seated).

Tom asks Paul what he plans to sing tomorrow. Paul, surprised at the question, says he hasn't sung in public in years, though he once took voice training, and doesn't plan to now.

Gemma is curious about what happened immediately after Harry shot himself; what the police did, etc.

TOM: Before the police came, Alice and I just sat in the hall outside the study. I wouldn't allow her to go back in. Once I'd seen . . . *(Beat.)* I helped her wash her face. She had some blood . . . She'd seen him do it—you knew that. So everything she does . . . I think we should remember that. *(Beat.)* I came in, and she was just sobbing. I pulled her into the hall. I called the police. They took out the body in a body bag; on a stretcher. I drove Alice in her car to the hospital behind the ambulance. I don't even have my license with me. *(Beat.)* A funeral director was called.

We met him in a room of the hospital. Alice liked him right away. He's about my age. Maybe a little younger. *(Beat.)* I'm just trying to recall if there's anything . . . It was the funeral director who gave us the name of the woman who did most of the cleaning up. Alice—Elizabeth knows this—found a few places she'd missed. You couldn't stop her. I couldn't have done it. There was a stain on the floorboards she couldn't get out or she didn't have the stuff in the house to get out. So Elizabeth—

ELIZABETH *(doing the puzzle):* I moved the carpet from one of the bedrooms. It's in the study now.

TOM: Where I'm supposed to sleep. *(He laughs.)*

Tom intends to stay up all night anyway. Elizabeth asks him about Alice, and Tom explains that Alice was married to his brother, who treated her shabbily. Alice and Tom ran into each other a couple of weeks ago in New York, had lunch, and Alice invited Tom for the weekend. (And finally the noise upstairs, which had started again, has stopped.) Elizabeth is uneasy about permitting Alice to make all the arrangements, etc.: "I don't know who she is. Or what she wants."

Sophie comes down, sleepily, having been disturbed by what she identifies as "a tree limb banging on the roof." She kisses Paul on the head, then goes to make herself some tea. Alice comes in, tactfully agreeing that she heard the tree limb too. She picks up a bottle, explaining that she met Alfred in the hall, and he wants a drink. She moves to leave, but Elizabeth stops her with questions about who's going to inherit all the furnishings and equipment, irrationally pursuing the subject to the point of mutual anger, even after Alice tells her to take whatever she wants.

ALICE: Is that what you want to ask me?!! Is it?!!! Or do you want to know why I . . . do you think I didn't know you could hear?! I've lived in this house for two years, and I know what can be heard!! But I didn't care! Why? Because I don't give one fuck what you—kids—think of me!! Why should I?!

ELIZABETH *(nearly in tears):* I don't know why I'm listening to this. What have I done?

TOM: I think we should stop before—

ELIZABETH *(to Alice):* What you don't understand is, I'm not interested in you, Alice. My question had to do with chairs, tables, there are lamps, rugs . . .

ALICE: He was so disappointed in all of you!!

ELIZABETH *(desperately trying to stay calm):* Books, there's his car, garden equipment—

TOM *(putting his hand on Elizabeth's arm):* I think you should talk about all of this in the morning.

ELIZABETH *(suddenly all of her anger comes out, directed at Tom):* Who the hell are you?! You little son of a bitch, you don't even belong here. This has nothing to do with you!! Shut up! Shut up! Shut up!

Elizabeth starts to sob. No one knows what to do.

Tom decides to remove himself and goes for a walk. Alice assures Elizabeth again that she can have everything that belonged to her father. Elizabeth repeats that this is really none of Tom's business anyhow (as Tom returns, unseen by anyone).

ELIZABETH: . . . . . You'd think he'd know he didn't belong.

ALICE: I put him in the study, for Christ's sake. You'd think he'd have taken the hint.

> *She laughs, as does Elizabeth. Then slowly they realize Tom is there and heard all this. No one knows what to say. Short pause.*

TOM: It's—raining. Outside. Just started. *(Beat.)* I think I'll go to bed now. Good-night. *(He goes.)*

> *Elizabeth sniffles. Alice takes a sip of her drink.*

ALICE: I'm drunk.

Scene 7

In the kitchen, an hour later, Elizabeth is looking through Harry's album, while Gemma sits quietly. Suddenly, from upstairs, there is the sound of a scream, and then another, "like a wounded animal." It's Alice, suddenly overtaken with the realization of what has happened. Alfred comes down, in his underpants, to get Alice's sleeping pills from her purse, then exits.

Tom comes in in his pajamas, apologizing for still being here: "There's no bus service at two in the morning." Elizabeth goes off for bed, and Gemma tries to make conversation with Tom, who tells her directly that he didn't ask to come here, Alice invited him, and after Harry's suicide he tried to get away but couldn't, partly because he didn't want to abandon Alice.

Gemma tries to keep talking about the theater—about how American actors have a way of "growling, spitting" as they perform. Tom tries to persuade her to go to bed, but Gemma has something she has wanted to tell someone ever since she got here, good news: she's engaged. He's part Mexican, but from an old American family. He works for Gemma's gardener and "doesn't know shit about art, music . . . . . a big dumb American like you see at the beach." Gemma talks right through additional screams from Alice upstairs. She told Harry this news yesterday on the phone. Her father was furious, believing Gemma was throwing away the culture and education Harry had been at some pains to give her.

GEMMA: . . . . . He just kept screaming at me: "Where have we gone wrong? Where have we gone wrong?" *(Beat.)* "How did we all get to here?" *(Beat.)* I didn't understand. But I'd never heard him shout like that—not at me. *(Beat.)* "The barbarians are sweeping over us, and all we do is kiss their ass." His words. I don't know what they mean. *(Beat.)* I tried to get him to calm down. Usually I could find a way, but this time it was impossible. It just kept coming out. The anger. At everything. At me . . . I warned him, Tom—if he did anything to himself, I'd hate him forever!

Mia Dillon (Elizabeth), Allison Janney (Gemma), Tom Irwin (Tom), Penny Fuller (Alice), Larry Bryggman (Alfred), Margaret Whitton (Sophie) and T. Scott Cunningham (Paul) in a scene from *New England*

Short pause.

This was yesterday—this conversation. When I called—he was in his study. He'd been reading, he said, and—I could hear—listening to music.

TOM: Yesterday afternoon?

Short pause.

GEMMA: At first, when Alice phoned with the news—I blamed myself. I even thought *I'd* killed him. *(Beat.)* I know that's unfair to me. I did nothing wrong. I was one thing maybe—a final straw to someone's . . . problem. It's taken me until now—to accept that it really had nothing to do with me.

A single scream from Alice in the distance.

(To Tom:) Did it?

TOM: No. I'm sure it didn't.

GEMMA *(suddenly relieved):* I've put myself through so much today. *(She stands.)* He should have been happy, dammit! With my news! I tried to tell him, Tom—we change. You have to. *(She starts to leave.)* Thank you. I'll try and go to sleep now. Goodnight. *(She goes.)*

TOM: Goodnight.

Short pause. Tom . . . . . heads into the hall, as Alice screams again.

Scene 8

The next morning in the kitchen, Alice, Alfred, Gemma, Elizabeth and Sophie are seated at the table, dressed in black suits and dresses, still amusing themselves with jokes and anecdotes highlighting eccentric aspects of the American character.

Paul comes in with the news that Tom plans to stay for the ceremony, for which Paul has loaned him one of Harry's black suits. Tom comes in and joins the group rather diffidently. He notices the urn containing Harry's ashes in the center of the table. Alice passes on some advice given her by the funeral director: "Be sure that when we throw the ashes—to keep our mouths closed."

Elizabeth passes around the photo album. Paul and Sophie have something they want cleared up: Yesterday, when Paul and Sophie arrived here at the house, Sophie moved toward Elizabeth to hug her, but Elizabeth brushed Sophie off to hug Paul.

PAUL: And this hurt Sophie. Correct? But Elizabeth, you didn't mean to hurt her. That too is correct?

ELIZABETH: No. Of course . . . why would I—?

PAUL *(to Sophie):* There. That has been addressed and dealt with.
         Beat.

ELIZABETH *(needing to explain):* I saw my brother. I wanted to hug him.

SOPHIE *(wanting help):* Paul.

PAUL: My Sophie is your sister-in-law. She wanted to console you. She wanted to be consoled herself. You should have let her do that. She has feelings too. Our father's death—upset her as well. Is that right, Sophie?

SOPHIE: Maybe this isn't the time to bring this up . . .

PAUL: You asked me—!

SOPHIE *(interrupting):* But I'm sure your sisters want to know these things.

Alice changes the subject, showing Alfred the picture in the album of the bathing suit Harry bought her. Alfred comments to the others, disingenuously, "None of you probably know this, but last night—Alice and I had the chance to spend some time together." And the upshot of it is, Alice has accepted Alfred's invitation to come visit him in Albuquerque. Alice assumes the others expect her to close or sell the house—none of them seems to want to live in it. The members of the family will discuss this, but some of them plan to leave very soon: Gemma tonight, Paul and Sophie tomorrow.

Alice reminds everyone to pretend to the guests that Harry loved teaching at the college. Then she opens a book she has been holding and reads a passage from Keats's *Ode on Melancholy* which she will also read at the ceremony. Paul feels that Harry would have liked him to sing *The British Grenadiers,* which he proceeds to do, with the enthusiastic support of others who remember how much Harry liked that song and used to sing it in the morning, while shaving.

All except Tom try to sing along, banging the table to the march beat.

EVERYONE *(sings):*

"Whene'er we are commanded
To storm the palisades,
Our leaders march with fuses,
And we with hand grenades."

ALICE *(to Tom):* Don't you know it?

TOM: A little.

GEMMA: Then sing!

EVERYONE *(sings):*

"We throw them from the glacis,
About the enemies' ears,
With a tow, row, row, row, row.
Row, the—"

SOPHIE *(shouts out):* French!!!

EVERYONE *(sings):*

"British Grenadiers!!!"

The family suddenly sings in a whisper, obviously as Harry used to do it.

"And when the siege is over,
We to the town repair,
The townsmen cry—

The family shout.

Hurrah boys, here comes a Grenadier;
Here comes the—"

ALICE: Sh-sh!!!

They stop singing. Beat. Alice goes and looks out.

It's a car. The guests are arriving.

Pause. Alice takes out a cigarette, lights it; takes one puff and puts it out. Everyone is straightening their clothes. Tom tries to straighten his.

SOPHIE *(to Tom):* You look good.

ELIZABETH: Paul, you better direct traffic. Tell everyone where to park.

He nods.

GEMMA: I can take their coats.

PAUL: I thought it was outside—

ELIZABETH: Until everyone comes.

They are on their way out.

ALICE: Just one thing I meant to tell you.

They stop.

You should know this. *(Beat.)* When people called—I told them it had just been an accident. That Harry was cleaning his gun.

She heads down the hall. The others look at each other and follow; Gemma tries to straighten out Tom's suit as they go. The urn is left alone on the table. Debussy's "The Girl With the Flaxen Hair" begins to play. Offstage, the sound of greetings, condolences, cars arriving, offers to take coats, car doors closing, directions where to park, etc. Curtain.

Best Play Citation

○○○
○○○
○○○
○○○
○○○
○○○ # VALLEY SONG

A Full-Length Play in One Act

BY ATHOL FUGARD

Cast and credits appear on page 318

ATHOL FUGARD was born June 11, 1932 in Middelburg in the semi-desert Karoo country of South Africa. His mother was an Afrikaner, his father of Irish and Huguenot descent. He studied motor mechanics at Port Elizabeth Technical College and philosophy at the University of Cape Town and spent three years in the Merchant Marine, mostly in the Far East. He married an actress, Sheila Meiring, and for a time they ran an experimental theater in Cape Town. His first play, No-Good Friday, *was produced in 1959 with an all-black cast, and his* Nongogo *(also 1959) had an American premiere in 1978 for 20 performances at Manhattan Theater Club.*

Fugard's The Blood Knot *premiered in Sophiatown, near Johannesburg, Sept. 3, 1961 and won him an international reputation extending to these shores in an off-Broadway production starring James Earl Jones, March 1, 1964 for 240 performances (it is about two black half-brothers, one light-skinned and one dark). His next play,* People Are Living There, *was done in Glasgow in 1968 and then in London during the 1971–72 season. His* Hello and Goodbye, *first produced in 1965, appeared off Broadway with Martin Sheen and Colleen Dewhurst Sept. 18, 1969 for 45 performances and was produced in London in 1972–73. His next,* Mille Miglia *(1968) was aired on BBC-TV (as was* The Blood Knot*). It was followed by* Boesman and Lena *(1969), done off Broadway with James Earl Jones, Ruby Dee and Zakes Mokae, June*

22, 1970 for 205 performances and named a Best Play of its season, a year before its London premiere.

Fugard's second Best Play, The Island, had strong mimetic as well as literary elements and is credited as a collaboration "devised" by the author and the actors who appeared in it, John Kani and Winston Ntshona. It reversed the direction of the previous Fugard Best Play by stopping in London before coming to New York, appearing under the auspices of the Royal Court Theater on a two-play program with Sizwe Banzi Is Dead by the same authors. These two plays then had their American premiere in tandem, first at the Long Wharf Theater in New Haven, Conn. in October 1974 and then in alternating repertory (Sizwe for 159 performances, Island for 52) beginning Nov. 13, 1974 in mini-Broadway productions at the Edison Theater, receiving Tony nominations for best play and for Fugard's direction.

Fugard's third Best Play, A Lesson From Aloes, first appeared on this side of the Atlantic at the Centaur Theater in Montreal Jan. 1, 1980; then was produced at the Yale Repertory Theater in New Haven March 26 and finally on Broadway Nov. 17 for 96 performances, winning the Critics Award as the best play of the season and Tony-nominated for best play, in all three cases under the author's direction. Fugard's fourth Best Play was Master Harold . . . and the Boys, which premiered at Yale Rep under its author's direction, in a production brought to Broadway May 4, 1982 for 344 performances, again Tony-nominated for both best play and direction; and a London production received the Evening Standard best-play citation.

Fugard's fifth Best Play, The Road to Mecca, took the same route under its author's direction through Yale Rep production in May 1984 to New York, opening off Broadway April 12, 1988 and playing for 172 performances. Ineligible for Tony consideration under a system that still stubbornly refuses to recognize that much of the theater's very best work appears in the smaller context of off Broadway, The Road to Mecca nevertheless won the broader-visioned citation of the Critics Circle as the best foreign play of the season (and The Blood Knot had emphasized the fallacy of the Tony policy when, in a 1986 Broadway revival, it was nominated for a Tony as best "new" play because it hadn't previously appeared uptown). The Road to Mecca has also been produced in London, by the National Theater.

Fugard's My Children! My Africa! was originally produced by the Market Theater in Johannesburg in June 1989. It made its U.S. debut Dec. 18 in an off-off-Broadway production under Fugard's direction by New York Theater Workshop, in a run limited to 28 performances by its production contract. It was cited as Fugard's sixth Best Play, in accordance with our policy of widening Best Play eligibility to include special cases of OOB production (i.e.: modern scripts which have already made their esthetic mark outside New York but for commercial reasons appear outside the defined limits of Broadway and off Broadway). Fugard's seventh Best Play is Valley Song, produced December 12 for 48 performances by Manhattan Theater Club and directed by Fugard following its August premiere in Johannesburg.

Other Fugard works appearing on our record of U.S. production have included Statements After an Arrest Under the Immorality Act *November 1978 for 35 performances at MTC;* The Drummer *at Actors Theater of Louisville in the 1979–80 season;* A Place With the Pigs *March 1987, premiering at Yale Rep; and* Playland *in 1993 for 24 performances at MTC. He is also the author of the plays* My Life, Orestes, Dimetos *and* The Coat; *and in 1992, following a revival of* Boesman and Lena *at MTC, he won the Obie Award for sustained achievement. In addition to his dual role in* Valley Song, *Fugard's performances in his own works have included those in* The Road to Mecca *and the movies* The Guest *and* Marigolds in August. *He has received honorary degrees from Yale, Natal and Georgetown Universities and the Universities of Rhodes and Cape Town, and he is an honorary member of the American Institute of Arts and Letters.*

Some of Fugard's training for what has turned out to be his triple profession of actor-director-writer was acquired in Rehearsal Room in Johannesburg's Dorkay House (the headquarters of South Africa's Union Artists, the organization that cares for the cultural interests of non-Europeans in the Transvaal). Later, as resident director of Dorkay House, he staged the work of many leading playwrights such as John Steinbeck and Harold Pinter. Since the mid-1960s he has been closely associated with Serpent Players of New Brighton, Port Elizabeth, a theater workshop for black Africans experimenting in collaborative "play-making" of works dealing with the contemporary South African scene. Fugard lives near Port Elizabeth with his wife, and they have a daughter, Lisa-Maria.

Time: The present

Place: The small town of Nieu-Bethesda in the Karoo, South Africa

SYNOPSIS: The Author, a white man in his 60s, enters with Veronica, a 17-year old girl. The Author shows the audience a handful of pumpkin seeds and describes the riches that spring from the earth under the hot Karoo sun in the Sneeuberg Mountains of South Africa.

The Author then describes Abraam Jonkers (known as "Buks"), the 70-year-old farmer who works this land, a so-called "coloured," a former corporal in the famous regiment the Cape Corps and the grandfather ("Oupa") of Veronica. As the Author speaks, he gradually becomes the character of Buks (both the Author and Buks are played by the same actor throughout).

After singing a marching song, Buks brings Veronica to attention, then orders her, "Platoon dismissed" as they revert to their easy, fond relationship of granddaughter and grandfather. Buks explains that he never shot anybody in the war (although he carried a loaded gun) because his duty was guarding Italian prisoners, and none of them ever tried to escape.

As Veronica sets out their lunch, Buks tells her of a development that disturbs him.

BUKS: . . . . . That Whiteman was back here again early this morning looking at the house and the land . . . our akkers.

VERONICA: So?

BUKS: I'm just saying. That's three times now.

VERONICA: That doesn't mean anything. Stop worrying about it, Oupa. Every few months there's another car full of white people driving around the village and looking at the old houses and talking about buying, and what happens? . . . They drive away in the dust and we never see them again. You watch and see: it will be just the same with this lot . . . nothing will happen!

BUKS: This one looks serious, my child. He even had the keys to get into the house.

VERONICA: Did he say anything to you?

BUKS: No. Just greeted me. Then walked around like a Whiteman and looked at everything.

VERONICA: Well, I still say you are worrying for nothing.

BUKS: Anyway, worry or not, there's nothing we can do about it, hey. If he buys the land he can tell me take my spade and my wheelbarrow and go, and that's the end of the story.

VERONICA: Don't say that, Oupa! That will make it come true!

Veronica changes the subject: she longs for adventure and romance, but nothing of that sort ever takes place in this neighborhood. Miracles happen here, Buks insists, and shows her pumpkin seeds as proof. What Veronica really wants to do is sing; that is, become a singer who performs to large audiences instead of in the church choir and in school. Veronica also makes up songs, and she has just made up a new one which she prepares to sing for Buks.

VERONICA: It's called "Railway Bus O Railway Bus."

BUKS: "Railway Bus"?

VERONICA: Yes. But you must say it two times with an "O" in between. "Railway Bus O Railway Bus."

BUKS: The Railway Bus that used to come from Graaff Reinet?

VERONICA: Yes yes yes! Wait for the song, Oupa. Then you'll understand. (*Sings.*)
    Railway Bus O Railway Bus
    Why don't you come no more.
    I want to travel fast, yes
    On the smooth tar road
    Far, far away,
    Far, far away,
    Far, far away
    Railway Bus O Railway Bus
    I want to get on board
    I want to see Big Cities

And strange places
Far, far away,
Far, far away,
Far, far away

Breaking off abruptly when she sees her song is disturbing her Oupa.

Veronica is hurt at Buks's dislike of her song, until she realizes that it's not the song that has upset Oupa, but the fact that it has brought back painful memories of the past. The Railway Bus made it all too easy for Oupa's daughter Caroline to run away from home to the big city with a boy friend named Harry Ruiters. Some time later they got a call from the hospital in Johannesburg, and Buks's wife Betty, Veronica's "Ouma," went to the city, found her daughter Caroline already dead and returned to the village with the infant Veronica in her arms. Possibly Ruiters was the father—Buks doesn't know: "Don't think about him, Veronica! He was rubbish, a disgrace to us coloured people, a good for nothing rubbish who led your mother into sin," a thief who was facing a court trial when he ran away.

Buks has a happy memory of those times: "After your Ouma got off the bus and we were walking home—I was carrying her suitcase and she was carrying you—you started to cry. And I thought . . . Oh heavens, this child is going to be difficult, I can hear that right now. And I said so to your Ouma. But she said, 'No, Buks. She's not crying. She's singing' . . . . . And so it was from then on. Your Ouma always used to say to me, 'If that child ever stops singing, Abraam Jonkers, then you must know there is something wrong with the world.' "

Betty cared for and loved Veronica, and after she died the only person to take care of Veronica was Buks himself. Veronica decided that she will sing no more songs that bring unhappy thoughts to her beloved Oupa. She marches off singing a military song.

Buks addresses his dead wife, the only person to whom he can tell his troubles. Veronica is happy and obedient, singing more than ever (he tells Betty), but she is getting restless. She looks very much like her mother Caroline and at 17 is beginning to be attracted to young men. And he's worried about the Whiteman looking at this property. He agrees that he must trust in the Lord. He has planted the pumpkin seeds and will ask Veronica to pray for rain. And if Betty can help in that direction, "That would also be very nice."

Veronica comes forward and talks to the audience about her life. She does the cooking and the washing and after supper sits under the bluegum tree reading from the Bible to her grandfather, who can't read. Veronica sleeps in the kitchen, and once Buks is fast asleep in the bedroom, "I get up and go quietly out of the house, and when I'm outside I run like hell to Mrs. Jooste's house—the big white one there on the corner in Martin Street. The old white woman doesn't know it, but she's my best friend. You see, she drinks whiskey and watches TV until late, late at night. And she's always got the curtains open, so if I stand on a box or something I can look over her head and see the whole TV. But the best thing of all is, that old white woman likes music—fast, slow, rhythm and blues, country, doesn't matter what kind, but that's what she looks for . . . ! *(She grabs her apple box and, standing on it, gives us the scene . . . mimicking the pop star she sees on the screen. Mike in hand, she sings to an audience of thousands . . . she sings loudly in a very soft voice.)"*

As Veronica finishes her song, she is startled by the sound of applause from the Author, who has witnessed this scene. Once recovered from her fright, Veronica tells him he didn't react enthusiastically enough.

VERONICA: . . . . . You must clap your hands and stamp your feet and shout and scream . . . Veronica! Veronica! . . . and then I come out again, you see, and sing some more. That's the way they're going to do it one day.

AUTHOR: When you're famous.

VERONICA: That's right. In Johannesburg and Durban and Cape Town . . . Veronica! Veronica! Give us more! We want to hear Veronica! . . . . .

AUTHOR: Go on. I want to hear more.

VERONICA: I'll be on TV. Ja. Then you can stand here on the porch and watch me singing. I'll be wearing a beautiful shiny green dress—that's my color—and green shoes with high, high heels and long gloves that go all the way up to my elbow and a fancy hair style with sparkles in it. You wait and see, my boy. You wait and see.

AUTHOR: So that's your dream.

VERONICA: Yes. Anything wrong with it?

AUTHOR: No. But it's a big one.

VERONICA: Of course. That's the only way to do it.

AUTHOR: Really?

VERONICA: Oh yes. What's the use of a little dream? A dream must be big and special. It must be the most special thing you can imagine for yourself in the whole world.

Veronica tells the Author about a friend named Alfred who foolishly dreams of working to earn a second-hand bicycle. He should be dreaming of a brand new one. The Author calls Alfred's dream "sensible," money and jobs being scarce here in the valley, but Veronica believes that if you dream big it will happen big. The Author observes wryly that many of his own dreams didn't come true, believe in them though he did.

Veronica sings a song about the bicycle dream. The Author quotes from the 24th Psalm, and as he does so becomes Buks, who sings a hymn with his granddaughter. Under the Bluegum tree, she tries to persuade her grandfather to believe that a Whiteman's purchase of this property won't happen, but Buks knows better. A friend overheard the Whiteman telling the people in the municipal office that he intended to buy this Landman house and land. None of the other villagers will come with him to work this land, Veronica assures Buks, "Everybody knows these are your akkers." Buks explains, "It's not our people I'm worried about, it's him, the Whiteman. If he buys the house and the land he's going to get a piece of paper that tells him those akkers are his. He can tell me to go any time he likes and get somebody else to work for him."

Veronica suggests that they might fight back by sending a petition to the government—which is "taking the land and giving it back to the people" in other places—signed by all the villagers. Buks's view is, "Government is trouble. I'll be very happy if they don't know where we are." Then Veronica will petition God in her prayers, she says, but Buks has a better idea: he'll speak to the Whiteman person to person. And, he adds, maybe there'll be a house cleaning position in it for Veronica. "No, no, no!" she reacts, her vehemence taking Buks by surprise.

VERONICA: I don't want to do housework, Oupa.

BUKS: But you do it in here every day, Veronica.

VERONICA: This is different, Oupa. This is our house. I'm doing it for us. I don't want to do it for other people. I don't want to do it for a living. Specially the Landman house.

BUKS: What is wrong with getting work there? Your Ouma cleaned that house.

VERONICA: Exactly, Oupa! That's what I been trying to say. Isn't it supposed to be different now?

BUKS: What must be different?

VERONICA: Everything. Our lives and . . . and everything. Isn't that why there was an election? . . . . . Here we are carrying on and talking just like the same old bunch of useless coloureds we've always been, bowing and scraping, frightened of the Whiteman, ready to crawl and beg him and be happy and grateful if we can scrub his floors.

Buks reproaches Veronica for what he takes as a slight on the memory of her Ouma, who came to the city to rescue her and saved her infant life. He adds, "As for this 'useless old coloured'—you're right—I've done a lot of crawling and begging in my life, and I'm ready to do it again for these few akkers. You want to know why, Veronica? So that I can grow food for you to eat, just as I grew food there for your mother and your Ouma to eat, and as my father grew food there for me to eat." Veronica, with tears in her eyes, apologizes.

The Author "*leaves the role of Buks*" and explains to the audience that he hadn't made up his mind to buy the Landman place, the house being in very bad disrepair, until he was preparing to return to Port Elizabeth. Buks comes up to him wheeling a barrow full of vegetables, introduces himself, points to the vegetables as evidence that at 76 he still does a full day's productive work. He has brought this barrowload as a present for the Author.

BUKS: . . . . . Master . . . ! I hear that Master is going to buy the Landman house . . . that's what I heard . . . Oh I see . . . Master is still thinking about it . . . I was just asking because if Master does buy it I was wondering what the Master's plans was going to be and if I could carry on there with my few akkers. I see, Master . . . yes, I see . . . but if Master does decide . . . all right, Master . . . we'll talk then because I was also going to tell Master that if Master does buy it and fixes up the house nicely and comes to live here in the village, I got a young granddaughter who . . . Okay . . .

Okay, Master . . . we'll talk then. Where does Master want me to put the vegetables . . . there by the motorcar? Okay, Master. Thank you, Master.

AUTHOR: The wheelbarrow load of vegetables did it. I mean, come on now, how could I pass up the chance to own a piece of my native Karoo earth that would allow me to brag and boast about "my own pumpkins," "my own beetroot," "my own potatoes"? And the timing was perfect! I was passing through a period of severe disenchantment with my supposed-to-be-glamorous life in the make-believe world of theater. I wanted to return to "essentials," to the "real" world, and here was my chance to do it.

Back at home, imagining what a peaceful, productive life he might enjoy as writer and farmer living on the Landman property, the Author wrote a check, and the land and the Title Deed were his. "But I would have felt a lot better if God had cosigned that Title Deed," he tells the audience. Buks first planted those "akkers" when he was only a few years old, after his father Jaap Jonkers, who worked for the Landmans, died and Buks took over his chores including farming a few acres for himself (it was Landman who had advised Jaap to do this). "His life is rooted now as deeply in that soil as the old walnut tree next to the windmill," the Author observes. "When it's like that between you and a piece of land, you end up being a part of it. Your soul wilts and withers with the young plants during the droughts. You feel the late frosts as if it was your skin that had been burnt black. And when it rains you rejoice and your heart swells with sweetness like the fruit on the trees. But Buks doesn't have a piece of paper with his name on it which says all these things, and so he has to come begging to me because I've got a piece of paper with my name on it which said that those akkers are mine."

Veronica now informs the audience, "I hate those akkers," because the land takes away their lives as it feeds them. Her mother turned her back on the land and ran away, but Buks is obsessed with it, it is now his whole life, apparently meaning even more to him than his granddaughter's future.

Veronica gets up onto her apple box preparing for another TV session, but—the Author informs her—the curtains are now closed because Mrs. Jooste is gone, dead of a heart attack. Probably she has become one of the village's "white ghosts," peering timorously at a world that no longer belongs to them. But, Veronica insists, the fact that the woman is dead doesn't mean that she will stop dreaming of being a rich and famous TV star. The Author warns her that the death of a big dream can be an exceedingly painful experience.

AUTHOR: . . . . . It's like your friend Alfred and that old second-hand bicycle he wants to buy. If he doesn't get it, it won't be too bad. The world is full of old second-hand bicycles. There'll be another chance one day. But if he takes your advice and starts dreaming—hard!—about a shiny brand-new one and believes—with all his might—that he is going to get it, and then doesn't because the only work he can find are occasional odd jobs that don't even pay enough for him to feed his family

LisaGay Hamilton as Veronica Jonkers and Athol Fugard as the Author
and Abraam Jonkers (a.k.a. Oupa and Buks) in Fugard's *Valley Song*

. . . That's a recipe for bitterness. And you're not dreaming about bicycles, Veronica.
You're dreaming about your life!

VERONICA: That's right, and that life isn't over like yours maybe is. If your
dreams didn't come true, that's your bad luck, not mine. Maybe you are ready to
be a ghost, I am not. You can't see into the future. You don't know what is going
to happen to me.

AUTHOR: That's true. I don't. But what I do know is that dreams don't do well in this Valley. Pumpkins, yes, but not dreams—and you've already seen enough of life to know that as well. Listen to me, Veronica—take your apple box and go home, and dream about something that has a chance of happening—a wonderful year for your Oupa on his akkers with hundreds of pumpkins—or dream that you meet a handsome young man with a good job . . .

VERONICA: You're wasting your breath.

AUTHOR: Okay, let's leave it at that. But for your sake I hope you don't remember tonight and what I've said to you in ten years time if like all the other women in the village you are walking barefoot into the veld every day with a baby on your back to collect firewood.

VERONICA: Never!

AUTHOR: Because you know what you'll be dreaming about then, don't you? . . . that I've given you a job scrubbing and polishing the floors of my nicely renovated old Landman house.

VERONICA: Never! Now you listen to me. I swear on the Bible, on my Ouma's grave, that you will never see me walk barefoot with firewood on my head and a baby on my back—you will never see me on my knees scrubbing a Whiteman's floor.

Veronica comes forward and talks to the audience as though it were white passers-by, sings a song about the windmills and produce of summer, holds out her hand for her reward, pockets it and then joins Buks, who is washing himself from a bucket of water.

Veronica tells her Oupa about an incident at the Post Office: the Brigadier came in after 12 o'clock to do some business, and the postmistress informed him that it was after closing time for the day. The Brigadier stood his ground and insisted on her making an exception for him. "This is no longer the old South Africa, Brigadier," she said. She went next door to the police station and came back with an officer who ousted the Brigadier, to the delight of the crowd that had gathered to see what would happen.

Veronica has also learned from the postmistress that there was a letter for her which she gave to Buks to deliver. Somewhat reluctantly, Buks hands over the letter. It has been opened—Buks did this, he admits, to find out what it said and gave it to a friend to read to him, but the friend couldn't read the handwriting either. Veronica sees that it's a letter from her friend Priscilla in Johannesburg. She pretends to read it to Buks, making up an innocuous and gossipy communication, but after only a few sentences she finds that she cannot keep on lying to Buks, who discerns immediately that she isn't telling him the truth. She apologizes for the lie, while charging that Buks had no right to open her letter. Buks feels that as long as she lives under his roof he has the right to know what she's about. Veronica finally reads Buks the true contents of the letter: Priscilla will be happy to have Veronica stay with her in Johannesburg, where there are plenty of jobs, "specially for a clever and good-looker like you."

Veronica plans to go to Johannesburg, she admits, and Buks immediately assumes she is following in her mother's footsteps: "Lies and secrets. And then stealing." He reminds Veronica that his daughter Caroline took all the money he'd been saving when she ran off to the city. Veronica protests vehemently that she would never do any such thing.

VERONICA: I got my own money.

BUKS: Your own money? *(Veronica is silent.)* What do you mean, "your own money"?

VERONICA: Money I save, Oupa.

BUKS: From where?

VERONICA: From what white people give me.

BUKS: You ask them for money?

VERONICA: No. I earned it. I sing my songs for them, and they pay me. *(Misinterpreting Buks's silence and thinking she can bring him over to her side.)* It's true. They all like my singing. They say I got a good voice and that I must go somewhere where there is a singing teacher so that I can take lessons and make it better. That's why I wrote to Priscilla. And you heard what she said in her letter, Oupa . . . There's plenty of jobs in Johannesburg, so I'll be able to get work and pay for my singing lessons—because if I become a very good singer, Oupa, I can make lots of money. People who sing on the TV and the radio get paid a lot of money. Just think, Oupa! You can even come up there as well then if you want to . . . forget about those old Landman akkers and come and live in Johannesburg in a proper house with a big garden . . .

> She takes a chance . . . fetching the tin with her savings, opening it and placing it trustingly on the table in front of her Oupa.

Look, Oupa—I nearly got half the price of a train ticket already. I'm doing it because I want Oupa to be proud of me. I want to give you something back for all you've given me. But I can't do it if I stay here. There's nothing for me in this Valley. Please try to understand what it is like for me. I'll die if I got to live my whole life here.

> Buks's devastation turns to rage. He grabs the tin and hurls it out into the night.

No, Oupa! No! It's mine!

BUKS: Devil's money.

VERONICA: It's not. I earned it. I earned it properly.

BUKS: I'm telling you it's Devil's money! That's where it comes from. Devil's money. He's trying to get you the way he got your mother. But this time I'm ready for him. Now you listen to me very carefully, Veronica. Don't ever let me catch you begging money from the white people again. And you can also forget all about Johannesburg. The family has already got one grave up there. There won't be another one. Whatever you might think, you are still a child, and I am your Oupa. If you try to run away, I'll have the police after you. I mean it. And I'll tell them to lock you up until you come to your senses.

That Sunday in church, Veronica goes with Buks but doesn't join him in singing the hymn. Buks points to the mountains as symbols of God's handiwork, and to the church as the house where God wants to hear Veronica sing, but she tells Buks, "You've killed the song in me."

In the winter, the Author tells the audience how he watches Buks going for a walk—"His little woolen cap is pulled down low over his ears, his hands buried deep in the pockets of his old jacket as he shuffles slowly past"—knowing that the old man is asking himself, "What did I do wrong?" to make Veronica stop the singing that used to fill their house with joy. Buks must be remembering (the Author tells the audience) how as a young lad his father Jaap told him that God would grant Buks a sweet life if Buks concentrated on hard work and love in the three all-important places of his existence: the akkers, the house and the church. Now Buks feels betrayed because he followed this advice, and yet his life has now become "as bitter as aloe juice."

As the Author moves into the character of Buks, Veronica moves toward him and hears him talking to his wife Betty about how he has kept his promise to care for and love Veronica. When Buks sees Veronica, he thinks she is his daughter Caroline come back to him, and he asks her, "What did I do wrong?" Veronica tries unsuccessfully to bring Buks back to the reality that Caroline and Betty are both long dead and gone. So to rescue her grandfather from his delusions, she breaks her silence.

VERONICA (sings):
>You plant seeds
>And I sing songs
>We're Oupa and Veronica
>Yes, Oupa and Veronica
>You work hard
>And I dream dreams
>That's Oupa and Veronica,
>Yes, Oupa and Veronica.

>Summer into autumn
>Winter into spring
>Planting seeds and singing songs
>It's Oupa and Veronica
>Veronica, Veronica, Veronica.

The song brings Buks back to reality, but also to the memory of how it was when Caroline left: the shame that Buks and his wife Betty felt, and the recurring question, "What did we do wrong? Because we loved her." Veronica knows that they loved Caroline, and she believes that Caroline knew it too.

VERONICA: You didn't do anything wrong, Oupa. You didn't do anything wrong with me, either . . . but I know my time is also coming.

BUKS: What do you mean?

VERONICA: You must let me go Oupa, otherwise I will also run away from you.

BUKS: No! You mustn't do that! I will let you go. But explain it to me. I want to understand.

VERONICA: Can Oupa explain to me how a little seed becomes a big pumpkin?

BUKS: No.

VERONICA: You said once it was a miracle.

BUKS: That's right.

VERONICA: You give it water and skoffel out the weeds, and it just grows. Isn't that so?

BUKS: Yes, that is so.

VERONICA: I think it is like that with me and my singing, Oupa. I also can't tell you how it happens. All I know is that when I sing, I'm alive. My singing is my life. I must look after it the way Oupa looks after his vegetables. I know that if I stay here in the Valley it will die. Does Oupa understand now?

BUKS: No . . . but that doesn't matter . . . . .

Buks is now prepared to give Veronica his blessing for whatever she decides to do.

Veronica sings a goodbye song to the Valley, promising to come back some day. When she is finished the Author joins her, and she tells him of the poignant sadness of parting with Oupa. The Author suggests that she should stay here with him, but Veronica is sure that she must go to Johannesburg and fulfill her destiny. She promises to write letters to Oupa weekly, letters which the schoolmaster can read to him.

The Author seems to approve of Veronica's decision, and she wonders why he so often argued that she should stay here. He was testing her, he informs her, and he is now certain that Veronica is strong enough to go through with her plan. He had a secret hope that she would fail the test, because her success would mean the Valley is changing, no longer "the unspoilt, innocent little world it was when I first discovered it. On all the late night walks that are left in my life, I want to find little Veronica Jonkers dreaming on her apple box." Also, he is a bit jealous of her youth and unlimited future. But he wishes her good luck anyway, as she prepares to leave.

AUTHOR: Wait! Can you hear it?

VERONICA: What?

AUTHOR: Listen. Close your eyes. "Veronica. Veronica. We want Veronica!"
    She leaves the stage.

And Buks? How do we leave him? Slumped in defeat and misery as we last saw him? I don't think so. That is what Buks himself would describe as a dishonorable discharge from life, and Buks is an honorable old soldier. The truth is, there was enough life left in him to yield to one last temptation . . . and I was the devil who did it! I found him in his house, sitting at the little kitchen table. When I entered he asked me "nicely" to sit down, but I said: No, I'm in a hurry . . . and so should you be! Come on, Buks. Onto your legs. Didn't you hear the rain last night? I'm telling you man, down at my end of the village came down so hard it sounded like that Sonderwater Military Band of yours was practicing on the tin roof. Think of it, Buks. Another spring has come, and we are still here! Still strong enough to go out there and plant!

   Nudging Buks and speaking softer.

Tell me the truth now, Buks. Think back to your young days and tell me . . . Did a woman ever smell as good as the Karoo earth after a good rain? Or feel as good? *(Another sly laugh.)* Ja, the ground is soft and wet and waiting. And look what I've got for you! *(A handful of shiny white pumpkin seeds.)* Pumpkin seeds! Imagine it, Buks. An akker full of shiny, flat, white, Boer pumpkins as big as donkey-cart wheels! *(The Devil laughs and starts to leave.)* Come . . . *(Looks back and beckons once more.)* Come . . . that's it! . . . COME!

   Curtain.

Critics, Lortel Awards

○○○
○○○
○○○
○○○
○○○
○○○ # MOLLY SWEENEY

A Play in Two Acts

BY BRIAN FRIEL

Cast and credits appear on page 317

BRIAN FRIEL was born January 9, 1929 in Omagh County, Tyrone. Educated at St. Patrick's, Maynouth, he became a schoolteacher but since 1960 has devoted himself entirely to writing. His short stories appeared in The New Yorker *beginning in 1959 and have been collected in volumes entitled* The Saucer of Larks *and* The Gold in the Sea.

Friel's first produced play was The Francophile *in 1958 in Belfast, followed by* This Doubtful Paradise, The Enemy Within *and* The Blind Mice *in Dublin, Belfast and London. His first far-flung international hit was* Philadelphia, Here I Come!, *produced in Dublin in September 1964, on Broadway Feb. 16, 1966 for 326 performances and a citation as Friel's first Best Play, and since then in every major theater center in Europe and America (it was revived on Broadway for 52 performances as recently as last season). A program of Friel one-acts,* Lovers, *was named his second Best Play at the time of its Lincoln Center engagement July 25, 1978 for 148 performances, and his third was* Translations, *produced off Broadway for 48 performances by Manhattan Theater Club April 7, 1981 after its premiere in Derry at the Field Day*

Theater Company, of which Friel was a co-founder with Stephen Rea. Translations *was also revived on Broadway last season, for 25 performances.* Aristocrats, *his fourth Best Play, was written in 1979 but did not reach New York until April 25, 1989, in a Manhattan Theater Club production for 186 performances. His fifth Best Play was* Dancing at Lughnasa, *which came from Dublin in the Abbey Theater production via the West End (where it won the Olivier Award as the best play of 1991) to Broadway October 24, 1991 (where it played 421 performances and won the Critics Award for best play regardless of category and three Tonys including the one for best play). His sixth is* Molly Sweeney, *which premiered at Dublin's Gate Theater, then moved on to the Almeida Theater in London before its off-Broadway production January 7 by Roundabout Theater Company, winning the Critics Award for best foreign play and the Lucille Lortel for best off-Broadway play.*

The succession of Friel's distinguished plays produced over the decades in Europe and America has included The Loves of Cass McGuire *(1966, reaching Broadway for 20 performances),* Crystal and Fox *(1968, reaching Los Angeles in 1970 and off Broadway in 1973),* The Mundy Scheme *(1969, reaching Broadway for 4 performances after a Dublin production),* The Gentle Island *(1971),* The Freedom of the City *(1973, which premiered simultaneously at the Royal Court and Abbey Theaters and was produced by the Goodman Theater in Chicago and on Broadway Feb. 17, 1974 for 9 performances),* Volunteers *(1975),* Living Quarters *(1977, OOB 1983) and* Faith Healer *(world premiere on Broadway for 20 performances April 5, 1979), a translation of Chekhov's* Three Sisters *(1981),* The Communication Cord *(1982), an adaptation of Turgenev's novel* Fathers and Sons *(1987),* Making History *(1988),* The London Vertigo *(1991), an adaptation of Turgenev's* A Month in the County *(1992) and* Wonderful Tennessee *(1993, reaching Broadway for 9 performances October 24, 1993).*

As his writing career began, Friel provided radio plays to the Belfast arm of the BBC in 1958 (and in 1989 BBC Radio devoted a six-play season to his work; he was the first living playwright to be so honored). In 1963 he spent six months with Tyrone Guthrie at the latter's regional theater in Minneapolis. Among his many awards is that of the Irish-American Cultural Institute, an honor bestowed annually but seldom to a dramatist, given to Friel in 1980 for his work on the Irish stage. He lives in Ireland, and he and his wife of more than 45 years are the parents of four daughters and a son.

Molly Sweeney *is constructed as a series of monologues alternating among three characters. To communicate as fully as possible the mood and characterizations of this work, the following synopsis appears as relatively long blocks of the text joined by relatively short connective narration.*

Time: The present

ACT I

SYNOPSIS: At curtain rise, three persons are seated in chairs onstage—Molly Sweeney, in her late 30s or early 40s at center, her husband Frank Sweeney, about the same age, at left and Mr. Rice, older, at right. Molly is almost blind but, *"Most people with impaired vision look and behave like fully sighted people. The only evidence of their disability is usually a certain vacancy in the eyes or the way the head is held . . . . . No canes, no groping, no dark glasses, etc."*

MOLLY: By the time I was five years of age, my father had taught me the names of dozens of flowers and herbs and shrubs and trees. He was a judge, and his work took him all over the county. And every evening, when he got home, after he'd had a few quick drinks, he'd pick me up in his arms and carry me out to the walled garden.

"Tell me now," he'd ask, "Where precisely are we?"

"We're in your garden."

"Oh, you're such a clever little missy!" And he'd pretend to smack me.

"Exactly what part of my garden?"

"We're beside the stream."

"Stream? Do you hear a stream? I don't. Try again."

"We're under the lime tree."

"I smell no lime tree. Sorry. Try again."

"We're beside the sundial."

"You're guessing. But you're right. And at the bottom of the pedestal there is a circle of petunias. There are about twenty of them all huddled together in one bed. They are—what?—seven inches tall. Some of them are blue-and-white, and some of them are pink, and a few have big, red, cheeky faces. Touch them."

And he would bend over, holding me almost upside down, and I would have to count them and smell them and feel their velvet leaves and their sticky stems. Then he'd test me.

"Now, Molly. Tell me what you saw."

"Petunias"

"How many petunias did you see?"

"Twenty."

"Color?"

"Blue-and-white and pink and red."

"Good. And what shape is their bed?"

"It's a circle."

"Splendid. Passed with flying colors. You *are* a clever lady."

And to have got it right for him and to hear the delight in his voice gave me such pleasure . . . . .

They would continue with his herb bed, other flower beds, trees. They'd then go in to a dinner prepared by Molly's mother (if she wasn't at the hospital being treated for her nervous disorder). On the way in, her father would whisper to Molly urgently, "I promise you, my darling, you aren't missing a lot; not a lot at all. Trust me." She didn't quite understand what he meant until much later in her life—after two years of marriage and her first eye operation.

Mr. Rice recalls the first time Molly and her husband Frank Sweeney came to consult him, bringing a thick folder of information Frank had compiled about Molly's case. Frank seemed full of energy, a devotee of causes like the protection of the whales and other wild life, charitable activities in Africa, etc.; with a major interest in the raising of goats and the making of cheese. Mr. Rice took a liking to Molly at once for her calm and independent bearing.

MR. RICE: ..... She had been blind since she was ten months old. She wasn't totally sightless; she could distinguish between light and dark; she could see the direction from which light came; she could detect the shadow of Frank's hand moving in front of her face. But for all practical purposes she had no useful sight. Other ophthalmologists she had been to over the years had all agreed that surgery would not help. She had a full life and never felt at all deprived. She was now forty-one, married just over two years, and working as a massage therapist in a local health club. Frank and she had met there and married within a month. They were fortunate they had her earnings to live on because he was out of work at the moment.

She offered this information matter-of-factly. And as she talked, he kept interrupting. "She knows when I pass my hand in front of her face. So there is some vision, isn't there?" Perhaps, I said. "And if there is a chance, any chance, that she might be able to see, we must take it, mustn't we? How can we not take it? She has nothing to lose, has she? What has she to lose?—Nothing! Nothing!"

And she would wait without a trace of impatience until he had finished, and then she would go on. Yes, I liked her at once .....

And when I talked to them on that first occasion I saw them together in my house, I knew that she was there at Frank's insistence to please him, and not with any expectation that I could help. And as I watched her sitting there, erect in her seat and staring straight ahead, two thoughts flitted across my mind. That her blindness was his latest cause and that it would absorb him just as long as his passion lasted. And then, I wondered, what then? But perhaps that was too stern a judgement.

And the second and much less worthy thought I had was this. No, not a thought; a phantom desire, a fantasy in my head; absurd, bizarre, because I knew only the barest outlines of her case, hadn't even examined her yet; the thought, the bizarre thought that perhaps, perhaps—up here in Donegal—not in Paris or Dallas or Vienna or Milan—but perhaps up here in remote Ballybeg was I about to be given— what is the vulgar parlance?—the chance of a lifetime, the one-in-a-thousand opportunity that can rescue a career—no, no, transform a career—dare I say it, restore a reputation? And if that opportunity were being offered to me, and if after all these years I could pull myself together and measure up to it, and if, oh my God if by some miracle pull it off perhaps ... *(He laughs in self-mockery.)* Yes, I'm afraid so. People who live alone frequently enjoy an opulent fantasy life.

Frank Sweeney is remembering how he imported Iranian goats for their high milk yield and discovered how much extra trouble it was to take care of them because they never adjusted to Irish time but lived out their lives on an Iranian time schedule. He explains that imprints on the memory—called "engrams"—provide us with instant recognition of people, objects, etc., and Molly's engrams were all of touch and smell, not of sight. A person whose sight had been restored after a lifetime of blindness (it has been argued for centuries) probably wouldn't be able to tell a cube from a sphere only by looking at them.

FRANK *(quoting Mr. Rice):* . . . . . Most of us are born with all five senses; and with all the information they give us, we build up a sight world from the day we are born—a world of objects and ideas and meanings. We aren't given that world, he said. We make it ourselves—through our experience, by our memory, by making categories, by interconnections. Now, Molly had only ten months of sight, and what she had seen in that time was probably forgotten. So, if her sight were restored, everything would have to be learned anew; she would have to *learn* to see. She would have to build up a whole repertory of visual engrams and then, then she would have to establish connections between these new imprints and the tactile engrams she already possessed. Put it another way; she would have to create a whole new world of her own . . . . .

Anyhow—anyhow. To go back for a second to our friend who knew what a cube was by touching it but couldn't identify it by sight alone. Rice talked a lot to Molly about all that stuff. He said neurologists had a word for people in that condition—seeing but not knowing, not recognizing what it is that they see. A word first used in this context by Freud, apparently. He said that people in that condition are called agnosic. Yes. Agnosic. Strange; because I always thought that word had to do with believing or not believing.

Molly has heard that Mr. Rice was an ophthalmologist of worldwide renown but went progressively downhill after his wife and children left him. He now has a job in the local hospital. She took to him especially because he didn't ask her questions about how it felt to be blind, only if she would be frightened at the possibility of regaining her sight. She doesn't regard herself as greatly disadvantaged but loves the world she lives in, including the sensations involved in swimming, which she believes she enjoys more than sighted people.

Mr. Rice, analyzing Molly's case, feels that she wasn't born clinically blind, with hopelessly useless retinas. In Molly's kind of blindness, she might have a very, very slight chance of recovery. He decides to give her some tests.

Frank admits that the moment he heard of even a slight chance, his mind burst with thoughts of the possibilities.

FRANK: . . . . . Molly was going to see! I knew it! For all his perhapses! Absolutely no doubt about it! A new world—a new life! A new life for both of us! . . . . .

I saw an Austrian psychiatrist on the television one night. Brilliant man. Brilliant lecture. He said that when the mind is confronted by a situation of overwhelming intensity—a moment of terror or ecstasy or tragedy—to protect itself from overload,

Jason Robards as Mr. Rice and Catherine Byrne as Molly in Brian Friel's *Molly Sweeney*

from overcharge, it switches off and focuses on some trivial detail associated with the experience.

And he was right. I know he was. Because that morning in that front room in the chilly bungalow—immediately after that moment of certainty, that explosion in the head—my mind went numb; fused; and all I could think of was that there was a smell of fresh whisky off Rice's breath. And at ten o'clock in the morning that seemed the most astonishing thing in the world, and I could barely stop myself from saying to Molly, "Do you not smell the whisky off his breath? The man's reeking of whiskey!"

Ridiculous . . .

Mr. Rice's tests revealed that Molly was suffering from cataracts and retinitis pigmentosa, but no present disease; so that if he operated, any gain of vision should be permanent.

It was on the morning of October 7 that the operation to remove a cataract and implant a lens was performed on Molly—Frank recalls—and he also remembers that he was offered a job that day, convoying food to Ethiopia. It was his first offer in months, but under these circumstances he couldn't accept it.

Mr. Rice, in his fantasy life, imagined himself phoning his most distinguished colleagues with the news that he plans to restore the sight of someone who has been blind for 40 years: "He is going to give her vision—the twenty-first recorded case in over a thousand years!" But he didn't; he wrote his daughters, had a few drinks and fell asleep in the armchair.

Molly remembers the celebration they had the night before the operation, lasting into the small hours of the morning—13 people including one baby and Molly's best friend, Rita Cairns, manager of the health club where she worked; but not Mr. Rice.

MOLLY: . . . . . Tom the fiddler played "The Lament for Limerick"! He played it softly, delicately. And suddenly, suddenly I felt utterly desolate. . . . . . And with sudden anger I thought: Why am I going for this operation? None of this is my choosing. Then why is this happening to me? I am being used. Of course I trust Frank. Of course I trust Mr. Rice. But how can they know what they are taking away from me? How do they know what they are offering me? They don't. They can't. And have I anything to gain? Anything? Anything?

And then I knew, suddenly I knew why I was so desolate. It was the dread of exile, of being sent away. It was the desolation of homesickness.

And then a strange thing happened. As soon as Tom played the last note of "The Lament for Limerick," I found myself on my feet in the middle of the sitting room and calling, "A hornpipe, Tom! A mad, fast hornpipe!" And the moment he began to play, I shouted—screamed, "Now watch me! Just you watch me!" And in a rage of anger and defiance I danced a wild and furious dance round and round that room; then out to the hall; then round the kitchen; then back to the room again and round it a third time. Mad and wild and frenzied. But so adroit, so efficient. No timidity, no hesitations, no falterings. Not a glass overturned, not a shoulder brushed. Weaving between all those people, darting between chairs and stools and cushions and bottles and glasses with complete assurance, with absolute confidence. Until Frank said something to Tom and stopped him playing.

God knows how I didn't kill myself or injure somebody. Or indeed how long it lasted. But it must have been terrifying to watch because, when I stopped, the room was hushed . . . . .

That night before the operation, Mr. Rice was at home, drinking and remembering that at the height of his powers, in Cairo, he received the phone call telling him that his wife was leaving him for another man, a colleague named Roger Bloomstein.

Frank remembers how much he regretted not being able to take the offered job in Ethiopia—"Bloody, bloody heartbreaking." But he knew he had to turn it down because "Molly was about to inherit a new world; and I had a sense—stupid, I know—I had a sense that maybe I was, too."

Molly remembers her first meeting with Frank, at the health club, introduced by Rita. Frank talked about a study he was doing on the blueback salmon, and Molly admired his enthusiasm.

After meeting Molly, Frank read everything he could find in the library on blindness. Considering how he might entertain her on a date, he decided that taking her dancing would be the thing to do.

FRANK: . . . . . In my heart of hearts I really didn't think she'd say yes. For God's sake, why should she? Middle-aged. No skill. No job. No prospect of a job. Two rooms above Kelly's cake shop. And not exactly Rudolf Valentino. And when she did speak, when she said very politely, "Thank you, Frank, I'd love to go." Do you know what I said? "All right then." Bloody brilliant! . . . . .

She had the time of her life. Knew she would. We danced every dance. Sang every song at the top of our voices. Ate an enormous supper. Even won a spot prize: a tin of shortbread and a bottle of Albanian wine. The samba, actually. I wasn't bad at the samba once.

Dancing. I knew. I explained the whole thing to her. She had to agree. For God's sake, she didn't have to say a word—she just glowed.

And after that night, Molly was aware that Frank would ask her to marry him. He was drawn to her partly because of her affliction: "He couldn't resist the different, the strange. I think he believed that some elusive off-beat truth resided in the quirky, the off-beat." And she knew that if he asked her she'd probably accept him.

MR. RICE: The morning of the operation. I stood at the window of my office and watched them walk up the hospital drive. It was a blustery morning, threatening rain.

She didn't have her cane, and she didn't hold his arm. But she moved briskly with her usual confidence; her head high; her face alert and eager. In her right hand she carried a gray overnight bag.

He was on her left. Now in the open air a smaller presence in a shabby raincoat and cap; his hands clasped behind his back; his eyes on the ground; his head bowed slightly against the wind so that he looked . . . passive. Not a trace of the assurance, the ebullience, the relentless energy.

And I thought: Are they really such an unlikely couple? And I wondered what hopes moved in them as they came toward me. Were they modest? Reasonable? Outrageous? Of course, of course they were outrageous.

And suddenly and passionately and with utter selflessness I wanted nothing more in the world than that *their* inordinate hopes would be fulfilled, that I could give them their miracle. And I whispered to Hans Girder and to Matoba and to Murnahan and to Bloomstein—yes, to Bloomstein too!—to gather round me this morning and steady my unsteady hand and endow me with all their exquisite skills.

Because as I watched them approach the hospital that blustery morning, one head alert, one head bowed, I was suddenly full of anxiety for both of them. Because I was afraid—even though she was in the hands of the best team in the whole world to deliver her miracle, because she was in the hands of the best team in the whole world—I was fearful, I suddenly knew that that courageous woman had everything, everything to lose.

Curtain.

ACT II

The morning in the hospital that Molly's bandages were to be removed, the nurse paid special attention to Molly's hair, dress and other details of her appearance. Molly didn't know what to expect when the bandages were taken off—not perfect vision, of course. She only hoped that Frank and Mr. Rice would be satisfied.

MOLLY: . . . . . For God's sake, of course I wanted to see. But that wasn't an expectation, not even a mad hope. If there was a phantom desire, a fantasy in my head, it was this. That perhaps by some means I might be afforded a brief excursion to this land of vision; not to live there, just to visit. And during my stay to devour it again and again and again with greedy, ravenous eyes. To gorge on all those luminous sights and wonderful spectacles until I knew every detail intimately and utterly—every ocean, every leaf, every field, every star, every tiny flower. And then, oh yes, then to return home to my own world with all that rare understanding within me forever . . . . .

When Mr. Rice did arrive, even before he touched me, I knew by his quick, shallow breathing that he was far more nervous than I was. And then as he took off the bandages his hands trembled and fumbled.

"There we are," he said. "All off. How does that feel?"

"Fine," I said. Even though I felt nothing. Were all the bandages off?

"Now, Molly. In your own time. Tell me what you see."

Nothing. Nothing at all. Then out of the void, a blur; a haze; a body of mist; a confusion of light, color movement. It had no meaning.

"Well?" He said. "Anything? Anything at all?"

I thought: Don't panic; a voice comes from a face; that blur is his face; look at him.

"Well? Anything?" . . . . .

A large, white moving object must be the nurse, Molly decided; she could see that. And a reddish blob was Mr. Rice's hand moving, easily identified by Molly as up-and-down movement. "Splendid!" exclaimed Mr. Rice, delighted by Molly's ability to see these things.

Frank sat at the hospital all morning, and it was almost noon before he was called in to see Molly. Mr. Rice and the staff nurse were exuberant at the "complete success" of the operation. Frank brought some flowers and handed them to Molly, who immediately identified the color of the flowers as blue and the paper they were wrapped in as yellow.

FRANK *(quoting Mr. Rice):* . . . . . Now—a really hard question, and I'm not sure I know the answer to it myself. What sort of flowers are they?

She brought them right up to her face. She turned them upside down. She held them at arm's length again. She stared at them—peered at them, really—for what seemed an age. I knew how anxious she was by the way her mouth was working.

"Well, Molly? Do you know what they are?"

We waited. Another long silence. Then suddenly she closed her eyes shut tight. She brought the flowers right up against her face and inhaled in quick gulps and at the same time, with her free hand, swiftly, deftly felt the stems and the leaves and the blossoms. Then with her eyes still shut she called out desperately, defiantly, "They're cornflowers! That's what they are! Cornflowers! Blue cornflowers! Centaurea!"

Then for maybe half a minute she cried. Sobbed, really . . . . .

That night when Frank came back to the hospital, Molly seemed thrilled that she could now see, could admire Frank's red necktie. But Frank still felt misgivings. He assured Molly that she looked beautiful, "but as I said good night I had a feeling she wasn't as joyous as she looked."

Mr. Rice muses on some of the major triumphs of his eye-surgery career, especially the Ballybeg triumph. After his wife left him he had sunk into a profound darkness, professionally as well as emotionally, and during the Molly Sweeney operation he felt miraculously restored, at least part way back into the light.

Molly returned to her job, acquired a brilliant scarlet beret and overcoat and managed to walk to the hospital three afternoons a week without a cane—sometimes for her a scary adventure. At home, Frank encouraged and tried to help her build new, visual engrams. It was an exciting time for Molly, with unexpected pleasures following each other in rapid succession.

Alfred Molina as Frank in *Molly Sweeney*

MOLLY: . . . . . But it was a very foreign world, too. And disquieting; even alarming. Every color dazzled. Every light blazed. Every shape an apparition, a specter that appeared suddenly from nowhere and challenged you. And all that movement—nothing ever still—everything in motion all the time; and every movement unexpected, somehow threatening. Even the sudden sparrows in the garden, they seemed aggressive, dangerous.

So that after a time the mind could absorb no more sensation. Just one more color—light—movement—ghostly shape—and suddenly the head imploded and the hands shook and the heart melted with panic. And the only escape—the only way to live—was to sit absolutely still; and shut the eyes tight; and immerse yourself in darkness; and wait. Then when the hands were still and the heart quiet, slowly open the eyes again. And emerge. And try to find the courage to face it all once more.

I tried to explain to Frank once how—I suppose how *terrifying* it all was. But naturally, naturally he was far more concerned with teaching me practical things.

And one day when I mentioned to Mr. Rice that I didn't think I'd find things as unnerving as I did, he said in a very icy voice, "And what sort of world did you expect, Mrs. Sweeney?"

Mr. Rice operated on the other eye about six weeks later, and the results were much the same as in the first operation. "She could now see," Mr. Rice reported, "from a medical point of view. From a psychological point of view she was still blind. In other words, she now had to learn to see."

Frank was soon aware that Molly had changed. It was explained to him by Jean O'Connor, a behavioral psychologist writing a book about Molly, that too many emotional swings from one mood to the other render a person "incapable of experiencing anything, feeling anything at all."

And Frank was disturbed by incidents of Molly's peculiar behavior: for example, proposing going for a swim in the ocean, in December, or changing hair styles in front of a mirror in which she couldn't see anything but a blur.

Mr. Rice noted that the hardest part for the patient is coming to terms with all the new challenges after the first wave of enthusiasm subsides.

Then, Frank noticed, Molly developed a condition in which she had dizzy spells, with the world seeming to become filled with thick fog. Frank consulted Mr. Rice about this and found that it was a recognized development in Molly's circumstances called "Gnosis." Then the condition disappeared as suddenly as it had come on.

Molly endured months of tests of all kinds. One day she bought a pot of flowers that looked attractive to her, without allowing herself to touch them. When she finally examined them closely at home, she found that they weren't nearly as pretty as she'd thought.

It was pointed out to Frank by Jean O'Connor that Molly was showing signs of withdrawal instead of the expected upsurge of personality.

FRANK: . . . . . And she was right. That's what happened. Molly just . . . withdrew.

Then in the middle of February she lost her job in the health club. And now Rita was no longer a friend. And that was so unfair—Rita kept making allowances for her long after any other boss would have got rid of her; turning in late; leaving early; maybe not even making an appearance for two or three days. Just sitting alone in her bedroom with her eyes shut, maybe listening to the radio, maybe just sitting there in silence . . . . .

Molly even neglected her scarlet coat and in fact never wore it outdoors again. And at this point Frank felt that there was nothing more he could do to help her.

Mr. Rice observed that Molly developed a condition called "blindsight," psychologically induced, in which the patient appeared to have lost sight entirely but actually was still receiving visual images which weren't reaching her consciousness.

Frank was approached by a journalist in a pub and indiscreetly talked freely with him for about an hour. The results were published in an article entitled "*Miracle Cure False Dawn. Molly sulks in darkness. Husband drowns sorrow in pub.*"

Molly remembers the three visits she made to her mother when the latter was hospitalized for her nerves. At one of them, Molly's mother and father had a heated argument over whether Molly should be sent to a school for the blind.

Molly's loss of confidence and self-sufficiency had become painfully evident to Mr. Rice during the last few months of treating her.

MOLLY: In those last few months I was seeing less and less. I was living in the hospital then, mother's old hospital. And what was strange was that there were times when I didn't know if the things I did see were real or was I imagining them. I seemed to be living on a borderline between fantasy and reality.

Yes, that was a strange state. Anxious at first; oh, very anxious. Because it meant that I couldn't trust any more what sight I still had. It was no longer trustworthy.

But as time went on, that anxiety receded; seemed to be a silly anxiety. Not that I began trusting my eyes again. Just that trying to discriminate, to distinguish between what might be real and what might be imagined, be guided by what Father used to call "excellent testimony"—that didn't seem to matter all that much, seemed to matter less and less. And for some reason the less it mattered, the more I thought I could see.

MR. RICE: In those last few months—she was living in the psychiatric hospital at that point—I knew I had lost contact with her. She had moved away from us all. She wasn't in her old blind world—she was exiled from that. And the sighted world, which she had never found hospitable, wasn't available to her any more.

My sense was that she was trying to compose another life that was neither sighted nor unsighted, somewhere she hoped was beyond disappointment; somewhere, she hoped, without expectation.

The last time he saw Mr. Rice, Frank was trying unsuccessfully to move a pair of badgers from one sett to another with his friend Billy Hughes while Mr. Rice was fishing nearby, dressed in oversized gear that made him look a bit like a circus clown.

FRANK: . . . . . Maybe he didn't annoy me that Easter Sunday afternoon because I knew I'd probably never see him again. I was heading off to Ethiopia in the morning.

We left the van outside Billy's flat, and he walked me part of the way home.

When we got to the courthouse I said he'd come far enough: we'd part here. I hoped he'd get work. I hoped he'd meet some decent woman who'd marry him and beat some sense into him. And I'd be back home soon, very soon, the moment I'd sorted out the economy of Ethiopia . . . the usual stuff.

Then we hugged quickly, and he walked away, and I looked after him and watched his straight back and the quirky way he threw out his left leg as he walked, and I thought, my God, I thought how much I'm going to miss that bloody man.

And when he disappeared round the corner of the courthouse, I thought, too— Abyssinia for Christ's sake—or whatever it's called—Ethiopia—Abyssinia—whatever it's called—who cares what it's called—who gives a damn—who in his right mind wants to go there, for Christ's sake? Not you. You certainly don't. Then why don't you stay where you are, for Christ's sake? What are you looking for?

Oh, Jesus . . .

Mr. Rice went to New York for a memorial service for Roger Bloomstein, killed in an airplane accident. Another of the world's four leading eye surgeons, Hans Girder, met Mr. Rice there and congratulated him on his achievement with Molly. Rice admitted to Girder that it didn't end well for Molly: she is now totally blind and psychologically afflicted. Girder comments, "They don't survive. That's the pattern. But they'll insist on having the operation, won't they? And who's to dissuade them?"

Mr. Rice saw his former wife at the memorial service—she looked as beautiful as ever and received him warmly in a gesture that he recognized as a final farewell. On his return to Ballybeg, Mr. Rice resigned from the hospital and packed up his things.

MR. RICE: . . . . . I called on Molly the night before I left. The nurse said she was very frail. But she could last forever or she could slip away tonight. "It's up to herself," she said. "But a lovely woman. No trouble at all. If they were all as nice and quiet . . ."

She was sleeping, and I didn't waken her. Propped up against the pillows; her mouth open; her breathing shallow; a scarlet coat draped around her shoulders; the wayward hair that had given her so much trouble now contained in a net.

And looking down at her I remembered—was it all less than a year ago?—I had a quick memory of the first time I saw her in my house, and the phantom desire, the insane fantasy that crossed my mind that day: Was this the chance of a lifetime that might pull my life together, rescue a career, restore a reputation? Dear God, that opulent fantasy life . . .

And looking down at her—the face relaxed, that wayward hair contained in a net—I thought how I had failed her. Of course I had failed her. But at least, at least for a short time she did see men "walking as if like trees." And I think, perhaps, yes I think she understood more than any of us what she did see.

In her hospital room, Molly reviews her situation: she can no longer distinguish between light and dark—as she could when she first consulted Mr. Rice—nor could she now see Frank's hand moving in front of her eyes. Despite the wasted effort to create new engrams, she seems to have less contact with the outside world than she did before.

She enjoys the many visits she receives from Billy Hughes (out of loyalty to Frank), from Rita (now her friend again) from her mother (who doesn't talk much but wanders through these surroundings so familiar to her). A 27-page letter from Frank revealed his great enthusiasm for and dedication to his new task—he's even found a species of African honey bee that he thinks would do well in Ireland.

She remembers Mr. Rice's last visit—she was awake and heard him say to her, "I'm sorry, Molly Sweeney, I'm so sorry," but the smell of whisky was so strong that she pretended to be asleep.

MOLLY: . . . . . And sometimes Father drops in on his way from court. And we do imaginary tours of the walled garden and compete with each other in the number of flowers and shrubs each of us can identify.

. . . . . I think I see nothing at all now. But I'm not absolutely sure of that. Anyhow, my borderline country is where I live now. I'm at home there. Well . . . at ease there. It certainly doesn't worry me any more that what I think I see may be fantasy, or indeed what I take to be imagined may very well be real—what's Frank's term?—external reality. Real—imagined—fact—fiction—fantasy—reality—there it seems to be. And it seems to be all right. And why should I question any of it any more?

Curtain.

Pulitzer, Tony, Critics Awards

○○○
○○○
○○○
○○○
○○○
○○○ RENT

A Musical in Two Acts

BOOK, MUSIC AND LYRICS BY **JONATHAN LARSON**

Cast and credits appear on pages 301–302

JONATHAN LARSON (book, music lyrics) was born February 4, 1960 in White Plains, N.Y., and grew up in Westchester County, where his father's business was marketing. His first encounter with La Boheme, *which inspired him to write his musical* Rent *about similar characters in similar circumstances in modern New York's Alphabet City, was in the form of a puppet show to which his parents took him. He was the star of his school plays and the composer of cabarets at Adelphi University, where he studied acting and decided after graduation to devote his energies to the theater.*

Like many young people who came before and will come after him, Larson supported himself for a decade waiting on tables while creating material for all media. In 1988 he won the Richard Rodgers Development Award for his rock musical Superbia, *which was staged at Playwrights Horizons. In 1989 he received the Stephen Sondheim Award from the American Music Theater Festival, contributing to the musical* Sitting on the Edge of the Future, *and Sondheim himself kept an advisory eye on the Larson career. It has branched into his score for the musical* J.P. Morgan Saves the Nation *presented in 1995 by En Garde Arts; his rock monologue* Tick, Tick ... BOOM! *which he performed at Second Stage, the Village Gate and New York Theater Workshop; and his scoring and song writing for various children's TV and film projects including* Sesame Street *and Stephen Spielberg's book-casettes* An American Tale *and* Land Before Time.

Larson finished the first draft of Rent *in 1992, and its subsequent development has taken place step by step at James C. Nicola's New York Theater Workshop. In 1994* Rent *won the Richard Rodgers Studio Production Award, which played for 7 performances of an experimental staging at the Workshop. The musical then went into production there at the off-off-Broadway level, opening January 26, 1996. It was enthusiastically received and converted to full off-Broadway status February 13 for a run of 56 performances, in which it was named a Best Play and won the Pulitzer Prize. It then moved to Broadway April 29 for an extended run in which it soon collected the New York Drama Critics Circle and Tony Awards for best musical. But its author had been noticeably unwell during the final week of rehearsals at the Workshop. On January 25, the day before the off-off-Broadway opening of his soon-to-be prizewinning musical, he died of an aortic aneurism, never knowing of the success he was destined to achieve, in a real-life tragedy of operatic dimensions.*

SYNOPSIS: The curtainless stage *"seems more like a pile of junk than a set,"* with three distinct areas, the center one being the apartment of two young men—Mark Cohen, a film maker, and Roger Davis, a musician—in the loft of an abandoned Lower East Side building. It is *"the top floor of what was once a music factory,"* walls decorated with old rock 'n' roll posters. *"Since the style of the piece is an operatic collage, the transitions between scenes should flow cinematically."*

On Christmas Eve at the loft, Mark is filming Roger struggling to write a song, using his guitar.

MARK *(sings):*
    December 24, 9 p.m.
    Eastern Standard Time
    From here on in
    I shoot without a script

    See if anything comes of it
    Instead of my old shit

    First shot—Roger
    Tuning his fender guitar
    He hasn't played in a year
ROGER *(sings):*
    This won't tune
MARK *(sings):*
    So we hear
    He's just coming back
    From a year of withdrawal

ROGER *(sings):*
>   Are you talking to me?

MARK *(sings):*
>   Not at all
>   Are you ready? Hold that focus—steady
>   Tell the folks at home what you're doing, Roger . . . ?

ROGER *(sings):*
>   I'm writing one great—
>   *The phone rings.*

They listen to the answering machine ("Voice Mail #1"). Mark's mother is calling to tell him she loves him and that she's sorry to hear that his girl friend Maureen has left him for a lesbian affair. Another call from a pay phone outside is from a close friend, Tom Collins, asking them to throw down the key (but before he can pick it up he is mugged). A third call is from Benjamin Coffin III (Benny), another friend who once lived there in the loft with Mark and Roger but is now the owner of their building. He is calling to demand last year's rent which he let go for a time but now wants paid.

A fuse blows and the men light candles, dancing in the moonlight and singing "Rent."

MARK *(sings):*
>   How do you document real life
>   When real life's getting more
>   Like fiction each day
>   Headlines—bread-lines
>   Blow my mind
>   And now this deadline
>   "Eviction—or pay"
>   Rent!

ROGER *(sings):*
>   How do you write a song
>   When the chords sound wrong
>   Though they once sounded right and rare
>   When the notes are sour
>   Where is the power
>   You once had to ignite the air

MARK *(sings):*
>   And we're hungry and frozen

ROGER *(sings):*
>   Some life that we've chosen

MARK and ROGER *(sing):*
>   How we gonna pay
>   How we gonna pay

How we gonna pay
Last year's rent! . . . . .

As the song continues, they warm themselves by throwing some of Mark's old manuscripts on the fire in their illegal, wood-burning stove. In other areas of this cinema-styled presentation, Benny is in his Range Rover on the phone complaining to a friend about Mark and Roger, Joanne Jefferson is at the pay phone telling Maureen Johnson that there's a little problem with the electrical equipment in the outdoor show Maureen is going to put on, and Collins is picking himself up off the ground after his mugging. Angel Schunard, a street drummer, happens to have set up nearby, and there is instant chemistry between the two men (expressed in the song "You Okay Honey"). Angel and Collins tell each other they both have AIDS. Angel invites Collins to a life support meeting that evening and takes him home to help him recover from the mugging.

Mark prepares to leave the apartment to join his ex-girl friend Maureen at her request. He tells the audience that Roger's girl friend left a note on the mirror telling Roger "We've got AIDS" and then slit her wrists. Roger has sunk into a depression and hasn't left the apartment in six months. Mark leaves. Alone, Roger picks at his guitar and expresses his frustration in "One Song Glory."

ROGER *(sings):*
One song
Glory
Before I go
Glory
One song to leave behind

Find one song
One last refrain
Glory
From the pretty boy front man
Who wasted opportunities . . . . .

Find glory
Beyond the cheap colored lights
One song
Before the sun sets
Glory—on another empty life

Time flies—time dies
Glory—one blaze of glory
One blaze of glory—glory

There is a knock on the door. Roger answers it. It's Mimi Marquez, a downstairs neighbor, requesting a light for her candle. Her smile reminds Roger of his dead girl friend, and he is clearly smitten by her. Roger lights her candle, but now Mimi seems to have dropped her drug stash. She gets down on all fours to look for it, then blows out the candle while singing "Light My Candle."

MIMI *(sings):*
   We could light the candle
   Oh won't you light the candle
      He lights it again, and gets down to help.
ROGER *(sings):*
   Why don't you forget that stuff
   You look like you're sixteen
MIMI *(sings):*
   I'm nineteen—but I'm old for my age
   I'm just born to be bad
ROGER *(sings):*
   I once was born to be bad
   I used to shiver like that
MIMI *(sings):*
   I have no heat—I told you
ROGER *(sings):*
   I used to sweat
MIMI *(sings):*
   I got a cold—
ROGER *(sings):*
   Uh huh—
   I used to be a junkie
MIMI *(sings):*
   But now and then I like to—
ROGER *(sings):*
   Uh huh
MIMI *(sings):*
   Feel good . . . . .

Though attracted to Mimi, Roger is wary of her because she's a junkie. Finding her stash, he tries to hide it. Mimi takes it out of his pocket and *"sexily exits."*

At Maureen and Joanne's, the phone rings, and the answering machine kicks in, announcing Maureen's performance—"Over the Moon"—at midnight that evening in the lot next door, a protest against the treatment of the homeless, some of whom live there. On the phone it's Joanne's parents, Mr. and Mrs. Jefferson, calling ("Voice Mail #2") to tell Joanne of their importantly busy lives and incidentally wishing her a Merry Christmas.

Later that night, Collins arrives at the loft with Angel, whom he introduces to Mark and Roger. Angel hands them all $20 bills—he just made $1,000 and explains how in "Today 4 U"

MODERN BOHEMIANS OF *RENT*: *Above left*, Mark (Anthony Rapp, *on phone*) and Roger (Adam Pascal, *with guitar*); *above right*, Roger with Mimi (Daphne Rubin-Vega); *below*, Joanne (Fredi Walker), Angel (Wilson Jermaine Heredia), Maureen (Idina Menzel) and Tom (Jesse L. Martin)

ANGEL *(sings):*

> It was my lucky day today on Avenue A
> When a lady in a limousine drove my way
> She said, "Dahling—be a dear—haven't slept in a year
> I need your help to make my neighbor's yappy dog
> Disappear
>
> "This Akita—Evita—just won't shut up
> I believe if you play non-stop, that pup
> Will breathe its very last high strung breath
> I'm certain that cur will bark itself to death"
>
> Today for you—tomorrow for me . . . . .

The woman promised a fee of $1,000 for the job and paid it when Angel played his drums until the dog jumped out of a window.

Benny (he married money and so is no longer considered a member of the artists' coterie) enters. Mark and Roger still can't pay what they owe. But Benny hasn't come to collect the rent. He's the new owner of the vacant lot next door, and (in the song "You'll See") he tells them he is going to develop it as Cyberarts, a multimedia studio. Mark can make films and Roger produce music here in the loft to their dreams' content, rent-free, if only they will persuade Maureen to cancel the performance she plans to put on in the lot that evening—it's the kind of demonstration that tends to scare investors.

Benny leaves, soon followed by Mark and Collins, leaving Roger alone once again with his music.

Joanne (Maureen's new lover) is working on the electrical equipment for Maureen's show, which will protest Benny's plan to evict the homeless and develop the lot. Mark offers to help her, and soon they are comparing notes, singing and dancing "Tango: Maureen."

MARK *(sings):*

> Honey, I know this act
> It's called the Tango: Maureen.
>
> The Tango: Maureen
> It's a dark, dizzy
> Merry-go-round
> As she keeps you dancing

JOANNE *(sings):*

> You're wrong

MARK *(sings):*

> Your heart she is mangling

JOANNE *(sings):*

> It's different with me

MARK *(sings):*
    And you toss and you turn
    Cause her cold eyes can burn
    Yet you yearn and you churn and rebound
JOANNE *(sings):*
    I think I know what you mean
MARK and JOANNE *(sing):*
    The Tango: Maureen . . . . .

    When you're dancing her dance
    You don't stand a chance
    Her grip of romance
    Makes you fall
MARK *(sings):*
    So you think, "Might as well"
JOANNE *(sings):*
    Dance a tango to hell
MARK and JOANNE *(sing):*
    "At least I'll have tangoed at all" . . . . .

Mark joins Collins and Angel at a support group (whose character names change at each performance of *Rent,* honoring friends of the company who have died of AIDS). In the number "Life Support" the group leader, Paul, asks one of the participants, Gordon, how he feels today. "Okay," Gordon replies, "best I've felt all year."

PAUL *(sings):*
    Then why choose fear?
GORDON *(sings):*
    I'm a New Yorker!
    Fear's my life!

    Look—I find some of what you teach suspect
    Because I'm used to relying on intellect
    But I try to open up to what I don't know
GORDON and ROGER *(sing):*
    Because reason says I should have died three years ago
ALL *(sing):*
    No other road
    No other way
    No day but today

In her apartment, Mimi is getting ready to go out, putting on makeup and singing to herself "Out Tonight."

MIMI *(sings):*

> In the evening I've got to roam
> Can't sleep in the city of neon and chrome
> Feels too damn much like home
> When the Spanish babies cry
>
> So let's find a bar
> So dark we forget who we are
> Where all the scars from the
> Nevers and maybes die
>> *She decides on an amazingly sexy dress.*
> Let's go out tonight
> Have to go out tonight
> You're sweet
> Wanna hit the street?
> Wanna wail at the moon like a cat in heat?
> Just take me out tonight
>> *She makes her way to Roger's door and ends the song in front of him.*
> Please take me out tonight
> Don't forsake me—out tonight
> I'll let you make me—out tonight
> Tonight—tonight—tonight

In the moonlight, Mimi finishes by kissing Roger, who recoils and protests, "Come back another day." Mimi persists, "No day but today."

ROGER *(sings "Another Day"):*

> Excuse me if I'm off track
> But if you're so wise
> Then tell me—why do you need smack?
>
> Take your needle
> Take your fancy prayer
> And don't forget
> Get the moonlight out of your hair
>
> Long ago—you might've lit up my heart
> But the fire's dead—ain't never ever gonna start
>
> Another time—another place
> The words would only rhyme
> We'd be in outer space
> It'd be another song
> We'd sing another way
> You wanna prove me wrong?
> Come back another day

MIMI *(sings):*
> There's only yes
> Only tonight
> We must let go
> To know what's right
> No other course
> No other way
> No day but today

The support group chimes in on this song, but Roger remains adamantly distant. Mimi finally gives up and exits. In spite of himself he has been moved by Mimi, though, and he can't now concentrate on composing. He gives up and goes out to join his friends.

Mark, Angel, Collins and the support group roam the lot. The conspicuous presence of Mark's camera stops three policemen from abusing a homeless woman, who is anything but grateful ("Who the fuck do you think you are?/I don't need no Goddamn help"). The company sings "Will I?" and "On the Street" and joins Collins in a wistful dream of moving out west and opening a restaurant there ("Santa Fe").

After Mark leaves, Angel and Collins express their love for each other in "I'll Cover You."

ANGEL *(sings):*
> I've been hearing violins all night.

COLLINS *(sings):*
> Anything to do with me?
> Are we a thing?

ANGEL *(sings):*
> Darling—we're *every*thing

> Live in my house
> I'll be your shelter
> Just pay me back
> With one thousand kisses
> Be my lover—I'll cover you

COLLINS *(sings):*
> Open your door
> I'll be your tenant
> Don't got much baggage
> To lay at your feet
> But sweet kisses I've got to spare
> I'll be there—I'll cover you

ANGEL and COLLINS *(sing):*
> I think they meant it
> When they said you can't buy love

Now I know you can rent it
A new lease you are, my love
On life—be my life . . . . .

In various locations, groups join in wondering about the future in a sort of round ("Will I?"). Joanne, at the pay phone and with a cellular phone in hand, is talking to both her parents and a friend, somewhat confusingly, at the same time ("We're Okay").

It's Christmas Eve at St. Mark's Place. A group of the homeless are singing "Christmas Bells." Vendors are selling their wares, including stolen goods, at an open air bazaar. Roger meets Mark, tells him about Mimi's visit that evening and points Mimi out to him—she and a group of junkies are trying to do business with a drug dealer. Roger pulls Mimi away, apologizes to her for the way he behaved and invites her to a dinner party with his friends after Maureen's show. She accepts, and Roger introduces her to Mark.

Benny comes through the square. He now knows that Maureen's protest show is not going to be called off.

Meanwhile, junkies, cops and homeless sing their versions of a Christmas message, while Angel buys Collins a new coat. Maureen enters on Joanne's motorcycle and takes her position in front of the microphone on stage. She launches into "Over the Moon," a sort of allegorical monologue in which Elsie the cow, forbidden to produce milk, is trying to make a "leap of faith" and jump over the moon, since "The only way out is up."

Following the performance, everyone gathers at the Life Cafe where Benny and one of his investors are meeting over a bottle of wine. Benny informs the artists that the Bohemia idea has had it: "Do you really want a neighborhood/Where people piss on your stoop every night?/Bohemia, Bohemia's/A fallacy in your head/This is Calcutta/Bohemia's dead." In response and in defiance, the artists celebrate their Bohemia with "La Vie Boheme," a mock funeral with Mark delivering the eulogy.

MARK *(sings):*
  . . . . . Here she lies
  No one knew her worth
  The late great daughter of Mother Earth
  On this night when we celebrate the birth
  In that little town of Bethlehem
  We raise our glass—you bet your ass to—La Vie Boheme
ALL *(sing):*
  La Vie Boheme
MARK *(sings):*
  To days of inspiration, playing hookey, making
  Something out of nothing, the need to express—to communicate
  To going against the grain, going insane, going mad . . . . .

To riding your bike, midday past the three-piece suits—
To fruits—to no absolutes—
To Absolut—to choice—to the *Village Voice*—to any
Passing fad

To being us—for once—
Instead of them—
La Vie Boheme . . . . .

Others contribute choruses to this song, and soon all are dancing and then doing solo bits which express their personalities. "*Mimi's beeper goes off. She takes out a bottle of pills and downs one. Roger's beeper goes off at almost the same time. He downs his.*" Mimi comments, "AZT break," and now both Mimi and Roger know that they are both under the same treatment—taking AZT pills on a regular schedule—and both HIV positive. "*They . . . . . hold hands and stare into each other's eyes lovingly.*" Soon they are singing "I Should Tell You," all inhibitions evaporated, trying to tell each other all about themselves.

ROGER and MIMI *(sing):*
. . . . . Who knows where
Who goes there
Who knows
Here goes

Trusting desire—starting to learn
Walking through fire without a burn
Clinging—a shoulder, a leap begins
Stinging and older, asleep on pins

So here we go . . . . .

Roger and Mimi exit. Joanne comes in to tell Maureen that her show started a riot in the Avenue B lot. Benny called the police and then padlocked their building. With Mark, Angel and Collins, all celebrate the tumultuous occasion with more of "La Vie Boheme."

COLLINS and MAUREEN *(sing):*
Revolution, justice, screaming for solutions,
Forcing changes, risk and danger making noise and making pleas
ALL *(sing):*
To faggots, lezzies, dykes, cross dressers too . . . . .
To you, and you and you, you and you
To people living with, living with, living with
Not dying from disease

Let he among us without sin
Be the first to condemn

La Vie Boheme . . . . .

MARK (sings):	ALL (sing):
Anyone out of the mainstream	La Vie Boheme
Is anyone *in* the mainstream?	La Vie Boheme
Anyone alive—with a sex drive	La Vie Boheme
Pull down the wall	
Aren't we all	

The opposite of war isn't peace . . .
It's creation

ALL (sing):

La Vie Boheme

MARK: The riot continues. The Christmas tree goes up in flames. The snow dances. Obliviously, Mimi and Roger exchange a small, lovely kiss.

ALL: Viva La Vie Boheme.

End of Act I.

ACT II

COMPANY (sings "Seasons of Love"):
Five hundred twenty-five thousand
Six hundred minutes
Five hundred twenty-five thousand
Moments so dear
Five hundred twenty-five thousand
Six hundred minutes
How do you measure—measure a year?

In daylights—in sunsets
In midnights—in cups of coffee
In inches—in miles
In laughter—in strife

In—five hundred twenty-five thousand
Six hundred minutes
How do you measure
A year in the life?

How about love?
How about love?
How about love?
Measure in love

Seasons of love

On New Year's Eve, the lot is now empty and fenced, and the loft building is still padlocked. Roger and Mimi alternate between trying to pry off the lock and celebrating the occasion with a bottle of champagne. Mark and then Maureen join them, followed by Joanne with rope and climbing gear and Collins and Angel with a bottle of their own in an ice bucket. Mark, Joanne and Maureen manage to climb in through a window, while Angel works on the door with a blow torch.

In Mark's apartment, the electricity mysteriously comes on, and the telephone answering machine delivers "Voice Mail #3," the first message being from Mark's mother.

MRS. COHEN *(sings):*
Mark, it's the Wicked Witch of the West
Your mother
Happy New Year from Scarsdale
We're all impressed that the riot footage
Made the nightly news
Even your father says Mazeltov—
Honey—call him
Love, Mom

The next message is from the TV producer Alexi Darling who saw Mark's footage of the riot and offers him a very large salary to work on her tabloid news program. As Maureen and Joanne head downstairs with Mark, the two women discuss planning another protest which Mark can film from the beginning. "It's nice to dream," Mark comments, but he distrusts the TV proposition.

Downstairs it's "Happy New Year" all over the place, in song and with paper hats and noisemakers. Benny comes in remarking, "I see that you've beaten me to the punch." He has come, he says, to make peace with his former friends. He suggests that Mark use his camera (he does) and ceremoniously hands Roger the key to this building "On behalf of Cyberarts." When Benny finds that Mark's camera battery is dead, he takes back the key, obviously wanting favorable publicity out of this.

Benny boasts that Mimi once came to his office dressed in "black leather and lace . . . . . My back is still sore," trying to annoy Roger, who dismisses the implication with "I'm not her boy friend." The artists continue their celebration, leaving Benny out. Finally Benny leaves.

All move to exit, but before he goes, Angel makes sure that Roger and Mimi are left there together. Roger leaves Mimi with a kiss. Alone, Mimi is approached by the drug dealer, who offers her stash.

Mark tells the audience, "Valentine's Day . . . Pan across the empty lot. Roger's down at Mimi's, where he's been for almost two months—though he talks about selling his guitar and getting out of here—still jealous of Benny . . . . . God knows where Collins and Angel are . . . Could be that new shantytown by the river, or a

Members of the cast of Jonathan Larson's musical *Rent* in their Alphabet City setting

suite at the Plaza . . . Maureen and Joanne are rehearsing." The women are also on the verge of a quarrel, arguing over one of the lines in their show.

MAUREEN: It just doesn't roll off my tongue. I like my version.
JOANNE: You—dressed as a groundhog—to protest the ground-breaking . . .
MAUREEN: It's metaphor!
JOANNE: It's . . . less than brilliant.
MAUREEN: THAT'S IT, MISS IVY LEAGUE.
JOANNE: What?
MAUREEN: Ever since New Year's I haven't said boo. I let *you* direct. I didn't pierce my nipples because it grossed *you* out. I didn't stay and dance at the Clit Club that night, cause *you* wanted to go home . . .
JOANNE: You were flirting with the woman in rubber.
MAUREEN: *That's* what this is about?? There will *always* be women in rubber— FLIRTING WITH *ME!!* Give me a break. (*Sings "Take Me or Leave Me"*):
    Every single day
    I walk down the street

I hear someone say
"Baby's so sweet"

Ever since puberty
Everybody stares at me
Boys—girls
I can't help it baby . . . . .

Take me for what I am
Who I was meant to be
And if you give a damn
Take me baby or leave me . . . . .

JOANNE *(sings):*
I look before I leap
I love margins and discipline
I make lists in my sleep
Baby what's my sin?

Never quit—I follow through
I hate mess—but I love you
What to do
With my impromptu baby . . . . .

Take me for what I am.

MAUREEN *(sings):*
A control freak

JOANNE *(sings):*
Who I was meant to be . . . . .

BOTH *(sing):*
Take me for what I am
Who I was meant to be
And if you give a damn
Take me baby or leave me
Take me baby
Or leave me

Guess I'm leavin'
I'm gone
        They part.

COMPANY *(sings "Seasons of Love"):*
In diapers—report cards
In spoke wheels—in speeding tickets
In contracts—dollars
In funerals—in births

In—five hundred twenty-five thousand
Six hundred minutes

How do you figure
A last year on earth?

Figure in love . . . . .
Measure in love
Seasons of love
Seasons of love

It is now the Easter season. Roger is seated on the bed in Mimi's apartment. Mimi enters and approaches Roger, in a hurry.

ROGER: Where *were* you?
MIMI: I'm sorry I'm late.
ROGER: You were with Benny. Weren't you?
MIMI: No.
ROGER: You were. (*Sings*):
    I'm sleeping upstairs tonight
    I have a song to write
        He grabs his guitar, kisses her on the cheek.
MIMI (*sings*):
    Wait!
    I should tell you I—
    Nothing
ROGER (*sings*):
    Happy spring
        Roger exits. Mimi reveals a just-purchased stash bag and angrily flings it across the room.

As Mimi sings the following ("Without You"), a stylized "musical beds" takes place symbolizing the situations in both the loft building and the hospital where Angel is a patient. By the end of the song, Roger and Mimi and Maureen and Joanne are reunited.

MIMI (*sings*):
    . . . . . The crowds roar
    The days soar
    The babies cry
    Without you

    The moon glows
    The river flows
    But I die
    Without you
ROGER (*sings*):
    The world revives

MIMI *(sings):*
  Colors renew
BOTH *(sing):*
  But I know blue
  Only blue
  Lonely blue
  Without me, blue . . . . .

  The mind churns
  The heart yearns
  The tears dry
  Without you
  Life goes on
  But I'm gone
  Cause I die
  Without you.

On Labor Day weekend, in "Voice Mail #4," Mark is still being propositioned by the TV producer. Angel is in the hospital. In "Contact" the couples thrash about, making love in a large bed, but they are dissatisfied with latex sex: "Fire fire burn—burn yes!/No latex rubber rubber/*Fire latex rubber latex bummer lover bummer.*" Then Angel appears in a spotlight, dancing wildly.

ANGEL *(sings):*
  Take me
  Take me

  Today me
  Today me

  Tomorrow you
  Tomorrow you
  Love
  You
  Love you . . . . .

Angel has died. At his funeral on Halloween, Collins sings an anguished reprise of "I'll Cover You." Mimi, Maureen and Mark participate in Angel's eulogy, a collection of affectionate memories. Mark remembers "that time he walked up to these tourists—and they were petrified because, A, they were obviously lost; B, had probably never spoken to a drag queen in their lives—and he . . . SHE just offered to escort them out of Alphabet City . . . And she let them take a picture with her—and said that she'd help 'em find the Circle Line . . ."

Mark has finally signed a contract with the TV producer, Alexi. As he shoots some footage of mourners leaving the church, he wonders about the cause and effect of it all in "Halloween."

MARK *(sings):*
      ..... Why are entire years strewn
      On the cutting room floor of memory
      When single frames from one magic night
      Forever flicker in closeup .....

      That's poetic
      That's pathetic

      Why did Mimi knock on Roger's door
      And Collins choose that phone booth
      Back where Angel set up his drums
      Why did Maureen's equipment break down

      Why am I the witness
      And when I capture it on film
      Will it mean that it's the end
      And I'm alone

Among those coming out of the church are Mimi, now with Benny; Roger, who informs Mimi that he's sold his guitar, bought a car and is moving to Santa Fe; and Maureen and Joanne, who join in the quarrel that develops. Mark ("Come on guys, chill!") and Collins ("Angel made us believe in love/I can't believe you disagree") manage to cool the others off. Joanne and Maureen embrace affectionately. Mimi gives Roger "*a look that says, 'can't we give it one more try like the others?'* " Roger turns away, so Mimi leaves with Benny and the others but comes back so that she overhears the developing quarrel between Roger and Mark ("Goodbye, Love"), Roger accusing Mark of not living up to his own standards of creativity and sensitivity, of using his work as a hiding place from life and its troublesome responsibilities. Mark in turn accuses Roger of deserting Mimi at a time when she still loves him and is pale and thin and seems to be getting very sick.

ROGER *(sings):*
      No more! Oh no!
      I've gotta go.
MARK *(sings):*
      For someone who's always been let down
      Who's heading out of town?
ROGER *(sings):*
      For someone who longs for a community of one's own

Who's with his camera, alone?
I'll call
> *Roger goes to shake Mark's hand. Mark refuses.*

I hate the fall
> *Roger begins to walk off and discovers Mimi.*

You heard?

MIMI *(sings):*
Every word
You don't want baggage without lifetime guarantees

You don't want to watch me die?
I just came to say
Goodbye, love
Goodbye, love
Came to say goodbye, love, goodbye

MIMI *(sings):*	ROGER *(sings):*
Just came to say	Glory
Goodbye, love	One blaze of
Goodbye, love	Glory
Goodbye love, goodbye	I have to find

Roger leaves and Benny returns, but Mimi pushes him away. Seeing that Mimi is really quite sick, Mark recommends a clinic he knows, and Benny offers to pay for her rehab there. The Pastor of the church throws Collins out, calling him a "queer." Collins comments in song, "That's no way to send a boy/To meet his maker/They had to know/We couldn't pay the undertaker." Benny takes out a check and hands it to Collins to pay for Angel's funeral, and the two go off to have a drink together.

Mark is at the phone, Roger at the wheel of his car, but both are reflecting on their lives in "What You Own."

ROGER *(sings):*
The filmmaker cannot see

MARK *(sings):*
And the songwriter cannot hear

ROGER *(sings):*
Yet I see Mimi everywhere

MARK *(sings):*
Angel's voice is in my ear

ROGER *(sings):*
Just tighten those shoulders

MARK *(sings):*
Just clench your jaw till you frown

ROGER *(sings):*
   Just don't let go
MARK *(sings):*
   Or you may drown
MARK and ROGER *(sing):*
   You're living in America
   At the end of the millennium
   You're living in America
   Where it's like the twilight zone

   And when you're living in America
   At the end of the millennium
   You're what you own

   So I own not a notion
   I escape and ape content
   I don't own emotion—I rent

   What was it about that night
   Connection—in an isolating age
   For once the shadows gave way to light
   For once I didn't disengage

Mark goes to the phone, reaches Alexi and tells her, "I need to do my own work/ I quit!" Roger sees Mimi in his mind's eye and finally hears his song: "One song: glory/Mimi/Your eyes."

In "Voice Mail #5," parents are leaving messages for Mark, Mimi, Joanne and Roger to get in touch, apparently to no avail.

In the loft on Christmas Eve, Mark is screening the movie he has made, which begins with the shot of Roger tuning his guitar the Christmas before. Roger has returned from Santa Fe and sold his car to retrieve his guitar. He found his song but hasn't been able to find Mimi since his return. Collins arrives and gives money to Mark and Roger which he got by rewiring the ATM machine at the Food Emporium to give money to whoever enters A - N - G - E - L.

From downstairs, Maureen calls frantically for help—she's found Mimi in the park, huddled and freezing, and is struggling to get her inside and warm. "We can buy some wood and something to eat," Mark observes. Collins adds regretfully, "I'm afraid she needs more than heat." She appears to be dying, as Roger plays and sings his glory song ("Your Eyes") to her.

ROGER *(sings):*
   Your eyes
   As we said our goodbyes
   Can't get them out of my mind
   And I find I can't hide . . . from . . .

Your eyes
The ones that took me by surprise
The night you came into my life
Where there's moonlight
I see your eyes

How'd I let you slip away
When I'm longing so to hold you
Now I'd die for one more day
'Cause there's something I should have told you
Yes, there's something I should have told you

When I looked into your eyes
Why does distance make us wise?
You were the song all along
And before the song dies

I should tell you, I should tell you
I have always loved you
You can see it in my eyes
      Roger plays the entire Puccini Theme, correctly and passionately.
Mimi!

MIMI *(as she weakly stirs):* I jumped over the moon!

ROGER: What?

MIMI: A leap of . . . Moooooooooooooooo—

JOANNE: She's back!

MIMI: I was in a tunnel. Heading for this warm, white light . . .

MAUREEN: OH MY GOD!

MIMI: And I swear Angel was there—and she looked GOOD! And she said, "Turn around, girl friend—and listen to that boy's song . . ."

COLLINS *(sings):*
    She's drenched

MAUREEN *(sings):*
    Her fever's breaking

MARK *(sings):*
    There is no future—there is no past

ROGER *(sings):*
    Thank God this moment's not the last

MIMI and ROGER *(sing):*
    There's only us
    There's only this
    Forget regret or life is yours to miss

ALL *(sing):*
    No other road, no other way
    No day but today

As the finale grows, the entire company makes their way onto the stage. Simultaneously, Mark's film resumes projecting onto the back wall, "Scenes" from "Rent."

WOMEN *(sing):*

I can't control
My destiny
I trust my soul
My only goal
Is just to be

Without you
The hand gropes
The ear hears
The pulse beats
Life goes on
But I'm gone
Cause I die
Without you

I die without you

MEN *(sing):*

Will I lose my dignity
Will someone care
Will I wake tomorrow
From this nightmare

There's only now
There's only here
Give in to love
Or live in fear
No other path
No other way

No day but today

No day but today

COMPANY *(sing):*

No day but today
        The end.

Best Play Citation

○○○
○○○
○○○
○○○
○○○
○○○ # A FAIR COUNTRY

A Play in Two Acts

BY JON ROBIN BAITZ

Cast and credits appear on pages 322–323

JON ROBIN BAITZ was born in Los Angeles in November 1961. His father was an executive in the international division of Carnation Milk, and at the time his son was 7 years old the family went on the move to Brazil for three years and then to South Africa for seven, not returning to California until young Baitz was 17 and ready to attend high school for one year, receiving his diploma in 1978. This was the extent of his formal education, but the experience of living abroad had inspired him to self-education, reading voluminously and beginning to write, in his early teens, with short stories ("A writer is a reader moved to emulation" is a Saul Bellow quote that Baitz likes to remember).

Listening to foreign languages, Baitz developed an ear for local dialects and expressions and returned to his native land with a special sensitivity to "the language under the surface of language" (he found the Watergate tapes particularly fascinating). In the early 1980s he apprenticed himself to the Padua Hills playwrights workshop in California, run by Sam Shepard and Murray Mednick. In 1985 his first formal production took place at L.A. Theater Works—Mizlansky/Zilinsky in repertory with a John Steppling play. His next, The Film Society, was produced January 22, 1987 at Los Angeles Theater Center and brought him national acclaim. The American Theater Critics Association cited it in The Best Plays of 1986–87 as one of the outstanding scripts of the cross-country season.

189

Baitz then moved to New York, where The Film Society *was produced OOB at Second Stage July 7, 1988, winning the Oppenheimer-Newsday Award, and where he became playwright-in-residence for the OOB group Stage and Film Company. The Mark Taper Forum in Los Angeles commissioned Baitz's* Dutch Landscape *and produced it in January 1989. That year he started work on* The Substance of Fire, *workshopping the first act at his own OOB group, Naked Angels, and the whole play the following year in New Haven in the Long Wharf Theater's workshop series. Playwrights Horizons produced it off Broadway March 17, 1991 for 120 performances in Baitz's New York professional theater debut and his first Best Play citation. His second is* A Fair Country, *produced off Broadway by Lincoln Center Theater February 19 after workshop viewings at New York Stage and Film, Naked Angels and Seattle Rep.*

Playwrights Horizons also produced Baitz's The End of the Day *April 7, 1992 for 64 performances, and Circle Rep put on his* Three Hotels *April 6, 1993 for 231 performances. And four of his one-acts—*It Changes Every Year, Four Monologues, Coq au Vin *and* Recipe for One—*were presented in New York Public Library Reading Room Readings April 18, 1994. Baitz has been the recipient of Rockefeller, Revson, N.E.A. and American Academy of Arts and Letters fellowships and the Oppenheimer and Humanitas (for* Three Hotels) *Awards. His screenplay for* The Substance of Fire *is to be released in 1996. He is a founding member of the Naked Angels theater company, a member of the Dramatists Guild Council and lives in New York City.*

ACT I

Scene 1: 1987. An archeological excavation in southern Mexico

SYNOPSIS: In a clearing near a rushing stream, Gil Burgess—a young man dressed for outdoor living—is brushing dirt off a ceremonial knife which he's uncovered. To his great surprise, his mother—Patrice Burgess—walks into the scene and joins him. She has tracked him down, he knows not how, because he gets no communications, even mail, here at the dig.

GIL: How did you get out here?

PATRICE: Some farmer.

GIL: Indian or white?

PATRICE: Indian.

GIL: You just got in his car?

PATRICE *(beat):* You're too thin, Gil.

GIL *(surprised):* I'm too thin, am I? Oh.

PATRICE: Harry died.

GIL: Well. I see. Oh.

PATRICE: I'm sorry to blurt it out. It's better that way.

GIL: Yeah, it is, isn't it? "Hi, been so long, your father is dead. Could I have a chair and a Fresca?" *(Beat.)* How did he die.

PATRICE: Not well.

GIL: *"Not well."*

PATRICE: Cancer.

GIL: All that red meat. The cigars. The boredom.

PATRICE: He was trying homeopathic—

GIL: I don't really need the details . . . . .

Gil suggests that a letter would have sufficed to bring him this news—he is clearly less than overjoyed to see his mother, after an absence of six years, and Patrice comments that there seems to be "no limit to the half-life of the anger of one's children." Gil corrects her: she has only one child now, he's the only one left. And he's alone here at the dig because the others on the team have gone on a mission to Mexico City; and Gil's boy friend has gone back to his girl friend in London: "I used to warn all my boy friends that I was on the rebound from you." This dig, an ancient Mayan settlement, looks promising if the team can prevent the Mexican government from burying it with a dam, and if Gil can hold off looters who invade the camp at night.

Gil informs his mother that there should be a truck at first light that can take her back, and in the meantime they have nine hours together. The lights fade on the scene.

Scene 2: 1978. Verandah of the Burgess home in Durban, South Africa

"It is late afternoon. The remains of a shattered Zulu pot are on the steps and the ground." Gil is joined by Hilton, a black gardener, carrying a bag of women's clothes. He has missed giving them to their owner, a servant named Edna, who has been carried off by the police.

Patrice comes in and asks Hilton to take over the kitchen, as a favor, and make them some tea. Hilton exits into the house, and Gil—who had heard Edna screaming and can deduce from the broken pot that she had been throwing things—wonders what happened to cause this household tempest.

PATRICE: The thing is, she and I had a little run-in. I may have forgotten the rules for a second. I may have forgotten that she is the maid and I am the mistress. Role confusion . . . . .

GIL: It's that Zulu rage, isn't it, Mom? It's that impenetrable African anger that you can't see through. You look at them and haven't got a clue as to what's going on.

PATRICE: Do you think that is a particularly *worthy* line to pursue, Gil?

GIL: *Um.*

PATRICE: Let's not make this into some sort of racial test-case here.

GIL: I'm not making—

PATRICE: No, no, no. You are making a critical mistake, sweetie, you are falling right into the traps. That Boer policeman. What he said just before he left: "That's the real African, they're not like your Sidney Poitier kind of native . . ."

GIL: I just said there *is this thing called* Zulu rage, that doesn't make me an Afrikaaner.

PATRICE: Well? What's the difference between your two points of view, then? It seems to me—

GIL *(highly agitated and confused):* But I saw how violent she was.

PATRICE: Yes. True. But listen. Look. I'm not going to do "the Kafir went mad." I will not lower, we will not lower ourselves. What this was, was merely a problem of two personalities clashing, Gil.

GIL: Okay. Big clashing personalities.

PATRICE: I mean, really clashing. Because, let's face it, she and I were not over the moon about each other. From the beginning. You had two people coming up against one another. Was it cultural? I'll give you that. Because I wouldn't play mistress to her put-upon servant, and I wouldn't play at being some goddamn lumpy-ankled white American housewife managing her every move, she resented me and she hated not being treated like shit.

GIL: But I don't know that she was geared up for a full-fledged insurrection, Mother.

As a matter of fact, there has been a stream of such servants through this Burgess household; none of them could get used to Patrice, who can remember none of their names. Gil's race-sensitivity may be influenced by his older brother Alec who has been visiting his family for the past two days. Alec (Allie) is characterized by Patrice as "the last bastion of the heroes of the left" who has been spending most of his visit so far, not at home, but talking to local people.

Patrice observes that the smashed pot was a rather rare Zulu objet d'art, so Edna's explosion was destructive of her own culture. She figures that all her neighbors heard the outburst and probably approved of the police intervention, which has left some of Edna's blood on her sleeve. Gil noticed that it was the black policeman who was directed by the Boer policeman to punch the black servant.

Hilton enters with the tea tray, and Patrice pulls Gil to his feet to dance to samba music emanating from a radio in the house, as the lights fade.

Scene 3: The same night. Togo Airport, West Africa

Harry Burgess (Gil's father and Patrice's husband) is looking over the passports of a dance troupe whose tour he is supervising. He is a cultural attache—exact position unnamed—in the U.S. foreign service. He is joined by Ellsworth Hodges, a fellow diplomat, who has been chasing Harry and has had difficulty catching up with him with such limited travel accommodations as are offered in this part of the African world. Hodges is Associate Director of Programs and Management stationed in Washington under the Carter administration. Hodges asks about the dancers waiting on their plane for Harry to join them.

HARRY *(a favorite subject, and still an amazement to Harry):* It's a company all descended from a single slave family in Tennessee. They have power. So it hits these people hard. And this tour . . . These kids talking all night. Mixing with audiences after. In Jo'burg, the homelands, Swaziland, everywhere, all over. We were in Sierra Leone . . . and the governments, they don't like it. Because it's all about not taking any crap. But: The People love it. I'm taking them to Durban. Look. Come with us. You'll have the great pleasure of seeing the South Africa police *vomiting with rage* on the sidelines. It will be . . . heaven. Heaven.

HODGES: The way you have cut through to the Africans. Astonishing. I'm so proud. All the years we were out in the cold; *"the art boys,"* they called us, like we were queers—well, now I'm the boss. Which is a lot of fun—to my surprise.

HARRY: It may be the enlightenment. But Ellsworth. I am still out here in the cold. So to speak. *(Pressing on.)* Two requests for transfer, and two polite responses asking me to please stay in South Africa. Two! And then silence.

HODGES *(simple, a shrug):* With the re-naming of the agency, we've been pre-occupied. We're still sorting it out. The systems are being reshuffled—

HARRY: Ellsworth, please. Not with me. Not that line. Why am I stuck? Should I start thinking about other things?

HODGES: You're a brilliant Africa hand. You have the trust, you have the ears of the Zulus, Xosas, Muslims. *Muslims,* for God's sake, man! . . . . .

Hodges suggests that Harry miss his flight and stick around here with him for the day. Harry can't—his son Alec is visiting, and if he missed his plane it might take him a couple of days to get another. Harry presses Hodges for a transfer, and Hodges admits there may be a European posting for the Voice of America: a producer-director for a magazine show, for which Harry would be ideal. But there's a problem with the Washington Old Guard. Harry's son Alec has been associating with "a group of exiled black South African kids in New York. Most of them are African National Congress. They're very vital, very powerful and quite secretive." There's reason to believe that new African leadership might emerge from this group, and they're the sort of people Allie will be looking up in Durban. Hodges emphasizes that his Washington people want access to them.

HARRY: So you're saying that I should use Allie to draw in his friends? No? Are you? Ellsworth? I'm misreading the situation, right?

HODGES: He is at the nexus. He has an extraordinary vantage point.

HARRY: Nexus. Nexus? Oh. *That word.* This smells. I can smell it. What? Did they come to you? I can't believe it.

HODGES: Harry.

HARRY: Is that the "Old Guard."

HODGES: It's a very low level of non-covert activity.

HARRY: You're asking me to take down names?

HODGES *(exasperated):* It's not like we're going to give the names to the South African government. It's for us! I'm just asking you to entertain your son's friends. Open a path. A road in. That's the real job. *(Tired, pleading.)* Just give 'em something. They'll approve you for VOA.

Harry is angered by Hodges's proposition: give the "Old Guard" some names in exchange for the job in Europe. Hodges in his turn accuses Harry of being soft, of being sorry for losers. "Did you think for a second I'd be your local fuck?" Harry asks, as the sound of his plane leaving for Durban is heard. Hodges replies, "I told them you wouldn't but I had to ask" and begs Harry's pardon as the scene ends.

Scene 4: The next morning. Verandah of the Burgess home

Gil and his older brother Allie enter from the house, arguing. Allie is concerned that their former servant, Edna, is languishing in jail. Gil is disturbed by Allie's pretense that he understands Africa well enough to make value judgments.

Allie is a journalist and asks Gil to give him a "chronology of events" regarding the incident. She worked here for five months, Gil tells him, neither happily nor unhappily, as far as he could tell. As happens from time to time in this country, because of all the hidden anger, she blew up suddenly for no apparent reason.

Allie has made an effort to talk with Edna and get to know her and others ("Their lives don't magically improve because you've befriended them on your little holiday," is Gil's comment). Allie has found that Edna has "an enormously complicated life." Gil is curious about the details.

ALLIE: But you're not, really. All that curious. I mean, if you had been, you'd have asked her.

GIL: And if I had, could I have been of any use? "Oh, a friendly ear?" Please. Allie. It does no good pretending these are your friends. Because they have to do certain things. For instance get paid. They have these *jobs. I* have been here since I was thirteen. I know something about it.

ALLIE: I would say you know a great deal about it. But what you don't have. What you lack, Gil. Is—you don't have distance. *(Beat.)* Something has happened to you. Something . . .

GIL *(quiet or scared):* Please don't tell me. Please don't come here and tell everybody where they don't measure up. Okay? Mother is terrified of you. You know that? Patrice is locked in her room. She's afraid you'll investigate her to death, and judge her, and she's not up for it!

ALLIE *(backing off):* Okay. You're right. It's unfair. I'm sorry.

Allie tells Gil about his rigorous life in New York—"dirt poor"—but suggests that his brother come back with him and finish high school in New York. They are interrupted by the arrival of Hilton bearing a coffee tray, assuring them that everything is under control both indoors and out ("Don't worry, someone new, someone very good is coming") and offering to make them anything special they want for breakfast, like French toast. Allie wants nothing, Gil asks for a papaya and a lime, and Hilton exits. Then Gil explains to Allie that he couldn't possibly go to New York with him.

Judith Ivey as Patrice and Matt McGrath as Gil in *A Fair Country* by Jon Robin Baitz

GIL: ..... What do you think? I could leave Mom here? Alone? In this house? Dad is away three quarters of the year. Do you think that'd be fair, Allie? "Oh, I'm going home now, with Allie, because it's wretched here . . ." No. No. Thank you.

ALLIE: Why was Mom arguing with Edna?

GIL: I have no idea.

ALLIE: Her niece's daughter was graduating from secondary school in the Transkei. The first person in their family to attend and complete their schooling. There was a graduation ceremony, not much, probably, from the sounds of it. She showed me a picture of the school, which is run by Jesuits. Mud and dead grass and a few sticks for the goal posts, all girls, field hockey and a cross on the roof, but the first in the family, and Edna wanted to go to the graduation but somehow had forgotten to give Patrice enough notice, so that when she asked to leave the next morning, for a seven-hour bus trip, Patrice declined.

GIL: I'm quite sure, I'm pretty sure it is more complicated than that.

Asked about his African school, Gil reports that he is a prefect and regarded by the other students as something special: an American. Again, Allie offers him "a futon and a blanket" in the East Village.

Harry enters looking very tired, greeting his sons Allie and Gil, asking about the Edna problem. Almost immediately Patrice enters dressed in a caftan and wearing large sunglasses, worrying about how Hilton has been doing with the breakfast. Harry takes her hand and assures her that they'll make out O.K.

Hilton comes in with the papaya and more coffee. He loses no time recommending his cousin Ginger for Edna's job.

HILTON: She is not like Edna. Nothing, don't worry . . .

HARRY: How do you mean, Hilton?

HILTON: She favors her employer.

HARRY: Edna . . . was . . . she had voiced to you some complaint of her treatment or her . . .

HILTON: She didn't talk to me. Different tribe. She is different. She is Xosa. I am Zulu. Different. I can not say what she was thinking.

HARRY: So, was there no warning here?

PATRICE: Could we, could I just, I would love that juice, Hilton. Maybe we could have breakfast, you know, and not do the post-game discussion for a few hours.

Hilton goes into the house.

HARRY: No, you're right, it's just, I can't get up to speed here, you know, I'm sorry, but I'm . . .

PATRICE: Just breakfast.

HARRY: Yes. I only—fine. Since everyone is okay. They—you keep seeing this sort of thing happen—since Soweto, the level of violence—

ALLIE: What sort of thing?

HARRY: Clashes.

ALLIE: Black and white. Servants, masters, that's what . . . you mean?

PATRICE *(drinks her coffee and speaks):* No, Allie. You see something else. You see people not being able to function very well. In any capacity, is what you see, employer or the employed, is what you see, you see. And I will add that you see it anywhere in the world where people work for other people. You simply hope that you're being quite reasonable in your treatment of one another.

ALLIE: Would you say that your treatment of Edna was reasonable?

HARRY: Really, really, let's not do this now, let's go somewhere get in the car and drive up the coast, or . . .

PATRICE: No, I can answer that. The answer, Allie, is, of course not. I do not think my treatment of Edna was reasonable. *(Beat.)* This situation is not reasonable.

Nothing about it exists within reason. No. And was Edna's treatment of *me* reasonable? No. There is no—cogent—Columbia School of Journalism, third-page editorial lesson for you to glean here, as much as I would love to supply one. Because that would be easy. *(Beat.)* Because that's not where we live now. Does that register?

Allie suggests that the problem could be eliminated by not having servants. Patrice reminds him that in their position they are required to please large groups of people by giving elaborate parties, so not employing help isn't an alternative.

At this point, Gil interjects the statement that he wants to go back to the U.S. with his brother. When his parents realize that he is talking about a longer stay than just a visit, Harry judges it "not practical." After their conversation about Edna, Patrice doesn't have enough energy left to take up another major family question. Gil adds the information that "I can't bear it here" and admits he liked seeing the policeman strike Edna—and he noticed that even his mother was smiling.

Patrice accuses Allie of widening the breach that is growing between him and his family by "lecturing people on their moral inferiority to you." Harry tries to stop her, but she goes on: "Who are you to come down here and play Che Guevara? Of the East Village? I read the pieces you send us, and you know what, you have yet to write a single thing that hasn't been said by minds far more unoriginal than your own. You have only smugness to fall back on. Only your own smugness, and it's the smugness of a young man who does not really know what life feels like. Only knows how to play on its disappointments to him. There. Now you know. Who are you to tell Gil? You know nothing of South Africa, baby."

The problem isn't South Africa, Allie insists, the problem is that Patrice uses everybody around her and sucks the life out of them. Allie tells his mother, "You stopped scaring me when I was twelve," and he wants to rescue Gil from her influence. He offers to end the visit and go back early, and that is fine with Patrice. When Allie mentions Edna as another of Patrice's victims, Patrice runs into the house, followed by Gil, apologizing.

Allie regrets having upset his mother, but he can't bring himself to go into the house and apologize, because he believes she behaved irresponsibly: "She called the police. On the maid. We don't do that." There's no point in Allie's trying to talk to his mother now, Harry observes, because Gil is in there with her, and between the two of them "It's a closed club."

Allie offers to leave early to take some of the pressure off, but Harry, understanding now that he must get Patrice and Gil away from Africa at all costs, replies, "No. No. No. I'm going to have us out of here within a few months" and tells Allie about the offer of a Voice of America job. In Europe, Patrice will be fine and Gil can go his own way. "It's not completely set," Harry admits, and Allie urges him, "Any sort of change is good. Do it!"

Allie picks up the bag full of Edna's belongings, to take them to her.

HARRY: Allie, make her bail.
>   *He hands Allie money. Allie exits. Hilton returns with his tray. Begins to*
>   *clear the table of the remains of the breakfast.*

HILTON: Ginger. Ginger is very adept. The butchers and Indian fruit men all know her and save the best for her. They wait for her. Her smile. *(Beat.)* Edna, you know, she was Xosa, those people are very bad. Everybody knows ... they come with bad trouble, always it happens. *(Beat.)* Ginger is very skilled. She also worked for the—what do you call the person who is the main teacher at the University of Natal? ...? The ...? They wear a black robe?

HARRY *(absently):* Uh-huh. Yeah. Here.

> *He places a cup on a tray for Hilton.*

A chancellor. A dean. A provost.

> *Hilton exits. Harry sits alone.*

A boss.

> *Curtain.*

ACT II

Scene 1: The Hague, Holland. The Burgess Living Room

It is New Year's Eve, 1980, and Patrice, in a dinner dress, is entertaining Van Eden, *"an elderly Dutch gentleman,"* dressed in black tie and sipping champagne. They are making conversation about Patrice's sons. It takes a more serious turn when Van Eden asks about Gil. Patrice's reaction somewhat discomfits Van Eden, though he keeps his cool excellently well like the ex-diplomat he is.

VAN EDEN: Has he settled on a ... future?

PATRICE: I think what you must be referring to is the scandal of his being caught *in flagrante delicto* with that seventeen-year-old boy from the other side of the building?

VAN EDEN: No.

PATRICE: Very attractive boy who looks rather like that actor you have—that actor with the eyes. Rutger Hauer. In the room where they store the bicycles. One can understand why one might—an attractive boy.

VAN EDEN: I'm not so familiar with that actor.

PATRICE: Then, of course, you were not part of that petition that was sent round to ask us to move out, to vacate?

> *Long pause.*

VAN EDEN: No.

PATRICE: Thank God. I didn't think you, a retired diplomat ... If you had seen the language they used. The committee. Tenants committee. *(Beat.)* I thought I saw your name, but perhaps it was a mistake.

VAN EDEN: I believe that my wife, before her illness, was on that body. She had not served for some time.

PATRICE: I can only assume it was a problem with translation. Words like "preying on" and "predatory perversion." These words must have other, alternative meanings in Dutch. I was surprised to see how bigoted and small minded our neighbors were. I thought this was a progressive culture where such things—

VAN EDEN *(cautious but interrupts):* I do not follow the various . . . comings and goings. Of the area. People are free to live their lives as they wish.

Changing the subject, Patrice comments that young people no longer live lives of service to the various institutions because they develop no respect for them. She doesn't hesitate to remind Van Eden—somewhat tactlessly—that the Dutch have lost Suriname, of which Van Eden was once governor. She wonders what kind of example the Dutch set there before they were thrown out. As for setting an American example, Patrice decries the kind of parties she and Harry are forced to give for visiting artists and the kind of shows he must put on: "Culture. 'American Culture Now.' Is the show. Different events each week. If it's theater, it's always some blue-collar thing with a porch and a broken dog. If it's art, it's always a sort of primitive thing with a despairing Laotian. And then they all come over here for a sweet and sour poo-poo platter."

Van Eden's reaction to this is noncommittal, and then Gil arrives, *"somewhat unsteady on his feet."* He reports that the New Year's Eve atmosphere in the bars is sedate but slightly more festive than usual. Gil and his mother are both speaking in a vein of sarcasm, and Van Eden is avoiding direct involvement.

VAN EDEN: May I have some more of this lovely champagne?

PATRICE: Like you guys did in Suriname, I lost a certain amount of credibility with Gil after I beat the shit out of our African maid. Didn't I, darling?

GIL: Yes. But she's very credible now.

PATRICE *(pours for Van Eden):* Well, Gil, maybe you can help from a young person's perspective.

GIL: I doubt it.

PATRICE: Perhaps you could shed some light?

GIL: Not likely.

PATRICE: Why is it the young dancers and the choreographers Harry brings around, and the poets, and the writers—the same trotting-out of their same six discoveries. "The story of me and my crisis." Part eight hundred and thirty-seven. The complaining, the lack of courage? The special pleading?

GIL: The young people I know don't complain much at all.

PATRICE *(a short laugh):* I'll bet they don't. We are aware of that. Everyone in the building is aware of that.

VAN EDEN *(suddenly understanding the nature of what he may be trapped in):* Do you think you might have anything stronger than champagne?

Patrice's attention reverts to her hostess duties. She thanks Van Eden for sharing New Year's Eve with the Burgess family, which will include Allie and his latest girl friend, due to arrive shortly.

Van Eden's late, beautiful wife died six weeks ago, before Patrice had a chance to really get to know her. Patrice asks Van Eden if he loved his wife very much. Then she leaves the room to get some caviar, and Gil is left to explain to Van Eden, "Sometimes she doesn't know that she's saying things which are not allowed." Van Eden declares himself not offended, and the two discuss Mondrian until Patrice returns and goes right back to the subject of Van Eden's wife: "How did she die?" She contracted malaria in Suriname, Van Eden replies, and after his retirement insisted on coming back to Holland where the climate was bad for her. He finishes, "Before she died, Mrs. Burgess, my wife said to me, 'Gerrit, there is no more harbor. No more port. We are sailors on the Flying Dutchman, ancient mariners on a boat, always at sea.'"

Harry arrives in the elevator—*"more gray, more expansive, more prosperous."* Allie and his girl have gone to look at a canal, and Gil descends in the elevator to fetch them.

Patrice introduces Harry to Van Eden, then asks about news from Washington. They are eagerly awaiting the release of the hostages in Iran, the minute the new President is inaugurated (and Patrice hands Harry the gold envelope that contains their invitation to the inauguration—apparently they are meeting with the new administration's approval).

Harry in his turn hands Patrice some hothouse tomatoes he has brought, and Patrice goes off to slice them, after mentioning that Van Eden's wife was on the committee that circulated the petition against the Burgesses. Van Eden quickly asserts that he knew nothing of it. Harry apologizes for Patrice's tactlessness.

VAN EDEN: Would you prefer it if I left? I do have several excuses at hand, you know. My Dalmatians require attention. My sadness at being with a happy family on New Year's Eve. One could slip away.

HARRY: It's a kind offer, but please stay.

VAN EDEN: In our line of work, where men spend so much of the day simply lying, I find the truth rather a tonic. She is not well, is she?

HARRY: Tonight it's worse. Our older boy arriving. Republicans move into the White House. She feels . . . that in particular agitates her.

VAN EDEN: But not you?

HARRY *(sitting):* I have learned, maybe a little late in life, the essential lesson for all diplomats: "Stay out of the way of the politicians."

VAN EDEN *(laughs):* Oh, yes.

HARRY: "Beware the wise men when they come limping into sight." One of those Chinese proverbs. I duck 'em. *(He laughs.)* It's so much cleaner that way. My wife likes to create a little fiction that I'm a closet-conservative. But I'm purely a *conservator.* Whoever's in charge, they're still gonna need a little culture . . . . .

The elevator is heard—it's the young people arriving. Allie enters with Carly (*"quite beautiful, quite blonde and quite strong looking"*), followed by Gil. Patrice enters, greets Allie, recognizes Carly, and Harry introduces Van Eden. Champagne is poured and toasts made.

Wondering why Allie's plane arrived so late, Patrice learns that her son came not from New York, as planned, but from Johannesburg. He sensed that there might be a story there, so he and Carly left the U.S. a few days early in order to go to South Africa, where he actually visited Durban. Carly looked at lions while Allie looked for a story. He tells Van Eden, "My girl friend told me she thought it was the most beautiful place she'd ever seen . . . . . She sees beauty. I see bodies."

Van Eden suddenly remembers that his Dalmatians need attention and departs. Allie continues: shortly after that visit to his family in Durban, his South African contacts in New York "dried up" and ceased speaking to him. He decided to stop over on his way to Europe to see if he could find out why from his friends in South Africa.

ALLIE: . . . . . And I found out exactly why. You met them all . . . . . Eight or so. That had been to our house. And we—if you recall—we had talked. Long into the nights, drinking, remember? Talk of the future?

PATRICE: Alec, what are you saying?

ALLIE: That those people are all either dead or in jail.

CARLY *(almost inaudible):* You didn't tell me that.

GIL: They were all taken in? Those exact people?

ALLIE: The ones who came to our house. And I was the only thing that all those people had in common. They weren't on lists—

HARRY: Everybody there is on a list.

ALLIE: Not together. Not the same ones. These people, they didn't know each other, they didn't run in the same circles, they were not all part of some cell . . . . . I was the only thing they had in common.

HARRY: Alec. You can't blame yourself.

ALLIE: I don't.

GIL: Therefore?

ALLIE: What did I tell you? What was the lesson? Journalism 101.

GIL: A chronology.

HARRY: Which leads to?

ALLIE *(simple, but heartbroken):* All roads lead to home, Harry. To Dad.

PATRICE: What are you saying, Allie?

HARRY: Wait. Why would that have anything to do with me?
       Beat.

ALLIE: Pop. Dad. Did you give our government a list?

Harry does not reply. Patrice's reaction is, "This is not a game to be played in our house ever again," and Gil's is, "He didn't, Allie. He wouldn't." Harry calls attention to his efforts both with his agency and the South Africans on behalf of "decent human behavior." Allie received death threats in Durban, but he hadn't realized until now where the betrayal came from. Harry asserts vigorously that he would never do anything to put anyone in danger. But Patrice perceives the truth and interrupts him.

PATRICE: Is that why you got promoted so suddenly, Harry? Because I have never figured it out. We were not on the fast track, my sweet. You were floundering. We were set for the Third World forever.

GIL: I refuse to believe this. I won't.

PATRICE *(beat):* Is that why they gave you Europe? Because you finally gave them something? Harry. Come on now.

HARRY: There never was a list. There were just conversations.

GIL: Dad.

HARRY: I had to get us out.

PATRICE: It's the end of the world, isn't it? Harry. Darling. *(Beat.)* We've done it.
    Alec stands there, sobbing. Lights fade.

Scene 2: A few hours later

Allie is sitting staring out of the window, listening to Harry's Voice of America broadcast (Appalachian singers and the New Year's ball ready to drop in Times Square). Gil enters to report that Carly is trying to get a cab. Patrice knows that Gil is leaving with Allie—he's all packed and ready to go.

Carly returns, having found a cab, and she and Gil manage to help Allie to his feet and point him towards the elevator. Harry comes in and makes one last plea to Allie.

HARRY: I was told we were offering help to people who would need it in the future.

ALLIE: Harry.

HARRY: In the future.

ALLIE: Harry. Don't you know? Look at me. You've killed me. Don't you understand that? Don't you want to say goodbye?

HARRY: I am not one of those men!

ALLIE: Clearly. They, Harry, are much better at it than you. If you had been one of "those men," I would have never found out.

HARRY: Allie, please. For God's sakes . . .

PATRICE *(entering):* Harry. They should go now. Let them. Just let them go.

ALLIE *(looks at Patrice and Harry):* Goodbye. Mom. *(Pause. She does nothing.)* It needn't have been, you know. There are so many other ways to live. *(He turns to Gil.)* Let's go.

GIL: I just have to . . .

ALLIE: Go ahead.
    Allie and Carly wait by the elevator.

GIL: Dad?

Laurence Luckinbill as Harry in *A Fair Country*

HARRY: I see how scared you are, but you will find moments where you have to take action. And who knows all the consequences. To examine every action. That would drive you mad. You cannot dwell. *(Beat.)* Gil. It's random and unknowable. But you still have to keep . . .

What Gil wants is not his father's blessing, but his father's spare coat to take with him—Gil's is at the cleaners. Gil's last words are an explanation to his mother that he can't serve her any longer, and then the three young people disappear into the elevator.

The Burgesses should never have gone abroad, Harry has decided, they should have stayed home in the little house they had, and Harry should have continued teaching.

PATRICE *(goes to him):* Let me put you to bed, Harry.

HARRY: Why? Do you still love me, Patrice? *(Beat.)* Maybe I'll just stay here for a bit. I'm not tired yet.

Harry walks over to the radio and turns it on. It's a Voice of America Announcer.

ANNOUNCER: "... the Carter-Reagan transition team still in a closed door session. There's no further word from Teheran. This has been a Voice of America news brief."

Music.

HARRY *(remote):* Poor Carter. Nothing he ever did worked. He could never do the right thing. And he just kept trying and trying and trying.

ANNOUNCER: "It is six p.m. in New York, six hours until the end of the year. This is the Voice of America."

Over The Hague there is a sudden flash of fireworks. The fireworks turn the sky red. Harry and Patrice look out.

HARRY: Happy New Year! Patrice!

Scene 3: 1987. The excavation

At the Mexican dig, as in the opening scene, it is almost dawn when Patrice and Gil hear a would-be looter making a noise in the surrounding bush. Gil scares him off by shouting into the darkness that he has a pistol.

By the light of a fire, Patrice and Gil are talking about the intervening years, how Harry was cared for by a girl friend, a waitress named Goldie, before he died, and how he always loved his sons. And Patrice managed to get her old job back.

PATRICE: ..... I work with people who are half my age. I like them. They're unafraid. They are fearless ... *(Beat.)* In this light, you look like Alec.

GIL *(shakes his head):* I hope not. He didn't look very ... the last time I saw him, he—

PATRICE: Tell me. Gil. I have to know.

GIL: You have to name it?

PATRICE: I have to name it.

GIL: You know it was a bullet ... *(Patrice nods.)* ... to the back of the neck behind a grocery store in Soweto. I imagine it was painless. So you don't have to worry about that. *(Beat.)* I think it was a simple assassination. I was in Kenya with him a few days before and begged him not to keep going down there. He knew there were many people with great, vast reasons to kill him. But he kept going anyway. It reached the point where I simply couldn't stop him. Even Carly couidn't stop him. God knows she stuck it out. *(Beat.)* He kept going back to South Africa again and again and again. They might have just let him fade away, but he wouldn't allow them. *(Beat.)* And that was that. At least in the end, he got what he wanted. *(Beat.)* I left Kenya, got to Jo'burg at four in the morning, went to their morgue, and I said, "Yes. This is my brother, Alec Dalton Burgess." They gave me his stuff. And I left.

There is a great, long silence. Neither can speak. Gil turns away.

PATRICE: If your father could have died in Alec's place, he would have done so without thinking.

Gil doesn't see how his mother can stand being with people; he himself needs solitude. They are waiting to flag a truck on its way north at dawn, to hitch a ride for Patrice to return to the U.S. In the meantime, contemplating the past, Patrice declares, "There is nothing, at a certain point, that I would not have done differently." And again they hear the would-be looter rustling in the bushes near them. Gil yells at him again, but it does no good. Gil asks Patrice to help him.

GIL: . . . . . You used to be the scariest white woman in Africa. *(Yells.)* Get out of here!

PATRICE *(shouts):* Listen you people, I swear to God, I'm giving you a minute to get out of here, and then we're coming after you. Did you hear me? *(Beat.)* I'm counting! I'm counting to three!

GIL: Oh, that's good. I remember that. That's scary.

PATRICE *(a roar):* One!

GIL and PATRICE: Two!

PATRICE: THREE!

> *Beat. Sound of footsteps running off.*

It worked. He's gone.

GIL: He'll be back. Tomorrow night.

PATRICE: What'll you do?

GIL: Well, we could scare him again.

PATRICE: We could.

GIL: It's getting lighter.

PATRICE: Is it?

> *Gil sits down by the fire, looks out. Patrice sits across the fire from him. The lights fade. Curtain.*

Critics Award

○○○
○○○
○○○
○○○
○○○
○○○ # SEVEN GUITARS

A Play in Two Acts

BY AUGUST WILSON

Cast and credits appear on page 295

AUGUST WILSON was born in 1945 in the Hill District of Pittsburgh, where his father worked as a baker and his mother determinedly introduced her son to the written word and had him reading at 4 years old. Despite his early acquaintance and continuing fascination with words, he didn't long pursue a formal education, leaving Central Catholic High School before graduating. He can clearly remember when he began to approach writing as a profession: it was April 1, 1965; he had just earned $20 writing a term paper for his sister, and he bought a typewriter which, he remembers, "represented my total commitment" because it took every penny he had. Lacking bus fare, he carried it home.

Wilson started with poetry. By 1972 he was writing one-acts. His first production was Jitney, *staged in 1978 by Black Horizons Theater, a group which he himself had founded in 1968.* Jitney *was repeated in 1982 by Allegheny Repertory Theater; meanwhile his* Black Bart and the Sacred Hill *was produced in 1981 by Penumbra Theater in St. Paul. After a staged reading at the O'Neill Theater Center in Waterford, Conn. in 1982 and production by Yale Repertory Theater April 3, 1984 (both organizations and the play itself being directed by Lloyd Richards), Wilson's* Ma Rainey's Black Bottom *was brought to Broadway October 11, 1984 for 275 performances, becoming its author's first full New York production, first Best Play, first Tony nominee and the winner of the New York Drama Critics Circle citation as the season's best play.*

All six of Wilson's New York productions have been named Best Plays, all figured prominently in the New York Critics' citations, and all have been directed by Richards. Wilson's second play, Fences, *was also developed at the O'Neill and premiered at Yale Rep on April 25, 1985, receiving the first annual American Theater Critics Association New Play Award, as recorded in* The Best Plays of 1985–86. *It was produced on Broadway March 26, 1987 for 526 performances and carried off the Critics best-of-bests citation, the Pulitzer Prize and the Tony Awards for both best play and direction. A year later,* Fences *was still running on Broadway when Wilson's* Joe Turner's Come and Gone *opened there March 27, 1988 after previous productions at Yale Rep and the Huntington Theater Company, Boston.* Joe Turner *won its author his third Best Play citation, third Critics Award for best-of-bests, playing 105 performances.*

During the 1987–88 season, Wilson's The Piano Lesson *received an O'Neill tryout, followed by a Goodman Theater, Chicago production cited by ATCA for its fourth annual New-Play Award. When it finally arrived on Broadway April 16, 1990 for a run of 329 performances,* The Piano Lesson *received its author's fourth Best Play citation, fourth Critics best-of-bests Award and second Pulitzer Prize. Wilson's* Two Trains Running *had already received the ATCA New-Play Award after four regional theater productions when it arrived on Broadway April 13, 1992 for 160 performances, its author's fifth straight Best Play and Critics Award winner (for best American play).*

About the same time as its opening on Broadway March 28, Wilson's Seven Guitars *received an ATCA 1995 runner-up citation, and its regional theater production history is detailed in its entry in the Season Around the United States section of this volume, together with a review of the play by Michael Grossberg, chairman of the ATCA Awards Committee. In New York,* Seven Guitars *now makes it an even half dozen Best Plays for Wilson and his fifth best-of-bests citation from the Critics. It is also the sixth full-length play in its author's cycle of plays about the life of black Americans through the decades:* Joe Turner *(the teens),* Ma Rainey *(1920s),* Piano Lesson *(1930s),* Seven Guitars *(1940s),* Fences *(1950s) and* Two Trains *(1960s). Reportedly, he's working on an expansion of his one-act* Jitney, *which is set in 1971 and may eventually be considered part of the cycle.*

Wilson is an alumnus of New Dramatists (which presented his The Mill Hand's Lunch Bucket *in staged readings in 1983 and 1984) and the Playwrights Center in Minneapolis. He is a Whiting Writers Award winner, a recipient of Bush, McKnight, Rockefeller and Guggenheim Fellowships and is a member of the American Academy of the Arts and Sciences and the American Academy of Arts and Letters. He is married to the costume designer Constanza Romero, has one daughter and makes his home in Seattle.*

The following synopsis of Seven Guitars *was prepared by Sally Dixon Wiener, who also prepared all five synopses of previous Wilson Best Plays.*

Time: Spring 1948

Place: Pittsburgh, the Hill District

ACT I

Scene 1: Wednesday afternoon

SYNOPSIS: The bleak back yard of a rundown but respectable stone and brick boarding house is the playing area. There are outside stairways leading to the first and second floor, and there is an entrance to the basement. A tiny garden plot is downstage right, with benches here and there. A table and a few chairs are center stage, and there are the ubiquitous clotheslines. A gateway leads upstage to the unseen street. The monochromatic industrial dinginess of the background towers over the stage. The telephone poles seem to be aspiring to high heaven, as are the inhabitants of this fenced-in world-unto-itself where the words are the music—and the music is the blues.

"*The lights come up in the yard. Canewell, Vera, Louise, Red Carter and Hedley have gathered in the yard. They are casual and relaxed, though dressed in their Sunday best. They have come from the cemetery where they have buried Floyd Barton.*" Canewell is gentle and appealing. Story-telling is like breathing to him. He's a harmonica player and a professional musician, as is Red Carter—they were both Floyd's sidemen. Red Carter, a drummer, is a more dapper and sporty character, but with stories of his own. Vera, who was the recently-killed Barton's much put-upon lady, is attractive, proud and far from naive, but her emotions can change in a trice. Louise is a cooler piece of work with a more generously womanly build and is wry and non-committal. Hedley, almost mythical, the idiot savant of the play, is older and grizzled, glowering and obsessive. "*There is lingering evidence of food and drink. Louise, in a much-needed affirmation of life, is singing a bawdy song.*"

Red Carter and Canewell are eating sweet potato pie as they talk about the police coming by and asking questions that morning and about the Reverend Thompson's "pretty" preaching at the funeral—"Floyd would have liked that," Canewell had thought at the time.

Vera claims to have seen angels at the cemetery. Canewell saw them, too. They were wearing black hats and suits, but they weren't from the funeral home, he's sure. One asked Canewell where Floyd's house was, and Red Carter admits someone had asked him that, too. Red Carter hadn't actually known where Floyd had been staying—he'd been in Chicago, sometimes here, sometimes there, Canewell didn't think it mattered.

Louise is having none of this—she didn't see any angels and doesn't think they did, either. Vera insists there were six, and that they came out of the sky. Just appeared, Canewell confirms, but they acted as if they'd been there all along. Hedley had seen them, too.

Canewell complains that when the time came to throw the dirt into the grave he'd had to push to get past them to throw down a handful, because he thought it was more proper than a stranger throwing it in. The angels carried Floyd "right on up in the sky," Vera believes. Red Carter had always sworn Floyd "was going straight to hell."

Not too long ago Floyd had asked Canewell what he thought of himself, and it struck him as odd.

CANEWELL: He asked me that, and I just look at him. I ain't said nothing at first. I told myself, "I have to think about this for a minute." What do I think of myself? I wonder why he wanna know? I ain't asked him what he think of himself. "That's a funny question to ask somebody."

RED CARTER: I'm quicker to tell you what I think of somebody else

CANEWELL: That's what I'm saying. I wanted to laugh, but he was looking at me too serious. I say, "He really do want to know."

RED CARTER: He asked me the same thing. He say, "Red, what do you think of yourself?" Just like that, "Red, what do you think of yourself?" That was a couple a days before he got killed. I asked myself now, "Did he know?"

CANEWELL: That's what I asked myself. Seem like he was trying to figure out if he thought the same thing as you did. That way he have a good yardstick on how right he was about everything before he died.

VERA: The Bible say some things ain't for you to know.

LOUISE: It say you know neither the day nor the hour when death come.

CANEWELL: He come like a thief in the night. And he don't go away empty. There's a song what go (*Sings*):

> He'll come to your house
> he won't stay long
> You look in the bed
> find your mother gone
> Your mother. Sister. Brother. Friend.

I don't believe he knew, but then again I do.

RED CARTER: I believe every man knows something but most times they don't pay attention to it.

VERA: I believe he knew something too.

LOUISE: Whether he did or not ain't done him no good. . . . .

Vera goes into the house and puts Floyd's record on. The sound of Floyd "Schoolboy" Barton singing "That's All Right" comes out of the kitchen window and envelops the yard. The music carries into the next scene, which moves backward in time to the week before Floyd's death.

Scene 2: The previous Tuesday

Floyd and Vera are dancing in the yard to Floyd's record playing on the radio inside. Floyd, in his mid-30s and several years older than Vera, is a tall, charismatic blues singer and moves well in his pin-striped suit. It's early in the evening, and intermittently a rooster can be heard crowing.

But Floyd's advances are not amusing Vera. The closer he holds her, the more she tries to back off, despite his promising, "I'll never jump back on you in life." He's proud of a letter he had sent her. It cost him 50 cents to have someone in the workhouse—where Floyd had recently been incarcerated—write it. Vera was not impressed with the lies: "I done told you my feet ain't on backwards." Floyd's not doing well trying to get back in her good graces.

Vera brings up the subject of Pearl Brown. Floyd claims she is nothing to him now, but it seems he had taken Pearl Brown to Chicago with him after saying he'd send for Vera when he got there. Now Floyd has to go back to Chicago—the record company has sent him a letter. He's just here in Pittsburgh to get his guitar out of the pawnshop. He may need to pawn his .38 —which is where he put it, Vera assures him. It's lucky he didn't have it when he was arrested. Apparently he had troubles enough when he'd asked a guard to show him where the back door was, in case of fire. He was told the jailhouse wouldn't burn. He'd prove different if he had a gallon of gasoline, he'd bragged. So when the judge was told he had threatened to burn down the jailhouse, he gave Floyd 90 days in the workhouse "for worthlessness."

Floyd is flaunting the letter from Chicago. It's addressed to Mr. Floyd Barton: "You get you a hit record, and the white folks call you Mister. Mister Floyd Barton." He asks Vera to read it aloud. If he's the same Floyd Barton who recorded "That's All Right" and is still in the business, they are interested in providing a chance for him to record for Savoy Records. "That's nice," Vera agrees—but she's not about to go to Chicago with him.

Floyd has written another song, "Good Rocking Tonight," and his manager, T.L. Hall, is working on setting up the recording date with Savoy. Vera doesn't think much of T.L. Hall. Floyd tells her, "Mr. T.L. Hall done fixed it up for me to play at the Hurricane Club. That's where I seen Muddy Waters. I was walking past this club, and I heard this music. People was pushing and crowding in the club, seem like the place was busting at the seams. I asked somebody, I say, 'Who's that?' They told me, 'That's Muddy Waters.' I took off my hat. I didn't know you could make the music sound like that. That told me say, 'The sky's the limit.' I told myself say, 'I'm gonna play like that one day.' I stayed there until they put me out. Mr. T.L. Hall asked me what I wanted to do. I told him I wanted to play at the Hurricane Club. He say he'd fix it."

Floyd, soft-soaping Vera again, recalls the first time he saw her, how pretty she looked.

FLOYD: .....You had on that blue dress. I believe it was pink and blue.

VERA: It was two different kinds of blue.

FLOYD: I had just got out the Army. They give me forty-seven dollars. Adjustment allowance or something like that. I come on up Logan Street, and I seen you. That's why I always say I had a pocket full of money when I met you. I seen you and said, "There go a woman." Whatever else you might say ... a pretty woman

... a nice woman a not-so-nice woman ... whatever else you might say you got to put that woman part in there. I say, "Floyd, there go a woman." My hands got to itching, and seem like I didn't know what to do with them. I put them in my pocket and felt them forty-seven dollars ... that thirty-eight under my coat ... and I got up my nerve to say something to you. You remember that? Seem like that was a long time ago.

VERA: I had just left my mama's house.

FLOYD: I knew you was just getting started. But what you don't know I was just getting started too. I was ready. You was just what I was looking for.

VERA: You was looking for anything you could find.

If she'll just give him one more try she won't have any regrets, Floyd pleads. She doesn't have any now, and she's leaving it at that. Again he assures her Pearl Brown means nothing to him. But it was something to Vera, his walking out on her. Didn't he wonder how she was doing? He had what he wanted, and she didn't. Floyd admits he was wrong, but it seemed as if Pearl believed in him more.

VERA: You supposed to believe in yourself.

FLOYD: A man that believe in himself still need a woman that believe in him. You can't make life happen without a woman.

VERA: I wanted to be that for you. Floyd. I wanted to know where you was bruised at. So I could be a woman for you. So I could touch you there. So I could spread myself all over you and know that I was a woman. That I could give a man only those things a woman has to give. And he could be satisfied. How much woman you think it make you feel to know you can't satisfy a man?

FLOYD: It ain't about being satisfied.

VERA: So he could say, "Yes, Vera a woman." That's what you say, but you never believed it. You never showed me all those places where you were a man. You went to Pearl Brown, and you showed her. I don't know what she did or didn't do, but I looked up, and you was back here after I had given you up. After I had walked through an empty house for a year and a half looking for you. After I would lay myself out on that bed and search my body for your fingerprints. "He touched me here. Floyd touched me here and he touched me here and he touched me here and he kissed me here and he gave me here and he took here and he ain't here he ain't here he ain't here, quit looking for him cause he ain't here, he's there! there! there! there!"

FLOYD: Come on. Vera ... don't do this ...

VERA: He's there. In Chicago with another woman, and all I have is a little bit of nothing, a little bit of touching, a little bit of myself left. It ain't even here no more what you looking for. What you remember. It ain't even here no more.

FLOYD: It's enough for me. It's all I ever wanted. Even if I couldn't see it. That's why I come back. That's why this time I want to take you with me. I told you about all that. I ain't never wanted to hurt you. Whatever you is, that's enough for me. Okay? Now I don't know what else to say. I ain't too good at talking all this out.

Come and go to Chicago with me. I need you real bad. That's all I know to say. I ain't never needed nobody like I need you. I don't want no hit record if I can't have a hit record with you. See? That's all I know to say about Pearl Brown . . . to say about Chicago . . . to say about Vera Dotsun. I don't want it if I can't have you with it.

VERA: Then you don't want it.

"Louise enters carrying a bag of groceries. There is immediate tension between her and Floyd." Louise asks what Vera's going to cook. Chicken, potatoes, green beans and cornbread, it seems. Louise reveals that her niece has gotten into trouble in Alabama and is coming to stay with her. ("Man trouble. What other kind of trouble a young woman get into?") Louise can't wait to beat Floyd at whist. He warns her he's gotten better at it. She claims she has, too. He's better at everything he does, Floyd tells Vera as Louise exits. Vera wonders how, since he hasn't had any practice. "Watch," he tells her, as they go inside. *" 'That's All Right' comes up on the radio."*

Scene 3: Wednesday morning

> *The lights come up in the yard the next morning. Hedley enters from the basement carrying a piece of corrugated tin. He begins to work at setting up a stand where he kills chickens. He makes several trips to the basement. Louise enters from the porch. The rooster crows intermittently throughout the scene.*

HEDLEY *(sings):*

> I thought I heard
> Buddy Bolden say
> Here go the money, King
> Take it away

LOUISE: Hey, Hedley. What kind of cigarettes you got? Give me a pack of Old Gold.

> *Hedley doesn't respond. He enters the basement and comes out carrying a crate of live chickens.*

Give me some cigarettes. What kind you got?

HEDLEY: Chesterfield.

> *Hedley enters the basement and carries out another crate of chickens which he stacks on top of the other.*

LOUISE: I want some Old Gold

But Chesterfields are what Hedley's got, and Chesterfields are what Louise will settle for. He hands her a pack and makes a note in his book. Louise knows Floyd is inside with Vera, but she thinks Vera would "be better off with the iceman . . . as ugly as he is." She's annoyed when Hedley claims she owes him $3.40. What about all the biscuits and collard greens she's fixed for him? And he's two days late paying

Left, Viola Davis as Vera and *above*, Michele Shay as Louise in August Wilson's play *Seven Guitars* cited among the year's best by both New York and cross-country drama critics

his rent. Hedley's not upset. He's going to make money tonight. She warns him not to leave a mess in the yard, but she's concerned about his health as well.

LOUISE: . . . . . Did you go down there and see the doctor? You need to go back and see the doctor. You sick. I called them and told them you need to go down there and get tested.

HEDLEY: Hedley not sick no more. I go see Miss Sarah Degree. She give me the root tea. I feel just fine.

LOUISE: You need to go see the doctor. You be spitting up blood. That don't sound like no job for Miss Sarah. You go to see Miss Sarah when you have a cold. You need to go back to that doctor and do what they tell you. They got medicine they can give you. That's what happened to George Butler. He didn't go back to the doctor. You need to get another chest X-ray. Miss Sarah can't do that.

HEDLEY: Miss Sarah a saint. She a saint if ever God made one. She can heal anything. She got a big power. She got her roots. She got her teas. She got her powders. I wonder do she have a man? Maybe next time I ask her. A woman need a man. That's what Hedley say. I knock on your door last night.

LOUISE: You can knock all you want. You go knock on the doctor's door before you come knocking on mine.

HEDLEY: You know a woman need a man.

LOUISE: I don't need none that bad. I got me a thirty-two caliber pistol up there. That be all the man I need. You need to go see the doctor. It ain't like it was before. They letting the colored people in the sanitarium now. You can get help. They can make you well. You don't have to die from T. B.

HEDLEY: Everybody got a time coming. Nobody can't say that they don't have a time coming. My father have his time. And his father have his time. Hedley is fifty-nine years old. His time come soon enough. I'm not worried about that.

Canewell appears with a Golden Seal plant he has brought for Vera. He'll bring his Bible next time, he tells Hedley. Canewell hollers to Floyd to come outside. Some neighborhood people have gone to see Miss Tillery and asked her to get rid of her rooster because it wakes people up. "That's what it's supposed to do," she'd told them.

Louise complains that they're playing Floyd's record on the radio more frequently, and she's tired of it. Canewell had told Floyd to get a cut of the profits, but they'd paid him a flat rate. Canewell has won a raffle at the Loendi Club, he admits; he won the radio he gave Vera. He was supposed to win $25 too, Louise insists, and she needs to buy some groceries. Canewell thinks somebody lied to her about that.

Floyd shows his letter from the record company to Canewell, but Canewell's not going back to Chicago where he was arrested for nothing.

FLOYD: You don't have to be in Chicago for them to arrest you for nothing. They arrested me in Pittsburgh. I ain't done nothing but walk down the street. Come home from the cemetery after burying my mama, was walking down the street—and they arrested me. That ain't got nothing to do with Chicago. What's that got to do with Chicago?

CANEWELL: I ain't going back there.

FLOYD: Mr. T.L. Hall gonna give us the money. It ain't gonna be like before.

CANEWELL: Put me in jail. Couldn't get a job. I don't need all that. I ain't going back up there. They never get me back in the Cook County jail.

LOUISE: What you went to jail for? You ain't told us all that. You just say you didn't like it. What you went to jail for?

CANEWELL: Nothing. I ain't done nothing. Ask Floyd. Singing. That's all I did. I was right down there on Maxwell Street waiting on Floyd. I started fiddling with my harmonica. I said if I'm gonna stand here and play I may as well throw my hat down . . . somebody might put something in it. The police said I was disturbing the peace. Soliciting without a license. Loitering. Resisting arrest and disrespecting the law. They rolled all that together and charged me with laziness and give me thirty days. I ain't going back up there.

LOUISE: I don't blame you. Where's Vera, Floyd?

FLOYD: She's in the house getting ready to go to work. Come on, Canewell, go over to the pawnshop with me. I got to see about getting my electric guitar out of pawn.

Hedley enters from the basement.

(Sings):

I thought I heard

Buddy Bolden say . . .

HEDLEY: What he say?

FLOYD: He said, "Wake up and give me the money."

HEDLEY: Naw. Naw. He say, "Come here, here go the money."

FLOYD: Well . . . what he give you?

HEDLEY: He give me ashes.

FLOYD: Tell him to give you the money.

The men laugh.

HEDLEY: Soon I going to be a big man. You watch. Buddy Bolden give me my father's money, I'm going to buy a big plantation. Then the white man not going to tell me what to do.

FLOYD: He ain't gonna tell me what to do either. And I ain't gonna have no plantation. I don't need nothing but that thirty-eight. I was up there in the work-house. The Captain say hurry . . . the Sergeant say run. I say if I had my thirty-eight I wouldn't do neither one.

HEDLEY: I gonna be a big man.

LOUISE: You ain't gonna be nothing.

There aren't any plantations in Pittsburgh, Louise points out, but Hedley's going to make one. He'll grow anything. Tobacco. Oats. Canewell suggests some sugar cane, but Hedley hates the sugar: "Sugar beat many a man." That's how Canewell got his name, Canewell reveals. His granddaddy cut sugar cane in Louisiana, and somebody said, "That boy can cane well"—otherwise his name would be cottonwell.

It will be a big plantation, Hedley insists, and Floyd encourages him.

Canewell wishes Floyd had heard Hedley the night before last. He was imbibing more than a bit and talking about Buddy Bolden, St. John the Divine, St. John the Revelator and St. Yolanda. He'd said his granddaddy was John the Baptist. Hedley corrects him—he said he was baptized by a man who called himself John the Baptist.

CANEWELL: We was talking about Zombies. Lazarus. Hey . . . hey, tell him Floyd, Jesus ain't had no business raising Lazarus from the dead. If it's God's will, then what he look like undoing it? If it's his Father's work then it's his Father's business, and he ought to have stayed out of it.

HEDLEY: His Father will him to do it. Jesus is the Obedient Son of the Father. He was a black man, you know. The Bible say his hair was like lamb's wool and his skin the color of copper. That's cause Mary was a Moabite.

CANEWELL: That ain't got nothing to do with Lazarus. What Mary being a Moabite got to do with Lazarus? I'm talking about you ain't supposed to go against nature. Don't care whether you the Son of God or not. Everybody know that. Lazarus even know that. When Lazarus was dying the second time . . . he was dying from pneumonia . . . somebody went up and got Jesus. Lazarus saw him coming and said, "Oh no, not you again!" See, all Jesus had done by raising him from the dead was to cause him to go through that much more suffering. He was suffering the pain of living. That's why the Bible say you supposed to rejoice when somebody die and cry when they come into the world.

Vera comes on from the house with Canewell's hat. It seems he left it there the other night. Floyd takes umbrage. Why is Canewell's hat in his house? If it's Floyd's house, Vera retorts, he can give her $25 for the rent.

Canewell gives Vera the Golden Seal and tells her to plant it. It will be all the doctor she needs. You can make a tea of the leaves, or use a little piece of the root. His grandmother made a tea or chewed the leaves to rub them on her chest, Hedley recalls. Louise insists Hedley must go to the doctor for real medicine. Canewell asks where she thinks the doctor gets his medicine from?

Canewell admits he's "looking to eat my breakfast in a brand new place." It seems he's not with Lulu Johnson now, he's drifting. Actually, he's staying on Clark Street—with someone he's helping out with her rent. They have an understanding, and he keeps his trunk packed. Vera opines that everybody keeps a trunk packed. That's what's the trouble: "Time to put two and two together and try and come up with four . . . they out the door."

Floyd wants Canewell to accompany him to get the 30 cents a day for working in the workhouse for 90 days so he can get his guitar out of the pawnshop. Vera suggests he can put some money down on the light bill before they cut it off, and to bring something to eat. Even people with a hit record have to buy groceries.

When Floyd goes into the house, Vera asks Canewell how much it costs to go to Chicago. It cost $17.40 the last time Canewell went there. Floyd returns with a guitar he once got from someone named Odell. He's going to pawn it, then visit his mother's grave. Hedley kills a chicken, as Floyd and Canewell exit.

Scene 4: Wednesday evening

Louise is talking about her niece, as she and Vera prepare food. The niece hasn't said when she's coming, but Louise assumes there's more to the story than she's been told. She doubts the niece—"with her fast little behind"—will stay long. Love is anything people want it to be, Louise opines. Maybe her niece had been in love, but now she's fortunate to be alive, with one man in her life dead and another in prison. Louise wants no part of love. She's "forty-eight going on sixty," and Hedley's as close to love as she wants to come. Vera reveals that Floyd wants her to go to Chicago. Why would she go? Louise wonders.

LOUISE: . . . . . Floyd don't mean nobody no good. He don't mean his own self no good. How he gonna mean you any good?

VERA: I believe Floyd means well. He just don't know how to do. Everything keeps slipping out his hands. Seems like he stumble over everything.

LOUISE: However it go, he make it go that way. He remind me of Henry. That man walked out on me, and that was the best thing that happened to me. When he left I told myself say if you have to say hello before you can say goodbye . . . I ain't got to never worry about nobody saying goodbye to me no more. I ain't never going through one of them goodbyes again. He was standing upstairs in the hallway. Told me say, "I'm leaving." I asked him what for? After twelve years. Why you gonna leave after all this time? After you done used me up. He say, "It's something I got to do." Then he went on and gathered up his things. He left a razor and a pair of shoes. They still up there.

VERA: That's like Floyd left his old guitar.

LOUISE: He got to the doorway, and I told him, "Leave your pistol. Don't leave me here by myself." He ain't said nothing. He took out his pistol and handed it to me. I told him say, "I ought to shoot you." We laughed, and then he kissed me goodbye. I ain't seen him since. I still got that pistol upstairs now. What I'm trying to tell you is, don't let no man use you up and then talk about he gotta go. Shoot him first.

VERA: Sometimes it seems like that more than they deserve.

If Vera goes to Chicago with Floyd, Louise predicts that in six weeks he'll be running from one woman to another, and Vera will be in the middle.

Floyd and Canewell come on. Floyd has the envelope but not the letter that was sent to him in the workhouse saying he was to be paid 30 cents for each day he was there. Now they're refusing to pay him because he hasn't got the letter itself. They told him to return the next day. He needs the money to get his guitar and to keep from being arrested for vagrancy and given another 30 days.

When Red Carter comes on, Floyd tells him they're going to Chicago to make another record. Red Carter isn't happy about going. It's a 15-hour-long bus ride, and if he wanted to go as far as that he could go visit his mother in Opelika, Alabama—"Down there where the women soft as cotton and sweet as watermelon." Floyd reminds him there are pretty women in Chicago. Red Carter agrees.

Vera asks Louise to show her how she cooks greens, but Canewell claims Louise doesn't know. He gives them his recipe which calls for three pounds each of turnip and mustard greens with the stems cut off. "Tear the greens up into little pieces. Don't cut them. That's where you mess up." In a big pot with water you add a quarter-pound of salt pork to the greens along with some red pepper seeds and cook them over a low fire for around six hours.

Red Carter's wife has just had another boy, and he's passing out cigars that Floyd complains are not only cheap but stale. That's because he's carried them around for nine months, he explains. They start a round of old rhymes and jokes, and Canewell ends up singing one about watermelons.

Hedley comes on, and Floyd goes into the Buddy Bolden routine with him. Canewell chimes in telling Hedley if Bolden doesn't give him the money he'll "cut him" for Hedley. He'll do it himself, Hedley replies. Told that Red Carter has a new son, Hedley hopes he'll grow up like Joe Louis. Maybe he'll have a son someday, Hedley muses. It seems Red Carter's wife has named the baby Mister. "White folks gonna have a fit with a nigger named Mister," Canewell thinks. "Mr. Mister Carter."

HEDLEY: . . . . . the Bible say Ethiopia shall rise up and be made a great Kingdom. Marcus Garvey say the black man is a king.

FLOYD: I don't want to hear nothing about no Bible.

RED CARTER: I'm with you, Floyd. If I want to hear that I'd go to church.

FLOYD: God is in his heaven and he staying there. He must be up there, cause a lot of things down here he don't know. He must not know about it. If he did, it seem like he would do something about it. Being that he God and everything ain't right in his kingdom. Wouldn't you want everything to be right if you was God? So I figure he don't know about it. That's why I don't want to hear nothing about no Bible. Ethiopia or nothing else.

HEDLEY: The black man is the conquering Lion of Judea, you know. He like Toussaint L'Ouverture. He is the king! Most people don't know that. Hedley know. He know himself what blood he got. They say Hedley, go on, you too serious with that. But! Hedley know the white man walk the earth on the black man's back.

RED CARTER: Ain't nobody walking on my back. I ain't gonna let nobody walk on my back.

FLOYD: All I want is you to get out my way. I got somewhere to go. See, everybody can't say that. Some people ain't got nowhere to go. They don't wanna go nowhere. If they wanted to go somewhere they would have been there. Time done got short, and it getting shorter every day. The only thing I want you to do is get out my way.

HEDLEY: You watch what Hedley say.

The talk turns again to being unfairly arrested and to the weapon each feels is his protection. You can't tell what they're going to do, and that's why Floyd has a .38 and Red Carter has a snub-nosed .32. Canewell has a professional-looking pocket knife that he claims "has a lot of niggers around here wearing Canewell's scars." Hedley has his big butcher knife, his chicken knife.

When someone almost trips over Floyd's old guitar, he bemoans not having his electric one.

FLOYD: . . . . . That will make me play better.

CANEWELL: Having a nice guitar don't make you play no better.

FLOYD: Not if you don't know how to play. But if you already know how to play good, a nice guitar will make you feel better about yourself. If you feel better about yourself, quite naturally you be able to play better. People see you with a nice guitar they know you put the music first. Even if you don't put the music first . . . it will work its way to the front. I know. I tried it many a time. I say, "Let me put this music down and leave it alone." Then one day you be walking along, and the music jump on you. It just grab hold of you and hang on. Ain't too much you can do then.

CANEWELL: If I could put the music down I would have been a preacher. Many a time I felt God was calling. But the Devil was calling too, and it seem like he call louder. God speak in a whisper, and the Devil shout.

RED CARTER: They say God have planned but the Devil have planned also.

FLOYD: Yeah, well I'm planning too . . . . .

Floyd plans to get his guitar, get the rest of the money from Mr. T.L. Hall and go to Chicago to make another hit record. But it seems Red Carter's drums are in the pawnshop too, and if it's Floyd's band, Floyd should be responsible for getting them out. It wasn't Red Carter's or Canewell's name on the record. It was Floyd's, and it will be this time too. Both Red Carter and Canewell are unhappy about the way things were in Chicago the last time and are wary of going again. "Twenty-five dollars and a bottle of whiskey do not make thirty-five dollars," Canewell reminds Floyd. Red Carter agrees. They were treated badly and want the money up front this time. Floyd assures them it will be different this time.

A music session gets underway when Canewell takes out his harmonica. Floyd tunes the old guitar and Red Carter begins to drum on a table with his drumsticks. Floyd is singing, and as the song ends Hedley has collected a two-by-four, chicken-wire, a hammer and nail. He's making a one-string, Canewell explains as Hedley hammers. Floyd is scornful, but Hedley claims it will make music. Hedley wraps wire on the nail and puts a rock under the string for added tension. He recalls, when he was small, asking his grandfather where his mother was. She was long gone, but his grandfather claimed he could hear her pray when he played a one-string. Hedley remembers playing it and trying to hear her. "Once. Maybe. Almost." As he plays, the others listen.

Floyd wishes he could hear his mother pray again, or sing. Floyd sings them The Lord's Prayer.

RED CARTER: Where your mother buried at, Floyd? My uncle's out in Greenwood.

FLOYD: That's where she at. She out there in Greenwood. I was out there today. Me and Canewell went out there. They got her buried over in the poor people part. Took me three hours to find the grave. They let the grass grow all over. I took and pulled up the grass and cleaned off her grave. Said I was gonna get her a marker. And that's what I'm gonna do. Cause when I leave this time I ain't planning on coming back. I get her that marker, and I won't owe nobody nothing.

Vera calls to Floyd that it's time for the fight—the Joe Louis-Billy Conn match for the world's heavyweight championship (which the playwright, exercising artistic license, has moved from June 19, 1946 to 1948). As everyone listens intently to the radio, Joe Louis, The Brown Bomber, wins by a knockout and is still the champ, and the men are circling the yard as they chant "The Brown Bomber." Red Carter begins to dance with Louise, to teach her the Joe Louis Shuffle, then goes to Vera, asking if she knows how to Jump Back. Vera doesn't know "all them little country dances." It's done everywhere, Red Carter tells her.

RED CARTER: Follow me now. Do what I say.
> *Red Carter puts his hand on his hip.*

Come on now. Put your hand back.
> *Vera puts her hand on her hip.*

Now just let it roll. You ain't got to worry about rocking it, it'll rock by itself. (*Sings*):
Jump Jump here
Jump Jump there
Jump Jump Jump
Everywhere
Jump Back Doo-ley
Jump Back Dooley when you really wanna blow your top
> *He jumps back and rolls his hip, in a subtle, suggestive way.*

See now, this the way we go . . . each time you got to do better than me. Better than whoever you dancing with. You got to outdo me. . . . .
> *Vera begins to do the dance. It is suggestive, and she loses herself in the science of it without realizing its full expression. Everyone watches. . . . .*
> *They kick up the dust. Canewell and Floyd become angry. Canewell tries to play his anger off so that it doesn't show. Floyd broods. His brooding darkens the stage.*

Go on, shake it out.

LOUISE: Go, Vera. That's right, girl. Shake it.

As Louise urges Vera on, Floyd can't control his jealousy and pulls a gun on Red Carter. Canewell and Louise are attempting to calm him down and get the card game started when Ruby, Louise's niece, arrives. At 25 she is charming and very pretty. "*She exudes a sensuality that is electric.*" She explains to Louise she couldn't let her know when she was coming—she'd had to wait until after the funeral and till she could get the money. Red Carter wonders if she needs help with her suitcase. She doesn't. She did need help at the bottom of the hill, she comments pointedly.

> *Ruby walks around the yard, already looking bored. She gets a pebble in her high heels and stumbles.*

RUBY: Got all these rocks around here.

LOUISE: Look at this old country gal with them fancy shoes complaining about rocks.

RUBY: I ain't country. Don't care where I come from. It's all in how you act, and I know I don't hardly act country.

Ruby sits down and takes off her shoes.

That's the longest hill I ever seen. I can't be walking up these hills getting all them muscles in my legs.

CANEWELL: For your information, in case you ain't figured it out yourself, this here is called the Hill District. That one of two things a woman coming into Pittsburgh need to know. The other thing is how to find me. My name is Canewell, and you can find me right down there on Clark Street. That's the same Clark like the candy bar. That's down in what the people call Little Haiti. Just ask anybody where Canewell lives, and they will tell you.

RED CARTER: Naw . . . don't pay him no mind. My name Red Carter but sometime people just call me Red. You can call me anything you want to. What you say your name was?

RUBY: My name is Ruby. I need me some water.

LOUISE: Go on in the house and get some. There's some in the house.

RUBY: Is it cold?

LOUISE: Go on in there and find out.

RUBY: Where to go?

LOUISE: Up them steps to the third floor. The door on the left. Don't go on the right. That's where Hedley live. Just go on up there.

Canewell and Red Carter vie for her suitcase but she takes it and goes upstairs, and the card game begins. Floyd muses about how he could get five years for punching a white man even if there aren't witnesses, but Joe Louis can get a million dollars for doing that in front of a hundred thousand people. Red Carter points out that Joe Louis has a license and Floyd doesn't. And he hasn't got his mind on the card game either, Louise notes. She asks Vera if she's going to make Mother's Day flowers. Vera will, if Floyd gets her the crepe paper. Canewell promises to get it for her the next day.

The rooster's crowing sets Canewell off on a long dissertation on how Alabama and Georgia and Mississippi roosters differ, adding that roosters didn't crow during slavery. The rooster only began crowing after the Emancipation Proclamation. The rooster's the king of the barnyard, Hedley insists. "He like the black man, he king."

There are more roosters in Chicago than in Pittsburgh, Canewell claims, but there are too many people there, and he isn't going to stay. He'll get another harmonica player then, Floyd retorts. When the rooster crows again, Floyd shouts and throws a stone across the fence. Hedley gets up and leaves the yard, and Vera rebukes Floyd for upsetting Hedley. Ruby comes on from upstairs and is asked to join the game, but she isn't interested in playing cards.

Hedley enters the yard carrying the rooster.

HEDLEY: God ain't making no more roosters. It is a thing past. Soon, you mark my words, when God ain't making no more niggers. They too be a done thing. This here rooster born in the barnyard. He learn to cock his doodle do. He see the sun he cry out so the sun don't catch you with your hand up your ass or your dick stuck in your woman. You hear this rooster you know you alive. You be glad to see the sun cause there come a time sure enough when you see your last day, and this rooster you don't hear no more.

> *He wrings the rooster's neck.*

That be for the living. Your black ass be dead like the rooster now. You mark what Hedley say.

> *He takes out a knife and cuts the rooster's throat.*

Ethiopia shall spread forth her wings, and every abomination shall be brought low.

> *He sprinkles the blood in a circle.*

This rooster too good live for your black asses.

> *He throws the rooster on the ground.*

Now he good and right for you.

> *Hedley exits the yard. Everyone is stunned.*

FLOYD: Hey Hedley . . . what you kill the rooster for?

VERA: Come on, leave him alone. He ain't right.

FLOYD: Hey, Hedley! Hey! What you do that for?

> *Curtain.*

ACT II

Scene 1: Thursday morning

Floyd's record is playing on the radio in the house as Hedley, who has turned his table in the yard into a grill, is making the last of the chicken sandwiches and putting them into a basket which also holds hard-boiled eggs, cigarettes and candy bars. Ruby comes on, asks for an egg and asks why Hedley killed the rooster. "Cause nobody want him," is Hedley's enigmatic reply. Ruby wonders if he could make her a mattress—"soft and low"—with the chicken feathers. He can make whatever she wants, as long as she's sure she wants it, he replies.

Hedley is singing about Buddy Bolden. Hedley's father named Hedley after King Buddy Bolden, it seems. Hedley's father was a trumpet player and never forgot the time he heard King Buddy Bolden play. His father's face lit up when he talked of hearing him, and "Something be driving him from inside, and it was a thing he love more than my mother." Hedley also reveals that he killed a black man once who wouldn't call him King. It had cost Hedley his "time with a woman," and since then he does not tell anybody his first name is King.

Hedley admits to being "not all right" in the head part of the time, but he's always wanted to be a big man, like Jesus, the Son of the Father. Maybe not as big as that, but he is the son of his father and wants to be big "for himself inside. That place where you live your own special life. I would be happy to be big there." Maybe if he had a son he would be big, like Moses, Hedley thinks, and could lead the black men out of bondage. Hedley's 59 years old and wants to father a child. Maybe Ruby is the woman for him, he ventures. Ruby claims Hedley's too old to have children and should put it out of his mind.

Floyd comes on, goes into Vera's place and returns with his guitar case. He offers to show Ruby around Pittsburgh. He'll tell people she's his cousin. Ruby agrees to go if he'll buy her a beer, and she goes off to change her shoes. Floyd is desperate for money, Buddy Bolden's or anybody else's, he complains to Hedley. But the Buddy Bolden money is Hedley's father's money that his father's sending to him. His father told him so in a dream, Hedley assures Floyd. Floyd assures Hedley Buddy Bolden will come with the money. Hedley'll be able to buy two plantations, and the white man won't tell him what to do.

Ruby is ready to go, but as she and Floyd start to leave, Hedley grabs Floyd's arm. Floyd's "the pick of the litter," he warns him, and they're going to say, "We gonna put a mark on this one." Floyd had better be careful, Hedley warns him.

Scene 2: Thursday afternoon

Louise and Vera are in the yard. Vera is making red and white crepe paper flowers. Louise is hoping Ruby will get a job. Vera confesses she might go to Chicago after all. Vera can do what she wants—Louise isn't going to tell her not to go. Vera would like to see Chicago. "Maybe I can be a different person up there," she thinks. Louise advises her to put that thought out of her head: "Wherever you go you got to carry you with you."

Ruby returns with a letter. Floyd's taken her around town, introducing her as his cousin. A man wanted to take her to Harlem. Louise is not impressed. That bunch couldn't take you around the corner. "Talking about Harlem," she sniffs. It seems Floyd has gone back to the pawnshop with Canewell. When they'd been there in the morning a waterline had broken, the street was blocked off and the pawnshop was closed. They expected it to be open this afternoon, however.

Ruby has a letter from Elmore, one of her ill-fated lovers. He's a jealous man, Ruby admits. "All men are jealous," Louise points out, "especially if you make them that way." Ruby claims he was always jealous, even when she met him. He doesn't understand, trying to hold onto someone ends up driving them away. He got mean, and she left him. Everyone saw Ruby and Leroy together and realized she'd left Elmore. Leroy didn't care if Elmore was jealous. The truth is she didn't love either of them, even though they were both "nice in their own way." She didn't belong to anybody, she told them when they fought. Later Elmore went to the barbershop and shot Leroy.

RUBY: . . . . . The problem with Elmore was, he never could get enough of me. He used to tell me he wanted to take it all so nobody else could have me. He wasn't gonna leave none for nobody else, to hear him tell it. That make you feel funny to be with a man want to use you up like that.

LOUISE: He don't mean you no good. That's for sure.

VERA: That when they say they got blood in their eyes for you. I tell them, if you got blood in your eye then you can't see good. What I want with a blind man?

RUBY: It was never enough for him. We lay down at night. In the morning. In the afternoon. Just stop what you doing . . . if you doing anything. Even that don't be enough. I told him one time say, "Baby, look in the mirror and count that as twice."

LOUISE: You sound like you complaining. You hear this, Vera? Child, I can think of ten women be happy to have a man look at them twice. They get mad if he get tired.

VERA: I'd rather that than to have somebody try to abuse you like that. They ain't loving you, they using you.

RUBY: That's what I'm trying to say.

LOUISE: I wonder what he using now. How much time he get?

RUBY: The judge told him he was gonna throw the book at him. He had the nerve enough to tell me to wait on him. He don't know I'm pregnant.

LOUISE: He ain't the only one don't know. Whose baby is it? Elmore's or Leroy's?

RUBY: I don't know. I got to wait to find out. I hope it's Leroy's.

Floyd and Canewell arrive. They are elated. Mr. T.L. Hall has arranged for the band to play at the Mother's Day dance at the Blue Goose. He also has the recording studio date and time set. He has agreed to give Floyd an advance tomorrow—"half the money up front." Floyd went to order a stone for his mother's grave—"a real nice one."

Hedley comes on with a letter. He is angry and keeps repeating, "Hedley don't go nowhere!" When he goes upstairs, Louise, who had called the Board of Health, explains that Hedley has tuberculosis but is refusing to go to the sanitarium. He's supposed to go there to be tested. "They letting colored in the sanitarium," Canewell reports, but Hedley sees it all as another plot against the black man. Floyd argues that Hedley has the right to not have anybody tell him what to do. Hedley has the choice as to whether he wants to live or die, Canewell sums up. "Then let him choose!" Floyd insists. Vera points out that Hedley doesn't believe he could be cured. Floyd is still arguing Hedley's case when Hedley comes down the stairs wearing a hat and coat. He goes off quickly.

Scene 3: Thursday Evening

When Floyd comes on he tells Canewell that he'd gone to the pawnshop by 9 o'clock where Mr. T.L. Hall had told him to meet him but he hadn't appeared. Nor has Floyd been able to find him any other place. Mr. T.L. Hall was to have given him advance money from the Blue Goose to get Floyd's guitar out of the pawnshop. Now it's been on the radio that they're playing for the dance, but Floyd "Schoolboy" Barton with the hit record doesn't even have a guitar. Red Carter's drums are still in the pawnshop too. Floyd had also promised to bring the rest of the money for his mother's gravestone. He'd hoped to get Vera a new dress as well.

Canewell carps about the money Floyd didn't get for having a hit record. Floyd should stand up for himself and demand a proper-sized piece of the pie. He should tell Mr. T.L. Hall, "You tired of him turning your big money into little money."

CANEWELL: . . . . . You can't go up to Chicago and be a poor man. A poor man have it rough. I might have to cut me somebody the first day. Vera don't want that.

FLOYD: How you know what Vera want?

CANEWELL: I know Vera longer than you have. I know what kind of woman she is. Vera a quiet woman. Chicago's a noisy city. Anybody can tell you the two don't fit together.

FLOYD: Chicago is what you make it. It got some quiet parts. It got whatever you want. That's why everybody go there. That's why I'm going there. I'm going to take advantage of the opportunity. I'm gonna put out some more records. I know what will make a hit record. I leave here on the Greyhound and I bet you in one year's time I be back driving a Buick. Might even have a Cadillac. If you come visit me you be able to use my telephone. I'm gonna have everything. Some nice furniture. The white man ain't the only one can have a car and nice furniture. Nice clothes. It take a fool to sit around and don't want nothing. I ain't no fool. It's out there for somebody, it may as well be out there for me. If Vera go up there with me and she don't like it I'll send her back. But at least she will have the chance to see the opportunities.

Red Carter comes on with the news that Mr. T.L. Hall has been arrested for selling over fifty thousand dollars worth of fake insurance. It's in the newspaper, with his picture too. Red Carter had thought Floyd and Canewell had heard about it.

FLOYD (*quietly*): I had seven ways to go. They cut that down to six. I say let me try one of them six. They cut it down to five. Every time I push . . . they pull. They cut it down to four. I say what's the matter? Everything can't go wrong all the time. They cut it down to three. I say three is better than two, I really don't need but one. They cut it down to two. See . . . I'm going to Chicago. If I have to buy me a graveyard and kill everybody I see. I am going to Chicago. I don't want to live my life without. Everybody I know live without. I don't want to do that. I want to live with. I don't know what you all think of yourself, but I think I'm supposed to have. Whatever it is. Have something. Have anything. My mama lived and died, she ain't had nothing. If it ain't nothing but peace of mind, then let me have that. My mama ain't had two dimes to rub together. And ain't had but one stick. She got to do without the fire. Some kind of warmth in her life. I don't want to live in a cold house. It a cold world, let me have a little shelter from it. That's all I want. Floyd Barton is gonna make his record. Floyd Barton is going to Chicago.

Floyd exits the yard.

Scene 4: Friday

Red Carter, sitting with Vera, Louise and Ruby, is carrying on about how corn-meal, eggs and milk, along with beans and rice, used to be enough to make a meal, how it used to be allowed to have a rooster, and how it used to be safe to leave your door open. Nothing's gone right for Red Carter since he broke a mirror three years ago, and he sees four more years of bad luck ahead. He's lost money gambling and has had to pawn his pistol now.

Vera, who's busy making her flowers, reports that the dogcatcher has told Miss Tillery she's got to have a license for her dog. Louise agrees—then you know he has an owner. Ruby doesn't see the need. "All you got to do is watch him and see where he go when he go home." Red Carter is discouraged with all this licensing—"Soon you need a license to walk down the street."

Vera's real concern is about Floyd, for whom she waited up until 4:30 a.m., but he never came home. Red Carter and Canewell have been looking for Floyd, and Red Carter claims Floyd said he was going to go to Chicago and nothing would stop him.

Some commotion in Miss Tillery's yard provokes Canewell and Red Carter to investigate. While they're gone, Hedley comes on singing. He's been drinking. He's been to see Joe Roberts—"The one hand wash the other, you know that saying?"—and he's in a fine mood and wants Louise to dance with him. He's going to be a big man soon, he tells the women. Vera is curious about what he has wrapped up in his apron.

VERA: What you got there?

HEDLEY: Where? Oh this? When I was a little boy I learn about Toussaint L'Ouverture in the school. Miss Manning. She say listen you little black as sin nig-gers, you never each and none of you amount to nothing, you grow up to cut the white man cane, and your whole life you never can be nothing as God is my witness, but I will tell you of a black boy who was a man and made the white man run from he blood in the street. Like that you know. Then she tell us about Toussaint L'Ou-verture. I say I going to be just like that. Everybody say that, you know. I go home, and my daddy he sitting there, and he big and black and tired of taking care of the white man's horses, and I say how come you not like Toussaint L'Ouverture, why you do nothing? And he kick me with him boot in my mouth. I shut up that day, you know, and then when Marcus Garvey come he give me back my voice to speak. It was on my father's death bed, with Death standing there I say to him father I sorry about the Toussaint L'Ouverture, Miss Manning say nobody ever amount to nothing, and I never did again try. Then Marcus Garvey come and say that it was not true and that she lied, and I forgive you, kick me, and I hope as God is with us now but a short time more that you forgive me my tongue. It was hard to say these things, but I confess my love for my father, and Death standing there say, "I already took him a half hour ago." And he cold as a boot, cold as a stone and hard like iron. I cried a river of tears, but he was too heavy to float on them. So I dragged him with

Ruben Santiago-Hudson (*left*) as Canewell and Roger Robinson as Hedley in *Seven Guitars*

me these years across an ocean. And then my father come to me in a dream, and he say he sorry he died without forgiving me my tongue, and that he would send Buddy Bolden with some money for me to buy a plantation. Then I get the letter from the white man who come to take me away. So I say, Hedley, be smart, go and see Joe Roberts. We sat and talked man to man. Joe Roberts is a nice man. I told him about Toussaint L'Ouverture and my father, and Joe Roberts smile, and he say he had something to give me. And he give to me this.

     He takes out a machete that is wrapped in his burlap apron.
Now Hedley ready for the white man when he come to take him away.

Scene 5: Late Friday night

    Hedley is brandishing his machete, ranting and raving and singing. He's not a dog, he insists, the black man isn't a dog. Ruby comes on from the stairs asking what's wrong with him and why he's making such a racket. He's a man, and the man to father her children, he pleads, but he won't crawl for her. He's offering her a kingdom and the "flesh of my flesh, my seven generations," but she laughs at him. He's offering her the chance to be Queen of Sheba, queen of the black man's kingdom.

> *Ruby goes over and takes the machete from Hedley. She lays it down on the bench. Hedley grabs her and kisses her violently. Hedley is feverish with lust. He tries to find an opening to touch flesh.*

RUBY: Slow down, baby. It's all right. Ruby help you. Here. Ruby help you.
> *She lifts her dress and gives herself to him out of recognition of his great need. The lights go down on the scene.*

Scene 6: Saturday evening

Floyd has just finished burying something in the garden plot and is smoothing the dirt. When he calls to Vera she comes to the window asking where he's been. He's been gone two days. Floyd's more interested in showing her his new guitar. It's the same kind Muddy Waters has. She'll hear how it sounds at the dance, and for the dance he has brought her a new dress. It's beautiful, Vera admits, but she's suspicious about where the guitar and dress have come from. He took a chance, Floyd shrugs. He didn't want to take a chance on not going back to Chicago. He's also paid off the gravestone man—the stone looked "so pretty"—and then he went to the Greyhound bus station.

> *He pulls some tickets out of his pocket.*

FLOYD: What that say? Pittsburgh to Chicago. I told the man to write your name on it . . . he said they didn't do that. I took a pencil and wrote it on there myself.
> *He shows the ticket.*

Then I made a long distance phone call . . . cost me three dollars and ten cents. I called Mr. Wilber H. Gardner, president of Savoy Records, and told him I would be there on the tenth of June. Then I called the Delaware Towers Hotel on State Street and told them to get ready their best room for Miss Vera Dotsun . . . soon to be Mrs. Floyd Barton. That is . . . if she say yeah.

VERA: I want to say yeah, but what am I saying yeah to? Another heartache? Another time for you to walk out the door with another woman?

FLOYD: You was there too, Vera. You had a hand in whatever it was. Maybe all the times we don't know the effect of what we do. But we cause what happens to us. Sometimes even in little ways we can't see. I went up to Chicago with Pearl Brown cause she was willing to believe that I could take her some place she wanted to go. That I could give her things that she wanted to have. She told me by that . . . it was possible. Even sometimes when you question yourself . . . when you wonder can you really make the music work for you . . . can you find a way to get it out into the world so it can burst in the air and have it mean something to somebody. She didn't know if I could do that. If I could have a hit record. But she was willing to believe it. Maybe it was selfish of her. Maybe she believed for all the wrong reasons. But that gave me a chance to try. So yeah . . . I took it. . . . .

Floyd remembers how frightened he was when the red lights were turned on in the recording studio, "like a bell ringing in the boxing match," but he'd called on his inner resources and done his best, as his mother had told him to do. When the record wasn't released, however, Pearl Brown had gone, thinking she'd been wrong in believing in him. Floyd didn't lose faith in himself, though.

After the record was released, then he could see he had only a hit record. He'd come back to Vera assuming she wouldn't turn down a man with a hit record, but she had, and he realized Vera wanted something more than Pearl Brown had. Now he's telling Vera he can give her that. Give him another try and he won't jump back on her, he asks. But Vera has been thinking, too, and she has gone to the bus station and has a ticket of her own. A one-way ticket from Chicago to Pittsburgh. She plans to put it in her shoe and walk around on it in Chicago. She hopes she won't need to use it.

Scene 7: Sunday, Mother's Day

Louise is dressed for the dance and grumbling to herself that the others ought to be ready too. She feels she's being driven crazy by everything that's been going on. When Vera comes on, Louise starts in on the subject of Ruby.

LOUISE: And don't you know, her and Hedley went to church. I liked to fell out. She say, "Aunt Louise, I'm going to church with Hedley." That child ain't set foot in a church since she was six years old on a Easter Sunday past the time ten years after I had quit going! Then on Thursday they going to the sanitarium. She talked him into going. You know Hedley wouldn't listen to nobody. I tried to talk him into going. You tried to talk him into going. Ain't no telling who else tried to talk him into going. He sit out here with a butcher knife. Sit out here with a machete ranting and raving and carrying on. She come along, and he's gonna up and run to the sanitarium. Act like he anxious to get there. I don't understand it.
VERA: Ruby seem like she got a way about her that the men take to.
LOUISE: I wouldn't be surprised if there wasn't something between them. I done seen stranger things. He told me himself. Say he was gonna go down there and get tested. I just looked at him. . . . .

Ruby enters and informs Louise that after she and Hedley left the church he'd gone to see a friend. Louise surmises he's gone for moonshine: "Talking about Ethiopia shall spread forth her wings and he won't be able to walk up the street." Ruby should have brought him back. And getting tested isn't going to do him any good, Louise remarks. He's been spitting up blood. Ruby hopes he'll live to see her baby born because she's going to let him think it's his. Hedley wants to be the father of the child, and the child needs that. Ruby isn't sure about the Messiah business, but if the baby's a boy, which she hopes it is, she's going to name him King after Hedley.

Canewell comes on with a newspaper that has a story about the neighbor's son being shot by the police, ostensibly fleeing from the scene of a crime (a robbery at the Metro Finance loan offices). The police reported the suspect fired twice at the officer who, returning the fire, struck him in the back. Canewell muses about how the police are the only people who can shoot straight. Everybody else misses. Williard Ray Tillery was a 27-year-old unemployed laborer, known in the District as Poochie, and when the police came to tell his mother about Poochie she started moaning and didn't stop for around eight hours. She wouldn't go inside the house until morning when her sister came from West Virginia and finally persuaded her to go in. Meanwhile, according to the paper, the police are looking for two other men, believed to be accomplices, who are said to have escaped with an undisclosed amount of cash. Canewell explains how this goes: the police take the money out of the hand of the man they shoot, stick it in their pockets and claim they're looking for the others that got away.

Poochie just wanted to be a bricklayer, Canewell eulogizes. "He laying bricks in hell now," Louise snaps. He might have gone to heaven, Canewell points out. The devil doesn't take all the people Louise thinks he should. Louise goes upstairs to see if Ruby's getting dressed, leaving Vera and Canewell alone.

VERA: Canewell, Floyd and me are gonna get married. See if we can make it.

CANEWELL: I always did believe in love. I felt like if you don't believe in love you may as well not believe in nothing. Even love that ain't but halfway is still love. And that don't make it no less cause it's only coming one way. If it was two ways it still be the same amount of love. Just like, say, I loved you and you didn't love me back. I can still say I'm all filled up with love for Vera. I go walking down the street, people can see that. They don't know what to call it but they can see something going on. Maybe they see a man who look like he satisfied with life and that make him walk more better. Make him walk like he got a million dollars in his pocket. If I loved you and this time you loved me back. I don't see where my love for you can get more bigger than it already was. Unless I walk like I got two million dollars. Sometime people don't count it if you ain't loved back. But I count it all the same. Some women make their bed up so high don't nobody know how to get to it. I know you ain't like that. You know how to make your bed up high and turn your lamp down low. That's why Floyd don't want to lose you. I think you and Floyd ought to go ahead and see what you all can make of it.

Red Carter comes on, and Vera wants to give him a flower to wear to the Mother's Day dance. He needs a red one, not a white one, he explains, because his mother is still alive.

It's time for the dance. Floyd comes on from the house in a white suit, carrying his guitar, and finally Ruby appears in a yellow dress, dazzling Floyd and Canewell. "Is these stockings straight?" she wonders.

Scene 8: Later Sunday night

Floyd, Vera, Louise and Canewell are returning from the Blue Goose where the dance seems to have been a huge success. There was an overflow crowd. People were yelling when Floyd got onstage. As for Canewell on the harmonica—"The way you was blowing on that thing!" Louise marvels. But she's angry at Red Carter. He'd acted as if he didn't even know her at the dance, she tells them before she goes off to bed.

Canewell sees the roots of the Golden Seal plant are uncovered, and he looks for one of Hedley's shovels. Floyd tells Vera they'll fix the plant and sends her into the house to wait for him. When he was singing "Good Rocking Tonight," didn't she know what he meant? Vera mentions she also likes another song, "Sixty Minute Man."

When Canewell's second shovelful of dirt turns up a handkerchief filled with $1,200 in tens and twenties, he picks it up. Floyd grabs at it, insisting that it's his. Canewell claims finder's keepers. He supposes it's Hedley's stash, since Hedley doesn't trust banks. Floyd argues that the money is his because he says it is, and Canewell doesn't need to know anything else. He pulls a gun on Canewell. Canewell is shocked, then realizes what's happened. "You and Poochie," he spells it out. Poochie and he had both taken a chance, Floyd admits. Canewell tells Floyd he understands, gives him the money and goes off.

Floyd, still in his white suit, is standing in a shaft of light as Hedley comes on and sees him.

> *Hedley . . . . . stops and rubs his eyes. He begins to laugh. It is an odd mixture of laughter and tears. He has waited many years for this moment.*

HEDLEY: Buddy . . . you come. You come, Buddy. Oh, how I wait for you. So long I wait for you. I think to myself many times, "Maybe I die before Buddy Bolden bring me my father's money." Maybe I'm not going to be a big man after all. Maybe my father don't forgive me, but I see you have the money. Give it to me.

FLOYD: Get out of here, Hedley. You been drinking that rotgut. Go on in the house.

HEDLEY: But I see I was wrong. I see you have the money. Give me the money, Buddy.

FLOYD: I ain't playing no game now. Go on in the house and go to bed.

HEDLEY: No, Buddy, give me the money. You say, "Come here . . . here go the money." Give it to me. It's my father's money. Give it to me.

FLOYD: Come on now! Watch it! Go on in the house.

> *Hedley attempts to take the money from Floyd. Floyd pushes him down on the ground.*

I told you to go on now!

> *Floyd helps Hedley get up.*

Here. Come on. Go on in the house now. I'll see you tomorrow.

> *Hedley gets up and exits up the stairs. Floyd . . . . . counts off some money and puts it in his pocket. He wraps the rest in the handkerchief as Hedley*

comes down the steps carrying the machete. Floyd, hearing him approach,
turns, and Hedley severs his windpipe with one blow.

HEDLEY: This time Buddy . . . you give me the money.

Scene 9: The following Wednesday afternoon

Everyone is gradually gathering in the yard after Floyd's funeral, as at the beginning of the play. We hear "That's All Right" playing on Vera's victrola in her apartment. Ruby comes on from the stairs complaining that a bathroom light bulb needs replacing, and she wants a beer. She eggs Red Carter on until he agrees to buy her two beers and whatever else she wants. Louise wants Red Carter to play pinochle, but he and Ruby go off. Louise offers to help Vera with the dishes, but Vera's mind is still on Floyd's burial.

VERA: I started walking away from there feeling bad. I turned to look back, and Floyd was floating up above the ground. Them six men was holding him up. He come right out the casket just like they laid him in there and was floating up in the air. I could see where they was carrying him. They was all floating up in the sky. I tried to call Floyd's name but wouldn't nothing come out my mouth. Seem like he started to move faster. I say the only thing I can do here is say goodbye. I waved at him, and he went on up in the sky.

> *Vera and Louise exit. Canewell and Hedley sit and stare at each other.*
> *The silence swells.*

CANEWELL *(sings):*

> I thought I heard
> Buddy Bolden say

HEDLEY: What he say?

CANEWELL: He say, "Wake up and give me the money."

HEDLEY: Naw. Naw. He say, "Come here, here go the money."

CANEWELL: What he give you?

HEDLEY: He give me ashes.

> *Hedley opens up his hands. There is $1,200 in bills. . . . .*

(Sings):

> I thought I heard
> Buddy Bolden say. . .
> I thought I heard
> Buddy Bolden say. . .
> I thought I heard
> Buddy Bolden say. . .
>
> *The lights go down to black. Curtain.*

Best Play Citation

○○○
○○○
○○○
○○○
○○○
○○○

THE SKRIKER

A Full-Length Play in One Act

BY CARYL CHURCHILL

Cast and credits appear on pages 327, 329

CARYL CHURCHILL is a native Londoner, born there September 3, 1938, but sent to school in Montreal at the Trafalgar School prior to receiving her B.A. at Lady Margaret Hall, Oxford, in 1960. The impressive roster of her stage credits began at Oxford in 1958 with Downstairs *and continued with productions in England of her* Having Wonderful Time, Easy Death, Schreber's Nervous Illness, *and* Owners, *her first major work, produced at the Royal Court Theater Upstairs in 1972 and off Broadway for 2 performances the following year. There followed* Perfect Happiness *(1974),* Moving Clocks Go Slow *(1975),* Objections to Sex and Violence *(Royal Court, 1975),* Vinegar Tom *(Monstrous Regiment, a touring feminist group, 1976),* Light Shining in Buckinghamshire *(1976, presented February 12, 1991 for 39 OOB performances by New York Theater Workshop),* Traps *(1977, presented OOB in the 1987-88 season) and* Cloud 9 *(1979, a transatlantic hit produced by the Joint Stock Company at the Royal Court and off Broadway for 971 performances in independent production May 18, 1981, Churchill's first Best Play, winning an Obie citation for playwriting).*

Since then, New York audiences have been treated to many more Churchill plays: Obie-winning Top Girls *December 29, 1982 for 129 performances and* Fen *May 24, 1983 for 43 performances, both at the Public in the same season;* Serious Money *(winner in London of the Olivier Award for best play, the Evening Standard Award*

235

*for best comedy and the Plays and Players Award, and in New York of an Obie)
December 3, 1987 for 30 performances at the Public, followed February 9, 1988 by a
15-performance Broadway engagement; the double bill of Churchill one-acts* Ice
Cream With Hot Fudge *OOB at New York Theater Workshop May 3, 1990 for 38
performances;* Mad Forest, *also at the Workshop, December 4, 1991 for 54 performances, Churchill's second Best Play, returning to New York the following season
October 1, 1992 at Manhattan Theater Club; and* Owners *and* Traps *in repertory
March 7, 1993 at the Workshop. This season Churchill returned to the Public May 12
with* The Skriker *for 17 performances and her third Best Play citation.*

Churchill's long list of produced stage plays also includes Three More Sleepless
Nights *(1980),* Softcops *(1984),* A Mouthful of Birds *(1986),* Lives of the Great
Poisoners *(1991) and* Thyestes. *She is the winner of Susan Smith Blackburn Awards
for 1984 and 1987 and the author of* The Ants *for radio,* The Judge's Wife *for TV
and many other works for both those media. Churchill is married and lives in London.*

Time: The present
Place: Mostly in London, England

SYNOPSIS: In the Underworld of this fantasy, "*Johnny Squarefoot, a giant riding
on a piglike man, throwing stones . . . . . goes off. The Skriker, a shapeshifter and
death portent, ancient and damaged,*" is declaiming at length a stream-of-conscious-
ness monologue in which, it appears, the very sound of each word leads to the next
thought, instead of the intellectual process of this strange and sinister speaker.

SKRIKER: Heard her boast beast a roast beef eater, daughter could spin span
spick and spun the lowest form of wheat straw into gold, raw into roar, golden lion
and lyonesse under the sea, dungeonesse under the castle for bad mad sad adders
and takers away. Never marry a king sized well beloved. Chop chip pan chap finger
chirrup chirrup cheer up off with you're making no headway. Weeps seeps deeps
her pretty puffy cream cake hole in the heart operation. Sees a little blackjack thin-
galingo with a long tale awinding. May day, she cries, may pole axed me to help her.
So I spin the sheaves shoves shivers into golden guild and geld and if she can't
guessing game and safety match my name then I'll take her no mistake no mister
no missed her no mist no miss no me no . . . . .
Revengeance is gold mine, sweet. Fe fi fo fumbledown cottage pie crust my heart
and hope to die. My mother she killed me and put me in pies for sale away and
home and awayday. Peck out her eyes have it. I'll give you three wishy washy. An
open grave must be fed up you go like dust in the sunlight of heart. Gobble gobble
says the turkey turnkey key to my heart, gobbledegook de gook is after you. Ready
or not here we come quick or dead of night night sleep tightarse.

In the "real" world—in which are found peculiar, intrusive creatures existing side by side with the human beings, some of whom are also behaving in peculiar ways—Lily, pregnant, is visiting her friend Josie in a mental hospital. Both are in their late teens. (With them in the scene, but taking no active part in it, is Kelpie, "*part young man, part horse.*") Josie has been sent here as punishment, but she feels much better now and hoping to be released. She wants to come to live with Lily and look after her. Lily is curious about a detail of Josie's life.

LILY: Was she being naughty?

JOSIE: You can't be naughty, a ten day old baby, can you. You really don't know anything about . . .

LILY: I just meant she might have annoyed you.

JOSIE: . . . it. What can a ten day old baby do that's naughty?

LILY: Like crying or—I don't know.

JOSIE: You wouldn't kill a baby because it annoyed you, would you.

LILY: I don't know.

JOSIE: Would *you?*

LILY: I don't know. You tell me.

JOSIE: Of course you wouldn't.
        Pause.

LILY: Was it difficult?
        Pause.

JOSIE: License to kill, seems to me.

LILY: You're in here.

JOSIE: They don't hang you.

LILY: They don't hang anyone.

JOSIE: It should have been me that died.

LILY: No. Why?

Josie doesn't answer. Once again she asks Lily to take her home, but Lily explains she's planning to leave home herself and go to London. Josie assures Lily she wouldn't hurt Lily's baby, and she tells Lily about a very, very old woman, who she first thought was a patient but now believes to be a mysterious creature. She offered to grant Josie a wish: "She'd like me to wish the baby back but I won't because she'd make it horrible." Lily is not much impressed with this tale, and, after a few more gestures of comfort to Josie, she exits.

> *Woman about 50 approches. Dowdy, cardigan, could be a patient. It is the Skriker.*

SKRIKER: I heard that.

JOSIE: What?

SKRIKER: You don't like me.

JOSIE: I'm thinking what you'd enjoy and you'd like her better than me. She's stronger, she's more fun. I'm ill, and I think you're ill and I don't think . . .

SKRIKER: You don't want me.

JOSIE: She'll have a baby and you'll like that.

SKRIKER: Please, please keep me.

>*Pause.*

I'll give you a wish.

JOSIE: I don't want a wish.

SKRIKER: I'll be nice.

JOSIE: It's cold all round you.

SKRIKER: I can get you out of here. Just say.

JOSIE: No. Where to? No.

SKRIKER: Josie.

JOSIE: All right, I'll have a wish.

SKRIKER: Yes? Wish.

JOSIE: I wish you'd have her instead of me.

>*Pause. Skriker turns away.*

Wait. I don't mind you any more.

SKRIKER: No, I'm not after you.

JOSIE: You won't hurt her? What do you want from her?

>*Skriker starts to go. A Man comes in carrying a white cloth and a bucket of water.*

Oh but I'll miss you now.

>*Skriker goes.*

The Man seems to be looking for just the right place to lay the cloth and place the bucket on it (throughout the following scene), and he finally does. The Kelpie exits. A character named Yallery Brown is playing music, to which a Passerby begins dancing after throwing Yallery a coin. A derelict woman is creating a disturbance in the street, when Lily enters. The derelict—who is in fact the Skriker—begs for Lily's help. Lily gives her money and hugs and kisses her. "There's a love. Off you go, Lily," the Skriker comments and exits, leaving Lily crying, "How do you know my name?—What? What's happening? My teeth. I'm sick. Help me. What is it? It's money. Is it? Out of my mouth?" And indeed, coins come out of Lily's mouth when she talks.

Lily goes, leaving the stage to a Young Girl, a Green Lady, a Bogle, the dancing Passerby and finally the returned Skriker, who changes herself into an American woman of about 40, tipsy, and joins Lily at a bar. Other patrons are a ten-foot-tall Spriggan (unseen by Lily) and the Kelpie drinking with a woman. A Brownie is cleaning up.

There's a TV in the bar, and the Skriker wants to know how it works. Lily has a vague idea and tries to explain about dots and lines going through the air on waves. But the Skriker—for all its command of shapeshifting—doesn't know what electricity is, doesn't "have much aptitude for science," can't understand what Lily is trying to tell her and believes Lily and others are deliberately withholding information on things like flight, massive explosions, the making of poison and other arcane matters.

Jayne Atkinson in one of the Skriker's shapes offers wine to Caroline Seymour as Josie, observed by two of the strange banqueters in the background, in the Underworld scene of *The Skriker* by Caryl Churchill

The Skriker informs Lily that she is in pain and dying. When Lily voices some concern, the Skriker does an about-face and insists she feels all right. She wants to be friends with Lily, she's curious about Lily's forthcoming baby, she proposes herself as its godmother. But Lily recognizes that this chance acquaintance is actually the supernatural being Josie told her about. The Skriker decides to explain herself to Lily: "I am an ancient fairy, I am hundreds of years old as you people would work it out, I have been around through all the stuff you would call history, that's Cavaliers and Roundheads, Henry the Eighth, 1066 and before that, back when the Saxons feasted, the Danes invaded, the Celts hunted, you know about any of this stuff? Alfred and the cakes, Arthur and the table, long before that, long before England was an idea, a country of snow and wolves where trees sang and birds talked and people knew we mattered, I don't to be honest remember such a time but I like to think it was so, it should have been, I need to think it, don't contradict me please. That's what I am, one of many, not a major spirit but a spirit." What's more, she's here (she says) to do good.

The Skriker has chosen Lily for her friendship "Because you're beautiful and good." The money coming from Lily's mouth is an example of the Skriker's favors. But Lily, half-skeptical and half-wary, suggests that Josie might better receive the Skriker's attentions because she is braver. The Skriker offers to give Lily a special ring if she'll divulge how the TV works, but Lily declines and exits, as does the Skriker, and the other characters go about their strange business.

As Josie is passing in the street, the Skriker resumes the derelict-woman shape and begs for money or a kiss. Josie, easily recognizing her for what she is, brushes her off with, "Get off, you stinking crazy—". But as Josie speaks, toads come out of her mouth.

Fair and Dark Fairies try unsuccessfully to take away a cake which the Man has made from some of the contents of his bucket. Meanwhile, Josie and Lily, who have met in the street in a stroke of good fortune, are seated on a sofa of which, unbeknownst to them, the Skriker is now a part. Lily explains that Josie was probably released from the hospital because Lily expressed a wish which the Skriker granted. Lily feels an icy coldness which, she correctly guesses, means the Skriker is present. All at once, Lily can see the Skriker as a fairy with gauzy wings, still invisible to Josie. Lily decides that this whole thing is just a dream she's having, but Josie assures her it's real. To bring an end to its nightmarish quality, Lily wishes for flowers, which rain down on her.

A Green Lady eats the Man's cake. RawHeadAndBloodyBones and the Spriggan tower over a row of small houses. In a small park, there are a Black Dog, a Girl With Telescope, Lily and, finally, a small child who is the Skriker in still another shape. Lily shows the child how to make a cat's cradle, while Josie enters and watches. The child tells Lily it wants a baby sister, and, having no mother, wants Lily to be its make-believe mother. Lily likes the child, but Josie doesn't.

JOSIE: She's horrible. There's something wrong with her.
> *Josie takes hold of Skriker to look at her.*
LILY: Leave her alone.
SKRIKER: Leave me alone, I'll tell my mum.
JOSIE: She's not your mum. You haven't got a mum.
SKRIKER: Mum! Mum!
LILY: Josie, stop it. It's all right, pet, she's just teasing.
JOSIE: Get out, you little scrounger. Leave Lily alone.
SKRIKER: Mum, don't let her hit me.
LILY: Josie.
JOSIE: I know you, you bastard. How you like toads? You like dirt in your mouth? Get away from us. You come in the house I'll put you in the fire, then we'll see what you look like.
> *Josie picks up dirt from the ground and stuffs it in the Skriker's mouth . . . . .*

Lily rescues the child. Josie has recognized her as the Skriker in a new shape, but Lily doesn't believe her. Angrily, Lily dismisses Josie, who moves away and watches

Lily taking the Skriker on her lap to comfort her. The Skriker calls Lily "fat" and hits Lily in the stomach, commenting, "Nasty baby." Lily warns her to be careful. The Skriker pleads with Lily to take her home with her. But the Skriker continues to behave in a way which endangers the baby, so Lily pushes her off her lap.

At first the Skriker lies on the ground crying and complaining in childish fashion, but under a scornful tongue-lashing by Josie is soon back in control of herself. But it's Lily whom she confronts: "You're stupid, aren't you, Lily. Josie knows." In fact, Josie not only recognizes the Skriker but offers to take her back. Though the Skriker now prefers Lily, she's flattered that both of them want to be her special friend. Lily warns Josie to reject the Skriker's friendship.

JOSIE: But when you've lost her you want her back. Because you see what she can do and you've lost your chance and it could be the only chance ever in my life to . . .

LILY: Josie, don't.

SKRIKER: I knew you were desperate, that's how I found you. Are you ready now?

LILY: Josie, I wish you wouldn't.

SKRIKER: You don't count any more.

Pause.

JOSIE: Yes.

> *Blackout. A horrible shriek like a siren that goes up to a very high sound and holds it. Gradually it relents little by little, breaking up into notes and coming down till it is pleasant and even melodious.*
>
> *Underworld. As Skriker and Josie arrive, it springs into existence. Light, music, long table with feast, lavishly dressed people and creatures such as Yallery Brown, Nellie Longarms, Jenny Greenteeth, the Kelpie, Black Dog, RawHeadAndBloodyBones, the Radiant Boy, Jimmy Squarefoot, Black Annis (with a blue face and one eye). It looks wonderful except that it is all glamor and here and there it's not working— some of the food is twigs, leaves, beetles; some of the clothes are rags; some of the beautiful people have a claw hand or hideous face. But the first impression is of a palace. Skriker is a fairy queen, dressed grandiosely, with lapses.*

The company breaks into song at Josie and the Skriker's arrival and will continue to sing, with only the two newcomers speaking. A Hag comes in looking for pieces of her body which were cooked for dinner, but the others drive her away. A Girl warns Josie not to touch the food: "I took one bite, and now I'm here forever." But when the Skriker offers Josie wine she drinks and then eats the food offered to her, making no distinction between cake and twigs.

A dance begins, and soon all are joined in it, some flying into the air. Then it disintegrates until only the Passerby is dancing. Josie is scrubbing the floor, near a fountain, watched by the Skriker in the form of a Monster, haranguing Josie in the weird linguistic style of the opening monologue: "When I go uppety, follow a fellow on a dark road dank ride and jump thrump out and eat him how does he taste? Toxic waste paper basket case, salmonelephantiasis, blue blood bad blood blue blood blad blood blah blah." The Skriker remembers how good her victims used to taste, but now they seem "Dry as dustpans, foul as shitpandemonium."

Josie would like to have the Skriker take her back on a visit to the real world, but she believes she has lived in the Underworld so long, longer than any earth life span, that there'd be no one left alive she knew.

SKRIKER: That doesn't bye bye a trip up. You're dry as dead leaves you behind.

JOSIE: Please.

SKRIKER: You'll never go home on the Range Rover's return again witless.

JOSIE: Why not, if I'm useless?

SKRIKER: When I'm weak at the need, you'll be a last tiny totter of whiskey whistle to keep my spirits to keep me stronger linger longer gaga. And while I'm await a minute, don't touch the water baby.

JOSIE: Don't touch the water in the fountain because I'll die.

>   *Skriker goes. Josie goes to the fountain and almost puts her hand in the water. She shrieks and plunges her hands in. A shrieking sound gets louder and louder. Darkness. Johnny Squarefoot throwing stones at Black Dog. Josie, Lily and the Skriker as child are exactly as they were in the park. Skriker runs off. The Black Dog is in the park. The Girl With the Telescope sits depressed. The Kelpie and the Woman who rode on his back stroll as lovers.*

LILY *(shouting after Skriker):* We're not scared of you. (*To Josie.*) It's just a child anyway.

JOSIE: Too bright. My eyes don't work. Hold me.

LILY: Now what?

JOSIE: You smell like people. Your hair's like hair. It was like putting a gun to my head because they always said I'd die if I did that. Liars, you hear me? I got away. Yah. Can't get me.

LILY: Stop. You can stop it.

JOSIE: I was ready to die. I thought I'd never get back.

LILY: Don't. It makes me lonely.

JOSIE: That's right, I'm not dead? We're not both dead? Lily, you didn't die while I was away?

Though it seemed to Josie that more than a lifetime passed while she was trapped in the Underworld, no such thing has happened; in fact, no real time has passed at all. People (some with Thrumpins riding them) and creatures come and go until the Skriker turns up as "*a smart woman in mid-30s.*" She is, she claims, "see if I care free and completely forgetmenot Lily and Josie" and moves off on other errands.

The two teenagers are seated with Lily's new baby, watched by RawHead-AndBloodyBones but not at this moment by the Skriker. They are still discussing

Josie's trip to the Underworld, Lily arguing that it was all imagined because she has been with Josie every second. Josie declares that the experience was as real to her as the baby is to Lily, even though it may have taken place in no time at all. The Underworld creatures need humans, Josie explains, they drink blood. And everything in the real world now seems flat "like a video" to Josie. And, she insists, they are being watched.

LILY: You want to go back?

JOSIE: I'm never going to be all right.

LILY: You know how they say, "Oh their little fingers," and of course they've got little fingers, they couldn't have fingers like us. But that's not what they mean. I mean look at her fingers.

JOSIE: She's a changeling.

LILY: She what?

JOSIE: That's not your baby. They've put one of theirs and taken yours off.

LILY: Don't say that, don't.

JOSIE: Changeling. Changeling.

LILY: I warn you, I'll kill you, don't say it.

JOSIE: You believe me, don't you?

LILY: I don't want, I don't believe you, no, but I . . .

JOSIE: Lucky for them.

LILY: . . . don't want to hear it.

JOSIE: They'll keep yours down there. It makes them stronger. They'll breed from it. And you'll always have this one watching you. Look at its little slitty eye.

LILY: Don't even think it. I'm not listening.

JOSIE: Shall I tell you what? If you want your own one back? You put the changeling on a shovel and put it in the fire, that's what they used to do. So we'd use the cooker and put it over the gas. And sometimes they turn into a cat and go up the chimney. How'd it get out of here? Round and round the walls. I'll open the window. Then you get your own one back in the cot.

LILY: I can't live with you if you're like this.

JOSIE: You've got to fight them. You say you love her and you won't even do something to get her back. This isn't human, I can tell.

In desperation, Lily calls upon the Skriker, though it is apparently not present here with them, to grant her wish that her friend Josie wasn't insane. Josie begins to feel a kind of pain, and soon she is suffering by remembering her own baby: "I killed her. Did I? Yes. I hadn't forgotten but. She was just as precious. Yours isn't the only. If I hadn't she'd still. I keep knowing it again, what can I do? Why did I? It should have been me. Because under that pain oh shit there's under that under that there's this other under that there's . . . . . Don't let me feel it. It's coming for me. Hide me. This is what. When I killed her. What I was frightened. Trying to stop when I. It's here."

Taking pity on Josie, Lily wishes her back the way she was, and Josie's pain vanishes. But Josie warns Lily, "Have you been wishing? Stupid. She'll get you now."

Lily has kicked off a shoe and is sitting on the sofa with the Skriker shapeshifted into a 30-year old man. Monster couples dance and then climb into a shoe which is an enlargement of the one Lily has just removed. The baby is in a carrycot. Josie finishes slicing vegetables and exits, while the Skriker converses with Lily about following her and watching her in the park, about the problem of going to sleep and the strange thoughts which intrude in the space between sleeping and waking. The Skriker has noticed an increase in "apocalyptic meteorological phenomena" recently and suggests they may be approaching an end to the comforting stability of nature: "Spring will return and nothing will grow."

The Skriker suggests they go on holiday together, bringing the baby—he senses that he and Lily are meant to stay together always.

SKRIKER: . . . . . You're the only good person I've ever met. Everyone else has tried to destroy me. But you wish me well. You wouldn't deny that.

LILY: No, I . . .

SKRIKER: No.

LILY: No, I . . .

SKRIKER: . . . . . I'm going to take care of you and the baby. You're coming with me. You don't have to worry about anything any more.

Josie comes in again.

LILY: I do like you. I can't look away from you. But a bit slower. It's no use getting angry because I can't . . .

SKRIKER: I hate it when I'm so unkind. This sometimes happens. I won't go into my childhood just now. I can't forgive myself. I feel terrible.

LILY: I didn't mean . . .

SKRIKER: I'm useless, I get something beautiful and I ruin it. Everything I touch falls apart. There are some people who deserve to be killed, and I believe it's important to be completely without remorse. I admire that if someone has no compassion because that's what it takes. But other people such as yourself. You won't want to see me again. How could I do that? I worship you. I'm so ashamed. I feel sick. Help me. Forgive me. Could you ever love me?

Josie attacks him with a knife, slashing his arm and chest. Blood on his shirt.

Do you love me? Do you love me?

LILY: Yes, yes I do.

He takes off his bloodstained shirt and tie. Underneath, identical clean ones.

SKRIKER *(to Josie):* You're getting into a lot of trouble. She loves me.

LILY: No I don't. What are you?

SKRIKER: But you do, you know. See you later.

He goes.

Green Lady, Bucket Man, Kelpie, Woman, Telescope Girl and other creatures (who intrude on their lives, Lily comments, only in connection with the Skriker) go about their grotesque activities. Josie exits. Lily is now accompanied by a young woman about her age pretending to be an old friend named Marie, but Lily is aware that this is just another of the Skriker's shapes. "Marie" reminisces with Lily about incidents in their youth and—feeling herself to be in some kind of danger—wants to stay here safe with Lily. But Lily tells her, "Go somewhere else . . . . . You're not Marie." She states definitely that she doesn't love or even like the Skriker and sends her away.

In the shape of a respectable 40-year-old man, the Skriker is now in the company of Josie and Black Dog. Josie is in the middle of recounting an incident.

JOSIE: She didn't know anyone. She didn't have anywhere to stay the night. I slipped a wire loop over her head.
>*Skriker laughs.*

So that'll do for a bit, yeh? You'll feel O.K. There's an earthquake on the telly last night. There's a motorway pileup in the fog.

SKRIKER: You're a good girl, Josie.

JOSIE: There's dead children.

SKRIKER: Tell me more about her.

JOSIE: She had red hair. She had big feet. She liked biscuits. She woke up while I was doing it. But you didn't do the carcrash. You'd tell me. You're not strong enough to do an earthquake.
>*Skriker coughs.*

I'll do terrible things, I promise. Just leave it to me. You don't have to do anything. Don't do anything. Promise.
>*Skriker coughs.*

You won't do anything to Lily?

SKRIKER: Who's Lily?

JOSIE: Nobody. Someone you used to know. You've forgotten her.
>*Skriker laughs.*

Have you forgotten her?
>*Skriker coughs,*

I think you'd like me to do something tomorrow.
>*Skriker coughs. The Bucket Man comes slowly in his wheelchair . . . . .*
>*He stops and dozes. The Telescope Girl comes in, she has bandaged*
>*wrists. RawHeadAndBloodyBones, Kelpie and Johnny Squarefoot rush*
>*across wildly, tangling with the Passerby, who keeps dancing.*

SKRIKER: Josie went further and murther in the dark, trying to keep the Skriker sated seated besotted with gobbets, tossing it giblets, to stop it from wolfing, stop it engulfing. But still there was gobbling and gabbling, giggling and gaggling, biting and beating, eating and hating, hooting and looting and lightning and thunder in the southeast northwest northeast southwest northsouth crisis. Lily doolalley was living in peacetime, no more friend, no more fiend, safe as dollshouses. But she worried

4B.

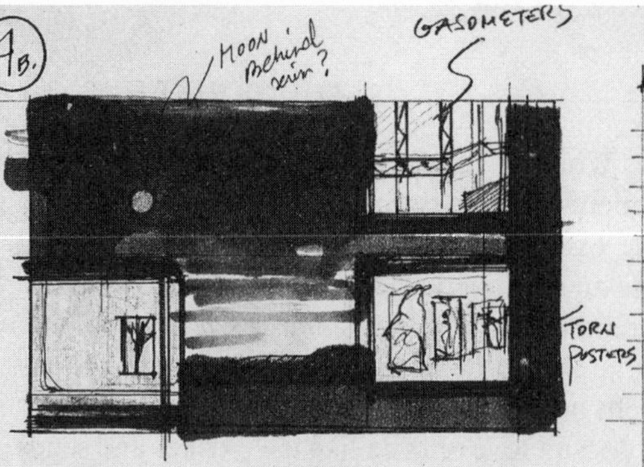

MOON Behind rain?   GASOMETERS

STREET

- U.S. TOP BOX HAS B+W PHOTO OF GASOMETERS
- U.S. BOX HAS TORN POSTERS ON PLYWOOD

- DERELICT WOMAN SHOUTS IN THE STREET
- LILY HAS MONEY COMING OUT OF HER MOUTH

TORN POSTERS

4C.

GASOMETERS

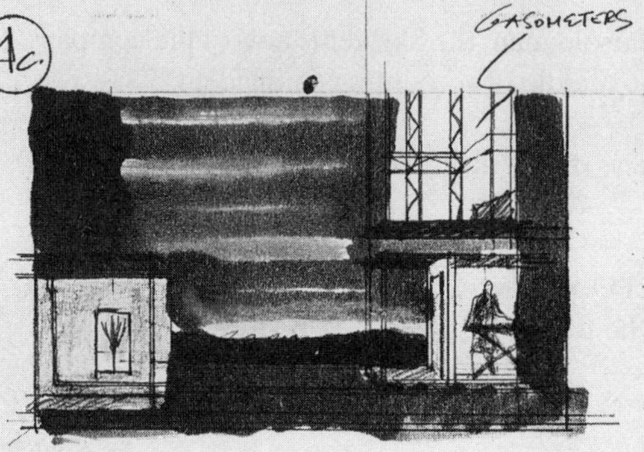

STREET

- U.S. BOX W/ PLYWOOD SLIDES OPEN TO REVEAL WOMAN IRONING (EX-TELESCOPE GIRL)
- LILY IS STILL IN THE STREET
- PASSERBY DANCING

4D

GASOMETERS

STREET

- D.S. BOX SLIDES AWAY
- CLEANING LADY SEES GREEN LADY DANCING W/ BOGLE
- PASSERBY DANCING
- LILY LEAVES

5.

TRANSITION

- SKRIEKER'S MONOLOGUE
- BROWNIE CLEANS (USES SINK)
- BAR IS SET UP

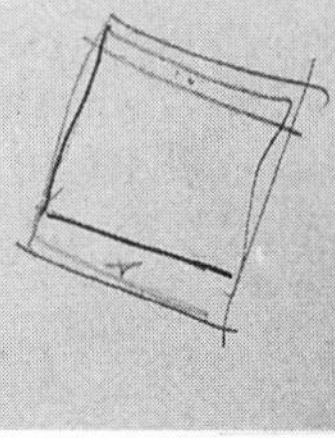

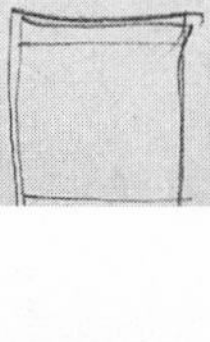

SINK

Examples of Marina Draghici's outstanding and imaginative scene and costume designs for *The Skriker* are pictured here: *on opposite page*, her sketches of the setting and its changes in the scene beginning with money coming out of Lily's mouth; *above*, her costume drawings for Black Annis and Kelpie

and sorried and lay far awake into the nightmare. Poor furry, she thought, pure feary, where are you now and then? And something drove her over and over and out of her mind how you go.

> *Black Annis has small houses in a glass aquarium. She slowly fills it with water.*

Lily, with her baby, comes to the hospital to visit a very old, ill woman—the Skriker's latest shape. Lily has come to tell the Skriker she'll go with her, she'll take care of her—if only the Skriker will promise to leave Josie and everyone else alone, especially the baby, who will be left behind. Lily assumes they'll be going to the Underworld, as Josie did, and so, no matter how long they stay there, Lily won't miss a moment with the baby because no time will have passed in the real world.

The Skriker jumps up, no longer an infirm patient, but full of energy. She lights a candle and gives it to Lily, telling her she is now in an enchanted wood. She's in the dark, with only the candle, while the song of a blackbird is heard. When Lily comes upon an Old Woman and Deformed Girl sitting together, the candle goes out and the Skriker elucidates.

SKRIKER: Lily appeared like a ghastly, made their hair stand on endless night, their blood run fast. "Am I in fairyland?" she wandered. "No," said the old crony, "this is the real world." Whirl whir wh wh what is this? Lily was solid flash. If she was back on earth, where on earth was the rockabye baby gone the treetop? Lost and gone for everybody was dead years and tears ago; it was another cemetery, a black whole hundred yearns. Grief struck by lightning. And this old dear me was Lily's granddaughter what a horror storybook ending. "Oh I was tricked tracked wracked," cried our heroine distress, "I hoped to save the worldly, I hoped I'd make the fury better than she should be." And what would be comfy of her now? She didn't know if she ate a mortal morsel she'd crumble to dust panic. Are you my grand great grand great are you my child's child's child's? But when the daughters grand and great greater greatest knew she was from the distant past master class, then rage raging bullfight bullroar.

The girl bellows wordlessly at Lily.

"Oh they couldn't helpless," said the granddaughter, "they were stupid stupefied stewpotbellied not evil weevil devil take the hindmost of them anyway." But the child hated the monstrous.

Girl bellows.

"Leave her alone poor little soul-o," said the grin drafter, "Cold in the headache, shaking and shocking. Have a what drink, wrap her in a blanket out, have a sand-which one would you like?" So Lily bit off more than she could choose. And she was dustbin.

The Old Woman holds out some food and Lily puts out her hand to take it. The Passerby stops dancing. Curtain.

Best Play Citation

○○○
○○○
○○○
○○○
○○○
○○○ # CURTAINS

A Play in Two Acts

BY STEPHEN BILL

Cast and credits appear on pages 341–342

*STEPHEN BILL was born and raised in Birmingham, England, where his father ran a small family artistic enameling business in the jewellery quarter. He was educated there, at Hansworth and Halesowen Grammar School, before going on to the Royal Academy of Dramatic Arts in London. He tells us, "I have written for as long as I can remember. As an actor I received an invaluable apprenticeship in the art and craft of the theater working in repertory theaters and in plays on the London fringe. I was working at The Crucible Theater, Sheffield, when they needed a play." Bill provided one—*The Final Wave—*which Crucible produced in 1979. "It worked well," he says, "and led to a Thames Television Writer-in-Residence Award—twelve months guaranteed employment that set me up as a professional writer." That year, 1980, saw the group producing his TV play* Lyndsey. *"Television and theater commissions followed," he recalls, "and the writing took over from the acting." But he credits working with Mike Leigh as an actor as one of the major influences on his work.*

There followed a spate of Bill plays produced by organizations in London and throughout England from 1979 to the present: The Old Order, Piggy Back Riders, Naked in the Bull Ring, The Bottom Drawer, Over the Bar, Crossing the Line, Girl Talk, Over a Barrel, Stitched Up, Cassie *and now* Curtains, *the first Bill play with an American production of* Best Plays *record, which opened an off-Broadway engagement May 21 and was named Bill's first Best Play.*

Bill formed Fair Game Films with Alan Dossor, a director, and Irving Teitelbaum, a producer, and his scripts for the movies include Fair Game, The Darling Buds of May *and* Broke. *He is married to the writer and actress Sheila Kelley, with two children, a boy and a girl. They live in Leamington Spa, near Stratford Upon Avon.*

The following synopsis of Curtains *was prepared by David Lefkowitz.*

Time: Spring 1987
Place: Birmingham, England

ACT I

Scene 1: Late afternoon

SYNOPSIS: *"In the rear living room of an inner-city, Victorian, villa-type house, there are two doors: one to the hallway and one to the kitchen. The room hasn't been properly redecorated for at least 30 years, though attempts have been made here and there to brighten things up . . . . . The light is fairly dingy. There are a lot of photographs covering several generations of family, and there are quite a lot of ornaments and pictures. The table is laid for a buffet birthday tea."* Joining *"tiny and frail"* Ida at her 86th birthday party are her daughters Katherine (53) and Margaret (50). *"Ida sits propped up with cushions, completely in her own world. Presents are piled on her lap."* Katherine's husband Geoffrey and son Michael are also in attendance. Margaret's husband Douglas, *"scruffier,"* is looking through an old tin can full of nails, screws and other junk. Margaret opens one of the presents for her mother.

MARGARET: Oh, and what's this? This one's from Jamie and Sue and baby John . . .
IDA: Where's Michael?
MICHAEL: I'm here.
KATHERINE: We're all here, Mom.
MARGARET: All the family, just for your birthday; you see how we care?
IDA: What day is it?
MARGARET: It's your birthday.
IDA: How quickly it's Friday.
KATHERINE: It's not Friday, Mom.
          They laugh.

Douglas is looking for a solid place on the wall to nail up a thermometer. Mrs. Jackson, a 70-year-old neighbor, enters. She's a friend and caregiver to Ida.

IDA: Where? Who's that?

MARGARET: Mrs. Jackson.

MRS. JACKSON: I've brought you a card, Ida. (*To the family.*) Is she behaving herself?

MARGARET: Oh yes, we're having a lovely birthday, aren't we, Mom? Shall I open it for you?

DOUGLAS: Where do you want it?

MARGARET: Oh Mom, where do you want the thermometer?

MRS. JACKSON: What's that?

GEOFFREY: It's a thermometer.

MRS. JACKSON: Oh . . .

MICHAEL: A present from Mom and Dad.

GEOFFREY: Well, we thought . . .

KATHERINE: They're advising all the old people to get them.

MRS. JACKSON: What for?

MARGARET: It'll be useful, won't it, Mom?

MRS. JACKSON: We had one once, told you the weather.

KATHERINE: Oh . . . this is a special one. Tells you when to turn the fire up.

MRS. JACKSON: Ohh . . .

DOUGLAS (*holding it against the wall*): There do you?

MARGARET: Not in a draught, Douglas.

DOUGLAS: In this house?

GEOFFREY: After last winter we thought . . .

MARGARET: That was hypothermia, that was.

KATHERINE: Her blood's like water, you see, Margaret.

Douglas moves the thermometer all around the wall. Each time Ida, dissatisfied, points to a different spot. After the thermometer is finally fixed to the wall, Katherine opens Mrs. Jackson's birthday card for Ida. In an aside to Katherine, Margaret mentions that there is no present from "you know who"—and there was nothing last Christmas either.

Katherine offers Ida a bit of tea, which gives Mrs. Jackson a chance to be useful and put the kettle on. Margaret tells why she used Dream Topping instead of double cream on the trifle—the latter might be too rich for Ida—but her effort to explain such distinctions to Ida is ultimately pointless.

KATHERINE: Has she had her tablets, Michael?

MRS. JACKSON: She's had everything she can until bedtime.

GEOFFREY: Does sitting up not help, perhaps?

MRS. JACKSON: It's all the same, Geoffrey. It's in her spine, see.

GEOFFREY: If she could keep moving . . .

KATHERINE: Don't be ridiculous.

GEOFFREY: I know, but if she could . . .

MICHAEL: Dad.

GEOFFREY: I mean, it's such a pity when she recovered so well from the surgery . . .

MARGARET: Oh, she's doing wonderfully, aren't you, Mom?

KATHERINE: Maybe we should move on to the cake.

Michael presents a cake with 86 little flowers on it. The group sings "Happy Birthday." Ida—"*the faintest of smiles lights her face*"—makes to blow out the single candle, and the others help her and congratulate her when the candle goes out.

MICHAEL: Speech, speech!

IDA: You're very kind. You're all very kind. I don't know why you bother, you shouldn't, you know.

GEOFFREY: Of course we should! It's our bounden duty!

KATHERINE: Of course.

GEOFFREY: Because we all love you very much!

Ida smiles.

MARGARET: You see—she's picking up, aren't you?

MRS. JACKSON: She's always brighter when there's people here.

Douglas climbs on a chair to get pictures of Katherine cutting the cake and Ida being served a slice. Soon after Ida starts eating the cake, she begins choking. She is in serious trouble, coughing up what looks like blood, but she manages to recover after Mrs. Jackson gives her some tea.

KATHERINE: Has she had any more trouble with the um . . .

MICHAEL: The ulcer?

KATHERINE: The tummy. I mean they don't know, do they, that she definitely has umm . . . ?

MICHAEL: How can they? Unless she goes in and has the old camera stuck down her throat, of course they don't know for certain, but the evidence . . .

KATHERINE: Better now, Mom?

MRS. JACKSON: Too much! She's not eating really, you see.

MICHAEL: Not unless you force her!

MARGARET: She must eat. I wish I could be here more often. Oh dear. She shouldn't be on her own.

MRS. JACKSON: Well, we do what we can.

MARGARET: Oh, Mrs. Jackson, you're marvellous.

MRS. JACKSON: I'm here more or less all the time! But I've got my own house, you see, to keep tidy, and I've only got one pair of hands . . .

GEOFFREY: Of course!

KATHERINE: It's not satisfactory, really.

MRS. JACKSON: No, it isn't. Well you see, when I'm watching *Young Doctors* of an afternoon, I can't hear a thing, so even if she knocked the wall . . .

David Cale (Douglas), Laura Esterman (Katherine), Jayne Haynes (Margaret), Frederick Weller (Michael), Lisa Emery (Susan), Kathleen Claypool (Ida), Betty Miller (Mrs. Jackson) and John Henry Cox (Geoffrey) as they appeared in *Curtains* by Stephen Bill

Margaret feels they can no longer "avoid the big question" and wants to turn the discussion, as she has so many times before, to finding a home for Grandma. Douglas won't hear of it and exits to the garden. Geoffrey wonders how Margaret and Douglas are doing on their farm. Fine, Margaret tells him, but he wonders how content Douglas can be after having spent exciting years as a Red Arrow in the Air Force.

Mrs. Jackson wheels Ida out, and the rest discuss getting Ida into Fairlawns or The Lavenders. Katherine has a real problem with the idea of incarcerating her mother. Ida had asked her to promise never to have her "put away," and Katherine argues, "Just moving them at all, it disorients them." Katherine once tried to take her mother into her home, but—her husband and son remind her—Ida hated it, and a repetition is out of the question.

Mrs. Jackson wheels Ida back in, Ida announcing that she's going to America. Her family humors her. Douglas returns pushing an old lawn mower. He wishes the mower had a motor, but he's willing to cut the grass with it anyway so that Grandma can go outside and enjoy the garden. Douglas oils the rusty mower, but it still won't work.

The doorbell rings. Michael assumes the vicar has come to offer birthday wishes, and everyone is shocked when Susan, Ida's other daughter, walks in. Susan, in her early 40s, carries a bunch of roses.

SUSAN: Oh, my God ... Well, well, well ... (*Silence, as she looks around taking in the faces.*) Katherine ... Margaret ... Douglas ...

DOUGLAS: Hello, stranger.

SUSAN: Geoffrey ... What's all this then, a party? (*Looks at Ida, who appears to be in her own world.*)

MARGARET: It's Mother's birthday.

SUSAN: Oh, I know, I know ... Hello, Mom.

IDA: What?

MARGARET: Susan ...

SUSAN: What?

MARGARET: She's ... listen; she's not well at all ...

SUSAN: I know. (*Stands looking at her mother. The others exchange glances.*)

MARGARET: Beg pardon?

SUSAN: I know.

MARGARET: Oh ... well ... How did you know?

SUSAN: I just knew. Sorry to take you all by surprise. I knew, and I knew I had to come. Mom ... it's Susan ...

IDA: Who's that?

SUSAN: It's Susan, I've come to see you. I've brought you some flowers. Happy birthday!

IDA: Who is it, Mrs. Jackson?

MRS. JACKSON: Um ... well, it's Susan ... you know ... your ... youngest, your daughter.

IDA: No.

MRS. JACKSON: It is. You remember!

IDA (*no recognition*): Do I? Right ...

MARGARET: You see? She won't take it in.

Susan tells those assembled she's been staying in Shepton Mallet, Somerset, with her daughter. On being told that her mother lives in constant pain from arthritis of the spine, Susan asks whether they should send for a doctor. Mrs. Jackson notes that the best one, the only one who'll make house calls, is "The black one ..... I call him Dr. Mucky-bee, but I don't know if that's correct."

Katherine and Margaret leave the room to phone the doctor. Geoffrey tells Susan of Ida's successful hip operation. Ida overhears mention of the hospital and becomes panicked at the idea of returning to such a place ever again: "Wicked people. Never again. Oh no!"

Susan begins getting reacquainted, chatting with Douglas about his son, who fought in what she calls "the Falklands fiasco." And again she tries to establish contact with her mother.

SUSAN: All right, Mom? I should have let you know I was coming, sorry Mom, but I didn't know what to say, and it was all very last minute.

IDA: What's going on dear, do you know?

SUSAN: Well ... where should I begin? It's your birthday, right? And do you remember, Mom, your youngest daughter Susan?

IDA: Who's this?

SUSAN: This is Susan.

IDA: I don't know anything any more, dear. I've had enough, I know that ... Who are you?

SUSAN: Susan. The one that went away.

IDA: I know; you did!

SUSAN: Right! I was a naughty girl!
>   *Ida just looks at her.*

Well, I wasn't all bad, I married the chap, you'll be pleased to know, when he finally got divorced. We had two children, then we went our different ways ... Then I had another little girl, well she's a big girl now. I've seen the world, Mom, you know? And now I've come back. I dreamt about you last night; you were poorly. My daughter woke me. She said, "Mom, you're crying." I thought I'd better come home.
>   *Ida is gripping Susan's hand tightly.*

Susan tells everyone how surprised she is that the neighborhood's changed so little since she left 25 years ago: "I passed houses with the same vase in the window as when I was a child." She learns that Michael has been living here at the house to save money and be close to the university.

Mrs. Jackson hands Ida one of Susan's roses, but the old woman doesn't have the control to hold it. Katherine and Margaret return and announce that the doctor, learning that Ida is 86, told them, "What do you expect—of course she'll be in pain!" and refused to come out here.

They speculate on the possibility of their reaching that great age, and Douglas gloomily notes that The Bomb will probably drop before that happens. Douglas gets up and *"tries out the mower. It works. He walks up and down in the very confined space in front of the fire. They all watch . . . . . Blackout."*

Scene 2: Evening

It's evening, dusk, with no lights turned on in the living room. Ida, *"well wrapped up,"* is wheeled into the room by Katherine. Ida grips Katherine's arm, saying, "You promised me," and Katherine tells her, "I don't know what you want, Mom." "You know," Ida insists, as Katherine, chattering away about Douglas and the events of the day, prepares a drink.

KATHERINE: Look, here's a lemon barley here. This must be yours.
>   *She hands her a glass.*

Are you uncomfortable?

She gets her pills from the wall-cupboard.

As it's your birthday. Just one more . . .

IDA: What's this?

KATHERINE: Your pills.

Katherine opens the bottle and puts it in Ida's hand.

Is that the right bottle?

Ida stares at Katherine.

Oh . . . I, I, I'm going to check the back door, all right. Did I lock it? I'm going to check the back door . . .

She heads for the kitchen. She stops by the kitchen door, not looking, just waiting. Ida starts to cram pills into her mouth. Katherine turns, sees what she's doing and turns away.

Oh, my God! Swallow, Mom, swallow!

She tries to help her.

Oh, God in heaven, help me! Drink some juice, drink some juice.

The pills are spat everywhere, as Ida convulses.

Drink, Mom! I can't do it, Mom, I can't!

IDA: Please!

Katherine tries to put a plastic bag over her head. It is ridiculously too big.

KATHERINE: Ohh . . .

She grabs the pillow and puts it over Ida's face. She lies her own body across, embracing mother, pillow and wheelchair.

Oh, God!

She remains like that for a considerable length of time. The front door slams.

Aghh!

She moves and sits on a chair, still holding the pillow. Geoffrey comes in. She looks away.

GEOFFREY: Anyone home? No light on . . .

He switches it on.

Oh . . . Oh, my God . . . Katherine . . . Katherine . . . What the . . . Is she . . . is she?

Katherine is not listening to him. Geoffrey checks Ida's pulse. As he does so, he spots the pills that are everywhere.

What are these? Oh, my Lor' . . . Katherine . . .

She can't look at him. She remains clutching the cushion.

Well . . .

He lays Ida's wrist down.

Well, I think she's . . .

Katherine looks at Ida for the first time. She goes over to her. She picks up the pills which are all over the blankets and clothes.

What happened? (*No reply.*) Katherine? You're shaking . . . .

Once Ida is cleaned up a bit, Katherine kisses her.

KATHERINE: Well, that's it.

Kathleen Claypool and Laura Esterman in a scene from *Curtains*

Geoffrey knocks on the wall to arouse Mrs. Jackson. As they wait for her to come in, Geoffrey notes that he's just come from a successful meeting: "We raised a hundred pounds tonight. Somalia, I think it's going to." That's as much small talk as he can muster, so Geoffrey again asks Katherine what happened. He worries about informing the authorities. Mrs. Jackson comes in, takes in the situation ("Oh dear, I knew, I knew . . . the minute you knocked"), calls it "a blessed release" and, with Katherine, wheels Ida out.

Geoffrey notices the empty pill bottle, picks it up and reads the label. Panicked, he puts it down, then picks it back up and wipes it thoroughly. Unsure where to hide the bottle, he drops it in the wastepaper basket and covers it with the trash that was already in it.

Katherine returns and tells Geoffrey that Mrs. Jackson's phoning the doctor. Geoffrey, highly agitated, all but pleads with Katherine to tell him what happened, but he doesn't really want to know. He observes that Mrs. Jackson seems to be taking death by natural causes for granted, and everyone in the family is still out, at the pub or elsewhere. And the doctor who will answer the call will probably be "the night-time relief. Some Iranian refugee." Geoffrey continues his queries.

GEOFFREY: . . . . . She'd asked to go into the garden, had she? And what happened? Did you just leave her in here for a while? (*Trying to lighten it.*) Where did all those pills come from? Isn't she a rogue! What did she do, just . . .

KATHERINE: Oh, for God's sake, Geoffrey!

GEOFFREY: I'm sorry, I'm sorry! Weren't there a lot of pills? It looked to me . . . tell me I'm wrong! But I have to know! Heavens, Katherine, when I came in here, if I didn't know you . . .

KATHERINE: What?

GEOFFREY: Shh ... It's all right; now look, everything's fine ...

Geoffrey goes across to comfort her. She shrugs him off. Mrs. Jackson comes in. Katherine goes out to the kitchen.

MRS. JACKSON: The doctor's on his way. Is she upset? She will be, it's always worse when the second one goes.

GEOFFREY: The second?

MRS. JACKSON: When both your parents ...

GEOFFREY: Oh. How did she look to you, Mrs. Jackson?

MRS. JACKSON: Not good.

GEOFFREY: Really?

MRS. JACKSON: Have you given her a drink?

GEOFFREY: Oh no, no ... I meant Mother.

MRS. JACKSON *(looking at him):* Ida? Well, I can't do any more ...

GEOFFREY: No.

MRS. JACKSON: Not till the doctor's been. There's nothing more I can do.

GEOFFREY: No, no, quite.

MRS. JACKSON: She's at peace now.

She picks up a pill off the floor.

Look at this ...

She picks another up.

GEOFFREY: What's that?

MRS. JACKSON: Look at this ... spits them out, you see. I find them in her pockets, down the bed.

She collects them.

If you don't take your pills, then what do you expect? Now where's the bottle gone?

She searches for the pill bottle

That was a new lot, have you seen it?

Geoffrey, for once, is speechless. He stands staring at her. Curtain.

ACT II: Late evening

Later that evening when Michael and Douglas come back to the house, they are talking about cuts in funding to Michael's department at the university. Geoffrey comes in to tell them of Ida's death. Douglas goes to check on Margaret. Mrs. Jackson joins Michael and Geoffrey, telling them confidentially that she saw Katherine taking pills out of Ida's mouth and tidying her up. Mrs. Jackson is still worried that she can't find the pill bottle anywhere. Fretful as she is, she can't help hinting that Ida may have committed suicide.

Geoffrey is wary of "putting two and two together and making six." Michael is sure he left the pill vial on the wall cupboard. He checks, but it's not there.

Margaret can be heard offstage commenting about her mother's death. Finally she comes into the living room, followed by Douglas.

MARGARET: She killed her.

GEOFFREY: What?

MARGARET: I don't care what anyone says, she's killed her! She was getting better!

DOUGLAS: No.

MARGARET: She was fine at tea time—she smiled!

DOUGLAS: Here, sit down . . .

MARGARET: She's killed her, Douglas! Mrs. Jackson, wasn't she picking up?

MRS. JACKSON: Oh, I don't . . . look, dear, I don't think we should go putting two and two together . . . and, and making four, you know?

MARGARET: If it wasn't for my sister!

DOUGLAS: Just calm down.

GEOFFREY: Yes, yes; let's just take it easy, shall we?

MARGARET: As soon as she came back, I knew! I knew!

GEOFFREY: Susan?

MARGARET: Yes!

GEOFFREY: Ah . . .

Susan has returned home driven by guilt for having ruined her life (Margaret observes) and instead of blaming herself, blames her mother. Margaret repeats her conclusion: "Mark my words, she's killed her . . . . . A shock like that, at her age!"

Katherine comes in and seems almost ready to confess. But the family interrupts with the usual "she's at peace now" platitudes. Michael brings up the subject of the pill bottle; both Katherine and Douglas are non-responsive. Margaret blurts to Katherine her theory about Susan, but Douglas intervenes: "Nobody has killed anyone!" Margaret remains unconvinced.

When Susan finally enters, Margaret accusingly asks where she's been. She says she'd made a phone call to the local pub, where she assumed Douglas and Michael had been. They weren't there, and she went out to look for them at two other pubs.

Ultimately, all eyes turn to Katherine. *"She shakes her head, unable to speak."* She walks around a bit, and there's a silence the moment when everyone truly realizes that Ida's dead. Susan becomes upset and reflects ruefully on her bad timing at coming home. She wonders whether her mother forgave her, or if Ida's death was some kind of revenge. She realizes, "I never said goodbye," and leaves the room to do so.

Michael starts looking for the pill bottle. Douglas ridicules the effort. Geoffrey tries to put a positive spin on things, as Mrs. Jackson brings everyone tea.

Margaret orders Douglas to check the attic first thing in the morning—she doesn't want Susan getting any of Ida's possessions. It may seem like junk, but it's Victorian junk, and there's money in it. There is more commiseration, with Mrs. Jackson soothing Margaret. And Katherine seems distracted, lost in her own sad thoughts.

Susan returns and reminisces with Douglas about riding in his old sports car. A doorbell signals the offstage arrival of the doctor. Geoffrey goes to let him in. Margaret looks down the hall and tells the others, "He's black." Mrs. Jackson tries to console Katherine, while Katherine, as tenderly as she can, tries to get Mrs. Jackson to go home and leave the family in peace. Mrs. Jackson finally takes the hint, though she promises to return, once the physician's gone.

Michael worries that he'll now have to move out, perhaps even leave the country, because he can't afford to pay rent. Katherine asks Geoffrey what he thinks the doctor's up to.

GEOFFREY: The doctor? Oh well, you know, he just has to, you know . . .

MICHAEL: Check she didn't swallow the pill bottle for a start-off!

GEOFFREY: Michael . . .

MICHAEL: Well, where is it? I wouldn't put it past her. I've searched the house. And it was her birthday, maybe she thought, I'll get 'em while they're all here!

MARGARET: It wasn't pills, Michael. That wasn't what killed her.

KATHERINE: Please, please!

GEOFFREY: Yes look, please, please; I'm sure the pill bottle will turn up and let's ha ha . . . not go giving the chap ideas, heh? Walls have ears, you know, so . . . ha ha! That's all we need, ha ha! Let's leave cause of departure to the professionals, shall we? Ha ha . . . that's his job, that's what he's paid for, and I'm sure . . .

KATHERINE: What have I done?

GEOFFREY: What?

KATHERINE: What have I done? I'm sorry, I'm sorry, everyone.

MARGARET: Why, what for?

KATHERINE: I'm sorry, Susan.

SUSAN: What for?

MARGARET: I don't see that you've got anything to be sorry for, Katherine. Have you? It wasn't you!

KATHERINE: Mother would be alive now, should be alive now . . .

MARGARET: Oh yes, she should! I know exactly; this is what I said—

SUSAN: All right, Margaret.

MARGARET: —it doesn't add up, it doesn't add up at all!

KATHERINE: No, no, no, it doesn't! You're right! I did it, all right?

GEOFFREY: Now, shh, sh, sh . . .

KATHERINE: No!

GEOFFREY: Dear, just let the doctor . . .

KATHERINE: Oh, shut up, Geoffrey! I did it, all right? O.K.? You're right—it doesn't add up, you're right. She could have gone on for years yet! She was picking up, wasn't she? But she didn't want to! She didn't want to, Margaret! She'd had enough, so . . . Oh, God . . .

MARGARET: So . . . what?

KATHERINE: I helped her.

GEOFFREY: Shhh . . .

MICHAEL: Not with the pills?

MARGARET: No?

KATHERINE: Yes.

GEOFFREY: No, no, no . . . now wait a minute, just all hold on a moment . . . Let's not get, you know . . . The doctor's in there now, and he'll umm, I mean we don't know . . .

KATHERINE: We do, Geoffrey, we do! Stop pussy-footing around, all right? You saw what happened.

GEOFFREY: Me?

KATHERINE: Yes, for God's sake!

GEOFFREY: I saw nothing!

KATHERINE: Didn't you? Oh, my God! Blind as well . . . I killed her . . . I . . .

GEOFFREY: No, no, no . . . I don't believe, not for an instant . . .

Katherine is tempted to go tell the doctor, but Geoffrey asks everyone to "just hold tight." The others, still unclear, try to fudge the line between what Katherine might have done and what she only thinks she might have done. Geoffrey keeps protesting that he wants "to be absolutely clear about this."

GEOFFREY: I mean, when things like this happen, it's all too easy to read things into things—we all naturally feel all sorts of things; a loved one, you know . . . and we feel distressed, guilty perhaps, confused, is that it, Katherine?

KATHERINE: No.

GEOFFREY: A feeling that you could have, should have, done more?

KATHERINE: More?

GEOFFREY: A feeling of inadequacy, such that you now think . . .

KATHERINE: O yes, oh yes; she wouldn't die! First the pills, she couldn't swallow the bloody things!

MARGARET: O, my God!

KATHERINE: Then the carrier bag—ridiculously too big.

MARGARET: What?

KATHERINE: Then the pillow . . . what have I done?

MARGARET: Katherine.

KATHERINE: She begged me! She begged me!

Geoffrey helps Katherine suppress another urge to run and tell all to the doctor. He and Margaret are more concerned with the "how" than the "why." Even Katherine acknowledges that if the pills or the suffocation killed Ida, it was only manslaughter. If it was the Sainsbury's bag, it was murder.

As everyone waits for the doctor's pronouncement, Katherine does give them the "why." Years ago, Ida made Katherine promise never to put her in a home. Once Ida started deteriorating physically and mentally, Katherine began reading up on euthanasia cases, even on the jail terms of participants. After Katherine tells them, "It was such a terrible mess! So squalid! She gagged and choked," Margaret admits she doesn't want to know any more.

Michael suggests that the law might require two doctors to certify a death like this, but Douglas assures them that's only in case of cremation, which is not planned for Ida. Susan still feels terrible guilt about her mother dying on the day she came back.

KATHERINE: It was nothing to do with you.

SUSAN: I find that difficult to believe.

MARGARET: So do I.

SUSAN: All right, Margaret. It's my fault, O.K.? I'll go and tell him, shall I? Cause of death . . .

GEOFFREY: Susan!

SUSAN: Yes. That's right!

GEOFFREY: What? Look. Listen. If we could keep to the point! I don't think she even knew it was you, actually.

KATHERINE: She did. Oh, she did.

SUSAN: Yes, and I think that's why . . .

KATHERINE: Yes, all right, yes, you could be right! Yes, O.K., yes, it did upset her—you were back, and you were seeing her in that state. If you looked her in the eye, you could see, for heaven's sake, that she knew exactly what was going on—and what was happening to her, and she'd had enough. She wanted to die. She wasn't afraid to die . . .

DOUGLAS: Of course she wasn't.

MARGARET: How do you know?

DOUGLAS: It's only us that aren't ready for it.

KATHERINE: Right! It was her choice, honestly!

DOUGLAS: That's the way it should be.

KATHERINE: Thank you, Douglas! Oh, thank you! I'm not a bad person, then, am I?

DOUGLAS: Don't be daft.

Nevertheless, Katherine and others worry about why the doctor's taking so long with Ida. Geoffrey and Margaret try to get the step-by-step facts of the killing correct. Katherine finally exclaims that she smothered Ida with a pillow. Geoffrey tries very hard to make the details reflect favorably on Katherine. Their son Michael is more interested in the truth. Margaret agrees with Michael, then panics at the thought that Katherine having told everyone about the crime makes them all accessories to it.

DOUGLAS (to Margaret): Do you want to know the truth, you and Michael?

MARGARET: I do, yes! Yes, I do, I can't believe, I can't start to imagine!

DOUGLAS: Well, the truth is, for a start-off, we're all as guilty as Katherine here, so . . .

KATHERINE: No!

MARGARET: Guilty?

DOUGLAS: Oh yes, yes we are, Katherine, believe me! So your mother's dead, why? Because we stopped forcing her to be alive! So don't you dare, Margaret . . .

MARGARET: We stopped . . .? She's dead because because Katherine . . .

DOUGLAS: It's nothing to do with Katherine! That's a mere technicality!

MICHAEL: Oh now, come on . . . . .

DOUGLAS: Why didn't you send her to the hospital weeks ago?

MICHAEL: Me?

DOUGLAS: How long has she been coughing blood?

GEOFFREY: We didn't want her mucked about, Douglas.

DOUGLAS: Quite right, too!

Katherine paces, she is restless.

It's all right, Katherine. But if she'd been a few years younger, you wouldn't let her cough blood, or dribble her antibiotics down her front, or spit out her tablets. If I was coughing blood, would you say, "I don't want him mucked about"?

KATHERINE: Please . . .

DOUGLAS: She was dying, Katherine. The pain was getting worse. All her infections were getting worse. We could have treated them, we have the technology, but no—we didn't want her mucked about—or kept alive any longer than was absolutely necessary—we were all letting her die! . . . . .

Praising Katherine's courage, ashamed she had to act alone, Douglas sees no moral difference between doing nothing or doing "something positive." Katherine admits she felt like crying out for assistance. Douglas notes that everyone's worried about blame, but the only one who shouldn't feel guilty is Katherine. The other day, even Margaret was heard to say, "If only Mother would die."

Geoffrey maintains the importance of telling the doctor nothing. Susan adds that they should all probably "be thinking up a bit of a whopper."

Katherine assures Susan that she and Geoffrey had tried many ways to help Ida before she died. Still, she wonders if she should have moved back home to look after her mom in her old age. Douglas reminds her of the time she and Geoffrey let Ida move into their home. "God, she hated it," Katherine remembers. "She left excrement all around the living room on purpose." Ida even drove Katherine to a breakdown—though Geoffrey always said she was merely "overtired." At that point they considered sending Ida to live with Margaret. Douglas notes that shuttling a sick woman around the country would have been no answer either.

They hear sounds outside the room indicating that the doctor may be finally leaving. Geoffrey goes to see him out. The others are on tenterhooks.

Geoffrey comes back in.

MARGARET: Geoffrey, where's he . . . ?

KATHERINE: He's not gone?

GEOFFREY: Well . . .

MICHAEL: Come on . . . what's happening, Dad?

GEOFFREY: Well, I have here a piece of paper . . .

KATHERINE: Has he gone?

GEOFFREY: The doctor has gone.

MARGARET: And is he coming back?

GEOFFREY: No.

KATHERINE: No?

MARGARET: You mean that's it?

GEOFFREY: Absolutely. That, Margaret, would appear to be it.

Katherine collapses into a chair and sobs into a cushion.

Katherine . . . Katherine . . . it's all right . . . Everything is hunky dory . . . he's gone!

Katherine runs out, continuing to bawl. Michael asks about cause of death, and Geoffrey replies that he didn't ask and the doctor didn't say: "There was no hint that he was anything but satisfied." Michael can't believe the doctor would be so lax about the details. Once more, Geoffrey tries to fob off the whole thing as "a very nasty little mixup," with Ida "having a seizure or a stroke or something."

Susan goes out to comfort Katherine. Michael keeps demanding the truth and insisting that Ida's death was no mixup but a deliberate act. He asserts that Katherine had no right to do what she did. Douglas comes to her defense. Michael cites the "Thou shalt not kill" Commandment, complaining that life is becoming cheap. Katherine and Susan come through and exit on their way to the kitchen, as Douglas continues the argument, challenging Michael to think about what he'll do when he gets old—will he simply let nature take its course, "leave it all in God's hands"? The likelihood that he'll have a problem is getting greater. "There's more and more people getting their telegrams now" from the Queen congratulating them on their 100th birthday.

DOUGLAS: . . . . . Forty years of retirement you could have now.

GEOFFREY: Oh, my God!

DOUGLAS: Twenty years, maybe, of senility.

GEOFFREY: Oh Lor'!

DOUGLAS: Ten years of double incontinence.

MICHAEL: Don't be ridiculous! Not necessarily!

DOUGLAS: Not necessarily, no. It's a lottery, of course. I didn't know you were a gambler—have you looked at the odds? Studied the form? Have you, by any chance, been to the homes of the losers? I have, Michael—I watched both my parents rot in homes full of decaying hulks, tried to talk to my mother only to be drowned out by the sound of the woman sitting next to her pissing on the plastic chair. Watched my father being kissed by another man who thought he'd just found his wife. I could go on. Will you really leave yourself happily in God's hands as you shit in the corridor on your way to communal lunch? Or will you beg someone to help you? Hoping to God they're not Christian! Beg someone to give you that final bit of dignity, to help you to a decent peaceful death . . .

GEOFFREY: It's difficult, isn't it?

DOUGLAS: I'll tell you what you'll do—you'll do what we're all doing—you'll leave it till it's too bloody late! Until your brain's gone or you've had a stroke and nobody understands your begging grunts!

About to respond vehemently, Michael brings his beer glass down on the table, shattering it and spreading both glass and beer. The conversation turns once again to worry about the doctor's conclusions while the family members move in and out of the living room bandaging Michael's cut hand, cleaning up the mess and offering various comments on the situation. Geoffrey tries to reassure Katherine that she won't be locked up. Douglas adds his feeling that the doctor secretly understood and tacitly approved of Katherine's actions—which only makes Katherine angry.

Margaret brings the conversation back to the what-do-we-do-now mode. A door slam announces the return of Mrs. Jackson—the last person Katherine wants around. Geoffrey manages to block her from coming in. Margaret goes upstairs with a migraine, Douglas promising to inform her if anyone comes to arrest the family. Once more Susan asks Katherine if her actions were, indeed, deliberate. The answer is emphatically yes.

KATHERINE: . . . . . It wasn't just that she was in pain, though that was terrible to watch, but more than that, you came back, and she couldn't even tell you to get out! Or tell you how much she loved you, or . . . when you can no longer express what you feel, because of the pain or whatever, then my God . . . it doesn't, you see, mean that you don't still feel it deep down. I know she was feeling, oh, feeling so much, and to express that, to be able to talk about what you feel, that's as much a part of being alive as having legs that work, isn't it?

DOUGLAS: Absolutely.

KATHERINE: And when that's gone, that ability to express, should we not have the right, one final right . . .

DOUGLAS: To a decent death.

KATHERINE: That's it—and that right must be hers, mustn't it? Oh God, mustn't it? (*She takes a deep breath, sighs and shakes her head.*) That we should come to this, Susan.

SUSAN: I have a feeling that wherever she is, she's laughing at us now.

KATHERINE: Yes, yes! Ha . . . it's all right for some! It's all right saying, "Help me, Katherine!" Bloody woman! What about Katherine? I wish I'd left home when you did, I tell you . . .

SUSAN: If I'd really left home, I wouldn't be here now, would I? . . . . . .

Katherine asks Susan how she could have abandoned the family for 25 years. Susan counters with, "Why did you never come looking for me?" Ida threw Susan out because she was pregnant and unmarried—but all that is best left in the past and forgotten, Douglas observes. "Just so long as you're happy," Katherine adds.

SUSAN: My second marriage has just broken up.

KATHERINE: Oh . . .

SUSAN: I'm homeless. My kids stubbornly refuse to grow up. My fault—I always told them not to. Forbade them to have any ambition, or soil their hands in the temple of Mammon, so . . .

DOUGLAS: They're not working?

SUSAN: God, no!

KATHERINE: What are their names?

SUSAN: Cloud . . .

KATHERINE: Sorry?

SUSAN: That's right. And Rain. At least you've saved me the trouble of trying to explain that one to Mom, thank you. Don't get me wrong—they're wonderful children . . . sorry; people—it just never occurred to me that it might one day be difficult for them, so . . . we're all at square one, them and me. Very exciting, all learning together, which is one reason why, I suppose, I'm back. But I certainly didn't . . . little did I . . . ohh . . .

Katherine and Susan embrace and cry, letting go at last.

When the emotion of the moment subsides, Douglas brings up Susan's future plans and invites her to stay at his farm; he'll be on his way there at dawn. "*They look at each other*" for a few moments of silent appraisal, then Susan finally decides, "I don't think that would be any answer, do you?"

Michael comes in with a tea towel wrapped around his hand and a question to pose: "Do we adapt what we believe to the way we live our lives, or should we adapt the way we live our lives to what we believe?" Douglas can't provide him with an answer. Mrs. Jackson comes through the room on her way to the kitchen, talking as she goes: "If I could just get the bowl and towel, I won't get in your way. I'll put a clean nightie on her though, dear, everything else can wait till morning, can't it? (*She picks up the rubbish basket.*) Oh, look at me . . . that's habit, that is! Every night I'd empty this, remove all matches and, you know, anything that might burn or spill. Oh, she was a terror. We never knew what we'd find in the morning, did we, Michael? She was supposed to be bedridden, but if she put her mind to something . . . Anyway . . . (*Going out.*) It's going to take a bit of getting used to."

Without Mrs. Jackson, everyone feels the quiet of the room: the crisis is passed, and life will go on as it did before. Margaret seems disappointed, and Douglas sneers, "What do you want—your pound of flesh?" Margaret feels that Douglas is taking out on her his anger at the difficulty of being a farmer.

Geoffrey plans to run home now, walk their dog Candy and then return here for the night. He suggests that it's time for bed, and there's room for everyone to sleep here in the house. But no one moves.

GEOFFREY: It did occur to me just by the by, before we all go our separate ways, we must arrange Christmas.

KATHERINE: What?

DOUGLAS: Shouldn't we arrange the funeral first?

GEOFFREY: Good point, good point!

KATHERINE: Shouldn't you go if you're going?

GEOFFREY: I suppose I must, unfortunately, if we don't want problems all over the kitchen floor . . . I'll be as quick as I can . . .

KATHERINE: Just go, Geoffrey.

GEOFFREY: I'm going, I'm going . . .

Mrs. Jackson comes in with a bowl of hot water and a towel.

All right, Mrs. Jackson?

MRS. JACKSON: I won't be long.

Mrs. Jackson goes. They watch her go through.

GEOFFREY: Right, then . . . And just in case . . . if anyone else should come, I'm sure they won't, but if the door was to go, are we a little clearer now . . . ?

KATHERINE: Perfectly! There is no confusion, Geoffrey! It's all perfectly clear, thank you very much, now go! Just go!

He can't. That was not the answer he wanted. He eventually sits down. Katherine grasps Susan's hand and holds it tight. Curtain.

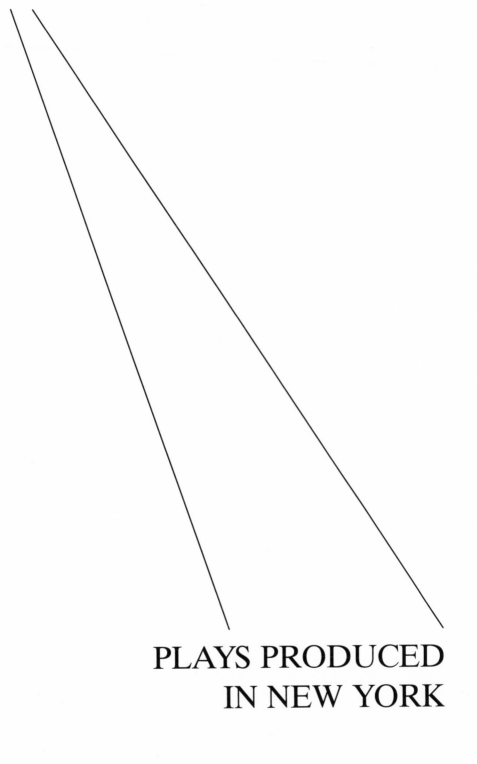

PLAYS PRODUCED
IN NEW YORK

PLAYS PRODUCED ON BROADWAY

Figures in parentheses following a play's title give number of performances. These figures do not include previews or extra non-profit performances. In the case of a transfer, the off-Broadway run is noted but not added to the figure in parentheses.

Plays marked with an asterisk (*) were still in a projected run June 1, 1996. Their number of performances is figured through May 31, 1996.

In a listing of a show's numbers—dances, sketches, musical scenes, etc.—the titles of songs are identified wherever possible by their appearance in quotation marks (").

HOLDOVERS FROM PREVIOUS SEASONS

Plays which were running on June 1, 1995 are listed below. More detailed information about them appears in previous *Best Plays* volumes of the years in which they opened. Important cast changes since opening night are recorded in the Cast Replacements section of this volume.

*Cats (5,697). Musical based on *Old Possum's Book of Practical Cats* by T.S. Eliot; music by Andrew Lloyd Webber; additional lyrics by Trevor Nunn and Richard Stilgoe. Opened October 7, 1982.

*Les Misérables (3,786). Musical based on the novel by Victor Hugo; book by Alain Boublil and Claude-Michel Schönberg; music by Claude-Michel Schönberg; lyrics by Herbert Kretzmer; original French text by Alain Boublil and Jean-Marc Natel; additional material by James Fenton. Opened March 12, 1987.

*The Phantom of the Opera (3,484). Musical adapted from the novel by Gaston Leroux; book by Richard Stilgoe and Andrew Lloyd Webber; music by Andrew Lloyd Webber; lyrics by Charles Hart; additional lyrics by Richard Stilgoe. Opened January 26, 1988.

*Miss Saigon (2,138). Musical with book by Alain Boublil and Claude-Michel Schönberg; music by Claude-Michel Schönberg; lyrics by Richard Maltby Jr. and Alain Boublil; additional material by Richard Maltby Jr. Opened April 11, 1991.

Crazy for You (1,622). Musical with book by Ken Ludwig; co-conceived by Ken Ludwig and Mike Ockrent; inspired by material (in the musical *Girl Crazy*) by Guy Bolton and John McGowan; music by George Gershwin; lyrics by Ira Gershwin. Opened February 19, 1992. (Closed January 7, 1996)

The Who's Tommy (900). Musical with book by Pete Townshend and Des McAnuff; music and lyrics by Pete Townshend; additional music and lyrics by John Entwistle and Keith Moon. Opened April 22, 1993. (Closed June 17, 1995)

Kiss of the Spider Woman (906). Musical based on the novel by Manuel Puig; book by Terrence McNally; music by John Kander; lyrics by Fred Ebb. Opened May 3, 1993. (Closed July 1, 1995)

Damn Yankees (533). Revival of the musical based on Douglas Wallop's *The Year the Yankees Lost the Pennant;* book by George Abbott and Douglas Wallop; music and lyrics by Richard Adler and Jerry Ross. Opened March 3, 1994. (Suspended performances December 31, 1994) Reopened March 12, 1995. (Closed August 6, 1995)

*Beauty and the Beast** (893). Musical with book by Linda Woolverton; music by Alan Menken; lyrics by Howard Ashman and Tim Rice. Opened April 18, 1994.

*Grease** (843). Revival of the musical with book, music and lyrics by Jim Jacobs and Warren Casey. Opened May 11, 1994.

*Show Boat** (694). Revival of the musical based on the novel by Edna Ferber; book and lyrics by Oscar Hammerstein II; music by Jerome Kern. Opened October 2, 1994.

*Sunset Boulevard** (649). Musical based on the Billy Wilder film; book and lyrics by Don Black and Christopher Hampton; music by Andrew Lloyd Webber. Opened November 17, 1994.

Love! Valour! Compassion! (249). Transfer from off Broadway of the play by Terrence McNally. Opened November 1, 1994 off Broadway where it played 72 performances through January 1, 1995; transferred to Broadway February 14, 1995. (Closed September 17, 1995)

*Smokey Joe's Cafe** (522). Musical revue with words and music by Jerry Leiber and Mike Stoller. Opened March 2, 1995.

Lincoln Center Theater. The Heiress (341). Revival of the play by Ruth and Augustus Goetz; suggested by Henry James's novel *Washington Square.* Opened March 9, 1995. (Closed December 31, 1995) **Arcadia** (173). By Tom Stoppard. Opened March 30, 1995. (Closed August 27, 1995)

*How to Succeed in Business Without Really Trying** (505). Revival of the musical based on the book by Shepherd Mead; book by Abe Burrows, Jack Weinstock and Willie Gilbert; music and lyrics by Frank Loesser. Opened March 23, 1995.

*Defending the Caveman** (361). Solo performance by Rob Becker; written by Rob Becker. Opened March 26, 1995.

Having Our Say (308). By Emily Mann; adapted from the book by Sarah L. Delany and A. Elizabeth Delany with Amy Hill Hearth. Opened April 6, 1995. (Closed December 31, 1995)

A Month in the Country (53). Revival of the play by Ivan Turgenev; translated by Richard Freeborn. Opened April 25, 1995. (Closed June 10, 1995)

Indiscretions (Les Parents Terribles) (221). Revival of the play by Jean Cocteau; translated by Jeremy Sams. Opened April 27, 1995. (Closed November 4, 1995)

The Rose Tattoo (73). Revival of the play by Tennessee Williams. Opened April 30, 1995. (Closed July 2, 1995)

Hamlet (91). Revival of the play by William Shakespeare. Opened May 2, 1995. (Closed July 22, 1995)

PLAYS PRODUCED JUNE 1, 1995—MAY 31, 1996

Buttons on Broadway (33). Solo performance by Red Buttons. Produced by Don Gregory at the Ambassador Theater. Opened June 8, 1995. (Closed July 16, 1995)

Musical director, Bryan Louiselle; scenery, Nancy Thun; lighting, Ken Billington; sound, Lewis Mead; production stage manager, J.P. Elins; stage manager, K. Dale White; press, Bill Evans Associates, Terry M. Lilly, Tom D'Ambrosio.

Songs and stand-up comedy in the Red Buttons style, presented in two parts.

Lincoln Center Theater. 1994–95 Broadway schedule concluded with **Chronicle of a Death Foretold** (37). Musical with book adapted by Graciela Daniele and Jim Lewis from the novel by Gabriel Garcia Marquez; music by Bob Telson; additional material by Michael John LaChiusa. Produced by Lincoln Center Theater, Andre Bishop and Bernard Gersten directors, by arrangement with INTAR Hispanic American Arts Center, at the Plymouth Theater, Opened June 15, 1995. (Closed July 16, 1995)

Santiago Nasar	George de la Pena	Bayardo San Roman	Alexandre Proia
Cristo	Julio Monge	Clotilde	Tonya Pinkins
Placida	Yolande Bavan	Flora	Lisa Leguillou
Victoria	Myra Lucretia Taylor	Faustino	Lazaro Perez
Divina	Monica McSwain	Xius	Norberto Kerner
Angela Vicario	Saundra Santiago	Col. Aponte	Nelson Roberto Landrieu
Pura Vicario	Ivonne Coll	Father Amador	Jaime Tirelli
Pablo Vicario	Luis Perez	Margot	Rene M. Ceballos
Pedro Vicario	Gregory Mitchell	Maria	Denise Faye

Orchestra: Steve Sandberg conductor, piano, synthesizer; Bob Telson piano, synthesizer; Gary Haase bass (acoustic/electric); Dominic Kanza guitar; Dan Reagan trombone; Yury Lemeshev accordion; Roger Squitero, Cyro Baptista percussion; Leroy Clouden drums.

Understudies: Mr. de la Pena—Edgard Gallardo, Julio Monge; Mr. Monge—Colton Green, Edgard Gallardo; Miss Bavan—Susan Pilar, Marina Chapa; Miss Taylor—Eyan Williams, Susan Pilar; Miss McSwain—Marianne Filali, Marina Chapa; Miss Santiago—Marina Chapa, Susan Pilar; Miss Coll—Rene M. Ceballos, Eyan Williams; Messrs. Luis Perez, Mitchell, Proia—Edgard Gallardo, Colton Green; Miss Pinkins—Eyan Williams, Susan Pilar; Miss Leguillou—Marianne Filali, Marina Chapa; Mr. Lazaro Perez—Colton Green, Edouard DeSoto; Mr. Kerner—Edouard DeSoto, Colton Green; Mr. Landrieu—Edouard DeSoto, Edgard Gallardo; Mr. Tirelli—Edouard DeSoto, Nelson Roberto Landrieu; Misses Ceballos, Faye—Marianne Filali, Eyan Williams.

Conceived, directed and choreographed by Graciela Daniele; musical direction and dance arrangements, Steve Sandberg; scenery, Christopher Barreca; costumes, Toni-Leslie James; lighting, Jules Fisher, Beverly Emmons; sound, Tony Meola; arrangements, Bob Telson; associate choreographer, Willie Rosario; casting, Daniel Swee; production stage manager, Leslie Loeb; stage managers, Valerie Lau-Kee, Robert Castro; press, Merle Debuskey, Susan Chicoine, Owen Levy.

Time: The past and present. Place: An isolated Latin American town. The play was presented without intermission.

Concentrating more on dance than song (there are no song numbers listed in the program), the musical moves back and forth in time to examine a murder, its causes and its consequences.

Roundabout Theater Company. Schedule of five revivals. **The Play's the Thing** (45). By Ferenc Molnar; adapted by P.G. Wodehouse. Opened July 9, 1995. (Closed August 17, 1995) **Company** (68). Musical with book by George Furth; music and lyrics by Stephen Sondheim. Opened October 5, 1995. (Closed December 3, 1995) **The Father** (52). By August Strindberg; adapted by Richard Nelson. Opened January 11, 1996. (Closed February 25, 1996) **The Night of the Iguana** (74). By Tennessee Williams. Opened March 21, 1996. (Closed May 19, 1996) And *A Thousand Clowns* by Herb Gardner scheduled to open 7/14/96. Produced by Roundabout Theater Company, Todd Haimes artistic director, Ellen Richard general manager, Gene Feist founding director, at Criterion Center Stage Right.

THE PLAY'S THE THING

Mansky ....Joe Grifasi	Ilona Szabo ....J. Smith-Cameron
Sandor Turai ....Peter Frechette	Almady ....Jeff Weiss
Albert Adam ....Alec Phoenix	Mr. Mell ....Keith Reddin
Johann Dwornitschek .... Paul Benedict	

Standbys: Messrs. Frechette, Weiss—Jonathan Bustle; Messrs. Grifasi, Benedict—George Hosmer; Messrs. Phoenix, Reddin—Jared Reed; Miss Smith-Cameron—Rebecca Wisocky.

Directed by Gloria Muzio; scenery, Stephan Olson; costumes, Jess Goldstein; lighting, Peter Kaczorowski; sound, Douglas J. Cuomo; casting, Pat McCorkle; production stage manager, Denise Yaney; press, Boneau/Bryan-Brown, Susanne Tighe.

Time: A Saturday in summer. Place: A room in a castle on the Italian Riviera. Act I: 3 a.m. Act II: 6 a.m. Act III: 7:30 p.m.

The last major New York revival of record of *The Play's the Thing* took place on Broadway 4/28/48 for 244 performances.

COMPANY

Robert .... Boyd Gaines	Amy ....Veanne Cox
Sarah ....Kate Burton	Paul .... Danny Burstein
Harry ....Robert Westenberg	Joanne .... Debra Monk
Susan ....Patricia Ben Peterson	Larry .... Timothy Landfield
Peter ....Jonathan Dokuchitz	Marta ....La Chanze
Jenny ....Diana Canova	Kathy ....Charlotte d'Amboise
David ....John Hillner	April ....Jane Krakowski

Orchestra: David Loud conductor, piano; James Moore associate conductor, keyboard; Les Scott, Dennis Anderson, John Winder woodwinds; Stu Sataloff trumpet; Bruce Bonvissuto trombone; Robert Renino bass; Bruce Doctor percussion.

Standbys: Messrs. Gaines, Dokuchitz, Burstein—James Chow; Messrs. Westenberg, Hillner, Landfield—Andy Umberger; Misses Ben Peterson, Canova, La Chanze, Krakowski—Colleen Fitzpatrick; Misses Cox, d'Amboise, Krakowski—Nancy Hess.

Directed by Scott Ellis; musical staging, Rob Marshall; musical direction, David Loud; scenery, Tony Walton; costumes, William Ivey Long; lighting, Peter Kaczorowski; sound, Tony Meola; orchestrations, Jonathan Tunick; projections, Wendall K. Harrington; musical coordinator, Seymour Red Press; fight direction, David Leong; assistant choreographer, Sarah Miles; casting, Pat McCorkle; production stage manager, Lori M. Doyle; stage manager, Matthew T. Mundinger.

Place: New York City.

Company was first produced on Broadway by Harold Prince 4/26/70 for 705 performances and was named a Best Play of its season and won the New York Drama Critics Circle and Tony Awards for best musical. This is its first major New York revival.

The list of musical numbers in *Company* appears on pages 328–9 of *The Best Plays of 1969–70.* The number "Marry Me a Little," the finale of Act II in the present production, is not listed among the numbers in the 1970 production.

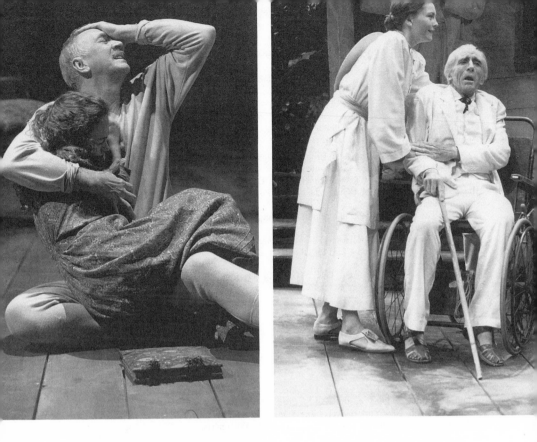

DUETS AT THE ROUNDABOUT—*Above left*, Frank Langella and Angela Bettis in Richard Nelson's new adaptation of Strindberg's *The Father*; *above right*, Cherry Jones and Lawrence McCauley in Tennessee Williams's *The Night of the Iguana*; *below*, Paul Benedict and Peter Frechette in the P.G. Wodehouse adaptation of Ferenc Molnar's *The Play's the Thing*

THE FATHER

The Captain	Frank Langella	Laura	Gail Strickland
The Pastor	Ivar Brogger	Doctor Ostermark	Tom Beckett
Orderly	William Verderber	Old Margaret	Irene Dailey
Nojd	Garret Dillahunt	Bertha	Angela Bettis

Understudies: Messrs. Langella, Brogger—William Verderber; Messrs. Verderber, Dillahunt, Beckett—Kyle Fabel; Miss Bettis—Stephanie A. Jones.

Directed by Clifford Williams; scenery, John Lee Beatty; costumes, Martin Pakledinaz; lighting, Kenneth Posner; sound, John Gromada; casting, Pat McCorkle; production stage manager, Jay Adler; stage manager, Charles Kindl.

Place: The Captain's house in a remote Swedish province. The play was presented in three acts with no intermission.

The last major New York revival of *The Father* was by Circle in the Square on Broadway in the Harry G. Carlson translation 4/2/81 for 29 performances.

THE NIGHT OF THE IGUANA

Maxine Faulk	Marsha Mason	Frau Fahrenkopf	Betsy Freytag
Pancho	Alfredo MacDonald	Hank	Scott Jaeck
Pedro	Diego Lopez	Judith Fellowes	Mary Beth Fisher
Rev. T. Lawrence Shannon	William Petersen	Hannah Jelkes	Cherry Jones
Hilda	Sinje Ollen	Charlotte Goodall	Paula Cale
Wolfgang	Lawrence Woshner	Nonno	Lawrence McCauley
Herr Fahrenkopf	Dan Frick	Jake Latta	Dennis Predovic

Directed by Robert Falls; scenery, Loy Arcenas; costumes, Susan Hilferty; lighting, James F. Ingalls; sound, Richard Woodbury; casting, Pat McCorkle; production stage manager, Ellen Richard.

The last major New York revival of *The Night of the Iguana* was by Circle in the Square on Broadway 6/26/88 for 81 performances. The play was presented in two parts.

*Moon Over Buffalo (276). By Ken Ludwig. Produced by Elizabeth Williams, Heidi Landesman, DLT Entertainment Ltd., Hal Luftig and Jujamcyn Theaters at the Martin Beck Theater. Opened October 1, 1995.

Ethel	Jane Connell	Charlotte Hay	Carol Burnett
Rosalind	Randy Graff	Eileen	Kate Miller
Howard	Andy Taylor	Paul	Dennis Ryan
George Hay	Philip Bosco	Richard Maynard	James Valentine

Standbys: Messrs. Bosco, Valentine—Richard Poe; Misses Burnett, Connell—Jane Trese; Misses Graff, Miller—Lannyl Stephens; Messrs. Taylor, Ryan—David Beach.

Directed by Tom Moore; scenery, Heidi Landesman; costumes, Bob Mackie; lighting, Ken Billington; sound, Tony Meola; fight staging, B.H. Barry; associate producers, Jack Cullen, James J. Jundt; casting, Johnson-Liff Associates; production stage manager, Steven Beckler; stage manager, Tom Capps; press, Boneau/Bryan-Brown, Adrian Bryan-Brown, Bob Fennell, Jackie Green, James Sapp.

Time and place: Onstage and backstage at the Erlanger Theater, Buffalo, N.Y., 1953. Act I: A mid-morning in June. Act II, Scene 1: Two hours later. Scene 2: Immediately following. Scene 3: Two hours later.

Comedy, a husband-and-wife acting team, past their prime, on tour in repertory.

Lynn Redgrave and Robert Goulet replaced Carol Burnett and Philip Bosco 3/5/96. Miss Burnett and Mr. Bosco replaced Miss Redgrave and Mr. Goulet 4/17/96.

*Circle in the Square. Schedule of five revivals. **Garden District** (31). Program of two plays by Tennessee Williams: *Something Unspoken* and *Suddenly Last Summer*. Opened October 10, 1995. (Closed November 5, 1995) **Holiday** (49). By Philip Barry. Opened December 3, 1995. (Closed January 14, 1996) **Bus Stop** (29). By William Inge. Opened February 22, 1996. (Closed March 17, 1996) ***Tartuffe: Born Again** (2). By Molière; adapted by Freyda Thomas. Opened May 30, 1996. And *Hughie* by Eugene O'Neill scheduled to open 7/25/96. Produced by Circle in the Square, Theodore Mann and Josephine R. Abady co-artistic directors, at Circle in the Square Theater.

GARDEN DISTRICT

Something Unspoken

Cornelia ....Myra Carter
Grace ....Pamela Payton-Wright
   Directed by Theodore Mann.
   Time: A late morning in November 1936.
Place: A house in the Garden District of New Orleans. The play was presented in two parts.

Suddenly Last Summer

Mrs. Venable ....Elizabeth Ashley

Dr. Cukrowicz ....Victor Slezak
Miss Foxhill ....Peggy Cosgrave
Mrs. Holly ....Celia Weston
George Holly .... Mitchell Lichtenstein
Catharine Holly ....Jordan Baker
Sister Felicity .... Leslie Lyles
   Directed by Harold Scott.
   Time: 1936, a late afternoon in spring. Place: The Garden District of New Orleans. The play was presented without intermission.

BOTH PLAYS: Standby: Misses Ashley, Payton-Wright—Maeve McGuire. Understudies: Miss Baker—Orlagh Cassidy; Misses Carter, Weston, Lyles—Peggy Cosgrave; Miss Cosgrave—Maeve McGuire; Messrs. Slezak, Lichtenstein—Neil Maffin.

Scenery and costumes, Zack Brown; lighting, Marc B. Weiss; composer, Kevin Farrell; sound, Bruce Cameron; dialects, K.C. Ligon; style and movement, Loyd Williamson; fight choreography, B.H. Barry; casting, Rosalie Joseph; production stage manager, Linda Harris; stage manager, Cheryl Zoldowski; press, Jeffrey Richards Associates, Kevin Rehac, Irene Gandy.

Garden District was first presented off Broadway during the 1957–58 season. *Suddenly Last Summer* was revived on an Equity Library Theater off-Broadway bill 10/30/64 with Arthur Miller's *A Memory of Two Mondays*. This is its first Broadway production.

HOLIDAY

Julia Seton .... Kim Raver
Henry ....Jim Oyster
Charles ....Reese Madigan
Johnny Case .... Tony Goldwyn
Linda Seton ....Laura Linney
Ned Seton ....Reg Rogers

Edward Seton .... Tom Lacy
Seton Cram ....Rod McLachlan
Laura Cram ....Becca Lish
Nick Potter .... Michael Countryman
Susan Potter ....Anne Lange

Understudies: Messrs. Goldwyn, Countryman, Madigan, Oyster—Christopher Cousins; Misses Linney, Lange—Allison Daugherty; Messrs. Rogers, McLachlan—Reese Madigan; Mr. Lacy—Jim Oyster; Misses Raver, Lish—Kim Sebastian.

Directed by David Warren; scenery, Derek McLane; costumes, Martin Pakledinaz; lighting, Donald Holder; sound and score, John Gromada; style and movement, Loyd Williamson; casting, Rosalie Joseph; production stage manager, Frank Marino; stage manager, Lori Lundquist.

Time: December 1928. Place: A room on the third floor and a room on the top floor of Edward Seton's house in New York City. The play was presented in three parts.

The last major New York revival of *Holiday* was in New Phoenix repertory on Broadway 12/26/73 for 28 performances.

BUS STOP

Elma Duckworth .... Patricia Dunnock
Grace Hoyland .... Kelly Bishop
Will Masters ....Scott Sowers
Cherie .... Mary-Louise Parker

Dr. Gerald Lyman ....Ron Perlman
Carl ....Michael Cullen
Virgil Blessing ....Larry Pine
Bo Decker .... Billy Crudup

Directed by Josephine R. Abady; scenery, Hugh Landwehr; costumes, Linda Fisher; lighting, Dennis Parichy; sound, Tom Gould; fight choreography, B.H. Barry; dialects, K.C. Ligon; casting, Rosalie Joseph.

Place: A street-corner restaurant in a small town about 30 miles west of Kansas City. Act I: A night in early March, 1 a.m. Act II: Early morning, about 5 a.m.

Bus Stop was first produced on Broadway March 2, 1955 for 478 performances. This is its first major New York revival of record.

TARTUFFE: BORN AGAIN

Tartuffe	John Glover	Maryann	Jane Krakowski
Cleante	Richard Bekins	Orgon	David Schramm
Mrs. Pernell	Patricia Conolly	Valere	T. Scott Cunningham
Elmire	Haviland Morris	Mrs. De Salle	Susie Duff
Dorine	Alison Fraser	Visitor	Peter Rini
Damis	Kevin Dewey	Production Assistant	Jeanne Hime

Understudies: Misses Morris, Fraser—Susie Duff; Miss Krakowski—Jeanne Hime; Messrs. Schramm, Rini—Tom Ligon; Messrs. Cunningham, Dewey—Peter Rini; Misses Conolly, Duff—Angela Pietropinto.

Directed by David Saint; scenery, Allen Moyer; costumes, Jess Goldstein; lighting, Jeff Davis; sound, John Kilgore; video, Ben Rubin; dialects, K.C. Ligon; casting, Rosalie Joseph; production stage manager, Frank Marino; stage manager, Robert Bennett; press, Jeffrey Richards Associates.

Place: Orgon's television studio in the American South.

Tartuffe as a TV evangelist in this adaptation. The last major New York revival of *Tartuffe* was by the Acting Company in the Richard Wilbur translation 4/26/83 for 4 performances.

Patti LuPone on Broadway (46). Solo performance by Patti LuPone; written by Jeffrey Richman. Produced by Jujamcyn Theaters, Paul Libin producing director, Jack Viertel creative director, at the Water Kerr Theater. Opened October 12, 1995. (Closed November 25, 1995)

The Mermen: Byron Motley, Josef Powell, Gene Van Buren, John West.

Musicians: Dick Gallagher conductor; Andrew Lippa, associate conductor, synthesizer; Rodney Jones guitar; Steve Bartosik drums; Bill Ellison bass; Mark Sherman percussion; Tom Christensen woodwinds.

Conceived and directed by Scott Wittman; musical direction, Dick Gallagher; musical arrangements, John McDaniel; lighting, John Hastings; additional musical arrangements, Steven D. Bowen, Dick Gallagher, Glen Roven, Marc Shaiman, Jonathan Tunick; music coordinator, John Monaco; production stage manager, George Darveris; press, Philip Rinaldi, James Morrison.

Concert of theater songs, many of them originated by Miss LuPone, introduced with anecdotes and accompanied by a male quartet. The performance was presented in two parts, Act I being a collection of standard, novelty and pop songs and Act II largely made up of hits from her own shows.

MUSICAL NUMBERS included "I Get a Kick Out of You," "Always," "Ain't Nobody Here But Us Chickens," "Moonshine Lullaby," "Calling You," "Get Here," "Surabaya Johnny," "I'm a Stranger Here Myself," "It Never Was You," "My Ship," "Lonely Heart," "Being Alive," "Looking for Love on Broadway," "Sleepy Man," "Don't Cry for Me Argentina," "Meadowlark," "As Long as He Needs Me," "I Dreamed a Dream," "Bewitched, Bothered and Bewildered," "Anything Goes," "As if We Never Said Goodbye."

Hello, Dolly! (118). Revival of the musical based on the play *The Matchmaker* by Thornton Wilder; book by Michael Stewart; music and lyrics by Jerry Herman; original production directed and choreographed by Gower Champion. Produced by Manny Kladitis, Magic Promotions and Theatricals, Pace Theatrical Group Inc. and Jon B. Platt at the Lunt-Fontanne Theater. Opened October 19, 1995. (Closed January 28, 1996)

Mrs. Dolly Gallagher Levi	Carol Channing	Minnie Fay	Lori Ann Mahl
Ernestina	Monica M. Wemitt	Irene Molloy	Florence Lacey
Ambrose Kemper	James Darrah	Mrs. Rose	Elizabeth Green
Horse	Sharon Moore, Michele Tibbitts	Rudolph	Steve Pudenz
Horace Vandergelder	Jay Garner	Stanley	Julian Brightman
Ermengarde	Christine DeVito	Judge	Bill Bateman
Cornelius Hackl	Michael DeVries	Court Clerk	Halden Michaels
Barnaby Tucker	Cory English		

Towspeople, Waiters, etc.: John Bantay, Desta Barbieri, Bill Bateman, Kimberley Bellmann, Bruce Blanchard, Stephen Bourneuf, Julian Brightman, Holly Cruikshank, Simone Gee, Jason Gillman, Milica Govich, Elizabeth Green, Donald Ives, Dan LoBuono, Jim Madden, Halden Michaels, Sharon Moore, Michael Quinn, Robert Randle, Mitch Rosengarten, Mary Setrakian, Clarence M. Sheridan, Randy Slovacek, Roger Preston Smith, Ashley Stover, Michele Tibbitts.

Swings: Kevin M. Burrows, Jennifer Joan Joy, John Salvatore, Matthew A. Sipress.

Orchestra: Jack Everly conductor; Lawrence Feldman, Robert Keller, Bill Meade, Frank Santigata reeds; Larry Pyatt, Jeff Parke, David Rogers trumpet; Dale Kirkland, Jack Schatz trombone; Masako Yanagita concert master; Ann Labin, Carlos Villa, Debbie Wong, Elizabeth Chang, Claudia Hafir-Tondi, Robert Lawrence violin; Daniel Miller, Ellen Westerman cello; Jeff Ganz bass; Joseph DeLuca drums; Ian Finkel percussion; Lise Nadeau harp; Steven Bargonetti guitar; Richard Riskin keyboard, assistant conductor.

Standby: Miss Channing—Florence Lacey. Understudies: Mr. Garner—Steve Pudenz; Miss Lacey—Mary Setrakian; Mr. DeVries—Jim Madden; Miss Mahl—Christine DeVito; Mr. English—Julian Brightman; Mr, Darrah—Dan LoBuono; Miss DeVito—Michele Tibbitts; Miss Wemitt—Elizabeth Green; Mr. Bateman—Halden Michaels; Messrs. Pudenz, Michaels—Roger Preston Smith; Miss Green—Milica Govich; Mr. Brightman—Matthew A. Sipress.

Directed and staged by Lee Roy Reams; musical direction, Jack Everly; assistant choreographer, Bill Bateman; scenery, Oliver Smith; costumes, Jonathan Bixby; lighting, Ken Billington; sound, Peter J. Fitzgerald; musical supervision, Tim Stella; orchestrations, Phillip J. Lang; dance arrangements, Peter Howard; scenic supervision, Rosaria Sinisi; casting, Mark Reiner; production stage manager, Thomas P. Carr; stage manager, Jim Semmelman; press, Boneau/Bryan-Brown, Dennis Crowley.

The last major New York revival of *Hello, Dolly!* took place on Broadway, starring Carol Channing in the Houston Grand Opera production, 3/5/78 for 145 performances.

The list of scenes and musical numbers in *Hello, Dolly!* appears on page 320 of *The Best Plays of 1963–64* and page 332 of *The Best Plays of 1975–76*.

Swinging on a Star (97). Musical revue written by Michael Leeds; music by various authors (see listing below); lyrics by Johnny Burke. Produced by Richard Seader, Mary Burke Kramer, Paul B. Berkowsky and Angels of the Arts at the Music Box. Opened October 22, 1995. (Closed January 14, 1996)

ACT I

Speakeasy—Chicago
Waiter .... Michael McGrath
Mame .... Terry Burrell
Reginald .... Lewis Cleale

Cleo .... Alvaleta Guess
Jeannie .... Denise Faye
Flora .... Kathy Fitzgerald
Ben .... Eugene Fleming

MUSICAL NUMBERS: "You're Not the Only Oyster in the Stew" (music by Harold Spina)—Cleo, Jeannie, Flora; "Chicago Style" (music by Jimmy Van Heusen)—Ben, Jeannie, Flora, Waiter; "Ain't It a Shame About Mame" (music by James Monaco)—Ben, Mame; "What's New" (music by Robert Haggart)—Jeannie; "Doctor Rhythm" (Monaco)—Cleo, Ben.

Choreography, Kathleen Marshall, Eugene Fleming.

Depression—The Bowery
Homeless Man .... Lewis Cleale

Polish Gentleman .... Michael McGrath
Housewife .... Kathy Fitzgerald

Street People: Alvaleta Guess, Denise Faye, Eugene Fleming, Terry Burrell. Suitors: Lewis Cleale, Michael McGrath, Eugene Fleming.

MUSICAL NUMBERS: "Pennies From Heaven" (music by Arthur Johnston)—Homeless Man; "When Stanislaus Got Married" (Van Heusen)—Polish Gentleman, Street People; "His Rocking Horse Ran Away" (Van Heusen)—Housewife; "Annie Doesn't Live Here Anymore" (lyrics by Burke, Young & Spina)—Suitors.

Radio Show—New York City
Announcer .... Lewis Cleale
Buddy .... Michael McGrath

Betty .... Denise Faye
Vicky Voyay .... Kathy Fitzgerald

Burkettes: Eugene Fleming, Alvaleta Guess, Terry Burrell.

MUSICAL NUMBERS: "Annie Doesn't Live Here Anymore" (Reprise)—Buddy, Betty, Announcer, Burkettes; "Scatterbrain" (by Burke, Kean, Bean & Masters)—Buddy; "One, Two, Button Your Shoe" (Johnston)—Betty, Buddy; "Whoopsie Daisy Day" (music by Burke)—Announcer, Burkettes; "What Does It Take to Make You Take to Me?" (Van Heusen)—Vicky Voyay; "Irresistible" (Spina)—Announcer, Vicky Voyay, Burkettes; "An Apple for the Teacher" (Johnston)—Company.

USO Show—The Pacific Islands		
Emcee	Michael McGrath	
Buzz Albright	Eugene Fleming	
Miss South Dakota	Kathy Fitzgerald	

Miss North Carolina	Denise Faye
Miss Rheingold	Terry Burrell
Lena George	Alvaleta Guess
Eddie	Lewis Cleale

MUSICAL NUMBERS: "Thank Your Lucky Stars and Stripes" (Van Heusen)—Emcee, Buzz; "Personality" (Van Heusen)—Misses South Dakota, North Carolina, Rheingold; "There's Always the Blues" (music by Joe Bushkin)—Lena; "Polka Dots and Moonbeams" (Van Heusen)—Eddie; "Swinging on a Star" (Van Heusen)—Company; "Thank Your Lucky Stars and Stripes" (Reprise)—Company.

ACT II

Ballroom—Hotel Roosevelt, Akron, Ohio	
Manager	Lewis Cleale
Coat Check Girl	Denise Faye
Waiter	Eugene Fleming

Vocalist	Terry Burrell
Man	Michael McGrath
Date	Kathy Fitzgerald
Woman Alone	Alvaleta Guess

MUSICAL NUMBERS: "Don't Let That Moon Get Away" (Monaco)—Waiter; "All You Want to Do Is Dance" (Johnston), "You Danced With Dynamite" (Van Heusen)—Date, Man; "Imagination" (Van Heusen)—Vocalist, Waiter, Coat Check Girl; "It Could Happen to You" (Van Heusen)—Woman Alone.

Road To—Paramount Studios, Hollywood	
Bing	Lewis Cleale
Bob	Michael McGrath
Dorothy	Kathy Fitzgerald

Sheik	Eugene Fleming
Girls	Denise Faye, Terry Burrell
Southern Woman	Alvaleta Guess

MUSICAL NUMBERS: "Road to Morocco" (Van Heusen)—Bing, Bob; "Apalachicola" (Van Heusen)—Bing, Bob, Dorothy; "Ain't Got a Dime to My Name" (Van Heusen)—Bing, Bob; "You Don't Have to Know the Language" (Van Heusen)—Bing, Bob, Girls; "Going My Way" (Van Heusen)—Bing; "Shadows on the Swanee" (lyrics by Burke & Young, Spina)—Southern Woman, Bing, Bob, Dorothy; "Pakistan" (Van Heusen)—Sheik, Dorothy, Bing, Bob; "Road to Morocco" (Reprise)—Bing, Bob, Dorothy.

Special advisor for "Road To" sequence—Dorothy Lamour.

Starlight Supper Club—Manhattan, the Present

Lovers: Denise Faye & Lewis Cleale, Alvaleta Guess & Michael McGrath, Terry Burrell & Eugene Fleming, Kathy Fitzgerald.

MUSICAL NUMBERS: "But Beautiful" (Van Heusen)—Burrell; "Like Someone in Love" (Van Heusen)—Faye; "Moonlight Becomes You" (Van Heusen)—Cleale; "If Love Ain't There" (Burke)—McGrath; "Sunday, Monday or Always" (Van Heusen)—Guess; "Misty" (Garner)—Fleming; "Here's That Rainy Day" (Van Heusen)—Fitzgerald; "Pennies From Heaven" (Reprise)—Company; "Swinging on a Star" (Reprise)—Company.

Orchestra: Barry Levitt conductor, piano; Ron Drotos associate conductor, synthesizer; Mark Minkler bass; Bill Easley saxophone; Gary Guzio trumpet; Brian Grice drums, percussion.

Understudies: Deborah Burrell-Cleveland, Naomi Naughton, Joe Joyce, Frantz Hall.

Directed by Michael Leeds; musical direction, orchestrations and vocal arrangements, Barry Levitt; choreography, Kathleen Marshall; scenery, James Youmans; costumes, Judy Dearing; lighting, Richard Nelson; sound, T. Richard Fitzgerald; dance music arrangements, Peter Howard; additional musical arrangements, Ron Drotos; video and projections, Batwin + Robin Productions; associate producers, David A. Rocker, Eleanor Gimon; casting, Pat McCorkle/Tim Sutton; production stage manager, Mary Porter Hall; stage manager, R. Wade Jackson; press, Keith Sherman & Associates, Jim Byk, Stuart Ginsberg.

Subtitled The Johnny Burke Musical, a showcase of the late lyricist's song numbers in a nostalgic revue context, previously presented in regional theater at the George Street Playhouse, New Brunswick, N.J. and the Goodspeed Opera House, East Haddam, Conn.

The Tempest (70). Transfer from off Broadway of the revival of the play by William Shakespeare. Produced by the Joseph Papp Public Theater/New York Shakespeare Festival, George C. Wolfe producer, at the Broadhurst Theater. Opened November 1, 1995. (Closed December 31, 1995)

Shipmaster	Avery Glymph	Caliban	Teagle F. Bougere
Boatswain	Adam Dannheisser	Ferdinand	Paul Whitthorne
Alonso	Miguel Perez	Adrian	Neal Huff
Gonzalo	MacIntyre Dixon	Trinculo	Ross Lehman
Sebastian	Graham Winton	Stephano	Mario Cantone
Antonio	Nestor Serrano	Iris	Midori Nakamura
Miranda	Carrie Preston	Ceres	Hilary Chaplain
Prospero	Patrick Stewart	Juno	Sybyl Walker
Ariel	Aunjanue Ellis		

Kuroko (Kabuki term for invisible onstage actors): Hilary Chaplain, Midori Nakamura, Sybyl Walker, David Costabile, Avery Glymph, Michael McGuigan, Seamas L. O'Brien, Adam Dannheisser, Marin Hinkle, Rainn Wilson, Michelle M. Robinson.

Musicians: Carlos Valdez, Moussa Diabate, Eric Kivnick percussion; Heather Paauwe percussion, violin; Curtis Woodside recorder, viola Da Gamba.

Understudies: Mr. Stewart—Miguel Perez; Miss Preston—Marin Hinkle, Sybyl Walker; Miss Ellis—Sybyl Walker, Midori Nakamura; Mr. Bougere—Avery Glymph; Mr. Whitthorne—Neal Huff, Avery Glymph; Messrs. Perez, Winton—Adam Dannheisser; Messrs. Dixon, Lehman—David Costabile; Mr. Serrano—Rainn Wilson, Neal Huff; Messrs. Cantone, Dannheisser, Glymph—Rainn Wilson; Mr. Huff—Michael McGuigan; Misses Nakamura, Chaplain, Walker—Michelle M. Robinson.

Directed by George C. Wolfe; scenery, Riccardo Hernandez; costumes, Toni-Leslie James; lighting, Paul Gallo; sound, Dan Moses Schreier; masks and puppets, Barbara Pollitt; composers, Carlos Valdez, Dan Moses Schreier; choreographer, Hope Clarke; artistic producer, Rosemarie Tichler; executive producer, Joey Parnes; associate producers, Kevin Kline, Morgan Jenness, Wiley Hausam; casting, Jordan Thaler, Heidi Griffiths; production stage manager, Bonnie Panson; stage managers, Buzz Cohen, Lisa Buxbaum; press, Carol R. Fineman, Thomas V. Naro.

This production of *The Tempest* was previously produced at the Delacorte Theater in Central Park in New York Shakespeare Festival's Shakespeare Marathon 6/22/95–7/19/95 for 22 performances; see its entry in the Plays Produced Off Broadway section of this volume.

*Victor/Victoria (249). Musical with book by Blake Edwards; music by Henry Mancini; lyrics by Leslie Bricusse; additional musical material by Frank Wildhorn. Produced by Blake Edwards, Tony Adams, John Scher, Endemol Theater Productions Inc. and Polygram Broadway Ventures Inc. at the Marquis Theater. Opened October 25, 1995.

Carroll Todd	Tony Roberts	Andre Cassell	Richard B. Shull
Richard Di Nardo	Michael Cripe	Jazz Singer	Devin Richards
Henri Labisse	Adam Heller	Norma Cassidy	Rachel York
Gregor; Juke	Casey Nicholaw	King Marchan	Michael Nouri
Mme. Roget; Chambermaid	Jennifer Smith	Squash (Mr. Bernstein)	Gregory Jbara
Victoria Grant	Julie Andrews	Street Singer	Tara O'Brien
Choreographer	Christopher Innvar	Sal Andretti	Ken Land
Miss Selmer	Cynthia Sophiea	Clam	Mark Lotito

Les Boys: Michael-Demby Cain, Angelo Fraboni, Darren Lee, Michael O'Donnell, Vince Pesce, Arte Phillips, Rocker Verastique. Jazz Hot Musicians: Michael-Demby Cain, Arte Phillips, Rocker Verastique. Jazz Hot Ensemble: Roxane Barlow, Caitlin Carter, Pascale Faye, Angelo Fraboni, Amy Heggins, Darren Lee, Aixa M. Rosario Medina, Casey Nicholaw, Michael O'Donnell, Cynthia Onrubia, Vince Pesce.

Louis Says Ensemble: Roxane Barlow, Michael-Demby Cain, Caitlin Carter, Pascale Faye, Angelo Fraboni, Amy Heggins, Darren Lee, Aixa M. Rosario Medina, Michael O'Donnell, Cynthia Onrubia, Vince Pesce, Arte Phillips, Devin Richards, Jennifer Smith, Cynthia Sophiea, Rocker Verastique. Apache Dancers: Angelo Fraboni, Darren Lee, Michael O'Donnell, Vince Pesce, Arte Phillips, Rocker Verastique. Norma's Girls: Roxane Barlow, Caitlin Carter, Pascale Faye, Amy Heggins, Aixa M. Rosario Medina, Cynthia Onrubia.

Victor/Victoria Ensemble: Roxane Barlow, Michael-Demby Cain, Caitlin Carter, Pascale Faye, Angelo Fraboni, Amy Heggins, Darren Lee, Aixa M. Rosario Medina, Tara O'Brien, Michael O'Donnell, Cynthia Onrubia, Vince Pesce, Arte Phillips, Devin Richards, Jennifer Smith, Rocker Verastique.

Orchestra: Ian Fraser conductor; Joseph Thalken associate conductor, keyboards; Dale Stucken-

THE TEMPEST—Carrie Preston (Miranda) and Patrick Stewart (Prospero) in the Broadway revival by New York Shakespeare Festival

bruck concertmaster; Rebekah Johnson, Karl Kawahara, Karen Karlsrud violin; Richard Spencer, Anne-Marie Bedney viola; Diane Barer cello; Richard Sarpola bass; Edward Joffe, Albert Regni, Dan Wieloszynski, Kenneth Dybisz, John Campo woodwinds; John Frosk, Danny Cahn, Bud Burridge trumpet; Jim Pugh, George Flynn trombone; Bob Rose guitar; Perry Cavari drums; Benjamin Herman percussion; Charlie Giordano accordion.

Standbys: Miss Andrews—Anne Runolfson; Mr. Roberts—Alex Wipf. Swings—Mark S. Hoebee, Elizabeth Mozer, Scott Taylor. Understudies: Miss Andrews—Tara O'Brien; Mr. Roberts—Ken Land; Mr. Nouri—Christopher Innvar; Miss York—Roxane Barlow, Caitlin Carter; Messrs. Jbara, Land—Mark Lotito; Mr. Heller—Casey Nicholaw; Mr. Cripe—Angelo Fraboni; Mr. Richards—Michael-Demby Cain; Miss O'Brien—Jennifer Smith.

Directed by Blake Edwards; musical direction and vocal arrangements, Ian Fraser; choreography, Rob Marshall; scenery, Robin Wagner; costumes, Willa Kim; lighting, Jules Fisher, Peggy Eisenhauer; sound, Peter Fitzgerald; orchestration, Billy Byers; dance and incidental music, David Krane; fight staging, B.H. Barry; music coordinator, John Miller; assistant director, Kirsten Sanderson; assistant choreographers, Cynthia Onrubia, Sarah Miles; executive producer, Robin De Levita; produced by Edwards-Adams Theatrical Inc., Metropolitan Theatrical Entertainment Inc.; co-producer, Jeff Rowland; associate producers, Joop Van Den Ende, Tina Vanderheyden, TDI, Ogden Entertainment; casting, Johnson-Liff Associates; production stage manager, Arturo E. Porazzi; stage manager, Bonnie L. Becker; press, Peter Cromarty.

Miss Andrews in a stage musical version of the role of a double impersonation—a woman masquerading as a man masquerading as a woman—which she created in the 1982 movie *Victor/Victoria,* written and directed by her husband Blake Edwards.

ACT I

Scene 4: Cassell's Nightclub
"Le Jazz Hot" .... Victor, Ensemble
Scene 5: Backstage at Cassell's
Scene 6: Left Bank Cafe
"The Tango" ....Victor, Norma
Scene 7: Paris hotel suites
"Paris Makes Me Horny"..Norma
"Crazy World" ....Victoria

ACT II

Scene 1: Cassell's Nightclub
"Louis Says" .... Victor, Ensemble
(music by Frank Wildhorn)
Scene 2: Victoria's dressing room
Scene 3: Paris hotel suites
"King's Dilemma" .... King
Scene 4: Chez Lui
"Apache"... Les Boys
"You & Me" .... Toddy, Victor
Scene 5: Small Square
"Paris by Night" (Reprise) .... Street Singer
Scene 6: Paris hotel suites
"Almost a Love Song".. King, Victoria
Scene 7: Chicago speakeasy
"Chicago, Illinois" .... Norma, Girls
Scene 8: Paris hotel suites
"Living in the Shadows" ....Victoria
(music by Frank Wildhorn)
Scene 9: Cassell's Nightclub
"Victor/Victoria" .... Victoria, Toddy, Company

Fool Moon (80). Revival of the comic performance program created by Bill Irwin and David Shiner. Produced by Pachyderm Entertainment in the James B. Freydberg, Kenneth Feld, Jeffrey Ash and Dori Berinstein production at the Ambassador Theater. Opened October 29, 1995. (Closed January 7, 1996)

With Bill Irwin, David Shiner.
The Red Clay Ramblers: Clay Buckner fiddle; Chris Frank piano, accordion, trombone, ukelele; Jack Herrick Bass, trumpet, mellophone, banjolin, tin whistle; Mark Roberts banjo, flute, oboe, tin whistle, keyboard; Rob Ladd drums, ukelele.
Scenery, Douglas Stein; costumes, Bill Kellard; lighting, Nancy Schertler; sound, Tom Morse; flying by Foy; producing associate, Nancy Harrington; associate producer, Daniel F. Kearns; production stage manager, Nancy Harrington; stage manager, Tami Toon; press, Boneau/Bryan-Brown, Chris Boneau.
The Irwin-Shiner active comedy performance of stunts, mime and sketches was first produced on Broadway 2/25/93 for 207 performances. The show was presented in two parts.

Sacrilege. (21). By Diane Shaffer. Produced by Alexander H. Cohen and Max Cooper at the Belasco Theater. Opened November 2, 1995. (Closed November 19, 1995)

Sister Grace .... Ellen Burstyn	Cardinal King .... Herb Foster
Crackerjack .... Brian Tarantina	Sister Virgilia .... Augusta Dabney
Ramon ....Giancarlo Esposito	Bishop Foley ....Reno Roop
Sister Joseph .... Jane Cecil	Monsignor Frigerio .... Frank Raiter
Father Jerome ....Damian Young	

Standby: Miss Burstyn—Carol Fox Prescott. Understudies: Messrs. Esposito, Tarantina—Al Espinosa; Misses Dabney, Cecil—June Squibb.

Directed by Don Scardino; scenery, John Arnone; costumes, Alvin Colt; lighting, Howell Binkley; sound, Aural Fixation; associate producer, Hildy Parks; casting, Meg Simon; production stage manager, Bob Borod; stage manager, Ira Mont; press, Merle Debuskey, Susan Chicoine, Patt Dale.

Time: Over the last six years. Place: In and around New York City and Washington, D.C. The play was presented in two parts.

A nun who works with the homeless provokes the Vatican by demanding that women be admitted to the priesthood.

*__Master Class__ (219). By Terrence McNally. Produced by Robert Whitehead & Lewis Allen and Spring Sirkin at the Golden Theater. Opened November 5, 1995.

Manny	David Loud	Stagehand	Michael Friel
Maria Callas	Zoe Caldwell	Sharon	Audra McDonald
Sophie	Karen Kay Cody	Tony	Jay Hunter Morris

Pianist—Emmanuel Weinstock.

Understudies: Misses Cody, McDonald—Lorraine Goodman; Mr. Loud—Gary Green; Messrs. Friel, Morris—Matthew Walley.

Directed by Leonard Foglia; scenery, Michael McGarty; costumes, Jane Greenwood; lighting, Brian MacDevitt; sound, Jon Gottlieb; musical supervision, David Loud; casting, Alan Filderman; production stage manager, Dianne Trulock; press, Bill Evans & Associates, Jim Randolph, Terry M. Lilly, Tom D'Ambrosio.

With time and place described simply as "A Master Class with Maria Callas," a detailed portrait of the volatile opera star as she coaches three students, one after the other, in the art of singing. The play was presented in two parts and was previously produced in regional theater by the Philadelphia Theater Company and the Mark Taper Forum, Los Angeles.

A Best Play; see page 103.

__Danny Gans on Broadway__ (6). Solo performance by Danny Gans. Produced by The Nederlander Organization at the Neil Simon Theater. Opened November 8, 1995. (Closed November 12, 1995)

The Band: Pat Caddick keyboards, vocals; Raphael Erardy drums, vocals; Tim Manfredi keyboards, guitar, vocals.

Lighting, John Featherstone, Fred Irish, Norm Schwab; sound, On Stage Audio, Tom Nicks; production supervisor, Chip Lightman; press, the Pete Sanders Group, Pete Sanders, Glenna Freedman.

Billed as The Man of Many Voices (more than 200 in his repertory) in a program of impressions and jokes. The show was presented without intermission.

__Radio City Music Hall.__ Schedule of two programs. __Radio City Christmas Spectacular__ (189). Spectacle originally conceived by Robert F. Jani. Opened November 8, 1995. (Closed January 7, 1996) __Radio City Spring Spectacular__ (27). Spectacle including *The Glory of Easter* pageant originally produced by Leon Leonidoff. Opened April 6, 1996. (Closed April 21, 1996) Produced by Radio City Productions, J. Deet Jonker executive producer, Howard Kolins producer, Penny Watkins-DiCamillo producer/director of Rockettes, at Radio City Music Hall.

RADIO CITY CHRISTMAS SPECTACULAR

Santa; Scrooge; Narrator	Charles Edward Hall	Ghost of Christmas Past	Heather McFadden, Melanie Malicote
Clara; Sarah Cratchit	Zoë Block, Lisa Rowe		
Bob Cratchit	Todd Eric Williams, Mason Roberts	Ghost of Christmas Present	Troy Magino, Lonnie Henderson
Scrooge's Nephew	Alan Bennett, Marty McDonough	Mrs. Cratchit; Mrs. Claus	Melinda Hull, Corinne Melançon
Marley's Ghost	Jim Testa, Brad Musgrove	Belinda Cratchit	Deborah Leamy, Keri Lee

Peter Cratchit ....Christopher Garneau, Graham Bowen	Thinker .... Kristoffer Elinder
	Tannenbaum .... Deborah Wilson
Tiny Tim ...... Michael Angarano, Ryan Tooher	Bartholomew ....Dwayne Wiseman
Poultry Man .... David Rosales, Dev Janki	Thumbs .... Leslie Stump-Vanderpool
Tinker .... Michael J. Gilden	Swings ....Steve Babiar, Marty Klebba

Skaters: Maradith Meyer, David Goodman, Laurie Welch, Randy Coyne.

Rockettes: Danielle Jolie Archer, Joy Andersen, Dottie Belle, Kiki Bennett, Linda Bloom, ElizaBeth Charney, Jennifer Clippinger, Eileen Collins, Renee Collins, Lillian Colon, Helen Conklin, Lori Ann Craig, Laurie Crochet, Kathy Dacey, Prudence Gray Demmler, MaryLee DeWitt-Baker, Joanne DiMauro, Susanne Doris, Rebecca Downing, Joyce Dwyer (Rockette Captain), Pamela Everett, Deanna Fiscus-Ford, Juliet Fischer, Jennifer Frankel, Toni Georgiana, Eileen Grace, Leslie Guy, Susan Heart, Cheryl Hebert, Vicki Hickerson, Ginny Hounsell, Stephanie James, Jennifer Jones, Debby Kole, Anne Kulakowski, LuAnn Leonard, Judy Little, Setsuko Maruhashi, Tabbatha Mays, Mary Frances McCatty, Patrice McConachie, Julie McDonald, Laraine Memola, MarQue Munday, Michelle O'Steen, Carol Toman Paracat, Kerri Pearsall, Renee Perry Lancaster, Laureen Repp Russell, Linda Riley D'Alessio, Lainie Sakakura, Maryellen Scilla, Jereme Sheehan, Trina Simon, Jane Sonderman, Terry Spano, Cindy Tennier, Karyn Tomzak, Rachel Tucker, Darlene Wendy, Kristin Willits, Elaine Winslow, Beth Woods, Eileen Woods, Deborah Yates, Ann Yocum, senior Rockette choreographer, Violet Holmes.

Ensemble: Barbara Angeline, Todd Bailey, James Allen Baker, Alan Bennett, Michelle Chase, Eric Christian, Michael Clowers, Kelly Cole, Randy Coyne, Nick Demos, John Dietrich, Carolyn Doherty, Jeff Elsass, Mark Esposito, Timothy Farley, Kevin Gaudin, David Goodman, Jamie Harris, Selena Harris, Lonnie Henderson, Mylinda Hull, Devanand Janki, Tom Kosis, Jennifer Krater, Deborah Leamy, Keri Lee, Ray Leeper, Michele Lynch, Bonnie Lynn, Troy Magino, Melanie Malicote, Joanne Manning, Michael McCaskey, Marty McDonough, Heather McFadden, Michael McGowan, Hannah Meadows, Corinne Melançon, Maradith Meyer, Stephanie Michels, Joan Mirabella, Brad Musgrove, Ginger Norman, Wendy Piper, Dirk J. Platzek, Mason Roberts, David Rosales, Tim Santos, Scott Spahr, Jim Testa, Amiee Turner, Laurie Welch, Todd Eric Williams, Christina Youngman.

Radio City Music Hall Orchestra: Don Pippin conductor; Bryan Louiselle associate conductor; Mary L. Rowell concertmaster; Andrea Andros, Carmine DeLeo, Michael Gillette, Joseph Kowalewski, Nannette Levi, Susan Lorentsen, Samuel Marder, Holly Ovenden violin; Barbara H. Vaccaro, Richard Spencer viola; Frank Levy, Sarah Carter cello; Dean Crandall bass; Kenneth Emery flute; Gerard J. Niewood, Richard Oatts, John M. Cipolla, Joshua Siegel, Kenneth Arzberger reeds; Russ Rizner, Nancy Schallert, French horn; Richard Raffio, Hollis Burridge, Zachary Schnek trumpet; John D. Schnupp, Thomas B. Olcott, Mark Johansen trombone; Andrew Rogers tuba; Thomas J. Oldakowski drums; Mario DeCiutiis, Maya Gunji percussion; Anthony Cesarano guitar; Susanna Nason, Henry Aronson piano; Jeanne Maier harp; George Wesner, Fred Davies organ.

Directed and choreographed by Robert Longbottom; musical direction, Don Pippin; scenery, Michael Hotopp; costumes, Gregg Barnes; lighting, Ken Billington, Jason Kantrowitz; associate producer, Steven Kelley; associate musical director, Bryan Louiselle; assistant choreographers, Tom Kosis, John MacInnis, John Dietrich; production stage manager, John Bonanni; stage managers, Tom Aberger, Tracy Crum, Travis DeCastro, Joel Elins, Doug Fogel, Mark Tynan; press, Annie Fort.

Special Credits: "Silent Night" arrangement by Percy Faith. Original Music—"Santa's Gonna Rock and Roll" and "I Can't Wait Till Christmas Day" music by Henry Krieger, lyrics by Bill Russell, arranged by Bryan Louiselle; "What Do You Want for Christmas" music by Larry Grossman, lyrics by Hal Hackady; "Christmas in New York" written by Billy Butt. Original orchestrations—Elman Anderson, Michael Gibson, Don Harper, Arthur Harris, Phillip J. Lang, Dick Lieb, Don Pippin, Danny Troob, Jonathan Tunick, Jim Tyler. Dance music arrangements: Marvin Laird, Peter Howard, Mark Hummel. Musical routines—Tony Fox, Bob Krogstad, Don Pippin, Don Smith. Writing—*Charles Dickens' A Christmas Carol* (play) by Charles Lisanby.

63d edition of the Music Hall's Christmas show, starring the Rockettes and including the traditional Nativity pageant, presented without intermission.

SCENES AND MUSICAL NUMBERS: Overture—Radio City Music Hall Orchestra (arrangement, Don Pippin, film score arrangement, Bryan Louiselle). Scene 1: Santa's Gonna Rock and Roll—Santa, Rockettes (choreography, Robert Longbottom; scenery, Michael Hotopp; costumes, Gregg Barnes; Rockette dance arrangement, Peter Howard). Scene 2: *The Nutcracker*—A Little Girl's Dream (choreography, Robert Longbottom; scenery, Michael Hotopp). Scene 3: The Parade of the Wooden Soldiers—Rockettes (restaged by Violet Holmes; scenery, Charles Lisanby). Scene 4: *Charles Dickens'*

A Christmas Carol (staged by Scott Salmon; scenery, Charles Lisanby). Scene 5: Christmas in New York—Rockettes, Orchestra, Ensemble (choreography, Marianne Selbert; Rockette choreography, Violet Holmes; scenery, Charles Lisanby; gowns and Rockette costumes, Pete Menefee). Scene 6: Ice Skating in the Plaza—Skaters. Scene 7: Santa's Toy Fantasy—Santa, Mrs. Claus, Elves (choreography, Scott Salmon, Linda Haberman; scenery, Charles Lisanby; costumes, Pete Menefee). Scene 8: Carol of the Bells—Rockettes, Ensemble (choreography, Scott Salmon; scenery, Charles Lisanby; costumes, Pete Menefee). Scene 9: The Living Nativity with One Solitary Life—"Silent Night," "O Little Town of Bethlehem," "The First Noel," "We Three Kings," "O Come All Ye Faithful," "Hark, the Herald Angels Sing" (restaged by Linda Lemac; scenery, Charles Lisanby; costumes, Frank Spencer). Jubilant, "Joy to the World"—Organ, Company.

RADIO CITY SPRING SPECTACULAR

Rabbit .... Dennis Callahan

Rockettes: Dottie Belle, Kiki Bennett, Julie Branam, Lillian Colon, Prudence Gray Demmler, MaryLee DeWitt-Baker, Susanne Doris, Rebecca Downing, Joyce Dwyer (Rockette Captain), Toni Georgiana, Eileen Grace, Susan Heart, Cheryl Hebert, Vicki Hickerson, Ginny Hounsell, Stephanie James, Jennifer Jones, Debby Kole, Anne Kulakowski, LuAnn Leonard, Judy Little, Mary Frances McCatty, Laraine Memola, Carol Toman Paracat, Kerri Pearsall, Renee Perry Lancaster, Laureen Repp Russell, Linda Riley-D'Alessio, Jereme Sheehan, Trina Simon, Jane Sonderman, Terry Spano, Leslie Stroud, Tracy Terstriep, Leigh-Anne Wenker, Darlene Wendy, Natalie Willes, Beth Woods, Eileen Woods. Senior Rockette choreographer: Violet Holmes.

Ensemble: Alan Bennett, Kevin M. Burrows, Michelle Chase, Michael Clowers, Lea Carmen Dellecave, Carolyn Doherty, Mamie Duncan-Gibbs, Kevin Gaudin, Chris Ghelfi, Peter Gregus, Lonnie Henderson, Shawnda James, Lenny Juliano, Carol Lee Meadows, Sharon Moore, Angela Piccinni, Keri Quinn, John Salvatore, Vincent Sandoval, Susan Taylor, Jim Testa, Kristin Tudor, Darius Williams, Christine Yasunaga. Swings: Barbara Angeline, Jim Osborne.

Brackney's Madcap Mutts: Tom Brackney, Bonnie Brackney.

Errol Manoff's Fantasy Factory: Geoffrey Bennett, Robert Johnson, Errol Manoff, Shawn Martin, Alejandro Zucchi.

Radio City Music Hall Orchestra: Don Pippin conductor; Bryan Louiselle associate conductor; Mary L. Rowell concertmaster; Andrea Andros, Carmine DeLeo, Michael Gillette, Joseph Kowalewski, Nannette Levi, Susan Lorentsen, Samuel Marder, Holly Ovenden violin; Barbara H. Vaccaro, Richard Spencer viola; Frank Levy, Sarah Carter cello; Dean Crandall bass; Kenneth Emery flute; Gerard J. Niewood, Richard Oatts, John M. Cipolla, Joshua Siegel, Kenneth Arzberger reeds; Russ Rizner, Nancy Schallert, French horn; Richard Raffio, Hollis Burridge, Zachary Shnek trumpet; John D. Schnupp, Thomas B. Olcott, Mark Johansen trombone; Andrew Rodgers tuba; Thomas Oldakowski drums; Mario DeCiutiis, Maya Gunji percussion; Anthony Cesarano guitar; Jeanne Maier harp; Susanna Nason, Robert Wendel piano; George W. Wesner III, Fred Davies organ.

Director and choreographer, Linda Haberman; musical direction and vocal arrangements, Don Pippin; scenery, Michael Hotopp, Eduardo Sicangco (Gershwin scenery and costumes, Erte); costumes, Frank Krenz, Bob Mackie, Pete Menefee, Eduardo Sicangco and Jose Lengson; orchestrations, Michael Gibson, Dick Lieb, Glenn Osser, Jim Tyler; dance music arrangements, Mark Hummel, Marvin Laird; associate musical director, Bryan Louiselle; Dancing in Diamonds staging, Violet Holmes; *The Glory of Easter* restaging, Linda Lemac; vocal solo recording, Marilyn Horne; assistant choreographers, Julie Branam, Dennis Callahan; scenic supervisor, John Farrell; original production directed and choreographed by Scott Salmon; production stage manager, Joe Bonanni; stage managers, Robin R. Corbett, Tom Aberger, Joe Onorato, Mark Tynan.

Original Music Credit: "Put a Little Spring in Your Step" music and lyrics by Jeffrey Ernstoff. Special Music Credits: "On the Sunny Side of the Street" and Rockettes' April Showers dance music by Mark Hummel; "Put on Your Sunday Clothes" music and lyrics by Jerry Herman; *La Cage aux Folles* music by Jerry Herman arranged by Gordon Lowry Harrell; "Dancing in Diamonds" and "There Are No Girls Like Showgirls" music by Don Pippin, lyrics by Sammy Cahn; "Encore" music by Stan Lebowsky, lyrics by Fred Tobias, arranged by Tom Bahler, orchestrated by Robert Freedman.

ACT I, Prologue: *The Glory of Easter* pageant. Overture: Radio City Music Hall Orchestra. Scene 1: Pure Imagination—Easter Rabbit. Scene 2: Put a Little Spring in Your Step—Rockettes, Singers, Dancers in Happy Feet. Scene 3: "On the Sunny Side of the Street"—Rabbit. Scene 4: Errol Manoff's

RADIO CITY SPRING SPECTACULAR—The Rockettes in the Happy Feet scene of the Easter show, set in a stylized version of the theater's famous marquee

Fantasy Factory (black light illusions). Scene 5: Rockettes' April Showers—Rockettes. Scene 6: With Gershwin—Singers, Dancers, Orchestra, Rockettes, music by George and Ira Gershwin.

ACT II: Entr'acte—Orchestra. Scene 1: Rockettes' Easter Parade—Rockettes, Rabbit. Scene 2: Brackney's Madcap Mutts. Scene 3: Dancing in Diamonds—Rockettes. Scene 4: Yesteryear—Easter Morning in the 1880s, Company.

Cinderella (12). Revival of the musical with book adapted by Steve Allen; based on the original book by Oscar Hammerstein II; adapted for the stage by Robert Johanson; music by Richard Rodgers; lyrics by Oscar Hammerstein II. Produced by New York City Opera, Christopher Keene general director, Mark J. Weinstein executive director, Donald Hassard managing director of artistic administration, at the New York State Theater. Opened November 9, 1995. (Closed November 19, 1995)

Fairy Godmother .... Sally Ann Howes	Little Girl .... Elizabeth Dietrich
Royal Herald ....Stephen Powell	Cinderella's Stepmother .... Jean Stapleton

Cinderella's Stepsisters:

Joy	Alix Corey
Portia	Jeannette Palmer
Cinderella	Rebecca Baxter
Dog	Andrew Pacho
Cat	Debbi Fuhrman
Queen	Jane Powell

King	George S. Irving
Royal Chef	Joel Sorenson
Royal Steward	John Lankston
Prince	George Dvorsky
Youngest Fairy	Stephanie Godino
Tiara Fairy	Irina Dvorovenko

Directed and choreographed by Robert Johanson; co-choreographer, Sharon Halley; conductor, Rob Fisher; orchestrations, Robert Russell Bennett; scenery, Henry Bardon; costumes, Gregg Barnes; lighting, Jeff Davis; sound, Abe Jacob; chorus master, Joseph Colaneri; children prepared by Mildred Hohner; assistant stage director, Paul L. King; musical preparation, John Beeson; press, Susan Woelzl.

Act 1, Prologue: Public square. Scene 1: The kitchen. Scene 2: Royal dressing room. Scene 3: Back in the kitchen. Scene 4: A magical place. Act II, Scene 1: The palace ballroom. Scene 2: A garden at the palace. Scene 3: The palace ballroom. Scene 4: Back in the kitchen. Scene 5: A garden at the palace. Scene 6: The palace ballroom.

This Rodgers & Hammerstein *Cinderella* was originally produced for CBS television March 31, 1957 by Richard Lewine with Julie Andrews in the title role and Howard Lindsay and Dorothy Stickney (King and Queen), Ilka Chase (Stepmother), Kaye Ballard and Alice Ghostley (Stepsisters) and Edie Adams (Fairy Godmother), under the direction of Ralph Nelson. Its only previous New York revival was by New York City Opera in this version 11/9/93 for 14 performances.

The list of musical numbers in *Cinderella* appears on page 418 of *The Best Plays of 1993–94.*

Note: New York City Opera also presented its repertory productions of *The Mikado* 3/3/96 for 4 performances and *The Merry Widow* 3/23/96 for 6 performances.

National Actors Theater. Schedule of two revivals. **The School for Scandal** (33). By Richard Brinsley Sheridan. Opened November 19, 1995. (Closed December 17, 1995) **Inherit the Wind** (45). By Jerome Lawrence and Robert E. Lee. Opened April 4, 1996. (Closed May 12, 1996) Produced by National Actors Theater, Tony Randall founder and artistic director, (*The School for Scandal* in association with Great Lakes Theater Festival, Gerald Freedman artistic director, by special arrangement with The Acting Company, Margot Harley producing director) at the Lyceum Theater.

THE SCHOOL FOR SCANDAL

Lady Sneerwell	Mary Lou Rosato
Snake; Moses	Norman Snow
Sneerwell Servant	Kevin Shinick
Joseph Surface	Simon Jones
Maria	Megan Dodds
Mrs. Candour	Jennifer Harmon
Mr. Crabtree	Philip Goodwin
Sir Benjamin Backbite	Matt Bradford Sullivan
Sir Peter Teazle	Tony Randall
Rowley	Ron Randell

Lady Teazle	Kate Forbes
Sir Oliver Surface	Ted Sorel
Moses	Norman Snow
Trip	Richard Topol
Charles Surface	Tom Hewitt
Careless	Ray Virta
Sir Harry Bumper	Allen Gilmore
Joseph's Servant	Derek Meader
Lady Teazle's Maid	Leslie Geraci

Charles's Friends: Anthony M. Brown, Matthew Edwards, Kevin Shinick. Servants: Katherine De Boda, Jennifer Chambers, Mony Damevsky, John Kinsherf, Brett LaRose, Judith Stambler, Mark C. Tafoya.

Understudies: Messrs. Jones, Hewitt—Ray Virta; Messrs. Sullivan, Snow—Richard Topol; Messrs. Gilmore, Topol—Matt Bradford Sullivan; Misses Forbes, Harmon—Leslie Geraci; Misses Dodds, Geraci—Heather Harlan; Messrs. Virta, Meader, Shinick—Matthew Edwards; Mr. Goodwin—Allen Gilmore; Messrs. Randell, Snow—Derek Meader.

Directed by Gerald Freedman; scenery, Douglas W. Schmidt; costumes, Theoni V. Aldredge; lighting, Mary Jo Dondlinger; sound, T. Richard Fitzgerald; music, Robert Waldman; executive producer, Manny Kladitis; associate producer, John Miller-Stephany; production stage manager, Maureen F. Gibson; stage manager, Richard Costabile; press, Springer Associates, John Springer, Gary Springer, Candi Adams.

Act I, Scene 1: Lady Sneerwell's house. Scene 2: Sir Peter Teazle's house. Scene 3: Lady Sneerwell's house. Scene 4: Sir Peter Teazle's house. Act II, Scene 1: Charles Surface's house. Scene 2: Joseph Surface's house. Scene 3: Sir Peter Teazle's house. Scene 4: Joseph Surface's house.

The last major New York revival of *The School for Scandal* was by City Center Acting Company off Broadway 9/27/72 for 12 performances.

INHERIT THE WIND

Rachel Brown	Kate Forbes	Mother	Alice Connorton
Meeker	Tom Stechschulte	Vendor	Robert Jimenez
Bertram Cates	Garret Dillahunt	Mrs. McLain	Prudence Wright Holmes
Mr. Goodfellow	Clement Fowler	Mrs. Blair	Joyce Lynn O'Connor
Mrs. Krebs	Marylouise Burke	Elijah	Ronn K. Smith
Rev. Jeremiah Brown	Tom Aldredge	E.K. Hornbeck	Anthony Heald
Sillers	John Griesemer	Hurdy Gurdy Man	Bill Corritore
Platt	Norman Snow	Matthew Harrison Brady	Charles Durning
Finney	Kevin McClarnon	Mrs. Brady	Bette Henritze
Timmy	Craig Lawlor	Reuter's Man	Dominic Cuskern
Cooper	Kenneth P. Strong	Mayor	Reathel Bean
Bannister	David Dossey	Tom Davenport	Herndon Lackey
Dunlap	Fred Burrell	Henry Drummond	George C. Scott
Howard	Paul F. Dano	Judge	Michael Lombard
Melinda	Allie Calnan	Harry Y. Esterbrook	J.R. Horne

Townspeople, Jurors, Scientists, etc.: Sam Andrew, Jeff Berry, Jennifer Chambers, Bill Corry, Katherine De Boda, Brad Fairbanks, Glenn Gehweiler, Joe Gioco, Rich Heraty, William York Hyde, Dawn Jamieson, John Kinsherf, Brett LaRose, Michael Lehr, John Lenartz, Charles Prior, Timothy Sozen, Judith Stambler, Mark C. Tafoya, Sewell Whitney.

Standby: Messrs. Scott, Heald—Tony Randall. Understudies: Mr. Durning—J.R. Horne; Mr. Dillahunt—Robert Jimenez; Messrs. Aldredge, Lombard, Bean—Norman Snow; Messrs. Stechschulte, Strong, Griesemer, Cuskern—Kevin McClarnon; Miss Henritze—Prudence Wright Holmes; Messrs. Lackey, Burrell, Dossey—Dominic Cuskern; Messrs. Smith, Horne, Jimenez—Kenneth P. Strong; Mr. Dano, Miss Calnan—Craig Lawlor; Mr. Lawlor—Allie Calnan; Mr. Snow—Fred Burrell.

Directed by John Tillinger; scenery, James Noone; costumes, Jess Goldstein; lighting, Ken Billington; sound, Aural Fixation; executive producer, Manny Kladitis; casting, Deborah Brown; production stage manager, Wm. Hare; press, Springer Associates, John Springer, Gary Springer.

Time: Summer, not too long ago. Place: A small town. The play was presented in two parts.

Inherit the Wind was first produced on Broadway 4/21/55 for 806 performances and was named a Best Play of its season. This is its first major New York revival.

A Christmas Carol (88). Return engagement of the musical based on the story by Charles Dickens; book by Mike Ockrent and Lynn Ahrens; music by Alan Menken; lyrics by Lynn Ahrens. Produced by Madison Square Garden at the Paramount Madison Square Garden Theater. Opened November 20, 1995. (Closed December 31, 1995)

Beadle	David Lowenstein	Lamplighter; Ghost of Christmas	
Mr. Smythe	James Judy	Past	Ken Jennings
Grace Smythe	Cara Horner, Joanna Howard	Blind Hag	Nicole Arrington
Scrooge	Terrence Mann	Mrs. Mops	Karen Murphy
Cratchit	Nick Corley	Ghost of Jacob Marley	Paul Kandel
Old Joe; Mr. Hawkins	Kenneth McMullen	Judge	Michael H. Ingram
Mrs. Cratchit	Robin Baxter	Scrooge at 8; Ignorance	Matthew Ballinger,
Tiny Tim	Zach London, Chris Marquette		Zachary Petkanas
Poulterer	Walter Willison	Fan at 6; Want	Diana Mary Rice,
Sandwichboard Man; Ghost of Christmas			Olivia Oguma
Present	Ben Vereen	Scrooge's Mother	Barbara Marineau
Fred	Steve Blanchard	Scrooge's Father;	
Jonathan	Jason Fuchs, Evan J. Newman	Undertaker	Michael X. Martin

Scrooge at 12	Paul Franklin Dano,	Young Marley; Undertaker	Ken Barnett
	Christopher Mark Petrizzo	Mrs. Fezziwig	Joy Hermalyn
Fan at 10	Eliza Atkins Clark,	Emily	Emily Skinner
	Nathalie Paulding	Sally	Stephanie Bast
Fezziwig	Michael Cone	Ghost of Christmas Future	Theara J. Ward
Scrooge at 18	Tom Stuart		

Charity Men: Robert Ousley, Wayne W. Pretlow, Walter Willison. Street Urchins: Matthew Ballinger, Zachary Petkanas, Paul Franklin Dano, Christopher Mark Petrizzo, Olivia Oguma, Diana Mary Rice. Lights of Christmas Past: Matthew Baker, Sean Thomas Morrissey, Rommy Sandhu, Tom Pardoe. Cratchit Children: Eliza Atkins Clark, Nathalie Paulding, Anthony Roth Costanzo, Bobby Steggert, Sean Thomas Morrissey.

Business Men, Gifts, Ghosts, People of London: Farah Alvin, Nicole Arrington, Matthew Baker, Ken Barnett, Stephanie Bast, Robin Baxter, Amy B. Blake, Steve Blanchard, Brad Bradley, Michael Cone, Candy Cook, Donna Dunmire, Peter Gregus, Jeffrey Hankinson, Melissa Haizlip, Joy Hermalyn, Michael H. Ingram, James Judy, David Lowenstein, Barbara Marineau, Michael X. Martin, Dana Lynn Mauro, Carol Lee Meadows, Sean Thomas Morrissey, Kenneth McMullen, Karen Murphy, Robert Ousley, Tom Pardoe, Gale Pennington, Angela Piccinni, Wayne W. Pretlow, Josef Reiter, Eric Riley, Pamela Remler, Sam Reni, Rommy Sandhu, Emily Skinner, Erin Stoddard, Tom Stuart, Tracy Terstriep, Theara J. Ward, Walter Willison.

Angels: P.S. 26 Chorus (Bronx), William Alexander Middle School 51 (Brooklyn), Roy H. Mann Concert Choir (Brooklyn), Park Middle School Chorus (Scotch Plains, N.J.).

Red Children's Cast: Matthew Ballinger, Jason Fuchs, Joanna Howard, Chris Marquette, Nathalie Paulding, Christopher Mark Petrizzo, Diana Mary Rice, Bobby Steggert.

Green Children's Cast: Eliza Atkins Clark, Anthony Roth Costanzo, Paul Franklin Dano, Cara Horner, Zach London, Evan J. Newman, Olivia Oguma, Zachary Petkanas.

Orchestra: Paul Gemignani conductor; Mark C. Mitchell assistant conductor, keyboards; Aloysia Friedmann concertmaster; Monica Gerard, Adria Benjamin violin; Clay Ruede cello; Charles Bergeron bass; David Weiss, Daniel Willis, Al Hunt, Kenneth Dybisz, John Winder woodwinds; Stu Sataloff, Phil Granger, Domenic Derasse trumpet; Phil Sasson, Dean Plank trombone; Nick Archer keyboards; Jennifer Hoult harp; Michael Berkowitz drums; Glenn Rhian percussion.

Directed by Mike Ockrent; choreography, Susan Stroman; musical direction, Paul Gemignani; scenery, Tony Walton; costumes, William Ivey Long; lighting, Jules Fisher, Peggy Eisenhauer; sound, Tony Meola; projections, Wendall K. Harrington; flying, Foy; orchestrations, Michael Starobin, Douglas Besterman; dance arrangements and incidental music, Glen Kelly; executive producer, Dodger Productions; producer, Tim Hawkins; casting, Julie Hughes, Barry Moss; production stage manager, Steven Zweigbaum; stage manager, Ara Marx; press, Cathy Del Priore; consultants, Boneau/Bryan-Brown.

Time: 1880. Place: London. The play was presented without intermission.

This *A Christmas Carol* was first produced last season on 12/1/94 for 71 performances. Its scenes and musical numbers, listed on page 319 of *The Best Plays of 1994–95,* differ somewhat from those in this return engagement, listed below.

MUSICAL NUMBERS

Scene 1: The Royal Exchange
"A Jolly Good Time" .... Charity Men, Smythe Family, Business Men, Wives, Children
"Nothing to Do With Me" .... Scrooge, Cratchit
Scene 2: The street
"You Mean More to Me" .... Cratchit, Tiny Tim
"Street Song (Nothing to Do With Me)" .... People of London, Scrooge, Fred, Jonathan, Sandwichboard Man, Lamplighter, Blind Hag, Grace Smythe
Scene 3: Scrooge's house
"Link by Link" .... Marley's Ghost, Scrooge, Ghosts
Scene 4: Scrooge's bedchamber
"The Lights of Long Ago" .... Ghost of Christmas Past
Scene 5: The law courts
"God Bless Us, Everyone" .... Scrooge's Mother, Fan at 6
Scene 6: The factory
"A Place Called Home" .... Scrooge at 12, Fan at 10, Scrooge

Scene 7: Fezziwig's Banking House
    "Mr. Fezziwig's Annual Christmas Ball" ....Fezziwig, Mrs. Fezziwig, Guests
    "A Place Called Home" (Reprise) ....Emily, Scrooge at 18, Scrooge
Scene 8: Scrooge and Marley's
    "The Lights of Long Ago" (Part II) .... Scrooge at 18, Young Marley, Emily, People From
                                                                                                    Scrooge's Past
Scene 9: A starry night
    "Abundance and Charity" ....Ghost of Christmas Present, Scrooge, Christmas Gifts
Scene 10: All over London
    "Christmas Together" ......Tiny Tim, Cratchits, Ghost of Christmas Present, Fred, Sally, Scrooge,
                                                                                                    People of London
Scene 11: The graveyard
    "Dancing on Your Grave" .... Ghost of Christmas Future, Monks, Business Men, Mrs. Mops,
                                                                                        Undertakers, Old Joe, Cratchit
Scene 12: Scrooge's bedchamber
    "London Town Carol" ....Jonathan
Scene 13: The street, Christmas Day
    "Nothing to Do With Me" (Reprise) ....Scrooge
    "Christmas Together" (Reprise) ....People of London
    "God Bless Us, Everyone" (Finale) ....Company

*Lincoln Center Theater. Schedule of two programs. **Racing Demon** (48). By David Hare; produced by arrangement with the Royal National Theater. Opened November 20, 1995. (Closed December 31, 1995) *A Delicate Balance** (46). Revival of the play by Edward Albee. Opened April 21, 1996. Produced by Lincoln Center Theater, Andre Bishop artistic director, Bernard Gersten executive producer, *Racing Demon* at the Vivian Beaumont Theater, *A Delicate Balance* at the Plymouth Theater.

RACING DEMON

Clergy:
Rev. Lionel Espy .... Josef Sommer
Rt. Rev. Charlie Allen ......George N. Martin
Rev. Tony Ferris .... Michael Cumpsty
Rev. Donald "Streaky"
    Bacon .... Paul Giamatti
Rev. Harry Henderson ....Brian Murray
Rt. Rev. Gilbert
    Heffernan ....John C. Vennema

Laity:
Frances Parnell ....Kathryn Meisle
Stella Marr .... Patrice Johnson
Heather Espy .... Kathleen Chalfant
Ewan Gilmour .... Denis O'Hare
Tommy Adair .... John Curless
Head Waiter ....Richard Clarke
Waiter .... Robert Gomes
Servers .... Ian Stuart, Richard Clarke

Synod Delegates: Tom Bloom, Alison Sheehy, Angela Thornton, Terri Towns.
    Understudies: Mr. Sommer—Ian Stuart; Messrs. Martin, Murray—Richard Clarke; Messrs. Cumpsty, O'Hare—Robert Gomes; Messrs. Giamatti, Vennema, Curless—Tom Bloom; Miss Meisle—Alison Sheehy; Miss Johnson—Terri Towns; Miss Chalfant—Angela Thornton.
    Directed by Richard Eyre; scenery and costumes, Bob Crowley; lighting, Mark Henderson; projections, Wendall K. Harrington; sound, Scott Myers; original music, George Fenton; casting, Daniel Swee; stage manager, Susie Cordon; press, Merle Debuskey, Susan Chicoine.
    Time: The present. Place: South London. The play was presented in two parts.
    Crises of faith and ethics among Church of England ministers and members of their congregations. A foreign play previously produced by London's Royal National Theater.

A DELICATE BALANCE

Agnes ....Rosemary Harris
Tobias ....George Grizzard
Claire ....,.....................Elaine Stritch

Harry .... John Carter
Edna ....Elizabeth Wilson
Julia ....Mary Beth Hurt

Standbys: Miss Harris—Patricia Kilgarriff; Messrs. Grizzard, Carter—William Cain; Misses Stritch, Wilson—Barbara Andres; Miss Hurt—Charlotte Maier.

Directed by Gerald Gutierrez; scenery, John Lee Beatty; costumes, Jane Greenwood; lighting, Pat Collins; sound, Aural Fixation; casting, Daniel Swee; stage manager, Michael Brunner; press, Philip Rinaldi.

Time: Now. Place: A large and well-appointed suburban house. Act I: Friday night. Act II, Scene 1: Early Saturday evening. Scene 2: Later that night. Act III: Early Sunday morning.

A Delicate Balance was first produced on Broadway 9/22/66 for 132 performances and was named a Best Play of its season and won the Pulitzer Prize. This is its first major New York revival.

Paul Robeson (11). Revival of the play with music by Phillip Hayes Dean. Produced by Eric Krebs and Anne Strickland Squadron at the Longacre Theater. Opened December 20, 1995. (Closed December 31, 1995)

Paul Robeson	Avery Brooks
Lawrence Brown	Ernie Scott

Directed by Harold Scott; musical direction and arrangements, Ernie Scott; lighting, Shirley Prendergast; sound, Tom Gould; original choreography, Dianne McIntyre; special arrangements and orchestrations, Eva C. Brooks; production stage manager, Doug Hosney; press, David Rothenberg Associates.

Incidents from the private life and public career of Paul Robeson, including the presentation of some of his popular song numbers. Previously produced on Broadway for 77 performances 1/19/78 and 11 performances 10/9/88 and at Crossroads Theater Company, New Brunswick, N. J. and presented now in association with Amas Musical Theater, Rosetta LeNoire artistic director.

The list of multiple scenes and characters in *Paul Robeson* appears on pages 361–362 of *The Best Plays of 1977–78.*

Riverdance—The Show (8). Dance and musical revue with music by Bill Whelan; poetry by Theo Dorgan. Produced by Moya Doherty at Radio City Music Hall. Opened March 13 1996. (Closed March 17, 1996)

Narrator ....John Kavanagh	Maria Pages, Tarik Winston, Daniel Wooten
Solo Dancers ....Jean Butler, Colin Dunne,	Solo Singer ....Ivan Thomas

With Anunas (choral group), Riverdance Irish Dance Company, Moscow Folk Ballet Company.

Directed by John McColgan; choreography, Michael Flatley, Jean Butler, Colin Dunne, Tara Little, Moscow Folk Ballet Company, Maria Pages, Tarik Winston; musical direction, David Hayes; scenery and painted projections, Robert Ballagh; costumes, Jen Kelly; lighting, Rupert Murray; sound, Michael O'Gorman; orchestrations, Nick Ingman, Bill Whelan; projections, Chris Slingsby; stage manager, Ann Mulvany; press, Merle Frimark, Marc Thibodeau.

Extravaganza featuring 30 Irish step-dancers as well as choral and solo songs and dances by European performers. A foreign show previously produced in Dublin and London. The show was presented in two parts.

Getting Away With Murder (17). By Stephen Sondheim and George Furth. Produced by Roger Berlind at the Broadhurst Theater. Opened March 17, 1996. (Closed March 31, 1996)

Martin Chisholm ....John Rubinstein	Gregory Reed ....Terrence Mann
Dossie Lustig .... Christine Ebersole	Dan Gerard ....Frankie R. Faison
Young Man .... William Ragsdale	Nam-Jun Vuong ....Jodi Long
Charmaine ....Michelle Hurd	Roberto .... Al Espinosa
Pamela Prideaux .... Kandis Chappell	Dr. Conrad Bering .... Herb Foster
Vassili Laimorgos .... Josh Mostel	

Standbys and understudies: Misses Ebersole, Chappell—Nancy Opel; Mr. Faison—Chuck Cooper; Misses Hurd, Long—Stephanie Park; Messrs. Foster, Mostel—Joel Kramer; Mr. Espinosa—Jesus Ontiveros; Mr. Ragsdale—Al Espinosa.

Directed by Jack O'Brien; scenery, Douglas W. Schmidt; costumes, Robert Wojewodski; lighting, Kenneth Posner; sound, Jeff Ladman; special effects design, Gregory Meeh; fight director, Steve Rankin;

GETTING AWAY WITH MURDER—John Rubinstein, Christine Ebersole, Josh Mostel and Terrence Mann in the Stephen Sondheim-George Furth comedy thriller

casting, Jay Binder; production stage manager, Jeff Lee; stage manager, Julie Baldauff; press, Bill Evans & Associates, Jim Randolph, Tom D'Ambrosio.

Time: The present, October. Place: A suite on the top floor of an old New York apartment building.

Comedy thriller, murder stalks a group of patients of a psychiatrist in a late-night therapy session from which the doctor seems to be unaccountably missing. Previously produced as *The Doctor Is Out* in regional theater at the Old Globe Theater, San Diego.

*Love Thy Neighbor (59). Solo performance by Jackie Mason; created and written by Jackie Mason. Produced by Jyll Rosenfeld and Abe Hirschfeld at the Booth Theater. Opened March 24, 1996.

Designed by Neil Peter Jampolis; production stage manager, Don Myers; press, Rubenstein Public Relations, Mitch Zamarin.

Fourth Broadway production of Jackie Mason's standup comedy comments on the social and political foibles of the day. The show was presented in two parts.

*State Fair (75). Musical based on the screen play by Oscar Hammerstein II and the novel by Phil Stong; book by Tom Briggs and Louis Mattioli; music by Richard Rodgers; lyrics by Oscar Hammerstein II. Produced by David Merrick in the Theater Guild production, Thomas Viertel executive producer, at The Music Box. Opened March 27, 1996.

Abel Frake	John Davidson	Wayne Frake	Ben Wright
Gus	James Patterson	David Miller; Judge Heppenstahl	Charles Goff
Melissa Frake	Kathryn Crosby	Eleanor	Susan Haefner

Margy Frake ....Andrea McArdle
Harry ....Peter Benson
Uncle Sam ....Michael Lee Scott
Fair Announcer; Clay ....J. Lee Flynn
Midway Cow .... Kelli Barclay
Midway Pig; Violet ....Jackie Angelescu
Hoop-La Barker .... Tim Fauvell
Emily Arden ....Donna McKechnie
The Astounding Stralenko; Chief
of Police .... Steve Steiner

Vivian ....Tina Johnson
Jeanne ....Leslie Bell
Mrs. Edwin Metcalf ......Jacquiline Rohrbacker
Pat Gilbert ....Scott Wise
Charlie ....Darrian C. Ford
Lem .... John Wilkerson
Hank Munson ....Newton R. Gilchrist
Roustabouts .....Michael Lee Scott, Scott Willis
Swings .... Julie Lira, John Scott

The Fairtones: Ian Knauer, James Patterson, Michael Lee Scott, Scott Willis. Barkers, Vendors, Judges, Fairgoers: Kelli Barclay, Leslie Bell, Linnea Dakin, Suellen Estey, Tim Fauvell, Amy Gage, Susan Haefner, Tina Johnson, Ian Knauer, James Patterson, Michael Lee Scott, Mary C. Sheehan, Steve Steiner, Scott Willis.

Orchestra; Kay Cameron conductor; Robert Berman associate conductor, keyboard; Pam Sumner keyboard; Richard Rosenzweig drums; Leon Maleson bass; Lou Oddo percussion; Peter Olstad, Gregory Gisbert, Phil Granger trumpet; Larry Farrell, Rock Cicarone trombone; Marcus Rojas tuba; David Wakefield, Leise A. Paer, French horn; Steve Kenyon, Charles Pillow, Scott Schachter, Don McGeen woodwinds; Rob Shaw, Cecelia Hobbs Gardner violin; Debra Shufelt viola; Daniel D. Miller cello; Park Stickney harp.

Understudies: Mr. Davidson—J. Lee Flynn; Miss Crosby—Suellen Estey; Mr. Wright—Ian Knauer; Miss McArdle—Susan Haefner; Miss McKechnie—Leslie Bell; Misses Angelescu (Violet), Haefner—Linnea Dakin; Miss Rohrbacker—Mary C. Sheehan; Mr. Benson—James Patterson; Mr. Fauvell—Tim Johnson; Misses Johnson, Bell—Kelli Barclay; Messrs. Gilchrist, Wilkerson, Goff—Tim Fauvell; Mr. Flynn—Steve Steiner; Messrs. Wise, Steiner—Scott Willis; Messrs. Ford, Patterson, Michael Lee Scott and Fairtones, Roustabouts—John Scott; Misses Barclay, Angelescu (Pig)—Julie Lira.

Directed by James Hammerstein and Randy Skinner; choreography, Randy Skinner; musical direction and vocal arrangements, Kay Cameron; scenery, James Leonard Joy; costumes, Michael Bottari, Ronald Case; lighting, Natasha Katz; sound, Brian Ronan; orchestrations, Bruce Pomahac; dance arrangements, Scot Woolley; music coordinator, John Miller; produced by Philip Langner, Robert Franz, Natalie Lloyd, Jonathan C. Herzog, Meredith Blair, Gordon Smith in association with Mark N. Sirangelo and the PGI Entertainment Company; casting, Caro Jones, Pat McCorkle; production stage manager, Warren Crane; stage managers, Donald Christy, Anita Ross; press, Susan L. Schulman.

Time: Five days in late August of 1946. Place: On the Frake farm in Brunswick, Iowa and at the Iowa State Fair in Des Moines.

Stage version of the movie musical about the Frake family going to the fair made in 1933 (with Will Rogers) and remade in 1945 and 1962, with the Rodgers & Hammerstein score.

ACT I

Scene 1: The Frake farm—a Tuesday afternoon in August
Opening ....Abel, Melissa, Wayne
"It Might As Well Be Spring" .... Margy
Scene 2: On the road to Des Moines—Wednesday morning before dawn
"Driving at Night" .... The Frakes
Scene 3: The midway at the Hoop-La booth—later that morning
"Our State Fair" ....Ensemble
Scene 4: The midway at the Temple of Wonder—later that morning
"That's for Me" ....Wayne
Scene 5: The beer tent—that afternoon
"More Than Just a Friend" ....Abel, Lem, Hank, Clay
Scene 6: Outside the Dairy Pavilion—later that afternoon
"Isn't It Kinda Fun?" .... Pat, Margy
Scene 7: The Starlight Dance Meadow—that night
"You Never Had It So Good" ....Emily Arden, The Fairtones
Scene 8: Camper's Hill—Thursday morning
"It Might As Well Be Spring" (Reprise) .... Margy
"When I Go Out Walking With My Baby" ....Abel, Melissa
Scene 9: Exhibition Hall—that afternoon

Scene 10: A nearby hillside—early that night
  "So Far" .... Wayne, Emily
Scene 11: The Starlight Dance Meadow—later that night
  "It's a Grand Night for Singing" .... Company

ACT II

Scene 1: Outside the Livestock Pavilion—Friday afternoon
  "The Man I Used To Be" .... Pat, Vivian, Jeanne
  "All I Owe Ioway" .... Abel, Company
Scene 2: Outside the Dairy Pavilion—early that night
  "The Man I Used To Be" (Reprise) .... Pat
  "Isn't It Kinda Fun?" (Reprise) .... Margy
Scene 3: The Starlight Dance Meadow—immediately following
  "That's the Way It Happens" .... Emily Arden, The Fairtones
Scene 4: The hillside—later that night
Scene 5: Camper's Hill—later that night
  "Boys and Girls Like You and Me" .... Abel, Melissa
Scene 6: On the midway—immediately following
  "The Next Time It Happens" .... Margy
Scene 7: The Frake farm—Saturday night after supper

*__Seven Guitars__ (72). By August Wilson. Produced by Sageworks, Benjamin Mordecai executive producer, Center Theater Group/Ahmanson Theater, Gordon Davidson artistic director, Herb Alpert/Margo Lion, Scott Rudin/Paramount Pictures and Jujamcyn Theaters, in association with the Goodman Theater, Huntington Theater Company, American Conservatory Theater and Manhattan Theater Club at the Walter Kerr Theater. Opened March 28, 1996.

Louise	Michele Shay	Hedley	Roger Robinson
Canewell	Ruben Santiago-Hudson	Floyd Barton	Keith David
Red Carter	Tommy Hollis	Ruby	Rosalyn Coleman
Vera	Viola Davis		

Understudy: Messrs. David, Santiago-Hudson—W. Allen Taylor.

Directed by Lloyd Richards; scenery, Scott Bradley; costumes, Constanza Romero; lighting, Christopher Akerlind; musical direction, Dwight Andrews; sound, Tom Clark; casting, Meg Simon; production stage manager, Jane E. Neufeld; stage manager, Narda Alcorn; press, Boneau/Bryan-Brown, Chris Boneau.

Time: Spring 1948. Place: Pittsburgh, the Hill District. The play was presented in two parts.

Events and episodes in a black Pittsburgh neighborhood, one of whose dwellers is trying to get to Chicago for a promised recording session. Previously presented at the O'Neill Center's National Playwrights Conference and in regional theater productions at the Goodman Theater, Chicago, the Huntington Theater Company, Boston, the American Conservatory Theater, San Francisco, and the Ahmanson Theater, Los Angeles.

A Best Play; see page 207.

__A Midsummer Night's Dream__ (65). Revival of the play by William Shakespeare. Produced by Terry Allen Kramer, James L. Nederlander, Carole Shorenstein Hays, the John F. Kennedy Center for the Performing Arts and Elizabeth Ireland McCann in the Royal Shakespeare Company production at the Lunt-Fontanne Theater. Opened March 31, 1996. (Closed May 26, 1996)

Theseus; Oberon	Alex Jennings	Peter Quince	John Kane
Hippolyta; Titania	Lindsay Duncan	Nick Bottom	Desmond Barrit
Philostrate; Puck	Barry Lynch	Francis Flute	Mark Letheren
Egeus	Alfred Burke	Tom Snout	Howard Crossley
Hermia	Monica Dolan	Snug	Kenn Sabberton
Lysander	Daniel Evans	Robin Starveling	Robert Gillespie
Demetrius	Kevin Robert Doyle	1st Fairy	Ann Hasson
Helena	Emily Raymond		

Fairies: Emily Button, Jane Colenutt, Howard Crossley, Robert Gillespie, Tim Griggs, John Kane, Mark Letheren, Darren Roberts, Kenn Sabberton.

Understudies: Mr. Jennings—Kevin Robert Doyle; Miss Duncan—Emily Button; Mr. Lynch—Kenn Sabberton; Messrs. Burke, Barrit—Howard Crossley; Miss Dolan—Ann Hasson; Mr. Evans—Mark Letheren; Messrs. Doyle, Crossley, Sabberton—Darren Roberts; Misses Duncan, Raymond, Hasson—Jane Colenutt; Messrs. Kane, Letheren, Gillespie—Tim Griggs.

Directed by Adrian Noble; assistant director, Piers Ibbotson; scenery and costumes, Anthony Ward; lighting, Chris Parry; music, Ilona Sekacz; movement, Sue Lefton; sound, Paul Slocombe, U.S. sound, Duncan Edwards; production supervisor, Alan Hall; press, Boneau/Bryan-Brown, Bob Fennell.

The last major New York revivals of *A Midsummer Night's Dream* took place at New York Shakespeare Festival 7/30/91 for 12 performances (in Portuguese translation) and 1/12/88 for 81 performances, the opening production of the Shakespeare Marathon. The play was presented in two parts.

*The King and I** (58). Revival of the musical based on the novel *Anna and the King of Siam* by Margaret Landon; book and lyrics by Oscar Hammerstein II; music by Richard Rodgers. Produced by Dodger Productions, The John F. Kennedy Center for the Performing Arts, James M. Nederlander, Perseus Productions with John Frost and the Adelaide Festival Center, in association with the Rodgers and Hammerstein Organization at the Neil Simon Theater. Opened April 11, 1996.

Captain Orton .... John Curless	Tuptim ....Joohee Choi
Louis Leonowens ....Ryan Hopkins	Lady Thiang .... Taewon Kim
Anna Leonowens ....Donna Murphy	Prince Chulalongkorn .... John Chang
Interpreter .... Alan Muraoka	Fan Dancer .... Kelly Jordan Bit
Kralahome ....Randall Duk Kim	Princess Yaowlak ....Lexine Bondoc
King of Siam .... Lou Diamond Phillips	Sir Edward Ramsey .... Guy Paul
Lun Tha ....Jose Llana	

Royal Wives, Slaves, Courtiers, Guards, Monks, English Guests, Market People: Tito Abeleda, John Bantay, Camille M. Brown, Benjamin Bryant, Meng-Chen Chang, Kam Cheng, Vivien Eng, Lydia Gaston, Margaret Ann Gates, C. Sean Kim, Shawn Ku, Doan Mackenzie, Paolo Montalban, Alan Muraoka, Paul Nakauchi, Tina Ou, Andrew Pacho, Mami Saito, Lainie Sakakura, Carol To, Yolanda Tolentino, Tran T. Thuc Hanh, Yan Ying, Kayoko Yoshioka, Greg Zane.

Royal Children: Kelly Jordan Bit, Lexine Bondoc, Kailip Boonrai, Jacqueline Te Lem, Erik Lin-Greenberg, Kenji Miyata, Brandon Marshall Ngai, Amy Y. Tai, Jenna Noelle Ushkowitz, Shelby Rebecca Wong, Jeff G. Yalun.

Small House of Uncle Thomas Ballet:	Little Eva .... Tran T. Thuc Hanh
Eliza ....Yan Ying	Topsy .... Tina Ou
Simon of Legree ....Tito Abeleda	Uncle Thomas ....Mami Saito
Angel George ....Meng-Chen Chang	

Dogs: John Bantay, Doan Mackenzie, Greg Zane. Guards: Andrew Pacho, C. Sean Kim, Shawn Ku. Propmen: Benjamin Bryant, Paolo Montalban, Alan Muraoka, Paul Nakauchi. Archers: Camille M. Brown, Vivien Eng, Lainie Sakakura, Kayoko Yoshioka. Singers: Kam Cheng, Margaret Ann Gates, Carol To, Yolanda Tolentino.

Orchestra: Michael Rafter conductor; Cherie Rosen associate conductor, keyboard; Helen Campo flute; Rich Dallessio oboe; Jon Manasse, Larry Guy, Anthony Bracket clarinet; Kim Laskowski bassoon; Alex Holten, Chuck Olsen trumpet; Kaitilin Mahoney, Alexandra Cook, French horn; Dick Clark, Jeff Caswell trombone; Martin Agee concertmaster; Roy Lewis, Darryl Kubian, Shinwon Kim violin; Crystal Garner viola; Stephanie Cummins, Sarah Carter cello; Bill Ellison bass; Victoria Drake harp; James Baker percussion.

Standby: Mr. Phillips—Raul Aranas. Understudies: Miss Murphy—Barbara McCulloh; Mr. Phillips—Paul Nakauchi; Mr. Llana—Benjamin Bryant, Paolo Montalban; Mr. Randall Duk Kim—Alan Muraoka, Paul Nakauchi; Mr. Paul—John Curless; Miss Choi—Kam Cheng, Carol To; Mr. Hopkins—Jonathan Giordano; Mr. Curless—Guy Paul; Miss Taewon Kim—Lydia Gaston, Yolanda Tolentino.

Swings: Jonathan Giordano, Devanand N. Janki, Susan Kikuchi, Joan Tsao. Partial Swings: Lydia Gaston, John Bantay.

Directed by Christopher Renshaw; choreography, Jerome Robbins, supervised by Susan Kikuchi;

musical staging and choreography for "Royal Dance Before the King" and "Procession of the White Elephant," Lar Lubovitch; musical direction, Michael Rafter; scenery, Brian Thomson; costumes, Roger Kirk; lighting, Nigel Levings; sound, Tony Meola, Lewis Mead; orchestrations, Robert Russell Bennett; musical supervision, Eric Stern; additional orchestrations, Bruce Coughlin; associate producers, Abbey Butler and Melvyn J. Estrin, Hal Luftig; casting, Jay Binder; production stage manager, Frank Hartenstein; stage manager, Karen Armstrong; press, Boneau/Bryan-Brown, Adrian Bryan-Brown, Susanne Tighe.

Time: The 1860s. Place: On the docks and in and around the Royal Palace in Bangkok. The play was presented in two parts.

The last major New York revival of *The King and I* was Yul Brynner's farewell appearance as the King of Siam 1/7/85 on Broadway for 191 performances.

The list of musical numbers in *The King and I* appears on page 361 of *The Best Plays of 1950–51.*

The Apple Doesn't Fall . . . (1). By Trish Vradenburg. Produced by Chase Mishkin and Jennie Blackton at the Lyceum Theater. Opened and closed at the evening performance April 14, 1996.

Kate Griswald	Margaret Whitton	Madge Wellington	Janet Sarno
Selma Griswald	Florence Stanley	Dr. Sam Gordon	Richard Cox
Jack Griswald	Lee Wallace	Lorna	Madeline Miller

Directed by Leonard Nimoy; scenery and projections, Kenneth Foy; costumes, Gail Cooper-Hecht; lighting, Ken Billington; sound, Tom Clark; original music, David Lawrence; casting, Stuart Howard/ Amy Schecter; production stage manager, K. Lee Harvey; stage manager, Robert Collins; press, Bill Evans & Associates, Jim Randolph, Tom D'Ambrosio.

Time: The past, the present and hopefully the future. Place: New York, Tenafly, Grand Canyon, Miami, Los Angeles, Washington, D.C. The play was presented in two parts.

Mother-daughter relationship in crisis brought on by mother's illness.

*A Funny Thing Happened on the Way to the Forum (51). Revival of the musical with book by Burt Shevelove and Larry Gelbart; music and lyrics by Stephen Sondheim. Produced by Jujamcyn Theaters, Scott Rudin/Paramount Pictures, The Viertel-Baruch-Frankel Group, Roger Berlind and Dodger Productions at the St. James Theater. Opened April 18, 1996.

Prologus; Pseudolus	Nathan Lane	Tintinabula	Pamela Everett
Hero	Jim Stanek	Panacea	Leigh Zimmerman
Philia	Jessica Boevers	The Geminae	Susan Misner, Lori Werner
Senex	Lewis J. Stadlen	Vibrata	Mary Ann Lamb
Domina	Mary Testa	Gymnasia	Stephanie Pope
Hysterium	Mark Linn-Baker	Erronius	William Duell
Lycus	Ernie Sabella	Miles Gloriosus	Cris Groenendaal

The Proteans: Brad Aspel, Cory English, Ray Roderick.

Orchestra: Edward Strauss conductor; Lawrence Yurman associate conductor, keyboards; Les Scott, Seymour Red Press, Virgil Blackwell, Ed Zuhlke, John Winder woodwinds; Stu Sataloff, Larry Lunetta, Kamau Adilifu trumpet; Bruce Bonvissuto, Jack Schatz trombone; Paul Riggio, French horn; Glenn Rhian, Rick Kivnick percussion; Lou Bruno bass; Beth Robinson harp; Ronald Oakland, Alexander Vselensky, Katsuko Esaki, Maura Giannini, Melanie Baker violin; Scott Ballantyne, Jeffrey Szabo cello.

Standby: Mr. Lane—Bob Amaral. Understudies: Mr. Stanek—Cory English, Kevin Kraft; Miss Boevers—Jennifer Rosin; Mr. Stadlen—MacIntyre Dixon, Kenneth Kantor; Miss Testa—Ruth Gottschall; Mr. Linn-Baker—Bob Amaral, Patrick Garner; Mr. Sabella—Bob Amaral, Patrick Garner, Kenneth Kantor; Miss Pope—Leigh Zimmerman; Mr. Duell—Patrick Garner, MacIntyre Dixon; Mr. Groenendaal—Kenneth Kantor. Swings: Michael Arnold, Kevin Kraft, Kristin Willis.

Directed by Jerry Zaks; choreography, Rob Marshall; musical supervision, Edward Strauss; scenery and costumes, Tony Walton; lighting, Paul Gallo; sound, Tony Meola; orchestrations, Jonathan Tunick; dance music arrangements, David Chase; musical coordinator, Seymour Red Press; associate choreographer, Sarah Miles; associate producers, Marc Routh, Perseus Productions, TV Asahi; casting, Johnson-Liff Associates; production stage manager, Arthur Gaffin; stage manager, Michael Pule; press, Boneau/ Bryan-Brown, Chris Boneau, Jackie Green.

A FUNNY THING HAPPENED ON THE WAY TO THE FORUM—Leigh Zimmerman and Nathan Lane in the revival of the Burt Shevelove-Larry Gelbart-Stephen Sondheim musical comedy

Time: Two hundred years before the Christian era, a day in spring. Place: A street in Rome in front of the houses of Erronius, Senex and Lycus.

The last major New York revival of *A Funny Thing Happened* took place on Broadway 3/30/72 for 156 performances.

The list of musical numbers in *A Funny Thing Happened* appears on pages 297–298 of *The Best Plays of 1961–62.*

Jack (12). Solo performance by Nicol Williamson; devised by Nicol Williamson and Leslie Megahey. Produced by John Heyman in association with Freddie Hancock, Meridian Theatrical Inc. and Geffen Playhouse at the Belasco Theater. Opened April 24, 1996. (Closed May 5, 1996)

Directed by Leslie Megahey; scenery, Bethia Jane Green; lighting, Richard Winkler; sound, Christopher Bond; production stage manager, Thomas P. Carr; stage manager, Newton Cole; press, Cromarty & Company, Peter Cromarty.

Williamson in a performance subtitled A Night on the Town With John Barrymore chronicling events in the great actor's life beginning with his first experiences in the theater. A foreign play previously produced in London and in Los Angeles.

*Bring in 'da Noise Bring in 'da Funk (42). Transfer from off Broadway of the musical performance piece based on an idea by Savion Glover and George C. Wolfe; conceived by George C. Wolfe; choreography by Savion Glover; book by Reg E. Gaines; music by Daryl Waters, Zane Mark and Ann Duquesnay. Produced by the Joseph Papp Public Theater/New York Shakespeare Festival, George C. Wolfe producer, Rosemarie Tichler artistic producer, Laurie Beckelman executive director, Joey Parnes executive producer, at the Ambassador Theater. Opened April 25, 1996.

Vincent Bingham	Raymond King
Jared Crawford	Jimmy Tate
Ann Duquesnay	Baakari Wilder
Savion Glover	Jeffrey Wright
Dule Hill	

Musicians: Zane Mark conductor, keyboards; Lafayette Harris keyboards; Zane Paul reeds; David Rogers trumpet; Vince Henry guitar, harmonica; Luico Hopper bass; Leroy Clouden drums.

Standbys: Miss Duquesnay—Lynette G. DuPré; Mr. Wright—Mark Gerald Douglas. Understudies: Mr. Glover—Baakari Wilder; Mr. Wilder—Dule Hill; Messrs. Bingham, Hill, Tate, Wilder—Omar A. Edwards, Derick K. Grant, Joseph Monroe Webb; Messrs. Crawford, King—David Peter Chapman.

Directed by George C. Wolfe; musical direction, Zane Mark; scenery, Riccardo Hernandez; costumes, Paul Tazewell; lighting, Jules Fisher/Peggy Eisenhauer; sound, Dan Moses Schreier; projection design, Batwin + Robin; musical supervision and orchestrations, Daryl Waters; vocal arrangements, Ann Duquesnay; musical coordinator, Seymour Red Press; associate producer, Wiley Hausam; artistic associate, Kevin Kline; casting, Jordan Thaler/Heidi Griffiths; production stage manager, Bonnie Panson; stage managers, Gwendolyn M. Gilliam, Rick Singer; press, Carol R. Fineman, Thomas V. Naro, Bill Coyle.

Evolution of the tap and hip-hop beat through the experience and creativity of the African-American people, expressed in song-and-dance and narrative. Previously produced off Broadway in this production 11/15/95 for 85 performances.

ACT I

In 'da Beginning: "Bring in 'da Noise Bring in 'da Funk"—Company; "The Door to Isle Goree"—Jeffrey Wright; "Slave Ships"—Ann Duquesnay, Savion Glover.

Som'thin' From Nuthin': "Som'thin' From Nuthin'/The Circle Stomp"—Baakari Wilder, Duquesnay, Company; "The Pan Handlers"—Jared Crawford, Raymond King.

Urbanization: "The Lynching Blues"—Wilder, Duquesnay, Company; "Chicago Bound"—Glover, Duquesnay, Company; "Shifting Sounds"—Wright; "Industrialization"—Glover, Wilder, Tate, Bingham, Crawford; "The Chicago Riot Rag"—Glover, Wilder, Tate, Bingham, Crawford; "I Got the Beat/Dark Tower"—Duquesnay, Wright, Company; "The Whirligig Stomp"—Company.

ACT II

Where's the Beat?: Voice—Wright; Chanteuse—Duquesnay; Kid—Hill; Grin & Flash—Tate, Bingham; Uncle Huck-a-Buck—Wilder; Li'l Dahlin'—Glover.

"Now That's Tap"	Grin & Flash
"The Uncle Huck-a-Buck Song"	Uncle Huck-a-Buck, Li'l Dahlin', Company
"Kid Go!"	Kid, Company
"The Lost Beat Swing"	Chanteuse, Company
Green, Chaney, Buster, Slyde	Glover

Street Corner Symphony: "1956, Them Conkheads"—Duquesnay, Company; "1967, Hot Fun"—Duquesnay, Wright, Company; "1977, Blackout"—Glover, Wilder, Tate, Bingham; "1987, Gospel/Hip Hop Rant"—Duquesnay, Wright, Glover.

Noise/Funk: "Drummin' "—Crawford, King; "Taxi"—Glover, Tate, Wilder, Bingham; "Conversations"—Crawford, King, Glover, Tate, Wilder, Bingham; "Hittin' "—Glover, Wilder, Tate, Bingham, Crawford, King, Wright; "Bring in 'da Noise Bring in 'da Funk" (reprise)—Company.

*Big (38). Musical based on the movie by Gary Ross and Anne Spielberg; book by John Weidman; music by David Shire; lyrics by Richard Maltby Jr. Produced by James B. Freydberg, Kenneth Feld, Laurence Mark and Kenneth D. Greenblatt in association with F.A.O. Schwartz Fifth Avenue at the Sam S. Shubert Theater. Opened April 28, 1996.

Cynthia Benson .... Lizzy Mack	Josh Baskin .... Daniel Jenkins
Young Josh .... Patrick Levis	Arcade Man; Lipton .... Frank Mastrone
Tiffany ....Samantha Robyn Lee	Matchless; Birnbaum .... Frank Vlastnik
Maggie .... Lori Aine Bennett	Paul ....Gene Weygandt
Mrs. Baskin .... Barbara Walsh	Susan .... Crista Moore
Mr. Baskin; Derelict; Larry Johnson;	MacMillan ....Jon Cypher
Tom .... John Sloman	Starfighter .... Brandon Espinoza
Mr. Kopecki; Panhandler; Nick ....Ray Wills	F.A.O. Sales Executive ....Joan Barber
Billy .... Brett Tabisel	Miss Watson .... Jan Neuberger
Mrs. Kopecki; Diane ....Donna Lee Marshall	Deathstarettes ....Joyce Chittick, CJay Hardy
Carnival Man; Barrett ....Clent Bowers	Abigail .... Jill Matson
Derek ....Alex Sanchez	Skatephone .... Spencer Liff
Zoltar ....Himself	Kid With Walkman .... Enrico Rodriguez
Voice of Zoltar .... Michel Bell	Skateboard Romeo .... Graham Bowen

Parents, Shoppers, Executives, Office Staff: Joan Barber, Clent Bowers, Joyce Chittick, CJay Hardy, Donna Lee Marshall, Frank Mastrone, Jill Matson, Jan Neuberger, Alex Sanchez, John Sloman, Frank Vlastnik, Ray Wills. The Big Kids: Lori Aine Bennett, Graham Bowen, Brandon Espinoza, Samantha Robyn Lee, Spencer Liff, Lizzy Mack, Enrico Rodriguez. Swings: Stacey Todd Holt, Joseph Medeiros, Corinne Melancon, Kari Pickler.

Understudies: Mr. Levis—Graham Bowen, Spencer Liff; Miss Walsh—Donna Lee Marshall, Joan Barber; Mr. Tabisel—Graham Bowen, Brandon Espinoza; Daniel Jenkins—Stacey Todd Holt, Frank Vlastnik; Mr. Weygand—Ray Wills, Frank Mastrone; Miss Moore—Jill Matson, Donna Lee Marshall; Mr. Cypher—Clent Bowers, Frank Mastrone; Messrs. Wills, Sloman—Frank Mastrone.

Orchestra: Paul Gemignani conductor; Nicholas Archer associate conductor; Suzanne Ornstein, Xin Zhao violin; Richard Brice viola; Clay Ruede cello; Charles Bergeron bass; Albert Regni, John Moses, Dennis Anderson, Eric Weidman, John Campo woodwinds; Ronald Sell, Michael Ishii, French horn; Joe Mosello, Danny Cahn, Dave Brown trumpet; Bruce Eidem, Dean Plank trombone; Nicholas Archer, Brian Besterman, Patrick Brady keyboards; Andrew Schwartz guitar; Paul Pizzuti drums; Thad Wheeler percussion.

Directed by Mike Ockrent; choreography, Susan Stroman; musical direction, Paul Gemignani; scenery, Robin Wagner; costumes, William Ivey Long; lighting, Paul Gallo; sound, Steve Canyon Kennedy; special effects, Gregory Meeh; orchestrations, Douglas Besterman; dance music arrangements, David Krane; electronic music, Brian Besterman; additional vocal arrangements, Patrick Brady; associate director, Steven Zweigbaum; assistant choreographer, Ginger Thatcher; associate producer, Daniel F. Kearns; producing associate, Michelle Leslie; casting, Johnson-Liff Associates; production stage manager, Steven Zweigbaum; stage manager, Clifford Schwartz; press, Boneau/Bryan-Brown, Chris Boneau.

As in the movie *Big,* a child magically and antically inhabits the body of a man.

ACT I

Scene 1: The neighborhood, New Jersey
"Can't Wait" ....Young Josh, Mrs. Baskin, Billy, Kids, Parents
"Talk to Her" .... Billy, Young Josh
"The Carnival" .... Company
Scene 2: The Baskin home
"This Isn't Me" ....Josh

Scene 3: Port Authority Bus Terminal
"I Want to Go Home" ....Josh
Scene 4: F.A.O. Schwartz
"The Time of Your Life" ....Kids
"Fun" .... McMillan, Josh, Company
Scene 5: The offices of McMillan Toys
"Dr. Deathstar" ....Deathstarettes
"Josh's Welcome" .... Susan, Paul, Executives
"Here We Go Again" .... Susan
Scene 6: Josh's loft
"Stars, Stars, Stars" ....Josh, Susan
Scene 7: A New York restaurant
"Tavern Foxtrot" ....Paul, Company
"Cross the Line" .... Josh, Kids, Company

ACT II

Scene 1: The mall
"It's Time" .... Billy, Kids
"Stop, Time" .... Mrs. Baskin
"Happy Birthday, Josh" ....Kids
Scene 2: Susan's office
"Dancing All the Time" .... Susan
"I Want to Know" ....Young Josh
Scene 3: The offices of McMillan Toys
"Coffee, Black" ....Josh, McMillan, Mrs. Watson, Birnbaum, Barrett, Lipton, Executives, Staff
Scene 4: An East Side apartment
"The Real Thing" ....Nick, Tom, Diane, Abigail
Scene 5: The roof terrace
"Our Special Man" .... Susan
Scene 6: The neighborhood
"When You're Big" ....Josh
"Skateboard Romance" ....Kids
Scene 7: A warehouse
"I Want to Go Home"/"Stars, Stars, Stars" (Reprise) ....Josh Susan

*Rent (36). Transfer from off Broadway of the musical with book, music and lyrics by Jonathan Larson. Produced by Jeffrey Seller, Kevin McCollum, Allan S. Gordon and New York Theater Workshop, James C. Nicola artistic director, Nancy Kassak Diekmann managing director, at the Nederlander Theater. Opened April 29, 1996.

Roger Davis .... Adam Pascal	Mrs. Jefferson; Woman With Bags;
Mark Cohen .... Anthony Rapp	Others ....Gwen Stewart
Tom Collins ....Jesse L. Martin	Gordon; The Man; Mr. Grey;
Benjamin Coffin III .... Taye Diggs	Others ....Timothy Britten Parker
Joanne Jefferson ....Fredi Walker	Man With Squeegee; Waiter;
Angel Schunard ....Wilson Jermaine Heredia	Others ....Gilles Chiasson
Mimi Marquez ....Daphne Rubin-Vega	Paul; Cop; Others .... Rodney Hicks
Maureen Johnson .... Idina Menzel	Alexi Darling; Roger's Mom;
Mark's Mom; Alison; Others .. Kristen Lee Kelly	Others .... Aiko Nakasone
Christmas Caroler; Mr. Jefferson; Pastor;	
Others ....Byron Utley	

The Band: Tim Weil conductor, keyboards; Steve Mack bass; Kenny Brescia guitar; Jeff Potter drums; Daniel A. Weiss keyboards 2, guitar 2.

Understudies: Messrs. Pascal, Rapp—Gilles Chiasson, David Driver; Mr. Martin—Darius de Haas, Byron Utley; Mr. Diggs—Darius de Haas, Rodney Hicks; Miss Walker—Shelley Dickinson, Simone; Mr. Heredia—Darius de Haas, Mark Setlock; Miss Rubin-Vega—Yassmin Alers, Simone; Miss Menzel—Yassmin Allers, Kristen Lee Kelly. Swings: Yassmin Allers, Darius de Haas, Shelley Dickinson, David Driver, Mark Setlock, Simone.

Directed by Michael Greif; choreography, Marlies Yearby; musical supervision and additional arrangements, Tim Weil; original concept and additional lyrics, Billy Aronson; scenery, Paul Clay; costumes, Angela Wendt; lighting, Blake Berba; sound, Kurt Fischer, musical arrangements, Steve Skinner; casting, Bernard Telsey Casting; film, Tony Gerber; production stage manager, John Vivian; stage manager, Crystal Huntington; press, Richard Kornberg & Associates, Richard Kornberg, Don Summa, Ian Rand.

Rock opera depicting the lifestyles of a group of artists in the modern East Village, New York, in the manner of *La Boheme*. Previously produced by New York Theater Workshop in a brief off-off-Broadway engagement 1/26/96 and in an off-Broadway engagement 2/13/96 for 56 performances.

A Best Play; see page 165.

ACT I

"Tune Up/Voice Mail #1" .... Mark, Roger, Mark's Mom, Collins, Benny
"Rent" .... Company
"You Okay Honey?" .... Angel, Collins
"One-Song Glory" .... Roger
"Light My Candle" .... Roger, Mimi
"Voice Mail #2" .... Mr. & Mrs. Jefferson
"Today 4 U" .... Angel
"You'll See" .... Benny, Mark, Collins, Roger, Angel
"Tango; Maureen" .... Mark, Joanne
"Life Support" .... Paul, Gordon, Company
"Out Tonight" .... Mimi
"Another Day" .... Roger, Mimi, Company
"Will I?" .... Company
"On the Street" .... Company
"Santa Fe" .... Collins, Company
"We're Okay" .... Joanne
"I'll Cover You" .... Angel, Collins
"Christmas Bells" .... Company
"Over the Moon" .... Maureen
"La Vie Boheme/I Should Tell You" .... Company

Act II

"Seasons of Love" .... Company
"Happy New Year/Voice Mail #3" ..... Mimi, Roger, Mark, Maureen, Joanne, Collins, Angel, Mark's
                                                          Mom, Alexi Darling, Benny
"Take Me or Leave Me" .... Maureen, Joanne
"Without You" .... Roger, Mimi
"Voice Mail #4" .... Alexi Darling
"Contact" .... Company
"I'll Cover You" (Reprise) .... Collins, Company
"Halloween" .... Mark
"Goodbye, Love" .... Mark, Mimi, Roger, Maureen, Joanne, Collins, Benny
"What You Own" .... Pastor, Mark, Collins, Benny, Roger
"Voice Mail #5" .... Roger's Mom, Mimi's Mom, Mr. Jefferson, Mark's Mom
Finale/"Your Eyes" .... Roger, Company

*Buried Child (36). Revival of the play by Sam Shepard. Produced by Frederick Zollo, Nicholas Paleologos, Jane Harmon, Nina Keneally, Gary Sinise, Edwin Schloss and Liz Oliver in the Steppenwolf Theater Company production at the Brooks Atkinson Theater. Opened April 30, 1996.

Bradley	Leo Burmester	Shelly	Kellie Overbey
Dodge	James Gammon	Halie	Lois Smith
Tilden	Terry Kinney	Vince	Jim True
Father Dewis	Jim Mohr		

Understudies: Miss Overbey—Patricia Jones; Miss Smith—David Lawrence; Messrs. Kinney, Burmester—Barton Tinapp; Mr. True—Connor Trinneer; Messrs. Gammon, Mohr—Christopher Wynkoop.

Directed by Gary Sinise; scenery, Robert Brill; costumes, Allison Reeds; lighting, Kevin Rigdon; sound, Rob Milburn; casting, Pat McCorkle; production stage manager, Laura Koch; stage manager, Franklin Keysar; press, Boneau/Bryan-Brown, Chris Boneau, Andy Shearer.

The first New York production of *Buried Child* took place off Broadway 12/5/78 for 152 performances and was awarded the Pulitzer Prize. This is its first major New York revival.

*An Ideal Husband (36). Revival of the play by Oscar Wilde. Produced by Bill Kenwright in the Peter Hall Company production at the Ethel Barrymore Theater. Opened May 1, 1996.

Sir Robert Chiltern ....David Yelland	Lady Basildon .... Valerie Leonard
Lady Chiltern .... Penny Downie	Mrs. Marchmont .... Allison Daugherty
Mabel Chiltern .... Victoria Hasted	Mr. Montford; Phipps ....Denis Holmes
Earl of Caversham ....Michael Denison	Mason .... Edmund C. Davys
Lord Goring .... Martin Shaw	James; Mr. Barford .... J. Paul Boehmer
Mrs. Cheveley ....Anna Carteret	Duchess of Maryborough ..... Angela Thornton
Lady Markby .... Dulcie Gray	Lady Jane Barford ....Cheryl Gaysunas
Vicomte de Nanjac ....Dominic Hawksley	

Standbys/Understudies: Messrs. Yelland, Holmes—Edmund C. Davys; Miss Downie—Allison Daugherty; Misses Hasted, Daugherty—Cheryl Gaysunas; Mr. Denison—Denis Holmes; Mr. Shaw—Dominic Hawksley; Miss Carteret—Valerie Leonard; Misses Gray, Leonard—Angela Thornton; Messrs. Hawksley, Davys—J. Paul Boehmer.

Directed by Peter Hall; designed by Carl Toms; lighting, Joe Atkins in association with Mike Baldassari; U.S. casting, Pat McCorkle; U.K. casting and assistant director, Gillian Diamond; production stage manager, David Hyslop; stage manager, Greg Schanuel; press, Philip Rinaldi.

Act I: The Reception Room in Sir Robert Chiltern's house in Grosvenor Square. Act II: The Morning Room in Sir Robert Chiltern's house. Act III: The library of Lord Goring's house in Curzon Street. Act IV: The Morning Room in Sir Robert Chiltern's house. The action of the play is completed within 36 hours. The play was presented in two parts with the intermission following Act II.

An Ideal Husband was first produced on Broadway by Daniel Frohman 3/12/1895 for 40 performances. Its only previous major New York revival of record took place 9/16/18 at the Comedy Theater for 80 performances.

PLAYS PRODUCED
OFF BROADWAY

Some distinctions between off-Broadway and Broadway productions at one end of the scale and off-off-Broadway productions at the other are blurred in the New York theater of the 1990s. For the purposes of *Best Plays* listing, the term "off Broadway" signifies a show which opened for general audiences in a mid-Manhattan theater seating 499 or fewer and 1) employed an Equity cast, 2) planned a regular schedule of 8 performances a week in an open-ended run (7 a week for solo shows) and 3) offered itself to public comment by critics after a designated opening performance.

Occasional exceptions of inclusion (never of exclusion) are made to take in visiting troupes, borderline cases and nonqualifying productions which readers might expect to find in this list because they appear under an off-Broadway heading in other major sources of record.

Figures in parentheses following a play's title give number of performances. These numbers do not include previews or extra non-profit performances.

Plays marked with an asterisk (*) were still in a projected run on June 1, 1996. Their number of performances is figured from opening night through May 31, 1996.

Certain programs of off-Broadway companies are exceptions to our rule of counting the number of performances from the date of the press coverage. When the official opening takes place late in the run of a play's regularly-priced public or subscription performances (after previews) we sometimes count the first performance of record, not the press date, as opening night—and in any such case in the listing we note the variance and give the press date.

In a listing of a show's numbers—dances, sketches, musical scenes, etc.—the titles of songs are identified wherever possible by their appearance in quotation marks (").

HOLDOVERS FROM PREVIOUS SEASONS

Plays which were running on June 1, 1995 are listed below. More detailed information about them appears in previous *Best Plays* volumes of appropriate date. Important cast changes since opening night are recorded in the Cast Replacements section of this volume.

*The Fantasticks (14,938; longest continuous run of record in the American theater). Musical suggested by the play *Les Romanesques* by Edmond Rostand; book and lyrics by Tom Jones; music by Harvey Schmidt. Opened May 3, 1960.

*Perfect Crime (3,750). By Warren Manzi. Opened October 16, 1987.

*Tony 'n' Tina's Wedding (2,922). By Artificial Intelligence. Opened February 6, 1988.

*Tubes (1,970). Performance piece by and with Blue Man Group. Opened November 17, 1991.

*Stomp (944). Percussion performance piece created by Luke Cresswell and Steve McNicholas. Opened February 27, 1994.

Three Tall Women (582). By Edward Albee. Opened April 5, 1994. (Closed August 26, 1995)

Jelly Roll (294). Solo performance by Vernel Bagneris; book by Vernel Bagneris; music and lyrics by Jelly Roll Morton. Opened August 9, 1994. (Closed July 2, 1995)

Manhattan Theater Club. After-Play (400). By Anne Meara. Opened January 31, 1995. (Closed March 5, 1995) Reopened May 15, 1995. (Closed April 28, 1996) Sylvia (283). By A.R. Gurney. Opened May 23, 1995. (Closed after 143 performances September 23, 1995) Reopened September 29, 1995. (Closed January 28, 1996)

Swingtime Canteen (294). Musical with book by Linda Thorsen Bond, William Repicci and Charles Busch; music and lyrics from Hit Parade songs of the 1940s. Opened February 24, 1995. (Closed November 26, 1995)

The Compleat Works of Wllm Shkspr (Abridged) (140). Revue by Adam Long, Daniel Singer and Jess Winfield. Opened February 27, 1995. (Closed July 1, 1995)

Death Defying Acts (407). Program of three one-act plays: *An Interview* by David Mamet, *Hotline* by Elaine May and *Central Park West* by Woody Allen. Opened March 6, 1995. (Closed February 25, 1996)

The Only Thing Worse You Could Have Told Me ... (175). Solo performance by Dan Butler; written by Dan Butler. Opened April 2, 1995. (Closed September 16, 1995)

London Suite (169). Program of four one-act plays by Neil Simon: *Settling Accounts, Going Home, Diana & Sidney* and *The Man on the Floor*. Opened April 9, 1995. (Closed September 3, 1995)

Travels With My Aunt (199). Adapted by Giles Havergal from the novel by Graham Greene. Opened April 12, 1995. (Closed October 1, 1995)

Party (366). By David Dillon. Opened May 11, 1995. (Closed March 24, 1996)

Coming Through (19). Adapted by Wynn Handman from recorded interviews of the Ellis Island Recorded History Project. Opened May 14, 1995. (Closed June 4, 1995)

Loose Lips (71). Comedy revue conceived and written by Kurt Anderson, Lisa Birnbach and Jamie Malanowski. Opened May 18, 1995. (Closed July 2, 1995)

Fortune's Fools (39). By Frederick Stroppel. Opened May 24, 1995. (Closed June 25, 1995)

PLAYS PRODUCED JUNE 1, 1995—MAY 31, 1996

john & jen (114). Transfer from off off Broadway of the musical with book by Andrew Lippa and Tom Greenwald; music by Andrew Lippa; lyrics by Tom Greenwald. Produced by the

Lamb's Theater Company and Carolyn Rossi Copeland at Lamb's Little Theater. Opened June 1, 1995. (Closed October 1, 1995)

john ....James Ludwig
jen ....Carolee Carmello

Musicians: Joel Fram conductor, piano; Matthew Szabo cello; Robert McEwan percussion.

Directed by Gabriel Barre; musical direction, Joel Fram; scenery, Charles E. McCarry; costumes, D. Polly Kendrick; lighting, Stuart Duke; orchestrations, Jason Robert Brown; production stage manager, Mary Ellen Allison; press, Kevin P. McAnarney.

Lives of a brother and sister. Previously produced in regional theater at the Goodspeed Opera House, Michael P. Price executive producer, and off off Broadway by the Lamb's Theater Company, Carolyn Rossi Copeland producing artistic director.

SCENES AND MUSICAL NUMBERS, ACT I: Prologue. Scene 1—"Welcome to the World." Scene 2—"Christmas." Scene 3—"Think Big." Scene 4—"Dear God." Scene 5—"Hold Down the Fort." Scene 6—"Timeline." Scene 7—"Out of My Sight," "Run and Hide." Epilogue.

ACT II: Scene 1—"Old Clothes." Scene 2—"Christmas" (Reprise). Scene 3—"Little League." Scene 4—"Just Like You," "Bye Room." Scene 5—"What Can I Do?" Scene 6—"Smile of Your Dreams." Scene 7—"Graduation." Scene 8—"The Road Ends Here," "That Was My Way," "Every Goodbye Is Hello."

Manhattan Theater Club. 1994–95 season concluded with **The Radical Mystique** (32). By Arthur Laurents. Produced by Manhattan Theater Club, Lynne Meadow artistic director, Barry Grove managing director, at City Center Stage II. Opened June 6, 1995. (Closed July 2, 1995)

Josie Gruenwald	Mary Beth Fisher	Tad Gruenwald	Kevin O'Rourke
Janice Catlett	Sharon Washington	Merriwell	Jake Weber
Parker Gruenwald	Oren J. Sofer		

Directed by Arthur Laurents; scenery, Thomas Lynch; costumes, Theoni V. Aldredge; lighting, Kenneth Posner; sound, Bruce Ellman; associate artistic director, Michael Bush; general manager, Victoria Bailey; casting, Nancy Piccione; production stage manager, Sandra Lea Carlson; stage manager, Alexis Shorter; press, Helene Davis, Barbara Carroll.

Time: The end of the Sixties. Place: The Gruenwald brownstone in Greenwich Village. The play was presented in two parts.

Comedy, affluent liberals face themselves and their lives in the course of organizing a benefit for the Black Panthers.

Brooklyn Academy of Music (BAM). 1994–95 season concluded with **Madame de Sade** (4). Revival of the play by Yukio Mishima; Swedish translation by Gunilla Lindberg-Wada and Per Eric Wahlund. Produced in the Swedish language in Ingmar Bergman's Royal Dramatic Theater of Sweden production, Lars Lofgren artistic director, by Brooklyn Academy of Music, Harvey Lichtenstein president and executive producer, at the BAM Carey Playhouse. Opened June 7, 1995. (Closed June 10, 1995)

Renee, Madame de Sade	Stina Ekblad	Baroness de Simiane	Margaretha Bystrom
Madame de Montreuil	Anita Bjork	Countess de Saint-Fond	Agnita Ekmanner
Anne	Elin Klinga	Charlotte	Helena Brodin

Directed by Ingmar Bergman; scenery and costumes, Charles Koroly; choreography, Donya Feuer; English translation, Donald Keene; readers of simultaneous translation, Tana Ross, Eva Engman; lighting, Sven-Eric Jacobsson; music, Ingrid Yoda; sound, Jan-Eric Piper; producer, Sofi Lerstrom; stage manager, Stephano Mariano; press, Heidi Feldman.

Act I: Late summer 1772, the drawing room in the house of Madame de Montreuil. Act II: Autumn 1778. Act III: Early spring 1790, twelve years after the second act and nine months after the outbreak of the French Revolution.

This Ingmar Bergman production of Mishima's play was previously presented by Brooklyn Academy of Music 5/20/93 for 3 performances.

THE RADICAL MYSTIQUE—Sharon Washington and Mary Beth Fisher in a scene from the play by Arthur Laurents

Lincoln Center Theater. 1994–95 off-Broadway schedule concluded with **Twelve Dreams** (69). Revival of the play by James Lapine. Produced by Lincoln Center Theater, Andre Bishop and Bernard Gersten directors, at the Mitzi E. Newhouse Theater. Opened June 8, 1995. (Closed August 6, 1995)

Charles Hatrick	Harry Groener	Sanford Putnam	Matthew Ross
Emma Hatrick	Mischa Barton	Dorothy Trowbridge	Donna Murphy
Jenny	Kathleen Chalfant	Miss Banton	Meg Howrey
Professor	Jan Rubes	Rindy	Brittany Boyd

Musicians: James Bassi musical direction, piano, celeste; Louis Bruno bass; Sue Evans percussion; William Kerr flute, clarinet, bass clarinet; Mia Wu violin, viola.

Understudies: Mr. Groener—Geoffrey Wade; Misses Barton, Boyd—Sylvana Opris; Misses Chalfant, Murphy—Anne Lange; Mr. Rubes—Mark Hammer; Mr. Ross—Grant James Varjas; Miss Howrey—Leslie Stevens.

Directed by James Lapine; scenery, Adrianne Lobel; costumes, Martin Pakledinaz; lighting, Peter Kaczorowski; sound, Dan Moses Schreier; original music, Allen Shawn; dance staging, Lar Lubovitch; casting, Daniel Swee; production stage manager, Beverley Randolph; stage manager, Thom Widman; press, Merle Debuskey, Susan Chicoine, Owen Levy.

Place: A university town in New England. Act I: December 1936. Act II: The following spring.

An author's note in the Playbill states: "*Twelve Dreams* was inspired by a case study of Carl Jung's as outlined in the book *Man and His Symbols*. The play takes those dreams as a starting point and all characters and events are fictional." It was previously produced off Broadway by New York Shakespeare Festival 12/22/81 for 48 performances.

*Second Stage Theater. Schedule of four programs. **Crumbs From the Table of Joy** (14). By Lynn Nottage. Opened June 20, 1995. (Closed July 1, 1995) **Sin** (23). By Wendy MacLeod. Opened October 11, 1995. (Closed October 29, 1995) **Oblivion Postponed** (35). By Ron Nyswaner; produced by special arrangement with Hal Luftig, Brent Peek, Richard Samson and Elizabeth Williams. Opened December 7, 1995. (Closed January 5, 1996) ***Dark Rapture** (10).

By Eric Overmyer. Opened May 23, 1996. Produced by Second Stage Theater, Carole Rothman artistic director, Suzanne Schwartz Davidson producing director, at Second Stage Theater.

CRUMBS FROM THE TABLE OF JOY

Ernestine Crump	Kisha Howard	Lily Ann Green	Ella Joyce
Ermina Crump	Nicole Leach	Gerte Schulte	Stephanie Roth
Godfrey Crump	Daryl Edwards		

Directed by Joe Morton; scenery, Myung Hee Cho; costumes, Karen Perry; lighting, Donald Holder; sound, Mark Bennett; associate producer, Carol Fishman; casting, Meg Simon; production stage manager, Delicia Turner; press, Richard Kornberg.

Black family moves from the rural South to Brooklyn in the 1950s. The play was presented in two parts.

SIN

Avery	Kelly Coffield	Helen	Camryn Manheim
Louis	Julio Monge	Fred	Tom Aulino
Michael	Bruce Norris	Jason	John Elsen
Jonathan	Steve Carell	Gerard	Jeffrey Hutchinson

Directed by David Petrarca; scenery, Scott Bradley; costumes, Allison Reeds; lighting, Robert Christen; music and sound, Rob Milburn; production stage manager, Nancy Harrington; stage manager, Elaine Bayless.

Time: 1989. Place: San Francisco. The play was presented in two parts.

Woman troubles herself and others by trying to set excessively high standards. Previously produced at the Goodman Theater, Chicago.

OBLIVION POSTPONED

David	David Aaron Baker	Patti	Mary Beth Hurt
Jeffrey	John Glover	Kyle	James Rebhorn
Vincenzo	Tony Gillan		

Directed by Nicholas Martin; scenery, Allen Moyer; costumes, Michael Krass; lighting, Michael Lincoln; sound, Randy Freed; associate producer, Carol Fishman; casting, Stephanie Klapper; production stage manager, Elise-Ann Konstantin; stage manager, Rebecca C. Monroe.

Two American couples—one gay, one straight—meet and interact while on a sightseeing trip to Rome.

DARK RAPTURE

Ray	Scott Glenn	Vegas; Bartender	Conan McCarty
Julia	Marisa Tomei	Ron; Waiter; Scones;	
Babcock; Nizam	Dan Moran	Lounge Singer	Bruce MacVittie
Danny; Tony	Derek Smith	Renee; Waitress	Jennifer Esposito
Lexington; Mathis	Joseph Siravo	Max	Ellen McElduff

Directed by Scott Ellis; scenery, Santo Loquasto; costumes, Jennifer Von Mayrhauser; lighting, Natasha Katz; sound, Tony Meola; original music, Jeremy Grody; fight direction, David Leong; associate producer, Carol Fishman; casting, Johnson-Liff Associates; production stage manager, Elise-Ann Konstantin; stage manager, Delicia Turner.

Mystery, a series of unfortunate events bedevils a screen writer. The play was presented in two parts.

New York Shakespeare Festival Shakespeare Marathon. Schedule of three revivals of plays by William Shakespeare. **The Tempest** (22). Opened June 22, 1995; see note. (Closed July 19,

1995 and transferred to Broadway; see its entry in the Plays Produced on Broadway section of this volume) **Troilus and Cressida** (27). Opened August 4, 1995; see note. (Closed September 3, 1995). **King Lear** (28). Opened January 25, 1996. (Closed February 18, 1996) Produced by New York Shakespeare Festival, George C. Wolfe producer, Rosemarie Tichler artistic producer, Joey Parnes executive producer, Laurie Beckelman executive director, Kevin Kline associate producer, *The Tempest* and *Troilus and Cressida* with the cooperation of the City of New York, Rudolph W. Giuliani Mayor, Peter F. Vallone Speaker of the City Council, Schuyler Chapin Commissioner of Cultural Affairs, Henry J. Stern Commissioner of Parks and Recreation, at the Delacorte Theater in Central Park; *King Lear* at the Joseph Papp Public Theater (Anspacher Theater).

THE TEMPEST

Shipmaster .... Tyrone Mitchell Henderson	Caliban .... Teagle F. Bougere
Boatswain .... Nathan Hinton	Ferdinand .... Kamar De Los Reyes
Alonso .... Larry Bryggman	Adrian .... Neal Huff
Gonzalo .... MacIntyre Dixon	Trinculo .... Bill Irwin
Sebastian .... Liev Schreiber	Stephano .... John Pankow
Antonio .... Nestor Serrano	Iris .... Midori Nakamura
Miranda .... Carrie Preston	Ceres .... Hilary Chaplain
Prospero .... Patrick Stewart	Juno .... Akwesi Asante
Ariel .... Aunjanue Ellis	

Ensemble: Akwesi Asante, Hilary Chaplain, Adam Dannheisser, Tyrone Mitchell Henderson, Nathan Hinton, Michael McGuigan, Midori Nakamura, Seamas L. O'Brien, Jodi Somers, Paul Whitthorne.

Musicians: Carlos Valdez, Moussa Diabate, Eric Kivnick percussion; Heather Paauwe percussion, violin; Beverly Au viola Da Gamba, recorder.

Understudies: Messrs. Stewart, Bryggman—Adam Dannheisser; Messrs. Bougere, Serrano—Nathan Hinton; Messrs. Huff, De Los Reyes, Schreiber—Paul Whitthorne; Messrs. Dixon, Pankow—Tyrone Mitchell Henderson; Mr. Irwin, Misses Chaplain, Asante—Michael McGuigan; Miss Preston—Jodi Somers; Miss Ellis—Midori Nakamura; Misses Chaplain, Asante, Ensemble Men—Seamas L. O'Brien; Messrs. Henderson, Hinton—Akwesi Asante.

Directed by George C. Wolfe; scenery, Riccardo Hernandez; costumes, Toni-Leslie James; lighting, Paul Gallo; sound, Dan Moses Schreier; choreography, Hope Clarke; mask and puppet design, Barbara Pollitt; composers, Carlos Valdez, Dan Moses Schreier; casting, Jordan Thaler/Heidi Griffiths; associate producers, Morgan Jenness, Wiley Hausam; production stage manager, Buzz Cohen; press, Carol Fineman.

The last major New York revival of *The Tempest* was by New York Shakespeare Festival in the Spanish language 8/27/91 for 12 performances. The play was presented in two parts.

TROILUS AND CRESSIDA

Prologue .... Victor L. Williams	Patroclus .... Phillip Christian
Troilus .... Neal Huff	Menelaus; Priam; Paris's
Pandarus; Calchas .... Stephen Spinella	Manservant .... Henry Stram
Aeneas .... Peter Francis James	Hector .... Boris McGiver
Cressida .... Elizabeth Marvel	Helenus .... Avery Glymph
Alexander .... David Costabile	Cassandra .... Catherine Kellner
Agamemnon .... Daniel Oreskes	Paris .... Bill Camp
Nestor .... Herb Foster	Diomedes .... Jeffrey Donovan
Ulysses .... Steven Skybell	Helen .... Tamara Tunie
Ajax .... Mark Kenneth Smaltz	Deiphobus; Margarelon .... Wood Harris
Thersites .... Tim Blake Nelson	Antenor .... Eddie Mitchell Morris
Achilles .... Paul Calderon	Andromache .... Elaina Davis

Soldiers, Servants, Trojan Bystanders, Myrmidons: Joel Carino, David Costabile, Robert Dolan, Olase Freeman, Avery Glymph, Wood Harris, Morley Kamen, Timothy McCracken, Eddie Mitchell Morris, Klea Scott, Victor L. Williams, Tracy Winston.

Musicians: Mark Bennett keyboards; Claire Daly saxophone, flute; Brian Johnson percussion; Willie Olenick trumpet, trombone.

Understudies: Messrs. Huff, Christian—Avery Glymph; Mr. Stram—Robert Dolan; Messrs. Spinella, James, Skybell—David Costabile; Messrs. Nelson, Donovan—Joel Carino; Miss Marvel—Catherine Kellner; Messrs. Oreskes, Foster—Timothy McCracken; Messrs. Smaltz, Calderon—Victor L. Williams; Messrs. Camp, McGiver—Wood Harris; Misses Tunie, Davis, Kellner—Klea Scott.

Directed by Mark Wing-Davey; choreography, Daniel Banks; scenery, Derek McLane; costumes, Catherine Zuber; lighting, Christopher Akerlind; sound, Dan Moses Schreier; original music, Mark Bennett; casting, Jordan Thaler/Heidi Griffiths; production stage manager, Rik Kaye; stage managers, Ron Nash, James D. Latus.

The last major New York production of *Troilus and Cressida* was by New York Shakespeare Festival 11/10/73 for 57 performances. The play was presented in two parts.

Note: Press date for *The Tempest* was 7/11/95, for *Troilus and Cressida* was 8/17/95.

KING LEAR

King Lear	F. Murray Abraham	Oswald	Francis Jue
Goneril	Margaret Gibson	King of France	Lee Mark Nelson
Regan	Elizabeth Marvel	Burgundy	Chris McKinney
Cordelia	Brienin Bryant	Kent	John Woodson
Albany	Armand Schultz	Gloucester	Thomas Hill
Cornwall	Ezra Knight	Edgar	Rob Campbell
Fool	Jeffrey Wright	Edmund	Jared Harris

Others: Joe Zaloom, Mel Duane Gionson, Jeff Stafford, Scott Brasfield, Paul Kielar, Jill Jaffe, Ed Zuhlke.

Directed by Adrian Hall; scenery, Eugene Lee; costumes, Catherine Zuber; lighting, Natasha Katz; sound, Dan Moses Schreier; music, Richard Cumming; fights, J. Steven White; casting, Jordan Thaler/Heidi Griffiths; production stage manager, Ruth Kreshka.

The last major New York revival of *King Lear* was by Roundabout Theater Company off Broadway 10/9/90 for 80 performances. This production was presented in two parts.

Note: New York Shakespeare Festival's Shakespeare Marathon is scheduled to continue through following seasons until all of Shakespeare's plays have been presented. *A Midsummer Night's Dream, Julius Caesar* and *Romeo and Juliet* were produced in the 1987–88 season; *Much Ado About Nothing, King John, Coriolanus, Love's Labour's Lost, The Winter's Tale* and *Cymbeline* were produced in the 1988–89 season; *Twelfth Night, Titus Andronicus, Macbeth* and *Hamlet* were produced in the 1989–90 season; *The Taming of the Shrew, Richard III* and *Henry IV, Part 1* and *Part 2* were produced in the 1990–91 season; *Othello* and *Pericles, Prince of Tyre* were produced in the 1991–92 season; *As You Like It* and *The Comedy of Errors* were produced in the 1992–93 season; *Measure for Measure, All's Well That Ends Well* and *Richard II* were produced in the 1993–94 season and *The Merry Wives of Windsor, The Two Gentlemen of Verona* and *The Merchant of Venice* were produced in the 1994–95 season.

Note: New York Shakespeare Festival and the Japan-U.S. Partnership for the Performing Arts presented Umekawa Rokuro and his Noh theater company Tagaki-Noh '95 at the Delacorte Theater in *Funa-Benkei,* a Noh drama of vengeance and thwarted love, and *Futari Daimyo,* the classic Kyogen farce, for 3 performances 9/8/95–9/10/95.

*Playwrights Horizons. Schedule of five programs. **The Springhill Singing Disaster** (14). Solo performance by Karen Trott; written by Karen Trott; developed by Norman Rene. Opened June 22, 1995. (Closed July 2, 1995) **The Monogamist** (24). By Christopher Kyle. Opened November 9, 1995. (Closed November 26, 1995). **Black Ink** (9). Program of four one-act plays: *Man in Polyester Suit* by Ed DuRante, *Life by Asphyxiation* by Kia Corthron, *Cover* by Beverly Smith-Dawson and *The Bodhisattva Locksmith* by Lynn Martin. Opened December 3, 1995. (Closed December 10, 1995) **Floyd Collins** (25). Musical with book by Tina Landau; music and lyrics by Adam Guettel; additional lyrics by Tina Landau. Opened March 3, 1996. (Closed March 24, 1996) ***Arts & Leisure** (13). By Steve Tesich. Opened May 19, 1996. Produced by

Playwrights Horizons, Don Scardino artistic director (through Dec. 31), Lynn Landis general manager, Leslie Marcus managing director, Tim Sanford associate artistic director and artistic director (as of Jan. 1) at Playwrights Horizons.

THE SPRINGHILL SINGING DISASTER

Directed by Norman Rene; scenery, Loy Arcenas; costumes, Walker Hicklin; lighting, Debra J. Kletter; sound, Joseph Robinson; production stage manager, Andrea J. Testani; press, Philip Rinaldi, James Morrison.

Vignettes and pitfalls of a life in the theater as portrayed by Karen Trott.

THE MONOGAMIST

Jasmine Stone	Caroline Seymour	Tim Hapgood	Timothy Olyphant
Dennis Jensen	Arliss Howard	Sky Hickock	Chelsea Altman
Susan Barry	Lisa Emery		

Directed by Scott Elliott; scenery, Derek McLane; costumes, Eric Becker; lighting, Peter Kaczorowski; sound Raymond D. Schilke; video, Mark McKenna; casting Janet Foster; production stage manager, John J. Harmon; stage manager, Alex Lyu Volckhausen.

Time: The Bush administration. Place: Various locations in Princeton, N.J. and New York City. The play was presented in two parts.

Poet loses faith in his work and his marriage with his longtime sweetheart, a college professor who has an affair with one of her students. The play was presented in two parts.

BLACK INK

Man in Polyester Suit

Deuce	David Eigenberg
Jack	Chad L. Coleman

Directed by Pamela Berlin; production stage manager, Michael McCormack.

Time: The present. Place: The back room of a bar in New York City.

Comedy, black man undergoes harrassment from his white friend who has decided to reveal that he is gay.

Life by Asphyxiation

JoJo	Ray Aranha
Nat Turner	Keith Randolph Smith
Andy	Stephen Mendillo
Katie	Lisa Weil
Paramedic	Chad L. Coleman

Directed by Gilbert McCauley; production stage manager, Caroline Ranald.

Time: The present. Place: Death Row.

Two black men on Death Row visited by the ghost of one of their victims. An intermission followed this play.

Cover

Man	Keith Randolph Smith
Woman	Anne Bobby

Directed by Gilbert McCauley; production stage manager, Caroline Ranald.

Time: Now . . . or later. Place: A man's home in a suburb, late night.

Comedy, a female officer in the witness-protection program visits one of her charges, a black man, intending to make sexual and racial adjustments.

The Bodhisattva Locksmith

May Eastman	Ellen Bethea
Nina	Melinda Wade
Locksmith	Kevin Geer

Directed by Pamela Berlin; production stage manager, Michael McCormack.

Time: The present, midnight. Place: May's apartment, New York City.

Two women and one man, a locksmith called to cope with problems with their apartment doors.

ALL PLAYS: Scenery, David Harwell; costumes, Mimi O'Donnell; lighting, Anne M. Padien; sound, Michael Clark; casting, Janet Foster.

FLOYD COLLINS

Floyd Collins	................Christopher Innvar	Homer Collins	...................Jason Danieley
Bee Doyle	...............Stephen Lee Anderson	Skeets Miller	......................Martin Moran
Ed Bishop	......................Rudy Roberson	H.T. Carmichael	.............Michael Mulheren
Jewell Estes	..........................Jesse Lenat	Cliff Roney; Reporter	.......Brian d'Arcy James
Lee Collins	.......................Don Chastain	Dr. Hazlett; Reporter	.........Matthew Bennett
Miss Jane	..........................Cass Morgan	Reporter; Con Man	............James Bohanek
Nellie Collins	................Theresa McCarthy		

Musicians: Ted Sperling conductor; Steve Marzullo piano, keyboards; Michael Nicholas violin; David Creswell viola, violin; Carlo Pelletieri, Peter Donovan bass; Kevin Kuhn guitar, banjo; Corrun Huddleston harmonica; Tom Parkinton percussion.

Directed by Tina Landau; musical direction, Ted Sperling; scenery, James Schuette; costumes, Melina Root; lighting, Scott Zielinski; sound, Dan Moses Schreier; orchestrations, Bruce Coughlin; consulting producer, Don Scardino; casting, Janet Foster, production stage manager, Erica Schwartz; press, James Morrison.

Time: January 30–February 16, 1925. Place: Barren County, Kentucky, Bee Doyle's farm.

Dramatization of the real-life individual tragedy and ironic exploitations of a man hopelessly trapped in a Kentucky cave.

ACT I

The Cave
"The Call"... Floyd
The Rescue
"Tween a Rock and a Hard Place" .... Ed Bishop, Jewell Estes, Bee Doyle
"Lucky" ....Nellie, Miss Jane
"Daybreak" .... Homer, Floyd
"I Landed on It" .... Skeets Miller
"Blue Eyes" .... Floyd
"Heart an' Hand" .... Miss Jane, Lee
"The Riddle Song" .... Homer, Floyd

ACT II

The Carnival
"Is That Remarkable?" ....Company
"The Carnival"..Company
"Through the Mountain" ....Nellie
"Git Comfortable" ....Homer
"Family Hymn" .... Nellie, Homer, Lee, Miss Jane
"The Dream" ....Company
"How Glory Goes" .... Floyd
"The Ballad of Floyd Collins" ....Homer

ARTS & LEISURE

Alex Chaney	........................Harris Yulin	Lenore	..........................Frances Conroy
Maria	...........................Randy Danson	Daughter	........................Elizabeth Marvel
Mother	............................Mary Diveny		

Directed by JoAnne Akalaitis; scenery, Douglas Stein; costumes, Susan Hilferty; lighting, Frances Aronson; sound, Bruce Odland; consulting producer, Don Scardino; casting, Janet Foster; production stage manager, Alan Fox.

Time: The present. Place: New York City. The play was performed without intermission.

A drama critic begins to regard and judge real life in the same manner that he regards and judges theatrical fiction.

Circle Repertory Company. 1994–95 season concluded with **Lonely Planet** (15). By Steven Dietz. Produced by Circle Repertory Company, Tanya Berezin artistic director, Milan Stitt executive director, Meredith Freeman managing director, at Circle Repertory. Opened July 12, 1995. (Closed July 23, 1995)

Carl .... Denis O'Hare
Jody .... Mark Shannon

Directed by Leonard Foglia; scenery, Michael McGarty; costumes, Markas Henry; lighting, Howard Werner; sound, One Dream Sound; production stage manager, Deborah Heimann; press, Jeffrey Richards Associates, Kevin Rehac.

Time: The present. Place: Jody's Maps, a small map store on the oldest street in an American city. The play was presented in two parts.

Bonds of friendship and overtones of death in the relationship of two gay men. Previously produced off off Broadway by the Barrow Group.

Pets (68). Musical revue written and/or composed by 17 authors (individual credits listed below). Produced by Leahy Productions in association with Arthur B. Brown at Theater East, Opened July 27, 1995. (Closed September 23, 1995)

Michelle Azar   Christopher Scott
Barbara Broughton   Jennifer Simard
Christopher Harrod

The Band: Albert Ahronheim conductor, keyboards; Sid Cherry keyboards; Kerry Meads drums, percussion.

Conceived, directed and choreographed by Helen Butleroff; musical direction, orchestrations and additional arrangements, Albert Ahronheim; scenery, Holger; costumes, Gail Cooper-Hecht; lighting, Phil Monat; sound, Ray Schilke, casting, Stephanie Klapper; production stage manager, D.C. Rosenberg; press, Cromarty & Company, Peter Cromarty.

Sketches, songs and dances on the subject of animals and the parts they play in our lives

SCENES AND MUSICAL NUMBERS, ACT I: Scene 1, Opening—"Pets" (music by Kim Oler, lyrics by Alison Hubbard). Scene 2, The Animal Shelter—"Take Me Home With You" (music and lyrics by Thomas Tierney); "Don't Worry 'Bout Me" (music by Ben Schaechter, lyrics by Dan Kael). Scene 3, Central Park—"I Walk Ze Dogs" (music by Jimmy Roberts, lyrics by June Siegel); "Just Do It Without Me" (music by Thomas Tierney, lyrics by Jane Brody Zales). Scene 4, The Home—"Cat in the Box" (music by Thomas Tierney); "There's a Bagel on the Piano" (music by Ben Schaechter, lyrics by Faye Greenberg); "Perpetual Care" (music by Ben Schaechter, lyrics by Adele Ahronheim); "Cool Cats" (music by Kim Oler, lyrics by Alison Hubbard); "Dear Max" (music by Carolyn Sloan, lyrics by Marion Adler and Carolyn Sloan); "First Cat" (introduction by Thomas Edward West, music and lyrics by Thomas Tierney).

ACT II: Scene 1, More Pets—"What About Us?" (music by Raphael Crystal, lyrics by Richard Engquist); "Peculiar" (music by Ben Schaechter, lyrics by Dan Kael); Bonus #1 (by Greer Woodward); "Franklin" (music by Ben Schaechter, lyrics by Faye Greenberg); "Mice of Means" (music by Ben Schaechter, lyrics by Dan Kael); Bonus #2 (by Greer Woodward); "Night of the Iguana" (music by Kim Oler, lyrics by Alison Hubbard); Bonus #3 (by Greer Woodward); "If You Can Stay" (music by Rick Cummins, lyrics by Greer Woodward). Scene 2, Heroes—"All in a Day's Work" (music and lyrics by Thomas Tierney). Finale "Pets" (Reprise).

We'll Meet Again (79). Musical revue conceived by Johnny King; written by Vicki Stuart; additional material by Ivan Menchell. Produced by Michael and Barbara Ross and Lois Teich at the 45th Street Theater. Opened July 27, 1995. (Closed October 1, 1995; see note)

Paul Katz   Vicki Stuart

Directed by Johnny King; scenery, James Morgan; lighting, Daniel Ettinger; costumes, Oleg Cassini; musical direction and arrangements, Paul Katz; sound, One Dream Sound; production stage manager, Michael J. Chudinski; press, Penny Landau.

Memories of World War II on the home front, with a selection of musical numbers of that era.

Note: *We'll Meet Again* reopened 5/23/96 under the auspices of the York Theater Company at the Theater at St. Peter's.

*The Food Chain (321). By Nicky Silver. Produced by Robert V. Straus, Randall L. Wreghitt, Annette Niemtzow and Michael Jackowitz in association with Evangeline Morphos and Nancy Richards at the Westside Theater Upstairs. Opened August 24, 1995.

Amanda	Hope Davis	Serge	Patrick Fabian
Bea	Phyllis Newman	Otto	Tom McGowan
Ford	Rudolf Martin		

Standbys: Miss Davis—Katie MacNichol; Miss Newman—Barbara Spiegel; Messrs. Martin, Fabian—Brendan Corbalis; Mr. McGowan—John Scurti.

Directed by Robert Falls; scenery, Thomas Lynch; costumes, William Ivey Long; lighting, Kenneth Posner; sound, Duncan Edwards, Ben Rubin; executive producer, Michael Rafael; associate producers, Kathleen O'Grady, Gilford/Freeley Productions, Andrew Barrett, Terrie Adams, Fanny M. Mandelberger, Richard Kornberg and Pope Entertainment Group; casting, Bernard Telsey; production stage manager, Allison Sommers; press, Richard Kornberg Associates, Ian Rand, Don Summa.

Scene 1: "Amanda"—New York City, the middle of the night. Scene 2: "Otto"—New York City, the same night. Scene 3: "Fatty and Skinny Lay in Bed . . ."—New York City, the next morning. The play was presented without intermission.

Various comic aspects of various forms of love—and the importance of avoiding being overweight.

Steven Skybell replaced Tom McGowan. Rob Leo Roy replaced Steven Skybell. Spencer Rochfort replaced Patrick Fabian. Marsha Dietlein replaced Hope Davis. Katie MacNichol replaced Marsha Dietlein. Joy Behar replaced Phyllis Newman 3/24/96. Veanne Cox replaced Katie MacNichol 4/30/96.

Too Jewish? (189). Transfer from off off Broadway of the solo performance by Avi Hoffman; conceived by Avi Hoffman. Produced by REL Productions, Judith Resnick, Paul Morer, Normand Kurtz and Steve Harris at the Westside Theater Downstairs. Opened September 7, 1995. (Closed February 18, 1996)

Musical direction, arrangements and accompaniment, Ben Schaechter; ballad by Faye Greenberg and Ben Schaechter; press, Richard Kornberg Associates.

Affectionate reminiscences of Yiddish comedy, history, vaudeville and songs. Previously produced off off Broadway 1/15/95.

*Grandma Sylvia's Funeral (275). Transfer from off off Broadway of the environmental theater piece conceived by Glenn Wein and Amy Lord Blumsack; created by Glenn Wein and Amy Lord Blumsack and the original company. Produced by Dana Matthow with Bonnie Loren and Amy Lord Blumsack at the Soho Playhouse. Opened October 4, 1995.

CAST: Glenn Wein, Paul Eagle, David Ellzey, Holgie Forrester, Ron Gilbert, Karen Ginsburg, Sheri Goldner, Sondra Gorney, Brooke Johnson, Marc Kamhi, Morgan Lavere, Simone Lazer, Janice Mautner, Brocton Pierce, David Eric Rosenberg, Joanna Rush, Tom Sarpi, Jim Simon, Stanley Allan Sherman, Helen Siff, Justine Slater, Barry Weinberger.

Directed by Glenn Wein; design, Leon Munier; costumes, Peter Janis; lighting, David J. Lander; production stage manager, Margaret Bodriguian; press, John Springer Associates, John Springer, Gary Springer.

Farcical treatment of a Jewish family coping with the details of a funeral, previously presented as an off off Broadway production for 167 performances 10/1/94—9/23/95.

1995 Young Playwrights Festival (31). Program of four one-act plays: *Guyworld* by Bret LaGree, *The King* by Denise Ruiz, *Proof Through the Night* by Clarence Coo and *This Is About a Boy's Fears* by Shaun Neblett. Produced by Young Playwrights Inc., Sheri M. Goldhirsch artistic director, Brett W. Reynolds managing director, at the Joseph Papp Public Theater's Martinson Hall. Opened October 4, 1995. (Closed October 29, 1995)

GRANDMA SYLVIA'S FUNERAL—Sheri Goldner and spectators in the interactive environmental theater piece conceived and created by Glenn Wein, Amy Lord Blumsack and the original off-off-Broadway company

Guyworld

Tom ....Jim Bracchitta
Ray .... Robert Montano
Bartender .... Gary Perez
Dave ....Ray Wills

Directed by Michael Breault; dramaturge, Lynn M. Thompson; stage manager, James Latus.
Satire, an ideal society inhabited exclusively by men.

The King

Ishmel .... Benny Nieves

Miguel .... Vincent Laresca
Rolando .... Robert Montano
Tuto .... Al D. Rodriguez
Guard; Priest .... David Wolos-Fonteno
Dito .... Gary Perez
Julio ....Jim Bracchitta
Prison Trustee (ok) ....Ray Wills
Mother .... Divina Cook

Directed by Susana Tubert; dramaturge, Charlie Schulman; stage manager, James Latus.
The rise and fall of a gang leader.

Proof Through the Night

Mavis ....Aleta Mitchell
Toby .... Sean Runnette

Directed by Richard Caliban; dramaturge, Ben Pesner; stage manager, Elise-Ann Konstantin.

Black comedy, two lonely people come together for a brief respite from their fading hopes.

This Is About a Boy's Fears

Marc ....Sharif

Enis ....Sean Thomas
Angela ....Aleta Mitchell
Jerry .... David Wolos-Fonteno

Directed by Mark Brokaw; dramaturge, Jeffrey D. MacCulloch; stage manager, Elise-Ann Konstantin.

Teen-ager feels he can't connect with his mother and older brother because of their preoccupation with sexual adventures.

Daniel O. Williams replaced Sean Thomas in mid-run.

ALL PLAYS: Scenery, Narelle Sissons; costumes, Karen Perry; lighting, Donald Holder; sound, Janet Kalas; casting, Alan Filderman, Michele Ortlip; press, Serino Coyne Inc., Terence Womble.

These four plays were selected from hundreds of entries in Young Playwrights Inc.'s 14th annual playwriting contest for authors 18 years of age or younger at the time of submission (all the above were 17 at that time). The program was presented in two parts.

Dangerous Corner (86). Revival of the play by J.B. Priestley. Produced by Atlantic Theater Company, Neil Pepe artistic director, Joshua Lehrer managing director, at the Atlantic Theater. Opened October 11, 1995. (Closed December 31, 1995)

Maud Mockridge .... Hilary Hinkle
Olwen Peel .... Rebecca Pigeon
Freda Chatfield .... Felicity Huffman
Betty Whitehouse .... Mary McCann

Charles Stanton ....David Pittu
Gordon Whitehouse .... Robert Bella
Robert Chatfield ....Jordan Lage

Directed by David Mamet; scenery, James Wolk; costumes, Laura Cunningham; lighting, Howard Werner; sound, Douglas Jaffe; production stage manager, Matthew Silver; stage manager, Michelle Bosch; press, Boneau/Bryan-Brown, Andy Shearer.

Dangerous Corner was first produced on Broadway 10/27/32 for 206 performances. It was revived on Broadway the following year for 90 performances and off Broadway in the seasons of 1945–46 and 1950–51. The play was presented in two parts.

Pomp Duck and Circumstance (147). Revue created by Hans-Peter Wodarz. Produced by MGM Grand, Dieter Esch producer, at Salon Zazou. Opened October 11, 1995. (Closed March 31, 1996)

"Restaurant Staff":
Ferdinand de Belair
    (Restaurateur) .... Denis H. Jaquillard
Maurice Fatale
    (Head Chef) ....Jean Michel Coll
Herr Lutz (Waiter) ....Lutz Jope
Miss Linda ....Francine Leonard
Matthias (Waiter) .... Matthias Krahnert
Gusti (Wine Steward) ...... Eduard Kaufmann
Hassan (Waiter) .... Hassan Celik
Rosa (Chamber Maid) ....Franziska Traub

Juliette (Waitress) ....Nathalie Tarlet
Arthur Senkrecht
    (Waiter Trainee) .... Arnd D. Schimkat
Acrobats, Other Performers:
Mr. P.P. (Restaurant Host) .....Timothy Tyler
Sophie Clutch (Waitress) .... Corey Shank
Conc (Waiter) .... Mark C. Colli
Ramon (Bartender, Magic Man) ..Ramon Saez
Pierette (Waitress) ....Danielle Trepanier
Ben Johnson (Journalist) .... Tim Ward
Jessica ....Sabine Hettlich

Other Performers: Les Barons Karamazoff (Sergej Karamazoff, Zoran Madzirov, Martin Gjakonovski), Kathryn Green, The Daidalos Brothers, Boxers (Christian Mrozek, Ronald Siegmund), The Chair Man (Vassili Dementchoukov), Mouvance—Carmen on the Trapeze (Helene Turcotte, Luc Martin).

Musicians: Rudi Mauser conductor, bass; Rich Laughlin trumpet; Rick Coleman piano; Hannes Schindler violin; Stephen Roger Buck saxophone; Robert Kopp drums.

Artistic director, Michel Dallaire; musical direction, Rudi Mauser; choreography, Ross Coleman; costumes, Dea Valmonte, Max Dietrich, Jurgen Blume, Nameck Gaud; lighting, Jason Kantrowitz, sound, Klaus Lohmann; assistant director, Stephane Laisne; stage manager, Christoph Wienecke; press, Keith Sherman, Jim Byk, Stuart Ginsberg.

Part comedy, part circus, part musical revue with a real restaurant staff (in addition to the fictional one) serving a real gourmet meal along with the show.

Bob Greenberg replaced Tim Ward; Victor Kee (acrobat-juggler) joined the performing troupe.

Moscow Stations (37). Solo performance by Tom Courtenay; written by Stephen Mulrine; adapted from the novel *Moscow to Petushi* by Venedikt Yerofeev. Produced by Julian Schlossberg, Brian Brolly, Alan J. Schuster and Mitchell Maxwell in the Traverse Theater Company production at the Union Square Theater. Opened October 15, 1995. (Closed November 26, 1995)

Directed by Ian Brown; scenery and costumes, Tim Hatley; lighting, Ian Sommerville; sound, John Irvine; production stage manager, John Vivian; press, Bill Evans.

Moscow anecdotes and observations by Courtenay as the author, Yerofeev, who has a compelling fondness for vodka. A foreign play previously produced in London.

Roundabout Theater Company. Schedule of three programs. **Moonlight** (72). By Harold Pinter. Opened October 17, 1995. (Closed December 17, 1995) **Molly Sweeney** (145). By Brian Friel; co-produced with the Gate Theater, Dublin, Michael Colgan director, and Emanuel Azenberg. Opened January 7, 1996. (Closed May 12, 1996) And *Grace & Glorie* by Tom Ziegler, scheduled to open 6/23/96. Produced by Roundabout Theater Company, Todd Haimes artistic director, Ellen Richard general manager, Gene Feist founding director, at the Laura Pels Theater.

MOONLIGHT

Bridget	Melissa Chalsma	Jake	Liev Schreiber
Andy	Jason Robards	Maria	Kathleen Widdoes
Bel	Blythe Danner	Ralph	Paul Hecht
Fred	Barry McEvoy		

Understudies: Messrs. Robards, Hecht—Christopher Wynkoop; Misses Danner, Widdoes—Deborah Kipp; Messrs. Schreiber, McEvoy—David Wiater; Miss Chalsma—Miranda Kent.

Directed by Karel Reisz; scenery, Tony Walton; costumes, Mirena Rada; lighting, Richard Pilbrow; sound, Tom Clark; casting, Pat McCorkle; production stage manager, Jay Adler; stage manager, Janet Beroza; press, Boneau/Bryan-Brown, Susanne Tighe.

A dying man and members of his family reflect on their troubled past relationships and attitudes. The play was presented without intermission. A foreign play previously produced at the Almeida Theater in London.

MOLLY SWEENEY

Molly Sweeney	Catherine Byrne	Frank Sweeney	Alfred Molina
Mr. Rice	Jason Robards		

Understudies: Mr. Robards—Malachy McCourt; Mr. Molina—Colin Lane.

Directed by Brian Friel; scenery and costumes, Joe Vanek; lighting, Mick Hughes; associate producer, Ginger Montel; casting, Jay Binder; production managers, Philip Cusack, John Vivian; press, Boneau/Bryan-Brown, Bill Evans & Associates.

Time: The present. The play was presented in two parts.

Doctor, an alcoholic, tries to restore the sight of a blind woman. A foreign play previously produced at the Gate Theater, Dublin and the Almeida Theater, London.

A Best Play; see page 149.

*Manhattan Theater Club. Schedule of six programs. **Full Gallop** (39). Solo performance by Mary Louise Wilson; written by Mark Hampton and Mary Louise Wilson. Opened October 18, 1995. (Closed November 19, 1995) **New England** (54). By Richard Nelson. Opened November 7, 1995. (Closed December 22, 1995) ***Valley Song** (68). By Athol Fugard; produced in association with the McCarter Theater. Opened December 12, 1995. (Closed January 21, 1996 after 48 performances) Reopened May 7, 1996. **Blue Window** (56). Revival of the play by Craig Lucas. Opened February 6, 1996. (Closed March 24, 1996) **Overtime** (48). By A.R. Gurney. Opened March 5, 1996. (Closed April 14, 1996) ***By the Sea by the Sea by the Beautiful Sea** (2). Program of three one-act plays: *Dawn* by Joe Pintauro, *Day* by Lanford Wilson and *Dusk* by Terrence McNally. Opened May 30, 1996. Produced by Manhattan Theater Club, Lynne Meadow artistic director, Barry Grove executive producer, Michael Bush associate artistic director, at City Center, *New England* and *Blue Window* at Stage I, *Full Gallop, Valley Song, Overtime* and *By the Sea* at Stage II.

FULL GALLOP

Directed by Nicholas Martin; scenery, James Noone; costumes, Michael Krass; lighting, David F. Segal; sound, Bruce Ellman; makeup design, Randy Houston Mercer; casting, Nancy Piccione; production stage manager, John Handy; press, Helene Davis, Barbara Carroll, Kevin McAnarney.

Understudy: Joan Rosenfels.

Time: 1971. Place: Diana Vreeland's Park Avenue apartment. The play was presented in two parts.

Mary Louise Wilson as the late Diana Vreeland, renowned former editor of *Vogue,* at the time when she had just been fired from that post. Previously produced in regional theater at the Old Globe Theater, San Diego.

NEW ENGLAND

Harry Baker, Alfred Baker .... Larry Bryggman	Paul Baker .... T. Scott Cunningham
Alice Berry .... Penny Fuller	Gemma Baker .... Allison Janney
Tom Berry ....Tom Irwin	Sophie Baker ....Margaret Whitton
Elizabeth Baker ....Mia Dillon	

Directed by Howard Davies; scenery, Santo Loquasto; costumes, Jennifer Von Mayrhauser; lighting, Richard Nelson; sound and arrangements, Mark Bennett; casting, Nancy Piccione; production stage manager, Franklin Keysar; stage manager, Scott LaFeber.

Time: Over a weekend. Place. A house in western Connecticut, just across the border from New York State.

Comedy, members of an English family condescend to live and work in the United States. An American play previously produced in London by the Royal Shakespeare Company. The play was presented without intermission.

A Best Play; see page 117.

VALLEY SONG

The Author, a White Man; Abraam (Buks)	Veronica Jonkers .... LisaGay Hamilton
Jonkers ....Athol Fugard	

Understudies: Mr. Fugard—Peter Walker; Miss Hamilton—Lisa Renee Pitts.

Directed by Athol Fugard; scenery and costumes, Susan Hilferty; lighting, Dennis Parichy; composer, DiDi Kriel; associate director, Susan Hilferty; casting, Elisa Myers, Paul Foquet, Nancy Piccione; production stage managers, Sandra Lea Carlson, Pamela Edington; restaging supervised by Lonny Price.

Time: The present. Place: The small town of Nieu-Bethesda in the Karoo, South Africa. The play was presented without intermission.

Grandfather and granddaughter, "coloreds," fear that a white buyer of their tenant farm might evict them, while she dreams of going to the city to become a singer, in present-day South Africa. A foreign play originally produced in 1995 by Mannie Manim Productions, Johannesburg, South Africa.

Marius Weyers replaced Athol Fugard 5/7/96.

A Best Play; see page 135.

BLUE WINDOW

Norbert	David Aaron Baker	Alice	Ellen McLaughlin
Emily	Johanna Day	Libby	J. Smith-Cameron
Griever	John Benjamin Hickey	Tom	David Warshofsky
Boo	Allison Janney		

Understudies: Messrs. Baker, Hickey, Warshofsky—Dylan McCormick; Misses Day, Janney—Amy Hohn; Misses McLaughlin, Smith-Cameron—Lee Brock.

Directed by Joe Mantello; scenery, Robert Brill; costumes, Laura Cunningham; lighting, Brian MacDevitt; sound, John Gromada; casting, Eve Battaglia; "The Same Thing (Office Girl's Lament)" words and music by William Bolcom; production stage manager, William Joseph Barnes; stage manager, Ira Mont.

Time: A Sunday evening, the present. Place: New York City. The play was presented without intermission.

Blue Window was originally produced off off Broadway 6/12/84 and was moved up to full off-Broadway status 12/9/84 for 96 performances and won its author the first annual George and Elisabeth Marton Award for playwriting. This is its first major New York revival of record.

OVERTIME

Portia	Joan McMurtrey	Jessica	Jill Tasker
Antonio	Rocco Sisto	Lorenzo	Willis Sparks
Bassanio	Jere Shea	Salerio	Robert Stanton
Gratiano	Michael Potts	Shylock	Nicholas Kepros
Nerissa	Marissa Chibas		

Directed by Nicholas Martin; scenery, John Lee Beatty; costumes, Michael Krass; lighting, Brian MacDevitt; sound, Aural Fixation; casting, Nancy Piccione; production stage manager, Ed Fitzgerald; stage manager, Scott LaFeber.

Time: Evening, today. Place: The grounds of Portia's estate in Belmont outside Venice. The play was presented in two parts.

The Merchant of Venice characters gather to celebrate their marriages, in a modern sequel to Shakespeare's play. Previously produced in regional theater at the Old Globe Theater, San Diego.

BY THE SEA BY THE SEA
BY THE BEAUTIFUL SEA

Act I: *Dawn*

Pat	Mary Beth Fisher
Veronica	Lee Brock
Quentin	Timothy Carhart

Daughter, son and son's wife come to the water's edge to dispose of mother's ashes at dawn.

Act II: *Day*

Ace	Timothy Carhart
Macy	Lee Brock
Bill	Mary Beth Fisher

Worker on lunch break is joined at the beach by his girl friend and another strange and calculating young woman.

Act III: *Dusk*

Dana	Mary Beth Fisher
Willy	Timothy Carhart
Marsha	Lee Brock

Attractive young fellow has the self-confidence to attempt to seduce two women at the same time.

ALL PLAYS: Directed by Leonard Foglia; scenery, Michael McGarty; costumes, Laura Cunningham; lighting, Brian MacDevitt; sound, One Dream Sound; production stage manager, Jill Cordle.

Time: Summer. Place: A beach.

Previously produced at Bay Street Theater, Sag Harbor, L.I.

Picasso at the Lapin Agile (249). By Steve Martin. Produced by Stephen Eich, Joan Stein and Leavitt/Fox Theatricals/Mages at the Promenade Theater. Opened October 22, 1995. (Closed May 26, 1996)

PICASSO AT THE LAPIN AGILE—Tim Hopper as Picasso and
Mark Nelson as Einstein in a scene from Steve Martin's play

Freddy .... Harry Groener	Sagot .... John Christopher Jones
Gaston .... Carl Don	Pablo Picasso .... Tim Hopper
Germaine .... Rondi Reed	Charles Dabernow
Albert Einstein .... Mark Nelson	Schmendiman .... Peter Jacobson
Suzanne; Countess;	Visitor .... Gabriel Macht
Female Admirer .... Susan Floyd	

Standbys/Understudies: Messrs. Groener, Don, Jones—William Keeler; Misses Reed, Floyd—Rebecca Creskoff; Mr. Nelson—Peter Jacobson; Messrs. Hopper, Jacobson, Macht—Jason Antoon.

Directed by Randall Arney; scenery, Scott Bradley; costumes, Patricia Zipprodt; lighting, Kevin Rigdon; sound, Richard Woodbury; associate producers, Jerry C. Bradshaw, George A. Schapiro/Yentl Productions; casting, Rosalie Joseph; production stage manager, Mark Cole; stage manager, Karen Evanouskas; press, Alma Viator, Michael S. Borowski, William Schelble.

Time: 1904 (a year before Einstein published *Special Theory of Relativity* and three years before Picasso painted *Les Demoiselles D'Avignon*). Place: A bar in Paris. The play was presented without intermission.

Comedy, a battle of ideas between the famous physicist and the famous painter during an imaginary chance meeting in a small Paris bistro. Previously produced in regional theater by Steppenwolf Theater Company, Chicago.

Zombies From the Beyond (72). Musical with book, music and lyrics by James Valcq. Produced by Colin Cabot at the Players Theater. Opened October 23, 1995. (Closed December 24, 1995)

Maj. Malone .... Michael Shelle	Mary Malone .... Claire Morkin
Rick Jones .... Robert Boles	Trenton Corbett .... Matt McClanahan
Charlene Osmanski .... Suzanne Graff	Zombina .... Susan Gottschalk
Billy Krutzik .... Jeremy Czarniak	

Musicians: Andrew Wilder conductor, keyboards; Andrew Burns percussion; Patricia Tregellas accordion.

Understudies: Misses Gottschalk, Graff, Morkin—Julie-Ann Liechty; Messrs. Boles, Czarniak, McClanahan, Shelle—Edward Prostak.

Directed and choreographed by Pam Kriger; musical direction, Andrew Wilder; scenery and costumes, James Schuette; lighting, Ken Billington; sound, Ivan Pokorny; production stage manager, Lisa Jean Lewis; press, Shirley Herz Associates, Sam Rudy.

Time: May 1955. Place: The Milwaukee Space Center and environs.

Spoof of science-fiction movie cliches.

ACT I

"The Sky's the Limit"	Maj. Malone, Rick, Charlie, Billy, Mary, Trenton
"The Rocket-Roll"	Rick, Mary
"Second Planet on the Right"	Trenton, Mary
"Blast off Baby"	Charlie, Rick, Trenton
"Atomic Feet"	Billy
"Big Wig"	Rick
"In the Stars"	Mary, Ensemble
"Secret Weapon"	Zombina
"Zombies From the Beyond"	Zombina, Rick, Zombettes

ACT II

"Dateline: Milwaukee"	Maj. Malone, Trenton, Mary, Billy
"Second Planet on the Right" (Reprise)	Trenton, Mary
"The American Way"	Trenton, Mary, Maj. Malone
"I Am a Zombie"	Rick, Company
"The Last Man on Earth"	Zombina
"Breaking the Sound Barrier"	Zombina, Company
"Keep Watching the Skies"	Maj. Malone, Company

*Mrs. Klein** (257). By Nicholas Wright. Produced by David Richenthal, Lucille Lortel, Anita Howe-Waxman and Jeffrey Ash at the Lucille Lortel Theater. Opened October 24, 1995.

Mrs. Klein	Uta Hagen	Melitta	Laila Robins
Paula	Amy Wright		

Directed by William Carden; scenery, Ray Recht; costumes, David C. Woolard; lighting, Chris Dallos; sound, Robert Auld; casting, Pat McCorkle; production stage manager, Lloyd Davis Jr.; stage manager, Matthew Farrell; press, Jeffrey Richards Associates, Kevin Rehac, Irene Gandy.

Time: The spring of 1934. Place: London. The play was presented in two parts.

Professional and personal controversies confronted by a pioneering child psychologist in a biographical drama of a real-life person portrayed by Uta Hagen. A foreign play previously produced in England (first in 1988) and off off Broadway.

A Best Play; see page 87.

National Youth Music Theater. Program of two musicals. **Pendragon** (3). By Peter Allwood, Joanna Horton, Jeremy James Taylor and Frank Whately. Opened October 25, 1995. **The Threepenny Opera** (3). Revival of the musical with book and lyrics by Bertolt Brecht; music by Kurt Weill. Opened October 26, 1995. (Both programs closed October 28, 1995) Produced by National Youth Music Theater, Jeremy James Taylor artistic director, supported by Andrew Lloyd Webber, at the City Center.

PENDRAGON

Uther Pendragon; Sir Malaigaunce	Nick Saich	Young Guinevere	Hannah Spearritt
Ygraine	Shula Keyte	Young Elaine	Sheridan Smith
The Merlin	Kyriacos Messios	Young Arthur Pendragon	Richard Stacey
Priest	Neil Abrahamson	Sir Kay	James Hoare
Nurse	Louise Potter	King Pellinore	Tom Chambers
Young Morgan Le Fay	Hayley Gelling	Will	Sonell Dadral

Thomas .... Hugo Sheppard
Kelemon ....Lara Pulver
Monk .... Irfan Ahmad
Raven .... Helen Power
Matt .... Daniel Beckett
Luke .... Joshua Deutsch
Older Morgan Le Fay .... Katie Wilson
Older Arthur Pendragon ....Timothy Fornara
Lady Angharad .... Angharad Reece
Lady Alice ....Michelle Thomas

Lady Margaret .... Sarah McMillan
Gawain ....Adam Knight
Sir Caradoc ....Maurice MacSweeney
Older Guinevere .... Rebecca Lock
Older Ekaine .... Charlotte Hoare
King Leodegraunce .... Reuben Jones
King Lot of Orkney ....Tom Sellwood
Ulfius ....Edmund Comer
Sir Gaynor ....Christian Coulson
Sir Lancelot ....Paul Cattermole

Band: Helen Ella flute; Andrew Jones horn; Adam Powell percussion; Alexander L'Estrange piano, Leon Skelton electric bass.

Directed by Joanna Horton, Jeremy James Taylor and Frank Whately; musical direction, Peter Allwood; design, Alison Darke; lighting, Richard House; sound, Simon Baker; stage manager, Vicki McLeod; press, Christian Jenner, Philip Rinaldi, James Morrison.

Time: During the Dark Ages. Place: Britain. The play was presented in two parts.

Musical version of episodes of the King Arthur legend. A foreign play previously produced in England by this group of 17, 18, 19, and a handful of 20 year old actors and musicians, here on a U.S. tour.

THE THREEPENNY OPERA

Ballad Singers; Narrators .... Nick Dutton,
                            Catherine Simmonds
Jeremiah Peachum ....Tim Steeden
Mrs. Peachum ....Kate Chesworth
Filch .... Kevin Pamplin
Macheath .... Laurence Taylor
Polly Peachum .... Jessica Watson
Lucy Brown .... Esther Shanson
The Gang:
    Matt of the Mint ....Jonathan Chesworth
    Crook Fingered Jake ....James Capewell
    Bob the Saw ....Barney Dillon
    Ned .... Jean-Paul Pfluger
    Jimmy Twitcher .... Delroy Anderson
    Dreary Walter .... Alex Bourne

Rev. Kimball .... Matthew Walton
The Police:
    Tiger Brown .... David Oyelowo
    Smith ....Matthew Gough
    Constable .... Chris Swift
The Whores:
    Jenny Diver .... Tiffany Gore
    Vixen .... Emma Sharnock
    Dolly .... Kelly Brett
    Coaxer ....Johanna Hewitt
    Brazen .... Carryl Thomas
    Suky Tawdry ....Hong-Van Laffer
    Betty ....Joanna Dunn
    Divine .... Fiona Finlow

Beggars, Policemen, Whores: (The Ensemble) Delroy Atkinson, Alex Bourne, Kelly Brett, James Capewell, Jonathan Chesworth, Kate Chesworth, Barney Dillon, Joanna Dunn, Fiona Finlow, Hong-Van Laffer, David Oyelowo Jean-Paul Pfluger, Emma Sharnock, Chris Swift, Carryl Thomas, Matthew Walton.

Band: Joanna Kenrick flute, piccolo; Eiusook Coh bassoon; Sandy Gibbons, Amy Pearce reeds; Pen Pearce trumpet I; Richard Payne trumpet II; Nerena Neathercoat trombone; Simon Maltby percussion; Emma Dengate timps; Chris Lambert piano; John Crockford harmonium, celeste; Louise Savill accordion; James Jervis guitar, banjo; Laura Moody cello; Polly Jones double bass.

Directed by Mark Pattenden; musical direction, Alison Berry; movement direction, Wendy Cook; design, Jason Denvir; lighting, Chris Davey; sound Simon Baker; stage manager, Maggie Ralston.

The last major New York revival of this work took place on Broadway under the title *3 Penny Opera* 11/5/89 for 65 performances.

The list of scenes and musical numbers in *The Threepenny Opera* appears on pages 372–3 of *The Best Plays of 1989–90*.

*Lincoln Center Theater. Schedule of two programs. **Northeast Local** (81). By Tom Donaghy. Opened October 29, 1995. (Closed January 7, 1996) ***A Fair Country** (119). By Jon Robin Baitz. Opened February 19, 1996. Produced by Lincoln Center Theater under the direction of Andre Bishop and Bernard Gersten at the Mitzi E. Newhouse Theater.

NORTHEAST LOCAL

Gi .... Mary Elizabeth Mastrantonio	Mair .... Eileen Heckart
Mickey .... Anthony LaPaglia	Jesse .... Terry Alexander

Standbys and understudies: Miss Mastrantonio—Theresa McElwee; Mr. LaPaglia—Ed Hodson; Miss Heckart—Mary Diveny; Mr. Alexander—Michael Genet.

Directed by Gerald Gutierrez; scenery, John Lee Beatty; costumes, Jane Greenwood; lighting, Brian MacDevitt; sound, Otts Munderloh; original music, Louis Rosen; casting, Daniel Swee; stage manager, Marjorie Horne; press, Merle Debuskey, Susan Chicoine.

Time: Over the course of 30 years, beginning in the early 1960s.

The troubled marriage and life of a blue-collar family.

A FAIR COUNTRY

Gil Burgess .... Matt McGrath	Ellsworth Hodges .... Jack Davidson
Patrice Burgess .... Judith Ivey	Alec Burgess .... Dan Futterman
Hilton .... Teagle F. Bougere	Gerrit Van Eden .... Richard Clarke
Togo Policeman; Victor .... Maduka Steady	Carly Fletcher .... Katie Finneran
Harry Burgess .... Laurence Luckinbill	

Directed by Daniel Sullivan; scenery, Tony Walton; costumes, Jane Greenwood; lighting, James F. Ingalls; original music, Robert Waldman; sound, Scott Lehrer; casting, Daniel Swee; stage manager, Roy Harris.

Act I, Scene 1: 1987, an archeological excavation site in southern Mexico. Scene 2: 1978, verandah of the Burgess home in Durban, South Africa. Scene 3: The same night, Togo Airport, West Africa. Scene 4: The next morning, verandah of the Burgess home. Act II, Scene 1: The Hague, Holland, the Burgess living room. Scene 2: A few hours later. Scene 3: 1987, the excavation.

Moral dilemma of a U.S. cultural representative trading sensitive information for promotion, and its effect on his wife and sons. Previously produced in workshop at New York Stage and Film, Naked Angels and Seattle Repertory Theater.

A Best Play; see page 189.

Rodgers & Hart Rediscovered. Concert series of two musical revivals. **I Married an Angel** (2). Book by Richard Rodgers and Lorenz Hart; adapted from the play by John Vaszary; music by Richard Rodgers; lyrics by Lorenz Hart; series opening introduction by Terrence McNally. Opened October 29, 1995. (Closed October 30, 1995) **America's Sweetheart** (2). Book by Herbert Fields; music by Richard Rodgers; lyrics and opening night introduction by Lorenz Hart. Opened December 10, 1995. (Closed December 11, 1995) Produced by Theater Off Park, Albert Harris artistic director, and Millenial Arts Productions, Inc./Paula Heil Fisher at Theater Off Park.

I MARRIED AN ANGEL

Narrator; Gen Lucash .... Edmund Lyndeck	Peter Mueller .... Robert Creighton
Major Domo; Valet de Chambre;	Count Willy Palaffi .... Jason Graae
2d Clerk .... Matthew Burnett	Countess Peggy Palaffi .... Kim Criswell
Guest; 1st Clerk .... Scott Beck	Anna Murphy .... Victoria Clark
Guest; Philomena .... Lauren Ward	Angel .... Marin Mazzie
Guest; 1st Vendeuse; Clarinda .... Karen Culp	Modiste; Duchess of Holstein-
Olga Madayn; 2d Vendeuse;	Kuhhoff .... Viola Harris
Lucinda .... Susan Owen	Harry Mischka Szigetti .... Brent Barrett

Directed by Albert Harris; musical direction, James Stenborg; lighting, Herrick Goldman; concert narration, Laurence Holzman, Felicia Needleman; "The Modiste" sequence staged by Joey McKneely; casting, Warren Pincus; stage manager, Alex Nicholas; press, Jim Randolph.

Time: 1938. Place: Budapest.

I Married an Angel was first produced on Broadway 5/11/38 for 338 performances. This is its first major New York revival of record.

MUSICAL NUMBERS, ACT I: Overture and Opening Ballet; "Did You Ever Get Stung"—Jason Graae, Kim Criswell, Robert Creighton; "I Married an Angel"—Graae; "The Modiste"—Graae, Marin Mazzie, Viola Harris, Karen Culp, Susan Owen; Honeymoon Ballet; "I'll Tell the Man in the Street"—Criswell, Brent Barrett; "How to Win Friends and Influence People"—Victoria Clark; Finale, Act I—Graae, Criswell, Ensemble. ACT II: "Spring Is Here"—Graae, Criswell; "Angel Without Wings"—Mazzie, Culp, Owen, Lauren Ward; "A Twinkle in Your Eye"—Criswell; "I'll Tell the Man in the Street" (Reprise)—Barrett; "Roxie Routine" (I'm Ruined)—Graae, Barrett, Criswell; "At the Roxy Music Hall"—Clark; Finale—Company.

AMERICA'S SWEETHEART

Waitress; Miss Mulligan; Georgianna; First Phone Girl ....Jennifer Piech	Paula; 2d Phone Girl ....Susan Owen
1st Wise Man; Eddie Lynch; Radio Voice ....Cordell Stahl	Dorith; Georgette ....Kerry O'Malley
2d Wise Man ....Clif Thorn	Larry Pitkin ....Guy Stroman
3d Wise Man ....Matthew Burnett	Madge Farrell ....Liz Larsen
Assistant Director; Albert Emery; Man at Radio ....David Jordan	Michael Perry ....Jarrod Emick
S.A. Dolan ....Ed Dixon	Geraldine March ....Darcie Roberts
	Denise Torel ....Alison Fraser
	Georgine ....Kerry O'Malley
	Larkin .... Jonathon Stewart

Directed by Albert Harris; musical direction, John McDaniel; lighting, A.C. Hickox; musical restoration, James Stenborg; casting, Warren Pincus; production stage manager, Alex Nicholas.

Time: 1931. Place: Hollywood.

America's Sweetheart was first produced on Broadway 2/10/31 for 135 performances. This is its first major New York revival of record.

MUSICAL NUMBERS, ACT I: Overture; Opening Act I; "Mr. Dolan Is Passing Through"—Ed Dixon, David Jordan, Ensemble; "In Californ-i-a"—Kerry O'Malley, Susan Owen, Ensemble; "My Sweet"—Liz Larsen, Guy Stroman; "I've Got Five Dollars"—Jarrod Emick, Darcie Roberts; "I've Got Five Dollars" (Reprise)—Emick, Roberts; "Sweet Geraldine"—O'Malley, Jennifer Piech; "There's So Much More"—Alison Fraser, Stroman; "We'll Be the Same"—Emick, Roberts; "I've Got Five Dollars" (Reprise)—Emick, Stroman; "How About It"—Larsen, Emick; "Innocent Chorus Girls of Yesterday"—O'Malley, Owen, Piech; "A Lady Must Live"—Fraser. ACT II: Opening Act II; "You Ain't Got No Savoir Faire"—Stroman, Larsen; "We'll Be the Same" (Reprise)—Roberts, Emick; "Two Unfortunate Orphans"—O'Malley, Owen; "I Want a Man"—Fraser; "How About It"—Owen, O'Malley, Jonathon Stewart, Clif Thorn; Finale, "We'll Be the Same"—Roberts, Emick, Ensemble.

Circle Repertory Theater. Schedule of three programs. **Riff Raff** (34). By Laurence Fishburne. Opened November 1, 1995. (Closed December 3, 1995) **The Hope Zone** (28). By Kevin Heelan. Opened January 4, 1996. (Closed February 4, 1996) **The Size of the World** (22). By Charles Evered. Opened March 20, 1996. (Closed April 7, 1996) Produced by Circle Repertory Theater, Austin Pendleton artistic director, Milan Stitt executive director, Andrew Chipok managing director, at Circle Repertory Theater.

RIFF RAFF

"20/20" Mike Leon ....Laurence Fishburne	Tony "The Tiger" Lee ....Heavy D
Billy "Torch" Murphy ....Titus Welliver	

Directed by Laurence Fishburne; scenery, Edward T. Gianfrancesco; costumes, Michael Krass; light-

RODGERS & HART REDISCOVERED—Performers in script-in-hand concert revivals of a pair of their shows included (*above*) Robert Creighton, Brent Barrett, Victoria Clark, Jason Graae, Kim Criswell and Marin Mazzie in *I Married an Angel* and (*left*) Alison Fraser and Guy Stroman in *America's Sweetheart*

ing, Dennis Parichy; sound, Darron L. West; fight director, Rick Sordelet; production stage manager, Greta Minsky; press, Jeffrey Richards Associates, Kevin Rehac, Irene Gandy.

Time: The present, All Hallows Eve, 9 p.m. Place: A corner third floor apartment in an abandoned building on New York's Lower East Side. The play was presented without intermission.

Criminals hiding out after an attempted drug heist in which they have killed an aide of an important drug lord.

THE HOPE ZONE

Countess	Olympia Dukakis	Newton	Craig Bockhorn
Fern	Barbara Caren Sims	Veeche	George Morfogen
Maureen	Anne Scurria		

Directed by Richard Jenkins; scenery, Eugene Lee; costumes, Walker Hicklin; lighting, Russell Champa; associate producer, Jerad Productions; production stage manager, Tom Stone.

Troubled daughter and mother who is a counselor of alcoholics. The play was presented in two parts. Previously produced in regional theater at Trinity Repertory, Providence, R.I.

THE SIZE OF THE WORLD

Vivian Merkle	Rita Moreno	Stan Merkle	Louis Zorich
Peter Hogancamp	Frank Whaley		

Directed by Austin Pendleton; scenery, Jeff Pajer; costumes, Walker Hicklin; lighting, Tom Sturge; sound, Raymond D. Schilke; stage manager, Tom Stone.

Parents who have lost their son take in a lodger who has lost his parents. The play was presented in two parts.

Splendora (14). Musical based on the novel by Edward Swift; book by Peter Webb; music by Stephen Hoffman; lyrics by Mark Campbell. Produced by Bay Street Theater, Murphy Davis producer, Norman Kline general manager, at the American Place Theater. Opened November 9, 1995. (Closed November 19, 1995)

Sue Ella Lightfoot	Evalyn Baron	Lucille Monroe	Susan Rush
Maga Dell Spivy	KT Sullivan	Jessica Gatewood	Nancy Johnston
Zeda Earl Goodrich	Laura Kenyon	Timothy John Coldridge	Michael Moore
Agnes Pullens	Kathy Robinson	Brother Leggett	Ken Krugman

Directed by Jack Hofsiss; musical staging, Robert La Fosse; musical direction, Sariva Goetz; scenery, Eduardo Sicangco; costumes, William Ivey Long; lighting, Richard Nelson; orchestrations, Michael Gibson; sound, Randy Freed; casting, Sarah Heming, Johnson-Liff Associates; production stage manager, Debora F. Porazzi; press, David Rothenberg Associates, David Gersten.

Young man returns to the East Texas town of Splendora to face his past, after a 15-year absence. The play was presented in two parts. Previously produced in this production by Bay Street Theater, Sag Harbor, L.I.

MUSICAL NUMBERS: "In Our Hearts," "How Like Heaven," "Don't Get Me Started," "Pretty Boy," "Home/Say Goodnight," "Poor Sad Thing," "A Hymn to Her," "Up at Dawn," "In Small and Simple Ways," "Warms My Soul," "Dear Heart," "How Little I Know/Had He Kissed Me Tonight/If He Knew," "Good Hearts, Rejoice," "What Is, Ain't," "Promise Me One Thing," "I Got Faith in You," "All the Time in the World," "A Man Named Dewey," "I Am Beauty," "Miss Crepe Myrtle," "Grateful," "My Name Is Timothy John."

The Joseph Papp Public Theater/New York Shakespeare Festival. Schedule of eight programs. **Bring in 'da Noise Bring in 'da Funk** (85) Musical performance piece based on an idea by Savion Glover and George C. Wolfe; conceived by George C. Wolfe; choreography by Savion Glover; text by Reg E. Gaines; music by Ann Duquesnay, Zane Mark, Daryl Waters. Opened November 15, 1995. (Closed January 28, 1996 and transferred to Broadway; see its entry in the Plays Produced on Broadway section of this volume) **WASP and Other Plays** (25). Program of four one-act plays by Steve Martin: *Guillotine, The Zig-Zag Woman, Patter for the Floating Lady* and *WASP.* Opened December 17, 1995. (Closed January 7, 1996) **Dancing on Her Knees** (22). By Nilo Cruz. Opened February 29, 1996. (Closed March 17, 1996) **Nude Nude Totally Nude** (29), solo performance by Andrea Martin, written by Andrea Martin, opened March 15, 1996; and **A Line Around the Block** (29), solo performance by Marga Gomez, written by Marga Gomez, opened March 22, 1996, presented in repertory. (Repertory closed April 28, 1996) **Venus** (22). By Suzan-Lori Parks; songs by Phillip Johnston; co-produced with Yale Repertory Theater, Stan Wojewodski Jr. artistic directer. Opened May 2, 1996. (Closed May 19, 1996) **The Skriker** (17). By Caryl Churchill. Opened May 12, 1996. (Closed May 26, 1996) **The Chang Fragments** (23). By Han Ong. Opened May 15, 1996. (Closed June 2, 1996) Produced by The Joseph Papp Public Theater/New York Shakespeare Festival, George C. Wolfe producer, Rosemarie Tichler artistic producer, Joey Parnes executive producer, Laurie Beckelman executive director, Wiley Hausam associate producer, Kevin Kline artistic associate, at the Public Theater.

BRING IN 'DA NOISE BRING IN 'DA FUNK

Vincent Bingham	Dule Hill
Jared Crawford	Raymond King
Ann Duquesnay	Jimmy Tate
Reg E. Gaines	Baakari Wilder
Savion Glover	

Musicians: Leroy Clouden drums; Lafayette Harris, Zane Mark keyboards; Vince Henry reeds; Luico Hopper bass.

Directed by George C. Wolfe; musical direction, Zane Mark; scenery, Riccardo Hernandez; costumes, Karen Perry; lighting, Jules Fisher, Peggy Eisenhauer; sound, Dan Moses Schreier; projection design, Batwin + Robin; musical supervision and orchestrations, Daryl Waters; vocal arrangements, Ann Duquesnay; musical coordination, Seymour Red Press; casting, Jordan Thaler, Heidi Griffiths; associate producer, Morgan Jenness; production stage manager, Gwendolyn M. Gilliam; stage manager, Rick Steiger; press, Carol R. Fineman, Thomas V. Naro, Eugenie Hero, Bill Coyle.

Evolution of the tap and hip-hop beat through the experience and creativity of the African-American people, expressed in song-and-dance and narrative.

ACT I

In 'da Beginning: "Bring in 'da Noise Bring in 'da Funk"—Company; "The Door"—Reg E. Gaines; "Slave Ships"—Ann Duquesnay, Savion Glover.

Som'thin' From Nuthin'—"Som'thin' From Nuthin'/The Circle Stomp"—Baakari Wilder, Dule Hill, Jimmy Tate, Vincent Bingham; "The Pan Handlers"—Jared Crawford, Raymond King.

Urbanization: "The Lynching Blues"—Wilder, Duquesnay, Company; "Chicago Bound"—Glover, Duquesnay, Company; "Shifting Sounds"—Gaines; "Industrialization"—Glover, Wilder, Tate, Bingham, King; "The Chicago Riot Rag"—Glover, Wilder, Tate, Bingham; "I Got the Beat/Dark Tower"—Duquesnay, Gaines, Company; "The Whirligig Stomp"—Company.

ACT II

Where's the Beat?: Voice—Gaines; Chanteuse—Duquesnay; Kid—Dule Hill; Grin & Flash—Tate, Bingham; Uncle Huck-a-Buck—Wilder; Li'l Dahlin'—Glover.

"Now That's Tap" .... Grin & Flash
"The Uncle Huck-a-Buck Song" .... Uncle Huck-a-Buck, Li'l Dahlin', Company
"Kid Go!" ....Kid, Company
"The Lost Beat Swing" .... Chanteuse, Company
Green, Chaney, Buster, Slyde .... Glover

Street Corner Symphony: "1956, Them Conkheads"—Company; "1967, Hot Fun"—Company; "1977, Blackout"—Glover, Wilder, Tate, Bingham; "1977, Gospel/Hip Hop Rant"—Gaines, Glover, Duquesnay.

Noise/Funk: "Drummin'/Taxi"—Crawford, King, Glover, Tate, Wilder, Bingham; "Hittin' "—Glover, Wilder, Tate, Bingham; "Bring in 'da Noise Bring in 'da Funk" (Reprise)—Company.

WASP AND OTHER PLAYS

Guillotine	Customer .... Don McManus	
Salesman .... Nesbitt Blaisdell	Maid .... Carol Kane	

Maid dusts the furniture in a suburban living room, which includes a guillotine with blade raised and ready.

The Zig-Zag Woman

Woman .... Amelia Campbell
Toni .... Peggy Pope
Older Man .... Nesbitt Blaisdell
Middle Man .... Don McManus
Billy Boy .... Kevin Isola

Woman takes extreme measures in an attempt to attract the attention of a young man in a bar-room.

Patter for the Floating Lady

Magician .... Don McManus

Angie .... Amelia Campbell
Assistant .... Carol Kane

A magician tries to bring on romance by levitating the woman who is the object of his desires.

WASP

Dad .... Don McManus
Mom .... Carol Kane
Sis .... Amelia Campbell
Son .... Kevin Isola
Female Voice .... Peggy Pope
Premier; Choirmaster;
    Roger .... Nesbitt Blaisdell
Satirical treatment of family life among white Anglo-Saxon Protestants.

ALL PLAYS: Directed by Barry Edelstein; scenery, Thomas Lynch; costumes, Laura Cunningham; lighting, Donald Holder; sound, Red Ramona; casting, Jordan Thaler/Heidi Griffiths; production stage manager, James Latus.

The program was presented in two parts with the intermission following *Patter for the Floating Lady*.

DANCING ON HER KNEES

Francine .... Luis Ramos
Ramona .... Franca Barchiesi
Federico .... Paul Calderon

Rosario Del Cielo .... Marianne Filali
Anuncio .... Julio Monge
Matthias .... Henry Stram

Directed by Graciela Daniele; scenery, Riccardo Hernandez; costumes, Toni-Leslie James; lighting, Peggy Eisenhauer; sound, Scott Stauffer; incidental music and music supervision, Carlos Valdez; casting, Jordan Thaler/Heidi Griffiths; production stage manager, Buzz Cohen.

Time: Late 1980s, November 2, All Soul's Day. Place: Miami Beach, Florida. The play was performed without intermission.

A tango-dancing couple, former champions, reaffirm their love in a mystical area between life and death.

NUDE NUDE TOTALLY NUDE

Directed by Walter Bobbie; scenery, Loren Sherman; costumes, Jane Greenwood; lighting, Brian MacDevitt; sound, John Gromada; special material, Bruce Vilanch; musical direction and piano, Seth Rudetsky.

Andrea Martin presents a galley of characters she has created in performance over the years and also explores her own life and personality. The performance was presented without intermission.

A LINE AROUND THE BLOCK

Directed by Corey Madden; scenery, Loren Sherman; costumes, Candice Cain; lighting, Brian MacDevitt; sound, John Gromada.

Marga Gomez enacts a tale set in the Manhattan Latino community in the 1960s, about a Cuban comedian and the daughter who follows in his footsteps, based on the life of Gomez's father, Willy Chevalier (a companion piece to Miss Gomez's *Memory Tricks*, the story of her dancer mother). The performance was presented without intermission. Previously produced by New World Theater at the University of Massachusetts and Mark Taper Forum, Los Angeles.

VENUS

Sartje Benjamin; Venus
    Hottentot .... Adina Porter
Man; Baron Docteur .... Peter Francis James

Brother; Mother Showman; Grade
    School Chum .... Sandra Shipley
Negro Resurrectionist .... Mel Johnson Jr.

Chorus of the 8 Human Wonders, Players of *For the Love of Venus,* Chorus of Spectators, Chorus of the Court, Chorus of the 8 Anatomists:

Fat Man; Others ....Cedric Harris
3-Legged Man; Others ....Ben Shenkman
Flame-Headed Man; Others ....Kevin Isola

Bride-to-Be; Others ....Lynn Hawley
Young Man; Others ....Thomas Jay Ryan
Mother; Others ....Adriane Lenox
Father; Others ....Rainn Wilson
Uncle; Others ....John Lathan

Directed by Richard Foreman; scenery, Richard Foreman; costumes, Paul Tazewell; lighting, Heather Carson; casting, Jordan Thaler/Heidi Griffiths; production stage manager, Lisa Porter.

Time: The early 1800s. Place: South Africa, England and France. The play was presented in two parts.

The story of the Venus Hottentot, renowned for the size of her buttocks. Previously produced at the Yale Repertory Theater, New Haven.

THE SKRIKER

Lost Girl ....April Armstrong
The Skriker ....Jayne Atkinson
Fair Fairy ....Marc Calamia
Green Lady ....Rene M. Ceballos
Black Dog ....Torrin T. Cummings
Hag ....Kate Egan
RawHeadAndBloody
Bones .... Philip Seymour Hoffman
Passerby .... Jodi Melnick

Dark Fairy .... Ric Oquita
Lily .... Angie Phillips
Dead Child .... Diana Rice
Black Annis .... Valda Setterfield
Josie ....Caroline Seymour
Man With Bucket ....Jack Shamblin
Kelpie .... Doug Von Nessen
Johnny Squarefoot .... Sturgis Warner

Yallery Brown, Woman Ironing, Brownie, Spriggan, Jennie Greenteeth, Radiant Boy, Nellie Longarms, Business Men with Thrumpins, Picnic Family, Granddaughter, Great-Great-Granddaughter, Others: Company.

Directed by Mark Wing-Davey; scenery and costumes, Marina Draghici; lighting, Christopher Akerlind; sound, John Gromada; composer, Judith Weir; additional music, John Gromada; musical direction, Martin Goldray; choreography, Sara Rudner; production stage manager, James Latus.

Time: The present. Place: Mostly in London, England. The play was presented without intermission.

Supernatural beings, including a Skriker, take control of the lives of two young English women. A foreign play previously produced in England.

A Best Play; see page 235.

THE CHANG FRAGMENTS

Ivan ....Darren Lee
Mr. Chang; James Takahashi .....Ernest Abuba
Flophouse Resident; Betty; Rita ....Tom Aulino
Roshumba; Flophouse Resident 2;
Ghost 1 .... Robin Miles

Flophouse Resident 3; Ghost 2 .... Stuart Rudin
Mrs. Chang ....Tina Chen
Lily ....Jennifer Kato
Bruce .... Daniel Dae Kim

Directed by Marcus Stern; scenery and costumes, James Schuette; lighting, Scott Zielinski; sound, John Huntington; casting, Jordan Thaler/Heidi Griffiths; production stage manager, Kristen Harris; stage manager, Gwendolyn D. Burrow.

Family, abandoned by the father, puts the pieces back together with the mother's efforts and guidance, while adjusting to life in America. The play was presented in two parts.

Note: In the Joseph Papp Public Theater there are many auditoria. *Bring in 'da Noise Bring in 'da Funk* and *The Skriker* played the Estelle R. Newman Theater, *WASP and Other Plays* and *Venus* played Martinson Hall, *Dancing on Her Knees* and *The Chang Fragments* played LuEsther Hall, *Nude Nude Totally Nude* and *A Line Around the Block* played the Anspacher Theater,

Jam on the Groove (100). Musical written and directed by GhettOriginal Productions (see note). Produced by Mitchell Maxwell, Alan J. Schuster and Margaret Selby in association with IMG at the Minetta Lane Theater. Opened November 16, 1995. (Closed February 11, 1996)

<table>
<tr><td>Peter "Bam Bam" Arizmendi</td><td>Antoine "Doc" Judkins</td></tr>
<tr><td>Leon "Mister Twister" Chesney</td><td>Risa Kobatake</td></tr>
<tr><td>Steve "Mr. Wiggles" Clemente</td><td>Adesola "D'Incredible" Osakalumi</td></tr>
<tr><td>"Crazy Legs"</td><td>Jorge "Fabel" Pabon</td></tr>
<tr><td>Gabriel "Kwikstep" Dionisio</td><td>Jerry "Flow Master" Randolph</td></tr>
<tr><td>Kenny "Ken Swift" Gabbert</td><td>Roger "Orko" Romero</td></tr>
<tr><td>Tamara Gaspard</td><td>Ereine "Honey Roc Well" Valencia</td></tr>
</table>

Directed and choreographed by GhettOriginal Productions; scenery, Andrew Jackness; lighting, Peter Kaczorowski; murals, Ernie Vales; sound, One Dream Sound; co-producers, Michael Skipper, Victoria Maxwell; associate producers, Susan Selby, James L. Simon; press, the Pete Sanders Group, Michael Hartman, Glenna Freedman.

Dance musical featuring hip-hop numbers introduced in vignettes. The show was presented without intermission.

Note: The GhettOriginal Productions Dance Company was formed by the members of the hip-hop troupes Magnificent Force, Rhythm Techniques and Rock Steady Crew. GhettOriginal has performed at Kennedy Center and elsewhere in the United States and in Vienna, Paris and Tokyo. It has received two choreographic grants from NEA and a 1991 Bessie Award for "an astonishing vocabulary of daring individual signatures and collective invention."

PROGRAM: Concrete Jungle—Company; The Shadow Knows—Ken Swift, Flow Master; Portrait of a Freeze—Crazy Legs, Ken Swift, Kwikstep, Flow Master; Puppet—Mr. Wiggles, Fabel; Who's the Mac—Company; Janitor—Kwikstep, Flow Master; Moments—Mr. Wiggles, Crazy Legs, Kwikstep, Ken Swift, Adesola, Fabel; Shaolin Temple of Hip-Hop—Company; Hip-Hop Ya Don't Stop—Company; Jam on the Groove—Company.

Nunsense (55). Revival of the musical with book, music and lyrics by Dan Goggin. Produced by The Triad, the *Nunsense* Theatrical Company in association with Joseph Hoesl, Bill Crowder and Jay Cardwell and Peter Martin and Nancy and Steve McGraw at The Triad. Opened November 17, 1995. (Closed December 31, 1995)

Sister Mary Regina	Nancy E. Carroll	Sister Mary Amnesia	Robin Taylor
Sister Mary Hubert	Jennifer Perry	Sister Mary Leo	Kim Galberaith
Sister Robert Anne	Lin Tucci		

Musicians: Michael Rice conductor, piano; John Ogden synthesizer.

Understudy: Teri Gibson.

Directed by Dan Goggin; musical direction, Michael Rice; musical staging and choreography, Felton Smith; scenery, Barry Axtell; lighting, Paul Miller; production stage manager, Paul J. Botchis; press, the Pete Sanders Group, Michael Hartman, Glenna Freedman.

First major New York revival of the long-run musical, 3,672 performances in its original run, which began on 12/12/85 and ended last season. The play was presented without intermission.

The list of musical numbers in *Nunsense* appears on pages 352-3 of *The Best Plays of 1985–86*.

American Place Theater. Schedule of three programs. **Spoonbread and Strawberry Wine** (28). By Norma Jean Darden. Opened November 21, 1995. (Closed December 10, 1995) **Spoke Man** (19). Solo performance by John Hockenberry; written by John Hockenberry. Opened March 3, 1996. (Closed March 24, 1996) **The Slow Drag** (31). By Carson Kreitzer. Opened April 17, 1996. (Closed May 12, 1996) Produced by American Place Theater, Wynn Handman artistic director, Susannah Halston executive director, at American Place Theater.

SPOONBREAD AND STRAWBERRY WINE

CAST: Norma Jean Darden, Jou Jou Papailler.

Directed by Josh Broder; scenery, Ken Rothchild; music, Jou Jou Papailler; press, Denise Robert.

Reminiscenses of family history recounted by a cookbook author who also served a Southern meal at each performance.

THE SLOW DRAG

Johnny Christmas	Peggy Shaw	Chester Kent	Vernel Bagneris
June Wedding	Ann Crumb		

Directed by Elise Thoron; choreography, Stormy Brandenberger; musical direction, James Mc-Elwaine; scenery, Joel Reynolds; lighting, Jane Reisman; sound, David Lawson; casting, Rebecca Taichman; production stage manager, Kate Broderick.

Female jazz artist posing as a man. The play was presented without intermission.

SPOKE MAN

Directed by Wynn Handman; scenery, Joel Reynolds; lighting, Chad McArver; stage manager, Judith M. Tucker.

John Hockenberry reflects on his lifestyle as reporter, commentator and activist while confined to a wheelchair after an accident at age 20. The performance was presented without intermission.

Dick Gregory Live (78). Solo performance by Dick Gregory. Produced by the Negro Ensemble Company, Susan Watson Turner and Carole Khan-White co-artistic directors, by special arrangement with Theater Legend at the Samuel Beckett Theater. Opened December 14, 1995. (Closed February 18, 1996)

Scenery, Michael Green; lighting, Marshall Williams; associate producer, Pamela Faith Jackson; press, Jeffrey Richards Associates, Irene Gandy.

The activist-comedian comments on political, social, ethical and even dietary aspects of contemporary life. The performance was presented in two parts.

Rendez-vous With Marlene (24). Solo performance of a play with music by Torill; created and written by Torill. Produced by Jerry Hammer and Pat DeRosa in association with Harold J. Newman at the 47th Street Theater. Opened December 14, 1995. (Closed January 5, 1996)

Directed by Frank Corsaro; scenery and lighting, Bruce Goodrich; costumes, Wong, Goff, Rodriguez; musical direction, Stan Freeman; associate producer, Jim Ellis; production stage manager, Jim Ring; press, Arthur Cantor Associates, Marianne Perback, David Cantor.

Norwegian actress-chanteuse Torill as the German movie star, previously produced in Los Angeles and San Francisco. The play was presented in two parts.

MUSICAL NUMBERS: "Falling in Love Again" by Sammy Lerner and Frederick Hollander; "Illusions" by Frederick Hollander; "Lola-Lola" by Frederick Hollander, Sammy Lerner and R. Liebman; "Jonny" by Frederick Hollander, English version by Edward Heyman; "You're the Cream in My Coffee" by Lew Brown, Ray Henderson and B.G. DeSylva; "Das Lied Ist Aus" by Young, Stolz, Reisch and Robinson, English lyrics by Torill; "Wer Wird Denn Weinen" by Hirsch and Hirsch Rebner, English by Torill; "The Laziest Gal in Town" by Cole Porter; "You Go to My Head" by J. Fred Coots and Haven Gillespie; "When the World Was Young" by Johnny Mercer and M. Philippe Gerard; "Look Me Over Closely" by M. Miller and T. Gilkyson; "Makin' Whoopee!" by Gus Kahn and Walter Donaldson; "Quand L'Amour Meurt" by Robin and Cremieux; "I've Grown Accustomed to Her Face" by Alan Jay Lerner and Frederick Loewe; "The Boys in the Backroom" by Frederick Hollander and Frank Loesser; "Go 'Way From My Window" by J.J. Niles; "You Little So-and-So" by Sam Coslow and Leo Robin; "Honeysuckle Rose" by Andy Razaf and Thomas "Fats" Waller; "Lili Marlene" by Norbert Schultze, Hans Liep, John Turner and Tommy Connoer; "Mutter Hast Du Mir Vergeben" by Niemen, Grau and Dietrich, English by Torill; "Well, All Right, Okay, You Win" by Sidney Wych and Mayme Watts; "Just a Gigolo" by Leonell Casucci and Irving Caesar.

Rent (56). Musical with book, music and lyrics by Jonathan Larson. Produced by New York Theater Workshop, James C. Nicola artistic director, Nancy Kassak Diekmann managing director, at New York Theater Workshop. Opened February 13, 1996 after a brief off-off-Broadway engagement beginning 1/26/96. (Closed March 31, 1996 and moved to Broadway; see its entry in the Plays Produced on Broadway section of this volume)

Mark Cohen .... Anthony Rapp	Mrs. Jefferson; Woman With Bags;
Roger Davis .... Adam Pascal	Others .... Gwen Stewart
Tom Collins .... Jesse L. Martin	Gordon; The Man;
Benjamin Coffin III .... Taye Diggs	Others .... Timothy Britten Parker
Joanne Jefferson .... Fredi Walker	Man With Squeegee; Cop;
Angel Schunard ...... Wilson Jermaine Heredia	Others .... Gilles Chiasson
Mimi Marquez .... Daphne Rubin-Vega	Paul; Cop; Others .... Rodney Hicks
Maureen Johnson .... Idina Menzel	Alexi Darling; Roger's Mom;
Mark's Mom; Alison; Others .. Kristen Lee Kelly	Others .... Aiko Nakasone
Christmas Caroler; Mr. Jefferson; Pastor;	
Others .... Byron Utley	

The Band: Tim Weil keyboards; Steve Mack bass; Kenny Brescia guitar; Jeff Potter drums; Daniel A. Weiss keyboards 2, guitar 2.

Directed by Michael Greif; choreography, Marlies Yearby; musical direction, Tim Weil; scenery, Paul Clay; costumes, Angela Wendt; lighting, Blake Burba; sound, Darron L. West; original concept and additional lyrics, Billy Aronson; arrangements, Steve Skinner; film, Tony Gerber; casting, Bernard Telsey Casting; production stage manager, Crystal Huntington; press, Richard Kornberg, Don Summa.

Rock opera depicting the lifestyles of a group of artists in the modern East Village, New York, in the manner of *La Boheme*.

A Best Play; see page 000.

ACT I

"Tune Up/Voice Mail #1" .... Mark, Roger, Mrs. Cohen, Collins, Benny	
"Rent" .... Company	
"You Okay Honey?" .... Angel, Collins	
"One Song Glory" .... Roger	
"Light My Candle" .... Roger, Mimi	
"Voice Mail #2" .... Mr. & Mrs. Jefferson	
"Today 4 U" .... Angel	
"You'll See" .... Benny, Mark, Collins, Roger, Angel	
"Tango: Maureen" .... Mark, Joanne	
"Life Support" .... Paul, Gordon, Company	
"Out Tonight" .... Mimi	
"Another Day" .... Roger, Mimi, Company	
"Door/Wall" .... Mark, Roger	
"On the Street" .... Company	
"Santa Fe" .... Collins, Company	
"I'll Cover You" .... Angel, Collins	
"Will I?" .... Company	
"We're Okay" .... Joanne	
"Christmas Bells" .... Company	
"Over the Moon" .... Maureen	
"La Vie Boheme/I Should Tell You" .... Company	

ACT II

"Seasons of Love" .... Company	
"Happy New Year/Voice Mail #3" .... Mimi, Roger, Mark, Maureen, Joanne, Collins, Angel, Mrs. Cohen, Alexi Darling, Benny	
"Take Me or Leave Me" .... Maureen, Joanne	
"Without You" .... Roger, Mimi	
"Voice Mail #4" .... Alexi Darling	
"Contact" .... Company	
"I'll Cover You" (Reprise) .... Collins, Company	

"Halloween" ....Mark
"Goodbye, Love" ....Mark, Mimi, Roger, Maureen, Joanne, Collins, Benny
"What You Own" ....Pastor, Mark, Collins, Benny, Roger
"Voice Mail #5" .... Roger's Mom, Mimi's Mom, Mr. Jefferson, Mrs. Cohen
"Finale/Your Eyes" .... Roger, Company

The Amazing Metrano (22). Solo performance by Art Metrano; written by Art Metrano and Cynthia Lee. Produced by Mitchell Maxwell and Victoria Maxwell in association with Workin' Man Theatricals Inc. and Fred H. Krones at the Union Square Theater. Opened February 15, 1996. (Closed March 3, 1996)

Directed by David Warren; scenery, James Youmans; lighting, Donald Holder; original music and sound, John Gromada; projections, Wendall K. Harrington; associate producer, Fine and Dandy Productions; production stage manager, Maureen F. Gibson; press, the Pete Sanders Group, Michael Hartman.

Subtitled An Accidental Comedy, an autobiographical account of the actor's fall from a ladder and painful recovery from his injuries. The play was presented without intermission.

Brooklyn Academy of Music. Schedule of four programs. **In the Loneliness of the Cottonfields** (9). By Bernard-Marie Koltes; presented in the French language with simultaneous English translation. Opened February 23, 1996. (Closed March 3, 1996) **Don Juan** (5) revival of the play by Molière, opened April 30, 1996 (closed May 5, 1996) and **The Inconstant Lovers** (La Double Inconstance) (5), revival of the play by Marivaux, opened May 7, 1996 (closed May 12, 1996); presented in the French language in the Comédie Française productions. And *The Misanthrope,* revival of the play by Molière in the Ingmar Bergman production, scheduled to open 6/8/96. Produced by Brooklyn Academy of Music, Bruce C. Ratner chairman of the board, Harvey Lichtenstein president and executive producer, at the BAM Opera House.

IN THE LONELINESS OF THE COTTONFIELDS

The Dealer ....Patrice Chéreau
The Client ....Pascal Greggory

Directed by Patrice Chéreau; scenery, Richard Peduzzi; costumes, Moidele Bickel; lighting, Jean-Luc Chanonat; sound, Philippe Cachia; choreography, Christophe Bernard; collaborators, Anne-Francoise Benhamou, Yves Boonen, Eva Desseker, Philippe Guegan, Stephanie Metge, Kuno Schlegelmilch; co-produced by the Odéon-Théâtre de l'Europe, Azor Films, La Biennale de Venezia and the Festival d'Automne à Paris; press, Heidi Feldman.

Verbal sparring between two articulate males with suggested but unnamed emotional objectives and consequences. A foreign play previously produced in Europe and presented without intermission.

DON JUAN

Don Louis; Voice of the	Don Alonse .... Olivier Dautrey
Commander .... Jacques Sereys	Elvire .... Jeanne Balibar
Pierrot .... Gérard Giroudon	Don Carlos .... Eric Ruf
Sganarelle ....Roland Bertin	Gusman; Franciscan; Monsieur
Charlotte ....Catherine Sauval	Dimanche .... Bruno Raffaelli
Mathurine .... Isabelle Gardien	La Violette ....Eric Theobald
Don Juan ....Andrzej Seweryn	Statue of the Commander ....Enrico Horn

Directed by Jacques Lassalle; scenery and costumes, Rudy Sabounghi; lighting, Frank Thévenon; sound, Jean Lacornerie; fight choreography, Francois Rostain; English titles, Francis Rizzo; American stage manager, Amy Richards.

The last major New York revival of Molière's play was by New York Shakespeare Festival at the Delacorte in the Donald M. Frame English translation 6/25/82 for 26 performances. This Comédie Française production was presented in five acts with one intermission.

COMEDIE FRANCAISE AT BAM—
Pictured in scenes from visiting French
productions are (*above*) Philippe Tor-
reton and Coraly Zahonero in Marivaux' *The Inconstant Lovers* (La Double
Inconstance), the first major New York
production of that play; and (*right*) An-
drzej Seweryn and Jeanne Balibar in
Molière's *Don Juan*

THE INCONSTANT LOVERS

Flaminia	Claire Vernet	Prince	Alain Lenglet
Lisette	Claude Mathieu	Trivelin	Michel Robin
Lord	Michel Favory	Silvia	Coraly Zahonero
Harlequin	Philippe Torreton		

Footmen: Mario Costa, Patrice Colombe. Chamber Maids: Florence Wasserman, Eline Rivière, Na-
thela Davrichewy.

Directed by Jean-Pierre Miquel; scenery, Pancho Quilici; costumes, Patrice Cauchetier; lighting,
Jean-Pierre Miquel; English titles, Francis Rizzo; American stage manager, Amy Richards.

Rustic lovers are seduced by a prince into enjoyment of palace amours and luxuries. This is the first
major production of this play in New York City. The play was presented in two parts.

The Green Bird (15) Revival of the play by Carlo Gozzi; translated by Albert Bermel and
Ted Emory. Produced by The New 42nd Street Inc. in the Theater for a New Audience
production, Jeffrey Horowitz artistic/producing director, Michael Solomon general manager.
Opened March 7, 1996. (Closed March 24, 1996)

Brighella	Trellis Stepter	Green Bird	Bruce Turk
Pantalone; Voice of Calmon	Andrew Weems	Ninetta	Kristine Nielsen
Smeraldina	Didi Conn	Tartaglia	Derek Smith
Truffaldino	Ned Eisenberg	Tartagliona; Statue of Treviso	Priscilla Shanks
Barbarina	Myriam Cyr	Pompea	Lee Lewis
Renzo	Sebastian Roche	Dancing Water	Erico Villanueva

Singing Apples: Sophia Salguero (soloist), Didi Conn, Myriam Cyr. Servants: Kristine Nielsen, Sophia Salguero, Erico Villanueva. Musicians: Liz Knowles, Bill Ruyle, Bruce Williamson. Puppeteers:
David Barlow, Stephen Kaplin, Katherine Profeta, Peggy Sullivan, Kathleen Tobin.

Directed and co-designed by Julie Taymor; scenery, Christine Jones; costumes, Constance Hoffman; lighting, Donald Holder; sound, Bob Belecki; original music ("Nygma Variations," "Mr. E's") by Elliot Goldenthal; musical direction, Richard Martinez; mask and puppet design, Julie Taymor; casting, Deborah Brown; production stage manager, Michele Steckler; stage manager, Amanda Sloan; press, Merle Debuskey, Susan Chicoine.

A *commedia del'arte* classic presented in two parts.

*Bein' With Behan (71). Solo performance by Michael L. Kavanaugh; written by Michael L. Kavanaugh. Produced by Edmund Gaines in association with Dublin Jackeen Productions at the Irish Repertory Theater. Opened March 10, 1996.

Directed by Bruce Heighley; press, David Rothenberg.
Portrayal of Brendan Behan, the Irish playwright, poet and political activist. A foreign play previously produced in Dublin.

*Forbidden Hollywood (93). Revue created and written by Gerard Alessandrini. Produced by John Freedson, Harriet Yellin and Jon B. Platt at the Triad Theater. Opened March 10, 1996.

Fred Barton	Christine Pedi
Toni DiBuono	Lance Roberts
Michael McGrath	

Directed and choreographed by Gerard Alessandrini and Phillip George; musical direction, Fred Barton; scenery, Bradley Kaye; costumes, Alvin Colt; additional choreography, Roxie Lucas; produced in association with Steve McGraw, Nancy McCall and Peter Martin; production stage manager, Elise-Ann Konstantin; press, the Pete Sanders Group; Pete Sanders, Glenna Freedman, Michael Hartman.

Satirical treatment of Hollywood movies and their stars, past and present, by the author-progenitor of and in a similar vein to the long-run *Forbidden Broadway*. The show was presented in two parts.

Nixon's Nixon (40). By Russell Lees. Produced by The Shubert Organization, Capital Cities/ABC, Jujamcyn Theaters and Robert LuPone and Bernard Telsey in the MCC Theater production. Opened March 12, 1996. (Closed May 12, 1996)

Richard M. Nixon .... Gerry Bamman
Henry Kissinger .... Steve Mellor

Understudies: Mr. Bamman—Joseph Culliton; Mr. Mellor—Ken Kliban.
Directed by Jim Simpson; scenery and lighting, Kyle Chepulis; costumes, Danielle Hollywood; sound, Mike Nolan; casting, Bernard Telsey Casting; production stage manager, Erica Blum; stage manager, Bernadette McGay; press, Merle Frimark, Erin Dunn.
Time: August 7, 1984, 10 p.m. Place: Lincoln Sitting Room, The White House.
The President and his Secretary of State meet in private the night before the President's resignation. Previously produced off off Broadway 10/4/95 in this production.

Below the Belt (68). By Richard Dresser. Produced by Julian Schlossberg, Meyer Ackerman and Anita Howe-Waxman at the John Houseman Theater. Opened March 14, 1996. (Closed May 12, 1996)

Hanrahan .... Judd Hirsch   Merkin .... Jude Ciccolella
Dobbitt ....Robert Sean Leonard

Understudies: Messrs. Hirsch, Ciccolella—Richard Zobel; Mr. Leonard—Michael Louden.
Directed by Gloria Muzio; scenery, Stephan Olson; costumes, Jess Goldstein; lighting, Peter Kaczorowski; sound, Martin R. Desjardins; fight director, Steve Rankin; associate producers, Georgia Frontiere, Michael Winter; casting, Stuart Howard/Amy Schecter; production stage manager, Denise Yaney; press, Bill Evans & Associates, Jim Randolph, Tom D'Ambrosio.
Place: An industrial compound in a distant land. The play was presented in two parts.
Comedy, three American businessmen operating and interacting in a world in which corporate authority and achievement is all. Previously produced in Actors Theater of Louisville's Humana Festival.

***Take It Easy** (82). Musical with book, music and lyrics by Raymond Fox. Produced by New Village Productions, Carol Polcovar artistic director, at the Judith Anderson Theater. Opened March 21, 1996.

John Graham	Emmet Murphy	Mary Taylor	Julianna Hahn
Fred Brown	Isaac Rockoff	Becky Winslow	Kristin Hughes
Joe Goldman	Christian Anderson	Winifred Taylor	Carrie Pollack
Susan Bradshaw	Stephanie Kurtzuba	Lt. Col. Robert Davidson	Tom Nigh

Standbys: Ash Curtis, Emily Sutton-Smith, Tanya Anderson. Understudies: Mr. Murphy—Randy Bobish; Mr. Rockoff—Jesse Raynes; Mr. Anderson—Billy Sharpe; Miss Kurtzuba—Robin Higginbotham; Miss Hughes—Suzanne Lindenblatt; Mr. Nigh—John Luke Mete.

Directed by Collette Black; choreography, Tom Ribbink; musical direction, William Zeffiro; musical staging, Robin Higginbotham; scenery, Eddie Krummins; costumes, Fiona Brook; lighting, Matt Berman; sound, Jeff Lin; orchestrations, Mario E. Sprouse; stage manager, Margarita G. Ruiz; press, Mark-Leonard Simmons.

On a college campus in 1944, three privates drafted into the Army's Specialized Training Program mix military business with co-ed college pleasures and find their share of romance.

ACT I

Overture and Victory March
Scene 1: Main Street, 1944
 "We're in the Army" ....Fred, Joe, John, Ensemble
 "Who Cares" .... Susan
Scene 2: The college dance, later that night
 "Take It Easy" .... Mary, Fred, Ensemble
Scene 3: The girls' dorm, the next day
 "An Old Time Girl" ....Ensemble
 "Just One More Time" ....Robert, Winifred
Scene 4: After the football game
 "It's All Right"..Fred, Susan
 "I Think I'm Falling for You" ....Joe, Becky
 "I'll Remember Spring" ....John, Mary
 "Funny" ....Winifred
 "Just One More Time" (Reprise) ....Winifred, Robert
Scene 5: The campus, one month later
 "It's All Right" (Reprise) .... Susan
Scene 6: The girls' dorm
 "The Night When We Were Young" ....Robert, Winifred
Scene 7: The Autumn Ball
 "Say Farewell" ....Becky, Ensemble

ACT II

Scene 1: The A.S.T.P. barracks
 "Worry About the Blues Tomorrow" .... John, Ensemble
Scene 2: The girls' dorm, morning, a few weeks later
 "The Home Front Farm Brigade" ....Ensemble
Scene 3: Later that same day
Scene 4: Christmas at the front and at home
 "Home for Christmas" ....John, Mary
Scene 5: At the front
Scene 6: The girls' dorm, six months later
 "Our Yesterday" ....Mary
Scene 7: The gym, April 1945
 "It's All Right" (Reprise) .... Susan
Scene 8: Memorial Day, one year later
 "Looking for the Sunshine" ....John, Mary

Encores! Great American Musicals in Concert. Schedule of three musical revivals presented in limited concert engagements. **One Touch of Venus** (4). Book by S.J. Perelman and Ogden Nash; music by Kurt Weill; lyrics by Ogden Nash; based on *The Tinted Venus* by F.J. Anstey. Opened March 28, 1996. (Closed March 30, 1996) **Du Barry Was a Lady** (4). Book by Herbert Fields and B.G. DeSylva; music and lyrics by Cole Porter. Opened February 15, 1996. (Closed February 17, 1996) **Chicago** (4). Book by Fred Ebb and Bob Fosse; music by John Kander; lyrics by Fred Ebb; based on the play *Chicago* by Maurine Dallas Watkins. Opened May 2, 1996. (Closed May 4, 1996) Produced by City Center 55th Street Theater Foundation, Judith E. Daykin president and executive director, at the City Center.

ALL PLAYS: Artistic director, Walter Bobbie; musical direction, Rob Fisher; scenery, John Lee Beatty; sound, Scott Lehrer, Daniel Bornstein; press, Philip Rinaldi.

ONE TOUCH OF VENUS

Whitelaw Savory .... David Alan Grier	Bus Starter .... Peter Flynn
Molly Grant .... Carol Woods	Mrs. Kramer .... Marilyn Cooper
Taxi Black .... Danny Rutigliano	Gloria Kramer .... Jane Krakowski
Stanley .... Kevin Chamberlin	Police Lieutenant .... Timothy Robert Blevins
Rodney Hatch .... Andy Taylor	Dr. Rook .... Keith Byron Kirk
Venus .... Melissa Errico	Matron .... Melinda Klump
Mrs. Moats .... Sheryl McCallum	

Directed by Leonard Foglia; choreography, Hope Clarke; lighting, Peter Kaczorowski; concert adaptation, Leonard Foglia; apparel coordinator, David C. Woolard; original orchestration, Kurt Weill; production stage manager, Patrick Ballard.

One Touch of Venus was first produced on Broadway starring Mary Martin 10/7/43 for 567 performances. This is its first major New York revival.

MUSICAL NUMBERS: "New Art Is True Art," "One Touch of Venus," "How Much I Love You," "West Wind," "Way Out West in Jersey," "I'm a Stranger Here Myself," "Foolish Heart," "The Trouble With Women," "Speak Low," "Dr. Crippen," "Very, Very, Very," "Catch Hatch," "That's Him," "Wooden Wedding."

DU BARRY WAS A LADY

Louis Blore; His Most Royal	Harry Norton; Captain of the
Majesty .... Robert Morse	King's Guard .... Scott Waara
May Daly; Mme. la Comtesse	Alice Barton; Mme. la Marquise Alisande de
du Barry .... Faith Prince	Vernay .... Liz Larsen
Vi Hennessey; Mme. la Duchesse	Florian; Zamore .... Eugene Fleming
de Villardell .... Ruth Williamson	Alex Barton; Alexandre .... Burke Moses
Bill Kelly; Le Duc de	Charley; His Royal Highness .. Michael McGrath
Choiseul .... Bruce Adler	Docteur Michel .... Dick Latessa

Directed by Charles Repole; choreography, Kathleen Marshall; lighting, Peter Kaczorowski; concert adaptation, David Ives, Walter Bobbie; apparel coordinator, Gregg Barnes; original orchestration, Hans Spielek; production stage manager, Perry Kline.

Du Barry Was a Lady was first produced on Broadway starring Ethel Merman and Bert Lahr 12/6/39 for 408 performances. This is its first major New York revival.

MUSICAL NUMBERS: "Ev'ry Day a Holiday," "It Ain't Etiquette," "When Love Beckoned (in Fifty-Second Street)," "Come On In," "Mesdames and Messieurs," "But in the Morning, No!", "Do I Love You?", "Du Barry Was a Lady," "Give Him the Oo-La-La," "Did You Evah!", "It Was Written in the Stars," "L'Apres-Midi d'un Boeuf," "Katie Went to Haiti," "Friendship."

CHICAGO

Velma Kelly	Bebe Neuwirth	Matron Morton	Marcia Lewis
Roxie Hart	Ann Reinking	Mary Sunshine	D. Sabella
Billy Flynn	James Naughton	Aaron	David Gibson
Amos Hart	Joel Grey	Judge	Jim Borstelmann

Directed by Walter Bobbie; choreography, Ann Reinking in the style of Bob Fosse; lighting, Ken Billington; concert adaptation, David Thompson; apparel coordinator, William Ivey Long; original orchestrations, Ralph Burns; production stage manager, Clayton Phillips.

Chicago was first produced on Broadway starring Gwen Verdon 3/6/75 for 898 performances. The list of musical numbers in *Chicago* appears on page 319 of *The Best Plays of 1975–76*.

I Do! I Do! (68). Revival of the musical based on *The Fourposter* by Jan de Hartog; book and lyrics by Tom Jones; music by Harvey Schmidt. Produced by Arthur Cantor at the Lamb's Theater. Opened March 28, 1996. (Closed May 12, 1996)

Michael	David Garrison
Agnes	Karen Ziemba

Musicians: Tim Stella, Valerie Gebert piano.

Directed by Will Mackenzie; choreography, Janet Watson; musical direction, Tim Stella; scenery, Ed Wittstein; costumes, Suzy Benzinger; lighting, Mary Jo Dondlinger; associate producer, Dan Shaheen; production stage manager, Ira Mont; press, Arthur Cantor Associates.

Time and place: Fifty years of a marriage beginning in 1898. The play was presented in two parts.

I Do! I Do! was first produced on Broadway 12/5/66 for 560 performances. This is its first major revival of record.

The list of musical numbers in *I Do! I Do!* appears on pages 375–6 of *The Best Plays of 1966–67*.

*Cowgirls (68). Musical conceived by Mary Murfitt; book by Betsy Howie; music and lyrics by Mary Murfitt. Produced by Denise Cooper, Susan Gallin, Rodger Hess and Suki Sandler at the Minetta Lane Theater. Opened April 1, 1996.

Jo Carlson	Rhonda Coullet	Mary Lou	Mary Murfitt
Rita	Mary Ehrlinger	Mo	Betsy Howie
Lee	Lori Fischer	Mickey	Jackie Sanders

Directed and choreographed by Eleanor Reissa; musical direction, Pam Drews Phillips; scenery, James Noone; costumes, Catherine Zuber; lighting, Kenneth Posner; sound, Scott Stauffer; arrangements, Mary Ehlinger; associate producers, Carollyne Ascher, Chanes/Shapiro; casting, Liz Woodman; production stage manager, William Joseph Barnes; stage manager, Beth Bornstein; press, Shirley Herz Associates, Sam Rudy.

Time: The present. Place: Hiram Hall, a country music hall in Rexford, Kansas.

Midwest country music hall owner, preparing his theater's gala reopening, books a classical trio instead of a country trio by mistake. Previously produced in regional theater in Florida (Caldwell Theater Company and Florida Studio Theater) and at Berkshire Theater Festival and Old Globe Theater, San Diego.

ACT I

Overture	Trio: Rita, Lee, Mary Lou
(Beethoven's Sonata Pathetique, Opus 13)	
"Three Little Maids"	Trio
(by Gilbert and Sullivan)	
"Jesse's Lullaby"	Trio
(music by Brahms)	
"Ode to Connie Carlson"	Mickey, Mo
"Sigma, Alpha, Iota"	Trio
"Ode to Jo"	Mickey, Mo

"From Chopin to Country" ....Trio
   (music by Chopin)
"Kingdom of Country" ....Jo, Trio
   (music by C. Converse and Mary Murfitt)
"Songs My Mama Sang" ....Jo, Mary Lou
   (traditional hymn, additional music by Mary Murfitt)
"Heads or Tails" .... Lee, Rita
"Love's Sorrow" .... Joe, Rita, Lee
   (music by Kreisler)
"Looking for a Miracle" ....Mary Lou, Jo, Company
   (additional music by Mozart)

ACT II

"Don't Call Me Trailer Trash" .... Mickey, Mo
"Honky Tonk Girl" ....Rita
"Every Saturday Night" ....Jo, Trio
"Don't Look Down" .... Lee, Rita
"They're All Cowgirls to Me" ....Jo, Trio
"Saddle Tramp Blues" ....Mary Lou, Rita, Lee
"It's Time to Come Home" ....Jo
"We're a Travelin' Trio" ....Trio
"Sunflower" ....Trio
"Concert Medley" ....Company
"House Rules" ....Jo, Company
"Cowgirls" ....Trio

The Shattering (16). By Mark R. Shapiro. Produced by Shelmar Productions at the Players Theater. Opened April 2, 1996. (Closed April 14, 1996)

Bea	Marge Redmond	Sid	Frank Vohs
Peg	Patricia Randell	Walt	Owen Hollander
Harry	Robert Hogan	Lester	Ray Aranha

Directed by Kenneth Elliott; scenery, Edward T. Gianfrancesco; costumes, Robert Mackintosh; lighting, Phil Monat; sound, Fox & Perla, Ltd.; casting, Irene Stockton; production stage manager, D.C. Rosenberg; press, Cromarty & Co., Peter Cromarty.

Time 1992. Place: A lower middle class suburb. Act I, Scene 1: Harry's home, May 20, 4:30 p.m. Scene 2: A street corner, July 12, 1 p.m. Scene 3: Harry's home, July 16, 9:50 a.m. Act II, Scene 1: Harry's home, September 30, 5:15 p.m. Scene 2: Walt's Bar, September 30, 11 p.m. Scene 3: Harry's home, October 1, 3:30 a.m.

Suburban family's reactions to the ups and down of a third-party Presidential candidate, suggested by the events of the Perot campaign.

Zombie Prom (12). Musical based on a story by John Dempsey and Hugh M. Murphy; book and lyrics by John Dempsey; music by Dana P. Rowe. Produced by Nat Weiss in association with Randall L. Wreghitt at the Variety Arts Theater. Opened April 9, 1996. (Closed April 19, 1996)

Delilah Strict	Karen Murphy	Joey	Marc Lovci
Toffee	Jessica-Snow Wilson	Jake	Stephen Bienski
Coco	Cathy Trien	Josh	Jeff Skowron
Ginger	Natalie Toro	Jonny	Richard Roland
Candy	Rebecca Rich	Eddie Flagrante	Richard Muenz

Directed by Philip William McKinley; choreography, Tony Stevens; musical direction, Darren R. Cohen; scenery, James Youmans; costumes, Gregg Barnes; lighting, Richard Nelson; sound, Abe Jacob; orchestrations, Michael Gibson; casting, Joseph McConnell; production stage manager, Joel P. Elins; press, Jeffrey Richards.

One-Actor
Performances
Off Broadway

Above, Len Cariou as Ernest Hemingway in *Pape*
by John deGroot; *left*, Michael L. Kavanagh a
Brendan Behan in his own *Bein' With Behan*; *be*
low left, Tom Courtenay in *Moscow Stations*, Ste
phen Mulrine's adaptation of the novel *Moscow to*
Petushi; *below, in wheelchair*, John Hockenberry
as himself in his autobiographical *Spoke Man*

Comedy-fantasy, girl in love with a member of the undead, in a situation influenced by its proximity to a nuclear power plant. The play was presented in two parts.

MUSICAL NUMBERS: "Enrico Fermi High," "Ain't No Goin' Back," "Jonny Don't Go," "Good as It Gets," "The C Word," "Rules, Regulations and Respect," "Blast From the Past," "That's the Beat for Me," "The Voice in the Ocean," "It's Alive," "Where Do We Go From Here," "Trio (Case Closed)," "Then Came Jonny," "Come Join Us," "How Can I Say Goodbye," "Easy to Say," "Expose," "Isn't It?", "Forbidden Love," "The Lid's Been Blown," "Zombie Prom."

The Boar's Carcass (17). By Stephanie Dickinson. Produced by The New American Stage Company, Cindy Webster executive producer, Michael Cambden Richards artistic director, at the Theater at St. Peter's Church. Opened April 14, 1996. (Closed April 28, 1996)

Pete	Sean Cullen	Ashley	Nadine Stenovitch
Dario	Michael Cambden Richards	Lorna	Diane Grotke

Understudy: Messrs. Cullen, Richards—Michael Aubele.
Directed by David Calvitto; scenery, Teresa Stroh; costumes, Moira Shaughnessy; lighting, Jeff Segal; sound, Rick Beenders; casting, Adrienne Stern; producing consultant, Darren Lee Cole; production stage manager, Christina Massie; press, Shirley Herz Associates.
Time: The present. Place: A seaside boarding house in New Jersey. Act I, Scene 1: Early evening in Pete's bedroom. Scene 2: Thirty minutes later. Scene 3: Two hours later. Scene 4: One hour later. Act II: 11:30 p.m. the same evening in another room in the house, formerly a doctor's office.
Results of a young man's placing an ad in the sex-wanted section.

Tovah: Out of Her Mind (43). Solo performance by Tovah Feldshuh; conceived by Tovah Feldshuh; chief writer, Larry Amoros. Produced by the Jewish Repertory Theater, Ran Avni artistic director, at Playhouse 91. Opened April 21, 1996. (Closed June 2, 1996)

Direction and musical staging, Sara Louise Lazarus; musical director and pianist, Scott Cady; visual consultant, Tony Walton; costume consultant, William Ivey Long; lighting, Matt Berman; sound, Robert Campbell; creative consultants, Gary Lyons, Jennifer Westfeldt; production stage manager, Ruth E. Kramer; press, Shirley Herz Associates, Wayne Wolfe.
The versatile Miss Feldshuh presenting a gallery of modern characters age 8 to 80, most of them comically accented and some of them inducing her to break into song.

*Papa (29). Solo performance by Len Cariou; written by John deGroot. Produced by Eric Krebs, Anne Strickland Squadron and Brian C. Smith at the Douglas Fairbanks Theater. Opened May 5, 1996.

Directed by John Henry Davis; scenery, Santo Loquasto; lighting, F. Mitchell Dana; sound, John Gromada, Christopher Todd; production stage manager, James Fitzsimmons; press, David Rothenberg.
Cariou as Ernest Hemingway during the latter part of his life and career.

*Curtains (13). By Stephen Bill. Produced by Edgar Lansbury, Everett King and Michael Mendelson in The New Group production, Scott Elliott artistic director, at the John Houseman Theater. Opened May 21, 1996.

Margaret	Jayne Haynes	Geoffrey	John Henry Cox
Ida	Kathleen Claypool	Douglas	David Cale
Michael	Frederick Weller	Mrs. Jackson	Betty Miller
Katherine	Laura Esterman	Susan	Lisa Emery

Understudies: Misses Claypool, Miller—Mildred Clinton; Mr. Weller—Jeff O'Malley; Messrs. Cox, Cale—Graeme Malcolm.
Directed by Scott Elliott; scenery, Kevin Price; costumes, Eric Becker; lighting, Peter Kaczorowski; sound, Raymond D. Schilke; executive producer, Claudia Catania; casting, Judy Henderson, Alycia Aumuller; production stage manager, John J. Harmon; press, James Morrison Public Relations, Kevin Gerstein, Tom D'Ambrosio.

Time: Spring 1987. Place: Birmingham, England. Act I, Scene 1: Late afternoon. Scene 2: Evening. Act II: Late evening.

Family copes with the assisted suicide of its hopelessly ill, desperately unhappy, 86 year old matriarch. Previously produced by The New Group off off Broadway in this production at INTAR for 23 performances 4/17/96-5/12/96.

A Best Play; see page 249.

CAST REPLACEMENTS AND
TOURING COMPANIES

Compiled by Jeffrey A. Finn

The following is a list of the major cast replacements of record in productions which opened in previous years, but were still playing in New York during a substantial part of the 1995–96 season; or were on a first-class tour in 1995–96.

The name of each major role is listed in *italics* beneath the title of the play in the first column. In the second column directly opposite appears the name of the actor who created the role in the original New York production (whose opening date appears in *italics* at the top of the column). In shows of the past five years, indented immediately beneath the original actor's name are the names of subsequent New York replacements, together with the date of replacement when available. In shows that have run longer than five years, only this season's or the most recent cast replacements are listed under the names of the original cast members.

The third column gives information about first-class touring companies. When there is more than one roadshow company, #1, #2, etc., appear before the name of the performer who created the role in each company (and the city and date of each company's first performance appears in *italics* at the top of the column). Their subsequent replacements are also listed beneath their names in the same manner as the New York companies, with dates when available.

AFTER-PLAY

	New York 1/31/95
Marty Guteman	Merwin Goldsmith
Terry Guteman	Rue McClanahan
	Anne Meara 5/16/95
	Jane Powell 3/1/96
Phil Shredman	Larry Keith
	Jerry Stiller 11/7/95
	Larry Keith 1/96
	Jerry Stiller 4/96
Renee Shredman	Barbara Barrie
	Rita Moreno 11/7/95
	Anne Meara 3/1/96

BEAUTY AND THE BEAST

	New York 4/18/94	*#1 Los Angeles 4/12/95* *#2 Minneapolis 11/7/95*
Beast	Terrence Mann	#1 Terrence Mann
	Jeff McCarthy	James Barbour 8/1/95
		#2 Frederick C. Inkley

343

Belle	Susan Egan	#1 Susan Egan
	Sarah Uriarte	Yvette Lawrence 3/27/96
	Christianne Tisdale	#2 Kim Huber
	Kerry Butler	
Lefou	Kenny Raskin	#1 Jaime Torcelinni
	Harrison Beal	#2 Dan Sklar
Gaston	Burke Moses	#1 Burke Moses
	Marc Kudisch	Stephen Bishop 12/26/96
		#2 Tony Lawson
Maurice	Tom Bosley	#1 Tom Bosley
	MacIntyre Dixon	#2 Grant Cowan
	Tom Bosley	
	Kurt Knudson	
Cogsworth	Heath Lamberts	#1 Fred Applegate
	Peter Bartlett	Gibby Brand 4/24/96
		#2 Jeff Brooks
Lumiere	Gary Beach	#1 Gary Beach
	Lee Roy Reams	#2 Patrick Page
	Patrick Quinn	
Babette	Stacey Logan	#1 Heather Lee
		#2 Leslie Castay
Mrs. Potts	Beth Fowler	#1 Beth Fowler
	Cass Morgan	Jeanne Lehman 9/26/95
	Beth Fowler	#2 Betsy Joslyn

CATS

	New York 10/7/82	*National tour 1/94*
Alonzo	Hector Jaime Mercado	William Patrick Dunne
	Hans Kriefall 4/24/95	Rudd Anderson 6/6/95
Bustopher	Stephan Hanan	Richard Poole
	Richard Poole 12/12/94	Andy Gale 7/11/95
		Bart Shatto 3/12/96
Bombalurina	Donna King	Helen Frank
	Marlene Danielle 1/9/84	Lori Longstreth 9/26/95
Cassandra	Rene Ceballos	Laura Quinn
	Ida Gilliams 5/22/95	Stephanie Lang
Coricopat	Rene Clemente	(not in tour)
	James Hadley 3/20/95	
Demeter	Wendy Edmead	N. Elaine Wiggins
	Mercedes Perez 6/17/94	Susan Lamontagne 6/6/95
		Jennifer Lynn Letteleir
		10/3/95
Grizabella	Betty Buckley	Mary Gutzi
	Liz Callaway 5/3/93	Jeri Sager
Jellylorum	Bonnie Simmons	Patty Goble
	Nina Hennessey 6/22/92	Kris Koop 12/26/95
Jennyanydots	Anna McNeely	Alice C. DeChant
	Carol Dilley 8/22/94	

Mistoffeles	Timothy Scott Gen Horiuchi 3/18/95	Christopher Gattelli Randy André Davis 3/12/96
Mungojerrie	Rene Clemente Roger Kachel 5/11/92	Gavan Palmer Billy Johnstone 5/16/95
Munkustrap	Harry Groener Keith Bernardo 9/20/93	Robert Amirante Randy Clements
Old Deuteronomy	Ken Page	John Treacy Egan Doug Eskew
Plato/Macavity	Kenneth Ard Karl Wahl 5/20/96	Steve Bertles Taylor Wicker
Pouncival	Herman W. Sebek Jacob Brent 10/24/94	Joey Gyondla Christopher Burks 3/12/96 Michael Barriskill 4/19/96
Rum Tum Tugger	Terrence Mann David Hibbard 9/20/93	Ron Seykell J. Robert Spencer 5/16/95
Rumpleteazer	Christine Langner Kristi Sperling 9/19/95 Maria Jo Ralabate 4/1/96	Jennifer Cody Dana Solimando 9/5/95
Sillabub	Whitney Kershaw Bethany Samuelson 8/8/94	Lanene Charters
Skimbleshanks	Reed Jones Eric Scott Kincaid 6/3/94	Carmen Yurich Blair Bybee
Tantomile	Janet L. Hubert Jill Nicklaus 12/19/94	(not in tour)
Tumblebrutus	Robert Hoshour Levensky Smith 8/29/94	Joseph Favolora Tim Hunter
Victoria	Cynthia Onrubia Nadine Isnegger 7/25/94	Tricia Mitchell Joyce Chittick 7/11/95 Melissa Miller 11/14/95

Note: Only this season's or the most recent cast replacements are listed above under the names of the original cast members. For previous replacements, see previous volumes of *Best Plays*.

CRAZY FOR YOU

	New York 2/19/92	Dallas 5/11/93
Polly Baker	Jodi Benson Karen Ziemba	Karen Ziemba Crista Moore Beverly Ward
Bobby Child	Harry Groener James Brennan 1/2/95	James Brennan Kirby Ward
Lank Hawkins	John Hillner Daren Kelly 8/95	Chris Coucill Daren Kelly
Tess	Beth Leavel Melinda Buckley	Cathy Susan Pyles
Bela Zangler	Bruce Adler John Jellison Bruce Adler	Stuart Zagnit Paul Keith

Irene Roth	Michele Pawk Kay McClelland Sandy Edgerton Kay McClelland Sandy Edgerton Pia Zadora 8/16/95	Kay McClelland Belle Callaway Riette Burdick
Mother	Jane Connell Ann B. Davis 8/16/95	Lanka Peterson Ann B. Davis
Everett Baker	Ronn Carroll Carleton Carpenter Roger Horchow Carleton Carpenter John Jellison Al Checco John Jellison	Carleton Carpenter Al Checco Raymond Thorne
Eugene	Stephen Temperley	Geoffrey Wade John Curless
Patricia	Amelia White Colleen Smith Wallnau	Jeanette Landis (part dropped)
Patsy	Stacey Logan Jill Matson Rebecca Downing Joan Leslie Simms	Sally Boyet Joan Leslie Simms

DEATH DEFYING ACTS

	New York 3/6/95
Dorothy/Carol	Linda Lavin Valerie Harper 8/15/95
Phyllis	Debra Monk Kelly Bishop 8/15/95 Cynthia Darlow 1/17/96
Attorney/Ken/Sam	Paul Guilfoyle John Rothman 8/15/95
Attendant/Dr. Russel/ *Howard*	Gerry Becker Brian Reddy 8/15/95 Paul O'Brien 12/31/95 Dan Desmond

THE FANTASTICKS

	New York 5/3/60
El Gallo	Jerry Orbach John Savarese
Luisa	Rita Gardner Jennifer Westfeldt Christine Long
Matt	Kenneth Nelson Darren Romeo Eric Meyersfield

Note: Only this season's or the most recent cast replacements are listed above under the names of the original cast members. For previous replacements, see previous volumes of *Best Plays*.

GREASE

	New York 5/11/94	*Syracuse 9/19/94*
Vince Fontaine	Brian Bradley Micky Dolenz Brian Bradley Joe Piscopo Brian Bradley	Davy Jones Micky Dolenz Don Most 8/95 Nick Santa Maria 11/95 Joe Piscopo 1/96 Brian Bradley Nick Santa Maria 4/96
Miss Lynch	Marcia Lewis Mimi Hines JoAnne Worley Dody Goodman Marcia Lewis	Sally Struthers Dody Goodman 6/95 Sally Struthers 9/95
Betty Rizzo	Rosie O'Donnell Maureen McCormick Brooke Shields Joely Fisher Tia Riebling Susan Moniz Jody Watley	Angela Pupello Wendy Springer 8/95 Angela Pupello 10/95 Debbie Gibson 11/95 Mackenzie Phillips 3/96
Doody	Sam Harris Ray Walker Ty Taylor	Scott Beck Ric Ryder 7/95 Roy Chicas 4/96
Kenickie	Jason Opsahl Douglas Crawford	Douglas Crawford Steve Geyer 10/95
Roger	Hunter Foster	Nick Cavarra Erick Buckley 5/95
Sonny Latierri	Carlos Lopez Brad Kane Nick Cavarra Danny Cistone Carlos Lopez	Danny Cistone Tom Richter 8/95
Frenchy	Jessica Stone Monica Lee Gradischek Beth Lipari	Beth Lipari Jennifer Naimo 1/96
Jan	Heather Stokes Marissa Jaret Winokur Heather Stokes	Robin Irwin Marissa Jaret Winokur 8/95
Marty	Megan Mullally Sherie Rene Scott Leah Hocking Deirdre O'Neil	Deirdre O'Neil Amanda Watkins 8/95
Danny Zuko	Ricky Paull Goldin Adrian Zmed Ricky Paull Goldin Jon Secada Jeff Trachta Joseph Barbara	Rex Smith Jon Secada 6/95 Adrian Zmed 7/95
Sandy Dumbrowski	Susan Wood Susan Moniz Lacy Hornkohl	Trisha M. Gorman Sutton Foster 11/95

Patty Simcox	Michelle Blakely Christine Toy Carrie Ellen Austin	Melissa Papp Leslie Jennings 9/95 Leanna Polk 2/96
Eugene Florczyk	Paul Castree	Christopher Youngsman Christopher Carothers 12/95 Ashton Byrum 2/95
Cha-Cha DiGregorio	Sandra Purpuro Jennifer Cody	Jennifer Cody Michelle Bombacie 3/95 Lori Lynch 5/96
Teen Angel	Billy Porter Mary Bond Davis Charles Gray Jennifer Holliday Charles Gray Al Jarreau Chubby Checker	Kevin-Anthony

HAVING OUR SAY

New York 4/6/95

Sadie Delany	Gloria Foster Frances Foster 10/95
Dr. Bessie Delany	Mary Alice Novella Nelson 10/95

THE HEIRESS

New York 3/9/95

Catherine Sloper	Cherry Jones
Dr. Austin Sloper	Philip Bosco Donald Moffat 4/25/95 Remak Ramsay 8/29/95
Lavinia Penniman	Frances Sternhagen
Morris Townsend	Jon Tenney Michael Cumpsty 4/15/95 Richard Thompson 10/17/95

HOW TO SUCCEED IN BUSINESS WITHOUT REALLY TRYING

	New York 3/23/95	*Baltimore 5/28/96*
J. Pierrepont Finch	Matthew Broderick John Stamos 11/13/95 Matthew Broderick 3/19/96	Ralph Macchio
Rosemary Pilkington	Megan Mullally Jessica Stone 1/30/96 Sarah Jessica Parker 3/12/96	Shauna Hicks

Betty Buckley as Norma Desmond in *Sunset Boulevard*

J.B. Biggley	Ronn Carroll	Richard Thomsen
Bud Frump	Jeff Blumenkrantz Brooks Ashmanskas 2/19/96	Roger Bart
Hedy LaRue	Luba Mason	Pamela Blair
Twimble/Wally Womper	Gerry Vicchi	Michael Cone
Smitty	Victoria Clark	Susann Fletcher
Miss Jones	Lillias White	Tina Fabrique

INDISCRETIONS

New York 4/27/95

| *George* | Roger Rees |
| *Leonie* | Eileen Atkins
  Sandra Shipley 7/31/95
  Dana Ivey 10/3/95 |

Yvonne	Kathleen Turner
Michael	Jude Law
Madeleine	Cynthia Nixon

LES MISERABLES

	New York 3/12/87	*Tampa 11/18/88*
Jean Valjean	Colm Wilkinson Frederick C. Inkley Philip Hernandez Craig Schulman	Gary Barker Ivan Rutherford 10/95 Robert Evan 4/96
Javert	Terrence Mann David Masenheimer	Peter Samuel Ron Baker 6/95 David McDonald 12/95 Robert Longo 4/96
Fantine	Randy Graff Jacquelyn Piro Melba Moore Susie McMonagle	Hollis Resnik Susie McMonagle 6/95 Lisa Capps 3/96
Enjolras	Michael Maguire Gary Mauer	Greg Zerkle Brian Noonan 12/95
Marius	David Bryant Tom Donoghue	Matthew Porretta Andrew Redeker 6/95
Cosette	Judy Kuhn Tamra Hayden	Jacquelyn Piro Gina Feliccia 9/95
Eponine	Frances Ruffelle Christeena Michelle Riggs	Michele Maika Christeena Michelle Riggs 11/95 Dawn Younker 2/96
Thenardier	Leo Burmester Drew Eshelman	Paul Ainsley J.P. Dougherty
Mme. Thenardier	Jennifer Butt Gina Ferrall	Linda Kerns Kelly Ebsary

Note: Only this season's or the most recent cast replacements are listed above under the names of the original cast members. For previous replacements, see previous volumes of *Best Plays*.

LONDON SUITE

New York 4/9/95

Kate Burton

Jeffrey Jones

Carole Shelley
Harriet Harris 8/8/95

Paxton Whitehead
Paul Hecht 6/29/95

LOVE! VALOUR! COMPASSION!

	New York *Off Broadway 11/1/94* *Broadway 2/14/95*
Gregory Mitchell	Stephen Bogardus
Arthur Pape	John Benjamin Hickey Richard Bekins 7/17/95
Perry Sellars	Stephen Spinella Anthony Heald 2/14/95 T. Scott Cunningham 7/17/95
John Jeckyll/James Jeckyll	John Glover
Buzz Hauser	Nathan Lane Mario Cantone 4/7/95
Bobby Brahms	Justin Kirk
Ramon Fornos	Randy Becker

MISS SAIGON

	New York 4/11/91	*#1 Chicago 10/12/93* *#2 Seattle 3/16/95*
The Engineer	Jonathan Pryce Francis Ruivivar 8/19/91 Jonathan Pryce 9/30/91 Francis Ruivivar 12/16/91 Herman Sebek Alan Muraoka Raul Aranas Luoyong Wang	#1 Raul Aranas Kevin Gray #2 Thom Sesma
Kim	Lea Salonga Leila Florentino 3/16/92 Rona Figueroa Emy Baysic (alt.) Joan Almedilla Roxanne Taga (alt.)	#1 Jennie Kwan Jennifer C. Paz (alt.) Jennifer C. Paz Hazel Raymundo (alt.) Melanie Mariko Tojio (alt.) #2 Deedee Lynn Magno Cristina Paras (alt.) Alex Lee Tano (alt.) 10/3/95
Chris	Willy Falk Sean McDermott 12/16/91 Chris Peccaro Jarrod Emick Eric Kunze Tyley Ross	#1 Jarrod Emick Eric Kunze Peter Lockyer #2 Matt Bogart Will Chase 4/16/96

THE ONLY THING WORSE YOU COULD HAVE TOLD ME. . .

	New York 4/2/95
	Dan Butler Greg Louganis 8/8/95

THE PHANTOM OF THE OPERA

	New York 1/26/88	#1 Los Angeles 5/31/90 #2 Chicago 5/24/90 #3 Seattle 12/13/92
The Phantom	Michael Crawford Davis Gaines	#1 Michael Crawford Frank D'Ambrosio 3/28/94 #2 Mark Jacoby Rick Hilsabeck #3 Frank D'Ambrosio Thomas James O'Leary 6/20/95
Christine Daae	Sarah Brightman Tracy Shayne Laurie Gayle Stephenson (alt.) Teri Bibb (alt.)	#1 Dale Kristien Lisa Vroman 12/2/93 Cristin Mortenson (alt.) #2 Karen Culliver Teri Bibb 12/19/95 Sandra Joseph (alt.) 2/27/96 Sandra Joseph 3/26/96 Kate Suber 3/26/96 #3 Tracy Shane Susan Facer (alt.) Adrienne McEwan 9/20/95 Diane Fratantoni 3/12/96
Raoul	Steve Barton Brad Little	#1 Reece Holland Aloysius Gigl 5/2/95 #2 Keith Buterbaugh Nat Chandler #3 Ciaran Sheehan John Schroeder

Note: Alternates play the role of Christine Daae Monday and Wednesday evenings. Only this season's or the most recent cast replacements are listed above under the names of the original cast members. For previous replacements, see previous volumes of *Best Plays*.

SWINGTIME CANTEEN

New York 3/14/95

Alison Fraser
   Charles Busch 8/24/95

Emily Loesser
   Maxene Andrews 9/12/95

SHOW BOAT

	New York 10/2/94	#1 Vancouver 12/3/95 #2 Chicago 3/24/96
Cap'n Andy	John McMartin John Cullum 1/30/96	#1 George Grizzard Ned Beatty 1/22/96 #2 John McMartin
Parthy	Elaine Stritch Carole Shelley 9/12/95	#1 Cloris Leachman #2 Dorothy Loudon

Magnolia	Rebecca Luker Sarah Pfisterer 2/96	#1 Teri Hansen #2 Gay Willis
Gaylord Ravenal	Mark Jacoby Hugh Panaro 11/95	#1 J. Mark McVey #2 Mark Jacoby
Julie	Lonette McKee Marilyn McCoo 9/26/95 Lonette McKee 2/13/96	#1 Valarie Pettiford #2 Marilyn McCoo
Frank	Joel Blum	#1 Keith Savage #2 Eddie Korbich
Ellie	Dorothy Stanley Beth Leavel 11/95	#1 Jacquey Maltby #2 Clare Leach
Queenie	Gretha Boston	#1 Anita Berry #2 Jo Ann Hawkins Whige
Steve	Doug LaBrecque Fred Love 9/26/95	#1 Todd Noel Kip Wilborn 3/29/96 #2 Todd Noel
Joe	Michel Bell André Solomon Glover 2/13/96	#1 Dan Tullis Jr. #2 Michel Bell

SUNSET BOULEVARD

	New York 11/17/94
Norma Desmond	Glenn Close Betty Buckley 7/4/95
Joe Gillis	Alan Campbell
Max von Mayerling	George Hearn
Betty Schaefer	Alice Ripley
Cecil B. DeMille	Alan Oppenheimer
Artie Green	Vincent Tumeo

THREE TALL WOMEN

	New York 4/5/94	*Boston 10/95*
A	Myra Carter Lucille Patton 5/23/95 Marian Seldes 6/13/95	Marian Seldes
B	Marian Seldes Joan Van Ark 5/19/95 Frances Conroy 7/17/95	Michael Learned
C	Jordan Baker Christina Rouner 6/13/95	Christina Rouner
The Boy	Michael Rhodes	Michael Rhodes

OTHER SHOWS
ON FIRST CLASS TOURS IN 1995–96

ANGELS IN AMERICA

Chicago 2/26/95

Roy Cohn	Jonathan Hadary
Louis Ironson	Peter Birkenhead
	Douglas Harmsen
	12/5/95
Prior Walter	Robert Sella
	Todd Weeks 12/5/95
Joe Pitt	Philip Earl Johnson
	Rick Holmes 9/5/95
Harper Pitt	Kate Goehring
	Sarah Underwood
	12/5/95
Belize	Reg Flowers
Angel	Carolyn Swift
Hannah Pitt	Barbara Robertson
	Pamela Burrell 9/5/95

CAROUSEL

Houston 2/2/96

Billy Bigelow	Patrick Wilson
Julie Jordan	Sarah Uriarte
Carrie Pipperidge	Sherry D. Boone
Enoch Snow	Sean Palmer
Nettie Fowler	Rebecca Eichenberger
Jigger Craigin	Brett Rickaby

DAMN YANKEES

Baltimore 9/25/95

Applegate	Jerry Lewis
Lola	Valerie Wright
Joe Hardy	David Elder
Joe Boyd	Dennis Kelly
Gloria Thorpe	Linda Gabler
Meg Boyd	Susan Bigelow

Sister	Amy Ryder Julie Prosser 3/26/96
Benny Van Buren	Joseph R. Sicari

AN INSPECTOR CALLS

Baltimore 10/17/95

Sybil Birling	Susan Kellerman
Edna	Kaye Kingston
Arthur Birling	Philip LeStrange Stacy Keach 5/7/96
Gerald Croft	David Andrew Macdonald
Sheila Birling	Jane Fleiss
Eric Birling	Harry Carnahan
Inspector Goole	Sam Tsoutsouvas John Lantz 1/16/96 Curt Hostetter 4/30/96 Kenneth Cranham 5/7/96
Boy	Jeffrey Force Zachary Freed 2/13/96

JOSEPH AND THE AMAZING TECHNICOLOR DREAMCOAT

#1 West Point, NY 1/13/95
#2 Toronto 5/31/95

Joseph	#1 Sam Harris Brian Lane Green 2/26/96 #2 Donny Osmond
Narrator	#1 Kristine Fraelich #2 Kelli James Chase Donna Kane 11/12/95
Jacob/Potiphar/Guru	#1 Russell Leib Steve Pudenz 2/25/96 #2 James Harms Gary Krawford 11/29/95 James Harms 3/31/96
Pharoah	#1 John Ganun Jeffrey Scott Watkins 1/12/96 #2 Johnny Seaton
Butler	#1 Glenn Sneed #2 J.C. Montgomery
Baker	#1 Paul J. Gallagher #2 Erich McMillan-McCall
Mrs. Potiphar	#1 Justine DiCostanzo Mindy Franzese #2 Carole Mackereth Julia Alicia Fowler 3/31/96

KISS OF THE SPIDER WOMAN

	Tampa 11/1/94
Molina	Juan Chioran Jeff Hyslop 7/95 Juan Chioran 8/95
Warden	Mark Zimmerman Michael McCormick 8/95
Valentin	John Dossett Dorian Harewood 8/95
Spider Woman/Aurora	Chita Rivera Carol Lawrence Chita Rivera
Molina's Mother	Rita Gardner Merle Louise 8/95
Marta	Juliet Lambert Lauren Goler-Kosarin 9/95

WEST SIDE STORY

	Detroit 9/5/95
Tony	H.E. Greer Scott Carollo 11/95
Maria	Marcy Harriell
Anita	Natascia A. Diaz
Riff	Jamie Gustis
Bernardo	Vincent Zamora

THE SEASON
OFF OFF BROADWAY

○
○
○

OFF OFF BROADWAY

○
　　By Mel Gussow
○
○

THIS SEASON, the news off off Broadway also became the news on Broadway. *Rent,* Jonathan Larson's rock opera based on *La Bohème,* opened at the New York Theater Workshop (after Larson died suddenly of an aortic aneurism) and went on to win all the major awards including the Pulitzer Prize for drama. The musical is fully discussed in the Broadway section of this book. It must also be regarded as a touchstone in the history of off off Broadway, which has increasingly served a significant purpose as a training ground for new talent that in some cases can have a broad popular appeal.

Nixon's Nixon, Russell Lees's acerbic, reconstructive look at Richard Nixon and Henry Kissinger on the eve of Nixon's resignation as President, came out of the MCC Theater, and, under the direction of Jim Simpson, moved into an off-Broadway engagement. Without looking like Nixon, Gerry Bamman caught the mania behind the man, seeing him as a kind of ham actor in thrall to his own image. Steve Mellor made Kissinger seem totally self-interested even when imitating Nixon at the suggestion of Nixon. The play, with full credit to Bamman's characterization, is cited as an outstanding 1996 OOB production. Also moving into an extended run off-Broadway was the New Group's production of *Curtains,* a dour dark comedy about Alzheimer's by the British playwright Stephen Bill. Actually, two of three nominations for the Pulitzer Prize began off off: *Rent* and *Old Wicked Songs,* Jon Marans's study of a pianist and a teacher (at the Jewish Repertory Theater), scheduled to return for an open-ended off-Broadway run. As a result of all this creative activity, more uptown producers can be found scouting shows in offbeat locations.

Rent brought the spotlight to the New York Theater Workshop, which, under the direction of James C. Nicola, has become one of the more valuable off-off companies, last year with Tony Kushner's *Slavs* and *The Family Business* by Ain and David Gordon, this year with Doug Wright's *Quills,* in addition to *Rent. Quills* was a Grand Guignol comedy about the incarceration at Charenton of that infamous Marquis de Sade. Though occasionally over the top, the play was marked by its revolutionary spirit, funniest when Lola Pashalinski was center stage as Mrs. de Sade, aka Satan's Bride. Poor thing: she is shunned by everyone in this "unending cavalcade of woe I'm doomed to call my life." Rocco Sisto was improperly insatiable as de Sade, a compulsive storyteller and intuitive performance artist. In one of Wright's artful stunts, in the denouement the dead de Sade's severed body parts were animated back into life.

Stage noir was most vividly represented by Eric Overmyer's *Dark Rapture,* an outstanding 1996 OOB production. Cited by ATCA in 1992–1993 and presented for the first time in New York at the Second Stage, *Dark Rapture* was loopy, polysyllabic and chimerical, in other words, prime Overmyer. Watching the devastation of his house in a massive California fire, the protagonist (Scott Glenn) said, "This is where we get our stories. Surviving catastrophe." He was, in fact, speaking for the author, who in plays like this, *On the Verge* and *Native Speech* has an unmatchable imagination. Moving in and out of plots and intrigue involving drugs, terrorism and the Bay of Pigs invasion, *Dark Rapture* left a trail of crazyquilt clues. Both Raymond Chandler and Elmore Leonard (in particular, *Get Shorty*) lurk in the background as Overmyer follows his own quirky, linguistic path. Scott Ellis's cinematic production was finely tuned to the author's sensibility, with especially choice performances by Marisa Tomei as a double dealer and Ellen McElduff as a shady woman named Max. In a typical Overmyer throwaway line, Max announces, "Before I was a drug dealer, I was an efficiency expert." The show was laden with lagniappes (author's word), offering more than a little something on the side.

Mac Wellman, Overmyer's kinsman as virtuoso verbalist, was the co-author with Len Jenkin of *Tallahassee,* a shaggy chamber musical drawn from Ovid. Although the events of the play were chaotic, the music by Elise Morris and Jim Ragland was sprightly in a *Hair*-like fashion. More interesting musically was *Bed and Sofa,* a "silent movie opera" by Polly Pen and Laurence Klavan. Based on Abram Room's celebrated 1927 film, *Bed and Sofa* peered into the domestic life of three Russians sharing an apartment (and a bed). A quaint cubicle of a musical, it had moments of charm as well as self-induced banalities. Ms. Pen, who wrote the wonderful *Goblin Market* several seasons ago, challenged herself with the question, how small can a musical be? Small, very small. *Bed and Sofa* would fit into a closet of *Rent;* and both have real estate as a subtext. Andre Ernotte gave *Bed and Sofa* the neat staging it deserved, with special credit for G. W. Mercier's design and Terri Klausner as a woman with an attachment to two men.

Elizabeth Swados returned to La Mama with two brief musicals *Doonesbury Flashbacks* and *The Emperor's New Clothes,* performed by her acting students at New York University. *Doonesbury Flashbacks* had moments but was not up to the level of Ms. Swados's Broadway *Doonesbury,* while *The Emperor's New Clothes* was a clever updating of an old tale.

The New Victory Theater on West 42d Street is a beautifully restored Broadway house, committed to theater for young audiences. One of its occupants was *The Green Bird,* as transformed by Julie Taymor into a spectacular canvas of magical surprises. Puppets, masks and panoply shared the stage. The play was too long and sprawling but was elevated by Ms. Taymor's restless inventiveness and Elliot Goldenthal's fanciful score. Earlier in the season, Andrei Serban took a different, equally valid view of *The Green Bird* at La Mama. As part of the season at the New

Victory, Bill Irwin curated a series of performance pieces, including one in which he appeared, *Hip-hop Wonderland,* an improvisational mix of clowning and street dancing.

With *An Epidog,* Lee Breuer revivified his animation cycle and wrote a post-prelude to *The Warrior Ant.* The story follows the life in death of the title dog and her involvement with a large bunny rabbit who looks like a drag queen. The convoluted play is destined to confuse: one ignores the plot and focuses on the play-fulness. Presented by Mabou Mines and the Gertrude Stein Repertory Theater at the Here theater, *Epidog* was a puppet extravaganza, fooling around with contemporary history, mythology and theater: a case of Breuer in a light-hearted mood. Rose, the dog, a lifelike creature, was manipulated Bunraku-style, with her voice supplied by Ruth Maleczech: a canny canine, or a dog that wags the tale. At one merry point, Rose did a pas de deux with Clove Galilee. Artistic points go to Julie Archer for the cybernetic set, Barbara Pollitt for her puppet direction and Ushio Torakai for the musical score.

In *Chinoiserie,* an outstanding OOB production, Ping Chong offered part two of his cycle of plays about East-West relations. Presented in the Next Wave Festival at the Brooklyn Academy of Music, *Chinoiserie* followed Chong's *Deshima* as a far-reaching contemplation/collage about racism, heritage and history. Reaching into his Asian ancestry, Chong as archivist probed such subjects as the Western obsession with tea, trade wars and Oriental immigration to the United States, along the way discovering lost stories of prejudice including a play entitled *Chinese Must Go.* With his customary humor, he wove a tapestry of story, song ("Take Me Out to the Ball Game" in Chinese) and slides. On stage as narrator, the author-director stimulated the audience with his visual dynamics and intellectual curiosity.

Robert Wilson returned to BAM with *Alice,* his own idiomatic and mysterious take on Lewis Carroll. The evening began with a chorus of Carrolls, then shifted to the author as photographer, seen zeroing in on Alice with a snake-like camera. Her fall into Wonderland was a perspective-distorting magic trick. As Alice grew smaller, the scenery grew larger: down and down she went into an inside-out world. The show was filled with brilliant touches: a self-puffing caterpillar, flying saucers for the pig and pepper scene. Tom Waits's score was Weill-tinged, mixing Lotte Lenya (and Marlene Dietrich) into the eclectic environment. Because the production came from Hamburg, the dialogue was in German and English (the songs were in English). Decidedly a hybrid, *Alice* was Wilsonian at its core, filled with his surrealistic picture-scapes.

While spreading his wings as director with Suzan-Lori Parks's *Venus* at the Joseph Papp Public Theater, Richard Foreman offered *The Universe* on his home ground, the Ontological Hysteric. Forget exegesis. Think power play. Is Tony Torn (in a Molière wig) a tempter from outer space? In this roundelay of dialectical vaudeville, Torn sounded like a W.C. Fields moving to Jimmy Durante like music, and here comes a chorus of beehived coneheads. *The Universe* is another dream of childhood, refraining favorite themes and motifs: tables that tip, a set strung with records, clocks and lampshades, everything emerging from Foreman's hyper-theatrical psyche.

Above, Jennifer Esposito and Scott Glenn in *Dark Rapture* by Eric Overmyer at Second Stage ("loopy, polysyllabic and chimerical"); *right*, Jonathan Fried, Kevin T. Carroll and Trazana Beverley in *Sleep Deprivation Chamber* by Adam and Adrienne Kennedy at Signature Theater ("a dramatic disturbance that resonated long after one left the theater"); *below*, Steve Mellor and Gerry Bamman in Manhattan Class Company's *Nixon's Nixon* by Russell Lees (an "acerbic, reconstructive look at Richard Nixon and Henry Kissinger on the eve of Nixon's resignation")

Michael Edo Keane, Shi-Zheng Chen, Ric Oquita and Aleta Hayes in Ping Chong's *Chinoiserie* in BAM's Next Wave Festival ("a far-reaching contemplation/collage about racism, heritage and history")

True Crimes was this season's contribution from Romulus Linney: a gnarled Gothic country tale about evil (disguised as piety), greed, revenge and murder. In other words, the play carried a heavy load, but it was done as a ballad, with twangy music and folk poetry. A lusty country boy reads True Crime stories then becomes enmeshed in violence through the unkind graces of his mother. The characters are unsavory, the writing assured and the acting earthily in tune with the subject. The source of the work, at a great remove, was Leo Tolstoy, transferred to a far corner of Appalachia. In *Antigone in New York,* Janusz Glowacki looked at New York's homeless immigrants. With the help of Steven Skybell, the play had occasional moments of gallows humor, but was mired in earnestness. Far funnier was a vignette about Polish workers that Glowacki contributed to an evening of ten minute plays at Primary Stages.

Among the worthy plays from abroad was *Sarachi* (at Japan House), written and directed by Shogo Ohta, a stubbornly original, uncompromising Japanese artist. Sweeping clean the slate of theater (and of society), he writes about the end of order in a post apocalyptical world. At the Ubu Repertory Theater, Francoise Kourilsky specializes in introducing audiences to modern European plays, this season with Jean-Yves Picq's *The Case of Kaspar Mayer* and Loleh Bellon's *Bonds of Affection,* among others. The latter, staged with subtlety by Shirley Kaplan, was a sensitive study of a mother and daughter over decades.

As usual, off off Broadway was marked by its diversity, with a range extending from a Ridiculous Theatrical romp (Everett Quinton's *Call Me Sarah Bernhardt*) to a musical version of *The Diary of Anne Frank (The Secret Annex)* to a further chapter in Theodora Skipitares's puppet history of medicine *(Under the Knife III)* to still another lost play by Shakespeare *(Cardenio).* Almost any night, one could find a work by Fassbinder, Schnitzler, Almodovar or J.B. Priestley. The Priestley was *Dangerous Corner,* as reinvented by David Mamet. With clever cutting and quick footwork, Mamet turned this mystery into a house of games. Presented by the Atlantic Theater, the play had a mid-Atlantic tone, without abandoning the original author: sounds like Mamet, but keeps Priestley. Mamet himself turned up at the Ensemble Studio Theater with an evening of five one-acts, directed by Curt Dempster. These were vignettes of "the things we say," and how we say them. Three of the plays were new. The two reprises were the sharpest, *A Sermon,* a diabolical spoof of ministerial blather, and the title piece, *No One Will Be Immune,* about an interrogation of a possible terrorist. David Rasche was superb in both.

Waiting for Godot was revived at the Jean Cocteau and *Endgame* (with an actress, Kathleen Chalfant, as Hamm) at the Classic Stage Company, which also devoted itself to Joe Orton. David Esbjornson, the artistic director of the CSC, staged a dry, suave production of *Entertaining Mr. Sloane.* Brian Murray was splendidly mock-dapper, capturing the affected high style of the author and Ellen Parker blossomed into the role of the predatory landlady.

Another notable revival was of *The Cocoanuts,* the Irving Berlin-George S. Kaufman musical forever indebted to the Marx Brothers, who played it on Broadway and then filmed it. Smartly staged by Richard Sabellico at the American Jewish Theater, *Cocoanuts* was a fresh breeze of vaudeville. As previously demonstrated at the Arena Stage in Washington, D.C., the only way to do this musical is to imitate the Marx Brothers, which the present company did with abandon. Michael McGrath proved to be a zany Groucho, even able to get laughs with puny puns. Peter Slutsker and Robert Sapoff cut up nostagically as Chico and Harpo, and Kirby Ward won laughs as the villain. Feet flew on this minuscule stage, and "Always," cut by Kaufman before the show opened, was wisely reinstated into this invigorating entertainment.

Clifford Odets's *Golden Boy* proved to have a surprising resilience in a production directed by Joanne Woodward for the new Blue Light Theater Company. The creakiness and the preachiness were temporarily obscured by the visceral acting of the large cast, especially by Greg Naughton in the title role of the violinist turned prizefighter. There were also sharp performances by Angie Phillips, James Naughton, Bruce MacVittie and Joe Grifasi. Blue Light also collaborated with the Potomac Theater Project in presenting Howard Barker's *Scenes From an Execution,* a provocative play about art and the state, and the question of censorship. One of the more persuasive performances was given by Greg Naughton as a painter of limited talent.

The estimable Signature Theater Company lost its home and took up temporary residence at the Public Theater, with a season devoted to Adrienne Kennedy. Though the work proved to be uneven, the festival helped to reestablish the playwright's reputation as an artist with a dreamlike, poetic talent. The revival of her best known play, *Funnyhouse of a Negro* (paired with *A Movie Star Has to Star in Black and White*) proved to be less interesting than the new work, *June and Jean in Concert* and, especially, *Sleep Deprivation Chamber,* cited as an outstanding 1996 OOB production. This harrowing story, a collaboration between Ms. Kennedy and her son Adam, was a reaction to the true story of the son's arrest and beating after being charged with a minor traffic violation. The son in the play is a light-skinned black who suffers repeated indignities under a system of injustice, in which one is "guilty until proven not guilty." The fact that the case was finally dropped does not mitigate the horror story. The play (directed by Michael Kahn) is a dramatic disturbance that resonated long after one left the theater.

Jonathan Marc Sherman's *Wonderful Time* (at the WPA) kept the author in the promising category with a sweet-tempered little romantic comedy about a young man trying to define himself. In the interesting but unsatisfying *Sabina,* Willy Holtzman placed Freud and Jung in love and war over a patient turned analyst; it was one of many plays this season to put historical figures on stage. Catherine Butterfield, who made her auspicious playwriting debut in New York with *Joined at the Head,* returned with *Where the Truth Lies,* a flawed but intriguing, double-edged play about abuse within marriage. Ron Nyswaner's *Oblivion Postponed* was heavy handed in its approach to skeletons in family closets. With *Frank Pig Says Hello,* the Irish writer Pat McCabe dramatized his novel, *The Butcher Boy.* This cautionary tale, about a maladjusted boy who becomes monstrous, lacked clarity on stage. The Holocaust preoccupied playwrights, as in Tim Blake Nelson's *The Grey Zone,* about the aftermath of Birkenau, and Donald Margulies's *The Model Apartment,* in which concentration camp memories haunt a couple in Florida.

With *Wally's Ghost* at the Soho Rep, Ain Gordon certified his originality, and his ability to turn life into comic art. In the rambling first act, Wally, a young gay man, is surrounded by ghosts, including Lady Astor who offers fascinating information about the history of New York real estate. The second act suddenly adds cohesiveness and turns into a story of urban angst. How does one get along in a world of officious waitresses, pushy realtors, murder and mayhem? Gordon has wry and sometimes moving things to say about life on Earth, while posing the question, where is home? Albert Macklin was splendid as Wally, perplexed but caring, a man who "haunts himself."

This busy season ended, as usual, with the Ensemble Studio Theater's annual Marathon of one-act plays, 12 plays presented in three productions. Although the work was marked by the usual high level of direction and performance, only a few were notable for their writing: Arthur Miller's *Elegy for a Lady* (about a man's dying love), Joyce Carol Oates's *The Adoption* (a black comic cartoon about the desperation of parents without children), Paul Selig's *Slide Show* (with the author evocatively playing a woman, the play's only role) and, especially, Howard Korder's *Geliebteh,* a daughter's monologue about a father she did not know. *Geliebteh* was movingly delivered by Lynn Cohen, following up her performance earlier this season in *The Model Apartment.*

Off off Broadway knows no boundaries: it appears in all boroughs of New York and in limitless locations, outdoors and indoors. Melanie Joseph's pioneering Foundry Theater troupe moved into the Anchorage under the Brooklyn Bridge with an environmental production of W. David Hancock's *Deviant Craft,* a mixture of *The Tempest* and *Marat/Sade.* Events happened in the lobby as well as on stage. An old woman pounding on a metal door and demanding to be admitted turned out to be an actress in the play. All false starts were intentional. At one performance, a theatergoer said, "This play is too interactive for me." In this case, the *place* was the thing: cavernous catacombs with high-vaulted ceilings, open brick walls and a feeling of permanent antiquity.

PLAYS PRODUCED
OFF OFF BROADWAY

AND ADDITIONAL N.Y.C. PRODUCTIONS

Compiled by Camille Dee

Here is a comprehensive sampling of off-off-Broadway and other experimental or peripheral 1995–96 productions in New York. There is no definitive "off-off-Broadway" area or qualification. To try to define or regiment it would be untrue to its fluid, exploratory purpose. The listing below of hundreds of works produced by more than 100 OOB groups and others is as inclusive as reliable sources will allow, however, and takes in all leading Manhattan-based, new-play producing, English-language organizations.

The more active and established producing groups are identified in **bold face type,** in alphabetical order, with artistic policies and the names of the managing directors given whenever these are a matter of record. Each group's 1995–96 schedule, with emphasis on new plays and with revivals of classics usually omitted, is listed with play titles in CAPITAL LETTERS. Often these are works-in-progress with changing scripts, casts and directors, sometimes without an engagement of record (but an opening or early performance date is included when available).

Many of these off-off-Broadway groups have long since outgrown a merely experimental status and are offering programs which are the equal in professionalism and quality (and in some cases the superior) of anything in the New York theater, with special contractual arrangements like the showcase code, letters of agreement (allowing for longer runs and higher admission prices than usual) and, closer to the edge of the commercial theater, a so-called "mini-contract." In the list below, all available data on opening dates, performance numbers and major production and acting credits (almost all for Equity members) is included in the entries of these special-arrangement offerings.

A large selection of lesser-known groups and other shows that made appearances off off Broadway during the season appears under the "Miscellaneous" heading at the end of this listing.

American Theater of Actors. Dedicated to providing a creative atmosphere for new American playwrights, actors and directors. James Jennings artistic director.

RICHARD II. By William Shakespeare. Director, James Jennings. June 1, 1995. With Jeff Sult, Pat Connelly, Tom Bruce, Kathleen Hogan, Courtney Everett, Ken Coughlin, Jeff Lynn.

RAVEN'S GATE. By Joseph Acosta. June 7, 1995. Director, Patrick Barnes. With Robert Airhart, Will Buchanan, James Hall, Heidi Lilly, Bill Timmins, Pat Waggoner.

AGAIN AND AGAIN. By Joseph Simone. June 14, 1995. Director, Michael Arzouane. With John Combs, Gil Grail.

LADIES WHO LUNCH. By C.C. Henley. July 5, 1995. Director, Jane Culley. With Melanie Robichaux, Julie Zimmermann, Ginger Masoud, Jane Cornell, Teresa Fischer.

DUET. By Jerry Kaufman. July 5, 1995. Director, Grethe Boe. With Gabriela May Ladd, Andrew Leher.

A SHORT VISIT. By Alex Menza. July 12, 1995. Director, David Logan. With Ed Mahler, Elaine Kussack.

TIMON OF ATHENS. By William Shakespeare. July 12, 1995. Director, James Jennings. With Tom Bruce, Jim Kosior, Abigail Walker, John Koprowski, Tom Delehanty, Zuri Wagner, Rob Cividanes.

TORNADO CHASER. Written and directed by James Jennings. August 9, 1995. With Cinda Lawrence, Jim Kosior, Abigail Walker.

MEASURE FOR MEASURE. By William Shakespeare. August 9, 1995. Director, Judith Caporale. With Alexandra Cremer, William Greville, Ken Coughlin, Jed Dent, Mark Schmetter, Mara Rixton, Diane Mostello, Lydia Russo.

MALIBU DUST. By Dan Socolov. August 30, 1995. Director, D.A.G. Burgos. With Brian Luna, Jonathan Webb, Dean Negri.

A SURPRISE VISIT. By Masayo Nishimura. August 30, 1995. Director, Catherine Lamm. With Kate Pak, Ron Contawe, Mark Neveldine, Brenda Lee, Garvie MacDiarmid, Toshifumi Toyota.

HOLIDAY MADNESS. By Carol Holland. September 6, 1995. Director, Ted Mornel. With Victoria Brooks, Mary Goggin, Karen Lawrence, Laura Morgan, Denise Mullen.

RICHARD III. By William Shakespeare. September 7, 1995. Director, James Jennings. With Ray Lando, Janine Cogelia, Tom Delehanty, Jorgi Knickrem, Zuri Wagner, Barbara Friend, Robert O'Malley, Mark Neveldine, Dan Gregry, David Tillistrand.

CEREMONIES OF PRAYER. By Evan Blake. September 27, 1995. Director, Greg Hubbard. With Alex Ceppi, Laura Ekstrand, Michael LaFetra, Carol Graziano.

PRIVATE PRACTICE. By Leonard Post. October 4, 1995. Director, Marc Thomas. With Alexander Lyras, Gary Carlson, Angela Nirvana, Sandra Parris.

CHANGING WOMAN. Written and directed by James Jennings. October 4, 1995. With Jim Kosior, Renata Rodriguez, Joe Iacona, Dean Negri, Alex Jordan, Rob Cividanes, David Kring.

OWLS. By Tom Labar. October 11, 1995. Director, John Koprowski. With Tom Bruce, Jerry Berk, Cinda Lawrence, Rachel Borut.

SWEETWATER. Written and directed by James Jennings. October 25, 1995. With Mark Schmetter, Amy de Lucia, Annette Sinclair.

HOOKERS' HAVEN. Written and directed by Tom Bruce. November 8, 1995. With Jerry Berk, John Koprowski, Jocelyn Druyan, Jeff Lynn, Adrian Lee, Courtney Everett, Jane Kennedy, Victor Mancini.

SCRO-O-O-GE. Adapted from Charles Dickens's *A Christmas Carol* and directed by Charles Scotland. December 21, 1995.

BILLY. Written and directed by James Jennings. January 10, 1996. With Derrick Begin, Dennis Kaiser, Stephanie Johnson, Judith Caporale Dean Negri, Zuri Wagner, Ray Trail.

STARGAZING. Written and directed by Nancy Chu. January 10, 1996. With Jaimee Young, David Leicht, Julienne Kim, Anton Strout.

MOUND DIGGERS. Written and directed by James Jennings. February 7, 1996. With Derrick Begin, Tracy Grinnell, Dean Negri, Mark Neveldine.

LOCATING THE PLANT. By Tim Marks. February 28, 1996. Director, David Hayden. With Tom Delehanty, Pat Waggoner, Judith Boxley, Zuri Wagner, Rosemary Serluca, J.P. Lavin, Dan Tatch.

POLES APART. By John Byrd. March 6, 1996. Director, Steven Boockvor. With Penrod Parker, William Greville, Willie Ann, Michael Boyle, David Kring, Curtis Deveraux, Harry Listig, Linda Sheridan.

EVERYTHING'S RELATIVE. By Scott Billings. March 6, 1996. Director, Jeff Lynn. With Ray Lando, Rob Cividanes, Janine Cogelia, Jorji Knickrem, Tom Fattoruso.

JOHN AND ELLEN. By Alex Menza. March 13, 1996. Director, Judith Caporale. With Barbara Friend, Joe Iacona.

BLOOD DUES. By Ed Musto. March 13, 1996. Director, Richard Galgano. With Ben Golden, Mick Hilgers, Frank Avoletta, Joanne McEvoy, Dannette Bock, Dana Watkins, Christopher Ridman, Blaine Lee Holtkamp.

THE GRAVITY OF DENISE. By Brandon Hawes. March 20, 1996. Director, Nathan Smith. With Jennifer Carpiniello, David Riedy, Brandon Hawes.

SINGIN' INSIDE THE HURRICANE. Written and directed by Nancy Kissam. March 27, 1996. With Susan DiGiulio, Kathryn Hahn, Cobey Mandarino, Steve Mize, Tina Posterli, Barbara Summerville.

ODE TO THE DRUMMERS. Written and directed by James Jennings. April 10, 1996. With James Kosior, Mark Schmetter, Jerry Berk, Tracy Grinnell, Dean Negri.

Circle Repertory Projects-in-Process. Program which is an essential part of the play development process. Austin Pendleton artistic director, Andrew Chipok managing director.

SAKURA: THE BANDIT PRINCESS (10). By Kikue Tashiro. November 3, 1995. Director, Penny Bergman; scenery, Shaun Motley; lighting, Darla J. Braswell; costumes, Elly Van Horne. With Kati Kuroda, Jolie Hatsuko Madigan.

THIS IS WHERE I GET OFF (14). By and with Beth Littleford. January 12, 1996. Director, Warren Etheredge; scenery, Shaun Motley; lighting, Anne Duston Cheney.

Classic Stage Company. Reinventing and revitalizing the classics for contemporary audiences. David Esbjornson artistic director, Mary Esbjornson executive director.

ENDGAME (34). By Samuel Beckett. October 5, 1995. Director, David Esbjornson; lighting, Kenneth Posner; costumes, Elizabeth Hope Clancy. With John Seitz, Kathleen Chalfant, Alan Manson, Irma St. Paule.

ENTERTAINING MR. SLOANE (41). By Joe Orton. February 21, 1996. Director, David Esbjornson; scenery, Narelle Sissons; lighting, Frances Aronson; costumes, Michael Krass; sound, John Kilgore. With Neil Maffin, Ellen Parker, George Hall, Brian Murray.

DON JUAN COMES BACK FROM THE WAR (34). By Odon von Horvath, translated by Ralph Manheim and Sean Allen. April 12, 1996. Directors, Annie-B Parson and Paul Lazar; scenery, Joanne Howard; lighting, David Moodey; costumes, Claudia Stephens; musical direction, Christopher Berg. With Katya Brue, Stacy Dawson, Lauren Hamilton, Deirdre Harrison, Molly Hickok, Anna Kohler, Chris McNally, Gwen Snyder, Irma St. Paule, Stephanie Weyman, Rebecca Wisocky. Co-produced by Cucharacha Theater.

En Garde Arts. Dedicated to developing the concept of "site-specific theater" in the streets, parks and buildings of the city. Anne Hamburger founder and producer.

J.P. MORGAN SAVES THE NATION (30). Book and lyrics, Jeffrey M. Jones; music, Jonathan Larson. June 15, 1995. Director, Jean Randich; choreography, Doug Elkins; scenery, Kyle Chepulis; lighting, Pat Dignan; costumes, Kasia Maimone; sound, David Meschter; musical direction, Jules Cohen. With James Judy, Stephen DeRosa, Buzz Bovshow, Julie Fain Lawrence, Robin Miles.

Ensemble Studio Theater. Membership organization of playwrights, actors, directors and designers dedicated to supporting individual theater artists and developing new works for the stage. Over 250 projects each season, ranging from readings to fully-mounted productions. Curt Dempster artistic director, Susan Jonas managing director.

HELL'S KITCHEN SINK (theatrical revue). Schedule included: TWO GUYS MOVING HEAVY STUFF by Dave Reidy, directed by Mark Roberts; THE MAMET WOMEN by Frederick Stroppel, directed by Mark Roberts; SECRETARY ON THE EDGE by Jamie Gorenberg, directed by Abigail Zealey; MAN ON THE MOON (a song from the Lullaby Project) with Janine Robbins, Rusty Magee; SERGEI BISGROVNY by and with Thomas McHugh, directed by Mark Roberts; ENGLISH, IT'S WHERE THE WORDS ARE by Peter Basch, directed by Jamie Richards; DAY JOB by and with Kevin Fisher, directed by Mark Roberts; DAS WOLFKIN by William Seabring, directed by Jamie Richards. February 5–25, 1996.

NO ONE WILL BE IMMUNE (FIVE PIECES FOR THEATER): A SERMON, SUNDAY AFTERNOON, JOSEPH DINTENFASS, ALMOST DONE and NO ONE WILL BE IMMUNE (18). By David Mamet. March 21, 1996. Director, Curt Dempster; scenery, Kert F. Lundell; lighting, Greg MacPherson; costumes, Barbara A. Bell; sound, Jeffrey Taylor. With David Rasche, David Margulies, Elaine Bromka, James Murtaugh, Kristina Lear, Byron Jennings.

MARATHON '96 (festival of one-act plays). CATS AND DOGS by Cherie Vogelstein, directed by Jamie Richards; GELIEBTEH by Howard Korder, directed by Matthew Penn; DEGAS, C'EST MOI by David Ives, directed by Shirley Kaplan; ELEGY FOR A LADY by Arthur Miller, directed by Curt Dempster; SLICE OF LIFE by Stuart R. Brown, directed by Pirie MacDonald; ENGLISH, IT'S WHERE THE WORDS ARE by Peter Basch, directed by Susann Brinkley; BEL CANTO by Will Scheffer, directed by Brian Mertes; LOVE LIKE FIRE (PART I) written and directed by Romulus Linney; THE ADOPTION by Joyce Carol Oates, directed by Kevin Confoy; HOME by Laura Cahill, directed by Jace Alexander; THE OBSERVATORY by Greg Germann, directed by Jim Simpson; SLIDE SHOW by Paul Selig, directed by Christopher A. Smith. May 8-June 16, 1996.

INTAR. Mission is to identify, develop and present the talents of gifted Hispanic American theater artists and multicultural visual artists. Max Ferra artistic director.

NEW LATINO VOICES (three plays in repertory): INKARRI'S RETURN by Henry Guzman, directed by Paulo Nunes-Ueno; FOREVER IN MY HEART by Oscar A. Colon, directed by Michael John Garces, music by Johnna Doty; IN THE LAND OF GIANTS by Roger Arturo Durling, directed by Eduardo Machado (22). March 10–30, 1996. Scenery, Van Santvoord; lighting, Traci Klainer-McDonnell; costumes, Mirena Rada; sound, Johnna Doty. With Victor Argo, Blanca Camacho, Maria Cellario, Ruben Gonzalez, Adriana Inchaustegui, Joe Quintero, Hechter Ubarry, Miriam Cruz, Doris Difarnecio, Michael John Garces.

RADIO MAMBO: CULTURE CLASH INVADES MIAMI (34). By and with Culture Clash (Richard Montoya, Ric Salinas, Herbert Siguenza). May 24, 1996. Director, Roger Guenveur Smith; scenery, Herbert Siguenza; lighting, Peter Edwards; sound, Mark Friedman.

Irish Repertory Theater. Aims to bring works by Irish and Irish American masters and contemporary playwrights to a wider audience and to develop new works focusing on a wide range of cultural experiences. Charlotte Moore artistic director, Ciaran O'Reilly producing director.

SAME OLD MOON (36). By Geraldine Aron. September 21, 1995. Director, Charlotte Moore; scenery, Bryan Johnson; lighting, Gregory Cohen; costumes, David Toser; sound, Aural Fixation. With Madeleine Potter, Aideen O'Kelly, Terry Donnelly, Risteard Cooper, John Keating, Ciaran O'Reilly, Paddy Croft, Aedin Moloney.

JUNO AND THE PAYCOCK. By Sean O'Casey. November 19, 1995. Director, Charlotte Moore. With Pauline Flanagan, W.B. Brydon, Aedin Moloney, John Keating, Risteard Cooper, Terry Donnelly, Fidelma Murphy.

IRISH REPERTORY THEATER—David Gorry and Sean
Rocks in *Frank Pig Says Hello* by Pat McCabe

FRANK PIG SAYS HELLO (24). By Pat McCabe. January 28, 1996. Director, Joe O'Byrne; scenery, Ian McNicholl. With David Gorry, Sean Rocks. (Co-Motion Theater Company production)

A WHISTLE IN THE DARK (32). By Thomas Murphy. February 29, 1996. Director, Charlotte Moore; scenery, David Raphel; lighting, Gregory Cohen; costumes, Monica Russell. With James Beecher, Ciaran O'Reilly, Jim Cunningham, Jean Parker, Denis O'Neill, Chris O'Neill, David Leary, Dara Coleman.

La Mama (a.k.a. LaMama) Experimental Theater Club (ETC). A busy workshop for experimental theater of all kinds. Ellen Stewart founder and artistic director.

Schedule included:

KEEP BACK 200 FEET. By Ray Thomas and Mel Williams. June 8, 1995. Director, Mel Williams. With Ray Thomas.

SAM'S TORMENTED ANGELS. By Albatross Theater of Sweden, adapted from Allen Ginsberg's poems. June 15, 1995. Director, Robert Jakobsson. With Albatross Theater of Sweden.

JAMES JOYCE: CARTA AL ARTISTA ADOLESCENTE. Adapted from James Joyce's *Portrait of the Artist As a Young Man* by Luis Mario Moncada and Martin Acosta. June 22, 1995. Director, Martin Acosta. With Alejandro Reyes, Arturo Reyes, Mario Oliver.

THE CRY OF SILENCE. Written and directed by Hans Falar. June 28, 1995. Choreography, Mihsen Hosseini.

DARK IS THE NIGHT. By Aleksandar Popovic, translated and directed by Ivana Askovic. September 21, 1995.

SONGS FOR MY SISTERS. By Abba Elethea. October 5, 1995. Director, Ozzie Rodriguez; music, Kate Dezina and Sheila Dabney.

A CHEKHOV TRIO: SUMMER IN THE COUNTRY, GRIEF and THE HARMFULNESS OF TOBACCO. By Anton Chekhov. October 11, 1995. With M.B. Ghaffari.

LOVE, THE GREATEST ENCHANTMENT by Calderon de la Barca, THE GOLDEN BIRD by Carlo Gozzi and LA DISPUTE by Pierre de Marivaux. October 12, 1995. Director, Andrei Serban; music, Bill Ruyle and Chris Wertenbaker.

ROSEL. By Harald Mueller, translated by Paul Costello. October 19, 1995. Director, Christian Schiaretti; music, Nino Rota. With Carla Cassola.

THE STRANGE GAMES. Written, directed and performed by Vladimir Olshansky. October 26, 1995.

STUPID FRENCH SONGS. By and with Nathalie Schmidt. November 2, 1995.

ONE ACT CORIOLANUS. Adapted from William Shakespeare's play and directed by Mervyn Willis. November 16, 1995. Music, William Norman. With Todd Theater Troupe.

FIRMAMENT. By The Winter Project. November 24, 1995. Director, Joseph Chaikin; music, Richard Peaslee and Gina Leishman. With Paul Zimet, Robbie McCauley, Roger Babb, Tina Shepard, Alyssa Bresnahan.

BIG DICKS, ASIAN MEN. By and with SLANT (Richard Ebihara, Wayland Quintero, Perry Yung). November 30, 1995. Music, Genji Ito. Reopened February 15, 1996.

THE LABOR OF LIFE. By Hanoch Levin, translated by Barbara Harshav. December 7, 1995. Directors, Victor and Geula Attar; music, Tamar Muskal.

TINY TIM AND THE SIZE QUEEN. Adapted from Charles Dickens's *A Christmas Carol* and directed by Daniel Haben Clark. December 14, 1995. With Brad Chandler, Joe Pichette.

TURANDOT. By Carlo Gozzi, translated by Albert Bermel and Ted Emory. December 28, 1995. Director, Joumana Rizk; music, Han Yong. Co-produced by Rushmore Festival.

PASTIME by Dawn Akemi Saito and PAPA BOY by Ernest Abuba (one-act plays). January 18, 1996. Director, Ernest Abuba.

THE LIVING CORPSE (REDEMPTION). Adapted from Leo Tolstoy's work and directed by Jonathan Schilder Brown. January 18, 1996. Music, Perry Hall.

UNDER THE KNIFE III. Created, designed and directed by Theodora Skipitares. January 18, 1996. Music, Virgil Moorefield.

HUA TIEN TSUO (Flower Field Folly). By and with Hai Lan Dance Drama Theater. February 15, 1996. Director, Lu-Yu.

THREE STORIES OF THE HONORABLE FLOWER. Libretto, Odile Marcel, translated by K. Alex Alatsis and Leslie Ann Wint; music, Maurice Ohana. February 15, 1996. Director, K. Alex Alatsis. With Stacy Fraser, Diana Solomon Glover.

KONSTANTIS AND ARETE. Conceived, directed and choreographed by Olga Zissi. February 22, 1996. Music, Gail Holst-Warhaft, Ross Daly.

POST TRAUMA. By and with Poppo and the Go-Go Boys. February 29, 1996.

BENITO CERENO. Adapted from Herman Melville's work by Robert Lowell. February 29, 1996. Director, Rich Crooks.

LOCOFOCO. Written and directed by Susan Mosakowski. February 29, 1996. With Mary Shultz.

THE THIRTEEN CLOCKS by James Thurber, JITTERS by Michael Garces and VENUS'S DIARY by Lynne McCollough. March 6, 1996. Direction and music, Tom O'Horgan. With La Mama 2000.

TOY GARDEN. By Kikuo Saito. March 14, 1996.

INTERFACING JOAN. By and with Louise Smith. March 14, 1996. Director and designer, Ping Chong.

THE HOUSE OF NANCY DUNN. By Steve Weisberg, Andy Craft and Howard Pflanzer. March 14, 1996. Director, John James Hickey.

AGUIRRE: THE SPIRAL OF THE WARRIOR. Adapted from Abel Posse's novel *Daimon,* directed and choreographed by Federico Restrepo. March 21, 1996.

BOX. Written and directed by Constantin Werner. March 28, 1996.

BAMBI LEVINE, PLEASE SHUT UP!. Written and directed by Stephen Holt. April 4, 1996.

MY KINGDOM FOR A HORSE. Adapted from William Shakespeare's *Richard III* and directed by Dario D'Ambrosi. April 11, 1996. Scenery, Jun Maeda. With Teresa Pascarelli, Bianca Ara.

SARAJEVO, MON AMOUR. Written, directed and performed by Turkar Coker. April 11, 1996.

THE FOURTEENTH WARD. Adapted from Henry Miller's play by Terry O'Reilly, Bill Raymond and Carter Burwell. April 18, 1996. Director, Terry O'Reilly; music, Carter Burwell.

UNTIL THE NEXT WHIRL. Conceived and directed by Zishan Ugurlu. April 25, 1996. Music, Genji Ito.

MISHIMA MONTAGE. Written and directed by Michael Rush. April 25, 1996.

WAYWARD WIND. Written and directed by Virlana Tkacz. May 9, 1996. Music, Genji Ito. With Yara Arts Group.

DOONESBURY FLASHBACKS book, music and lyrics by Elizabeth Swados, based on Garry Trudeau's comic strip and THE EMPEROR'S NEW CLOTHES book, music and lyrics by Elizabeth Swados, based on Hans Christian Andersen's fairy tale. May 9, 1996. Director, Elizabeth Swados.

THE FAIRGROUND BOOTH. By Alexander Blok, translated by Michael Green. May 9, 1996. Directors, Roger Babb and Rocky Bornstein; scenery, Ralph Lee; lighting, Pat Dignan; costumes, Gabriel Berry; music, Neal Kirkwood. With Otrabanda Company (Nancy Alfaro, Roger Babb, Tim Cummings, Dan Hurlin, Jennifer Miller, Lenard Petit, Mary Shultz).

DANCE CARD. Written and directed by Harold Dean James. May 23, 1996.

TAKING CARE OF BUSINESS: BETTY'S GARAGE by Carmen Rivera; HANDS OF STONE and JUAN PACHANGA by Candido Tirado. May 23, 1996. Director, Gloria Zelaxa. With Latino Experimental Fantastic Theater.

The Club

ONE WOMAN SHOE reopened June 8, 1995.

TILT. By and with Orlou. October 5, 1995.

VOICE CROSSING. By and with Joshua Fried. October 27, 1995.

ALL ABOUT JEEZ, OR THE SACRED SQUIRT. Written and directed by Assurbanipal Babilla. November 2, 1995. Lighting, Howard Thies; sound, One Dream Sound. With Purgatorio Ink Theater (Assurbanipal Babilla, David Cote, Jennie Crotero, Leyla Ebtehadj, Suzanne Elizabeth Fletcher, Lynne Kanter, Bill Martin).

LOOKING FOR MR. AMERICA. By and with George Birimisa. November 9, 1995.

THE BALLAD OF JUNE COOL (one-woman show). By and with Laura Kenyon. November 20, 1995.

POLLY'S PANIC ATTACK. By Sebastian Stuart. November 30, 1995. Director, Everett Quinton. With Chris Tanner, Richard Spore, Bobby Reed, Irene Shea, Eureka, Nicole Zaray.

JAIL BABES. By and with Duelling Bankheads (David Ilku and Clark Render). January 4, 1996. Reopened March 14, 1996.

THE DEAD MAN. By George Bataille, translated by Austryn Wainhouse. January 18, 1996. Music, Achim Gieseler.

LEMUEL (rap opera). By Lonnie Carter. February 1, 1996. Director, Andre De Shields.

ALICE UNDERGROUND. Adapted from Lewis Carroll's *Alice's Adventures in Wonderland* and *Through the Looking Glass* by Charles Drew; music, Janice Lowe. March 4, 1996.

THE PORTRAIT SERIES: A QUARTET OF MEN by and with Warren Lehrer, music by Brian Lehrer; performance piece by Judith Sloan. March 11, 1996.

THE HARDY BOYS AND THE MYSTERY OF WHERE BABIES COME FROM by Christopher Durang; THE TRICK by Perry Laylon Ojeda; CREDO by Craig Lucas. April 11, 1996. Director, Randy Gener.

INFIDELS: THE BLANCO DANCES. April 25, 1996. Director, R. Michael Blanco; choreography, Carol Blanco; music, David Lawson.

LANA LYNX: PASSPORT, PISTOL AND PASSION. By Ruth Fuglistaller. May 6, 1996. Director, Tina Johnson.

THE LAST HAND LAUNDRY IN CHINATOWN. Book and lyrics, Alvin Eng; music and direction, John Dunbar. May 9, 1996.

THE KNIVES AND FORKS OF LANA LYNX. By Ruth Fuglistaller. May 13, 1996. Director, Tina Johnson.

THE LARYNX CHALET. Book, music, lyrics and direction, Rebecca Moore. May 23, 1996. With Larry Miller, Jessica Liebman, Mary McBride, Richard Scheinmel.

Mabou Mines. Theater collaborative whose work is a synthesis of motivational acting, narrative acting and mixed-media performance. Collective artistic leadership. Frederick Neumann, Terry O'Reilly, Ruth Maleczech, Lee Breuer artistic directors.

AN EPIDOG (29). Written and directed by Lee Breuer. January 13, 1996. Scenery, lighting and puppets, Julie Archer; costumes, Mary Pat Bishop; sound, Edward Cosla; music, Ushio Torakai; co-produced with Gertrude Stein Repertory Theater. With Ruth Maleczech, Frederick Neumann, Clove Galilee, Leslie Mohn, Xin Zhang, Barbara Pollitt, Terry O'Reilly, Basil Twist, Bina Sharif, Samantha Hack, Kathy Shaw, Carrie Cantor, Emily Weiner, Marymay Impastato, Crystal Scott, Maria Hurley, Jessica Smith, Jenny Subjack, Lute Ramblin'.

MCC Theater. Dedicated to the promotion of emerging writers, actors, directors and theatrical designers. Robert LuPone and Bernard Telsey executive directors.

NIXON'S NIXON (53). By Russell Lees. September 29, 1995. See its entry in the Plays Produced Off Broadway section of this volume.

THE GREY ZONE (47). By Tim Blake Nelson. January 5, 1996. Director, Douglas Hughes; scenery, Neil Patel; lighting, Michael Chybowski; costumes, Catherine Zuber; music and sound, David Van Tieghem. With Christopher McCann, Edward Dougherty, Gus Rogerson, Matthew Sussman, Michael Stuhlbarg, David Chandler, Henry Stram, Abigail Revasch.

THREE IN THE BACK, TWO IN THE HEAD (42). By Jason Sherman. May 18, 1996. Director, Pamela Berlin; scenery, Neil Patel; lighting, Howard Werner; costumes, Michael Krass; sound, David Van Tieghem. With Fred Burrell, Alma Cuervo, Byron Jennings, Ben Shenkman, Nick Wyman.

Music-Theater Group. Pioneering in the development of new music-theater. Lyn Austin producing director, Diane Wondisford general director.

YOU DON'T MISS WATER (4). Book, Maureen Shea and Cornelius Eady, based on Cornelius Eady's poems; music, Diedre Murray. November 2, 1995. Director, Maureen Shea; choreography, Susan Dibble; scenery, Vanessa James; lighting, David Weiner; costumes, Eve Sandler; sound, Richard Jansen; musical direction, Richard Harper. With Alaiye Agemo, Jeannine Otis, James Randolph, Charles Thomas, Sean Conly, Eli Fountain, Richard Harper, Diedre Murray. Co-produced by Aaron Davis Hall's New Faces/New Voices/New Visions.

New Dramatists. An organization devoted to playwrights; member writers may use the facilities for anything from private cold readings of their material to public script-in-hand readings. Elana Greenfield director of artistic programming, Jana Jevnikar director of finance, Paul A. Slee executive director.

Readings:

IN WALKS ED. Written and directed by Keith Glover. September 6, 1995.

TURN OF THE SCREW. By Jeffrey Hatcher. September 14, 1995. Director, Greg Leaming.

ECSTASY. By Ramon Griffero. September 20, 1995. Director, Eduardo Machado.

COMING OF THE HURRICANE. By Keith Glover. September 20, 1995. Director, Marion McClinton.

SCAR. By Murray Mednick. September 28, 1995. Director, Vivian Sorenson.

FEDUNN. Written and directed by Murray Mednick. September 29, 1995.

BEDFELLOWS. Written and directed by Herman Daniel Farrell III. October 2, 1995.

THE NEGRO OF PETER THE GREAT. By Carlyle Brown. October 6, 1995. Director, Peter Francis James.

WAITING WOMEN. By Sylvia Gonzalez S. October 16, 1995. Directors, Dan Green and Sylvia Gonzalez S.

I CAN'T EAT GOATHEAD. By Sylvia Gonzalez S. October 17, 1995. Directors, Dan Green and Sylvia Gonzalez S.

WITHOUT QUALITIES. By Ana Maria Simo. October 24, 1995. Director, David Greenspan.

TRUTH. By Ana Maria Simo. October 24, 1995. Director, Damien Gray.

TRIP'S CINCH. By Phyllis Nagy. October 25, 1995. Director, JoAnne Akalaitis.

THE STRIP. By Phyllis Nagy. October 25, 1995. Director, Len Jenkin.

QUINLY AGONISTES. Book and lyrics, Quincy Long; music, Michael Silversher. October 26, 1995. Director, Kathleen Dimmick.

THE JOY OF GOING SOMEWHERE DEFINITE. By Quincy Long. October 26, 1995. Director, Lisa Peterson.

AS IT IS IN HEAVEN. By Joe Sutton. October 27, 1995. Director, Douglas Hughes.

THE WRONG KIND OF KISS. By Joe Sutton. October 27, 1995. Director, Kenneth Elliott.

OCEANO PACIFICO. By Roger Arturo Durling. November 6, 1995. Director, Eduardo Machado.

YELLOW MOON RISING. By Carlyle Brown. November 11, 1995. Director, Walter Dallas.

COVERED DISHES. By Deborah Baley. November 22 and December 10, 1995. Director, Jim Simpson.

WAITING FOR GODOT TO LEAVE. By Oana-Maria Hock Cajal. December 1, 1995. Director, Damien Gray.

THE ENDURING LEGEND OF MARINKA PINKA AND TOMMY ATOMIC. By Oana-Marie Hock Cajal. December 1, 1995. Director, Damien Gray.

THE SWORD OF CAZARAN. Written and directed by Keith Glover. December 3, 1995 and February 21, 1996.

THE JUDGMENT OF THE WHORE. By Jonathan Pascoe. December 6, 1995. Director, Jim Simpson.

LANDSCAPE OF DESIRE. By Barry Jay Kaplan. December 10, 1995. Director, Alison Summers.

SECOND-HAND SMOKE. By Mac Wellman. December 13, 1995. Director, Jim Simpson.

INFRARED. By Mac Wellman. December 14, 1995. Director, Jim Simpson.

BUFFALO HAIR. By Carlyle Brown. January 12, 1996. Director, Jim Simpson.

CUBA AND THE NIGHT. By Eduardo Machado. January 17, 1996. Director, Jim Simpson.

ELEPHANT PLAY. By Dmitri Lipkin. January 19, 1996. Director, Tim Cunningham.

SWITCHBACK. By Murray Mednick. January 22, 1996. Director, Damien Gray.

JOE AND BETTY. By Murray Mednick. January 26, 1996. Director, Alison Summers.

TRIGGER LOVE. By August Baker. January 30, 1996. Director, Jim Simpson.

SQUEEZED AVOCADOS. By Sylvia Gonzalez S. February 13, 1996. Director, Gail Noppe-Brandon.

THE SHRINKING WIFE. By Sylvia Gonzalez S. February 14, 1996. Director, Bruce Katzman.

STICK WITH ME, KID, etc. By Tony Peltier. February 15, 1996. Director, Damien Gray.

BANANAS AND WATER. By Barry Jay Kaplan. February 22, 1996. Director, Stephen Haff.

ROCK AND ROY. Book and lyrics, Barry Jay Kaplan; music, Stephen Weinstock. February 26, 1996.

DREAM HOUSE. By Darrah Cloud. February 29, 1996. Director, Elizabeth Theobald.

BRIDE STRIPPED BARE. By Kate Robin. March 11, 1996. Director, Tim Cunningham.

DEMONOLOGY. By Kelly Stuart. March 14, 1996. Director, Alison Summers.

TAXIDANCE. By Kelly Stuart. March 18, 1996. Director, Stephen Haff.

COYOTE GOES SALMON FISHING. Book and lyrics, Deborah Baley; music, Scott D. Richards. March 20, 1996. Director, Christopher Grabowski.

TO MANDELA. By Herman Farrell. March 28, 1996. Director, Clinton Turner Davis.
WANTS. By Lenora Champagne. April 1, 1996. Director, Liz Diamond.
MR. MELANCHOLY. By Matt Cameron. April 10, 1996. Director, Karen Kohlhaas.
TEAR FROM A GLASS EYE. By Matt Cameron. April 18, 1996. Director, Alison Summers.
ROCK AND ROY. Book and lyrics, Barry Jay Kaplan; music, Stephen Weinstock. April 19 and May 14, 1996. Director, Alison Summers.
DEMONOLOGY. By Kelly Stuart. April 22, 1996. Director, Stephen Haff.
WITHOUT QUALITIES. By Ana Maria Simo. April 24, 1996. Director, David Greenspan.
ESSEX GIRLS. By Rebecca Pritchard. May 1, 1996. Director, Alison Summers.
THERE. By Herman Daniel Farrell III. May 3, 1996. Director, Seth Gordon.
THE SLOW DEATH OF ECSTASY. By Rebecca Pritchard. May 13, 1996. Director, Stephen Haff.
DRIVER, PAINTER. By Hillel Mitelpunkt. May 16, 1996. Director, Lawrence Sacharow.
THE HOUSE MOTHER. By Hillel Mitelpunkt. May 21, 1996. Director, Alison Summers.
THE SINGING. By Lenora Champagne; music, Daniel Levy. May 22, 1996. Director, Matthew Maguire.
THE LIGHT OUTSIDE. By Kate Robin. May 23, 1996. Director, Stephen Haff.

New Federal Theater. Dedicated to presenting new playwrights and plays dealing with the minority and Third World experience. Woodie King Jr. producing director.

FOR COLORED GIRLS WHO HAVE CONSIDERED SUICIDE/WHEN THE RAINBOW IS ENUF. Written and directed by Ntozake Shange. June 22, 1995. Choreography, Mickey Davidson; scenery, Chris Cumberbatch; lighting, William H. Grant III; costumes, Judy Dearing; sound, Tim Schellenbaum; music, Craig Harris. With Catrina Ganey, Yvette Ganier, Deidra LaWan Johnson, Dorcas M. Johnson, Patrice Johnson, Tamika Lamison, Brenda Phillips. Reopened August 16, 1995 for 36 performances.

BLACK GIRL (29). By J.E. Franklin. November 9, 1995. Director, Anderson Johnson; scenery, Kent Hoffman; lighting, Antoinette E. Tynes; costumes, Vassie Welbeck-Browne; sound, Genji Ito. With Leslie Uggams, Sabrina DePina, Justin West, TraLynn Husbands, Lynn Dandridge, Maggie Henderson, Marlene Chavis, Arthur French, Adam Wade.

CHECKMATES (30). By Ron Milner. April 10, 1996. Director, Woodie King Jr.; scenery, Felix E. Cochren; lighting, Antoinette E. Tynes; costumes, Vassie Welbeck-Browne; sound, Tim Shellenbaum. With Ruby Dee, Arthur French, Amy-Monique Waddell, Peter Jay Fernandez.

New York Shakespeare Festival/Joseph Papp Public Theater. Schedule of special projects, in addition to its regular off-Broadway productions. George C. Wolfe producer, Rosemarie Tichler, Kevin Kline associate producers.

Schedule included:

TAKIGI NOH '95 (3). September 8, 1995. With Umewaka Rokuro and Company.

WAKE UP CALL (one-person shows, performance art and cabaret acts): WAKE UP, I'M FAT by and with Camryn Manheim; THE LIMBAUGH LOVER'S SONG BOOK: SONGS THE WAY THEY OUGHTA BE by and with Wayne Lammers; THE BIBLE BELT AND OTHER ACCESSORIES by and with Paul Bonin-Rodriguez; THE WHITE GUY by and with Stephen Hunt; LIVING IN FLAMES by and with Todd Alcott; YELLOW PERIL (Asian American rap artists) with performances by Bertrand D. Wang and John A. Stewart; WITHOUT SKIN OR BREATHLESSNESS by and with Tanya Barfield; CHRONICLES OF A COMIC MULATTA: AN OREO/CHOREOPOEM by and with Josslyn Luckett; A TATTLE TALE (work-in-progress) by Judith Sloan and Warren Lehrer. November 9–26, 1995.

NEW WORK NOW! (festival of staged readings). Schedule included NECESSARY TARGETS written and directed by Eve Ensler; MR. MELANCHOLY by Matt Cameron, directed by Karin Coonrod; GHOSTS IN THE COTTONWOODS by Adam Rapp, directed by Barry Edelstein; SCHADENFREUD by Carlos A. Murillo, directed by David Greenspan; ICARUS by Edwin Sanchez, directed by Melia Bensussen; IKEBANA by Alice Tuan, directed by Liz Diamond; GROOMED written and directed by Don Cheadle; HEDWIG AND THE ANGRY INCH by and with John Cameron Mitchell; NATURAL KNEES by Keith Josef Adkins, directed by Ken Johnson; HALF LIVES by Chay Yew; THE POPPY GARDEN by Timothy Lea, directed by Jean Randich; LITTLE FISH book, music and lyrics by Michael John LaChiusa, directed by Kirsten Sanderson. May 7–20, 1996.

New York Theater Workshop. Produces new theater by American and international artists and encourages risk and stimulates experimentation in theatrical form. James C. Nicola artistic director, Nancy Kassak Diekmann managing director.

QUILLS (47). By Doug Wright. November 27, 1995. Director, Howard Shalwitz; scenery, Neil Patel; lighting, Blake Burba; costumes, James Schuette; sound, Darron L. West. With Daniel Oreskes, Kirk Jackson, Lola Pashalinski, Jefferson Mays, Rocco Sisto, Katy Wales Selverstone.

RENT (68). Book, music and lyrics by Jonathan Larson. January 26, 1996. Director, Michael Greif; choreography, Marlies Yearby; scenery, Paul Clay; lighting, Blake Burba; costumes, Angela Wendt; sound, Darron L. West; musical direction, Tim Weil. With Anthony Rapp, Adam Pascal, Jesse L. Martin, Taye Diggs, Fredi Walker, Wilson Jermaine Heredia, Daphne Rubin-Vega, Idina Menzel, Kristen Lee Kelly, Byron Utley, Gwen Stewart, Timothy Britten Parker, Gilles Chiasson, Rodney Hicks, Aiko Nakasone. Also see its entries in the Plays Produced on and off Broadway sections of this volume.

JUST ADD WATER FESTIVAL: NOTHING FOREVER and YESTERDAY'S WINDOW. By Chiori Miyagawa. April 6, 1996. Director, Karin Coonrod; scenery and lighting, Darrel Maloney; costumes, Myung Hee Cho; music and sound, Fabian Obispo; lyrics, Mark Campbell. With Dawn Akemi Saito, Lenora Champagne, Bobby Daye.

A PARK IN OUR HOUSE (37). By Nilo Cruz. May 24, 1996. Director, Loretta Greco; scenery, Robert Brill; lighting, Allen Lee Hughes; costumes, Anne Patterson; sound, Stephen G. Smith. With Vanessa Aspillaga, Franca Barchiesi, James Colby, Shawn Elliott, Gary Perez, Joe Quintero.

Pan Asian Repertory Theater. Celebrates and provides opportunities for Asian American artists to perform under the highest professional standards and to create and promote plays by and about Asians and Asian Americans. Tisa Chang artistic/producing director.

PRIVATE LIVES (27). By Noel Coward. October 27, 1995. Director, Ron Nakahara; scenery, Robert Klingelhoefer; lights, Richard Schaefer; costumes, Terry Leong; sound, Ty Sanders. With Elizabeth H. Piccio, Michael Gee, Sam Ardeshir, Fay Rusli, Christen Villamor.

CAMBODIA AGONISTES (5). Text and lyrics, Ernest Abuba; music, Louis Stewart. November 22, 1995. Director, Tisa Chang; scenery, Robert Klingelhoefer; lighting, Deborah Constantine; costumes, Juliet Ouyoung; sound, Jim van Bergen. With Lydia Gaston, Jason Ma, John Baray, Moly Chan Sam, Richard Ebihara, Constance George, Sam-Oeun Tes, Eileen Rivera, Hai Wah Yung.

FRIENDS (28). By Kobo Abe, translated by Donald Keene. April 19, 1996. Director, Ron Nakahara; scenery, Robert Klingelhoefer; lighting, Richard Schaefer; costumes, Maggie Raywood; sound, Peter Griggs. With James Saito, Kati Kuroda, Monique Holt, Dawn Akiyama, Philip Baltazar, Josie Chavez, Eleonora Kihlberg, Matthew Lai, Alvin Lum, Les Mau, Christen Villamor.

Primary Stages Company. Dedicated to new American plays by new American playwrights. Casey Childs artistic director, Margaret Chandler general manager, Janet Reed associate artistic director, Seth Gordon associate producer.

THE MODEL APARTMENT (34). By Donald Margulies. October 24, 1995. Director, Lisa Peterson; scenery, Neil Patel; lighting, Paul Clay; costumes, Katherine Roth; music and sound, David Van Tieghem. With Lynn Cohen, Paul Stolarsky, Roberta Wallach, Akill Prince.

THE PRESERVATION SOCIETY (11). By William S. Leavengood. January 21, 1996. Director, Casey Childs; scenery, Bob Phillips; lighting, Deborah Constantine; costumes, Rodney Munoz; sound, Jim van Bergen. With Laurie Kennedy, Nina Humphrey, Deirdre Lovejoy, Bryan Clark, Larry Pine, Kevin Geer.

N. Y. THEATER WORK-SHOP—The 1995–96 production schedule at the *Rent*-producing group also included *(above) A Park in Our House* by Nilo Cruz, with Franca Barchiesi, Shawn Elliott, James Colby and Vanessa Aspillaga; and *(right) Quills* by Doug Wright, with Katy Wales Selverstone *(in background)*, Jefferson Mays and Rocco Sisto

VIRGINS AND OTHER MYTHS (one-man show) (70). By and with Colin Martin. January 24, 1996. Director, Bruce Blair; scenery, Bob Phillips; lighting, Deborah Constantine; sound, Tim Coyle. Reopened April 23, 1996 at the Atlantic Theater.

SABINA (54). By Willy Holtzman. March 19, 1996. Director, Melia Bensussen; scenery, Judy Gailen; lighting, Dan Kotlowitz; costumes, Claudia Stephens; music and sound, David Van Tieghem. With Marin Hinkle, David Adkins, Kenneth L. Marks, George Bartenieff.

ANCIENT HISTORY (33). By David Ives. May 21, 1996. Director, John Rando; lighting, Deborah Constantine; costumes, Rodney Munoz; sound, Jim van Bergen. With Vivienne Benesch, Michael Rupert.

Puerto Rican Traveling Theater. Professional company presenting bilingual productions primarily of Puerto Rican and Hispanic playwrights, emphasizing subjects of relevance today. Miriam Colon founder and producer.

Schedule included:

BOMBER JACKETS. By Rob Santana. March 13, 1996. Director, Alba Oms. With Alex Furth, Marc Geller.

ONE HOUR WITHOUT TELEVISION. By Jaime Solon. May 16, 1996. Director, Miriam Colon. With Christina Sanjuan, Alfredo Huereca.

The Ridiculous Theatrical Company. The late Charles Ludlam's comedic troupe devoted to productions of his original scripts and new works in his style. Everett Quinton artistic director, Adele Bove managing director.

MURDER AT MINSING MANOR: A NANCY BOYS MYSTERY. By Michael Simon and Richard Simon. October 24, 1995. Director, Chuck Brown; scenery, Tom Greenfield; lighting, Richard Currie; costumes, Kaye Voyce; sound, Raymond D. Schilke. With Grant Neale, Cory Lippiello, Christa Kirby, Tom Deroesher, Everett Quinton, Kyle Kennedy, Jason Williams, Lenys Sama, Wilfredo Medina, Dave Murray.

CALL ME SARAH BERNHARDT. By Everett Quinton. March 14, 1996. Director, Eureka; scenery, Kerry Sharps; lighting, Richard Currie; costumes, Ramona Ponce; sound, Dean Meyers. With Everett Quinton, Lenys Sama, Richard Scheinmel, Dave Murray, Beth Dodye Bass, Peggy Oldfield, Jimmy Szezepanek, Christa Kirby.

Signature Theater Company. Dedicated to the exploration of a playwright's body of work. James Houghton artistic director, Thomas Proehl managing director.

FUNNYHOUSE OF A NEGRO and A MOVIE STAR HAS TO STAR IN BLACK AND WHITE (one-act plays) (31). By Adrienne Kennedy. September 22, 1995. Directors, Caroline Jackson-Smith and Joseph Chaikin; scenery, E. David Cosier; lighting, Jeffrey S. Koger; costumes, Teresa Snider-Stein and Jonathan Green; sound, Bruce Ellman; music, Cathy Elliot. With Ellen Bethea, Caroline Clay, Lisa Renee Pitts, Robert Jason Jackson, Cleve Lamison, Wendy vanden Heuvel, Sanaa Lathan, Joyce Lynn O'Connor, Simon Jutras, Joan Harris, Michael Early, Wayne Maugans, Tim Michael, Jennifer Gibbs.

JUNE AND JEAN IN CONCERT (30). By Adrienne Kennedy, based on her autobiography, *People Who Led to My Plays* (30). November 10, 1995. Director, James Houghton; scenery, E. David Cosier; lighting, Jeffrey S. Koger; costumes, Mary Myers; music and musical direction, Loren Toolajian. With Eisa Davis, Alicia Rene Washington, Lisa Renee Pitts, Nicole Parker, Cedric Turner, Angela Bullock.

THE ALEXANDER PLAYS . . . SUZANNE IN STAGES (one-act plays): DRAMATIC CIRCLE, OHIO STATE MURDERS and MOTHERHOOD 2000 (13). By Adrienne Kennedy. April 19, 1996. Director, Robbie McCauley; scenery, E. David Cosier; lighting, Jeffrey S. Koger; costumes, Teresa

Snider-Stein and Jonathan Green; sound, Jim van Bergen. With Leon Addison Brown, Tom Gerard, Jake-Ann Jones, Sanaa Lathan, Seret Scott, Ned Van Zandt, Jennifer Wiltsie, Craig Wroe.

SLEEP DEPRIVATION CHAMBER (31). By Adam Kennedy and Adrienne Kennedy. February 23, 1996. Director, Michael Kahn; scenery, E. David Cosier; lighting, Jeffrey S. Koger; costumes, Teresa Snider-Stein and Jonathan Green; sound, Jim van Bergen. With Glynis Bell, Trazana Beverley, Willie C. Carpenter, Kevin T. Carroll, Jonathan Fried, Paul Geier, Ben Hersey, Leslie Silva, Grafton Trew, Mark Gorman, Bo Smith, Jacques Henri Taylor.

Soho Rep. Dedicated to new and avant-garde American playwrights. Julian Webber artistic director, Christine Arnold development director.

SUMMER CAMP: SODOMY by Dan McMullin, directed by Pam McKinnon; THE HOLE by Wendy Hammond; GINGER & MARYANN by Sue Kenny and Catherine Weidner; SUBTERRANEANS by Carlos Murillo, directed by David Greenspan; MALIBU by Carl Gadjusek, directed by Matt Wilder; THE GUEST by Marina Schron, directed by Tim Farrell. July 7–30, 1995.

DARK RIDE (25). By Len Jenkin. January 4, 1996. Director, Julian Webber; scenery, Anthony MacIlwaine; lighting, Adam Silverman; costumes, Anita Yavich; sound, Chris Todd. With Reed Birney, Marylouise Burke, Leslie Lyles, Bruce MacVittie, Joseph McKenna, Joanna P. Adler, Angie Phillips, Keith Reddin, Frank Wood, Frank Deal, Ray Norberto, Michael La Fetra.

WALLY'S GHOST (25). By Ain Gordon. April 13, 1996. Director, Ain Gordon and Michael Sexton; scenery, Neil Patel; lighting, John-Paul Szczepanski; costumes, Ain Gordon. With Albert Macklin, Mitchell Lichtenstein, Alison Tatlock, John McAdams, Tim Michael, Norma Fire.

Theater for the New City. Developmental theater and new American experimental works. Crystal Field executive director.

Schedule included:

CONTRACT (13). Book, lyrics and direction by Crystal Field. August 5, 1995. Scenery, Anthony Angel; costumes, Flo Kerr and Allan Charlet; sound, Paul Garrity. With Joseph C. Davies, Cheryl Gadsden, Crystal Field, Michael-David Gordon, Jerry Jaffe, Terry Lee King, Mark Marcante, Craig Meade.

DER SIGNAL by Vladimir Gorschin, music, Martin Bresnick; SYNOECISM (COMING TOGETHER) by Robert Bresnick and Leslie Weinberg, music, Brian Johnson. September 7, 1995. Director, Robert Bresnick; scenery, Karl G. Ruling; lighting, John Carr; puppets and projections, Leslie Weinberg. With Azdak's Garden/Puppetsweat Theater.

ANYPLACE BUT HERE (12). By Caridad Svich. September 21, 1995. Director, Maria Irene Fornes; scenery, Mark Tambella; lighting, Tyler Micoleau. With Mary Forcade, Joseph Goodrich, Jerry Jaffe, Suzanne E. Fletcher.

SHROVE TUESDAY. Written and directed by Frank Biancamano. September 28, 1995. Scenery, Ian Gordon; lighting, Mark Grossman; sound, David Scott. With Bob Adrian, Alice Barden, Joseph C. Davies, Jessy Ortiz, Ana Maria Jomolca, Michael Luggo, Mark Marcante, Anthony Pick.

TRAGEDY FOR THREE AND ONE OBSERVER (12). Adapted from Monica Volonteri's book *Some Often Repeated Echoes,* and directed by Arcadio Ruiz-Castellano. October 12, 1995. Choreography, Noreen Pietri; music, Jose Halac. With Noreen Pietri, Scott Geyer, Richard Alger, Dan Thorens, Nancy Rose Alamo.

ABSTINENCE. Book and lyrics, Tom Attea; music, Arthur Abrams. November 12, 1995. Director, Mark Marcante; choreography, Craig Meade, Crystal Field. With Paul Hoover, Pamela Cecil, Nancy St. Alban, Ray Cullom.

BROTHER MARX NATIVITY. By and with Bread and Puppet Theater. November 30, 1995. Director, Peter Schumann.

RUBY AND PEARL: A CLASS ACT (16). By Laurence Holder. December 28, 1995. Director, Rome Neal; scenery, Anie Blackburn; lighting, Zdenek Kriz; costumes, Marcel Christian; sound,

David Wright; music, Christopher Cherney. With Arlana Blue, Randi Pannell, Julie Adams, John DiBenedetto, Jerry Jaffe, Theo Polites.

PUTAMA MOKSHA (11). By Leslie Mohn. December 22, 1995. Director, Lee Breuer. With Leslie Mohn, Mio Morales, Bina Sharif.

TRUE CRIMES (16). Written and directed by Romulus Linney. December 31, 1995. Scenery, E. David Cosier; lighting, Jeffrey S. Koger; costumes, Jonathan Green. With David Johnson, Heather Melton, Cheryl Haas, Christine Parks, Daniel Martin, Fred Burrell, Rebecca Harris, Mark Alan Gordon, Erin Hill.

THE EMERGING PLAYWRIGHTS' PROJECT, SERIES II: TELL ME SOMETHING I DON'T ALREADY KNOW . . . by Liana Rosario, directed by Liana Rosario and Margaret Cabrera; BAR NONE by Peter Arbour, directed by Rae C. Wright; THE HANGED MAN by Robert J. Kornfeld, directed by Melanie S. Armer. January 11, 1996. Scenery, Peter Arbour; lighting, Ian Gordon; sound, David Scott.

VOICES, INSISTENT VOICES (12). By Stuart McCarrell. January 28, 1996. Director, Lee Gundersheimer; scenery, Murphy Gigliotti; lighting, Alexandra Radrocchia; costumes, Jerry Hsieh; music, Nina Bates. With Atli Kendall, Victoria Boosma, James Caulfield, Thomas Cote, Jack Frankel, Paul Garrett, Ruth Jaffe, Atli Kendall, Penelope Richards, John Taylor, George Vlachos.

SEXUAL PSYCHOBABBLE (12). By Lissa Moira and Richard West. February 15, 1996.

HAPHAZARD (12). By Anthony Patton. February 29, 1996. Director, Ken Terrell; scenery, Jerry Dolan and W. Craig Hutchison; lighting, Michael Cole. With Andy Bruno, Jenna Kellard, Theron T. Hudgins, Luke Sabis, Michael Canaan.

MR. BUDDHO'S LETTER OF RESIGNATION FROM THE I.M.F. (50 YEARS IS ENOUGH) (14). By and with Bread and Puppet Theater. March 13, 1996. Director, Peter Schumann.

WILDERNESS OF MIRRORS (12). By Ralph Pezzullo. March 21, 1996. Director, Mark Marcante; scenery, John Paino; lighting, Ian Gordon; sound, David Adrian Scott. With Claudia J. Arenas, Chris De Oni, John Doman, Craig Meade, Valentina Quinn, Jesse Sparks.

SPINNEN UN SPINNEN (12). By Beverly Taylor. April 11, 1996. Director, Walter Cohen; scenery, Iosif Yusupov; lighting, Alison Brummer; costumes, Seth Hanson. With Amy Braverman, Jill Helene, Jennifer Maxx, Robert Manganaro, Eddie Kehler, Jacqueline Sydney, Andy Bruno, Dennis Horvitz, Phil Hochman.

JIM THE LIONHEARTED (24). By Rene Kalisky, translated by David Willinger and Luc Deneulin. April 11, 1996. Director, David Willinger; scenery, Clark Fidelia; lighting, Thaddeus Strassberger; costumes, E. Shura Pollatsek; music, Arthur Abrams. With Anthony Greenleaf, Donald Brooks, Caesar Paul Del Trecco, Jerry Jaffe, Mark Lang, Kevin Martin, Mari Prentice, Katy Winn.

RELUCTANT ANGEL (one-woman show) (12). By Margo Lee Sherman and Kate Mennone. May 2, 1996. Director, Kate Mennone; lighting, Katy Orrick. With Margo Lee Sherman.

PRISM (12). By Alex McDonald. May 23, 1996. Direction, scenery and costumes, Jonathan Silver; lighting, Easton O. Nelson Jr.; sound, David Roche. With Rome Neal, Jesse Wilson.

WHATEVER HAPPENED TO REST ON THE SEVENTH DAY? (12). Book, music and lyrics, Michael Vazquez and David Adrian Scott. May 23, 1996.

WATCH YOUR STEP (12). Book, Harry B. Smith, adapted by Robert Dahdah; music and lyrics, Irving Berlin. May 25, 1996. Director, Robert Dahdah; choreography, Carol La Madrid; scenery, Christian Roy; costumes, Allan Charlet; musical direction, Arthur Abrams. With Judy Ayres, John Beebout, Dennis Carrig, John Cloutman, Brian James Grace, Vincenetta Gunn, Carla Hall, Quanda Johnson, Martha McMahon, John Patrick Schutz, Jack Sullivan, Frank Shattuck, Debra Weiner, Peggy Williams.

Ubu Repertory Theater. Committed to acquainting American audiences with new works by contemporary French-speaking playwrights from around the world. Francoise Kourilsky artistic director.

NIGHT JUST BEFORE THE FOREST (7). By Bernard-Marie Koltes, translated by Timothy Johns. October 11, 1995. Director, Susan Einhorn; scenery, Watuko Ueno; lighting, Greg Mac-Pherson; costumes, Carol Ann Pelletier; sound, David M. Lawson. With David Weynand.

THE CASE OF KASPAR MAYER (15). By Jean-Yves Picq, translated by Michael Feingold. November 8, 1995. Director, Andre Ernotte; scenery, Watuko Ueno; lighting, Greg MacPherson; costumes, Carol Ann Pelletier; sound, David M. Lawson. With Ian Kahn, Kurt Rhoads, Brad Morris, Stelio Savante.

ALWAYS TOGETHER (14). By Anca Visdei, translated by Stephen J. Vogel. February 14, 1996. Scenery, Watuko Ueno; lighting, Greg MacPherson; costumes, Carol Ann Pelletier; music, Genji Ito. With Maria Deasy, Thea Mercouffer.

BONDS OF AFFECTION (14). By Loleh Bellon, translated by Barbara Bray. March 13, 1996. Director, Shirley Kaplan; scenery, Watuko Ueno; lighting, Greg MacPherson; costumes, Carol Ann Pelletier; music, Genji Ito. With Kathryn Rossetter, Kristin Griffith, Paul Hoover, George Hosmer.

NO EXIT (14). By Jean-Paul Sartre, translated by Richard Miller. April 17, 1996. Director, Francoise Kourilsky; scenery, Watuko Ueno; lighting, Greg MacPherson; costumes, Carol Ann Pelletier; music and sound, Genji Ito. With Ronald Guttman, Michel Moinot, Colette Berge, Genevieve Schartner.

Staged Readings:

ALL IT TAKES IS SOMETHING SMALL. By Martine Drai, translated by Stephen J. Vogel. October 16, 1995. Director, Elyse Singer.

THE SIFTER. By Michel Azama, translated by Judith G. Miller. October 23, 1995. Director, Ted Altschuler.

MADAME BERTIN'S TESTIMONY. By Fatima Gallaire, translated by Jill McDougall. November 13, 1995. Director, Shirley Kaplan.

THE APOLLO OF BELLAC. By Jean Giraudoux, translated by Alex Szogyi. November 20, 1995. Director, Stephanie Klapper.

LAPIN LAPIN. By Coline Serreau, translated by Barbara Wright. March 18, 1996.

MOBIE-DIQ. By Marie Redonnet, translated by Dan McGillicuddy. March 25, 1996.

The Vineyard Theater. Multi-art chamber theater dedicated to the development of new plays and musicals, music-theater collaborations and innovative revivals. Douglas Aibel artistic director, Barbara Zinn Krieger executive director, Jon Nakagawa managing director.

POR'KNOCKERS (27). By Lynn Nottage. November 19, 1995. Director, Michael Rogers; scenery, G.W. Mercier; lighting, Phil Monat; costumes, Candice Donnelly; sound, Aural Fixation. With Ray Ford, Sanaa Lathan, Ramon Melindez Moses, Earl Nash, Afemo Omilami, Daniel Zelman.

BED AND SOFA (52). Libretto, Laurence Klavan, based on Abram Room's film; music, Polly Pen. February 1, 1996. Director, Andre Ernotte; scenery and costumes, G.W. Mercier; lighting, Phil Monat; sound, Aural Fixation; musical direction, Alan Johnson. With Terri Klausner, Jason Workman, Michael X. Martin.

ANTIGONE IN NEW YORK (31). By Janusz Glowacki. April 23, 1996. Director, Michael Mayer; scenery, William Barclay, lighting, Christopher Akerlind; costumes, Michael Krass; music and sound, David Van Tieghem. With Priscilla Lopez, Steven Skybell, Ned Eisenberg, Monti Sharp.

The Women's Project and Productions. Nurtures, develops and produces plays written and directed by women. Julia Miles founder and artistic director.

CROCODILES IN THE POTOMAC (22). By Wendy Belden. October 23, 1995. Director, Suzanne Bennett; scenery and lighting, Roger Hanna; costumes, Elizabeth Fried; sound, Mark Bruckner. With Tristine Skyler, Gretchen Eglof, Firdous Bamji, Kristin Griffith, Brad Bellamy.

WPA Theater. Produces new American plays and neglected American classics in the realistic idiom. Kyle Renick artistic director, Lori Sherman managing director.

RIDICULOUS THEATRICAL COMPANY—Everett Quinton and Christa Kirby in a scene from Quinton's play *Call Me Sarah Bernhardt*

SONGS FOR A NEW WORLD (musical revue) (27). Music and lyrics, Jason Robert Brown. October 26, 1995. Director, Daisy Prince; choreography, Michael Arnold; scenery, Stephan Olson; lighting, Craig Evans; costumes, Gail Brassard. With Billy Porter, Brooks Ashmanskas, Jessica Molaskey, Andrea Burns.

WONDERFUL TIME (33). By Jonathan Marc Sherman. January 11, 1996. Director, Tim Vasen; scenery, Henry Dunn; lighting, Jeremy Stein; costumes, Mimi Maxmen; sound, Aural Fixation. With Josh Hamilton, Anney Giobbe, Silas Weir Mitchell, Marin Hinkle, Daniel Zelman.

BRINE COUNTY WEDDING (one-man show) (28). By and with Christopher V. Alessi. March 5, 1996. Director, Henry Polic II; scenery, Alistair Wandesforde-Smith; lighting, Jack Mehler; scenery, Kurt B. Kellenberger.

THE BOYS IN THE BAND (42). By Mart Crowley. June 3, 1996. Director, Kenneth Elliott; scenery, James Noone; lighting, Phil Monat; costumes, Suzy Benzinger; sound, John Kilgore. With David Drake, Jeff Woodman, James Lecesne, Sean McDermott, David Bishins, William Christian, Scott Decker, David Greenspan, Robert Bogue.

York Theater Company. Specializing in producing new works, as well as in reviving unusual, forgotten or avant-garde musicals. Janet Hayes Walker producing director, James Morgan associate artistic director.

STANDING BY (26). By Norman Barasch. September 14, 1995. Director, Alex Dmitriev; scenery, James Morgan; lighting, Jerold R. Forsyth; costumes, Beba Shamash; sound, Jim van Bergen. With Gregg Edelman, Cynthia Watros.

MATA HARI (12). Book, Jerome Coopersmith; music, Edward Thomas; lyrics and direction, Martin Charnin. January 25, 1996. Choreography, Michele Assaf; scenery, James Morgan; lighting, Mary Jo Dondlinger; costumes, Jennifer Arnold; sound, Jim van Bergen; musical direction, Keith Levenson. With Kirk McDonald, Allen Fitzpatrick, Marguerite MacIntyre.

Miscellaneous

In the additional listing of 1995–96 off-off-Broadway productions below, the names of the producing groups or theaters appear in CAPITAL LETTERS and the titles of the works in *italics*. This list consists largely of new or reconstituted works. It includes a few productions staged by groups which rented space from the more established organizations listed previously.

ACTORS COMPANY THEATER. *The Man Who Came to Dinner* by Moss Hart and George S. Kaufman. October 2, 1995. Directed by Scott Alan Evans; with Larry Keith, Maia Danziger, Cynthia Harris, Greg Salata, David Staller, Guy Paul. *Fashion* by Anna Cora Mowatt. November 13, 1995. Directed by Scott Alan Evans; with Cynthia Harris, David Staller, Larry Keith, Greg Salata, James Murtaugh, Lyn Wright, Alec Phoenix. *The Beauty Part* by S.J. Perelman. January 20, 1996. Director, Scott Alan Evans. With Ivy Austin, Greg Salata, James Murtaugh, Greg McFadden, Merwin Goldsmith, Lyn Wright, Tom Stewart, David Staller, Marc Kudisch, Cynthia Harris. *The Women* by Clare Boothe Luce. April 29, 1996. Director, Scott Alan Evans; with Lauren Mitchell, Lynn Vogt, Anne Swift, Kim Hunter, Joan Buddenhagen, Delphi Harrington, Kay Walbye.

ADOBE THEATER COMPANY. *The Eight: Reindeer Monologues* by Jeff Goode. November 28, 1995. Directed by Jeremy Dobrish; with Erin Quinn Purcell, Christopher Marobella, Molly Renfroe, Kathryn Langwell.

ALCHEMY THEATER COMPANY. *Speed-the-Plow* by David Mamet. May 6, 1996. Directed by Robert Saxner; with Rick Kaplan, Michael Daly, Gretchen Eglof.

ALTERED STAGES. *Screwdrivers & Sunday Brunch* by Suzanne Bachner. October 27, 1995. Directed by Patricia Minskoff; with Laura Lee Ash, Ethan Flower, Patrick Hillan, John Kooi, Monica McCormack. *Whatever the Matter May Be* by and with Misi Lopez Lecube. November 5, 1995. *Mouthful* by Suzanne Bachner. November 6, 1995. Directed by Colette Duvall. *Orpheus on West Fourth St.* by and with Michael Schwartz. November 8, 1995. Directed by Patricia Minskoff. *Jump Start* by and with David Bush. November 13, 1995.

AMERICAN JEWISH THEATER. *The Warm-Up* by Sammy Shore and Rudy DeLuca. November 19, 1995. Directed by Martin Landau; with Sammy Shore. *The Yiddish Trojan Women* by Carole Braverman. January 22, 1996. Directed by Richard Sabellico; with Joanna Merlin, Marilyn Pasekoff, Lori Wilner, Laura Esterman, Hugh O'Gorman. *Working Title* by Andrew Bergman. March 19, 1996. Directed by Max Mayer; with Susan Blackwell, David Chandler, Jerry Grayson, Stephen O'Reilly, John Seitz, Gia Carides, Douglas Weston. *The Cocoanuts* book by George S. Kaufman; music and lyrics by Irving Berlin. May 12, 1996. Directed by Richard Sabellico; with Michael McGrath, Peter Slutsker, Robert Sapoff, Celia Tackaberry, Kirby Ward.

ARDEN PARTY. *Victor, or Children Take Over* by Roger Vitrac, translated by Aaron Etra, Karin Coonrod, Frederic Maurin and Esther Sobin. March 21, 1996. Directed by Karin Coonrod; with Mary Christopher, Paula Cole, Linda Donald, Jan Leslie Harding, Gretchen Krich, Patrick Morris, Randolph Curtis Rand, Steven Rattazzi, T. Ryder Smith.

ATA. *Reality* by Morgan Doninger. June 26, 1995. Directed by Maureen Rahill. *The Window* and *In an Infinite Universe* (one-act plays) by Sheldon Woodbury. September 21, 1995. Directed by Sue Lawless; with Hamilton Clancy, Michael Collins, Eliza Ventura.

AXIS THEATER COMPANY. *Rockland County No Vaudeville* by Randy Sharp and Michael Gump. February 22, 1996. Directed by Randy Sharp; with Robert Ierardi, Michael Gump, Wren Arthur, Paul Dawson, Max Hernandez, Vivian Jordan, Sue Ann Molinell.

THE BARROW GROUP. *Old Wicked Songs* by Jon Marans. November 5, 1995; see its entry under Jewish Repertory Theater in this section.

BLUE LIGHT THEATER COMPANY. *Golden Boy* by Clifford Odets. November 27, 1995. Directed by Joanne Woodward; with James Naughton, Greg Naughton, Angie Phillips, Joe Grifasi, Yusef Bulos, Peter Gregory, Spiro Malas, Emily Wachtel, James Matthew Ryan, Lee Wilkof, Bruce MacVittie, P.J. Brown, Alex Draper, Jon Rothstein. *Scenes From an Execution* by Howard Barker.

February 27, 1996. Directed by Richard Romagnoli; with Greg Naughton, Alex Draper, Naomi Jacobson, Jon Rothstein, Alan Wade, Francesca Di Mauro. Co-produced by Potomac Theater Project. *Treasure Island* adapted by Vernon Morris from Robert Louis Stevenson's novel. May 5, 1996. Directed by B.H. Barry; with Greg Naughton, Alex Draper, Joe Grifasi, Jon Rothstein, James Matthew Ryan, Lee Wilkof, Charlie Hofheimer, Larry Pine.

BOSAKOWSKI THEATER. *Bad Language* by Dusty Hughes. October 8, 1995. Directed by Kent Paul.

BOUWERIE LANE THEATER. *Homo Americanus* written and directed by Assurbanipal Babilla. June 4, 1995. With Assurbanipal Babilla, Andrew Costell, David Cote, Jennie Crotero, Leyla Ebtehadj, Suzanne Fletcher, Georgia Hodes, Lynne Kanter, Bill Martin, Jason McKay, Laurie Wickens.

BROOKLYN ACADEMY OF MUSIC. *Next Wave Festival.* Works included *Alice,* adapted and directed by Robert Wilson from Lewis Carroll's *Alice's Adventures in Wonderland* and *Through the Looking Glass,* book by Paul Schmidt; music and lyrics by Tom Waits and Kathleen Brennan. October 6, 1995. With Annette Paulmann, Stefan Kurt, Jorg Holm, Dirk Ossig, Sven-Eric Bechtolf. *Salome* by Oscar Wilde. October 17, 1995. Directed by Steven Berkoff; with Zigi Ellison, Steven Berkoff, Jolyon Baker, Richard Clothier, Carmen Du Sautoy, Peter Brennan, Christopher Brand, Jeremy Peters. *Chinoiserie* conceived and directed by Ping Chong; text and lyrics by Michael Matthews, Ping Chong, Regina Anna Seckinger and Ric Oquita; music by Guy Klucevsek. November 11, 1995. With Ping Chong, Shi-Zheng Chen, Aleta Hayes, Michael Edo Keane, Ric Oquita. *The Duchess of Malfi* by John Webster. December 6, 1995. Directed by Declan Donnellan; with Cheek by Jowl (Anastasia Hille, Matthew Macfayden, George Anton, Paul Brennen, Scott Handy, Nicola Redmond, Shaun Parkes, Avril Clark, Matthew Bowyer, Sean Hannaway, Christopher Kell, Terence Maynard, Guy More, Peter Moreton).

CAMILLA'S. *Brutality of Fact* by Keith Reddin. May 4, 1996. Directed by Casey Childs; with Leslie Lyles, Rebecca Nelson, Scotty Bloch, Samantha Brown, Greg Stuhr, Kathryn Meisle, Marcus Giamatti, Beth Littleford, Beatrice Rose.

CASTILLO THEATER. *A Season in the Congo* by Aime Cesaire. September 15, 1995. Directed by Fred Newman; with Emmitt H. Thrower. *Controluce* by Graziella Martinoli and Fred Newman. October 27, 1995. Directed by Graziella Martinoli.

CENTER STAGE. *Come in From the Rain* by David Mauriello. June 9, 1995. Directed by Mark Harborth; with Eric Martin Brown, John Gasdaska, Russell Elder.

CHELSEA PLAYHOUSE. *Two, Nikita* by Jeffrey Hatcher. October 5, 1995. Directed by John Morrison; with T. Ryder Smith, Michael MacCauley, Suzanne von Eck. *The Fall of the House of Usher* adapted from Edgar Allan Poe's story by Linda Manning. December 10, 1995. Directed by Douglas Wagner; with Michael Pinney, Linda Manning, Derek Stearns. *When the Bell Tolls: The Rose and Crown* and *Riders to the Sea* (one-act plays) by J.B. Priestley. April 25, 1996. Directed by Clinton Bond Jr. and Joan Matthiessen; with Helen Gallagher.

DIXON PLACE. *Hunger and Lightning* by and with Kestutis Nakas. August 2, 1995. *An Evening of Black Magic: Songlines and Dreamtracks* by Philip Brown and Deborah Long. February 2, 1996. Directed by Ilaan Egeland; with Philip Brown. *Faux Blonde Fiesta* by and with We Are Not Blondes (Jane Setteducato and Nancy Alfaro). April 10, 1996.

ECLECTIC THEATER COMPANY. *Identical Twins From Baltimore* book by Marc Mantell; music and lyrics by Dan Alvy. June 25, 1995. Directed by Bill Castellino; with Adriane Lenox, Mary Stout.

FOOLS COMPANY SPACE. *The Zalmar Boys* by Matthew Ramsay. November 24, 1995.

FOUNDRY THEATER. *Deviant Craft* by W. David Hancock. July 13, 1995 Developed and directed by Melanie Joseph.

GREENWICH ST. THEATER. *The Countess* by Gregory Murphy. December 7, 1995. Directed by Ludovica Villar-Hauser; with James Riordan, Jennifer Woodward, Matthew Dudley.

GROVE ST. PLAYHOUSE. *The Tragic and Horrible Life of the Singing Nun* written and directed by Blair Fell. March 27, 1996. With Suzanne Schuckel, Lucy Avery Brooke, Nick DeMarco, Craig Archibald, Eileen O'Connor, Karen Wright, Laura Desmond, Chicklet.

HAMLET OF BANK ST. THEATER. *Cross Your Heart* by Brian Connors. May 5, 1996. Directed by A. Dean Irby; with Dylan Chalfy, Erika Burke, Jonathan Teague Cook, Alice McLane.

HERE. *Love in the Void (alt.fan.c-love)* by and with Carolyn Baeumler. September, 1995. Directed by Elyse Singer. *Floating Rhoda and the Glue Man* by Eve Ensler. September 14, 1995. Directed by Ariel Orr Jordan; with Dylan McDermott, Myriam Cyr, Harry O'Reilly, Priscilla Shanks, Tara Hauptman, Matthew Dixon, Debbon Ayer, Joseph Taylor. *Bikini* by and with Linda Mancini. February 11, 1996. Directed by Michael Mackenzie. *The Corner Bar's My Lover Since You Ran Out on Me* by Patrick Fahey. March 1, 1996. Directed by Jason Rosenbaum; with Mike Danner, Janet Girardeau, Antonia Beamish, Jeremy Ryan Brisiel, Janet Gilbert, David Morgan O'Connor. *Sunset Salome* libretto and lyrics by Peter Wing Healey; music by Max Kinberg. April 7, 1996. Directed by Laurence J. Geddes; with Michael McQuary, Janet Norquist, Rochelle Mancini, Brannon Hall-Garcia, Chris Knoblock, Elaine Valby, Joe Gately, John Higenbotham, Sherri Parker Lee, Felicia Norton, Jordanna Tobak, Jim Boutin, Richard Storm, Janie Brendel. *Caught in the Act* (one-act plays): *The Visit* by Juan Antonio Castro; *Katzelmacher* by Rainer Werner Fassbinder; *The Blind Men* by Michel de Ghelderode; *Let's Eat Hair* by Carl Laszlo. May 13, 1996.

HUDSON GUILD THEATER. *Shivaree* by William Mastrosimone. March 6, 1996.

IBIS. *The Magic Carpet Revue* conceived and directed by Samiha Koura D'Aiuto. November 16, 1995.

INTAR THEATER. *The Price of Madness* by Catherine Filloux. January 28, 1996. Directed by Donna Moreau-Cupp; with Jane Altman, Ronald Guttman, Liza O'Keeffe, Tom Schall, Nicola Sheara. *Curtains* by Stephen Bill. April 17, 1996. Directed by Scott Elliott; with David Cale, Kathleen Claypool, John Henry Cox, Laura Esterman, Lisa Emery, Frederick Weller, Jayne Haynes, Betty Miller. Also see its entry in the Plays Produced Off Broadway section of this volume.

INVISIBLE THEATER. *Do Something With Yourself: The Life of Charlotte Bronte* by Linda Manning. February 14, 1996. Directed by Douglas Wagner; with Linda Manning, Michael Pinney.

IRONDALE ENSEMBLE PROJECT. *A Family Affair* by Alexander Ostrovsky, translated by Nick Dear. November 14, 1995. Directed by Jim Niesen; with Yvonne Brechbuhler, Georgina Corbo, Michael-David Gordon, Kathryn Grant, Terry Greiss, Alan Hunkins, Jacqueline Kleefield, Steven Satta. *The Bundle* by Edward Bond. April 20, 1996. Directed by Jim Niesen.

JEAN COCTEAU REPERTORY. *Waiting for Godot* by Samuel Beckett. September 1, 1995. Directed by Eve Adamson; with Craig Smith, Harris Berlinsky, Abner Genece, Kennedy Brown, Peter William Dunn. *Nathan the Wise* by Gotthold Ephraim Lessing. October 15, 1995. Directed by Scott Shattuck; with Kennedy Brown, Craig Smith, Patrick Hall. *The Lady From the Sea* by Henrik Ibsen, translated by Rolf Fjelde. November 26, 1995. Directed by Tom Prewitt; with Harris Berlinsky, Elise Stone, Christopher Black, Molly Pietz. *Major Barbara* by George Bernard Shaw. January 21, 1996. Directed by Robert Hupp; with Angela Vitale, Craig Smith, Kennedy Brown, Will Leckie. *Tartuffe* by Molière, translated by Richard Wilbur. March 17, 1996. Directed by Scott Shattuck; with Craig Smith, Harris Berlinsky, Abner Genece, Angela Vitale, Elise Stone, Glenn Cruz, Molly Pietz, Joseph Small, Will Leckie. *Orphee* by Jean Cocteau, translated by Carl Wildman. May 19, 1996. Directed by Eve Adamson; with Kennedy Brown, Elise Stone, Harris Berlinsky.

JEWISH REPERTORY THEATER. *Old Wicked Songs* by Jon Marans. November 5, 1995. Directed by Seth Barrish; with Hal Robinson, Michael Stuhlbarg. (Barrow Group production) *Sheba* book and lyrics by Sharleen Cooper Cohen; music by Gary William Friedman. January 21, 1996. Directed by Tony Stevens; with Tamara Tunie, Joseph Siravo. *Tovah: Out of Her Mind* (one-woman show) conceived and performed by Tovah Feldshuh; also see its entry in the Plays Produced Off Broadway section of this volume.

JEWISH THEATER OF NEW YORK. *The Beggar of Borough Park* by Tuvia Tenenbom. March 10, 1996. Directed by Sasha Nanus; with Herb Klinger, Mark Jupiter, Russell Costen, Sally Frontman, Steve Flum, Jeff Kronson.

JOHN HOUSEMAN THEATER. *Lust* book, music and lyrics by the Heather Brothers, adapted from William Wycherley's *The Country Wife*. July 13, 1995. Directed by Bob Carlton; with Denis Lawson, Robert McCormick, David Barron, Jennifer Lee Andrews, Lee Golden, Judith Moore. *Time and the Wind* (musical revue) music by Galt MacDermot; lyrics by Norman Matlock. August 9, 1995.

Directed by Louis Johnson; with Johnetta Alston, Russell Joel Brown, Carol Denise, Suzanne Griffin, Carl Hall, Christopher Jackson. *Wasting Time With Harry Davidowitz* by and with Dani Maseng. November 19, 1995. Directed by Julia Carey.

JOYCE THEATER. *Constant Stranger* (one-man show) by and with John Kelly. October 10, 1995.

JUDITH ANDERSON THEATER. *A Musical: Madame Bovary* book, music and lyrics by Paul Dick, adapted from Gustave Flaubert's novel. November 17, 1995. Directed by Ed Setrakian; with Jennifer Little, Henry Grossman, Brett Hamilton, David Jordan, Patrick Sullivan. *Mud* by Maria Irene Fornes. December 2, 1995. Directed by Mary Forcade; with Joseph Goodrich, John O'Keefe, Wendy vanden Heuvel. *The Magic Formula* by Sidney Morris. December 20, 1995. With Michael Dunn Litchfield, Mark Robert Gordon.

LINCOLN CENTER. *Serious Fun!* Schedule included *Hamlet: A Monologue* adapted from William Shakespeare's play by Wolfgang Wiens and Robert Wilson. July 6, 1995. Directed and performed by Robert Wilson. *I Was Looking at the Ceiling and Then I Saw the Sky* libretto by June Jordan; music by John Adams. July 12, 1995. Directed by Peter Sellars; with Sophia Salguero, Harold Perrineau Jr., Welly Yang, Kennya J. Ramsey, Darius de Haas, Kaitlin Hopkins, Michael Christopher Ness. Lincoln Center Out of Doors: *C'est la Vie* conceived and directed by Veronique Gillaud, dialogues by Lucy Grealy, Gil Kofman, Ann Nocenti, Peter Steinfeld and Rob Singer. August 3, 1995.

LIVING THEATER. *Utopia* by Hanon Reznikov. January 10, 1996. Directed by Judith Malina.

LOVE CREEK PRODUCTIONS. *The Wallenberg Mission* by Nicholas Wenckheim. September 5, 1995. Directed by Francine L. Trevens; with Philip Albanese, Gil Grail, Roslyne Hahn, Scott Sparks, Jeff P. Weiss, Larry Weissman. *8th Annual One-Act Festival: The Hero* by Josh Ben Friedman, directed by David Guttman; *Betty Boob* by Sally Dixon Wiener, directed by Leslie Morris; *Lunch in the Afternoon* by Gordon Osmond, directed by Howell Mayer. September 29, 1995.

McGINN/CAZALE THEATER. *Bonhoeffer 1945* by D. Paul Thomas. July 19, 1995. Directed by Albert Sinkys; with D. Paul Thomas, Nicholas Hormann.

MANHATTAN CENTER. *Lypsinka! As I Lay Lip-Synching* created and performed by John Epperson. June 24, 1995. Directed by Kevin Maloney.

MINT THEATER. *King James and the Indian* by Tony Howarth. July 12, 1995. Directed by William Roudebush; with Gabriel Barre, Gil Silverbird, Kristin Flanders, Sioux Madden, William Groth, Mark Alan Gordon, Robert Emmett, Jim Sterling, Patricia Kelley. *Working Class* (one-man show) by and with Richard Hoehler. September 14, 1995. Reopened January 17, 1996. *Two Men/Two Women* (two plays in repertory): *The Grabelski Concertos* by Tommy Swerdlow, directed by Stephen DiMenna; *Kind Eyes* by S.W. Stout, directed by K.G. Wilson. December 5, 1995–January 7, 1996. With Mark Lane, Sam Sedar, Lisa M. Bostnar, Lynn Niederman Silver. *Murphy* by Jack Frankel. March 14, 1996. Directed by Herman Babad; with Frank Biancamano, Jonathan Halyalkar, Jasper McGruder, Lenore Wolf. *Mouthbook* by Eben Hewitt. May 3, 1996. Directed by Andrew Frank.

MIRANDA THEATER COMPANY. *The Soul of an Intruder* by Steve Braunstein. June 7, 1995. Directed by Frank Cento; with Darby Townsend, Patrick Skelton, Jeffrey Spolan. *The Brooch* by Emily Whitesell. January 31, 1996. With Celeste Holm.

MUSICAL THEATER WORKS. *Cardenio* attributed to William Shakespeare, adapted by Kermit Christman and Kevin Crawford, based on Charles Hamilton's text. March 17, 1996. Directed by Kermit Christman; with William D. Michie, Mather Zickel.

NATIONAL ASIAN AMERICAN THEATER COMPANY. *The School for Wives* by Molière, translated by Richard Wilbur. June 21, 1996. Directed by Stephen Stout; with Ron Nakahara, Arloa Reston, Daniel Dae Kim, Jojo Gonzalez, Eileen Rivera, Richard Eng, Mel Duane Gionson, Ching Gonzalez.

NEW GEORGES. *Frank, Frank* written and directed by Randolyn Zinn and Jennifer McDowall. June 3, 1995. With Susan Hall, Doug Krizner, Maria Lakis, Jean McDade, Randolyn Zinn. *Nice Chair* by Susan Bernfield. May 24, 1996. Directed by Jessica Bauman; with Barbara Pitts, Richard Topol, Greer Goodman.

NEW PERSPECTIVES THEATER. *Jihad* by Ann Chamberlin. April 26, 1996. Directed by Melody Brooks; with Albert Michael Goudy, Charles Loflin, Collette Wilson.

NEW YORK DEAF THEATER. *Language of One* by Drew Emery and Lewis Merkin. September 6, 1995. Directed by Drew Emery; with Lewis Merkin, Teri Sweeney, Jon Wolfe Nelson, Laura Conviser, Michael P. Ralph, Margaret Arnold, Helen Slayton-Hughes, Lenore Pemberton, Hal Panchansky.

NEW YORK GILBERT AND SULLIVAN PLAYERS. *The Sorcerer* and *Trial by Jury.* October 15, 1995. *Patience.* December 29, 1995. Directed by Albert Bergeret and Daryl Gray; with Stephen O'Brien, Keith Jurosko, Michael Niemann, Susan Case, Lisa Pierce. *H.M.S. Pinafore.* January 4, 1996. Directed by Albert Bergeret; with Pat Carroll.

NEW YORK PUBLIC LIBRARY FOR THE PERFORMING ARTS READING ROOM READINGS. *The Blues Are Running* written and directed by Michael Cristofer. October 16, 1995. With Kevin O'Rourke, Adam LeFevre. *The Smell of the Kill* by Michele Lowe. November 13, 1995. Directed by Alice Jankell; with Siobahn Fallon, Laura Hughes, Ellen McElduff, Jonathan Wade, Scott Sherman, Tony Cucci. *Caravaggio* by Richard Vetere. December 11, 1995. Directed by Alice Jankell; with Jonathan Wade, Valerie Stevens, Dan Grimaldi, Robert LuPone, Sean Patrick Reilly, Michael Ingram. *Tongue of a Bird* written and directed by Ellen McLaughlin. February 5, 1996. With Allison Janney, Debra Monk, Sloane Shelton, Elizabeth Marvel, Angela Goethals. *The Hollow Lands* by Howard Korder. March 4, 1996. Directed by David Chambers; with Reg Rogers, Dan Futterman, Brendan Corbalis, Susan Cremin, Tom Mardirosian, John Christopher Jones, David Batiste, Chris McCann, Matt McGrath, Paul Giamatti, Jerry Grayson, Welker White. *A Question of Mercy* by David Rabe. April 15, 1996. Directed by Doug Hughes; with Daniel Von Bargen, John Gould Rubin, John Benjamin Hickey, Michael Kell, Annabella Sciorra. *The Merit System* by Edwin Sanchez. May 13, 1996. Directed by Marya Mazor; with Divina Cook, Socorro Santiago, Nelson Vasquez.

NEXT STAGE! *Colombina's Suite* by Ludmilla Petrushevskaya. October 11, 1995. Directed by Linda Lees; with Ludmila Bokievsky, Antoinette LaVecchia, Alice O'Neill, Michael Rudko, Stephen Turner.

NEXT STAGE COMPANY. *White People* by J.T. Rogers. April 22, 1996. Directed by Gus Reyes; with John Bader, Cynthia Vance, John Ottavino.

NUYORICAN POETS CAFE. *Outrageous: Cold Beer, Paper Toilet* and *Sideshow* (one-act plays) by Miguel Pinero. October 28, 1995. Directed by Rome Neal and Dadi Pinero. *Hubba City* by Ishmael Reed. January 28, 1996. Directed by Rome Neal; with Vinie Burrows, Neil Harris, Jim Ganser, Tom Southern.

OHIO THEATER. *Blink of an Eye* written and directed by Jeremy Dobrish. September 10, 1995. With Arthur Aulisi, Vin Knight, Kathryn Langwell, Arthur Halpern, Henry Caplan, Erin Quinn Purcell, Christopher Marobella.

ONE DREAM THEATER. *A Candle in the Window* by Tom Gilroy. June 14, 1995. Directed by Michael Imperioli; with Maggie Low. *Wolf at the Door* by Erik Ehn. May 16, 1996. Directed by Matthew Earnest; with Trish Hawkins, Grant James Vargas, Karen Lee Pickett, Walton Wilson, Trae Hicks, Kathryn Graybill, John Di Benedetto.

ONTOLOGICAL-HYSTERIC THEATER. *The Universe (I.E.: How It Works)* written, directed and designed by Richard Foreman. January 4, 1996. With Mary McBride, Tony Torn, James Urbaniak.

ONYX THEATER COMPANY. *A Laying of Hands* by Michele Maureen Verhoosky. February 14, 1996. Directed by Veona Thomas; with Patrice Joyner, Dee Dixon, Kai M. Reevey, Timothy Joyner, David Hoxter.

PARAMOUNT THEATER. *Born to Sing! (Mama 3)* book, music, lyrics and direction by Vy Higginsen and Ken Wydro. March, 1996. With Shirley Caesar, CeCe Winans, Stacy Francis, Shanna.

PEARL THEATER COMPANY. *A Doll's House* by Henrik Ibsen, translated by William Archer. September 17, 1995. Directed by Grey Johnson; with Robin Leslie Brown, Michael Butler, Carol

Schultz, Kurt Ziskie, Robert Hock. *Antigone* by Sophocles. November 5, 1995. Directed by Shepard Sobel. *When Ladies Battle* by Eugene Scribe and Ernest Legouve, translated by Michael Feingold. December 24, 1995. Directed by John Rando; with Joanne Camp, Arnie Burton, Bradford Cover, Patricia Jones, Mark LaMura, William Stiles. *The Winter's Tale* by William Shakespeare. February 11, 1996. Directed by Kathryn Long; with Arnie Burton, Joanne Camp, Patricia Jones. *Life Is a Dream* by Calderon de la Barca. March 31, 1996. Directed by Rob Bundy; with Joanne Camp, Sean Pratt.

PERFORMANCE SPACE 122. *Kitty Killer* by and with Keith Levy. June 10, 1995. Directed by Joshua D. Rosensweig. *The Island of Lost Shoes* by Ray Dobbins. September 7, 1995. Directed by Bette Bourne; with Bloolips (Lavinia Co-op, Bella Bechstein, Naughty Nickers, Harmony). *The Moxie Show* by and with Queen Esther. November 2, 1995.

PLAYHOUSE 91. *Radical Radio* book, music and lyrics by Steve Underwood, Karmo Sanders and Jerry Sanders. October 1, 1995. Directed by Brian P. Allen. *The Secret Annex* book and lyrics by Robert K. Carr; music by Charles Baton. September 12, 1995. Directed by Dom Ruggiero; with Patricia Ann Gardner, Don Frame.

PLAYQUEST THEATER. *In a Different Light* by Robert Fannin. March 11, 1996. Directed by Hilary Fannin; with Ger Campbell.

PLAYWRIGHTS' COLLECTIVE. *Between the Sheets* book and lyrics, Eduardo Machado; music, Mike Nolan and Scott Williams. April 20, 1996. Directed by Tim Cunningham; with Josie de Guzman, George de la Pena, Philip Anthony, Erin Hill.

PLAYWRIGHTS' PREVIEW PRODUCTIONS. *Blues for Miss Buttercup* by L.E. McCullough. June 12, 1995. Directed by Patricia R. Floyd. *Tiny Tim Is Dead* by Barbara Lebow. November 28, 1995. Directed by Frank Wittow. *Minor Demons* by Bruce Graham. March 17, 1996. Directed by Richard Harden.

PRODUCERS' CLUB. *Blanca: Monologue for Mice, A Twitch in the Sun* written and directed by Nitza Henig and *Hamlet Variations* by Nitza Henig, directed by Ching Valdes-Aran. In repertory April 24–June 15, 1996.

RORSCHACH GROUP. *I Am Yours* by Judith Thompson. October 23, 1995. Directed by Andrew Frank; with Brian Gaskill, Sung Yun Cho, Lisa Benavides, Caroline McGee, David Wells, Shea Whigham.

SAMUEL BECKETT THEATER. *Brotherly Love* by John Fedele. September 20, 1995. Directed by Robert Mariah; with Robert Arcaro, John Fedele, John LaGioia, Rosalina Macisco, Tara Leigh. *Glory Girls* by Jan Buttram. October 27, 1995. Directed by Cathey Crowell Sqwyer. *Gender Wars* by Joseph Krawczyk. April 12, 1996. Directed by Vincent Apollo.

SANCTUARY THEATER. *Strangers in the Land of Canaan* by Paul Alexander. January, 1996. Directed by Rip Torn; with Angelica Torn, David John Dean, Robert P. Juergens, Stephen Largay.

SIX FIGURES THEATER COMPANY. *Alabama Rain* by Heather McCutchen. April 11, 1996. Directed by Rachel Wineberg; with Ellen Bernfeld, Suzanne Bradbeer, Kate Hoffman, Andria Laurie, Susan P. Vaughn.

SYLVIA AND DANNY KAYE PLAYHOUSE. *An Italian Straw Hat* by Eugene Labiche and Marc Michel, translated by Niki Wenger, adapted and directed by Kenneth Albers. September 21, 1995. With National Theater of the Deaf.

SYNCHRONICITY SPACE. *Like Two Eagles* by Tuvia Tenenbom. October 19, 1995. Directed by Robert Kalfin. *Promised Land* by Harvey Huddleston. April 12, 1996. Directed by Mark Roberts; with Jerry Ball, Janet Girardeau, William Hill, Edward Cannon, Tristan Fitch, Kezia Norton.

THEATER AT ST. CLEMENT'S. *Marlowe's Eye* by Naomi Iizuka. March 14, 1996. Directed by Moises Kaufman; with Jerry Ball, Jermaine Chambers, Sarah Gunnell, Bruce McKenzie, Maude Mitchell, Maria Striar, John Douglas Thompson, Wallace Wilhoit Jr.

THEATER OFF PARK—Michael Curry and Robert Gomes in *2 Boys in a Bed on a Cold Winter's Night* by James Edwin Parker

THEATER AT ST. PETER'S CHURCH. *A Captured Claus* book and lyrics by Nick Raposo, based on a story by L. Frank Baum; music by Joe Raposo. November 30, 1995. Directed by Michael John Murnin; with John Funk, Doreen Montalvo, Steve Steiner, Susan Stringer, Robert Zanfini, Jonathan Giordano.

THEATER AT 224 WAVERLY PLACE. *Like a Brother* by T.E. Klunzinger. October 22, 1995. Directed by Jeff Brenner. *Shayquan's Picture* written and directed by Stephen F. Kelleher. March 17, 1996. With Deann Halper, Kofi, Erik Kraus, Joe Masi, Minerva Scelza, Cezar Williams.

THEATER EAST. *Have a Nice Day* (musical satire) conceived by Rick Lewis. April 22, 1996. Directed by Frank Latson.

THEATER OFF PARK. *2 Boys in a Bed on a Cold Winter's Night* by James Edwin Parker. July 16, 1995. Directed by Thomas Caruso; with Robert Gomes, Michael Curry. *Reinventing Daddy* by Gary Bonasorte. September 25, 1995. Directed by Susana Tubert; with Meg Kelly, Jeff Robins, Crayton Robey. *I Married an Angel* book by Richard Rodgers and Lorenz Hart; music by Richard Rodgers; lyrics by Lorenz Hart; October 29, 1995; and *America's Sweetheart* book by Herbert Fields; music by Richard Rodgers; lyrics by Lorenz Hart; December 10, 1995; see their entries in the Plays Produced Off Broadway section of this volume. *A Trip to the Beach* by David Van Asselt. January 14, 1996. Directed by David Dorwart; with Jack Koenig, Kristina Lear, Mick Weber, Stuart Zagnit,

Chris Hietikko, Arija Barekis. *CarPool* by Laura Hembree. April 14, 1996. Directed by Laura Josepher; with William Severs, Davis Csizmadia, Frank Girardeau, John Tormey, Bob Dillon. *The Wilde Spirit* (one-man show) by and with Kerry Ashton. May 21, 1996. Directed by Robert Kalfin.

THEATER ROW THEATER. *The Lobster Reef* by Eda LeShan. June 6, 1995. With Marilyn Chris. *The Principality of Sorrows* by Keith Bunin. December 28, 1995. Directed by Elizabeth Gottlieb; with Joanna Going, David Lansbury, Robert Sean Leonard. *Oh, That Wily Snake!* by Martin Dockery, directed by Beth Lincks; *Where I'm Headed* by Leah Ryan, directed by John Rue; *Finding Rose* ... by Bonnie Morgan, directed by Thomas Edward West; in repertory January 18-February 11, 1996.

THEATER TEN TEN. *Engaged* by W.S. Gilbert. May 3, 1996. Directed by Allan Gilbert; with Hal Blankenship, Joanna Brown, Janet Anderson, Diana Lynn Drew, Jeffrey Eiche, David Kroll, Jason Hauser, Judith Jarosz, Jay Nickerson, Dana White.

THEATER 22. *Seascape* by Edward Albee. August 31, 1995. Directed by Terese Hayden; with Jacqueline Brookes, James Stevenson, Charles D. Cissel, Vanessa Parise.

28TH STREET THEATER. *Her Majesty's Visit* by Onukaba A. Ojo. October 12, 1995. Directed by Loni Berry; with Louise Mike, Todd Anthony-Jackson, Robin Miles.

29th STREET REPERTORY THEATER. *Lion in the Streets* by Judith Thompson. February 23, 1996. Directed by Abby Epstein; with Paula Ewin, Leo Farley, Tim Corcoran, Elizabeth Elkins, Charles Willey.

30TH STREET THEATER. *Two Cities: The Bells of Nagasaki* and *The Mask of Hiroshima* (one-act plays) by Ernest Ferlita, S.J. March 7, 1996. Directed by Ken Lowstetter; with Gregory Zaragoza, Mark Hattan.

WATERMARK THEATER. *Waiter, Waiter* by David Simpatico. October 16, 1995. Directed by Nela Wagman; with Karl Herlinger, Amy Lammert, Sue-Anne Morrow, Chris Prizzi, Patricia Randell, M.W. Reid, Cheryl Rogers, Melissa Schaffer, D.L. Shroder, Jane Young. *Wordfire Festival '96* (solo performances): *Haiku Tunnel* by Josh Kornbluth; *My Left Breast* by Susan Miller; *Characters in Motion* by Dael Orlandersmith; *Underground Goddess: Wings of Glass* by Abigail Gampel; *Ask Aunt Charlene* by Leonard Jacobs and Kelly Main; *Excuse My Dust* by Barbara Pitts; *Loveland* by Ann Randolph; *Inconclusive Gazes* by David Rothenberg; *Self Defense* by Michael Scasserra; *James Bond's Old Girl Friends* by Toni Schlessinger; *Denial of the Fittest* by Judith Sloan. February 1–18, 1996.

WEISSBERGER THEATER GROUP. *Where the Truth Lies* by Catherine Butterfield. April 16, 1996. Directed by Evan Yionoulis; with Catherine Butterfield, Brittany Boyd, Ellen Dolan, Mischa Barton, Taylor Stanley, Michael Countryman, Armand Schultz.

WEST END THEATER. *Get a Wonderful Life* by David DeWitt and Bill Phillips. December 6, 1995. Directed by Victoria Clark.

WESTBETH THEATER CENTER. *Dammit, Shakespeare!* by Seth Panitch. May 15, 1996. Directed by Matt Conley; with Rainard Rachele, Michael Butler, David Snizek, Eva Lowe.

WILLOW CABIN THEATER. *A Child's Christmas in Wales* adapted from Dylan Thomas's story by Jeremy Brooks and Adrian Mitchell. December 18, 1995. Directed by Edward Berkeley; with Laurence Gleason, Fiona Davis, Ken Forman. *The Ends of the Earth* by Morris Panych. March 4, 1996. Directed by Edward Berkeley; with John Bolger, Laurence Gleason, Ken Forman, Angela Nevard, Maria Radman. *The Killing of Sister George* by Frank Marcus. May 6, 1996. Directed by Jimmy Bohr; with Maria Radman, Tasha Lawrence, Fiona Davis, Christine Radman.

THE WOOSTER GROUP. *The Hairy Ape* by Eugene O'Neill, adapted by The Wooster Group. January 24, 1996. With Willem Dafoe, Peyton Smith, Kate Valk, Jill Clayburgh, Elizabeth LeCompte. *Dupe* (multimedia performance) by and with Roy Faudree. May 23, 1996.

WORKHOUSE THEATER—Calista Flockhart
and Austin Pendleton in a scene from *The Impostor* by J. Dakota Powell

WORKHOUSE THEATER. *Tallahassee* book by Len Jenkin and Mac Wellman, based on Ovid's
Metamorphoses; music and lyrics by Elise Morris and Jim Ragland. October 6, 1995. Directed by
Damien Gray; with Joseph Klosek Jr., Michael Louden, Patty Cornell. *The Impostor* by J. Dakota
Powell. January 3, 1996. Directed by John David Coles; with Calista Flockhart, Austin Pendleton,
Clark Gregg, Katherine Leask, Melinda Wade, Matthew Weiss.

WORTH STREET THEATER. *The Coyote Bleeds* by Tony DiMurro. November 2, 1995. Directed
by Jeff Cohen; with Peter Appel, Anthony Mangano.

THE SEASON
AROUND
THE UNITED STATES

OUTSTANDING NEW PLAYS CITED BY AMERICAN THEATER CRITICS ASSOCIATION

and

A DIRECTORY OF NEW-PLAY PRODUCTIONS

THE American Theater Critics Association (ATCA) is the organization of over 250 leading drama critics in all media in all sections of the United States. One of this group's stated purposes is "To increase public awareness of the theater as a *national* resource" (italics ours). To this end, beginning in 1974 ATCA has annually cited three outstanding new plays produced around the U.S., to be represented in our coverage by excerpts from each of their scripts demonstrating literary style and quality. And one of these—*Amazing Grace* by Michael Cristofer—has been designated 1995's 11th annual New Play Award winner of $1,000.

Two other 1995 ATCA citations went to *Seven Guitars* by August Wilson as the critics' second choice and *Jungle Rot* by Seth Greenland as their third. And the third annual Elizabeth Osborn Award for an emerging playwright was voted to Richard Kalinoski for *Beast on the Moon.*

Other plays nominated by individual ATCA members for the attention of the awards committee this year were, from the 1994–95 season, *The Killing of Michael*

Malloy by Erik Jendresen, *The Coming of the Hurricane* by Keith Glover, *In the Heart of the Wood* by Tod Jefferson Moore, *Counterfeits* by Shanny Mow, *Voir Dire* by Joe Sutton, *Clean* by Edwin Sanchez, *Counting Days* by Marie Kohler, *War Stories From the 20th Century* by Wayne Frank and *Neil's Garden* by Geoffrey Hassman; and, from the 1995–96 season, *An Almost Holy Picture* by Heather McDonald, *With and Without* by Jeffrey Sweet and *Birth and Afterbirth* by Tina Howe.

The process of selection of these outstanding plays is as follows: any ATCA member may nominate a play which has been given a production in a professional house. It must be the first full professional production of a finished play (not a reading or an airing as a play-in-progress) during the *calendar* year. Nominated scripts were studied and discussed by an ATCA play-reading committee chaired by Michael Grossberg of the Columbus *Dispatch* and comprising Misha Berson of the Seattle *Times,* Lawrence Bommer of the Chicago *Reader, Tribune* and Windy City *Times,* Christine Dolen of the Miami *Herald,* Dennis Harvey of the San Francisco Bay *Guardian,* Catherine Stadem of the Anchorage *Daily News* and alternates Michael Phillips of the San Diego *Union-Tribune* and Beatrice MacLeod of the Ithaca *Journal.*

These committee members made their choices on the basis of script rather than production, thus placing very much the same emphasis as the editors of this volume in making the New York Best Play selections. If the timing of nominations and openings prevents some works from being considered in any given year, they will be eligible for consideration the following year if they haven't since moved to New York.

We offer our sincerest thanks and admiration to the ATCA members and their committee for the valuable insights into the 1995 theater year around the United States which their selections provide for this *Best Plays* record, in the form of excerpts from the outstanding scripts, and most particularly in the introductory reviews by Christopher Rawson (*Amazing Grace*), Michael Grossberg (*Seven Guitars*) and Marianne Evett (*Jungle Rot*).

1995 ATCA Award

○○○
○○○
○○○
○○○
○○○
○○○ # AMAZING GRACE

A Play in Two Acts

BY MICHAEL CRISTOFER

Cast and credits appear on page 449

MICHAEL CRISTOFER was born in Trenton, N.J. Jan. 22, 1946 and grew up there and in Princeton as Michael Procaccion. He attended Catholic University in Washington, D.C. but dropped out to become an actor and playwright, taking the stage name Cristofer. His early produced plays included Plot Counter Plot *at St. Clements Space,* The Mandala *at Theater of the Living Arts Workshop in Philadelphia and* Americommedia *in a street theater production that toured during the Presidential campaign of 1972.*

The following year Cristofer began to practice both his arts at the Mark Taper Forum in Los Angeles (his first credit of record there was as an actor in a new play in October 1973; in August 1974 he was billed as Michael Ivan Cristofer in a production of Savages*). Cristofer played the leading role of Colin in the first American production of David Rudkin's British play* Ashes *at the Mark Taper a few months after his own play* The Shadow Box *had its first production there Oct. 30, 1975 under Gordon Davidson's direction. This play was subsequently produced at the Long Wharf Theater in New Haven, Conn. Jan. 21, 1976, again under Davidson's direction, then proceeding to its author's Broadway playwriting debut and winning a Best Play citation and the Pulitzer Prize.*

Cristofer's New York debut in 1977 was a double one: while his The Shadow Box *was bowing on Broadway, he was taking his first New York bows as an actor playing Trofimov in* The Cherry Orchard *at Lincoln Center. His long list of acting credits includes other Mark Taper Forum stints, repertory credits with Arena Stage in Washington, D.C. and A Contemporary Theater in Seattle, many TV appearances and the movie* An Enemy of the People.

Cristofer has also made a name for himself as a director, but it is as a playwright that he established the major share of his national and international reputation. His canon includes Ice *(Mark Taper 1975–76 season, Manhattan Theater Club 1979, 28 performances)*, Black Angel *(Mark Taper 1978, Circle Repertory 1982, 25 performances)*, The Lady and the Clarinet *(Mark Taper 1980, off Broadway 1983, 39 performances)*, Love Me or Leave Me *(River Arts, Woodstock, N.Y., 1989–90 season)*, Execution of the Caregiver *(Intiman Theater, Seattle staged reading 1993–94 season)*, Breaking Up *(Old Globe Theater, San Diego 1992, OOB at Primary Stages 1993, 24 performances) and, in 1995, the ATCA Award-winning* Amazing Grace *at Pittsburgh Public Theater and a 48 performance revival of* The Shadow Box *which was a major enhancement of last year's Broadway season.*

INTRODUCTION: *Amazing Grace* is a very American tale of personal lovelessness and spiritual hope. Though a sensational drama about the circuitous journey of a condemned serial killer, it is no less realistic than the stories of O.J. Simpson, Susan Smith or the Menendez brothers.

Most immediately, it's an engaging story. We meet Selena Goodall tending her senile mother. The poison she administers seems almost inadvertent, almost understandable. We learn more about Selena in byplay with her caustic friend, Vivian (her vivid counterpoint throughout), and in tentative flirtation with Vivian's brother, John.

The story of Selena's murders proceeds with basic chronological naturalism and occasional ribald humor. But something else accumulates, some intimation of spiritual despair. The atmosphere is speckled with Southern evangelical oratory. Bible verses slice through Selena's increasingly frantic conviction of sin. We catch a glimpse of its source, the "rats in the cellar" of her past that poison her life, but Cristofer never trivializes character with easy explanation.

In Act II, we follow Selena to trial and prison, where Cristofer astonishes us with totally unexpected visitations of grace. Selena receives a gift of love that she (and a timid audience) can barely recognize, and she develops a power that tests credulity. Then Cristofer abruptly returns us to legal reality. The ending is emotionally ambivalent, leaving the audience to sort out its feelings. *Amazing Grace* deserves a detailed theological reading, but it justifies its title: The grace it asserts and dispenses is amazing indeed.

Selena's character is never unraveled, but how can we expect a mere playwright to know all? Although Cristofer may never tell us as much about her as we'd like, it is more important that he never tells us more than we need. This is playwriting for grown-ups, assuming we can follow a complex story without having important details outlined in neon.

Attending the progress of the story is an ensemble, "the Witnesses," which functions as a character itself, providing a faintly menacing context of straitened gentility. Individuals from it play significant roles, but mainly it comes and goes in silent witness—witness both religious and legal. At play's end, a coolly cynical press aide forces us to accept our own involvement; Vivian tests our capacity for forgiveness, and the Witnesses attend Selena's execution, completing a ritual of crime and punishment with deep communal significance.

Though oppressed and delusive, Selena bubbles with life. A compulsive actor, always hiding from herself, she moves slowly toward clarity and knowledge. In the premiere at the Pittsburgh Public Theater, Marsha Mason's performance was long on stamina and utterly devoid of self-indulgence, but in one scene she unleashed a chilling cry that would befit King Lear. Under the caring direction of Edward Gilbert, the company's artistic director, the ensemble never hit a false note. Laurie Kennedy's Vivian was emotionally immediate, Larry John Meyers's warden was a perfect miniature of punctilious concern, and nothing was more astonishing than Adina Porter's Georgia, Selena's black John the Baptist and lover.

The play answered two questions. Does Cristofer's new play have the heart, soul and brains to match his 1977 Pulitzer Prize-winning *The Shadow Box?* And could this Pittsburgh theater stage it with the vision, care and technique needed? The answers to both were resoundingly affirmative, Gilbert's impeccable direction precisely matching Cristofer's unadorned storytelling.

Cristofer describes the advent of *Amazing Grace* this way: "It was inspired by an interview I saw of a woman on death row in North Carolina—she was about to be executed for killing five or six people who were in her care and related to her. She was so ordinary and seemed like my own grandmother, not in any way the stereotyped notion of a psychotic serial killer. I have that interview on tape and showed it to the cast—it was the jumping-off point."

Amazing Grace is too tautly spare and grim—even though lit with an aurora of redemption—for easy popularity. Cristofer says, "A lot of other theaters were hemming and hawing, saying, 'It's so big, so dark.' But Eddie [Gilbert] was passionate about it." Now that it's launched, its dramatic maturity should earn it attention among the regional professional companies that are America's true national theater.

—CHRISTOPHER RAWSON

Excerpts From *Amazing Grace*

Selena's trial having driven home the truth of what she's done, she tells her lawyer she wants no more appeals. Then a radio preacher touches a deep chord of repentance, leaving her on her knees, asking forgiveness.

SELENA *(very fast):* Oh, Lord Jesus, my own savior who died for my sins, forgive me. Forgive me. Forgive me.

PITTSBURGH PUBLIC THEATER—Marsha Mason (Selena) and
Stephen Bradbury (Preacher) in Michael Cristofer's *Amazing Grace*

She remains on her knees. One female Witness enters to play Georgia.
She looks suspiciously at Selena. Finally . . .

GEORGIA: Honey, if you're down there waiting for some suckable dick to come along—I can tell you right now, you're at the wrong bus stop. (*No response*). Hello? Anybody home? Or are we running on empty here? Yo, bitch. I'm talking to you.

Selena looks at her.

That's better. Now, you want to get up off the floor? Or you want a bucket and a mop so you can make yourself look useful?

SELENA: Oh. Georgia?

GEORGIA: Yeah. It's me.

SELENA: I was just listening to the radio.

GEORGIA: And I was just on my way to Elizabeth Arden. That's why I got these roller blades on. Just get up. Get up before you start causing trouble for all of us.

SELENA: I don't think I can get up. I'm stuck.

Georgia offers a hand. Selena takes it.

GEORGIA: Your hands are burning up. You got a fever or what?

She feels Selena's forehead.

SELENA: It was a gospel station.

GEORGIA: Your head ain't hot.

SELENA: One of those. . .

GEORGIA: It's just your hands. . .

SELENA: . . . religious preacher programs. I guess I got carried away by it.

GEORGIA: I guess you did.

SELENA: He was going on about God and Jesus.

GEORGIA: Yeah. I know. I know. Jesus loves you, so send me four dollars.

SELENA: I don't think he was asking for money.

GEORGIA: Ain't nobody talks about God without asking for something. If it ain't your money, it's your soul. And if it ain't your money or your soul—then look out, 'cause the only other thing they could possibly be after is your pussy.

SELENA: He was talking about something else.

GEORGIA: Uh-huh. Well, let it go.

SELENA: Yes.

GEORGIA: Peddling that shit in here. If they're looking for money, they're broadcasting to the wrong bitches. Aint' they?

SELENA: I heard something. It was so clear. Like a bell going off inside my brain.

GEORGIA: Oh, yeah. I heard that one, too. Bells in the brains. You know what that is? That's every thought you're thinking bouncing off these concrete walls. Making you stranger than you already know you are. Else why else would you be here in the first place? Let it go, bitch. There ain't no help no way coming in here from outside. That's a hope you just got to let die. Otherwise it will kill you. That's what hope is for. To kill you. Hope is the killing thing. You know? I ain't here. I ain't gonna be here long. I shall be released. I ain't really who I am. I ain't really done what I done. Just a great load a shit that you got to get out of your insides. The sooner you flush it down the toilet, the cleaner the air will smell. And you can get on with what little bit of miserable life you got left. Now are you getting up or ain't you?

SELENA *(laughs):* My legs are like pudding ...

GEORGIA *(trying to help her up):* Somebody sees you like this ...

SELENA: ... and my heart is racing away from itself.

Georgia suddenly drops to her knees next to Selena.

GEORGIA: Ow! What in hell ... ? Now look, sister. You got to get up or let go of me, 'cause your hands are getting too hot to hold. What's the matter with you?!

SELENA: I feel ... I don't know. I feel it in my heart. What is it? My stomach, too. Oooh ...

Selena puts Georgia's hands on her body.

GEORGIA: Jesus! Jesus Christ Almighty! Let go of me!

SELENA: You feel something?

GEORGIA: You're burning in my hands!

SELENA: What is it?! My insides are on fire ...

GEORGIA: Let go! Let go!!! Let go!!!

Selena lets go. Georgia pulls away. Selena clutches her belly.

SELENA: I feel it, too. I feel it. Here. Here. Here.

Blood starts to flow from between her legs, staining her dress—bright red. Selena is more confused than scared. She touches the wetness, looks at the blood on her hands.

GEORGIA: Selena ... ?

SELENA: What? What did I do? What did I do . . . ?

Blackout. Lights up immediately on Georgia.

GEORGIA: Well, you can believe this or disbelieve it, I don't care. Most everybody now don't hardly mention it when they talk about her. That is because they cannot make any kind of sense out of it, no matter which way they try.

Selena enters—frail, walking as if on eggs. A soft breeze could knock her down. One Witness comes down to Selena. Selena holds the Witness's hands for a moment. Then slowly, almost like slow motion, the Witness's hand carries Selena's hand to the Witness's shoulder. The Witness turns so that Selena is embracing the Witness from behind with one arm around the Witness's waist and one hand on the Witness's hand which in turn is on the Witness's shoulder.

GEORGIA: But the truth is there weren't no sense in it. And unless you're prepared to talk about miracles—which most people ain't—there just ain't a hell of a lot to say about it. Belinda Coyne, she was the first. She had pain in her left shoulder, you would not believe the pain. There was no joint left. Those bones were knit right together, she could not move that arm. Sometimes, at night . . .

WITNESS (BELINDA) AND GEORGIA *(together):* . . . sometimes at night, I (she) roll over in my (her) sleep, roll on top of that shoulder. Oh, God. Oh, God, the pain is like razors . . .

BELINDA: . . . razors inside cutting their way out.

SELENA: Oh, what a terrible thing.

BELINDA: And they won't give me nothing for it. "Nothin' we can do. You take some aspirin."

SELENA: You leave it to them, they'd give you aspirin for a flat tire.

They all laugh.

BELINDA: Yes, they would.

BELINDA AND GEORGIA: Oh, yes they would.

SELENA *(still holding Belinda):* Where is it? Here?

BELINDA: Yes. There it is.

SELENA: Right here?

BELINDA: That heat feels good. What is that?

SELENA: That's just my hand. It gets hot.

Selena slides her hand up and down Belinda's arm.

Does that feel good?

BELINDA: Yes. But be careful . . .

SELENA: I am careful. I am *full* of care.

BELINDA: 'Cause I can't move that arm . . .

SELENA: I know that.

BELINDA: I can't even move it but one inch that it don't hurt . . .

SELENA *(lifting her arm slightly):* You mean like this?

BELINDA: Yes. Like that.

SELENA: Like this?

BELINDA: This is what hurts.

SELENA: I don't think so.

BELINDA: What are you doing?

> *Belinda's arm starts to rise.*

SELENA: I ain't doing nothing.

BELINDA: Oh my, you must be doing something.

SELENA: I'm just holding your hand. See? See?

> *Belinda's arm continues to rise. Selena lets go of the hand. No pain.*

BELINDA: Oh . . . oh . . . oh . . .

GEORGIA: And that arm just floated on up to heaven. And it weren't no hypnosis trance neither . . .

BELINDA: . . . because to this day, there ain't no pain in that arm. Once it was gone, it was gone. They wanted to do X-rays and such. But I said, "No thank you." I said, "You leave well enough alone." And when they said, "But how could this happen?"—I said, "Well, it must have been the aspirin."

> *She laughs and goes to join the Witnesses. Selena and Georgia sit down and start playing cards. Selena's movements are strange, tentative, fragile—like a baby or a very old person. At the same time, there is a growing clarity in her eyes and spirit.*

GEORGIA: Well, after that, the bitches was lining up to get themselves touched, to get the "laying on of the hands," you know? Everything from the cancer and the HIV, all the way down to headaches, backaches and your ordinary diarrhea.

SELENA *(smiles):* I can't do anything about that.

GEORGIA: You don't know, do you? Not for sure.

SELENA: I guess I don't—not for sure, anyway. But still . . .

GEORGIA: Yeah. I know. For one thing, you got to figure out, for that one, just where you gonna lay your hands. (*She laughs.*)

SELENA: Oh, you. I used to have a friend was just like you. She had a mind on her . . . just like yours.

GEORGIA: Ain't nobody got a mind like mine.

SELENA: You see? That's just the kind of thing she would say.

GEORGIA: Oh, yeah? Well, that's one bitch I'd like to meet.

SELENA: I can hardly imagine the two of you in the same room. The walls would just explode. And anyway, I lost her. She's gone.

GEORGIA: Was she one of "yours"?

SELENA: Oh, no, no, no. I lost her in a different way.

GEORGIA *(lays down her cards):* That's gin.

SELENA: Oh, boy. Ten, twenty, five, seven—thirty-two.

> *Georgia shuffles and deals. They play again through the following.*

GEORGIA: You ain't thinking straight.

SELENA: No.

GEORGIA: You're tired.

SELENA: It takes it out of me.

GEORGIA: I bet.

SELENA: Like a spigot opens and my insides rush out.

GEORGIA: Every time?

SELENA: Maybe it's more like burning fuel, burning up the fuel supply. Because of the heat. And because I feel so cold after.

GEORGIA: You know when you had your hands on Red Ryan's back, did you know, when you finished, did you know you went out cold?

SELENA: That's what it is. Going out cold.

GEORGIA: Did you realize?

SELENA: No.

GEORGIA: I didn't think you knew.

SELENA: Going out cold.

GEORGIA: And when you was healing that bitch with the ovarian cyst and she was screaming bloody murder . . .

SELENA: I remember that.

GEORGIA: You was out that time almost three days.

SELENA: Yes. I do remember that.

GEORGIA: So what do you think?

SELENA: About what?

GEORGIA: About how much of this shit you got in you. About how much it takes to get it out of you. About how much time you got to go on burning up the fuel supply before you go out cold for good. I mean, is that a possibility?

SELENA: I don't know.

GEORGIA: Because maybe you should think of saving a little for yourself, you know? Just to keep yourself alive.

SELENA: You don't have to worry about me.

GEORGIA: Well, I know I don't *have* to. But I do. I do worry. Don't you see that?

SELENA: I do now.

GEORGIA: Well, good. You ain't the best looking bitch in this joint. Not by a long shot. And there's plenty others deserve my attention. So when I express my concern and my affection—don't you brush it aside like you're shooing flies off a piece of pie.

SELENA: No. I don't . . . I wouldn't.

GEORGIA: I ain't asking for nothing. I never have.

SELENA: I know that. You are my very best friend.

GEORGIA: And I ain't asking for nothing now either. Except that you take enough care of yourself so as to be available in the future for the continuance of these all-too-exciting card games. Gin.

Selena reaches across the table and takes the inmate's hands.

SELENA: What I believe is this. I believe that I asked for God's forgiveness and he heard me, and I believe that this little power in my hands is his answer. I believe that it is his love burning up my body and doing whatever good I can do. And I believe that whatever happens to me in the service of his love is not for me to question. Because the joy that he has put inside my heart is bigger than life itself. And the more I can give of his love, the greater that joy will be.

GEORGIA: Well. I'm glad *one* of us is happy.

SELENA: And you are not?

GEORGIA: Let me say this. There's give and there's take. You know what I'm saying? There's them that give and give and give. And there's them that take, take, take. And them that give, everybody thinks, oh, them's the good people. And them that take, well, they just selfish, no good people. But the truth is something entirely different from that. Now you, you're used to the give, give, give. And I ain't making judgments, but the truth is, you got yourself into deep shit with that philosophy. And I would say you are living proof of how wrong a person can go with that way of thinking. And even now—maybe you been blessed and forgiven and whatever else you think happened to you—and now God's love may be shooting out of you like fireworks on the Fourth of July. So you got even more to give and give and give. But I ain't impressed. Because until you learn to take some, take some of the love that is being offered you—and I ain't just talking about me. I'm talking about all the love that's been coming your way all your life—no matter how strange and sad and small and unlike anything you may have expected—until you face that love and don't run from it or hide from it or kill it—until you learn to take some kind of love from some kind of living human being—well, honey, you can die happy and holy and blessed, but I'm here to tell you, you ain't never really lived.

SELENA: Do you . . . do you have love for me?

GEORGIA: Honey, I dream every night about the heat coming out of you. I dream about getting my hands on it. Getting my mouth on it. And sucking it down inside me. And then when you go all cold, all tired and used up, whenever you might need it, I dream of putting my lips back on your body and blowing that heat right back into you, right back through your skin and into your heart. I dream of putting the life back into you. I dream of doing that for you. I dream of you letting me do that.

SELENA: Well . . .

GEORGIA: Yeah. Well, I must be getting old.

SELENA: Why?

GEORGIA: I never ever had to do *this* much talking to get a bitch into bed.

Selena kisses her hands. Georgia kisses Selena.

SELENA: She used to lay her hands on me. She'd say, "What's this?" And I'd say, "That's my arm." Then she'd say, "Yes. And what is this?" "Well, that is my neck." "Yes," she'd say, "and what are these?"

Georgia leaves her as she speaks and goes to join the Witnesses. During the following, the Witnesses give Georgia a suitcase and an overcoat.

"Well, that's my chest," I'd say. "No," she'd say. "A chest is something with drawers in it." Well, all right, it's my bosom. "Bosom is for old ladies," she'd say. "Now you tell me what these are because I ain't going to let go of them till you say it." "All right," I'd say, "they are breasts. They are my breasts." And we laughed. She says she'll accept that, but what she really wants to hear is . . . And then she'd use one, two, three words that I just couldn't say. I still can't say them. I laugh. And then she grabs me between my legs and she says, "What is this? Huh? What's this? You say what this is. 'Cause I ain't going to let you go until you say it." And I said, "Well then, I ain't never going to say it. Never. Never. Never."

Georgia walks down to Selena carrying a suitcase and wearing an overcoat.

And when I was cold, she made me warm. Just like she said. And then in January, I was put into the infirmary . . .

WITNESS: What happened to you?

SELENA: Oh, it was nothing. It was a flu that turned into pneumonia—she was right. I never did know how to take care of myself.

WITNESS: Did you still have this heat in your hands? This power to heal?

SELENA: Oh, yes. I still had the gift. I have it now. I just couldn't do anything about myself.

WITNESS: And when you got out of the infirmary . . .

SELENA: She was gone. Transferred. And I never got to say goodbye. And I missed my chance to say thank you.

Georgia exits.

I missed her. I still do. You know, I believe in angels. I believe that sometimes in your life, you are on a track that is somehow going in the wrong direction. And someone comes along, some human being who sometimes you don't even know, and they cross your path maybe just for an instant. And something is said or something is done or something just happens and in that split second your life is changed. I believe those people are sent to us. I believe they are angels. I believe she was one of them.

Amazing Grace *was first produced at the Pittsburgh Public Theater October 12, 1995 under the direction of Edward Gilbert.*

1995 ATCA Citation

○○○
○○○
○○○
○○○
○○○
○○○ SEVEN GUITARS

A Play in Two Acts

BY AUGUST WILSON

Cast and credits of the opening regional theater production appear on
page 457 of *The Best Plays of 1994–95* and of the 1996 New York
production on page 295 of this volume

AUGUST WILSON'S Seven Guitars, *the sixth in his cycle of plays about the life and
times of black Americans in this century, was cited by ATCA as one of 1995's outstanding plays produced in regional theater simultaneously with its opening in New
York and citation as one of the Best Plays of the 1995–96 season. A biographical
sketch of the author and a synopsis of the script appear in the Best Plays section of
this volume. A review by Michael Grossberg of its production in regional theater
appears below.*

SEVEN GUITARS: August Wilson soulfully sings the blues in *Seven Guitars,* his
sixth major play about black Americans. Like *Ma Rainey's Black Bottom,* Wilson's
first Broadway play about the 1920s blues singer, *Seven Guitars* chronicles the exploitation of black musicians and ends with the death of one black at the enraged,
frustrated hands of another. Unlike *Ma Rainey* and Wilson's Pulitzer-winning dra-
mas, *Fences* and *The Piano Lesson, Seven Guitars* strongly favors texture and character over plot. The setting is 1948 in the Pittsburgh Hill District—the same neighborhood and decade of Wilson's childhood.

Lyrical dialogue has rarely seemed more like lyrics. Even more of an ensemble
piece than Wilson's *Joe Turner's Come and Gone, Guitars* is a sprawling symphony
about the urgent dreams and bitter disappointments of blacks who migrated from
the South to the North to better themselves. Many fought in World War II, affirming

a tacit promise of integration and opportunity that *Guitars* reveals as tragically premature.

Wilson's central "melody" mourns and celebrates a struggling, 35-year-old blues guitarist who dies on the brink of a career breakthrough. Floyd "Schoolboy" Barton, arrested for vagrancy while returning home from his mother's funeral, is determined to succeed in a white man's world. Ironically, Barton was arrested for playing his guitar on a public sidewalk, with his hat at his feet for spare change—an innocent action which would not have caused trouble in the South. Another irony: In the workhouse, Floyd hears on the radio that he has a hit record. When his white producers invite him to cut another, Floyd must find a way to raise money for his mother's gravestone, his hocked guitar and his band's trip to Chicago.

Floyd's tale is interlaced with the bluesey riffs of six characters who gather in the half-urban, half-rural backyard of a Pittsburgh boarding house: Red Carter, a drummer and womanizer who wants to get his drums out of hock; Canewell, a harmonica player and singer who dreams of a rural respite; Vera, Floyd's ex-girlfriend, whom he hopes to win back; Louise, the earth mother who runs the boarding house; Ruby, Louise's sexy niece and a pregnant Alabama refugee; and Hedley, a tubercular prophet and madman whose haunted persona has appeared with variations in each Wilson work.

The seven "guitars" are the seven characters, with Wilson as the guitarist singing a folk ballad suffused with poetic language, bittersweet humor, bloody violence, seemingly improvisatory dialogue and riff-like side stories involving offstage characters such as Floyd's cheating manager.

Framed by the opening and closing scenes in which the others mourn Floyd's death, this three-hour two-act play is largely a flashback to their interactions during Floyd's final days. They eat, drink, talk, fight, make love or make music and listen to the Joe Louis-Billy Conn boxing match on the radio in that backyard, which evokes a cemetery and a garden. Finally, the backyard becomes a metaphoric arena for their struggle—not so much against an oppressive society, but inside each soul for self-worth. The blues, conceived as a response to slavery, become a source of power and faith in this rich tapestry of conversations, monologues, prayers, songs, symbolism, lofty dreams and petty schemes. The numerology extends from the seven characters to the "seven birds sitting on that fence" and "seven ways" for Floyd to go.

Although Wilson's dark elegy qualifies as an American tragedy, in the highest tradition of Eugene O'Neill and Arthur Miller, Wilson's emphasis is on the earthy spirituality of his flesh-and-bloodied characters, not the harsh social limitations that left their dreams unfulfilled. His tone is as lyrical as an Irish wake, as meandering as the bustling urban under-currents in Elmer Rice's *Street Scene*. Wilson's ultimate theme is transcendence: He favors the soul—if a choice must be made—over the body, heroic remembrance over angry victimization. At the wake, Floyd's friends mention seeing him ascend into heaven, lifted from the grave by six men in black who might be angels or funeral parlor employees. Americans of all races dream of the future, but we are haunted by the past.

HUNTINGTON THEATER COMPANY, BOSTON—Ruben Santiago-
Hudson (Canewell), Michele Shay (Louise) and Keith David (Floyd) in a
regional theater production of August Wilson's *Seven Guitars*

Wilson, the onstage poet of black America, has won the American Theater Critics
Association's New Play Award more than anyone—for *Fences* (1986), *The Piano
Lesson* (1989) and *Two Trains Running* (1991). With *Seven Guitars,* Wilson has
passed the halfway mark in his ambitious life-plan to write a cycle of plays about
the black experience in each decade of the 20th century.

Some critics have described his ghost-filled style as magical realism. While magical realism grew out of South American culture, Wilson's vision is rooted in the
American South. Perhaps a better term for his approach is *spiritual* realism—the

compassionate clarity of an old soul who understands that living and dreaming with honor is more important than winning, losing or dying.

—MICHAEL GROSSBERG

After a workshop staging under the direction of Lloyd Richards at the Eugene O'Neill National Playwrights Conference, Seven Guitars *was first produced January 23, 1995 at the Goodman Theater in Chicago under Walter Dallas's direction. Subsequent regional theater productions directed by Richards took place at the Huntington Theater Company, Boston, the American Conservatory Theater, San Francisco, and the Ahmanson Theater, Los Angeles, prior to its New York production March 28, 1996 at the Walter Kerr Theater, also directed by Richards. It was named a Best Play (see its synopsis in the Best Plays section of this volume) and won the Critics Award for the best play of the 1995–96 New York season.*

1995 ATCA Citation

○○○
○○○
○○○
○○○
○○○
○○○ **JUNGLE ROT**

A Play in Two Acts

BY SETH GREENLAND

Cast and credits appear on page 460 of *The Best Plays of 1994–95*

SETH GREENLAND has written for all three dramatic media. His ATCA Citation-winning play Jungle Rot, *about events in the Congo in 1960 when Patrice Lumumba was its prime minister, was workshopped in Cleveland Play House's Discovereads Series in 1991 and The New York Shakespeare Festival's Public Hearings series in 1992, prior to its production in 1995 at Cleveland Play House. His other plays are* Girls in Movies, Partners in Crime *and* Red Memories, *the latter presented at Circle Repertory's Projects in Progress series for 2 performances in November 1993.*

For television, Greenland provided a series of monologues entitled The Love Doctor *on MTV networks as well as several pilots. His screen plays are* Bad With Numbers *(1993) and* Who's The Man? *(1995). Greenland is married, with children, and lives in upstate New York.*

INTRODUCTION: Seth Greenland's *Jungle Rot* makes you laugh out loud, even on the page. Yet its characters and basic situation come straight from the real Cold War shenanigans of the CIA.

Greenland discovered the nugget for the play in an interview with Miles Copeland, one of the founders of the CIA, published in *Rolling Stone* magazine in 1986.

Copeland, who had by then left the agency, mentioned that the CIA Head of Station in Leopoldville in 1960 got a message from the White House ordering him to assassinate Congolese Prime Minister Patrice Lumumba, whose professed neutrality and left-wing sympathies made Washington foresee a possible Communist takeover. At first, the agent was outraged by the idea; but he appeared stuck at a mid-level desk job in Africa, and his wife thought that the assassination would be a great career move. A CIA chemist specializing in untraceable poisons was dispatched to help in the assassination, but the attempt failed.

Greenland turns this historical situation into political farce by presenting it straight, with all its Alice-in-Wonderland logic and skewed morality. The play moves with cinematic rapidity—there are 15 scenes in Act I and 11 in Act II. In the fast-paced and funny Cleveland Play House production, directed by Roger T. Danforth, designer James Noone's simple set pieces whizzed in and out with their own comic rhythms.

Jungle Rot exposes the arrogance and ignorance that leads Americans to assume that other countries want to be just like us—a mind-set that still influences our foreign policy. On another level, it is a study of ambition, of murder seen as career advancement. This theme is wittily sounded at the beginning, when three mysterious African figures chant the opening lines from *Macbeth.* Hailing the CIA agent, John Stillman, as "the man who shall be supreme chief," they tell him to "Be on the lookout for a sign."

Stillman is no Macbeth, however. He is passive; an intelligent, decent man who is appalled by the idea of killing (it's one reason he has not gotten very far in his career). His wife, Patience, however, is a real Lady Macbeth knock-off. A Foxcroft graduate languishing in darkest Africa, ignored by the ambassador's wife (who is merely a grocer's daughter), Patience yearns for success, glamour and a good dry cleaner. Give her a chance and she'll engineer giving Lumumba a fatal kiss without turning a hair.

Around the Stillmans revolves a circle of mind-boggling comic types, each with a foot squarely planted in reality. Stillman's new assistant, Walter Clark, may be too green to manage his elusive Congolese "joe" (spy), but he's clearly going to grow up to be Bob Haldeman, or maybe even Oliver North. A company man, he obeys orders, whatever they are. And there's Dr. Felix Bender, the CIA poison specialist who arrives to engineer the assassination. Bender has devised a lipstick that becomes fatal when combined with wine (remember the CIA plan to poison Fidel Castro's cigars?), a little toy he is dropping off before joining his wife and kids on vacation. In his tropic whites, rotund actor Robert Machray looked like a sinister Moby Dick.

Bender's plan is simple. The Stillmans will invite Lumumba to a party. He'll have a glass of wine; Bender's voluptuous assistant, Miss Rendelbaker, will entice him into kissing her; and later, after the party is all over, he will have what will look like a fatal heart attack.

Stillman's life is further interrupted by Bud Bradshaw, an auto parts salesman from Schenectady who has come to Leopoldville with his wife, Alice, to search for their daughter Debbie. She has run off with an exchange student from the Congo, who has turned out to be a Marxist revolutionary.

Greenland brings both plots together in a frenetic climax. Miss Rendelbaker gets sick and Patience agrees to administer the fatal kiss herself. Her tryst with Lumumba is interrupted by his bodyguards, however, and she learns further bad news: He doesn't drink. Lumumba, who has been lured to the party with a false promise— that he can talk privately to the U.S. ambassador—grows restless. When the irate Bradshaw shows up, Patience tries to pass Bud off as the missing ambassador, but the ruse doesn't work. Lumumba leaves, Patience faints and Bud (who has had a glass of wine) tries to revive her with mouth-to-mouth resuscitation, not suspecting that he has completed the fatal combination.

The play ends at the airport the next morning. Patience is leaving John to go back to Washington. John is leaving the CIA, pleading a total nervous breakdown. Walter will take charge of the Congo station and is smuggling his native joe to America as promised—in Bud's coffin. The three Africans have the last word, however, reminding us that although Lumumba escaped from the CIA, he was soon murdered "by other mad men."

Although this political satire gives us a look at a dark, crazy world, Greenland maintains a light, comic tone and never gives us much chance to think about it. Until, of course, it's over.

—MARIANNE EVETT

Excerpts From *Jungle Rot*

John and Walter are in their office. Dr. Bender enters, carrying his medical bag. He looks nervously over his shoulder.

JOHN: Can I help you, sir? This isn't a public room.

BENDER: Who's Stillman?

JOHN: I am.

BENDER: Prove it.

JOHN: Excuse me?

WALTER: What's your business, sir?

BENDER: Hello, Mr. Clark.

JOHN: Walter, is this guy one of yours?

WALTER: I've never seen him before. How do you know who I am?

BENDER: Meticulous research. (*To John.*) John Stillman. B.A. University of New Hampshire, M.A. Harvard, posts have included Bucharest and Algiers, hobby is tennis.

JOHN: Who are you?

BENDER: Joe from Paris. I believe you're expecting me.

JOHN: It's you?

BENDER: Delightful city we're in, but I can't find a dry cleaner. Any idea where I can get a suit pressed?

Bender pokes around the office for a moment, searching the desk and light fixtures for bugs.

WALTER: They don't have them here.

BENDER: I had really planned on being able to get a suit cleaned. I can't stand working when I don't look neat. I've always believed a natty appearance is paramount.

JOHN: We're clean.

BENDER: Can't be too safe. Dr. Felix Bender, Psychopharmaceutical Division. Pleasant place you gentlemen have. Care to tell me what's on the agenda down here? Embassy bugs, infiltration, the usual covert ops?

JOHN: You know how it works.

BENDER: If only that sort of thing could really do the job.

JOHN: It always has.

BENDER: Until now. I appreciate your romantic notions, Stillman, but alas, the world of chivalry and fair play is but a faint memory. Strap yourselves down, gentlemen. Bender is going to crank up the excitement level.

JOHN: Wait a minute . . .

BENDER: You got the cable, didn't you?

JOHN: We haven't explored the feasibility of the operation yet and as far as I know . . .

BENDER: This comes from the White House. Ike wants it done. We can't have loose cannons like Lumumba running around the countryside gumming up the works for everyone. If Ivan gets a toehold in the Congo, pretty soon all of Africa is dancing to the balalaika!

WALTER: Did Ike give the order?

BENDER: Of course not! He's the President. He doesn't give those kind of orders.

JOHN: I thought political assassination had fallen out of favor.

BENDER: It seems to be making a comeback. Unfortunately, too many do-gooder types in positions of power often forget that a well-timed assassination is a healthy alternative to war. One life is taken, countless are saved.

JOHN: The guy was elected! The military is running the show now anyway, and if we kill Lumumba, it's going to give them an excuse to stay in power.

BENDER: That's how we put them on the path to democracy.

JOHN: By establishing a military dictatorship?

BENDER: What is the point of having free elections if the man who wins ties on a bib, orders some sweet and sour sauce . . . and eats the loser?

JOHN: First, there are no cannibals in Leopoldville.

BENDER: I could swear my cabdriver was smacking his lips as I paid him.

JOHN: And second, the man who wins has won an election.

BENDER: Lumumba's a wild card. We have no idea what he'll do.

JOHN: But he was elected! That's the whole point!

BENDER: You can't teach these people democracy any more than you can put it in a hypodermic needle and inject it. Which brings me back to the purpose of my visit. Believe me, Stillman, I'm perfectly aware that this is an odious business, but assassination is in the twenty-first century now. If we want to remove someone we don't do it like the Mafia. They're not shot down in a restaurant in Brooklyn somewhere between the linguine and the calamari. We're in the pharmaceutical age. (*To Walter.*) How many types of assassination are there?

WALTER: Two. One kind looks like natural death and the second only serves its purpose if it looks intentional.

BENDER: Precisely. Now what shall we do with Comrade Lumumba?

JOHN: Why don't you go back to your hotel, get settled and then in a few days we can . . .

BENDER (*placing his medical bag on the desk*): I'm afraid we're going to have to get the planning done now, as I'm due in Havana next week for a repeat performance. And then I'm off to Thailand for a little R & R with the wife and kiddies. I believe we'll be going for death by natural causes here, so we've got a variety of options. We can get him by placing a little bit of this . . . (*Holds up a small vial.*) . . . on an envelope. When he's sending in his dues to the Comintern, he licks the envelope, it seeps into his body and suddenly—BANG—his nervous system feels like a Fourth of July celebration. An unfortunate side effect is everyone else who touches it drops dead too. It's very popular in Asia.

JOHN: Dr. Bender . . .

BENDER (*holds up a tube*): This is noxious toothpaste. Simply induce him to brush with it and he'll never again have to worry about plaque, and his last breath will be a refreshing spearmint. But of course, the technique I'm partial to is the two-pronged approach. Here we introduce into the body of our victim two separate substances at different times. They're harmless in themselves, but when one mixes them together . . . let's just say the party ends early.

He sees a framed picture on John's desk.

Is this your lovely wife?

JOHN: Yes.

BENDER: We've got killer lipstick.

He removes another container from his bag.

There's something in the cosmetic that makes the person allergic to wine. We would serve Lumumbavitch a pleasant Bordeaux and have an agent wearing the lipstick kiss him goodnight later in the evening, thereby inducing a massive thrombosis. And as thromboses go, I can assure you, that's the best kind. Then he dies peacefully in his sleep of what looks like a bad ticker.

JOHN: How do you intend to get him to do any of this?

BENDER: I'm sorry. I've neglected to tell you. You're having him to dinner. We'll be sending him a note on the ambassador's stationery inviting him to a dinner being held at your house. Talk to your wife. We'll need her assistance. Why don't we try for tomorrow night? I'll take care of the invitations.

JOHN: Where does my wife fit in?

BENDER: We'll need a hostess.

JOHN: Would you mind telling me how you're going to accomplish this?

BENDER: Miss Rendelbaker is going to kiss him to death.

JOHN: Who is Miss Rendelbaker?

BENDER: My assistant.

WALTER: Is she diseased?

BENDER: It's all in the lipstick.

JOHN: Where is she now?

BENDER: Resting. She just threw up in her hat.

JOHN: I can't imagine why.

BENDER: Poor thing. Bad ratatouille. We'll chat in the morning. Must dash!
> *He closes his bag and exits.*

WALTER: John, this is really exciting.

JOHN: I'm not a hit man, Walter. Just because we live under a rock, doesn't mean we have to act like vermin . . . . .

John and Walters's conference is interrupted by a couple from America, Alice and Bud Bradshaw, whose daughter Debbie has run off to Katanga with a Congolese exchange student whom she intends to marry. They want to go find her and bring her back. Walter advises them against it.

WALTER: It's not very safe.

BUD: When can we leave?

WALTER: I'm obligated to advise you not to make this trip.

BUD *(rising from his chair):* We're Americans, dammit! We'll go where we want. This little rat stole our daughter! I try and be open minded, and what do I get? Some congobongo swipes my kid! Listen, mister, I was at Guadalcanal. I killed Japs with my bare hands! I know how to handle myself. Now, if you'll just give us a map.

JOHN: I sympathize with you, Mr. Bradshaw, but we're not a missing persons service.

BUD: You clowns couldn't find bullshit in a cow pasture! Come on, Alice.
> *Alice rises.*

ALICE *(sincerely):* Thank you for your help.

JOHN: It's a pleasure.
> *The Bradshaws exit.*

WALTER: What are we going to do about Lumumba?
> *Three natives appear.*

NATIVES: Hail to John Stillman! The man who will be chief!
> *Lights down on the natives. John scribbles something on a piece of paper and hands it to Walter.*

JOHN: Take this to communications. I'm cabling Washington.

WALTER: What does it say?

JOHN: Joe from Paris arrived. Operation go.

Walter writes a postcard to his fiancée, Emily, back in Indiana; the Bradshaws head into the jungle to look for Debbie and are captured by revolutionaries.

Lights up revealing Patience in her living room. A large suitcase is nearby . . . . . John enters. He appears slightly distracted.

JOHN: Would you make the drinks tonight?

PATIENCE: I'd be happy to.

> *She rises and crosses to the liquor trolley where she prepares two gin and tonics.*

How was your day?

JOHN: Dreadful.

> *He takes off his jacket and slumps on the sofa.*

PATIENCE: I'm sorry to hear that.

JOHN: What's the suitcase doing out?

PATIENCE *(handling him his drink):* I'm leaving you. Tchin tchin.

> *She drinks, he doesn't.*

JOHN: You're doing what?

PATIENCE: I'm leaving you, Johnny.

JOHN: Am I missing something here? Shouldn't we be discussing this, or is it a fait accompli?

PATIENCE: I don't see what there is to discuss. It no longer works.

JOHN: Patience, this is absurd. How can you say that?

PATIENCE: Because I dwell in the house of truth. I've reserved a seat on a flight that leaves in a couple of hours. I only waited because I wanted to tell you in person.

JOHN: That was very considerate.

PATIENCE: I never lose sight of my manners.

JOHN: I thought we had a reasonable facsimile of a successful marriage.

PATIENCE: If your idea of a successful marriage is fifteen years of my being a slave to the ebbs and flows of your none-too-wonderful career, I'd say it was a resounding triumph.

JOHN: I was under the impression you loved me.

PATIENCE: Of course I love you. I just don't respect you any more, and I can't be married to a man I don't respect. I'm simply not cut of a cloth to be a vice-consul's wife. I intend to assault Washington while I still have a few good years left. I'm tired of reading six-week-old copies of the *Post* and seeing all the names of all the girls I went to Foxcroft with while I languish helplessly in some tropical back-water with nothing to look forward to except the cocktail hour, which, I must confess, is hovering dangerously near lunch.

JOHN: Why didn't you ever tell me this?

PATIENCE: I did. I got tired of hearing myself whine. I was raised to ask and be given. Whining is for those who don't get. It ill becomes me. Of course I love you, and we'll always be chums, but that's rather beside the point.

> *A car horn honks.*

That's the taxi. I suppose I had better go. Call me when you're in Washington, and we'll reminisce. I don't think there's any point in filing for a divorce right away.

> *She kisses him on the cheek.*

JOHN: First, they want me to assassinate Lumumba, and now you're leaving. Have a good flight.

PATIENCE: Lumumba?

JOHN: The former Prime Minister of the Congo. He was just fired by the President. Then Colonel Mobutu staged a military coup. I don't think *Vogue* covered it.

PATIENCE: They want you to assassinate him?

JOHN: Not only do they want me to assassinate him, but they've sent a psychopath down from headquarters to help. You wouldn't believe this guy. He's a nightmare. Well, I'm sorry you want to leave.

A long pause.

PATIENCE: John, this is wonderful news! It's a vote of confidence in you, darling! Someone in Washington has taken note of the work you've been doing, and when this job came up they decided John Stillman was their man. This is the most exciting thing that's happened to us in years!

JOHN: Patience, you're kidding, right?

PATIENCE: Don't you see? You do this and your star goes straight up. You're just a CIA man now, but if you come through for them you can set your cap for the State Department.

JOHN: Are you serious? They want me to kill a man.

PATIENCE: It's a great career move. It's the opportunity we've been waiting for.

JOHN: I thought you were leaving.

PATIENCE: Not now, honey. Why go to Washington as a 40-ish divorcee when I can go as Mrs. Foggy Bottom?

JOHN: I just don't know if I can do it.

PATIENCE: It's your job, Johnny. It's your patriotic duty. And if you want this marriage to work, it's your obligation. All the years I've given you, the bloom of my youth, and you don't know if you can assassinate an enemy of the United States Government? How do they want you to do it? I'm sure you don't have to crawl into his bedroom at night and strangle him.

JOHN: They want me to invite him to a dinner party here and poison him.

PATIENCE: A dinner party? Here? *(She lets out a little yelp of joy.)* I finally get to entertain! My God, how much good news can I take at one time? This is just a little example of how when skies are cloudy and gray, happiness and sunshine can be just around the corner. Five minutes ago I was a miserable expatriate bordering on dipsomania, and now my husband comes home from the office with just about the greatest news I've ever heard. And some people don't believe in kismet.

The car horn honks again and she crosses to the door.

Go away! Allez! Allez! No need for taxi! *(Turning to John.)* I misjudged you and I apologize.

JOHN: I don't know if I can kill this man.

PATIENCE: I thought they sent you a little helper.

JOHN: A "little helper"? He's a lunatic from the Third Reich! I'm the one who has to do it. I'm the responsible party.

PATIENCE: And I get to give a dinner. Perhaps we can have the Ambassador's wife and kill her too. Oh, I'm joking. But if they want you to do this Lumumba business, what's wrong with that?

JOHN: There's a thing called morality.

PATIENCE: But that's a relative thing, isn't it? He's a Communist. It's not like they're asking you to kill an American.

JOHN: And you don't mind being party to this?

PATIENCE: Whenever a wife can help her husband in his work, it's a blessing. John, I am blessed.

She kisses him deeply.

The Bradshaws, tied to stakes, are about to be shot when Debbie, who has joined the revolutionaries, enters and saves them.

The Stillman living room. Patience sits on the sofa leafing through a cookbook. John stares out a window.

PATIENCE: This is awful.

JOHN: Isn't it?

PATIENCE: It's too early to serve *boeuf bourguignon.* Do you think lobster newburg would be more *soigné*? *(No response.)* Johnny?

JOHN: Hmm? Sorry. What?

PATIENCE: Do you think I should serve lobster newburg?

JOHN: Fine.

PATIENCE: Good. I was hoping you'd agree. Listen to the menu. Shrimp bisque. A small salad to cleanse the palate. I saw the most wonderful tomatoes in the market yesterday. Lobster newburg, assuming I can get the right ingredients for the sauce.

The phone rings.

And the phone is working! I'm not sure I can digest all this good fortune at once.

John crosses to the phone and answers it.

JOHN: Yes? *(Pause.)* I see. Is she going to be all right? *(Pause.)* Well, perhaps it's just a twenty-four-hour bug. You're sure? I'm sorry to hear that. Tell her I hope she feels better. I suppose it's off then? *(Pause.)* My wife? Don't be ridiculous. Isn't it enough that she's the hostess? I know there's a time problem. Can't someone fly in? I see. I'll ask her. No. I'll call you back.

He hangs up the phone and turns to face Patience.

PATIENCE: Were you talking about me? My ears were burning.

JOHN: Patience, do you remember that cat you had when you were growing up?

PATIENCE: How could I forget Mousie?

JOHN: What happened to Mousie?

PATIENCE: I've told you. She was run over by a Good Humor truck.

JOHN: Do you remember how you felt?

PATIENCE: Like Camille.

JOHN: Because Mousie's death was a tragic thing.

PATIENCE: It was heartbreaking. That cat had a great life.

JOHN: And death is difficult to comprehend and somewhat painful.

PATIENCE: It sure was for Mousie. The poor thing was squished all over Wayside Lane.

CLEVELAND PLAY HOUSE—Robert Machray (Bender), Leon Addison Brown (Lumumba), Kay Walbye (Patience), David Atkins (Walter) and Richmond Hoxie (John) in a scene from Seth Greenland's *Jungle Rot*

JOHN: So you were sad?

PATIENCE: Well, of course I was. Johnny, what are you getting at?

JOHN: Miss Rendelbaker is ill.

PATIENCE: I'm sorry to hear that. Who is Miss Rendelbaker?

JOHN: She was supposed to play a key role in the operation.

PATIENCE: What are you going to do?

JOHN: I can't even tell you.

PATIENCE: Johnny, we've been married for fifteen years. You can tell me.

JOHN: That was my "little helper" on the phone. He wants to know if you'll take her place.

PATIENCE: Sure I will.

JOHN: Don't you want to know what you'll be doing?

PATIENCE: Tell me.

JOHN: He's going to want you to kiss Lumumba.

PATIENCE: Where?

JOHN: On the lips, I suspect.

PATIENCE: At the dinner party?

JOHN: That's right.

PATIENCE: He's a negro, isn't he?

JOHN: Yes. He is.

> *Patience turns away from her husband, and we see a frisson of excitement surreptiously play on her face. She then turns back to him.*

PATIENCE: If kissing a negro person on the lips is going to advance my husband's career and further the interests of my country, then, damn the torpedoes!

JOHN: I won't hold it against you if you refuse to take part.

PATIENCE: John, I said I'd do it.

JOHN: It's an extraordinary imposition, and this fruitcake's idea of coercing you into participating is extremely irregular.

PATIENCE: I don't mind. What the heck. When the Stillmans give a party, they pull out all the stops. You know, Johnny, when my mother was entertaining . . . and I can tell you, she knew how to do it . . . do you know what her motto was? Knock 'em dead!

JOHN: She'll be very proud.

PATIENCE: But I have a problem.

JOHN: I know. It's excruciating to live in a moral twilight where the difference between right and wrong is so vague.

PATIENCE: No, not that.

JOHN: What is it, then?

PATIENCE: I don't have anything to wear.

JOHN: How can you worry about your wardrobe when you're going to be kissing a man to death?

PATIENCE: What do you mean?

JOHN: He's going to give you tainted lipstick that will interact with the wine. For Mr. Lumumba, the combination will prove fatal.

PATIENCE: Really?

JOHN: You can change your mind. Personally, I find the whole business revolting.

PATIENCE: I'm an American, sweetheart. My lips belong to my country.

JOHN: That's very touching.

PATIENCE: He'll die?

JOHN: Irrevocably.

> *Lights shift and we see the three natives.*

PATIENCE: This is going to be some party.

Jungle Rot *was first produced at the Cleveland Play House January 17, 1995 under the direction of Roger T. Danforth.*

A DIRECTORY OF NEW-PLAY PREMISES PRODUCTIONS

○
○
○

Professional productions June 1, 1995–May 31, 1996 of new plays by leading companies around the United States who supplied information on casts and credits at Camille Dee's request, plus a few reported by other reliable sources, are listed here in alphabetical order of the locations of 66 producing organizations. Date given is opening date, included whenever such information was available. Most League of Resident Theaters (LORT) and other regularly-producing Equity groups were queried for this comprehensive Directory, and all ATCA-nominated productions which opened within the above time frame are included, with their citations noted. Theater companies not listed here either did not offer new or newly-revised scripts during the period under review or had not responded to our query by press time. Most productions listed below are world premieres; a few are American premieres, new revisions, second looks or scripts not previously reported in *Best Plays.*

Abingdon, Va.: Barter Theater

(Richard Rose artistic director; Pearl Hayter business manager)

THE TIE THAT BINDS. By Frank Lowe. April 18, 1996. Director, Richard Rose; scenery, Daniel Ettinger; costumes, Amanda Aldridge; lighting, John McLain; sound, Jakima King, Scott Koenig; original music, Scott Koenig.

The Family:
Sean Phelan .... Dan Ziskie
Joyce Phelan ....Lisa Bansavage
David Phelan ....Jordan Mott
John Phelan ....Jamie Bennett

Stonega Management and Families:
Richard Lacey .... William Langan
Frank Mullins .... Hardy Rawls
Lucille Mullins .... Katherine Levy
Peggy Mullins .... Jenny Maguire
United Mine Workers Staff:
Ben Myers ....Randall Rapstine
Miners and Families:
Al Pennington ....Mark Harris
Inez Pennington .... Jennifer Rau

Calvin Stallard ....Michael Rudko
Will Bledsoe ....Robert Anglin
Lester Callahan .... Michael Linstroth
Clara Figgins ....Charlotte Nolan
Place: Roda, a colliery in the mountains of southwestern Virginia. Act I: autumn 1937, summer months 1937. Act II: Summer/fall 1937, autumn 1937, winter 1943, autumn 1949, late autumn 1953.

THE ANGEL'S SHARE. By Joseph Kline. May 23, 1996. Director, Richard Rose; scenery, Crystal

Tiala; costumes, Amanda Aldridge; lighting, Richard Rose; music and sound, Scott Koenig.
One ....Randall Rapstine
Two ....Susanne Boulle
Three ....Victoria Boothby
Four ....John Hardy
Five ....Jay Apking
Place: The Institute for Plant Studies, Leningrad. Act I: August-December 1941. Act II: Winter 1942.

Ashland, Ore.: Oregon Shakespeare Festival

(Henry Woronicz, Libby Appel artistic directors)

MOLIERE PLAYS PARIS. By Molière; translated and contrived by Nagle Jackson. February 16, 1996. Director, James Edmondson; scenery, Michael Ganio; costumes, Deborah M. Dryden; lighting, Robert Peterson; music, Todd Barton.
The Illustrious Theater Company:
Molière (Jean-Baptiste Poquelin) .. Ray Porter
Béjart ....Sandy McCallum
Madeleine Béjart .... Kirsten Giroux
Armande Béjart ....Cindy Basco
La Grange ....Ted Deasy
Brécourt .... Robert Vincent Frank
De Croisy .... U. Jonathan Toppo
La Thorillière .... Derrick Lee Weeden
Gros-Rene .... David Kelly
Petit-Rene ....Jesse Petrick
Marquise-Thérèse Du Parc .... Cindy Lu
Beauval .... Steve Cardamone
Baron ....Karl Backus
The Court:
King Louis XIV ....Karl Backus
Herald .... Steve Cardamone
Alphonse ....Jesse Petrick
In The Love Doctor by Molière; Gorgibus—Béjart; Lucinda—Armande Béjart; Sabine—Madeleine Béjart; Valère—La Grange; Sganarelle—Molière; Dr. Toxin—La Thorillière; Dr.

Prophylactus—Brécourt; Dr. Mortice—Gros-Rene; Dr. Snot—De Croisy; Notary—Beauval.
In The Forced Marriage by Molière: Alcantor—Béjart; Dorimène—Armande Béjart; Page, Pancras—Gros-Rene; Lycaste—La Grange; Sganarelle—Molière; Geronimo—La Thorillière; Alcidas—Brécourt; Marphurias—De Croisy; La Comtesse—Madeleine Béjart.
Time: October 24, 1658. Place: Salle des Gardes of the old Louvre, Paris. One intermission.

STRINDBERG IN HOLLYWOOD. By Drury Pifer. February 25, 1996. Director, Pat Patton; scenery, William Bloodgood; costumes, Claudia Everett; lighting, Marcus Dilliard; music, Todd Barton; sound, Douglas K. Faerber.
August Strindberg .... Philip Davidson
Harriet Bosse .... Kirsten Giroux
Micki Kidde .... Karole Foreman
Otis De Marco .... Douglas Markkanen
One intermission.

Unstaged Readings:

FORDLANDIA. By Coleen Hubbard. March 15, 1996.
HITLER'S HEAD. By John Lee. March 29, 1996. Director of readings, Cynthia White.

Atlanta: Alliance Theater Company

(Kenny Leon artistic director; Edith H. Love managing director)

ONCE MORE WITH HART: THE MUSIC OF RODGERS AND HART. Musical revue conceived by David H. Bell. Music by Richard Rodgers; lyrics by Lorenz Hart. November 1, 1995. Director, David H. Bell; musical direction and arrangements, Christopher Cannon; scenery, Dex Edwards; costumes, Jeff Cone; lighting, Diane Ferry Williams.

With Christopher Cannon, Crystal R. Fox, Kurt Johns, Jeffrey Johnson, Heather McKenney.
Time: Just before 8 p.m., November 23, 1943. Place: A storage room/rehearsal hall/library owned by Rodgers and Hart, above Broadway.

THE ART OF SWINDLING. By Susana Tubert and Lorenzo Mans; translated and adapted from

OREGON SHAKESPEARE FESTIVAL, ASHLAND—Ray Porter (Sgana-relle), Cindy Basco (Dorimene) and David Kelly (Page) in *Molière Plays Paris*, translated and contrived by Nagle Jackson

Los Intereses Creados by Jacinto Benavente y Martinez. February 28, 1996. Director, Susana Tubert; music composed by Mauricio Beltran; lyrics by Lorenzo Mans; scenery, James Leonard Joy; costumes, Mariann Verheyen; lighting, Ann G. Wrightson; sound, Brian Kettler.

Harlequin .... Pedro Porro
Crispin .... Mauricio Bustamente
Leandro .... Brad Sherrill
Innkeeper; Risela .... Bill Murphey
Captain .... Peter Thomasson

Dona Sirena; Puppeteer .... Olivia Negron
Columbine .... Lisa Benavides
Silvia .... Elizabeth D. Wells
Polichinela .... Gonzalo Madurga
Judge .... Sharlene Ross

Time and place: A small town in provincial Spain in the 17th century where a troupe of actors is putting on a farce, *The Art of Swindling,* which takes place in a small town in provincial Spain. Act I, Scene 1: The town plaza. Scene 2: Dona Sirena's garden. Act II: A suite at the inn.

Baltimore: Center Stage

(Irene Lewis artistic director; Peter W. Culman managing director)

THE LOVER. By Elizabeth Egloff. February 16, 1996. Director, Irene Lewis; scenery, Christopher Barreca; costumes, Paul Tazewell; lighting, Pat Collins; sound, David Budries; fight consultant, J. Allen Suddeth.

Tanya .... Colleen Quinn
Nicholas Artyomevich Stahov .... James Noah
Pavel Yakovlevich Shubin .... William Youmans

Andrei Petrovich Bersyenev;
Rendic .... Jefferson Mays
Elena Nikolayevna Stahov .... Kali Rocha
Anna Vassilyevna Stahov .... Patricia Hodges
Dmitri Nikanorovich Insarov .... Reg Rogers
Landlady .... Colleen Quinn

Household Staff: Janel Bosies, Kathryn Falcone, Liam Hughes, Brad Reiss.

Time: March 1854, the eve of the Crimean War. Place: Moscow and Venice. Acts I and II: The family home of Elena Nikolayevna Stahov.

Coda: A hotel room in Venice, on the other side of the world.

Berkeley, Calif: Aurora Theater Company

(Barbara Oliver artistic director)

THE PANEL. By Dorothy Bryant. February 1, 1996. Director, Barbara Oliver; scenery and lighting, Rick Oliver; costumes, Cassandra Carpenter; sound, Matthew Spiro; fights, Joan Mankin.
Spirit of Simone Weil .... Lura Dolas

Marsha Lee .... Louahn Lowe
Prof. Nathan Schneider .... Allan Droyan
Sister Cecilia Vero .... Joan Mankin
William Bettencourt .... Terry Lamb
One intermission.

Berkeley, Calif.: Berkeley Repertory Theater

(Sharon Ott artistic director)

BALLAD OF YACHIYO. By Philip Kan Gotanda. November 8, 1995. Director, Sharon Ott; scenery, Loy Arcenas; costumes, Lydia Tanji; lighting, Peter Maradudin; music, Dan Kuramoto; sound, Stephen LeGrand; puppets, choreography, Bruce Schwartz; co-commissioned and co-produced with South Coast Repertory, Costa Mesa, Calif.
Yachiyo Matsumoto ....Sala Iwamatsu
Hiro Takamura ....Lane Nishikawa

Papa .... Sab Shimono
Mama ....Dian Kobayashi
Okusan ....Emily Kuroda
Willie Higa .... Greg Watanabe
Osugi Chong ....Annie Yee
    Koken, Puppeteers: Michelle Camaya, Si Hwa Noh, Tomomi Itakura.
    Time: 1919. Place: Kauai, Hawaiian Islands. One intermission.

Cambridge, Mass.: American Repertory Theater

(Robert Brustein artistic director; Robert J. Orchard managing director; Ron Daniels associate artistic director)

UBU ROCK. Musical based on Alfred Jarry's *Ubu Roi*; book by Shelley Berc and Andrei Belgrader; music and lyrics by Rusty Magee. June 7, 1995. Director, Andrei Belgrader; musical direction, Rusty Magee; scenery, Andrei Both; costumes, Catherine Zuber; lighting, John Ambrosone; sound, Christopher Walker.
Pa Ubu ....Charles Levin
Ma Ubu ....Francine Torres
Capt. Trash; Gen. Lasky .... Thomas Derrah
    Others: Kevin Waldron, Will LeBow, Adrianne Krstansky, Ajay Naidu, Scott Ripley, Kerri Aldrich, J.C. Mirad, Marni Ratner, Monique Wegele, John-Andrew Morrison.
    MUSICAL NUMBERS: "The Opening Song," "Get What You Want," "The Feast," "I'm Screwed," "Count of Sandomir," "We'll Kill Him Good," "My Son," "Song of the Ancestors," "I Am the Diktator," "We Love Pa Ubu," "Wrong Is Just the Same," "I Am Everything," "Song of

the Peasants," "The Rat Sarabande," "Let's Go to War," "Ubu Aria," "Ma Ubu Tango," "Button Song," "Limb Symphony," "Back Together Again," "Peasant Uprising," "A New Land Is Waiting."

ALICE IN BED. By Susan Sontag. April 14, 1996. Director, Bob McGrath; scenery, Laurie Olinder, Fred Teitz; costumes, Susan Anderson; lighting, John Ambrosone; sound, Christopher Walker; music, James Farmer; film, Bill Morrison.
Alice James .... Stephanie Roth
Nurse ....Steve Harper
Henry James .... Thomas Derrah
Father; Mother .... Will LeBow
Margaret Fuller ....Deborah Breitman
Emily Dickinson ....Blair Sams
Myrtha, Queen of the Wilis .... Erica Yoder
Kundry .... Kwana Martinez
    Others: Kevin Bergen, Brian Lamphier. No intermission.

Chicago: Court Theater

(Charles Newell artistic director; Sandra Karuschak managing director)

CELIMENE AND THE CARDINAL. Adapted by Ranjit Bolt from the play by Jacques Rampal. September 15, 1995. Director, Charles Newell; scenery and lighting, John Culbert; costumes, Nan Cibula-Jenkins.

Celimene ....Hollis Resnik
Alceste .... Kevin Gudahl
Time: 1686, twenty years after the events of *The Misanthrope.* Place: Celimene's house in Paris. No intermission.

KING HENRY IV: THE SHADOW OF SUCCESSION. By Charles Newell and David Bevington; adapted from *King Henry IV, Parts 1 and 2* by William Shakespeare. January 5, 1996. Director, Charles Newell; scenery and costumes, Anita Stewart; lighting, Marcus Dilliard.
The Court:

King Henry IV ....John Reeger
Prince Henry ....Raymond Fox
Nurse to King Henry ....Shannon Cochran
Prince John ....Shawn Douglass
Duke of Clarence ....Michael Cargill
Duke of Gloucester .... Doran Schrantz
Earl of Westmorland ....Kevin Gudahl
The Rebels:
Earl of Worcester .... Tony Dobrowolski
Earl of Northumberland ...... Wilson Cain III
Hotspur ....Josh Stamberg
The Douglas .... Ned Mochel

The Tavern:
Sir John Falstaff ....William Brown
Mistress Quickly ....Shannon Cochran
Peto ....Michael Cargill
Poins ....Shawn Douglass
Bardolph .... Wilson Cain III
Doll Tearsheet .... Doran Schrantz
Chief Justice ....Tony Dobrowolski
Pistol ....Josh Stamberg
Justice Shallow .... Kevin Gudahl

THE BARBER OF SEVILLE. New translation by Gilbert Pestureau and Anne Wakefield of the play by Pierre-Augustin Caron de Beaumarchais. March 13, 1996. Director, Charles Newell; scenery, Todd Rosenthal; costumes, Nan Zabriskie; lighting, John Culbert; composer and sound designer, Charles Berigan.

Figaro ....Diego Matamoros
Count Almaviva ....Byron Stewart
Rosine ....Kate Fry
Dr. Bartholo ....William Brown
Youthful; Notary ....Bradley Mott
Wakeful; Alcalde ....Chad Kelderman
Don Bazile ....Hollis Resnik
Time: Over the course of one day and night, 1775. Act I, Scene 1: Outside the house of Dr. Bartholo in Seville. Scene 2: Within Dr. Bartholo's home. Act II: Within Dr. Bartholo's home.

Chicago: Goodman Theater

(Robert Falls artistic director; Roche Schulfer executive director)

ANOTHER MIDSUMMER NIGHT. Musical with book and lyrics by Arthur Perlman; music by Jeffrey Lunden. June 26, 1995. Director, Michael Maggio; choreography, Danny Herman; musical direction, Bradley Vieth; scenery, Linda Buchanan; costumes, Catherine Zuber; lighting, Robert Christen; sound, Richard Woodbury; orchestrations, Bruce Coughlin; flying, Foy; video design, Christopher C. Derfler.

Larry .... Michael Rupert
Dan ....Jim Walton
Heather .... Kathleen Rowe McAllen
Helen ....Jessica Molaskey
Nicki Patos ....Hollis Resnik
Pete .... David Coronado
Fran ....Ora Jones
Reporter .... Robert D. Mammana
Puck .... Jim Corti
Cobweb ....Jennifer Rosin
Peaseblossom .... Lisa Menninger
Oberon; Director .... Nick Wyman

Titania; Actress ....Mary Ernster
Time: Today, a midsummer night. Place: A city park. One intermission.
MUSICAL NUMBERS: "Another Midsummer Night," "We Call on the Fairies," "Wake Up," "Aching," "Follow Me," "This Is Wrong," "Fairyland," "Lullaby," "It's Love—I Think," "The Music of Love," "What Fools They Be," "How Sweet Is the Taste of Revenge," "I Never Guessed," "Transform-ed," "What a Mess," "Everything's Changed," "A Midsummer Dream."

BLACK STAR LINE. By Charles Smith. January 22, 1996. Ditector, Tazewell Thompson; scenery, Joseph P. Tilford; costumes, Kay Kurta Silva; lighting. T.J. Gerckens; sound and music composition, Fabian Obispo.
Henrietta Vinton Davis;
Sarah ....Crystal Laws Green
Issac Allen; Willis .... Rick Worthy
Valet; Pres. Charles King .... Jacson Laroc

Valet; Ellis; Johnson ....Leonard Roberts
Maid; Anne .... Lynn M. House
Amy Ashwood .... Ora Jones
Cyril Briggs; Fight
    Captain .... A Benard Cummings
George Harris .... Ron Cephas Jones
John E. Nail; Rev. Easton .... Ernest Perry Jr.
Austin Norris; Simon;
    Edward Smith ....Paul Oakley Stovall
Steven Mare ....Craig Spidle
Jess Binga .... A.C. Smith
Mme. C.J. Walker .... Cheryl Lynn Bruce
John Abbott; Harry Daugherty; Pickens; Aide
    to Clarke; Jailer .... Dan Mooney
Marcus Mosiah Garvey ..Todd Anthony-Jackson
Amy Jacques .... Shanesia Davis
Emmett Scott ....Allan Louis
Aide to W.E.B. DuBois;
    Julius Clarke .... Lee Sellars
Gordon Phillips; J. Edgar
    Hoover ....Joe Van Slyke
W.E.B. DuBois .... Christopher B. Duncan
Jim Davis .... Tim Decker
    Roustabouts: Rick Worthy, Ernest Perry Jr.,
Christopher B. Duncan. Other Aides, Guards,
Nurses, etc.: Company.

Time: 1916–1940: Place, Act I: A rented ball-room in Harlem, a field in Sedalia, Miss., a hotel room, the office of W.E.B. DuBois, the UNIA office in Harlem, a Harlem street corner, the steps of the courthouse in Harlem, backstage at Madison Square Garden. Act II: A sugar plantation in Cuba, the UNIA office in Harlem, a hotel room in Niagara Falls, Briggs's apartment, the UNIA office in Harlem, the office of the FBI, the office of the Grand Imperial Wizard, Julius Clarke, a small room in Harlem, a jail cell, the train heading west.

Goodman Studio

UNJUSTIFIABLE ACTS. By Aaron Iverson. February 12, 1996. Director, Harry J. Lennix; scenery, Robert C. Martin; costumes, Laura Cunningham; lighting, Diane Ferry Williams; sound, Rob Milburn.
Reporter ....Rengin Altay
Police Captain .... Mart Wohlgenant
Rev. A.M. Powers ....Ellis Foster
James Lucas .... Tim Rhoze
Christine Vogel ....Amy Morton
Jack Boyle ....David New
Janet Wells .... Sylvia Carter
    One intermission.

Chicago: Lookingglass Theater Company

(Laura Eason artistic director; David Catlin managing director)

S/M: A DREAM BIOGRAPHY. By Mary Zimmerman; based on the lives and writings of the Marquis de Sade and Leopold von Sacher-Masoch. January 24, 1996. Director, Mary Zimmerman; scenery and lighting, John Culbert; costumes, Mara Blumenfeld; sound, Michael Bodeen; music, Michael Bodeen, Miriam Stern.
Gaufridy; Young Masoch .... Thomas J. Cox
Fanny von Pister; Rose Keller ......Joy Gregory
Sade's Father; Older Masoch .... David Kersnar
Stage Manager ....Jennifer Smith
Dolmance; Inspector Marais;
    Justine's Father ....Philip R. Smith

Eugenie; Juliette; Actual
    Wanda ....Heidi Stillman
Mme. de Montreuil ....Lisa Tejero
Sade's Mother; Sade's Wife;
    Laura de Sade ....Tracy Walsh
Abbe de Sade; Imaginary
    Wanda ....Margaret Werry
Sade .... Andrew White
Justine .... Meredith Zinner
    Others: The Company. No intermission.

Chicago: Next Theater

(Steve Pickering artistic director; Peter Rybolt managing director)

ALMOST BLUE. By Keith Reddin. September 19, 1995. Director, Steve Pickering; scenery, Rebecca Hamlin; costumes, Linda Roethke; lighting, Peter Gottlieb; sound, Phil Lavine.
Liz ....Soseh Kevorkian
Blue ....William J. Norris
Phil .... Thomas Kelly
Steve .... Michael Park Ingram
    No intermission.

LOSING FATHER'S BODY. By Constance Congdon. November 7, 1995. Director, Sarah

Tucker; scenery, Scott Cooper; costumes, Linda Roethke; lighting, Andrew Meyers; sound, Michael O'Toole.
Kim ....Marguerite Hammersley
Scott .... Tim Decker
Pauline .... Maureen Gallagher
Cecil; Dr. Ryan ....John Dunleavy
George .... G. Scott Thomas
Jerri; Felicia .... Susannah Kavanaugh
Dorothea .... Rosemary Rock
Clarence; Todd .... Dale Rivera

*Reflections of the Past
On Chicago Stages*

COURT THEATER—*Above*, William Brown (Falstaff), Raymond Fox (Prince Hal) and John Reeger (Henry IV) in *King Henry IV: The Shadow of Succession*, a new adaptation of Shakespeare

STEPPENWOLF THEATER COMPANY—*Below*, John Malkovich as John Wilmot, 2d Earl of Rochester, with Mariann Mayberry in *The Libertine* by Stephen Jeffreys

GOODMAN THEATER—Todd Anthony-Jackson as Marcus Garvey and Christopher B. Duncan as W.E.B. DuBois in a scene from *Black Star Line* by Charles Smith

Alice; Michelle .... Dado
One intermission.

YELLOW HEAT: VINCENT VAN GOGH IN ARLES. By Allan Bates. February 9, 1996. Director, Peter Rybolt.

Vincent Van Gogh .... Bruce Orendorf
Joseph Roulin .... Ralph Flores
Madame Ginoux .... Patti Hannon
Rachel .... Amy Landecker
Paul Gaugin .... Yasen Peyankov

Chicago: Steppenwolf Theater Company

(Randall Arney artistic director; Stephen Eich managing director)

AS I LAY DYING. Adapted by Frank Galati from the novel by William Faulkner. July 9, 1995. Director, Frank Galati; scenery and costumes, John Paoletti; lighting, James F. Ingalls; sound, Rob Milburn.

Addie .... Cynthia Baker
Jewel .... Ian Barford
Cash .... Christopher Bauer
Dr. Peabody .... Robert Breuler
Mrs. Armstid; Mrs. Bundren II .. Dana Eskelson
Armstid .... Neil Flynn
Cora Tull .... Marilyn Dodds Frank
Little John; Jody .... Pat Healy
Houston; Skeet MacGowen .... Steve Key
Vardaman .... Jay Kiecolt-Wahl
Dewey Dell .... Mariann Mayberry
Quick .... Bill McGough
Lafe .... Nick Offerman
Darl .... Jeff Perry
Eustace .... Robert Radkoff-Ek
Uncle Bill .... Michael Sassone
Vernon Tull .... Craig Spidle
Eula .... Heidi Stillman
Brother Whitfield .... Marc Vann
Anse .... Will Zahr
Time: July 1929. Place: Rural Mississippi. One intermission.

THE LIBERTINE. By Stephen Jeffreys. February 25, 1996 (American premiere). Director, Terry Johnson; scenery, Derek McLane; costumes, Virgil C. Johnson; lighting, Kevin Rigdon; sound, Richard Woodbury; musical coordination, Bradley Vieth; choreography, Bea Rashid; fights, Robin McFarquhar.

John Wilmot (2d Earl of
Rochester) .... John Malkovich
George Etherege; Jacob
Huysmans .... Alan Wilder
Charles Sackville .... Marc Vann

Billy Downs .... Steve Key
Jane .... Mariann Mayberry
Mrs. Will Ufton .... Lisa Nicholls
Tom Alcock .... Ian Barford
Elizabeth Barry .... Martha Plimpton
Harry Harris .... Si Osborne
Molly Luscombe .... Carole Gutierrez
Elizabeth Malet .... Missi Pyle
Charles II .... Francis Guinan
Staff .... Christopher Hainsworth
Pike .... Pat Healy
Others: Playgoers, Whores, Clients, Guards.
Act I, Scene 1: Will's Coffee House, 1675, morning. Scene 2: Dorset Gardens Theater, the same day. Scene 3: St. James's Park, the next morning. Scene 4: Dorset Gardens Theater, that afternoon. Scene 5: Dog and Bitch Yard, that night. Scene 6: Rochester's London home, the next day. Scene 7: Whitehall Gardens, that night. Act II, Scene 8: Windsor Great Park, 1676. Scene 9: Epsom, the next day. Scene 10: The East End of London, a few weeks later. Scene 11: Dorset Gardens Theater, several weeks later. Scene 12: Adderbury, a few days later.

SUPPLE IN COMBAT. By Alexandra Gersten. May 19, 1996. Director, Max Meyer; scenery, Narelle Sissons; costumes, Laura Cunningham; lighting, Kevin Rigdon; sound, Rob Milburn, Michael Bodeen.

Teresa .... Martha Lavey
Bill .... John Mahoney
Ma .... Linda Stephens
Tony .... Ron Dean
Waiter .... David Alan Novak

New Plays Lab Staged Readings:

NETHERBONES. By Adam Rapp.
GIVEN FISH. By Melissa James Gibson.
LOCK DOWN HOME. By Daniel J. Rubin.

Chicago: Victory Gardens Theater

(Dennis Zacek artistic director; John Walker managing director)

WITH AND WITHOUT. By Jeffrey Sweet. November 10, 1995. Director, Sandy Shinner; scenery, Bill Bartelt; costumes, Margaret Morettini; lighting, Chris Phillips; sound, Galen G. Ramsey.

Jill .... Annabel Armour
Mark .... James Sherman
Shelly .... Linnea Todd
Glen .... Marc Vann

Time: The present, summer. Place: On a deck at a country cottage overlooking a lake. One intermission. Nominated for the ATCA Award.

UNMERCIFUL GOOD FORTUNE. By Edwin Sanchez. January 19, 1996. Co-produced with Northlight Theater, Evanston, Ill. and AT&T Onstage; see its listing in the Northlight entry in this section.

LEMUEL. By Lonnie Carter. April 25, 1996. Director, Dennis Zacek; scenery, Nic Dimond; costumes, Serena Zahnke; lighting, Andrew Meyers; original music, Michael Keck, Andre De Shields;

additional music and musical direction, Andre Pluess, Ben Sussman.

Cast: Jelly Belly, Lemuel Louis Gulliver, Ee-pop Shazzaji—E. Milton Wheeler; Papa, Noodles, Java, Adolphus Savage—Carl Barnett; Pee Wee, Brother Sorat, RFK/MJK, Willie Morton—Sephus Booker; Big Mamy Ruth Booth, Eunice Beecher, Policeman in Miranda Rights, Authorine—Felicia Ann Bradley; Mr. Johansson, Father John Millington Synge, Robert Fitzgerald Kennedy, Jim E. Ray—Alan Kopischke; Mama, Ingrid, J. Wyatt—Audrey Morgan; Melanctha Volontiers, Ee-mom Shazzaji, Stateless Person—Lisa Tejero; Manny Saperstein Sr., Cab Driver, August—Jordan Teplitz; Esther Fein, Barbara, Policeman in Miranda Rights—Sarah Willis.

Time: 1942–1983. Place: Chicago and elsewhere. The play was presented in two parts.

Cincinnati: Cincinnati Playhouse in the Park

(Edward Stern producing artistic director)

AN ASIAN JOCKEY IN OUR MIDST. By Carter W. Lewis. January 11, 1996. Director, Brian Kulick; scenery and costumes, Mark Wendland; lighting, Kevin Adams; sound, David B. Smith.
Nathan Timmons; Yoshio
Nokumura .... Daryl Edwards

Alice Timmons; Junko
Nokumura .... Pamela Isaacs
Cody; Haiku Nokumura .... Kaipo Schwab
Grady Tayler; Ichitaro Yamamoto ......Ray Xifo
One intermission.

Cleveland: Cleveland Play House

(Peter Hackett artistic director; Dean Gladden managing director)

THE ENCHANTED MAZE. By Murphy Guyer. January 23, 1996. Director, Peter Hackett; scenery, costumes and lighting, Pavel Dobrusky; sound, Robin Heath.
Old Man ....Donald Christopher
Avery Adamson ....Perry Laylon Ojeda
Kingsley Commoner .... Murphy Guyer
Gus Woolly .... Mike Hartman
Danger ....Rainee Day of Winston
Sincerity McLavish .... Kay Walbye

Atticus Garrett .... Donald Berman
Marion Kind .... Rebecca Waxman
Leander Plummet .... Michael Connor
Gladys Doomcracker .... Nancy Franklin
Little Girl .... Allana Janell Romansky
Little Boy .... John R. Magaro
Victor Boson ....Donald Christopher
Berkeley Malison .... Evan Thompson
Time: A beautiful spring day. Place: The Enchanted Maze. One intermission.

Cleveland: Great Lakes Theater Festival

(Gerald Freedman artistic director; Anne B. DesRosiers managing director)

THE DYBBUK. By S. Ansky; new adaptation by Gerald Freedman. February 9, 1996. Director, Gerald Freedman; choreography, Mauricio Wainrot; scenery, John Ezell; costumes, Barbara Kessler; lighting, Mary Jo Dondlinger; score devised by Gerald Freedman; additional music, John Morris; sound, Tom Mardikes.
Channon ....Michael Berresse
Hennakh; Mikhol .... Danny Gurwin

Asher; Martyred Bridegroom .....Mark Tomasic
Messenger .... John Buck Jr.
Meyer .... Reuben Silver
Leye .... Nina Goldman
Frade .... Dorothy Silver
Gittel ....Amy Tarachow
Elderly Woman .... Evangelia Constantakos
Reb Sender ....John LaGioia
1st Batlon; Reb Mendel ....Richard Lear

2d Batlon ...........................O.V. Vargas
3d Batlon; Nakhman; Spirit of
    Nissen ....Daniel Pardo
Martyred Bride ....Anita Intrieri
Menashe ....Alex Lubliner
Reb Azrielke ....Max Jacobs
Reb Shimshon ....Jonathan Brody
    Ensemble: Jeanette L. Buell, Susana Weingar-

ten De Evert, Dennis Johnston, Edwina King, Daniel Wright.

Time and place: What is really happening, and what is imagined or hallucinatory, or taking place in another reality, is ambiguous. Act I, Scene 1: An old synagogue with blackened walls. Scene 2: A public square of Brinnits, between the old synagogue and Sender's house.

Costa Mesa, Calif.: South Coast Repertory

(David Emmes producing artistic director; Martin Benson artistic director; Paula Tomei managing director)

Mainstage

SHE STOOPS TO FOLLY. By Tom Murphy. September 1, 1995. Director, Barbara Damashek; scenery, Ralph Funicello; costumes, Shigeru Yaji; lighting, Peter Maradudin; incidental music and sound, Nathan Birnbaum; songs, Barbara Damashek; choreography, Sylvia C. Turner.
Vicar ....Jim Norton
Mrs. Primrose ....Jane Carr
George ....Scott Denny
Olivia ....Devon Raymond
Sophy .... Jennifer Parsons
Moses .... Christopher DuVal
Dick ....Aaron Cohen, Anthony Petrozzi
Bill ....Andrew Wood, Jason Lau
Mr. Burchill .... Richard Doyle
Mr. Thornhill .... Douglas Sills
Rev. Jenks ....Ron Boussom
Maid; Landlady; Lady Blarney .....Lynne Griffin
Miss Wilmot; Mrs. Skeggs ....Emily Chase
Rev. Wilmot; Flamborough; Gaoler ..Don Took
Landlord; Butler .... Art Koustik
Timothy Baxter ....Todd Fuessel
    Time: 18th century England. Place: A debtor's prison. One intermission.
    MUSICAL NUMBERS: "Toorrallee" lyrics by Tom Murphy; "Death and the Lady" music and lyrics traditional; other lyrics from the poetry of Oliver Goldsmith.

BALLAD OF YACHIYO. By Philip Kan Gotanda. January 5, 1996. Co-commissioned and co-produced with Berkeley, Calif Repertory Theater; see its entry in the Berkeley listing.

Second Stage

THE THINGS YOU DON'T KNOW. By David Hollander. September 19, 1996. Director, Martin Benson; scenery, John Iacovelli; costumes, Todd Roehrman; lighting, Paulie Jenkins; sound, Garth Hemphill.
Annie ....Fran Bennett
Louis .... Tom Chick
Andrew; Eric; Rev. Worth; Policeman;
    Waiter; Bus Driver .... Michael McFall

Louis age 12 ....Jonathan Hunt Ficcadenti,
                                    Alexander Knox
Dan ....Hal Landon Jr.
Phyliss .... Julie Fulton
    Time: The present and nine years ago. Place: Pittsburgh, Pa. One intermission.

THE INTERROGATION OF NATHAN HALE (By Capt. John Montresor of HRM Expeditionary Forces). By David Stanley Ford. October 31, 1995. Director, Diane Wynter; scenery, Cliff Faulkner; costumes, Julie Keen; lighting, Anne Militello; sound, Garth Hemphill; fight direction, Christopher Duval.
Capt. John Montresor .... Richard Doyle
Capt. Nathan Hale .... Matt Keeslar
Sergeant .... Ron Rapp
    Time: The morning of September 2, 1776. Place: The tent of Capt. John Montresor. No intermission.

A MESS OF PLAYS BY CHRIS DURANG. By Christopher Durang. April 23, 1996. Director, David Chambers; scenery, Michael C. Smith; costumes, Todd Roehrman; lighting, Tom Ruzika; sound and video design, Garth Hemphill; video sequences conceived by David Chambers and Christopher Durang.
    With Robert Patrick Benedict, Amanda Carlin, Hal Landon Jr., Howard Shangraw, Jodi Thelen.
    One intermission.

NewSCRipts Readings:

THREE DAYS OF RAIN. By Richard Greenberg. October 23, 1995. Director, Evan Yiannulis.
COLLECTED STORIES. By Donald Margulies. December 11, 1995. Director, Lisa Peterson.
CRUMBS FROM THE TABLE OF JOY. By Lynn Nottage. February 5, 1996. Director, Seret Scott.
EDEN. By Jennifer Maisel. April 15, 1996. Director, Bill Rauch.
BIG HUNK O' BURNING LOVE. By Prince Gomolvilas. May 13, 1996. Director, Timothy Douglas.

Dallas: Dallas Theater Center

(Richard Hamburger artistic director; Robert Yesselman managing director)

THE UNMENTIONABLES and THE SNOB. By Carl Sternheim; new adaptation by Melissa Cooper, Paul Lampert and Kate Sullivan of the translation by Paul Lampert and Kate Sullivan. January 16, 1996. Director, Richard Hamburger; scenery, Christopher Barreca; costumes, Katherine B. Roth; lighting, Mark L. McCullough; sound, Bruce A. Richardson.

The Unmentionables

Ted Mask .... Norman Browning
Louise Mask ....Jurian Hughes
Trudy Wink .... Charis Leos
Monsieur Scarron ....Reno Roop
Mr. Mandelstam .... Bruce DuBose
   Time: The 1950s. Place: Ted & Louise's house

in Levittown, Long Island. Scene 1: Friday afternoon. Scene 2: The next day. Scene 3: That evening. Scene 4: The following afternoon.

The Snob

Christian Mask, Son of Ted
   & Louise .... David Manis
Sybil Husk .... Leslie Hendrix
Ted Mask .... Norman Browning
Louise Mask ....Jurian Hughes
Adirondack Lodge Van
   Morgan III ....Joan Buddenhagen
Trudy Wink .... Charis Leos
   Time: The 1980s. Place: Christian Mask's apartment in Manhattan. Scene 1: One morning. Scene 2: Two years later. Scene 3: A year later.

Denver: The Changing Scene

(Al Brooks and Maxine Munt executive producers)

*Summerplay X Program of One-acts,
July 20–30, 1995*

DOG STAR. By Werner Trieshmann. Director, Trace Oakley.
Shep ....Kelly Koreau
Skip .... Jordan Sher
Franz .... Kent Shelton
THE HALLS OF MENTAL SCIENCE. By Moss Kaplan. Director, Patricia Madsen.
Josh .... Josh Hartwell
Martin ....Nicholas Martinez
Louise .... Betsy Grisard
Addy ....David Miller
FATHER, SON AND TRINITY SITE. By James B. Hemesath. Director, Jeremy Cole.
Dad .... Michael Katt
John .... Adam DeChar
   Scenery, Kent Shelton; lighting, Eric Bruce; music and sound, Chuck Rhodes. One intermission.

A PICNIC IN THE GARDEN. By Trista Conger. October 5, 1995. Director, Jeff Pavek; scenery, Dana Seymour; costumes coordinated by Patricia Robertson; lighting, Michael Bybee.
Stagehand (Spirit of
   Bob Dylan) ....Robert Hainline
Thomas Merton at 53 ....George Berlin
Thomas Merton at 20 ... Matthew Boylan Smith
Thomas Merton at 9 ....Alex Horne,
                                   Hunter Combs
Grace ....Lynn Hamilton, Ali Frick
Carrie .... Carol Anne Lopez
Sister Mark; Ann ..Becky Peters, Hunter Combs

Bill .... Charles Kocher
   One intermission.

AMERICAN STANDARD. By Kevin Barry. November 22, 1995. Director, Trace Oakley; scenery, Denis Horvath; costumes, Patricia Robertson; lighting, Jeremy Cole.
Sam ....Art Ecoff
Edie .... Betsy Grisard
Richie .... Matthew Boylan Smith
Mona .... Amber Leigh Florest
Mrs. Rocket .... Sandra Shipley
Mr. Putnam ....Arthur Payton
   Time: Christmas Eve. Place: Queens. One intermission.

*Colorado Quickies III: Ten-minute Plays
January 18, 1996*

THE FORGOTTON ONE. Written and directed by Pat Gabidge.
Jasper Whitney ....Wade P. Wood
Charlie Biggs .... Antoinette LeCouteur
WAITING TO WIN. Written and directed by Mark Ogle.
Hal .... Michael Katt
Ruth ....Cynthia A. Voigt
Laura .... Jennifer Tawse
BRIGHT RED PARADIGM SHIFT. Written and directed by D.J. Jones.
Nick .... Carl Kline
Angela .... Antoinette LeCouteur
Erica .... Mary Ann Amari
Bradley ....Mark Cecelones
THE CURSE OF MUMBO JUMBO. Written and directed by Steve Hunter.

Professor Harrison ....James O'Leary
Mumbo ....Rebecca Lloyd
Polk ....Penny Quinn
THE BOOBY PRIZE. Written and directed by
Wesley Webb.
Mr. Y ....Michael Katt
Bobby ....Christopher Berliner
Mr. X ....Jeff Miller
CAGED. Written and directed by Jeannene L.
Bybee.
Woman ....Jennifer Tawse
LIVER FOR DINNER. Written and directed by
Tami Canaday.
Frank ....Steven Divide
Gabby ....Mary Ann Amari
Cousin Samantha ....Monica Schuster
A VIEW FROM THE ROOM. Written and di-
rected by Ken Crost.
Alan ....Jeff Miller
Margaret ....Mary Valenti
ASSORTED ENDINGS TO AN UNWRITTEN
PLAY. Written and directed by Leroy Leonard.
Stacy ....Luanne Nunes
Charles ....Christopher Berliner

Scenery and lightning, Michael A. Bybee. One
intermission.

CHEAP SKY. By Gary Guillot. February 15,
1996. Director, Edward Osborn; production de-
sign, Dennis Bontems; lighting and sound, Katrina
Geesaman; produced in collaboration with the
Community College of Denver Theater.
Janet ....Lynn Drebes
Mike ....Zeke Bielby
Arthur ....David M. Payne
No intermission.

VIEWS OF THE LION. By Larry Loebell. March
7, 1996. Director, Patricia Anne Madsen; scenic
artists, Eric Bien, Tom Jones; costumes, Trina Es-
campia; lighting, Lisa Kurtz; sound, Chuck
Rhodes.
David Williamson ....Gary Cupp
Reese ....Tony Accetta
Helen Williamson ....Cynthia Ergenbright
Annie Williamson ....Monica Schuster
Act I: Williamson's club, mid-afternoon. Act
II: Williamson's den, that evening. Act III: Wil-
liamson's den, the next morning. One intermission
between Acts II and III.

Denver: Denver Center Theater Company

(Donovan Marley, artistic director)

BEETHOVEN 'N' PIERROT. Conceived and
written by Pavel Dobrusky and Pere-Olav Soren-
son. November 30, 1995. Directors and designers,
Pavel Dobrusky and Pere-Olav Sorenson; music
adapted, arranged or composed by Larry Delin-
ger; choreography, Leslie Watanabe; sound, Jason
F. Roberts.
Napoleon Bonaparte ....Taro Alexander
Josephine Brunsvik ......Jacqueline Antaramian
Beethoven's Mother; Empress ...Yolande Bavan
Pierrot ....Bill Bowers
Mephisto ....Mark Boyett
Princess of Austria;
    Dancer ....Paula Leggett Chase
Alabaster Princess ....Stephanie Cozart
Anton; Dancer ....Carl J. Danielson
Bettina Brentano ....Sally Groth
Therese Brunsvik; Dancer ......Sharahn La Rue
Ludwig van Beethoven ....Anthony Powell
Countess Maria Erdody ....Luan Schooler
Emperor ....William Whitehead
Marionettist (Karl, Beethoven's
    Nephew) ....Vit Horejz
    Ensemble: Rolls Andre, Peter J. Crosby, Elsie
Ly Escobar, Michael Porter, Christa Scott-Reed,
Peter Starrett.
No intermission.

APPALACHIAN STRINGS. Musical by Randal
Myler and Dan Wheetman; includes authentic

songs and stories from the people of Appalachia.
May 2, 1996. Director, Randal Myler; choreogra-
phy, Suzanne Girardot; scenery, Andrew V. Ye-
lusich; costumes, Patricia A. Whitelock; lighting,
Michael Gilliam; sound, David R. White.
    With Molly Andrews, Kathleen M. Brady,
Dale Dickey, Suzanne Girardot, Tony Marcus,
L.J. Slavin, Archie Smith, Dan Wheetman.
    One intermission.

PRELUDE TO LIME CREEK. Devised by Anthony Zerbe; excerpts from novel and poem by
Joe Henry; songs by Joe Henry and Gary Burr.
May 9, 1996. Director, Anthony Zerbe; scenery,
Bill Curley; costumes, Patricia A. Whitelock; lighting, Charles R. MacLeod; sound, Jason F. Roberts;
produced in association with Poetry in Motion.
    With Anthony Zerbe, Greg Barnhill.
    One intermission.

Staged Readings:

LOS VIAJES DE LOS ANGELES (The Jour-
neys of the Angels). By Roy Conboy. November
8, 1995. Director, Tom Szentgyorgyi.
AXIS SALLY'S LAST BROADCAST. By Nagle
Jackson. February 9, 1996. Director, Nagle Jackson.
THE WOLF. By Ferenc Molnar; translated by
Andrew S. George and Tom Szentgyorgyi. February 16, 1996. Director, Tom Szentgyorgyi.

East Farmingdale, N.Y.: Arena Players

(Frederic De Feis producer/director)

THE BROTHER AND WEINBERG. By William Missouri Downs. February 15, 1996. Director, Frederic De Feis; designer technician, Fred Sprauer; costumes, Lois Lockwood.

Arlen Weinberg ....Stephen T. Wangner
Iranola Aldridge ....Ron Stroman
    Act I: Noon—a hot June day. Act II: The action is continuous.

East Haddam, Conn: Goodspeed Opera House

(Michael P. Price executive director)

Goodspeed-at-Chester Productions:

(Sue Frost associate producer; Warren Pincus casting director; Michael O'Flaherty resident music director)

THE GIG. Musical based on the motion picture by Frank D. Gilroy; book, music and lyrics by Douglas J. Cohen. August 10, 1995. Director, Victoria Bussert; choreography, Daniel Stewart; musical direction, David Evans; scenery, James Morgan; costumes, Tom Reiter; lighting, Mary Jo Dondlinger; orchestrations, Michael Gibson.

Marty .... William Parry
Jack ....James Judy
Georgie; Vince Amati ....David Brummel
Aaron ....Stuart Zagnit
Gil .... Charles Pistone
Arthur .... Michael McCormick
Marshall ....Don Mayo
Abe Mitgang .... Stephen Berger
Donna ....Alison Bevan
Lucy .... Donna English
Ricki Valentine .... Ilene Kristen
    Time: August 1982. Place: New York and the Catskills.

MUSICAL NUMBERS, ACT I: Opening Sequence, "Farewell Mere Existence, Hello Jazz" (original piano arrangement by Robert Elhai), "Four Hours Away From Paradise/Time Out," "Departures," "A Real Nice Trip—Part I," "A Real Nice Trip—Part II," "Play Nice," "Drifting," "Benny Goodman," "Drifting" (Reprise). ACT II: "Biff-Bam-Bang!" (original piano arrangement by Robert Elhai), "Beautiful," "Beautiful" (Reprise), "Ricki Is Back in Town!", "Time to Put the Toys Away," "Choices," "I Can't Live Without Your Horn," "Biff-Bam-Bang!" (Reprise).

SILVER DOLLAR. Musical with book and lyrics by Mary Bracken Phillips; music by Jack Murphy. November 2, 1995. Director, John Shuck; choreography, Karen Azenberg; musical direction, Paul Ascenzo; scenery, Peter Harrison; costumes, Charlotte Yetman; lighting, Victor En Yu Tan; sound, Jay Hilton; orchestrations, Kim Scharnberg.

    Cast: Elizabeth Bonduel McCourt "Baby

Doe" Tabor—Elizabeth Richmond; 1st Man, Harvey Doe, Riche, Waiter, Reporter/Photographer, Henry—Jeff Gurner; Augusta Pierce Tabor—Mary Bracken Phillips; Mr. Doe, Mr. Pierce, Jake Sands, Father Chapelle, Doctor—Bob Freschi; Mr. McCourt, Hook, William Jennings Bryan—Nick Jolley; Peter McCourt, Uncle Dave, Jason—Don Stephenson; Horace Austin Warner Tabor—George Ball; Bill Bush—Tom Demenkoff.

    Townsmen, Prospectors, Miners, Restaurant Patrons, Bellhops, Footmen, Friends, Priests, Con Men, Moving Men, etc.: Bob Freschi, Jeff Gurner, Nick Jolley, Don Stephenson.

    Time: September 18, 1935. Place: "Baby Doe" Tabor's cabin atop the Matchless Mine in Leadville, Colo.

    MUSICAL NUMBERS, ACT I: "Hole in the Ground," "Demon on the Ice," "Whirling and Whirling/More Than a Prayer," "Way Out There," "Ordinary Days," "Way With Numbers," "More Than a Prayer" (Reprise), "Silver Queen," "Be Careful," "Love in the Shadows/Never Mind," "Silver Queen Rag," "Closeness," "Hell to Pay." ACT II: "The Wedding of the Century," "The Carriage Race," "Mea Culpa/Kyrie," "Take the Money and Run," "Words to Learn," "Love Turns," "Love Turns" (two Reprises), "Silver Dollar."

BATTLE CRY OF FREEDOM. Musical conceived and dramatized by Jack Kyrieleison; music by various authors (see listing below). May 16, 1996. Director, Ron Holgate; musical staging, Karen Azenberg; musical direction, Jay Atwood; scenery, Peter Harrison; costumes, Jane Finnell; lighting, Donald Holder; musical supervision and vocal arrangements, Michael O'Flaherty; orchestrations, Andrew Wilder; sound, Jay Hilton.
Mr. Hawk's Company:
Cassie Drumwright ....Sheryl McCallum
Harry Hawk .... Gary Marachek
Hannibal Drumwright ....James Stovall

GOODSPEED AT CHESTER—Elizabeth Richmond as Baby Doe and George Ball as Horace Tabor in the Mary Bracken Phillips-Jack Murphy musical *Silver Dollar*

Augustin Lovecraft ....David Eric
Cordelia Hopewell ...Donna Lynne Champlin
Tom Trudgett ....Michael Moore
Time: 1880. Place: A theater.

MUSICAL NUMBERS, ACT I: "Link o' Day" (traditional), "Ring de Banjo" (by Stephen Foster), "The Liberty Ball/Lincoln and Liberty" (words, Jesse Hutchinson, music, traditional), "High-Toned Southern Gentleman" (words, anonymous, music, traditional); "May God Save the Union" (words, Rev. G. Douglass Brewerton, music, Carl Wolfsohn), "Abraham's Daughter" (by Septimus Winner), "Home, Sweet Home" (by Henry R. Bishop), "Marching Along" (by William B. Bradbury), "Oh Comrades, Fill No Glass for Me" (by Stephen Foster), "All Quiet on the Potomac" (words, Ethel L. Beers, music, John Hill Hewitt), "We'll Fight for Uncle Abe" (words, C.E. Pratt, music, Frederick Buckley), "Better Times Are Coming" (by Stephen Foster), "We Are Coming, Father Ab'ram" (words, James Sloan Gibbons, music, L.O. Emerson) "Wake Nicodemus" (by Henry Clay Work), "Pat Murphy of the Irish Brigade" (anonymous), "Marching Along" (Reprise), "O, Wasn't Dat a Wide River" (traditional), "Battle Cry of Freedom" (by George F. Root), "Heav'n Bound Soldier" (traditional).

ACT II: "Der Deitcher's Dog" (by Septimus Winner), "John Brown's Body" (traditional), "Somebody's Darling" (words, Marie Ravenal de la Coste, music, John Hill Hewitt), "Grafted into the Army" (by Henry Clay Work), "Weeping Sad and Lonely" (words, Charles C. Sawyer, music, Henry Tucker), "Tenting on the Old Camp Ground" (by Walter Kittredge), "McClellan Is the Man" (by Will Shakespeare Hays), "Marching Through Georgia" (by Henry Clay Work), "Beautiful Dreamer" (by Stephen Foster), "Steal Away" (traditional), "Hard Times Come Again No More" (by Stephen Foster).

Evanston, Ill: Northlight Theater

(Russell Vandenbroucke artistic director; Richard Friedman managing director)

UNMERCIFUL GOOD FORTUNE. By Edwin Sanchez. January 19, 1996. Director, Susana Tubert; scenery, Mary Griswold; costumes, Claudia Boddy; lighting, Todd Hensley; sound and original music, Lindsay Jones; co-produced with Victory Gardens Theater, Chicago, and AT&T Onstage.

Fatima Garcia	Denise Casano
Maritza Cruz	Sol Miranda
Pito	Ernesto Gasco
Luz	Carmen Roman
Paul Leslie	Jim Catafio
Jeremy Kirkwood	Clifton Williams
Prison Guard	Bob Bills

Time: The present. Place: The Bronx, N.Y. One intermission.

MARK TWAIN AND THE LAUGHING RIVER. Musical with book, music and lyrics by Jim Post. February 28, 1996. Director, Brian Russell; scenery, Stephen R. White; costumes, Dawn Dewitt; lighting, B. Emil Boulos; sound, Bruce Holland.

Mark Twain	Jim Post

Guitar, banjo, fiddle—Jenny Armstrong; piano, guitar, bass, accordion—Luke Nelson.

MUSICAL NUMBERS, ACT I: "Mighty Big River," "Uncle John's Farm," "Steamboats A-Comin'," "Hannibal," "The Cat in the Box," "Huckleberry Finn." ACT II: "Naked Little Boy," "Riverboat Honeymoon," "Steal Away/Swing Low, Sweet Chariot," "Elegy," "Riverboat Man," "Mighty Big River" (Reprise).

Gloucester, Mass.: Gloucester Stage Company

(Israel Horovitz artistic director)

BARKING SHARKS. By Israel Horovitz. August 20, 1995. Director, Michael Allosso; scenery, Charles F. Morgan; costumes, Jane Alois Stein; lighting, John Ambrosone; sound, Jeff Benish.

With Richard McElvain, Joseph McIntyre, Ja-

mey Dereshinsky, Jennifer Brule, Ted Kazanoff, Jane Nichols, Dori May Kelly, John Fiore, Mick Verga.

One intermission.

Hartford, Conn.: Hartford Stage

(Mark Lamos artistic director; Stephen J. Albert managing director)

I AIN'T YO' UNCLE: THE NEW JACK REVISIONIST UNCLE TOM'S CABIN. By Robert Alexander. November 17, 1995. Director, Reggie Montgomery; scenery, Edward Burbridge; costumes, Karen Perry; lighting, Donald Holder; mask and puppet design, Barbara Pollitt; music, Alva Nelson; choreography, Leslie Arlette Boyce.

George Harris	Sam Wellington
Topsy; Aunt Chloe; Mann	Michele Morgan
Eliza; Young Shelby	Simi Junior
Harriet Beecher Stowe; Marks;	
Miss Ophelia	Marylouise Burke
Uncle Tom	Byron Utley
Shelby; Jane; Skeggs; Dream Chloe;	
Sambo	Jesse L. Martin
Haley; Simon Legree	Edward J. Hyland
Phineas; Marie St. Clare;	
Cassy	Kena Tangi Dorsey
Loker; Augustine St. Clare	Mace Perlman
Little Eva; Emmaline	Kristin Flanders
Heavy G	Alva Nelson

Musicians: Alva Nelson keyboard, percussion; Kwe Yao Agyapon percussion.

One intermission.

GHOSTS. By Henrik Ibsen; new translation by Gerry Bamman and Irene B. Berman. March 29, 1996, Director, Mark Lamos; scenery, Chris Barreca; costumes, Susan Hilferty; lighting, Chris Akerlind; sound, David Budries.

Engstrand	Robert Breuler
Mrs. Alving	Kathleen Chalfant
Pastor Manders	Richard Easton
Regina	Fiona Gallagher
Osvald	Ian Kahn

Kansas City, Mo.: Unicorn Theater

(Cynthia Levin producing artistic director; Atif Rome artistic director)

JACK AND JILL GO UP THE HILL. By Jane Martin. June 7, 1995. Director, Cynthia Levin; scenery and costumes, Atif Rome; lighting, Art Kent; sound, Roger Stoddard.

Jack .... William Harper
Jill .... Cheryl Weaver
    Dressers: Sarah Jane Barnum, Milly Hands, John P. Mulvey, Emmie Hsu.
    One intermission. Also see its listing in the Louisville entry in this section.

ARMS AND LEGS. By Ron Simonian. October 25, 1995. Director, Julie Nessen; scenery, Jarrett S. Bertoncin; costumes, Tina Brodeur; lighting, Victor En Yu Tan; sound, Roger Stoddard.

Dad .... Phil Fiorini
Mom; Prosecutor .... Jan Rogge
Bobby .... Matt Rapport
Grandma; *Variety* Reporter .... Nora Denney
Parker .... Terry O'Reagan
Flavia .... Celia Grinwald
Grandpa; Doctor; Senator, etc. .... Rick Truman
Bernie; Interviewer;
    Reporter, etc. .... Daniel Ruch
Announcer's Voice .... Walter Coppage
    One intermission.

La Jolla, Calif: La Jolla Playhouse

(Michael Greif artistic director; Terrence Dwyer managing director)

AN ALMOST HOLY PICTURE. Solo performance by David Morse; written by Heather McDonald. September 12, 1995. Director, Michael Mayer; scenery, Michelle Riel; costumes, Norah L. Switzer; lighting, Kevin Adams; sound and original music, Mitchell Greenhill.

Samuel Gentle .... David Morse
    Time: The present. Place: The grounds of a cathedral and other places. Part 1: Sighs too Deep for Words. Part 2: The Grace of Daily Obligation. Part 3: An Almost Holy Picture. Part 4: The Garden in Winter. One intermission. Nominated for the ATCA Award.

FAUST. Musical with book, music and lyrics by Randy Newman. September 19, 1995. Director, Michael Greif; choreography, Lynne Taylor-Corbett; musical direction, Joseph Church; scenery, James Youmans; costumes, Mark Wendland; lighting, Christopher Akerlind; sound, Steve Canyon Kennedy; orchestrations, Michael Roth; projections, Alex W. Papalexis.

The Lord .... Ken Page
The Devil .... David Garrison
Henry Faust .... Kurt Deutsch
Margaret .... Bellamy Young
Martha .... Sherie Rene Scott
Angel Rick .... Christopher Sieber
    Others: Brian Evers, Melissa Jones, Lindsay Marie Sablan, Michael Hune, Daphne Rubin-Vega, Michael Potts, Andre Carthen, Jonathan Brody, Erin Hill, Henry Aronson, Joshua W. Coleman, H. Clent Bowers, Shelley Dickinson, Melissa Haizlip, Marissa Perez.
    MUSICAL NUMBERS: "Pass on Over/Glory Train," "Can't Keep a Good Man Down," "Each Perfect Day," "Best Little Girl," "Bless the Children of the World," "Little Island," "Eastertime," "March of the Protestants," "The Man," "Lovetime," "Relax, Enjoy Yourself," "When Love Is in the Air," "Gainesville," "How Great Our Lord," "Life Has Been Good to Me," "My Hero," "It Was Beautiful," "Hard Currency," "Feels Like Home," "Bleeding All Over the Place," "Sandman's Coming."

Lansing, Mich: BoarsHead Michigan Public Theater

(John Peakes artistic director)

Staged Readings:

THE OYSTER BED. By Kate Hawley. October 14, 1995.

SOLIDARITY. By Gus Kaikkonen. April 24, 1996.

Little Rock: Arkansas Repertory Theater

(Cliff Fannin Baker producing artistic director)

Second Stage

LEE ROY AND DONNA AND THE BIG GRANDADDY. By Byron Tidwell. November 9, 1995. Director, Brad Mooy; scenery, Tom Kagy; costumes, Verda Davenport; lighting, Danny Brissey; sound, Jon K. Keck.

Denise .... Fran Austin
Allison .... Angel Bailey
Donna ....Sandy Baskin
Sean Michael .... David Holt
Lamar ....Luke Kramer

Lee Roy ....John Potter
    Time: The present. Place: Humidity, Alabama. One intermission.

A WOMAN'S KNEES. Compiled and adapted from writings of various authors by Sarah Frey and Brad Mooy. January 11, 1996. Director, Brad Mooy; scenery, Tom Kagy; costumes, Don Bolinger; lighting, Lisa Katz; sound, Jon K. Keck.

Second Stage Staged Reading:

DEL RAY'S NEW MOON. By Charles Portis. April 18, 1996.

Los Angeles: East West Players

(Tim Dang artistic director)

TWELF NITE O WHATEVA! Adapted by James Grant Benton from *Twelfth Night, or What You Will* by William Shakespeare. June 2, 1995. Director, Brian Nelson; choreography, Keali'i Ceballos; scenery, Patrick Plamondon; costumes, Ken Takemoto; lighting, Frank McKown.

Prince Amalu .... Jim Ishida
Kawika .... Kipp Shiotani
Alika; Kohala ....Donald Sager
Lahela ....Jennifer Fujii
Fisherman ....Jack Newalu
Kukana ....Janice Terukina
Count Opu-Nui .... Benjamin Lum
Sir Andrew Waha .... Radmar Agana Jao
Lope .... Casey Kono
Princess Mahealani .... Kellye Nakahara
Malolio ....Alberto Isaac

Koa ....Jack Newalu
Loka .... Shaun Shimoda
Kahuna ....Ken Takemoto
Musician ....Tim "Kimokeo" Holtwick
    Time: A while back, brah. Place: O'ahu, da kine like 'Ewa side, eh?

WHITELANDS. Trilogy by Chay Yew: Part I, *Porcelain*, March 16, 1996; Part II, *A Language of Their Own*, March 16, 1996; Part III, *Half Lives*, March 14, 1996, presented in repertory. Director, Tim Dang.

    With Tsai Chin, John Cho, Art Desliyo, Tom Donaldson, Tom Jameson, Radmar Agana Jao, Dana Lee, Alec Mapa, Phil Oakley, Steve Park, William Peden, Joanne Saketa, Ben Shepard, Eric Steinberg, Thomas Weber.

Los Angeles: L.A. Theater Works

(Susan Albert Loewenberg producing director; Gale Cohen managing director)

Live Radio Theater Series

BOGAAZAN! THE CHILD ON THE BATTLESHIP YAMATO. By Akira Hayasaka; translated by Ichiko Flynn and Robert Solomon. June 28, 1995. Director, Mako; music by Raymon Guarna.

    With June Angela, Francois Chau, Shizuko Hoshi, Jim Ishida, Dana Lee, James Saito, Shaun Shimoda, B.D. Wong, Keone Young.

MURDER IN THE FIRST. By Dan Gordon. July 12, 1995. Director, Steve Albrezzi.

    With Edward Asner, Kate Asner, David Birney, Ron Byron, William Frankfather, Arye Gross, Andrew Hawkes, Cynthia Mace, Eric Poppick, John Randolph, Gil Segel, Bill Smitrovich.

THIS TOWN. By Sidney Blumenthal. October 11, 1995. Director, Ron West; music by Ray Guarna.

    With Gerrit Graham, Richard Kind, Jane Lanier, David Lewman, Joe Liss, Gates McFadden, Paul Mercier, John Randolph, John Vickery, Alan Wilder.

ON LOS ANGELES STAGES—*Above*, Anna Gunn, Richard Libertini and David Margulies in *Hysteria* by Terry Johnson at the Mark Taper Forum; *right*, Edward Asner and Ron West in Mark Harris's *The Southpaw*, adapted by Eric Simonson, at L.A. Theater Works

THE SOUTHPAW. By Mark Harris; adapted by Eric Simonson. November 28, 1995. Director, Eric Simonson.

With Edward Asner, Kate Asner, Earl Brown, Evan Gore, Henry Harris, Armando Ortega, Amy Pietz, Tom Virtue, Ron West, Rugg Williams, Eric Winzenreid.

MIMI'S GUIDE. By Doris Baizley. March 6, 1996. Director, Belita Moreno; original music by Ray Guarna.

With Powers Boothe, Frances Conroy, Ping Wu.

Los Angeles: Mark Taper Forum

(Gordon Davidson artistic director; Charles Dillingham managing director; Robert Egan producing director)

HYSTERIA. By Terry Johnson. July 16, 1995. Director, Phyllida Lloyd; scenery and costumes, Mark Thompson; lighting, Chris Parry; sound, Jon Gottlieb; original music, Karl Fredrik Lundeberg.

Sigmund Freud	David Margulies
Jessica	Anna Gunn
Abraham Yahuda	Kenneth Mars
Salvador Dali	Richard Libertini

Others: Jack Axelrod, Fiona Hale, BobbyRuth Mann, Kenneth Mars, Liann Pattison, Marra Racz, Katherine Talent. Voice of Anna Freud: Liann Pattison.

Time: 1938. Place: London. One intermission.

Taper Lab 1995–96
New Work Festival Workshops:

A PREFACE TO THE ALIEN GARDEN. By Robert Alexander. October 28, 1995. Director, L. Kenneth Richardson.

G Roc	Dwayne L. Barnes
Candi	Natalie Venetia Belcon
Ice Pick	Kevin Hunter
Slick Rick	Monte Russell
Crazy Mike	Cedrick Terrell
Lisa Body	Bahni Turpin
Sheila	Persia White
B Dog	Troy Winbush

Time: The present. Place: A crack house in the middle of America's heartland. One intermission.

PLAY OF FATHER AND JUNIOR. Written, directed and performed by Han Ong. October 30, 1995.

No intermission.

THE SEDUCTIONS OF JOHNNY DIEGO. By Guillermo Reyes. November 8, 1995. Director, Tony Plana.

Johnny Diego	David Barrera
Mrs. Zeveda	Bibi Besch
Bonita Zeveda	Maria Canals
Arnie Zeveda	Ronald Garcia
Teresa Zeveda	Ruth Livier
Luis	William Marquez
Jake Sanders	David Watts

Act I, Scene 1: East L.A., kitchen of the Zeveda home, 1967. Scene 2: Hollywood, kitchen of the new Zeveda home, 1968. Act II, Scene 1: Same as Act I. Scene 2: 1970.

FISHES. By Diana Son. November 11, 1995. Director, Jessica Kubzansky.

Mom	Tsai Chin
Lionel	Alan Mozes
Junebug	Sandra Oh
Amelia	Alina Phelan
Pop	Winston J. Rocha

Act I: The Mom and Pop Pet Store. Act II: The Mom and Pop Pet Store eight years later.

MULES. By Winsome Pinnock. November 15, 1995. Director, Lisa Peterson.

Allie; Lyla	Patrice Pitman Quinn
Lou; Olu; Sammie	Bahni Turpin
Bridie; Rose; Piglet	Sharon Washington

Time: The present. Place: In and around London, and Jamaica's trench town. One intermission.

YOUNG VALIANT. By Oliver Mayer. November 18, 1995. Director, Robert Egan.

Dad	Stephen Macht
Mama	Ada Maris
Boy	Mario Rendon Jr.

No intermission.

INSURRECTION: HOLDING HISTORY. By Robert O'Hara. December 9, 1995. Director, Timothy Douglas.

Ron	Demitri Corbin
T.J.	Gregory Wallace
Mutha Wit; Mutha	Juanita Jennings
Gertha; Clerk Wife; Mistress Mo'tel	Cleo King
Octavia; Katie Lynn	Kimberleigh Aarn
Nat Turner; Ova' Seea' Jones	Ellis E. Williams
Clerk Son; Izzie Mae; Sheriff	Regina Byrd Smith
Reporter; Cop; Clerk Husband; Buck Naked; Detective	Edward Nattenberg
Hammet	Robert Barry Fleming

Time: Now and then. Place: Here and there. One intermission.

THE BALLAD OF GINGER ESPARZA. By Diane Rodriguez and Luis Alfaro. December 13, 1995. Music written and performed by Maria Fatal.

No intermission.

THE MYSTERIOUS MRS. NIXON. By Donald Freed. December 13, 1995. Director, Robert Egan; performed by Salome Jens.

Time: After the fall, midnight. Place: Richard M. Nixon's study. No intermission.

THE LAST SURVIVOR. By Eleanor Reissa. December 16, 1995. Director, Gordon Davidson.

The Man; Grandfather ....Mike Nussbaum
Daughter .... Dinah Manoff
The Man's Father; The Man's Brother; Last
  Survivor ....Nehemiah Persoff
The Man's Brother; Translator; Cousin;
  Thom ....Joel Polis
The Man's Mother; Lover; Daughter-in-Law;
  Mindy .... Susan Merson
The Man (Young); Boy; Bill .... Mark Arnott
Man's Brother; Boy (Young) .... Max Casella

Dr. Wrightson; Office Man .... Nick Ullett
One intermission.

Taper Lab 1995–96
New Work Festival Readings:

THE JOY OF GOING SOMEWHERE DEFINITE. By Quincy Long. October 29, 1995. Director, Lisa Peterson.

THE SONG OF GRENDELYN. By Russell Davis. October 30, 1995. Director, Corey Madden.

THE MAGIC FIRE. By Lillian Garrett-Groag. December 1, 1995. Director, Lillian Garrett-Groag.

THE ROSENBERG JUDGE. By Wendy R. Leibowitz. December 2, 1995. Director, Corey Madden.

TONGUE OF A BIRD. By Ellen McLaughlin. December 3, 1995. Director, Lisa Peterson.

THE HUNGRY WOMAN: A MEXICAN MEDEA. By Cherrie Moraga. December 3, 1995. Director, Lisa Wolpe.

Louisville: Actors Theater of Louisville

(Jon Jory producing director)

20th Humana Festival of New American Plays
February 27-April 6, 1996

ONE FLEA SPARE. By Naomi Wallace. February 27, 1996. Director, Dominic Dromgoole.

Morse .... Erin F. Joslyn
Bunce .... Richard Thompson
Mr. William Snelgrave ....William McNulty
Mrs. Darcy Snelgrave .... Peggy Cowles
Kabe .... Fred Major
  Time: 1665. Place: A comfortable house in Axe Yard, off King Street, Westminster, in London. One intermission.

MISSING MARISA and KISSING CHRISTINE (one-acts). By John Patrick Shanley. March 2, 1996. Director, Douglas Hughes.
Missing Marisa
Terry .... Christopher Evan Welch
Eli ....Daniel Oreskes
  Time: End of day, some daylight, some twilight. Place: Eli's kitchen.
Kissing Christine
Larry .... Christopher Evan Welch
Christine ....Laura Hughes
Server .... Elaine C. Bell
  Time: The present. Place: A Thai restaurant.

THE BATTING CAGE. By Joan Ackermann. March 6, 1996. Director, Lisa Peterson.
Julianna ....Veanne Cox
Wilson .... Babo Harrison
Bobby .... Justin Hagan

Peg ....Carol Morley
  Time: The present. Place: A Holiday Inn hotel room in St. Augustine, Florida. One intermission.

CHILEAN HOLIDAY. By Guillermo Reyes. March 10, 1996. Director, Lillian Garrett-Groag.
Digna ....Isabel Keating
Cecilia .... Rose Portillo
Don Pablo ....Bob Burrus
Lautaro .... Bobby Canavale
Dona Conchita .... Divina Cook
Dona Irma .... Suzan Mikiel
  Time: Prologue, September 11, 1973; rest of play, two years later. Place: The patio of a small house in the working class district of Conchali in Santiago, Chile. One intermission.

JACK AND JILL. By Jane Martin. March 14, 1996. Director, Jon Jory.
Jack ....John Leonard Thompson
Jill .... Pamela Stewart
  Changers: David A. Baecker, Elizabeth Dwyer, Heather LaFace, Sean McNall.
  Time: The present. One intermission. Also see its listing in the Kansas City entry in this section.

FLESH AND BLOOD. By Elizabeth Dewberry. March 17, 1996. Director, Mark Brokaw.
Charlotte ....Karen Grassle
Dorris .... Adale O'Brien
Judd ....V Craig Heidenreich
Crystal ....Liann Pattison
  Place: Dorris's backyard, kitchen and den

somewhere in the present-day suburban South. One intermission.

GOING, GOING, GONE. Conceived by Anne Bogart; created by the Saratoga International Theater Institute. March 20, 1996. Director, Anne Bogart; assistant director, Devorah Herbert.
Woman .... Ellen Lauren
Man .... Tom Nelis
Guests ..... Karenjune Sanchez, Stephen Webber
No intermission.

Humana Festival Designers: Scenery, Paul Owen; costumes, Nanzi Adzima, Jeanette deJong, Kevin R. Mcleod; lighting, T.J. Gerckens, Mimi Jordan Sherin; sound, Michael Rasbury, Martin R. Desjardins, Darron L. West.

Ten-Minute Plays, March 29 & 31, 1996:

TRYING TO FIND CHINATOWN. By David Henry Hwang. Director, Paul McCrane; original violin music, Derek Reeves.
Benjamin .... Richard Thompson
Ronnie .... Zar Acayan
Time: The present. Place: A street corner on the Lower East Side, New York City.

WHAT I MEANT WAS. By Craig Lucas. Director, Jon Jory.
Fritzie .... Allen Jeffrey Rein
J. Fred .... Bob Burrus
Helen .... Peggy Cowles
Nana .... Adale O'Brien
Time: 1968. Place: A dinner table in Columbia, Maryland.

REVERSE TRANSCRIPTION. By Tony Kushner. Director, Tony Kushner.
Hautflote .... John Leonard Thompson
Aspera .... Jennifer Hubbard
Biff .... Christopher Evan Welch
Happy .... Daniel Oreskes
Ottoline .... Fanni Green
Flatty .... Fred Major
Time: In December, near midnight. Place: A cemetery on Abel's Hill, Martha's Vineyard.

CONTRACT WITH JACKIE. By Jimmy Breslin. Director, Frazier W. Marsh.
Jackie .... Divina Cook
Newt .... William McNulty
Time: 1980. Place: A hospital room in Atlanta.

Madison, N.J.: Playwrights Theater of New Jersey

(John Pietrowski producing artistic director; Buzz McLaughlin founding director)

GENESIS and MARK'S GOSPEL. Solo performance by Max McLean of Bible stories adapted by Max McLean; *Genesis* co-adapted by Buzz McLaughlin. November 30, 1995. Director, John Pietrowski.

Workshop Productions:

I SEE MY BONES. By Kitty Chen. September 28, 1995. Director, John Pietrowski.
Peter Kuo .... Les J.N. Mau
Cynthia Potts .... Peg Small
Anna Perkins .... Georgia Southcotte
Helen Buckler .... Virginia Downing
Time: The present, spanning about a year. Place: Far View Village, a total-care community for the elderly. One intermission.

SISTER CALLING MY NAME. By Buzz McLaughlin. May 2, 1996. Director, John Pietrowski.
Michael .... Timothy Wahrer
Sister Anne .... Ann Kittredge
Lindsey .... Bethany Larson
Time: The present, various times in the past and out of time altogether. Place: Sisters of Mercy's home for women, a private institution for the developmentally disabled in Fairmont. Minn. and

various other places in the minds of the characters.

THE LOWER CORTEX. By Robert Clyman. May 4, 1996. Director, Joseph Megel.
Tom .... Chris Clavelli
Summerlin .... Greg Zerkle
Jen .... Kristina Lear
Act I: The present, midday, an office of the psychology department of a university. Act II: One year later, evening, a small drawbridge over a river.

Designers: scenery, Rod Kadri, Bruce Goodrich; costumes, Bruce Goodrich; lighting, Christopher Gorzelnik.

Concert & Staged Readings:

THUNDER KNOCKING ON THE DOOR. By Keith Glover. August 1995.
AN ASIAN JOCKEY IN OUR MIDST. By Carter W. Lewis. September 15, 1995.
THE SECRET WIFE. By Y York. October 20, 1995.
TAR RIVER LOVE STORY. By Jett Parsley. November 10, 1995.
THE SEDUCTIONS OF JOHNNY DIEGO. By Guillermo Reyes. April 5, 1996.

Madison, Wis.: Broom Street Theater

(Joel Gersmann artistic director)

UNPLUGGED: THE KURT COBAIN STORY. By Paul Wells. June 9, 1995. Director, Paul Wells; scenery, Richard Swaback; lighting, Scooter.

Cast: Kurt Cobain—Scott M. Christensen; Mourner, Lumberjack, Aunt Mary, Billy, Stoner, Cheerleader, Prairie's Mom, School Administrator, Tracy, Amanda Jones, MTV Stage Manager, Lynn Hirschberg—Jessica Callahan; Roger, Dave Grohl, Drummer—Dunes; Wendy Cobain, Cheerleader, Tad's Stomach, Axl Rose—Pamela Jahn; Cheerleader, Courtney Love—Amanda Jones; Mourner, Uncle Chuck, Buzz Osbourne, Bob, Gary Gersh—Paul Kreitz; SPIN Reporter, Don Cobain, Henry Rollins, Jonathan Poneman, Tad, Sam Bayer—Matthew P. Poulson; Mourner, Relative, Howie, Stoner, Matt, Rikki Rachtman, Eddie Vedder, Coffehouse Waiter—Eric Premeau; Electrician, Lumberjack, Doctor, Pat, Chris Novoselic—Pete J. Selbo; Andy, Butch Vig—Scooter; Mourner, Lumberjack, Aunt Sally, Flight Attendant, Cheerleader, Silent Stoner, Lorelei, Employer, Jenny, Nurse, MTV VJ—Amy Solberg.

Musicians—Paul Kreitz, Dunes, Pete J. Selbo.

Time: The 1960s, 70s, 80s and 90s. Place: Aberdeen, Wash.; the Pacific Northwest; both coasts; Europe. One intermission.

BUCK MULLIGAN'S REVENGE. By Marty Mulhern. September 15, 1995. Director, Marty Mulhern; scenery, Mike Matheson, Joey Cammerano; lighting, Frank Furillo.

The Mulligans:

Gramps	Phil Strowman
Aunt Philomena	Siobhan Edge
Buck	Callen Harty
Caroline	Carie Novitzke
Maurice	Pete J. Selbo
Maggie	Maureen Grogan
Joseph Patrick	Bob Moccero
Joseph Michael	Adam Seeger
Sadie	Sarah Austin
Shane	Ben Mayo Mulhern

The Quigleys:

Ian	Mark J. Peters
Maud	Marcy Weiland
Ronan	Buck Hakes
Cromwell	Jesse Lyne
Vincent	Brad DeLange
Rose	Jennie Capellaro
Grandpapa; Seamus O'Rourke	D.W. Wanberg

Musicians: Tommy Dean fiddle, guitar; Jan Ingram guitar, recorder; Bob Wolske tin whistle.

Time and place: Three years in modern-day Westport, Ireland. One intermission.

THE ABORTIONIST: THE STORY OF A WOMAN AGAINST THE LAW. Adapted by Joel Gersmann from the biography of Ruth Barnett by Rickie Solinger. November 10, 1995. Director, Joel Gersmann; scenery, Richard Swaback; costumes, Carie Novitzke; lighting, D. W. Wanberg; sound, Richard Vorndran.

Cast: Jesus, Dirk Smith, Bill Holbrook, Dr. Clegg, Bartender, Maude Van Alstyme, Supreme Court Justice 1, Bob the Cop, John Tull, Dr. K.C. Bagby—Nate Beyer; Frank Converse, Miss Allen, The Tull Boy—Steve Carstensen; Ned Grange, Don Rogers, Arnold, Dr. Ed Stewart, Hank the Cop, Joseph, Carl Budd Scott, Dr. James Jordan, Ralph, Dr. Sam Norris, Supreme Court Justice 2—Jeff Ferguson; William Steele, Betsy, Evil Abortionist, Estelle, The Scott Girl—David Gapen; Dr. William Pancoast, Dr. Alys Bixby Griff, Rex Rankin, Ed, Film Narrator, Deputy Sheriff Darryl Howard—Callen Harty; Marshall Banks, Ruth Barnett, Supreme Court Justice 3, Kathy Tull—Shelley Johnson; Virgin Mary, Maggie Barnett, Suzanne Tyler, Mrs. Connie Scott, Mrs. Debra Stone—Clare Mayo Sorman; Abel Stone, Dr. George Watts, Old Zero, Leo Levenson, Judge John Grossett; A Baby—Joe Wiener; Shelley Duvall, Peter Fields, Dr. Marie Equi, Dorothy Taylor, Judge, John E. Sampson—Brian Wild.

Time: 1884–1995. Place: Portland, Ore. and the West Coast. One intermission.

Miami, Fla.: Coconut Grove Playhouse

(Arnold Mittelman producing artistic director)

Encore Room Theater

MAMA'S LAST WALTZ. By Rafael V. Blanco. December 1, 1995. Director, Rafael V. Blanco; scenery, Stephen M. Lambert; costumes, Ellis Tillman; lighting, David Goodman.

Lucy	Eleanor Garth
Amanda	Judith Delgado
Bea	Elayne Wilks
Father Valladares	Tyrone Tait Murphy
Elena	Yolandi Hughes

Time: The present. Place: The living room of a modest, well-kept home in an old section of Miami. Act I, Scene 1: A Sunday morning early in the month of May. Scene 2: Monday. Scene 3:

Tuesday. Act II, Scene 1: The last Monday in May. Scene 2: The following weekend.

MARJORY. Solo performance by Joan Turner; written by Evelyn Wilde Mayerson. February 23, 1996. Director, Gail Garrisan; scenery, Stephen M.

Lambert; costumes, Ellis Tillman; lighting, Todd Wren.

Marjory .... Joan Turner
Time: A span of eight weeks during 1979. Place: Coconut Grove, Florida. One intermission.

Milford, N.H.: American Stage Festival

(Matthew Parent producing director; David Henderson general manager)

ALICE REVISITED. Musical conceived by Joan Micklin Silver and Julianne Boyd; music and lyrics by various authors (see listing below); includes material from A . . . My Name Is Alice and A . . . My Name Is Still Alice. August 17, 1995. Director, Julianne Boyd; choreography, Hope Clarke; musical direction, Joel Framm; scenery, Jim Noone; costumes, Kim Krumm Sorenson; lighting, Dennis Parichy; sound, Phil Cassidy; co-produced by Barrington Stage Company and the Foxborough Regional Center for the Performing Arts.

With Barbara Walsh, Heather Mac Rae, Cheryl Howard, Gwen Stewart, Marguerite McIntyre.

SCENES AND MUSICAL NUMBERS: ACT I—"All Girl Band" (music by Doug Katsaros, lyrics by David Zippel); A . . . My Name Is Alice Poems by Marta Kaufman and David Crane; "At My Age" (music by Glen Roven, lyrics by June Siegel); "Trash" (music by Michael Skloff, lyrics by Marta Kaufman and David Crane); For Women Only Poems by Marta Kaufman and David Crane; "Sensitive New Age Guys" (music and lyrics by Christine Lavin and John Gorka); "Welcome to Kindergarten, Mrs. Johnson" (music by Michael Skloff, lyrics by Marta Kaufman and David Crane); "I Sure Like the Boys" (music by Lucy Simon, lyrics by Steve Tesich); Demigod by Richard LaGravanese; "Watching All the Pretty Young

Men" (music by Lucy Simon, lyrics by Susan Birkenhead); Ida Mae Cole Takes a Stand by Lynn Nottage; "The Portrait" (music and lyrics by Amanda McBroom); "I'm Bluer Than You" (music by David Evans, lyrics by Winnie Holzman).

ACT II: "Painted Ladies" (sketch, music and lyrics by Douglas Bornstein and Denis Markell); Nonbridaled Passion by Kate Shein; "Wheels" (music and lyrics by Amanda McBroom); "The French Monologue and Song" (monologue by Art Murray, music and lyrics by Don Tucker); Hot Lunch by Anne Meara; A Lovely Little Life by Steve Tesich; "Once and Only Thing" (music and lyrics by Michael John LaChiusa); "Honeypot" (sketch and lyrics by Mark Saltzman, music by Stephen Lawrence); "Friends" (music by David Mettee, lyrics by Georgia Holoff); "Lifelines" (music by Carolyn Sloan, lyrics by Marion Adler).

Early Stages Readings:

THE VEIL. By Henry Slesar. July 1, 1995.
THE WELL FRONT—THE STORY OF TUCK. By Paul Mroczka. July 15, 1995.
SUMMER FEET HEARTS. By Lynn Martin. July 29, 1995.
BAILEY. By Larry Maness. August 19, 1995.
AMICI CURIAE. By Steven P. Bann. August 26, 1995.

Millburn, N.J.: Paper Mill Playhouse

(Robert Johanson artistic director)

COMFORTABLE SHOES. Musical with book by Clint Holmes; music and lyrics by Clint Holmes and Nelson Kole. February 14, 1996. Director, Robert Johanson; musical direction, Nelson Kole; choreography, John Carrafa; scenery, Michael

Anania; costumes, Gregg Barnes; lighting, Tim Hunter.

With Clint Holmes, La Chanze, Nancy Ringham, Adam Wade, Scott Irby-Ranniar.

Milwaukee: Milwaukee Repertory Theater

(Joseph L. Hanreddy artistic director; Dan Fallon managing director)

SILENCE. Adapted by Stephen Dietz from the novel by Shusaku Endo. September 10, 1995. Directors, Joseph Hanreddy, Ganshi Murata; scenery and lighting, E. Kent Dorsey; costumes,

Kiichi Arai; sound, Rob Milburn, Shiro Yamakita; music, Toru Ueda; co-produced with the Subaru Acting Company.

Kichijiro ....Ryuji Mizuno
Inoue ....Hiroyuki Nishimoto
Interpreter ....Yukihiro Yoshida
Mokichi ....Yuichi Nakamura
Monica ....Shinobu Sato
Ichizo ....Yoshiyuki Kaneko
Guard; Sailor ....Ren Iwamatsu

Concubine; Prisoner ....Chiaki Nemoto
Rodrigues .... Lee E. Ernst
Garrpe ....Torrey Hanson
Valignano ....Peter Silbert
Ferreira ....Marco Baricelli
Acolyte .... Matt Penn
No intermission.

Minneapolis: Cricket Theater

(William Partlan artistic director)

WHAT'S THE MATTER WITH MOLLY? By
Nancy Bagshaw-Reasoner; September 20, 1995.
Director, Nancy Bagshaw-Reasoner; scenery,
Steve Krahnke; costumes, Bill Ingram; lighting,
Paul Epton; sound, Craig Schumacher.
Redhat .... Camilla D'Ambrose
Davis .... Gretchen Douma
Kim .... Lia Rivamonte
Cassandra ....Susan Fuller
Mrs. Darrell ....Shirley Venard
Chris ....Grant Richey
Russ ....Jay Reilly

One intermission.

SECOND-STORY MAN. By Richard Strand.
November 1, 1995. Director, William Partlan;
scenery, Kirby Moore; costumes, Kathleen Egan;
lighting, Michael Burgoyne; sound, Michael Cro-
swell.
Alex .... Christopher Bloch
Kate .... Cathy Anastasion
Ellen .... Mary Grant
Mary ....Heidi Ricks
No intermission.

Minneapolis: Tyrone Guthrie Theater

(Garland Wright artistic director; Edward A. Martenson executive director)

K: IMPRESSIONS OF THE TRIAL. Adapted by
Garland Wright from Franz Kafka's novel The
Trial. September 26, 1995. Director, Garland
Wright; scenery, Garland Wright; costumes, Susan
Hilferty; lighting, Marcus Dilliard.
    With Christopher Bayes, Nathaniel Fuller,
June Gibbons, Richard S. Iglewski, Charles Jan-
asz, Isabell Monk, Richard Ooms, Stephen Pelin-
ski, Brenda Wehle, Sally Wingert, Stephen
Yoakam.
    One intermission.

BABES IN ARMS. Musical with original book by
Lorenz Hart; new book by Ken LaZebnik; music
by Richard Rodgers; lyrics by Lorenz Hart. Feb-
ruary 15, 1996. Director, Garland Wright; musical
direction, David Bishop; choreography, Liza Gen-
naro; scenery, John Arnone; costumes, Susan Hil-
ferty; lighting, Howell Binkley; sound, Stephen L.
Bennett.
Billy Valentine ....James Ludwig
Bobbie McGuire ....Erin Dilly
Gus Fielding ....Kevin Kahoon
Sally Jones ....Kristin Chenoweth
Henry Hunnicut ....Harold Cromer
Baby Lou ....Sandrea Bianchi
Pocket ....Marshall L. Davis Jr.
Molly ....Aussa Kramer

Millie .... Heidi Kramer
Bo; Policeman ....Tif Luckenbill
Doc ....Eric Millegan
Linka ....Kiki Moritsugu
Kiko ....David Norona
Pinky ....Max Perlman
Peter; Grocer .... Thom Christopher Warren
Harry; Mr. Happy Feet ......John Paul Gamoke
Francois; Mr. Zitz ....Wayne Meledandri
Frederick Morgan; Mr.
    Goldwyn ....Jay Hornbacher
Tess .... Laura Kirkeby
Josh ....Devin Malone
Posy ....Pamela McMoore
P.J. ....Kevin Redmon
Violet ....Ellyn A. Wright
Wealthy Woman; Radio
    Announcer ....Laurel Lynn Collins
Maid .... Regina Ahlgren
Magician .... Tony Vierling
Comedian ....John Soroka
    Harmonaires: Michael Matthew Ferrell, John
Soroka, Tony Vierling. Chorines: Regina Ahlgren,
Shari Berkowitz, Myra Browning, Laurel Lynn
Collins. Pedestrians, Photographers, Others: Rob-
ert Bruce-Brake, Robert W. DeMars, Elizabeth
Erickson, Delta Rae Giordano, Ryan Goodell,
Bettina Gronning, Christopher Heineman, Nan

Langevin, Patricia Nieman, Surya J. Pierce, Jennifer Tillson, Jennifer Weston.

Time: 1938. Place: New York City. Act I, Scene 1: The streets near Broadway. Scene 2: A deserted alleyway. Scene 3: The stage of an old vaudeville theater. Scene 4: Frederick Morgan's office. Scene 5: The theater. Scene 6: Another part of the theater. Scene 7: The alley by the stage door. Scene 8: A street. Scene 9: The theater, onstage. Act II, Scene 1: The theater, two days before opening. Scene 2: The theater, final dress rehearsal. Scene 3: Baby Lou's dressing room. Scene 4: Another part of the theater. Scene 5: A corner of the theater, day before opening. Scene 6: A street, opening day. Scene 7: Dressing room, half hour before opening night curtain. Scene 8: The theater, onstage, curtain time. Scene 9: Backstage, opening night. Scene 10: Onstage, opening night. Scene 11: The theater, the wings and onstage, opening night.

Montgomery: Alabama Shakespeare Festival

(Kent Thompson artistic director)

THE MOVING OF LILLA BARTON. By John MacNicholas. November 24, 1995. Director, Susan Willis; scenery, Robert James Stapley; costumes, Mark Hughes; lighting, Michael Rourke; sound, Kirsten R. Kuipers.

Lilla Barton .... Anne Swift

Bishop Harold Clarke ....Roger Forbes
Luwanna Harp ....Rose Stockton
Jonas Mabry .... Barry Boys
Matt Parker ....Greg Thornton
Sheriff Jackson Tate .... Raphael Nash
    One intermission.

New Brunswick, N.J.: George Street Playhouse

(Gregory S. Hurst producing artistic director; Diane Claussen managing director; Wendy Liscow associate artistic director)

ENTRIES. By Bernardo Solano. January 20, 1996. Director, Lou Jacob; scenery, G.W. Mercier; costumes, Caryn Neman; lighting, Frances Aronson; composer, Carlos Valdez; sound, Jeff Willens.

Sam ....Candy Buckley
Jorge ....Johnny Garcia
Celestino .... Ric Oquita
Tim ....T. Ryder Smith
    Music performed by Michael Sirotta.
    Time: The present. Place: Caparu, in the Colombian rain forest. One intermission.

LOVE COMICS. Musical with book by Sarah Schlesinger and David Evans; music by David Evans; lyrics by Sarah Schlesinger. October 28, 1995. Director, Rod Kaats; musical direction, Tom Fay; scenery and costumes, Eduardo Sicangco; lighting, Phillip Monat; sound, Jeff Willens; orchestrations, Michael Gibson; produced in association with Daryl Roth, Scott Allyn and The Touring Artists Group.

Andrea ....Liz Larsen
Kyle ....Clif Thorn
Felice .... Jennifer Simard
Troy .... Peter Reardon
Editor ....Terry Layman
    MUSICAL NUMBERS, ACT I: "Searching for Love," "The Boy," "True Love," "Love Doctor's Credo," "Cha-Cha," "A Piano Has Fallen on My Heart," "Absolute Angel," "Going No-

where," "Tragedy." ACT II: "Haunted," "Felice's Turn," "The Heart Throb," "In Here," "Happy Ending," "Four Hearts."

CHEAP SENTIMENT. By Bruce Graham. February 4, 1996. Produced in association with Philadelphia Festival Theater for New Plays; see its entry in the Philadelphia listing in this section.

Stage II Workshop:

LET'S DO IT. Musical with book by A.R. Gurney; partially suggested by the Franz Lehar operetta *The Count of Luxembourge;* music and lyrics by Cole Porter. April 9, 1996. Director, John Tillinger; choreography, David Marques; musical direction and arrangements, Tom Fay.

Max ....Gregory Mitchell
Society Sue ....Maureen Moore
Ruby; Cynthia Drinkwater .. Jennifer Clippinger
Gloria .... Jennifer Frankel
Mike; Louie .... Sean Martin Hingston
Maisie ....Shannon Lewis
June ....Kimberly Lyon
Nick Cameron .... Steve Barton
Jenny Brown .... Caroline McMahon
Roddy Biltmore ....Robert Cary
Binky Biltmore ....Donald Grody
Bertha Biltmore ....Ruth Williamson
    Time: The early 1930s. Place: In and around Max's night club and gambling casino in Palm Beach, Florida.

New Haven, Conn.: Long Wharf Theater

(Arvin Brown artistic director; M. Edgar Rosenbloom executive director)

DENIAL. By Peter Sagal; December 6, 1995. Director, Arvin Brown; scenery, Marjorie Bradley Kellogg; costumes, David Murin; lighting, Richard Nelson; sound, Jim van Bergen; fights, Michael Giansanti.

Stephanie	Starla Benford
Prof. Bernard Cooper	Max Wright
Abigail Gersten	Bonnie Franklin
Adam Ryberg	Geoffrey P. Cantor
Noah Gomrowitz	Alan Mandell
Nathan	Sol Frieder

Time: The present. Place: A law office in Southern California. One intermission.

ALMOST ALL IN THE TIMING. By David Ives; program of six one-act plays including *Degas, C'Est Moi* (American premiere). April 10, 1996. Director, Gordon Edelstein; scenery, James Youmans; costumes, Candice Donnelly; lighting, Donald Holder.

Degas, C'Est Moi

Ed	Tim Choate
Doris	Julia Gibson

Ensemble: Richard Nagel, Eve Michelson, Martin Garcia, Robert Sella, Ann McDonough.

New Haven, Conn.: Yale Repertory Theater

(Stan Wojewodski Jr. artistic director; Victoria Nolan managing director)

PENTECOST. By David Edgar. November 9, 1995 (American premiere). Director, Stan Wojewodski Jr.; scenery, Michael Yeargan; costumes, Jane Greenwood; lighting, Matthew E. Adelson; sound, David Budries; fight choreographer, Dale Anthony Girard; associate artistic director, Mark Bly.

Oliver Davenport	Graeme Malcolm
Gabriella Pecs	Miriam Healy-Louie
Teenage Girl; Toni Newsome	Brandy Zarle
Soldier; Commando 2	Victor Khodadad
Father Petr Karolyi	John Hines
Father Sergei Bojovic	Kenneth Gray
Pusbas; Nico	Boris McGiver
Mikhail Czaba	Patrick Boll
Czaba's Secretary; Fatima	Lulu D'Agostino

Leo Katz	David Chandler
Anna Jedlikova; Marina	Elzbieta Czyzewska
Raif	Steven Memran
Antonio	Obi Ndefo
Abdul	John Ortiz
Yasmin	Nina Landey
Grigori Kolorenko	Christopher McHale
Cleopatra	Priscilla Garita
Amira	Svetlana Efremova
Tunu	Kavitha Ramachandran

Others: Company. One intermission.

VENUS. By Suzan-Lori Parks; songs by Phillip Johnston. March 21, 1996. Co-produced by New York Shakespeare Festival; see its entry in the Plays Produced Off Broadway section of this volume.

Philadelphia: Philadelphia Festival Theater for New Plays

(Sally de Sousa producing director; Stephen Goff managing director; Bruce Graham interim artistic director)

CHEAP SENTIMENT. By Bruce Graham. February 4, 1996. Director, Thomas Bullard; scenery, Richard Hoover; costumes, Kim Krumm Sorenson; lighting, Donald Holder; sound, Jeff Willens; co-produced with George Street Playhouse, New Brunswick, N.J.

David Connors	Evan Pappas
Em Kowalski	Mary Fogarty
Meg Van Dyke	Reiko Aylesworth
Giddy Rourke	Roger Serbagi
Leonard Korn	Allen Swift

One intermission.

VILNA'S GOT A PROBLEM. By Ernest Joselovitz. May 5, 1996. Director, Lou Jacob; scenery, David P. Gordon; costumes, Janus Stefanowitz; sound, Eileen Tague.

Zebi	David Ingram
Zavel	Benjamin Lloyd
Zeizel	Ray Xifo
Enzo	Michael Nichols
Isaac	Charlie Fersko
Isador	Ben Lipitz
Basha	Debora Cahn
Shulamis	Tamir

Musician: John S. Lionarons.

One intermission.

ON NEW HAVEN STAGES—*Above*, Bonnie Franklin and Max Wright in *Denial* by Peter Sagal at the Long Wharf Theater; *below, in foreground*, David Chandler, Graeme Malcolm and Nina Landey with other cast members in a scene from the American premiere of David Edgar's *Pentecost* at Yale Repertory Theater

Philadelphia: Walnut Street Theater

(Bernard Havard executive director)

BLOOD MONEY. By The Heather Brothers. September 27, 1995 (American premiere). Director, Mark Clements; scenery, Chris Crosswell; costumes, Kevin E. Ross; lighting, Chris Ellis; incidental music, David Roper; sound, Scott Smith. fights, Payson H. Burt.

Mike Mason	Alan Feinstein
Sue Thompson	Juliette Dunn
Elizabeth Mason	Kathleen Doyle
Julie Campbell	Patricia Hodges
Awards Show Host	Nancy Glass

Time: The present. Place: The lounge of the Masons' home in New Hope, Pa. Act I, Scene 1: The lounge, late afternoon. Scene 2: The Emmy Awards ceremony, the same day. Act II, Scene 1: The following morning. Scene 2: Later that afternoon. Scene 3: Late that night.

Studio 3

BART & FAY. By Michael Bamberger. March 26, 1996. Director, William Roudebush; scenery, David Peterson; costumes, Lani Apperson; lighting, Juliet A. Hampel; sound, Eileen Tague.

Bart Giamatti	Tom Teti
Fay Vincent	Tom McCarthy

One intermission.

Staged Readings:

WALKING ON WATER. By Paul Minx. October 30, 1995. Director, William Roudebush.
HOW I SPENT MY LIFE'S VACATION. By Rita Nachtman. December 4, 1995. Director, Kenny Finkle.
A REBEL BORN. By Cleveland Morris. February 26, 1996.

Philadelphia: Wilma Theater

(Blanka and Jiri Zizka artistic and producing directors; Teresa Eyring managing director)

BIRTH AND AFTER BIRTH. By Tina Howe. September 6, 1995. Director, Paul Berman; scenery, Jerry Rojo; costumes, Maxine Hartswick; lighting, Paul M. Fine; sound, Eileen Tague.

Sandy Apple	Kate Skinner
Bill Apple	David Ingram
Nicky Apple	Rob Leo Roy
Jeffrey Freed	Greg Wood
Mia Freed	Jessica Sager

Time: A few years ago. Place: The Apples' kitchen-playroom-dining room-living room. One intermission. Nominated for the ATCA Award.

RENDEZVOUS WITH REALITY. By Murphy Guyer. November 29, 1995. Director, Jiri Zizka; scenery, David P. Gordon; costumes, Hillary Guenther; lighting, Jerold R. Forsyth; sound, Eileen Tague; original music, John Hodian.

Little	Cory Einbinder
Trena	Juliette Dunn
Oleta	Alix D. Smith
Chelsea McKinnon	Jill Brennan
Todd Albright	David Ingram
Wesley	Kevin Del Aguila
Colin Claymore	Scott Hoxby
Lionel MacCory	Hank deLuca

Time: The present. Place: The mountains of Northern Idaho. One intermission.

Pittsburgh: Pittsburgh Public Theater

(Edward Gilbert artistic director; Stephen Klein managing director)

AMAZING GRACE. By Michael Cristofer. October 20, 1995. Director, Edward Gilbert; scenery, David Sumner; costumes, Martha Hally; lighting, Tom Sturge; sound, James Capenos.

Selena	Marsha Mason
John; Preacher	Stephen Bradbury
Esther; Witness	Frances Chaney
Lawyer; Witness	Aaron Eckhart
Vivian; Prosecutor; Witness	Laurie Kennedy
Warden; Witness	Larry John Meyers
Georgia; Witness	Adina Porter
Mrs. Fennel; PR Woman; Witness	Kate Young

One intermission. Winner of the 1995 ATCA Award; see introduction to this section.

Portland, Me.: Portland Stage Company

(Greg Leaming artistic director; Tom Werder managing director)

THE TURN OF THE SCREW. Adapted by Jeffrey Hatcher from the novel by Henry James. January 11, 1996. Director, Greg Leaming; scenery and costumes, Judy Gailen; lighting, Dan Kotlowitz; sound, JR Conklin. Produced in association with Stage West, Springfield, Mass.

The Woman ....Susan Appel
The Man ....Joey L. Golden
Time: 1872. Place: Essex, England. The play was presented without intermission.

7th Annual Little Festival of the Unexpected, April 24–27, Staged Readings:
AS BEES IN HONEY DROWN. By Douglas

Carter Beane. Director, Mark Brokaw.
UNDER THE SKIN. By Susan Yankowitz. Director, Greg Leaming.
BLOOD SHOCK BOOGIE. By Daniel Alexander Jones. Director, Laurie Carlos.
THE FLOOD. Solo performance by Anne Galjour.
MEN DIE SOONER. Solo performance by Tom Cayler.

Princeton, N.J.: McCarter Theater

(Emily Mann artistic director; Jeffrey Woodward managing director)

A PARK IN OUR HOUSE. By Nilo Cruz. June 6, 1995. Director, Loretta Greco; scenery, Robert Brill; costumes, Catherine Homa-Rocchio; lighting, Christopher Gerzelnik; sound, Steve Smith.

Pilar ....Vanessa Aspillaga
Ofelina ....Franca Barchiesi
Dimitri ....James Colby
Fifo ....Angel David
Hilario ....Shawn Elliott
Camilo ....Joe Quintero
One intermission.

VALLEY SONG. By Athol Fugard. October 24, 1995. Directed by Athol Fugard; associate director, scenery and costumes, Susan Hilferty; lighting, Dennis Parichy; original songs, DiDi Kriel; produced in association with Manhattan Theater Club.

Author, a White Man; Abraam
Jonkers ....Athol Fugard
Veronica Jonkers .... LisaGay Hamilton
Time: The Present. No intermission.

GREENSBORO: A REQUIEM. By Emily Mann. February 6, 1996. Director, Mark Wing-

Davey; scenery, Robert Brill; costumes, Catherine Homa-Rocchio; lighting, Pat Collins; projection design, John Boesche; composer, Baikida Carroll; musical direction and vocal arrangements, Carl Maulsby; additional material, Sally Bermanzohn.

Cast: Interrogation Officer, Dr. Paul Bermanzohn, Lewis Pitts, Skinhead—Michael Countryman; Edward Dawson—Jeffrey De Munn; Roland Wayne Wood, David Duke, Goldberg's Lawyer, Judge, Virgil Griffin—Jon DeVries; Sally Bermanzohn—Lisa Eichhorn; Signe Waller, Mrs. Waller, Dr. Marty Nathan, Jane—Deborah Hedwall; David Matthews, Anonymous Klansman, FBI Agent Goldberg, Chapman, Minister—Philip Seymour Hoffman; Rev. Nelson Johnson, Big George—Robert Jason Jackson; Interrogation Officer, Demonstrator, Amir, Minister—Stanley Wayne Mathis; Interviewer—Angie Phillips; Ronnie, Floris Cauce Weston, Doris Gordon, Joyce Johnson—Myra Lucretia Taylor; Rose—Carol Woods.

Time: The present and the remembered past. One intermission.

Providence, R.I.: Trinity Repertory Company

(Oskar Eustis artistic director; Patricia Egan managing director)

THE RETURN OF DON QUIXOTE. Adapted by Kira Obolensky from *The Adventures of Don Quixote de la Mancha, Part II* by Miguel de Cervantes. February 2, 1996. Director, Brian Kulick; scenery, Mark Wendland; costumes, William Lane; lighting, Kevin Adams.

Fake Don Quixote; Printer;
Quixote #2 ....Brian McEleney
Farmer; Head; Quixote #3; Lope Tocho;
Lionkeeper ....Stephen Berenson
Sancho Panza ....William Damkoehler
Mrs. Housekeeper; Girl #3;
Doctor ....Barbara Meek
Innocenta; Girl #1 .... Brooke Simpson

Sampson Carrasco;
Quixote #1 ....Fred Sullivan Jr.
Don Quixote .... Timothy Crowe
Teresa Panza; Girl #2; Aldonza ...... Phyllis Kay
Small Boy ....Elise Fargnoli, Liana Stillman
Guards: Fred Sullivan Jr., Lance Axt, Jeff Anthony Miller. One intermission.

Workshop:

SKIING TO NEW ENGLAND, OR IT'S A SLIPPERY SLOPE. Solo performance by Spalding Gray; written by Spalding Gray. November 30, 1995.

St. Louis: Repertory Theater of St. Louis

(Steven Woolf artistic director; Mark D. Bernstein managing director)

MISSISSIPPI SUGAR. Conceived and adapted by Randy Redd from short stories by Lewis Nordan. October 25, 1995. Director, Martin LaPlatney; musical direction and arrangements, Christopher Drobny; scenery, Arthur Ridley; costumes, Clyde Ruffin; lighting, Glenn Dunn; choreography, Dana Lewis.

Cast: Sugar Mecklin—Randy Redd; Delta Legend, Mrs. Meyers, W.C. Handy, Sweet Runa—Paula Newsome; Marlboro Man, Tex Ritter, Mr. Gibbs, Po Pilkington, Big G.B.—Ken Triwush; Mama—Lori Putnam; Gilbert Mecklin—Bernie Sheredy; Red Rooster, Talker at Freak Show, G.B. Jr.—Spike McClure.

Time: Now and then (the 1970s). Place: Here and there—the Mississippi Delta.

GHOSTS. By Henrik Ibsen; adapted by Anthony Clarvoe. April 7, 1996. Director, John Dillon; scenery and costumes, Lindsay W. Davis; lighting, Max De Volder.

Regina ....Pilar Witherspoon
Engstrand ....Robert Elliott
Parson Manders ....Joneal Joplin
Mrs. Alving ....Peggy Friesen
Oswald ....Matthew Rauch

Time: 1890. Place: Mrs. Alving's country estate near a large fjord in western Norway.

Imaginary Theater Company

THE GIFT OF THE MAGI. By Michael Erickson; based on a story by O. Henry. December 16, 1995 (touring November 27, 1995). Director, Kathleen Singleton; scenery, Aaron Black; costumes, J. Bruce Summers; musical arrangements, David Horstman.

Rodney the Mouse; The Boss ... Eric J. Connors
Jim .... Steve Isom
Della .... Laura McConnell
Velda; Davy; Glenda ....Andree E. Petersen

JACK AND THE BEANSTALK. By Barbara Field; music by Hiram Titus. March 30, 1996 (touring October 16, 1995 and January 16, 1996). Director, Susan Gregg; scenery, Nick Kryah; costumes, J. Bruce Summers;
Jack .... Eric J. Connors
Mother; Ogre .... Steve Isom
Peddler; Flim Flammer .... Laura McConnell
Mrs. O. ....Andree E. Petersen

Lab Project:

KUDZU, THE MUSICAL. Book by Doug Marlette and Jack Herrick; music and lyrics by Jack Herrick and Bland Simpson. February 23, 1996. Director, Susan Gregg.

San Diego: Old Globe Theater

(Jack O'Brien artistic director; Craig Noel executive producer; Tom Hall managing director)

PILGRIMS. By Stephen Metcalfe. July 2, 1995. Director, Thomas Bullard; scenery, Greg Lucas, Robin Sanford Roberts; costumes, Michael Krass; lighting, Ashley York Kennedy; sound, Jeff Ladman.
Ed Cook .... William Anton
Jilly O'Brien .... Tracey Middendorf
Dan Hackett ....David Mann
Frank D'Angelo .... Gregory Vignolle
Dee D'Angelo .... Dann Florek
Roy Ferguson ....John Paul Saurine
John Toole ....Gary Brownlee
Marcia Miller .... Elisa Llamido
Act I: November 1969. Act II: June 1970.

OVERTIME. By A.R. Gurney. July 9, 1995. Director, Nicholas Martin; scenery, Robert Morgan; costumes, Michael Krass; lighting, Kenneth Posner; sound, Jeff Ladman.
Portia .... Joan McMurtrey
Bassanio .... Bo Foxworth

Nerissa .... Angela Lanza
Gratiano .... Sterling Macer Jr.
Jessica .... Wendy Kaplan
Lorenzo ....David Aaron Baker
Antonio .... Tom Lacy
Shylock .... Nicholas Kepros
Salerio ....David Ledingham
Time: Evening, today. Place: The grounds of Portia's estate in Belmont. One intermission.

UNCOMMON PLAYERS, OR WAITING IN THE WINGS: A SHAKESPEARE CELEBRATION. Created and adapted by Dakin Matthews. September 3, 1995. Director, Dakin Matthews; scenery, Robin Sanford Roberts; costumes, Andrew Y. Yelusich; sound, Jeff Ladman; "Fear No More the Heat of the Sun" composed by Carl Smith.
Larry ....Jonathan McMurtry
Ellen ....Lillian Garrett-Groag
Charley ....Katherine McGrath

Ned .... Richard Easton
 Time: Whitsunday. Place: The undiscovered country. One intermission.

THE DOCTOR IS OUT (later entitled GETTING AWAY WITH MURDER). By Stephen Sondheim and George Furth. September 10, 1995. Director, Jack O'Brien; scenery, Douglas W. Schmidt; costumes, Robert Wojewodski; lighting, Kenneth Posner; sound, Jeff Ladman; fights, Steve Rankin.

Martin Chisholm ....John Rubinstein
Dorothea (Dossie) Lustig .....Becky Ann Baker
Young Man .... William Ragsdale
Couple in Bar ....Elisa Llamido,
                            Nestor G. Carbonell
Charmaine .... Crystal Allen
Pamela Prideaux .... Kandis Chappell
Vassili Laimorgos .... Josh Mostel
Gregory Reed ....Terrence Mann
Dan Gerard ....Chuck Cooper
Nam-Jun Vuong ....Takayo Fischer
Roberto .... Nestor G. Carbonell
Dr. Conrad Bering ...................F.J. O'Neil
 Time: The present, October. Place: A suite on the top floor of an old New York apartment building. One intermission.

THE GATE OF HEAVEN. By Lane Nishikawa and Victor Talmadge. March 7, 1996. Director, Benny Sato Ambush; scenery, Ralph Funicello; costumes, Susan Snowden; lighting, Kevin Rigdon; sound, Jeff Ladman; movement, Yuriko Doi; projections, Linda Batwin, Robin Silvestri.
"Sam" Yamamoto ....Lane Nishikawa
Leon .... Victor Talmadge

TIME AND AGAIN. Musical based on the novel by Jack Finney; book by Jack Viertel; music and lyrics by Walter Edgar Kennon. May 4, 1996. Director, Jack O'Brien; choreography, Kathleen Marshall; musical direction, Tom Helm; scenery, John Conklin; costumes, Catherine Zuber; lighting, Peter Kaczorowski; sound, Jeff Ladman; orchestrations, Chris Walker; projections, Wendall K. Harrington; special effects, Chic Silber.

Opera Singer ....Anne Allgood
Teacher ....Terry Burrell
Frank; Felix .... Danny Burstein
Dr. Danziger .... John Carpenter
Sandra; Fanny ....Susan Cella
Mr. Carmody .... George Dvorsky
Paperboy; Tavern Singer .... Marc Heller
Dance Teacher ....Nancy Hess
Trolleyman ....Joseph Kolinski
Julia Charbonneau ....Rebecca Luker
Danziger's Father .... John MacInnis
Si Morley .... Howard McGillin
Danziger's Mother .... Elizabeth Mills
Kate Mancuso; Mrs. Carmody .. Jessica Molaskey
Aunt Eva ....Roxann Parker
Ruben Prine; Jake Pickering ...... William Parry
Hypnotist .... Jacquelyn Piro
Joyce; Apple Mary .... KT Sullivan
Mr. Harriman .... Andy Umberger
Megaphone Man ....John Leslie Wolfe
 Ensemble: Anne Allgood, Terry Burrell, Danny Burstein, Susan Cella, George Dvorsky, Sean Grant, Marc Heller, Nancy Hess, JoAnne M. Hunter, Joseph Kolinski, John MacInnis, Elizabeth Mills, Roxann Parker, Luis Perez, Jacquelyn Piro, KT Sullivan, Andy Umberger, John Leslie Wolfe.
 Time 1982 & 1882. Place: New York City. One intermission.

San Francisco: Magic Theater

(Mame Hunt artistic director; Jane E. Brown managing director)

A HUEY P. NEWTON STORY. Solo performance by Roger Guenveur Smith; created by Roger Guenveur Smith. October 24, 1995. Scenery and lighting, David Welle; sound, Marc Anthony Thompson; projected images from original photography by Huey P. Newton; produced in association with Oakland Ensemble Theater.
 No intermission.

San Jose, Calif.: San Jose Repertory Theater

(Timothy Near artistic director)

LA POSADA MAGICA. Play with music with book and lyrics by Octavio Solis; music by Marcos Loya. December 8, 1995. Director, Norma Salvidar; musical direction, David Silva; scenery, Michelle Riel; costumes, Lydia Tanji; lighting, Ashley York Kennedy; sound, Jeff Mockus.
Horacio ....Eduardo Robledo
Consuelo; Widow ....Wilma Bonet

Caridad; Widow .... Tessa Koning-Martinez
Mom; Mariluz .... Vilma Silva
Refugio; Buzzard .... Jesus Mendoza
Popi; Josecruz .... Soren Oliver
Eli; Lauro; Bones .... Phillip Rodriguez
Gracie ....Dina Martinez
Musicians: David Silva, Russell Rodriguez.
One intermission.
MUSICAL NUMBERS: "Vamos Todos a Belen," "Vamos a Pie," "Down and Out on Christmas Eve," "Este Canto Mio," "Quieres Chocolate?", "Lovin' Santa," "Searching," "Christmas Memories of Home," "Dirge," "Corridio de Los Muertos," "Sacred Child," Finale.

MIRANDOLINA. By Carlo Goldoni; translated and adapted by Stephen Wadsworth. January 12, 1996. Director, Timothy Near; scenery, Michelle Riel; costumes, B. Modern; lighting, Derek Duarte; sound, Jeff Mockus; fights, John McCluggage.
Marchese of Forlipopoli .... Ken Grantham
Count of Albanorita .... Dan Hiatt
Fabrizio ....Jesus Mendoza
Cavaliere of Ripafratta .... Kurt Rhoads
Mirandolina .... Melissa King
Cavaliere's Servant ....Luis Oropeza
Ortensia .... Kimberly King
Desianza ....Adria Woomer-Stewart
Count's Servant; New Boy ....Josh Miyaji
Serpetta ....Jennifer Fagundes
Others: Alpha Schramm, Michele M. Trimble.
One intermission.

Seattle: Intiman Theater

(Warner Shook artistic director; Laura Penn managing director)

NINE ARMENIANS. By Leslie Ayvazian. August 16, 1995. Director, Christopher Ashley; scenery, Loy Arcenas; costumes, Gabriel Perry; lighting, Donald Holder; sound, Steven M. Klein; composer, George Mgrdichian; associate artistic director, Victor Pappas.
Marie; Non .... Barbara Andres
Armine; Mom .... Charlotte Colavin
Ani .... Julie Dretzin
Ari ....Benjamin Fels
John; Dad .... Sherman Howard
Antry; Pop ....Bernard Kates
Aunt Louise .... Lauren Klein
Virginia; Ginya .... Mallery MacKay-Brook

Uncle Garo ....Martin Shakar
Musician .... George Mgrdichian
No intermission.

New Voices at Intiman: Reading Series:

SMASH. By Jeffrey Hatcher. July 24, 1995. Director, Victor Pappas.
HUSH!! A MUSICAL EVENING OF THEATER. By Tamara Madison-Shaw. August 21, 1995. Director, Jacqueline Moscou.
A SMOKING LESSON. By Julia Jordan. October 30, 1995. Director, Michael Olich.
THE MAGIC FIRE. By Lillian Garrett-Groag. December 4, 1995. Director, Victor Pappas.

Seattle: Seattle Repertory Theater

(Daniel Sullivan artistic director; Benjamin Moore managing director)

THE CIDER HOUSE RULES, PART I. By Peter Parnell; adapted from the novel by John Irving. March 2, 1996. Directors, Tom Hulce, Jane Jones; scenery, Eugene Lee; costumes, David Zinn; lighting, Greg Sullivan; music and musical direction, Dan Wheetman.
Dr. Wilbur Larch .... Michael Winters
Homer Wells ....Neal Huff
Melony; Foster Mother ....Jillian Armenante
Others: Tom Beyer, Sarah Brooke, Rebecca Chace, James Chesnutt, Christopher Collett, Beth Dixon, Dougald Park, Myra Platt, Salim Rahman, Stephanie Shine, Jeff Steitzer, Jayne Taini, Brenda Wehle, David-Paul Wichert.
Two intermissions.

PSYCHOPATHIA SEXUALIS. By John Patrick Shanley. March 13, 1996. Director, Daniel Sullivan; scenery, Andrew Wood Boughton; costumes, Jane Greenwood; lighting, Pat Collins; sound, Steven M. Klein.
Arthur ....Matt Servitto
Howard ....Daniel Sullivan
Dr. Block ....John Aylward
Ellie .... Talia Balsam
Lucille .... Park Overall
One intermission.

INTIMAN THEATER, SEATTLE—Barbara Andres, Julie Dretzin *(in background)* and Charlotte Colavin in *Nine Armenians* by Leslie Ayvazian

Sharon, Conn.: Sharon Stage

(Michael Gill managing director)

TWICE REMOVED. By Mark Rosin and Barry Glasser. June 20, 1995. Director, David Saint; scenery, Paul Wonsek; costumes, Lee J. Austin; lighting, Kenneth Posner; sound, Abe Jacob; produced in association with Jerrold J. Ziman.

Michelle "Mickey" Bell .... Estelle Parsons
Gwyneth Bell .... Carol Kane
Katherine "Kiki" Hotchkis ...... Deborah Rush
Halloran .... Michael Genet
Stark .... Mark Nelson
Rutledge .... Jerry Lanning

Time: Halloween. Place: An old, once elegant mansion in Poughkeepsie, New York. Act I, Scene 1: Late morning. Scene 2: A few hours later. Scene 3: Late that afternoon. Act II: One hour later.

THE WOMAN WHO LAUGHED. By Joyce Carol Oates. August 15, 1995. Director, Don Amendolia; scenery, Eric Lowell Renschler; costumes, Lee J. Austin; lighting, Susan Chute.

Nell Ryder .... Lucie Arnaz
Gil Pollack .... Jack Koenig
Clive Tuttle .... Bill Lewis
Madge Harkness .... Lianne Kressin
Jim Towers .... Ken Parker
Mrs. Eaton .... Edith Meeks
Randolph Pitts .... Mitchell Greenberg
Joey Eaton .... Jordan D. Gochros
Waitress .... Francine Hughes
Young Woman .... Audra White

Party Guests: Harry Colley II, Ed Hayden, Sandra Sherrard, Mindy Utay. Students: Michael Baldwin, Eleanor Casson, Ashleigh Lynn Catsos, Jason Kassirer, Ryan Jones, Alison Levitch, Katharine Luckinbill, Chelsea Miller, Katie Spero, Jillian Sprance, Virginia Sprance.

Time: The present. Place: The small fictitious town of East Oracle, Mich. One intermission.

Springfield, Mass.: Stage West

(Albert Ihde producing director)

THE TURN OF THE SCREW. Adapted by Jeffrey Hatcher from Henry James. February 10, 1996. Produced in association with Portland Stage Company, Greg Leaming artistic director, Tom Werder managing director; see its listing in the Portland, Me. entry in this section.

Stockbridge, Mass.: Berkshire Theater Festival

(Arthur Storch artistic director; Kate Maguire managing director)

KAFKA'S WICK. By Alan Bennett. August 17, 1995 (American premiere). Director, Arthur Storch; scenery, Michael Miller; costumes, Pamela Scofield; lighting, Phil Monat; sound, James Wildman.

Kafka .... Peter Bartlett

Brod .... Steve Routman
Linda .... Susan Greenhill
Father .... Ron Randell
Sydney .... Bill Kux
Hermann K .... David Sabin
One intermission.

Syracuse, N.Y.: Syracuse Stage

(James A. Clark producing director)

DEAR. By Rosalyn Drexler. September 26, 1995. Director, Worth Gardner; original music, Fabian Obispo Jr.; musical direction, Worth Gardner; scenery, Myung Hee Cho; costumes, Ashley R. Smith; lighting, Dennis Parichy; sound, Bianchi & Smith.

George Culp .... Andrew Boyer

Perry Como .... Romain Fruge
Perry's Girls . Rebecca Hirsch, Wendy Perelman
Louise Culp .... Heather Robison
Jessie Culp .... Margo Skinner
Time: June 1955. Place: The home of Jessie Culp in Queens, N.Y. and NBC-TV Studio. One intermission.

Washington, D.C.: Arena Stage

(Artistic director, Douglas C. Wager; producing director, Kyle Donnelly; executive director, Stephen Richard)

DANCE OF DEATH. By August Strindberg; translated by Bill Coco and Peter Stormare. February 16, 1996. Director, JoAnne Akalaitis; scenery, John Conklin; costumes, Gabriel Berry; lighting, Jennifer Tipton; original music and sound, Bruce Odland.
Edgar .... Henry Strozier
Alice .... Tana Hicken
Jenny; Margaret .... Cecelia Riddett
Curt .... Gary Sloan
Sentry .... Paul Takacs
Time: Autumn. Place: An Island. One intermission.

PlayQuest Workshop

RIP YOUR HEART OUT. By Ernest Thompson. January 12, 1996. Director, Nick Olcott; scenery, Alice Andreini; costumes, Anne Kennedy; lighting, Michele M. McDermott; sound, Paco Aguilar.
Julie .... J. Fred Shiffman

Basil .... John Elko
Kale .... Rob Sullivan
Sonny .... Paul Morella
Canecki .... Richard Lopez
Wolf .... Christopher Lane
Lola .... Emily Townley
Rogers; Torre; Sister
Charlie .... Robert Wayne White
One intermission.

PlayQuest Readings

AMERICAN MEDEA. By Silas Jones. July 19, 1995. Director, L. Kenneth Richardson.
THE MAD DANCERS. By Yehuda Hyman. February 1, 1996. Director, Darryl V. Jones.
THREE NIGHTS IN TEHRAN. By John Strand. February 9, 1996. Director, Kyle Donnelly.
THE SECRET WIFE. By Y York. February 16, 1996. Director, Kyle Donnelly.

STAGE WEST, SPRINGFIELD, and PORTLAND STAGE COMPANY—
Susan Appel and Joey L. Golden in Jeffrey Hatcher's adaptation of Henry
James's *The Turn of the Screw*

Waterbury, Conn.: Seven Angels Theater

(Semina De Laurentis artistic director)

BEFORE YOU GO. By Jim McGinn. March 9, 1996. Director, Bill Castellino; scenery, Robert John Andrusko; costumes, Rosalind Spann; lighting, Peter Petrino; sound, John Keil.

Bill .... R. Bruce Connelly

Jerry .... Joe Pacheco
Celia .... Priscilla Pointer
Mac .... Robert Symonds
Penny .... Denise Taylor
    One intermission.

Waterford, Conn.: Eugene O'Neill Theater Center

(Lloyd Richards artistic director; George C. White president)

1995 National Playwrights Conference Readings, July 2–29:

ALL AMERICANS. By Jamie Baker.
INTO THE FIRE. By Deborah B. Bailey.
FLORIDA. By Marcia Cebulska.
EURYDICE'S RETURN. By Alexander Detkov.
THE GUY UPSTAIRS. By Mark Eisman.
THERE. By Herman Daniel Farrell III.
BETWEEN MEN AND CATTLE. By Richard Kalinoski.
A LOVE OF THE GAME. By Kevin Kane.
THE PRESERVATION SOCIETY. By William S. Leavengood.

THE NICKEL CHILDREN. By Eric John Litra.
STAND. By Toni Press.
THE OLD SETTLER. By John Henry Redwood.
THE SECOND-STORY MAN. By Richard Strand.

Directors: Casey Childs, William Partlan, Amy Saltz, Oz Scott. Dramaturges: Philip Barry, Tony Converse, Corinne Jacker, Edith Oliver, Ernest Schier, Gay Smith, Dan Sullivan, Max Wilk. Designers: Charles McClennahan, G.W. Mercier, Spencer Mosse.

Worcester, Mass.: Worcester Foothills Theater Company

(Marc P. Smith artistic director and executive producer)

BACKSTAGE CONFIDENTIAL. Musical with book by Marc P. Smith; music and lyrics from works by Noel Coward, Otto Harbach and Karl Hoschna. February 1, 1996. Director, Marc P. Smith; musical direction and performance, Steven Bergman; choreography, Denise Day; scenery, Richard Russell; costumes, Ted Giammona; lighting, Annmarie Duggan; sound, Andrew Skomorowsky.

With Natalie Brown, Mark S. Carter, Stephen Murray, Chip Phillips, Deborah Stein.

Time: The present. One intermission.

MUSICAL NUMBERS: "Don't Put Your Daughter on the Stage, Mrs. Worthington," "Why Must the Show Go On?", "I've Been Invited to a Party" (by Noel Coward); "Every Little Movement" (music by Karl Hoschna, lyrics by Otto Harbach).

FACTS AND
FIGURES

LONG RUNS ON BROADWAY

The following shows have run 500 or more continuous performances in a single production, usually the first, not including previews or extra non-profit performances, allowing for vacation layoffs and special one-booking engagements, but not including return engagements after a show has gone on tour. In all cases, the numbers were obtained directly from the show's production offices. Where there are title similarities, the production is identified as follows: (p) straight play version, (m) musical version, (r) revival, (tr) transfer.

THROUGH MAY 31, 1996

(PLAYS MARKED WITH ASTERISK WERE STILL PLAYING JUNE 1, 1996)

Plays	Number Performances	Plays	Number Performances
A Chorus Line	6,137	The Voice of the Turtle	1,557
Oh! Calcutta! (r)	5,959	Barefoot in the Park	1,530
*Cats	5,697	Brighton Beach Memoirs	1,530
*Les Misérables	3,786	Dreamgirls	1,522
42nd Street	3,486	Mame (m)	1,508
*The Phantom of the Opera	3,484	Same Time, Next Year	1,453
Grease	3,388	Arsenic and Old Lace	1,444
Fiddler on the Roof	3,242	The Sound of Music	1,443
Life With Father	3,224	Me and My Girl	1,420
Tobacco Road	3,182	How to Succeed in Business Without	
Hello, Dolly!	2,844	Really Trying	1,417
My Fair Lady	2,717	Hellzapoppin	1,404
Annie	2,377	The Music Man	1,375
Man of La Mancha	2,328	Funny Girl	1,348
Abie's Irish Rose	2,327	Mummenschanz	1,326
Oklahoma!	2,212	Angel Street	1,295
*Miss Saigon	2,138	Lightnin'	1,291
Pippin	1,944	Promises, Promises	1,281
South Pacific	1,925	The King and I	1,246
The Magic Show	1,920	Cactus Flower	1,234
Deathtrap	1,793	Sleuth	1,222
Gemini	1,788	Torch Song Trilogy	1,222
Harvey	1,775	1776	1,217
Dancin'	1,774	Equus	1,209
La Cage aux Folles	1,761	Sugar Babies	1,208
Hair	1,750	Guys and Dolls	1,200
The Wiz	1,672	Amadeus	1,181
Born Yesterday	1,642	Cabaret	1,165
The Best Little Whorehouse in		Mister Roberts	1,157
Texas	1,639	Annie Get Your Gun	1,147
Crazy for You	1,622	Guys and Dolls (r)	1,144
Ain't Misbehavin'	1,604	The Seven Year Itch	1,141
Mary, Mary	1,572	Butterflies Are Free	1,128
Evita	1,567	Pins and Needles	1,108

Plays	*Number Performances*	*Plays*	*Number Performances*
Plaza Suite	1,097	Blood Brothers	839
They're Playing Our Song	1,082	You Can't Take It With You	837
Grand Hotel (m)	1,077	La Plume de Ma Tante	835
Kiss Me, Kate	1,070	Three Men on a Horse	835
Don't Bother Me, I Can't Cope	1,065	The Subject Was Roses	832
The Pajama Game	1,063	Black and Blue	824
Shenandoah	1,050	Inherit the Wind	806
The Teahouse of the August		Anything Goes (r)	804
Moon	1,027	No Time for Sergeants	796
Damn Yankees	1,019	Fiorello!	795
Never Too Late	1,007	Where's Charley?	792
Big River	1,005	The Ladder	789
The Will Rogers Follies	983	Forty Carats	780
Any Wednesday	982	Lost in Yonkers	780
A Funny Thing Happened on the Way		The Prisoner of Second Avenue	780
to the Forum	964	M. Butterfly	777
The Odd Couple	964	Oliver!	774
Anna Lucasta	957	The Pirates of Penzance (1980 r)	772
Kiss and Tell	956	Woman of the Year	770
Dracula (r)	925	My One and Only	767
Bells Are Ringing	924	Sophisticated Ladies	767
The Moon Is Blue	924	Bubbling Brown Sugar	766
Beatlemania	920	Into the Woods	765
The Elephant Man	916	State of the Union	765
Kiss of the Spider Woman	906	Starlight Express	761
Luv	901	The First Year	760
The Who's Tommy	900	Broadway Bound	756
Chicago (m)	898	You Know I Can't Hear You When the	
Applause	896	Water's Running	755
*Beauty and the Beast	893	Two for the Seesaw	750
Can-Can	892	Joseph and the Amazing Technicolor	
Carousel	890	Dreamcoat (r)	747
I'm Not Rappaport	890	Death of a Salesman	742
Hats Off to Ice	889	For Colored Girls, etc.	742
Fanny	888	Sons o' Fun	742
Children of a Lesser God	887	Candide (m, r)	740
Follow the Girls	882	Gentlemen Prefer Blondes	740
City of Angels	878	The Man Who Came to Dinner	739
Camelot	873	Nine	739
I Love My Wife	872	Call Me Mister	734
The Bat	867	West Side Story	732
My Sister Eileen	864	High Button Shoes	727
No, No, Nanette (r)	861	Finian's Rainbow	725
Song of Norway	860	Claudia	722
Chapter Two	857	The Gold Diggers	720
A Streetcar Named Desire	855	Jesus Christ Superstar	720
Barnum	854	Carnival	719
Comedy in Music	849	The Diary of Anne Frank	717
Raisin	847	I Remember Mama	714
*Grease (r)	843	Tea and Sympathy	712

Plays	Number Performances	Plays	Number Performances
Junior Miss	710	The Happy Time (p)	614
Last of the Red Hot Lovers	706	Separate Rooms	613
The Secret Garden	706	Affairs of State	610
Company	705	Oh! Calcutta! (tr)	610
Seventh Heaven	704	Star and Garter	609
Gypsy (m)	702	The Mystery of Edwin Drood	608
The Miracle Worker	700	The Student Prince	608
That Championship Season	700	Sweet Charity	608
Da	697	Bye Bye Birdie	607
The King and I (r)	696	Irene (r)	604
Cat on a Hot Tin Roof	694	Sunday in the Park With George	604
*Show Boat (r)	694	Adonis	603
Li'l Abner	693	Broadway	603
The Children's Hour	691	Peg o' My Heart	603
Purlie	688	Street Scene (p)	601
Dead End	687	Flower Drum Song	600
The Lion and the Mouse	686	Kiki	600
White Cargo	686	A Little Night Music	600
Dear Ruth	683	Agnes of God	599
East Is West	680	Don't Drink the Water	598
Come Blow Your Horn	677	Wish You Were Here	598
The Most Happy Fella	676	Sarafina!	597
The Doughgirls	671	A Society Circus	596
The Impossible Years	670	Absurd Person Singular	592
Irene	670	A Day in Hollywood/A Night in the	
Boy Meets Girl	669	Ukraine	588
The Tap Dance Kid	669	The Me Nobody Knows	586
Beyond the Fringe	667	The Two Mrs. Carrolls	585
Who's Afraid of Virginia Woolf?	664	Kismet (m)	583
Blithe Spirit	657	Gypsy (m, r)	582
A Trip to Chinatown	657	Brigadoon	581
The Women	657	Detective Story	581
Bloomer Girl	654	No Strings	580
The Fifth Season	654	Brother Rat	577
*Sunset Boulevard	649	Blossom Time	576
Rain	648	Pump Boys and Dinettes	573
Witness for the Prosecution	645	Show Boat	572
Call Me Madam	644	The Show-Off	571
Janie	642	Sally	570
The Green Pastures	640	Jelly's Last Jam	569
Auntie Mame (p)	639	Golden Boy (m)	568
A Man for All Seasons	637	One Touch of Venus	567
Jerome Robbins' Broadway	634	The Real Thing	566
The Fourposter	632	Happy Birthday	564
The Music Master	627	Look Homeward, Angel	564
Two Gentlemen of Verona (m)	627	Morning's at Seven (r)	564
The Tenth Man	623	The Glass Menagerie	561
The Heidi Chronicles	621	I Do! I Do!	560
Is Zat So?	618	Wonderful Town	559
Anniversary Waltz	615	Rose Marie	557

Plays	Number Performances	Plays	Number Performances
Strictly Dishonorable	557	Biloxi Blues	524
Sweeney Todd, the Demon Barber of		Irma La Douce	524
Fleet Street	557	The Boomerang	522
The Great White Hope	556	*Smokey Joe's Cafe	522
A Majority of One	556	Follies	521
The Sisters Rosensweig	556	Rosalinda	521
Sunrise at Campobello	556	The Best Man	520
Toys in the Attic	556	Chauve-Souris	520
Jamaica	555	Blackbirds of 1928	518
Stop the World—I Want to Get Off	555	The Gin Game	517
Florodora	553	Sunny	517
Noises Off	553	Victoria Regina	517
Ziegfeld Follies (1943)	553	Fifth of July	511
Dial "M" for Murder	552	Half a Sixpence	511
Good News	551	The Vagabond King	511
Peter Pan (r)	551	The New Moon	509
Let's Face It	547	The World of Suzie Wong	508
Milk and Honey	543	The Rothschilds	507
Within the Law	541	*How to Succeed in Business Without	
Pal Joey (r)	540	Really Trying (r)	505
What Makes Sammy Run?	540	On Your Toes (r)	505
The Sunshine Boys	538	Sugar	505
What a Life	538	Shuffle Along	504
Crimes of the Heart	535	Up in Central Park	504
Damn Yankees (r)	533	Carmen Jones	503
The Unsinkable Molly Brown	532	The Member of the Wedding	501
The Red Mill (r)	531	Panama Hattie	501
Rumors	531	Personal Appearance	501
A Raisin in the Sun	530	Bird in Hand	500
Godspell (tr)	527	Room Service	500
Fences	526	Sailor, Beware!	500
The Solid Gold Cadillac	526	Tomorrow the World	500

LONG RUNS OFF BROADWAY

Plays	Number Performances	Plays	Number Performances
*The Fantasticks	14,938	Jacques Brel	1,847
*Perfect Crime	3,750	Forever Plaid	1,811
Nunsense	3,672	Vanities	1,785
*Tony 'n' Tina's Wedding	2,922	You're a Good Man Charlie	
The Threepenny Opera	2,611	Brown	1,597
Forbidden Broadway 1982–87	2,332	The Blacks	1,408
Little Shop of Horrors	2,209	One Mo' Time	1,372
Godspell	2,124	Let My People Come	1,327
Vampire Lesbians of Sodom	2,024	Driving Miss Daisy	1,195
*Tubes	1,970	The Hot l Baltimore	1,166

Plays	*Number* Performances	Plays	*Number* Performances
I'm Getting My Act Together and Taking It on the Road	1,165	Scuba Duba	692
Little Mary Sunshine	1,143	The Foreigner	686
Steel Magnolias	1,126	The Knack	685
El Grande de Coca-Cola	1,114	The Club	674
The Proposition	1,109	The Balcony	672
Beau Jest	1,069	Penn & Teller	666
Tamara	1,036	America Hurrah	634
One Flew Over the Cuckoo's Nest (r)	1,025	Oil City Symphony	626
The Boys in the Band	1,000	Hogan's Goat	607
Fool for Love	1,000	Beehive	600
Other People's Money	990	The Trojan Women	600
Cloud 9	971	The Dining Room	583
Sister Mary Ignatius Explains It All for You & The Actor's Nightmare	947	Krapp's Last Tape & The Zoo Story	582
*Stomp	944	Three Tall Women	582
Your Own Thing	933	The Dumbwaiter & The Collection	578
Curley McDimple	931	Forbidden Broadway 1990	576
Leave It to Jane (r)	928	Dames at Sea	575
The Mad Show	871	The Crucible (r)	571
Scrambled Feet	831	The Iceman Cometh (r)	565
The Effect of Gamma Rays on Man-in-the-Moon Marigolds	819	The Hostage (r)	545
A View From the Bridge (r)	780	What's a Nice Country Like You Doing in a State Like This?	543
The Boy Friend (r)	763	Forbidden Broadway 1988	534
True West	762	Frankie and Johnny in the Clair de Lune	533
Isn't It Romantic	733	Six Characters in Search of an Author (r)	529
Dime a Dozen	728	All in the Timing	526
The Pocket Watch	725	Oleanna	513
The Connection	722	The Dirtiest Show in Town	509
The Passion of Dracula	714	Happy Ending & Day of Absence	504
Adaptation & Next	707	Greater Tuna	501
Oh! Calcutta!	704	A Shayna Maidel	501
		The Boys From Syracuse (r)	500

NEW YORK DRAMA CRITICS CIRCLE AWARDS, 1935–36 TO 1995–96

Listed below are the New York Drama Critics Circle Awards from 1935–36 through 1995–96 classified as follows: (1) Best American Play, (2) Best Foreign Play, (3) Best Musical, (4) Best, regardless of category (this category was established by new voting rules in 1962–63 and did not exist prior to that year).

1935–36—(1) Winterset

1936–37—(1) High Tor

1937–38—(1) Of Mice and Men, (2) Shadow and Substance

1938–39—(1) No award, (2) The White Steed

1939–40—(1) The Time of Your Life

1940–41—(1) Watch on the Rhine, (2) The Corn Is Green

1941–42—(1) No award, (2) Blithe Spirit

1942–43—(1) The Patriots

1943–44—(2) Jacobowsky and the Colonel

1944–45—(1) The Glass Menagerie

1945–46—(3) Carousel

1946–47—(1) All My Sons, (2) No Exit, (3) Brigadoon

1947–48—(1) A Streetcar Named Desire, (2) The Winslow Boy

1948–49—(1) Death of a Salesman, (2) The Madwoman of Chaillot, (3) South Pacific

1949–50—(1) The Member of the Wedding, (2) The Cocktail Party, (3) The Consul

1950–51—(1) Darkness at Noon, (2) The Lady's Not for Burning, (3) Guys and Dolls

1951–52—(1) I Am a Camera, (2) Venus Observed, (3) Pal Joey (Special citation to Don Juan in Hell)

1952–53—(1) Picnic, (2) The Love of Four Colonels, (3) Wonderful Town

1953–54—(1) The Teahouse of the August Moon, (2) Ondine, (3) The Golden Apple

1954–55—(1) Cat on a Hot Tin Roof, (2) Witness for the Prosecution, (3) The Saint of Bleecker Street

1955–56—(1) The Diary of Anne Frank, (2) Tiger at the Gates, (3) My Fair Lady

1956–57—(1) Long Day's Journey Into Night, (2) The Waltz of the Toreadors, (3) The Most Happy Fella

1957–58—(1) Look Homeward, Angel, (2) Look Back in Anger, (3) The Music Man

1958–59—(1) A Raisin in the Sun, (2) The Visit, (3) La Plume de Ma Tante

1959–60—(1) Toys in the Attic, (2) Five Finger Exercise, (3) Fiorello!

1960–61—(1) All the Way Home, (2) A Taste of Honey, (3) Carnival

1961–62—(1) The Night of the Iguana, (2) A Man for All Seasons, (3) How to Succeed in Business Without Really Trying

1962–63—(4) Who's Afraid of Virginia Woolf? (Special citation to Beyond the Fringe)

1963–64—(4) Luther, (3) Hello, Dolly! (Special citation to The Trojan Women)

1964–65—(4) The Subject Was Roses, (3) Fiddler on the Roof

1965–66—(4) The Persecution and Assassination of Marat as Performed by the Inmates of the Asylum of Charenton Under the Direction of the Marquis de Sade, (3) Man of La Mancha

1966–67—(4) The Homecoming, (3) Cabaret

1967–68—(4) Rosencrantz and Guildenstern Are Dead, (3) Your Own Thing

1968–69—(4) The Great White Hope, (3) 1776

1969–70—(4) Borstal Boy, (1) The Effect of Gamma Rays on Man-in-the-Moon Marigolds, (3) Company

1970–71—(4) Home, (1) The House of Blue Leaves, (3) Follies

1971–72—(4) That Championship Season, (2) The Screens (3) Two Gentlemen of Verona (Special citations to Sticks and Bones and Old Times)

1972–73—(4) The Changing Room, (1) The Hot l Baltimore, (3) A Little Night Music

1973–74—(4) The Contractor, (1) Short Eyes, (3) Candide

1974–75—(4) Equus (1) The Taking of Miss Janie, (3) A Chorus Line

1975–76—(4) Travesties, (1) Streamers, (3) Pacific Overtures

1976–77—(4) Otherwise Engaged, (1) American Buffalo, (3) Annie

1977–78—(4) Da, (3) Ain't Misbehavin'

1978–79—(4) The Elephant Man, (3) Sweeney Todd, the Demon Barber of Fleet Street

1979–80—(4) Talley's Folly, (2) Betrayal, (3) Evita (Special citation to Peter Brook's Le Centre International de Créations Théâtrales for its repertory)

1980–81—(4) A Lesson From Aloes, (1) Crimes of the Heart (Special citations to Lena Horne: The Lady and Her Music and the New York Shakespeare Festival production of The Pirates of Penzance)

1981–82—(4) The Life & Adventures of Nicholas Nickleby, (1) A Soldier's Play

1982–83—(4) Brighton Beach Memoirs, (2) Plenty, (3) Little Shop of Horrors (Special citation to Young Playwrights Festival)

1983–84—(4) The Real Thing, (1) Glengarry Glen Ross, (3) Sunday in the Park With George (Special citation to Samuel Beckett for the body of his work)

1984–85—(4) Ma Rainey's Black Bottom

1985–86—(4) A Lie of the Mind, (2) Benefactors (Special citation to The Search for Signs of Intelligent Life in the Universe)

1986–87—(4) Fences, (2) Les Liaisons Dangereuses, (3) Les Misérables

1987–88—(4) Joe Turner's Come and Gone, (2) The Road to Mecca, (3) Into the Woods

1988–89—(4) The Heidi Chronicles, (2) Aristocrats (Special citation to Bill Irwin for Largely New York)

1989–90—(4) The Piano Lesson, (2) Privates on Parade, (3) City of Angels

1990–91—(4) Six Degrees of Separation, (2) Our Country's Good, (3) The Will Rogers Follies (Special citation to Eileen Atkins for her portrayal of Virginia Woolf in A Room of One's Own)

1991–92—(4) Dancing at Lughnasa, (1) Two Trains Running

1992–93—(4) Angels in America: Millennium Approaches, (2) Someone Who'll Watch Over Me, (3) Kiss of the Spider Woman

1993–94—(4) Three Tall Women (Special citation to Anna Deavere Smith for her unique contribution to theatrical form)

1994–95—(4) Arcadia, (1) Love! Valour! Compassion! (Special citation to Signature Theater Company for outstanding artistic achievement)

1995–96—(4)Seven Guitars, (2) Molly Sweeney, (3) Rent

NEW YORK DRAMA CRITICS CIRCLE VOTING 1995–96

The New York Drama Critics Circle named August Wilson's *Seven Guitars* the best play of the season regardless of category in a fourth, run-off ballot between the Wilson play and Brian Friel's *Molly Sweeney*. Having named an American play best of bests, the Critics proceeded to name *Molly Sweeney* the best foreign play of the season on a second point-weighted ballot in which Athol Fugard's *Valley Song*, Stephen Bill's *Curtains* and David Hare's *Racing Demon* were in contention. And in the voting for best musical, the late Jonathan Larson's multi-award-winning *Rent* won easily with most of the Critics' first-choice votes on the first ballot.

Seventeen of the Circle's 21 members were present and two more were voting by proxy, on the first rounds only. First-round best play votes were distributed as follows: *Racing Demon* 5 (Mary Campbell, Jeremy Gerard, Jacques le Sourd, David Sheward, Linda Winer), *Molly Sweeney* 4 (Alexis Greene, Howard Kissel, Donald Lyons, David Patrick Stearns) Terrence McNally's *Master Class* 3 (Greg Evans, Robert Feldberg, Ken Mandelbaum), *Seven Guitars* 3 (John Heilpern, Michael Kuchwara, Michael Sommers), Christopher Kyle's *The Monogamist* 2 (Frank Scheck, Jan Stuart) and 1 each for Jon Marans's *Old Wicked Songs* (Clive Barnes) and Adrienne Kennedy's *June and Jean in Concert* (Michael Feingold).

After two more ballots which included the Critics' second and third choices and were scored on points weighted 3 for first choice, 2 for second and 1 for third, no play had accumulated enough points for victory under the Circle's rules, but *Seven Guitars* and *Molly Sweeney* were the leaders. According to the rules, they went head to head on the fourth ballot, the former winning by 11 votes to 6.

The vote for best musical was also a matter of simple individual preference, *Rent* winning a big majority on the first ballot with 12 votes (Barnes, Campbell, Evans, Feldberg, Gerard, Kuchwara, Lyons, Mandelbaum, Scheck, Sheward, Sommers, Stearns) to 3 for the Savion Glover-George C. Wolfe-Reg E. Gaines tap dance revue *Bring in 'da Noise Bring in 'da Funk* (Heilpern, Kissel, Winer) and the Laurence Klavan-Polly Pen *Bed and Sofa* (Feingold, Greene, le Sourd) and 1 for the Tina Landau-Adam Guettel *Floyd Collins* (Stuart). The voting for best foreign play was more closely contested, going to a second ballot when no play received a majority of first choices. To win on this point-weighted ballot which includes second and third choices as well as first, a play must collect a point total of three times the number of members present, divided by two, plus one—27 this year. *Molly Sweeney* filled the bill on this ballot (see below) with 34 points to 24 for *Racing Demon*, 23 for *Valley Song*, 20 for *Curtains* and 1 for *Scenes From an Execution*.

Absent Circle members were Greg Evans of *Variety*, Jack Kroll of *Newsweek*, Frank Scheck of the *Christian Science Monitor* and John Simon of *New York*.

SECOND BALLOT FOR BEST FOREIGN PLAY

Critic	*1st Choice (3 pts.)*	*2d Choice (2 pts.)*	*3d Choice (1 pt)*
Clive Barnes *Post*	Racing Demon	Molly Sweeney	Curtains
Mary Campbell AP	Racing Demon	Molly Sweeney	Valley Song
Michael Feingold *Village Voice*	Molly Sweeney	Curtains	Valley Song
Robert Feldberg Bergen *Record*	Molly Sweeney	Valley Song	Curtains
Jeremy Gerard *Variety*	Racing Demon	Valley Song	Molly Sweeney
Alexis Greene *Theater Week*	Molly Sweeney	Valley Song	Curtains
John Heilpern *Observer*	Molly Sweeney	Valley Song	Curtains
Howard Kissel *Daily News*	Molly Sweeney	Curtains	Valley Song
Michael Kuchwara AP	Racing Demon	Curtains	Molly Sweeney
Jacques le Sourd Gannett Papers	Racing Demon	Valley Song	Curtains
Donald Lyons *Wall St. Journal*	Molly Sweeney	Valley Song	Scenes From an Execution
Ken Mandelbaum *Theater Week*	Valley Song	Molly Sweeney	Racing Demon
David Sheward *Back Stage*	Racing Demon	Curtains	Valley Song
Michael Sommers Newhouse Group	Curtains	Molly Sweeney	Valley Song

David Patrick Stearns *USA Today*	Molly Sweeney	Racing Demon	Curtains
Jan Stuart *Newsday*	Molly Sweeney	Curtains	Valley Song
Linda Winer *Newsday*	Racing Demon	Valley Song	Curtains

CHOICES OF SOME OTHER CRITICS

Critic	*Best Play*	*Best Musical*
Donald Burman *Entertainment Tonight*	Master Class	Rent
Casper Citron TV Program	An Ideal Husband	Rent
Matthew Diebel *Post*	Racing Demon	Bring in 'da Noise
Sherry Eager *Back Stage*	The Model Apartment	Rent
Martin Gottfried *N.Y. Law Journal*	A Fair Country	Floyd Collins
John Harris *Theater Week*	Quills	Rent
Ralph Howard WINS Radio	Master Class	Rent
Stewart Klein WNYW-TV	Seven Guitars	Bring in 'da Noise
Roma Torre NY1 News	Seven Guitars	Rent
Ross Wetzsteon *Village Voice*	Quills	Rent
John Willis *Theater World*	Seven Guitars	Victor/Victoria

PULITZER PRIZE WINNERS 1916–17 TO 1995–96

1916–17—No award

1917–18—Why Marry?, by Jesse Lynch Williams

1918–19—No award

1919–20—Beyond the Horizon, by Eugene O'Neill

1920–21—Miss Lulu Bett, by Zona Gale

1921–22—Anna Christie, by Eugene O'Neill

1922–23—Icebound, by Owen Davis

1923–24—Hell-Bent fer Heaven, by Hatcher Hughes

1924–25—They Knew What They Wanted, by Sidney Howard

1925–26—Craig's Wife, by George Kelly

1926–27—In Abraham's Bosom, by Paul Green

1927–28—Strange Interlude, by Eugene O'Neill

1928–29—Street Scene, by Elmer Rice

1929–30—The Green Pastures, by Marc Connelly

1930–31—Alison's House, by Susan Glaspell

1931–32—Of Thee I Sing, by George S. Kaufman, Morrie Ryskind, Ira and George Gershwin

1932–33—Both Your Houses, by Maxwell Anderson

1933–34—Men in White, by Sidney Kingsley
1934–35—The Old Maid, by Zoe Akins
1935–36—Idiot's Delight, by Robert E. Sherwood
1936–37—You Can't Take It With You, by Moss Hart and George S. Kaufman
1937–38—Our Town, by Thornton Wilder
1938–39—Abe Lincoln in Illinois, by Robert E. Sherwood
1939–40—The Time of Your Life, by William Saroyan
1940–41—There Shall Be No Night, by Robert E. Sherwood
1941–42—No award
1942–43—The Skin of Our Teeth, by Thornton Wilder
1943–44—No award
1944–45—Harvey, by Mary Chase
1945–46—State of the Union, by Howard Lindsay and Russel Crouse
1946–47—No award
1947–48—A Streetcar Named Desire, by Tennessee Williams
1948–49—Death of a Salesman, by Arthur Miller
1949–50—South Pacific, by Richard Rodgers, Oscar Hammerstein II and Joshua Logan
1950–51—No award
1951–52—The Shrike, by Joseph Kramm
1952–53—Picnic, by William Inge
1953–54—The Teahouse of the August Moon, by John Patrick
1954–55—Cat on a Hot Tin Roof, by Tennessee Williams
1955–56—The Diary of Anne Frank, by Frances Goodrich and Albert Hackett
1956–57—Long Day's Journey Into Night, by Eugene O'Neill
1957–58—Look Homeward, Angel, by Ketti Frings
1958–59—J.B., by Archibald MacLeish
1959–60—Fiorello!, by Jerome Weidman, George Abbott, Sheldon Harnick and Jerry Bock
1960–61—All the Way Home, by Tad Mosel
1961–62—How to Succeed in Business Without Really Trying, by Abe Burrows, Willie Gilbert, Jack Weinstock and Frank Loesser

1962–63—No award
1963–64—No award
1964–65—The Subject Was Roses, by Frank D. Gilroy
1965–66—No award
1966–67—A Delicate Balance, by Edward Albee
1967–68—No award
1968–69—The Great White Hope, by Howard Sackler
1969–70—No Place To Be Somebody, by Charles Gordone
1970–71—The Effect of Gamma Rays on Man-in-the-Moon Marigolds, by Paul Zindel
1971–72—No award
1972–73—That Championship Season, by Jason Miller
1973–74—No award
1974–75—Seascape, by Edward Albee
1975–76—A Chorus Line, by Michael Bennett, James Kirkwood, Nicholas Dante, Marvin Hamlisch and Edward Kleban
1976–77—The Shadow Box, by Michael Cristofer
1977–78—The Gin Game, by D.L. Coburn
1978–79—Buried Child, by Sam Shepard
1979–80—Talley's Folly, by Lanford Wilson
1980–81—Crimes of the Heart, by Beth Henley
1981–82—A Soldier's Play, by Charles Fuller
1982–83—'night, Mother, by Marsha Norman
1983–84—Glengarry Glen Ross, by David Mamet
1984–85—Sunday in the Park With George, by James Lapine and Stephen Sondheim
1985–86—No award
1986–87—Fences, by August Wilson
1987–88—Driving Miss Daisy, by Alfred Uhry
1988–89—The Heidi Chronicles, by Wendy Wasserstein
1989–90—The Piano Lesson, by August Wilson
1990–91—Lost in Yonkers, by Neil Simon
1991–92—The Kentucky Cycle, by Robert Schenkkan
1992–93—Angels in America: Millennium Approaches, by Tony Kushner
1993–94—Three Tall Women, by Edward Albee
1994–95—The Young Man From Atlanta, by Horton Foote
1995–96—Rent, by Jonathan Larson

THE TONY AWARDS, 1995–96

The American Theater Wing's Antoinette Perry (Tony) Awards are presented annually in recognition of distinguished artistic achievement in the Broadway theater. The League of American Theaters and Producers and the American Theater Wing present the Tony Awards, founded by the Wing in 1947. Legitimate theater productions opening in eligible Broadway theaters during the eligibility season of the current year —May 4, 1995 to May 1, 1996—were considered for Tony nominations.

The Tony Awards Administration Committee appoints the Tony Awards Nominating Committee which makes the actual nominations. The 1995–96 Nominating Committee consisted of Jon Robin Baitz, playwright; Donald Brooks, costume designer; Marge Champion, choreographer; Betty L. Corwin, theater archivist; Gretchen Cryer, composer; Thomas Dillon, administrator; Brendan Gill, historian and writer; Jay Harnick, artistic director; Charles Hollerith, producer; Barnard Hughes, actor; Ming Cho Lee, set designer; Robert McDonald, union administrator; Douglas Watt, critic; and George White, administrator.

For the third time, because of the large number of revivals that opened on Broadway, the category of best revival was split in two (for play and musical).

The Tony Awards are voted from the list of nominees by the members of the governing boards of the five theater artists' organizations: Actors' Equity Association, the Dramatist Guild, the Society of Stage Directors and Choreographers, the United Scenic Artists and the Casting Society of America, plus the members of the designated first night theater press, the board of directors of the American Theater Wing and the membership of the League of American Theaters and Producers. Because of the fluctuation within these boards, the size of the Tony electorate varies from year to year. In the 1995–96 season, there were 720 qualified Tony voters.

The list of 1995–96 nominees follows, with winners in each category listed in **bold face type.**

BEST PLAY (award goes to both author and producer). *Buried Child* by Sam Shepard, produced by Frederick Zollo, Nicholas Paleologos, Jane Harmon, Nina Keneally, Gary Sinise, Edwin Schloss, Liz Oliver; *Master Class* by **Terrence McNally,** produced by **Robert Whitehead, Lewis Allen, Spring Sirkin;** *Racing Demon* by David Hare, produced by Lincoln Center Theater, Andre Bishop, Bernard Gersten; *Seven Guitars* by August Wilson, produced by Sageworks, Benjamin Mordecai, Center Theater Group/Ahmanson Theater, Gordon Davidson, Herb Alpert/ Margo Lion, Scott Rudin/Paramount Pictures, Jujamcyn Theaters, Goodman Theater, Huntington Theater Company, American Conservatory Theater, Manhattan Theater Club.

BEST MUSICAL (award goes to the producer). *Bring in 'da Noise Bring in 'da Funk* produced by the Joseph Papp Public Theater/ New York Shakespeare Festival, George C. Wolfe, Joey Parnes; *Chronicle of a Death Foretold* produced by Lincoln Center Theater, Andre Bishop, Bernard Gersten, INTAR Hispanic Arts Center; *Rent* produced by **Jeffrey Seller, Kevin McCollum, Allan S. Gordon, New York Theater Workshop;** *Swinging on a Star* produced by Richard Seader, Mary Burke Kramer, Paul B. Berkowsky, Angels of the Arts.

BEST BOOK OF A MUSICAL. *Big* by John Weidman; *Bring in da Noise Bring in 'da Funk* by Reg E. Gaines; *Chronicle of a Death Foretold* by Graciela Daniele, Jim Lewis, Michael John LaChiusa; *Rent* by **Jonathan Larson.**

BEST ORIGINAL SCORE (music & lyrics) WRITTEN FOR THE THEATER. *Big,* music by David Shire, lyrics by Richard Maltby Jr.; *Bring in 'da Noise Bring in 'da Funk,* music by Daryl Waters, Zane Mark, Ann Duquesnay, lyrics by Reg E. Gaines, George C. Wolfe, Ann Duquesnay; *Rent,* music and lyrics by **Jonathan Larson;** *State Fair,* music by

Richard Rodgers, lyrics by Oscar Hammerstein II (only four songs in the score eligible for nomination).

BEST LEADING ACTOR IN A PLAY. Philip Bosco in *Moon Over Buffalo*, **George Grizzard** in *A Delicate Balance*, George C. Scott in *Inherit the Wind*, Martin Shaw in *An Ideal Husband*.

BEST LEADING ACTRESS IN A PLAY. Carol Burnett in *Moon Over Buffalo*, **Zoe Caldwell** in *Master Class*, Rosemary Harris in *A Delicate Balance*, Elaine Stritch in *A Delicate Balance*.

BEST LEADING ACTOR IN A MUSICAL. Savion Glover in *Bring in 'da Noise Bring in 'da Funk*, **Nathan Lane** in *A Funny Thing Happened on the Way to the Forum*, Adam Pascal in *Rent*, Lou Diamond Phillips in *The King and I*.

BEST LEADING ACTRESS IN A MUSICAL. Julie Andrews in *Victor/Victoria*, Crista Moore in *Big*, **Donna Murphy** in *The King and I*, Daphne Rubin-Vega in *Rent*.

BEST FEATURED ACTOR IN A PLAY. James Gammon in *Buried Child*, Roger Robinson in *Seven Guitars*, Reg Rogers in *Holiday*, **Ruben Santiago-Hudson** in *Seven Guitars*.

BEST FEATURED ACTRESS IN A PLAY. Viola Davis in *Seven Guitars*, **Audra McDonald** in *Master Class*, Michele Shay in *Seven Guitars*, Lois Smith in *Buried Child*.

BEST FEATURED ACTOR IN A MUSICAL. **Wilson Jermaine Heredia** in *Rent*, Lewis J. Stadlen in *A Funny Thing Happened on the Way to the Forum*, Brett Tabisel in *Big*, Scott Wise in *State Fair*.

BEST FEATURED ACTRESS IN A MUSICAL. Joohee Choi in *The King and I*, Veanne Cox in *Company*, **Ann Duquesnay** in *Bring in 'da Noise Bring in 'da Funk*, Idina Menzel in *Rent*.

BEST DIRECTION OF A PLAY. **Gerald Gutierrez** for *A Delicate Balance*, Peter Hall for *An Ideal Husband*, Lloyd Richards for *Seven Guitars*, Gary Sinise for *Buried Child*.

BEST DIRECTION OF A MUSICAL. Michael Greif for *Rent*, Christopher Renshaw for *The King and I*, **George C. Wolfe** for *Bring in 'da Noise Bring in 'da Funk*, Jerry Zaks for *A Funny Thing Happened on the Way to the Forum*.

BEST SCENIC DESIGN. John Lee Beatty for *A Delicate Balance*, Scott Bradley for *Seven Guitars*, **Brian Thomson** for *The King and I*, Anthony Ward for *A Midsummer Night's Dream*.

BEST COSTUME DESIGN. Jane Greenwood for *A Delicate Balance*, **Roger Kirk** for *The King and I*, Allison Reeds for *Buried Child*, Paul Tazewell for *Bring in 'da Noise Bring in 'da Funk*.

BEST LIGHTING DESIGN. Christopher Akerlind for *Seven Guitars*, Blake Burba for *Rent*, **Jules Fisher/Peggy Eisenhauer** for *Bring in 'da Noise Bring in 'da Funk*, Nigel Levings for *The King and I*.

BEST CHOREOGRAPHY. Graciela Daniele for *Chronicle of a Death Foretold*, **Savion Glover** for *Bring in 'da Noise Bring in 'da Funk*, Susan Stroman for *Big*, Marlies Yearby for *Rent*.

BEST REVIVAL OF A PLAY (award goes to the producer). **A *Delicate Balance*** produced by **Lincoln Center Theater, Andre Bishop, Bernard Gersten;** *A Midsummer Night's Dream* produced by Terry Allen Kramer, James L. Nederlander, Carole Shorenstein Hays, The John F. Kennedy Center for the Performing Arts, Elizabeth Ireland McCann, The Royal Shakespeare Company; *An Ideal Husband* produced by Bill Kenwright; *Inherit the Wind* produced by National Actors Theater, Tony Randall.

BEST REVIVAL OF A MUSICAL (award goes to the producer). *A Funny Thing Happened on the Way to the Forum* produced by Jujamcyn Theaters, Scott Rudin/Paramount Pictures, The Viertel-Baruch-Frankel Group, Roger Berlind, Dodger Productions; *Company* produced by Roundabout Theater Company, Todd Haimes, Ellen Richard; *Hello, Dolly!* produced by Manny Kladitis, Magic Promotions and Theatricals, Pace The-

ON THE MUSICAL AWARDS LISTS—*Above*, Lisa Leguillou, Rene M. Ceballos, Monica McSwain, Tonya Pinkins, Denise Faye and Alexandre Proia in *Chronicle of a Death Foretold*, nominated for best musical and for Graciela Daniele's book and choreography in the Tony competition sponsored by the League of American Theaters and Producers; *below*, Theresa McCarthy, Cass Morgan, Don Chastain, James Bohanek, Brian d'Arcy James and Matthew Bennett in *Floyd Collins*, named best musical in the Lucille Lortel competition sponsored by the League of Off-Broadway Theaters and Producers

atrical Group, Inc., Jon B. Platt; *The King and I* produced by **Dodger Productions, The John F. Kennedy Center for the Performing Arts, James M. Nederlander, Perseus Productions, John Frost, The Adelaide Festival Center, The Rodgers and Hammerstein Organization.**

SPECIAL TONY AWARD. Regional Theater Award to **The Alley Theater,** Houston, Texas.

TONY AWARD WINNERS, 1947–1996

Listed below are the Antoinette Perry (Tony) Award winners in the categories of Best Play and Best Musical from the time these awards were established until the present.

1947—No play or musical award
1948—Mister Roberts; no musical award
1949—Death of a Salesman; Kiss Me, Kate
1950—The Cocktail Party; South Pacific
1951—The Rose Tattoo; Guys and Dolls
1952—The Fourposter; The King and I
1953—The Crucible; Wonderful Town
1954—The Teahouse of the August Moon; Kismet
1955—The Desperate Hours; The Pajama Game
1956—The Diary of Anne Frank; Damn Yankees
1957—Long Day's Journey Into Night; My Fair Lady
1958—Sunrise at Campobello; The Music Man
1959—J.B.; Redhead
1960—The Miracle Worker; Fiorello! and The Sound of Music (tie)
1961—Becket; Bye Bye Birdie
1962—A Man for All Seasons; How to Succeed in Business Without Really Trying
1963—Who's Afraid of Virginia Woolf?, A Funny Thing Happened on the Way to the Forum
1964—Luther; Hello, Dolly!
1965—The Subject Was Roses; Fiddler on the Roof
1966—The Persecution and Assassination of Marat as Performed by the Inmates of the Asylum of Charenton Under the Direction of the Marquis de Sade; Man of La Mancha
1967—The Homecoming; Cabaret
1968—Rosencrantz and Guildenstern Are Dead; Hallelujah, Baby!
1969—The Great White Hope; 1776
1970—Borstal Boy; Applause
1971—Sleuth; Company

1972—Sticks and Bones; Two Gentlemen of Verona
1973—That Championship Season; A Little Night Music
1974—The River Niger; Raisin
1975—Equus; The Wiz
1976—Travesties; A Chorus Line
1977—The Shadow Box; Annie
1978—Da; Ain't Misbehavin'
1979—The Elephant Man; Sweeney Todd, the Demon Barber of Fleet Street
1980—Children of a Lesser God; Evita
1981—Amadeus; 42nd Street
1982—The Life & Adventures of Nicholas Nickleby; Nine
1983—Torch Song Trilogy; Cats
1984—The Real Thing; La Cage aux Folles
1985—Biloxi Blues; Big River
1986—I'm Not Rappaport; The Mystery of Edwin Drood
1987—Fences; Les Misérables
1988—M. Butterfly; The Phantom of the Opera
1989—The Heidi Chronicles; Jerome Robbins' Broadway
1990—The Grapes of Wrath; City of Angels
1991—Lost in Yonkers; The Will Rogers Follies
1992—Dancing at Lughnasa; Crazy for You
1993—Angels in America, Part I: Millennium Approaches; Kiss of the Spider Woman
1994—Angels in America, Part II: Perestroika; Passion
1995—Love! Valour! Compassion!; Sunset Boulevard
1996—Master Class; Rent

THE LUCILLE LORTEL AWARDS

The Lucille Lortel Awards were established in 1985 by a resolution of the League of Off-Broadway Theaters and Producers, which administers them and has presented them annually since 1986 for outstanding off-Broadway achievement. Eligible for the 11th annual awards in 1996 were all off-Broadway productions which opened between March 1, 1995 and March 31, 1996 except any which had moved from an off-Broadway to a Broadway theater. The 1995 selection committee was composed of Clive Barnes, Howard Kissel, Alvin Klein, Jack Kroll, Michael Kuchwara, John Simon, Linda Winer and Miss Lortel.

PLAY. *Molly Sweeney* by **Brian Friel.**

MUSICAL. *Floyd Collins* book by **Tina Landau,** music and lyrics by **Adam Guettel.**

REVIVAL. *Entertaining Mr. Sloane* produced by **Classic Stage Company.**

ACTOR IN A PLAY. **Jim Dale** in *Travels With My Aunt.*

ACTRESS IN A PLAY. **Uta Hagen** in *Mrs. Klein.*

ACTOR IN A MUSICAL. **Jason Workman** in *Bed and Sofa.*

ACTRESS IN A MUSICAL. **Melissa Errico** in *One Touch of Venus.*

DIRECTOR. **Scott Elliott** for *The Monogamist.*

SET DESIGN. **Tony Walton** for *A Fair Country.*

LIGHTING DESIGN. **Michael Chybowski** for *The Grey Zone.*

COSTUME DESIGN. **Jane Greenwood** for *Sylvia.*

BODY OF WORK. **Athol Fugard.**

SPECIAL ACHIEVEMENT. **Cora Cahan** and **Theaterworks USA.**

LIFETIME ACHIEVEMENT. **Gene Feist.**

LIFETIME DEDICATION TO OFF BROADWAY. **Edith Oliver.**

LORTEL AWARD WINNERS, 1986–96

Listed below are the Lucille Lortel Award winners in the categories of Outstanding Play and Outstanding Musical from the time these awards were established until the present.

1986—Woza Africa!; no musical award
1987—The Common Pursuit; no musical award
1988—No play or musical award
1989—The Cocktail Hour; no musical award
1990—No play or musical award
1991—Aristocrats; Falsettoland

1992—Lips Together, Teeth Apart; And the World Goes 'Round
1993—The Destiny of Me; Forbidden Broadway
1994—Three Tall Women; Wings
1995—Camping With Henry & Tom; Jelly Roll!
1996—Molly Sweeney, Floyd Collins

ADDITIONAL PRIZES AND AWARDS, 1995–96

The following is a list of major prizes and awards for achievement in the theater this season. In all cases the names of winners appear in **bold face type** and the titles of winners appear in **bold face italics.**

11th ANNUAL ATCA AWARDS. For outstanding new plays in cross-country theater, voted by a committee of the American Theater Critics Association. 1995 New Play Award: *Amazing Grace* by Michael Cristofer. 1995 Citations: *Seven Guitars* by August Wilson; *Jungle Rot* by Seth Greenland. 1995 Elizabeth Osborn Award for an emerging playwright: **Richard Kalinoski** for *Beast on the Moon.*

15th ANNUAL WILLIAM INGE FESTIVAL AWARD. For distinguished achievement in American theater. **August Wilson.**

18th ANNUAL SUSAN SMITH BLACKBURN PRIZE. For a play of outstanding quality written by a woman for the English-speaking theater, selected by a committee comprising Richard Coe, Heidi Landesman, James MacDonald, Sharon Ott, Fiona Shaw and Charles Spencer, *One Flea Spare* by Naomi Wallace. Runners-up: *Nine Armenians* by Leslie Ayvazian; *Disappeared* by Phyllis Nagy.

1995 ELIZABETH HULL-KATE WARRINER AWARD. To the playwright whose work dealt with controversial subjects involving the fields of political, religious or social mores of the time, selected by the Dramatists Guild Council. **Emily Mann** for *Having Our Say: The Delany Sisters' First Hundred Years.*

12th ANNUAL GEORGE AND ELISABETH MARTON AWARD. To an American playwright, selected by a committee of Young Playwrights, Inc. **Chay Yew** for *A Language of Their Own.*

1995 THEATER HALL OF FAME FOUNDERS AWARD. For outstanding contribution to the theater. **Harvey Sabinson.**

18th ANNUAL KENNEDY CENTER HONORS. For distinguished achievement by individuals who have made significant contributions to American culture through the arts. **Jacques d'Amboise, Marilyn Horne, B.B. King, Sidney Poitier, Neil Simon.**

GEORGE JEAN NATHAN AWARD. For dramatic criticism, administered by the Cornell University English department. **Robert Hurwitt.**

4th ANNUAL ROBERT WHITEHEAD AWARD. For an outstanding new theater producer. **Randall L. Wreghitt.**

11th ANNUAL MR. ABBOTT AWARDS. For lifetime achievement, presented by the Stage Directors and Choreographers Foundation. **Gordon Davidson; Bernadette Peters; The Really Useful Group.**

1996 AMERICAN THEATER WING DESIGN AWARDS. For design originating in the U.S. voted by a committee comprising Tish Dace (chair), Jeremy Gerard, Alexis Greene, Henry Hewes, Jeffrey Sweet and Joan Ungaro. Scenic design: **Christopher Barreca** for *Chronicle of a Death Foretold.* Costume design: **Angela Wendt** for *Rent.* Lighting design: **Jules Fisher** and **Peggy Eisenhauer** for *Bring in 'da Noise Bring in 'da Funk.* Noteworth unusual effects: **Karen Ten Eyck** for projections and **Julie Archer** for Rose the Dog and Sri Moo in *An Epidog.*

1995 SUSAN STEIN SHIVA AWARD. For an artist who, having started a career in the theater, has gone on to achieve fame and popularity in film and television, while remaining committed to the stage; presented by New York Shakespeare Festival. **Morgan Freeman.**

51ST ANNUAL CLARENCE DERWENT AWARDS. For the most promising male and female performers on the metropolitan scene.

Ruben Santiago-Hudson for *Seven Guitars;* **LisaGay Hamilton** for *Valley Song.*

52d ANNUAL *THEATER WORLD* AWARDS. For outstanding new talent in Broadway and off-Broadway productions during the 1995–96 season, selected by a committee comprising Clive Barnes, Frank Scheck, Michael Sommer, Douglas Watt and John Willis. **Jordan Baker** in *Suddenly Last Summer,* **Joohee Choi** and **Lou Diamond Phillips** in *The King and I,* **Karen Kay Cody** in *Master Class,* **Viola Davis** in *Seven Guitars,* **Kate Forbes** in *The School for Scandal,* **Michael McGrath** in *Swinging on a Star,* **Alfred Molina** in *Molly Sweeney,* **Timothy Olyphant** in *The Monogamist,* **Adam Pascal** and **Daphne Rubin-Vega** in *Rent,* **Brett Tabisel** in *Big.*

62d ANNUAL DRAMA LEAGUE AWARDS. For distinguished achievement in theater. Play: *Seven Guitars.* Musical: *Rent.* Revival: *A Delicate Balance.* Distinguished performance: **Uta Hagen.** Distinguished achievement in musical theater: **George C. Wolfe.** Unique contribution to theater: **42d Street Development Project.**

41st ANNUAL DRAMA DESK AWARDS. For outstanding achievement in the 1995–96 season, voted by an association of New York drama reporters, editors and critics from nominations made by Robert Feldberg, Peter Filichia, Alexis Greene, Frank Scheck, David Sheward, Michael Sommers and David Patrick Stearns. New play: *Master Class.* New musical: *Rent.* Revival of a play: *A Delicate Balance.* Revival of a musical: *The King and I.* Actor in a play: **Frank Langella** in *The Father.* Actress in a play: **Zoe Caldwell** in *Master Class.* Actor in a musical: **Nathan Lane** in *A Funny Thing Happened on the Way to the Forum.* Actress in a musical: **Julie Andrews** in *Victor/Victoria.* Featured actor in a play: **Martin Shaw** in *An Ideal Husband.* Featured actress in a play: **Elaine Stritch** in *A Delicate Balance.* Featered actor in a musical: **Wilson Jermaine Heredia** in *Rent.* Featured actress in a musical: **Rachel York** in *Victor/Victoria.* Solo performance: **Mary Louise Wilson** in *Full Gallop.* Book, lyrics and music of a musical (three awards): **Jonathan Larson** for *Rent.* Direction of a play: **Gerald Gutierrez**

for *A Delicate Balance.* Direction of a musical: **Christopher Renshaw** for *The King and I.* Choreography: **Savion Glover** for *Bring in 'da Noise Bring in 'da Funk.* Scenery of a play: **Scott Bradley** for *Seven Guitars.* Scenery of a musical: **Brian Thomson** for *The King and I.* Costumes: **Roger Kirk** for *The King and I.* Lighting: **Jules Fisher** and **Peggy Eisenhauer** for *Bring in 'da Noise Bring in 'da Funk.* Sound: **Dan Moses Schreier** for *Floyd Collins.* Orchestration: **Steve Skinner** for *Rent.*

41st ANNUAL *VILLAGE VOICE* OBIE AWARDS. For outstanding achievement in off- and off-off Broadway Theater, chosen by a panel of judges chaired by Ross Wetzsteon. Distinguished performance: **Julie Archer** and **Barbara Pollitt** in *An Epidog,* **Gerry Bamman** in *Nixon's Nixon,* **LisaGay Hamilton** in *Valley Song,* **Terri Klausner** in *Bed and Sofa,* **Tom McGowan** in *The Food Chain,* **Mark Nelson** in *Picasso at the Lapin Agile,* **Adina Porter** in *Venus,* **Marty Pottenger** in *City Water Tunnel #3,* **Virginia Rambal** in *Troya de Merica/La Dama Duende,* **Rocco Sisto** in *Quills,* **Steven Skybell** in *Antigone in New York,* **Derek Smith** in *The Green Bird,* **James Urbaniak** in *The Universe,* **Mary Louise Wilson** in *Full Gallop;* **the cast** of *Curtains;* **the cast** of *Rent.* Sustained excellence: direction, **Ingmar Bergman;** performance, **Kathleen Chalfant, Henry Stram;** lighting design, **Jeffrey S. Koger;** set design, **Neil Patel;** music, **David Van Tieghem.** Direction, **Scott Elliott** for *Curtains,* **Michael Greif** for *Rent,* **Doug Hughes** for *The Grey Zone.* Orchestration: **Bruce Coughlin** for *Floyd Collins.* Choreography/Dance: **Savion Glover** for *Bring in 'da Noise Bring in 'da Funk.* Playwriting: **Ain Gordon** for *Wally's Ghost,* **Donald Margulies** for *The Model Apartment,* **Suzan-Lori Parks** for *Venus,* **Doug Wright** for *Quills.* Music: **Adam Guettel** for *Floyd Collins,* **Polly Pen** for *Bed and Sofa.* Book, lyrics and music, **Jonathan Larson** for *Rent.*

Other awards and grants: **Repertorio Espanol** for its New Voices Series; **New Georges; Uta Hagen** for sustained achievement; **TEBA Teatro Experimental Blue Amigos; Adrienne Kennedy** for *June and Jean in Concert* and *Sleep Deprivation Chamber.*

46th ANNUAL OUTER CRITICS CIRCLE AWARDS. For outstanding achievement in the 1995–96 season, voted by an organization of critics on out-of-town periodicals and media. Broadway play: *Master Class.* Broadway musical: *Victor/Victoria.* Off-Broadway play: *Molly Sweeney, Picasso at the Lapin Agile* (tie). Off-Broadway musical: *Rent.* Revival of a play: *Inherit the Wind.* Revival of a musical: *The King and I.* Direction of a play: **Lloyd Richards** for *Seven Guitars.* Direction of a musical: **Jerry Zaks** for *A Funny Thing Happened on the Way to the Forum.* Choreography: **Savion Glover** for *Bring in 'da Noise Bring in 'da Funk.* Actor in a play: **George C. Scott** in *Inherit the Wind.* Actress in a play: **Zoe Caldwell** in *Master Class.* Actor in a musical: **Nathan Lane** in *A Funny Thing Happened on the Way to the Forum.* Actress in a musical: **Julie Andrews** in *Victor/Victoria.* Solo Performance: **Patti LuPone** in *Patti LuPone on Broadway.* Debut of an actor: **Lou Diamond Phillips** in *The King and I.* Debut of an actress: **Karen Kay Cody** in *Master Class.* Design: *The King and I.*

John Gassner Award for an American play: *Picasso at the Lapin Agile.* Special achievement awards: **Carol Channing** for *Hello, Dolly!;* **Betty Corwin** as founder of the New York Public Library's Theater on Film and Tape Archive; **the cast** of *Seven Guitars* for ensemble performance.

1995–96 CONNECTICUT CRITICS CIRCLE AWARDS. For outstanding achievement in Connecticut theater during the 1995–96 season. Production of a play: **Hartford Stage** for *Blues for an Alabama Sky* by Pearl Cleage. Production of a musical: **Goodspeed Opera House** for *Sweeney Todd.* Actor in a play: **Neil Stewart** in *Butley;* **Max Wright** in *Denial.* Actress in a play: **Marian Seldes** in *Three Tall Women.* Actor and actress in a musical: **Timothy Nolen** and **Barbara Marineau** in *Sweeney Todd.* Director of a play: **Mark Lamos** for *Romeo and Juliet* and *The Rivals.* Director of a musical: **Gabriel Barre** for *Sweeney Todd.* Choreography: **Craig North** for *42nd Street.* Set design: **Michael Yeargan** for *Pentecost* and *Romeo and Juliet.* Lighting design: **Hugh Hallinan** for *Blackbirds of Broadway.* Costume design: **Jess Goldstein** for *The Rivals.* Sound design: **David Budries** for

Ghosts, Romeo and Juliet, The Rivals and *Pentecost.* Ensemble performance: **Tim Choate, Martin Garcia, Julia Gibson, Ann McDonough, Eve Michelson, Richard Nagel, Robert Sella** in *Almost All in the Timing.*

Tom Killen Award: **Mark Lamos.** Lucille Lortel Debut Award: **Alex Woods** in *Moonshadow.* Special Achievement Award: **Joyce Ebert.**

3d ANNUAL BOSTON THEATER AWARDS (formerly Elliot Norton Awards). For outstanding contribution to the theater in Boston, voted by a committee comprising Skip Ascheim, Carolyn Clay, Iris Fanger, Arthur Friedman, Joyce Kulhawik, Jon Lehman, Bill Marx, Ed Siegel, Caldwell Titcomb. Large visiting company—Production: *Three Tall Women.* Designer: **Ian MacNeil** for the sets of *An Inspector Calls.* Small visiting company—Production: *The Diary of Anne Frank.* Large resident company—Production: *A Raisin in the Sun.* Director: **Kenny Leon** for *A Raisin in the Sun.* Actor: **Ralph Waite** in *The Young Man From Atlanta.* Actress: **Patti Allison** in *The Threepenny Opera* and *Iolanthe.* Small resident company—Production: *All in the Timing.* Director: **Spiro Veloudos** for *Sweeney Todd* and *Anything Goes.* Designer: **John Malinowski** for the lighting of *Weldon Rising.* Actor and actress: **Doug Stender** and **Karen MacDonald** in *Who's Afraid of Virginia Woolf?* Local fringe company—Production: *Jeffrey.*

Script in its local premiere: *Seven Guitars.* Lifetime Achievement Award: **Uta Hagen.** Elliot Norton Prize for Sustained Excellence: **Alvin Epstein.** Special citations: **John Langstaff** for his 25 years as inspiration and impresario of seasonal celebrations combining ritual theater, dance and music from around the world; **Shakespeare & Company** for continued excellence in illuminating the works of Shakespeare, Wharton and others, and for the vitality of its education program.

12th ANNUAL HELEN HAYES AWARDS. In recognition of excellence in Washington, D.C. area theater, presented by the Washington Theater Awards Society. Resident productions—Play: *The Pitchfork Disney.* Musical: *Bessie's Blues.* Actor in a play: **Wallace Acton** in *The Pitchfork Disney.*

Actress in a play: **Tana Hicken** in *Long Day's Journey Into Night.* Actor in a musical: **Steven Cupo** in *Cabaret.* Actress in a musical: **Dahd Sfeir** in *Mano a Mano.* Supporting actor in a play: **Henry Strozier** in *A Month in the Country.* Supporting actress in a play: **June Kyoko Lu** in *The Waiting Room.* Supporting actor and actress in a musical: **David A. St. Louis** and **Roz White** in *Bessie's Blues.* Director of a play: **Douglas Wager** for *Long Day's Journey Into Night.* Director of a musical: **Thomas Jones II** for *Bessie's Blues* and **James Petosa** for *Jacques Brel* (tie). Choreography: **Patdro Harris** for *Bessie's Blues.* Musical direction: **Dave Ferguson** for *Bessie's Blues.* Set design: **James Kronzer** for *Conversations With My Father.* Lighting design: **Howell Binkley** for *Henry V.* Costume design: **Anita Stewart** for *Love's Labour's Lost.* Sound design: **Daniel Schrader** for *The Pitchfork Disney.*

Non-resident productions: Play or musical: *Angels in America, Part I: Millennium Approaches.* Actor: **Jonathan Hadary** in *Angels in America.* Actress: **Zoe Caldwell** in *Master Class.*

Charles MacArthur Award for New Play: *The Psychic Life of Savages* by **Amy Freed.**

27th ANNUAL JOSEPH JEFFERSON AWARDS. For achievement in Chicago Theater during the 1994-95 season, selected by a 40-member Jefferson Awards Committee from 109 Equity productions offered by 45 producing organizations. Resident productions—Play: *Angels in America, Parts 1 and 2.* Musical: *Hello, Dolly!, Pope Joan* (tie). Revue: *Forever Plaid.* Actor in a principal role, play: **Jonathan Hadary** in *Angels in America.* Actress in a principal role, play: **Nan Martin** in *Three Tall Women.* Actor in a principal role, musical: **Andrew J. Lupp** in *Singin' in the Rain.* Actress in a principal role, musical: **Alene Robertson** in *Hello, Dolly!* Supporting actor, play: **Brad Armacost** in *Faith Healer.* Supporting actress, play: **Barbara Robertson** in *Angels in America.* Supporting actor and actress, musical: **Marshall Titus** and **LaTonya Holmes** in *Dreamgirls.* Actor in a revue: **John Steven Crowley** in *Doo Wop Shoo Bop,* **Kurt Johns** in *Rodgers and Hammerstein's A Grand Night for Singing* (tie). Actress in a revue: **Velma Austin** in

The Colored Museum, **Hollis Resnik** in *The World Goes 'round,* **Nancy Voights** in *Falling in Love With Love* (tie). Ensemble: *Forever Plaid.* Director, play: **Michael Mayer** for *Angels in America.* Director, musical: **David Zak** for *Pope Joan.* Director, revue: **Stuart Ross** for *Forever Plaid.* New work or adaptation (multiple votes permitted): **Gloria Bond Clunie** for *North Star,* **Christopher Moore** for *Pope Joan,* **Mary Zimmerman** for *Journey to the West.* Original music: **Joseph Shabalala** for *Nomathemba.* Scene design: **Robert Brill** for *A Clockwork Orange.* Costume design: **Allison Reeds** for *Journey to the West.* Lighting design: **Kevin Rigdon** for *A Clockwork Orange.* Sound design: **Michael Bodeen** and **Rob Milburn** for *A Clockwork Orange.* Choreography: **Jim Corti** for *Singin' in the Rain.* Musical direction: **Kevin Cole** for *Forever Plaid.*

Touring productions—Production: *Kiss of the Spider Woman.* Actor in a principal role: **Juan Chioran** in *Kiss of the Spider Woman.* Actress in a principal role: **Petula Clark** in *Blood Brothers.* Supporting actor: **Savion Glover** in *Jelly's Last Jam,* **Richard Kinsey** in *Les Miserables* (tie). Supporting actress: **Jessica-Snow Wilson** in *Les Miserables.*

Special Awards: **Diane Rudall, WTTW** and the **Special Collections Department of the Chicago Public Library** for outstanding contributions to Theater Year Chicago; **Nicholas Rudall** whose vision, commitment and energy transformed the Court Theater into a vital professional company.

27th ANNUAL LOS ANGELES DRAMA CRITICS AWARDS. For distinguished achievement in Los Angeles Theater during 1995 (since they do not designate "bests," there can be multiple recipients, or none, in any category). Production: *Beauty and the Beast, The Homecoming, Wit.* Writing: **Margaret Edson** for *Wit,* **Brad Fraser** for *Unidentified Human Remains and the True Nature of Love,* **Deborah Rogin** adaptation of Maxine Hong Kingston's *The Woman Warrior.* Original music: **Ron Abel** for *Twist of Fate.* Lead performance: **Zoe Caldwell** in *Master Class,* **Megan Cole** in *Wit,* **Julie Hagerty** in *Raised in Captivity,* **Charles Hallahan** in *Endgame,* **Gregory Itzin** and **W. Morgan Sheppard** in *The Homecoming,* **Marcia Mitzman** and **Sean**

Smith in *Chess.* Featured performance: **Jane Carr** and **Douglas Sills** in *She Stoops to Folly,* **Tsai Chin** in *The Woman Warrior,* **Jane Kaczmarek** in *Raised in Captivity.* Direction: **Martin Benson** for *Wit,* **Andrew J. Robinson** for *Endgame* and *The Homecoming.* Scenic design: **Ralph Funicello** for *She Stoops to Folly,* **Stan Meyer** for *Beauty and the Beast.* Lighting design: **Paulie Jenkins** for *Wit,* **Natasha Katz** for *Beauty and the Beast.* Costume design: **Ann Hould-Ward** for *Beauty and the Beast,* **Shigeru Yaji** for *She Stoops to Folly.* Musical direction: **Ron Abel** for *Twist of Fate.* Choreography: **Rob Marshall** for *Damn Yankees.*

Special Awards—Lifetime achievement: **Carol Channing.** Ted Schmitt Award: **Margaret Edson** for *Wit.* Margaret Harford Award: **A Noise Within** theater company. Angstrom Lighting Award: **Robert W. Zentis.** Natalie Schafer Award: **Bonita Friedericy.**

1995 LOS ANGELES OVATION AWARDS. Peer-judged by Theater LA, an association of more than 130 theater companies and producers, as "bests" from 183 entries. Writing of a world premiere play: **Lee Murphy** for *Catch a Falling Star.* New translation/adaptation: *Medea* by **Kenneth Albers.** In a larger theater—Musical: *Beauty and the Beast.* Play: *Master Class.* In a smaller theater—Franklin R. Levy Award for musical: *Sweeney Todd.* Play: *Counsellor-at-Law.* Lead actor and actress in a musical: **Sean Smith** and **Marcia Mitzman** in *Chess.* Lead actor in a play: **Joe Garcia** in *The Puppet Master of Lodz.* Lead actress in a play: **Zoe Caldwell** in *Master Class.* Featured actor in a musical: **Radmar Agana Jao** in *Sweeney Todd.* Featured actress in a play: **Reg Flowers** in *Angels in America.* Featured actress in a musical: **Beth Fowler** in *Beauty and the Beast.* Featured actress in a play: **Audra McDonald** in *Master Class.* Director of a musical: **Tim Dang** for *Sweeney Todd.* Director of a play: **Leonard Foglia** for *Master Class.* Choreography: **Joey McKneely** for *Smokey Joe's Cafe.* In a larger theater—Lighting design: **Brian MacDevitt** for *Master Class.* Set design: **John B. Wilson** for *Man of La Mancha.* Costume design: **Ann Hould-Ward** for *Beauty and the Beast.* Sound design: **Jon Gottlieb** for *Master Class.* In a smaller theater—Lighting design: **G. Shizuko Herrera** for *Sweeney Todd.* Set design: **Chris Tashima** for *Sweeney Todd.* Costume design: **Barbara Ayers** for *Counsellor-at-Law.* Sound design: **John Rubinstein** for *Counsellor-at-Law.*

Lifetime achievement: **Martin Benson, David Emmes.**

THE THEATER HALL OF FAME

The Theater Hall of Fame was created to honor those who have made outstanding contributions to the American theater in a career spanning at least 25 years. Members are elected annually by the nation's drama critics and editors (names of those so elected in 1995 and inducted January 22, 1996 appear in ***bold face italics***).

GEORGE ABBOTT

MAUDE ADAMS

VIOLA ADAMS

STELLA ADLER

EDWARD ALBEE

THEONI V. ALDREDGE

IRA ALDRIDGE

JANE ALEXANDER

WINTHROP AMES

JUDITH ANDERSON

MAXWELL ANDERSON

ROBERT ANDERSON

MARGARET ANGLIN

HAROLD ARLEN

GEORGE ARLISS

BORIS ARONSON

ADELE ASTAIRE

FRED ASTAIRE

BROOKS ATKINSON

PEARL BAILEY

GEORGE BALANCHINE

WILLIAM BALL

ANNE BANCROFT

TALLULAH BANKHEAD

RICHARD BARR

PHILIP BARRY

ETHEL BARRYMORE

JOHN BARRYMORE

LIONEL BARRYMORE

NORA BAYES

S.N. BEHRMAN

NORMAN BEL GEDDES

DAVID BELASCO

MICHAEL BENNETT

RICHARD BENNETT

IRVING BERLIN

SARAH BERNHARDT

LEONARD BERNSTEIN

EARL BLACKWELL

KERMIT BLOOMGARDEN

JERRY BOCK

RAY BOLGER

EDWIN BOOTH

JUNIUS BRUTUS BOOTH

SHIRLEY BOOTH

ALICE BRADY

FANNIE BRICE

PETER BROOK

JOHN MASON BROWN

BILLIE BURKE

ABE BURROWS

RICHARD BURTON

MRS. PATRICK CAMPBELL

ZOE CALDWELL

EDDIE CANTOR

MORRIS CARNOVSKY

MRS. LESLIE CARTER

GOWER CHAMPION

FRANK CHANFRAU

CAROL CHANNING

RUTH CHATTERTON

PADDY CHAYEFSKY

INA CLAIRE

BOBBY CLARK

HAROLD CLURMAN

LEE J. COBB

GEORGE M. COHAN

JACK COLE

CY COLEMAN

CONSTANCE COLLIER

BETTY COMDEN

MARC CONNELLY

BARBARA COOK

KATHARINE CORNELL

NOEL COWARD

JANE COWL

LOTTA CRABTREE

CHERYL CRAWFORD

HUME CRONYN

RUSSEL CROUSE

CHARLOTTE CUSHMAN

JEAN DALRYMPLE

AUGUSTIN DALY

E.L. DAVENPORT

OSSIE DAVIS

RUBY DEE

ALFRED DE LIAGRE JR.

AGNES DEMILLE

COLLEEN DEWHURST

HOWARD DIETZ

DUDLEY DIGGES

MELVYN DOUGLAS

ALFRED DRAKE

MARIE DRESSLER

JOHN DREW

MRS. JOHN DREW

WILLIAM DUNLAP

MILDRED DUNNOCK

ELEANORA DUSE

JEANNE EAGELS

FRED EBB

FLORENCE ELDRIDGE

LEHMAN ENGEL

MAURICE EVANS

ABE FEDER

JOSE FERRER

CY FEUER

DOROTHY FIELDS

HERBERT FIELDS

LEWIS FIELDS

W.C. FIELDS

JULES FISHER

MINNIE MADDERN FISKE

CLYDE FITCH

GERALDINE FITZGERALD

HENRY FONDA

LYNN FONTANNE

HORTON FOOTE

EDWIN FORREST

BOB FOSSE

RUDOLF FRIML

CHARLES FROHMAN

GRACE GEORGE

GEORGE GERSHWIN

IRA GERSHWIN

JOHN GIELGUD

JACK GILFORD

WILLIAM GILLETTE

CHARLES GILPIN

LILLIAN GISH
JOHN GOLDEN
MAX GORDON
RUTH GORDON
ADOLPH GREEN
PAUL GREEN
CHARLOTTE GREENWOOD
JOEL GREY
JOHN GUARE
TYRONE GUTHRIE
UTA HAGEN
LEWIS HALLAM
OSCAR HAMMERSTEIN II
WALTER HAMPDEN
OTTO HARBACH
E.Y. HARBURG
SHELDON HARNICK
EDWARD HARRIGAN
JED HARRIS
JULIE HARRIS
ROSEMARY HARRIS
SAM H. HARRIS
REX HARRISON
KITTY CARLISLE HART
LORENZ HART
MOSS HART
TONY HART
HELEN HAYES
LELAND HAYWARD
BEN HECHT
EILEEN HECKART
THERESA HELBURN
LILLIAN HELLMAN
KATHARINE HEPBURN
VICTOR HERBERT
JERRY HERMAN
JAMES A. HERNE
AL HIRSCHFELD
RAYMOND HITCHCOCK
CELESTE HOLM
HANYA HOLM
ARTHUR HOPKINS
DE WOLF HOPPER
JOHN HOUSEMAN
EUGENE HOWARD
LESLIE HOWARD
SIDNEY HOWARD
WILLIE HOWARD
BARNARD HUGHES
HENRY HULL
JOSEPHINE HULL
WALTER HUSTON
WILLIAM INGE

BERNARD B. JACOBS
ELSIE JANIS
JOSEPH JEFFERSON
AL JOLSON
JAMES EARL JONES
ROBERT EDMOND JONES
RAUL JULIA
JOHN KANDER
GARSON KANIN
GEORGE S. KAUFMAN
DANNY KAYE
ELIA KAZAN
GENE KELLY
GEORGE KELLY
FANNY KEMBLE
JEROME KERN
WALTER KERR
MICHAEL KIDD
SIDNEY KINGLSEY
JOSEPH WOOD KRUTCH
BERT LAHR
BURTON LANE
LAWRENCE LANGNER
LILLIE LANGTRY
ANGELA LANSBURY
CHARLES LAUGHTON
ARTHUR LAURENTS
GERTRUDE LAWRENCE
JEROME LAWRENCE
EVA LE GALLIENNE
ROBERT E. LEE
LOTTE LENYA
ALAN JAY LERNER
SAM LEVENE
ROBERT LEWIS
BEATRICE LILLIE
HOWARD LINDSAY
FRANK LOESSER
FREDERICK LOEWE
JOSHUA LOGAN
PAULINE LORD
LUCILLE LORTEL
ALFRED LUNT
CHARLES MACARTHUR
STEELE MACKAYE
ROUBEN MAMOULIAN
RICHARD MANSFIELD
ROBERT B. MANTELL
FREDRIC MARCH
JULIA MARLOWE
ERNEST H. MARTIN
MARY MARTIN
RAYMOND MASSEY

SIOBHAN MCKENNA
TERRENCE MCNALLY
HELEN MENKEN
BURGESS MEREDITH
ETHEL MERMAN
DAVID MERRICK
JO MIELZINER
ARTHUR MILLER
MARILYN MILLER
HELENA MODJESKA
FERENC MOLNAR
LOLA MONTEZ
VICTOR MOORE
ZERO MOSTEL
ANNA CORA MOWATT
PAUL MUNI
THARON MUSSER
GEORGE JEAN NATHAN
MILDRED NATWICK
NAZIMOVA
JAMES M. NEDERLANDER
ELLIOT NORTON
CLIFFORD ODETS
DONALD OENSLAGER
LAURENCE OLIVIER
EUGENE O'NEILL
GERALDINE PAGE
JOSEPH PAPP
OSGOOD PERKINS
BERNADETTE PETERS
MOLLY PICON
CHRISTOPHER PLUMMER
COLE PORTER
ROBERT PRESTON
HAROLD PRINCE
JOSE QUINTERO
JOHN RAITT
MICHAEL REDGRAVE
ADA REHAN
ELMER RICE
LLOYD RICHARDS
RALPH RICHARDSON
CHITA RIVERA
JASON ROBARDS
JEROME ROBBINS
PAUL ROBESON
RICHARD RODGERS
WILL ROGERS
SIGMUND ROMBERG
HAROLD ROME
LILLIAN RUSSELL
GENE SAKS
WILLIAM SAROYAN

JOSEPH *SCHILDKRAUT*
ALAN SCHNEIDER
GERALD SCHOENFELD
ARTHUR SCHWARTZ
GEORGE C. SCOTT
MARIAN SELDES
SAM SHEPARD
ROBERT E. SHERWOOD
J.J. SHUBERT
LEE SHUBERT
HERMAN SHUMLIN
NEIL SIMON
LEE SIMONSON
EDMUND SIMPSON
OTIS SKINNER
MAGGIE SMITH
OLIVER SMITH
STEPHEN SONDHEIM
E.H. SOTHERN
KIM STANLEY

MAUREEN STAPLETON
ROGER L. STEVENS
ELLEN STEWART
DOROTHY STICKNEY
FRED STONE
LEE STRASBERG
ELAINE STRITCH
JULE STYNE
MARGARET SULLAVAN
JESSICA TANDY
LAURETTE TAYLOR
ELLEN TERRY
TOMMY TUNE
GWEN VERDON
ELI WALLACH
JAMES WALLACK
LESTER WALLACK
TONY WALTON
DOUGLAS TURNER WARD
DAVID WARFIELD

ETHEL WATERS
CLIFTON WEBB
JOSEPH WEBER
MARGARET WEBSTER
KURT WEILL
ORSON WELLES
MAE WEST
ROBERT WHITEHEAD
THORNTON WILDER
BERT WILLIAMS
TENNESSEE WILLIAMS
LANFORD WILSON
P.G. WODEHOUSE
PEGGY WOOD
IRENE WORTH
ED WYNN
VINCENT YOUMANS
STARK YOUNG
FLORENZ ZIEGFELD

MUSICAL THEATER HALL OF FAME

This organization was established at New York University on November 10, 1993. Names of those elected in 1995 appear in *bold face italics.*

HAROLD ARLEN
IRVING BERLIN
LEONARD BERNSTEIN
EUBIE BLAKE
GEORGE GERSHWIN
IRA GERSHWIN

OSCAR HAMMERSTEIN II
E.Y. HARBURG
LARRY HART
JEROME KERN
BURTON LANE
ALAN JAY LERNER

FREDERICK LOEWE
COLE PORTER
ETHEL MERMAN
JEROME ROBBINS
RICHARD RODGERS

MARGO JONES
CITIZEN OF THE THEATER
MEDAL

Presented annually to a citizen of the theater who has made a lifetime commitment to the encouragement of the living theater in the United States and has demonstrated an understanding and affirmation of the craft of playwriting.

1961 LUCILLE LORTEL
1962 MICHAEL ELLIS
1963 JUDITH RUTHERFORD
    MARECHAL
    GEORGE SAVAGE
    (University Award)
1964 RICHARD BARR,
    EDWARD ALBEE &
    CLINTON WILDER
    RICHARD A. DUPREY
    (University Award)
1965 WYNN HANDMAN
    MARSTON BALCH
    (University Award)
1966 JON JORY
    ARTHUR BALLET
    (University Award)
1967 PAUL BAKER
    GEORGE C. WHITE
    (Workshop Award)

1968 DAVEY MARLIN-JONES
    ELLEN STEWART
    (Workshop Award)
1969 ADRIAN HALL
    EDWARD PARONE &
    GORDON DAVIDSON
    (Workshop Award)
1970 JOSEPH PAPP
1971 ZELDA FICHANDLER
1972 JULES IRVING
1973 DOUGLAS TURNER
    WARD
1974 PAUL WEIDNER
1975 ROBERT KALFIN
1976 GORDON DAVIDSON
1977 MARSHALL W. MASON
1978 JON JORY

1979 ELLEN STEWART
1980 JOHN CLARK DONAHUE
1981 LYNNE MEADOW
1982 ANDRE BISHOP
1983 BILL BUSHNELL
1984 GREGORY MOSHER
1985 JOHN LION
1986 LLOYD RICHARDS
1987 GERALD CHAPMAN
1988 NO AWARD
1989 MARGARET GOHEEN
1990 RICHARD COE
1991 OTIS L. GUERNSEY JR.
1992 ABBOT VAN NOSTRAND
1993 HENRY HEWES
1994 JANE ALEXANDER
1995 ROBERT WHITEHEAD

1995–96 PUBLICATION OF
RECENTLY-PRODUCED NEW PLAYS
AND NEW TRANSLATIONS/ADAPTATIONS

Alice's Adventures Under Ground. Adapted by Christopher Hampton and Martha Clark. Faber & Faber.
Angels in America: One Volume Edition. Includes *Millennium Approaches* and *Perestroika.* Tony Kushner. TCG.
Arcadia. Tom Stoppard. Faber & Faber (acting edition).
Break of Day, The. Timberlake Wertenbaker. Faber & Faber (paperback).
Brutality of Fact. Keith Reddin. Dramatists (acting edition).
Camping with Henry & Tom. Mark St. Germain. Samuel French (acting edition).
Case of Kaspar Mayer, The. Jean-Yves Picq, translated by Michael Feingold. UBU Repertory (paperback).
Cell Mates. Simon Gray. Faber & Faber (paperback).
Changing Room, The. David Storey (revised version). Methuen USA (paperback). Random House. Penguin (paperback). Samuel French (acting edition).
Cheever Evening, A. A.R. Gurney. Dramatists (acting edition).
Cherry Orchard, The. Anton Chekhov, adapted by Robert Brustein. Ivan R. Dee (paperback).
Communicating Doors. Alan Ayckbourn. Faber & Faber (paperback).
Dancing on Moonlight. Keith Glover. Dramatists (acting edition).
Das Barbecu. Jim Luigs and Scott Warrender. Samuel French (acting edition).
Don Juan in Chicago. David Ives. Dramatists (acting edition).
Food Chain, The. Nicky Silver. Dramatists (acting edition).
Fragments: A Sit-Around. Edward Albee. Dramatists (acting edition).
Harry and Me. Nigel Williams. Faber & Faber (paperback).
Having Our Say. Emily Mann. Dramatists (acting edition).
Indian Ink. Tom Stoppard. Faber & Faber (paperback).
Inside Out. Libretto by Doug Haverty et al. Samuel French (acting edition).
J.P. Morgan Saves the Nation. Jeffrey M. Jones. Sun & Moon (paperback).
Kindertransport. Diane Samuels. Plume/N.A.L. (paperback).
Land Beyond the Forest: Dracula and Swoop. Mac Wellman. Sun and Moon (paperback).
Laura Dennis. Horton Foote. Dramatists (acting edition).
Life in the Trees. Catherine Butterfield. Samuel French (acting edition).
Love! Valour! Compassion! and *A Perfect Ganesh.* Terrence McNally. Penguin.
Master Class. Terrence McNally. New American Library (paperback).
Middle-Aged White Guys. Jane Martin. Samuel French (acting edition).
Molly Sweeney. Brian Friel. N.A.L. (paperback).
My Head Was a Sledgehammer. Richard Foreman. Overlook (also paperback).
Pentecost. David Edgar. Nick Hern (paperback).
Phaedra. Matthew Maguire. Sun & Moon (paperback).
Professional, The. Dusan Kovacevic. Samuel French (acting edition).
Raised in Captivity. David Silver. TCG (paperback).
Sanctuary. David Williamson. Currency Press (paperback).
Simpatico. Sam Shepard. Random House (paperback).
Skylight. David Hare. Faber & Faber (paperback).
Slice of Saturday Night, A: The 60's Musical. Heather Brothers (acting edition).
Someone Who'll Watch Over Me. Frank McGuiness. Faber & Faber (paperback, also acting edition).
Stanley. Pam Gems. Nick Hern (paperback).
Uncle Bob. Austin Pendleton. Dramatists (acting edition).
Unexpected Tenderness. Israel Horovitz. Samuel French (acting edition).
Watbanaland. Doug Wright. Dramatists (acting edition).
Whoop-Dee-Doo! Howard Crabtree. Samuel French (acting edition).
You Should Be So Lucky. Charles Busch. Samuel French (acting edition).

A SELECTED LIST OF OTHER PLAYS PUBLISHED IN 1995-96

Actor's Book of Gay and Lesbian Plays, The. Eric Lane and Nina Shengold, editors. Penguin (paperback).

Alan Ayckbourn: Plays 1. Faber & Faber (paperback).

Alan Bennett: Plays 1. Faber & Faber (paperback).

Classic Plays From the Negro Ensemble Company. Paul Carter Harrison and Gus Edwards, editors. University of Pittsburgh (paperback).

Collected Plays 1980-1995. Jane Martin. Smith & Kraus (also paperback).

Collected Plays: Volume I, The. Steven Berkoff. Faber & Faber (paperback).

Collected Plays: Volume II, The. Steven Berkoff. Faber & Faber (paperback).

Collected Works: Volume II. Israel Horovitz. Smith & Kraus (also paperback).

Contemporary Plays by Women of Color: An Anthology. Kathy A. Perkins and Roberta Uno, editors. Routledge (trade paperback).

Court Masques: Jacobean and Caroline Entertainments 1605-1640. David Lindley, editor. Oxford (paperback).

Decade of New Comedy: Plays From the Humana Festival, A. Volume I. Michael Bigelow Dixon and Michele Volansky, editors. Heinemann (paperback).

Decade of New Comedy: Plays From the Humana Festival, A. Volume II. Michael Bigelow Dixon and Michele Volansky, editors. Heinemann (paperback).

Doll Trilogy, The. Ray Lawler. Currency Press (paperback).

Eleutheria. Samuel Beckett, translated by Michael Brodsky. Foxrock.

Faust: Parts I and II. Johann Wolfgang Von Goethe, translated by Howard Brenton. Nick Hern (paperback).

Modern Arabic Drama: An Anthology. Salma Khadra Jayyusi and Roger Allen, editors. Indiana University Press (paperback).

National Black Drama Anthology, The. Woodie King Jr., editor. Applause (paperback).

Nine Early Plays 1961-1973. A.R. Gurney. Smith & Kraus (paperback).

Plautus: The Comedies–Volumes I,II,III,IV. David R. Slavitt and Palmer Bovie, editors. Johns Hopkins University Press (paperback).

Portable Arthur Miller: Revised Edition, The. Revised by Arthur Miller with Christopher Bigsby. Penguin (paperback).

Raisin in the Sun, A./Sign in Sidney Brustein's Window, The. Lorraine Hansberry. Random House (paperback).

Recruiting Officer and Other Plays, The. George Farquhar, newly edited by William Myers. Oxford (paperback).

Richard and Anne: A Play in Two Acts. Maxwell Anderson. McFarland.

Selected Plays of Jerome Lawrence and Robert E. Lee, The. Alan Woods, editor. Ohio State University Press.

Sidney Kingsley: Five Prizewinning Plays. Nena Couch, editor. Ohio State University Press.

Sight Unseen and Other Plays. Donald Margulies. TCG (paperback).

Something Cloudy, Something Clear. Tennessee Williams. New Directions.

Three Plays by Mart Crowley. Alyson (paperback).

Timberlake Wertenbaker: Plays 1. Faber & Faber (paperback).

Trevor Griffiths: Plays 1. Faber & Faber (paperback).

Tom Stoppard: Plays I. Faber & Faber (paperback).

Twelve Plays of the Noh and Kyogen Theaters. Karen Brazell, editor. Cornell University (paperback).

Unseen Hand & Other Plays, The. Sam Shepard. Random House (paperback).

Women of Troy/Hecuba/Helen. Euripides, translated by Kenneth McLeish. Absolute (paperback).

NECROLOGY

MAY 1995—MAY 1996

PERFORMERS

Abbott, John (90)—May 24, 1996
Anderson, Thomas Charles (90)—January 12, 1996
Andrews, Maxene (75)—October 21, 1995
Balsam, Martin (76)—February 13, 1996
Barwiolek, Alan (43)—April 17, 1996
Beltrán, Lola (mid-60s)—March 24, 1996
Beradina, John (79)—May 19, 1996
Bissell, Whitner (89)—March 5, 1996
Blackburn, Clarice (74)—August 5, 1995
Blackwell, Charles (65)—June 2, 1995
Blackwood, Caroline (64)—February 14, 1996
Blaine, Vivian (74)—December 13, 1995
Blanc, James Daniel (36)—May 11, 1996
Bremer, Lucille (79)—April 16, 1996
Brett, Jeremy (59)—September 12, 1995
Bronson, Lillian (92)—August 1, 1995
Brooks, Phyllis (80)—August 1, 1995
Burns, George (100)—March 9, 1996
Butler, Ethel (82)—April 9, 1996
Calkins, Michael (47)—October 16, 1995
Carew, Peter (73)—August 9, 1995
Cash, Rosalind (56)—October 31, 1995
Chaplin, Lita Grey (88)—December 30, 1995
Christopher, Dale (47)—September 27, 1995
Clair, Ethlyne (91)—February 27, 1996
Clark, Alexander (94)—September 30, 1995
Costello, Tom (58)—February 18, 1996
Craven, John (79)—November 24, 1995
Crosby, Gary (62)—August 24, 1995
Daniel, Pebble (48)—December 4, 1995
Daniels, Jerry Franklin (79)—November 7, 1995
Darden, Severn (65)—May 26, 1995
Deane, Edna (90)—November 22, 1995
Dickson, Dorothy (102)—September 25, 1995
Dilian, Irasema (71)—April 16, 1996
Doyle, Mary (63)—June 8, 1995
Edwards, Vince (67)—March 11, 1996
Farrar, David (87)—August 31, 1995
Forristal, John (37)—June 29, 1995
Foshko, Julia Adler (97)—June 3, 1995
Gabor, Eva (74)—July 4, 1995
Garson, Greer (92)—April 6, 1996
Gee, Kevin John (40)—August 3, 1995
Gordon, Gale (89)—June 30, 1995
Grayson, Arlene (45)—June 1, 1995
Grenier, Larry (46)—January 31, 1996
Groves, William (Harlow) (74)—January 21, 1996

Guardino, Harry (69)—July 17, 1995
Harris, Phil (89)—August 11, 1995
Healy, David (64)—October 25, 1995
Helmore, Tom (91)—September 12, 1995
Hemphill, Essex Charles (38)—November 4, 1995
Henry, Deborah (44)—February 6, 1996
Herbert, Ralph (86)—October 21, 1995
Heyman, Barton (59)—May 15, 1996
Hurd, Hugh (70)—July 15, 1995
Hyman, Phyllis (45)—June 30, 1995
Hyson, Dorothy (81)—May 21, 1996
Irving, Val (86)—May 19, 1995
Jenkins, Timothy (44)—September 21, 1995
Johnson, Ben (77)—April 8, 1996
Johnston, Johnny (81)—January 6, 1996
Kambert, Isabel (103)—January 31, 1996
Keane, George (78)—October 10, 1995
Keighley, Genevieve Tobin (93)—July 31, 1995
Kellin, Sally Moffet (63)—May 8, 1995
Kelly, Gene (83)—February 2, 1996
Kimbrough, Clinton (63)—April 9, 1996
Kindle, Tom (47)—February 12, 1996
Kirby, George (71)—September 30, 1995
Knowles, Patric (84)—December 23, 1995
Lahr, Mildred Schroeder (88)—December 6, 1995
Lamott, Nancy (43)—December 13, 1995
Landes, Gloria Wills (69)—August 4, 1995
Lane, Ziggy (75)—November 2, 1995
LaPrise, Larry (83)—April 4, 1996
Larsen, William (68)—January 21, 1996
LaRue, Lash (79)—May 29, 1996
Lawrence, Rodha (71)—July 30, 1995
Laye, Evelyn (95)—February 17, 1996
Leonard, William Patrick (38)—March 21, 1996
Lindfors, Viveca (74)—October 25, 1995
Lipson, Paul (82)—January 3, 1996
Lishner, Leon (82)—November 21, 1995
Locke, Katherine (85)—September 12, 1995
Lorimer, Louise (97)—August 12, 1995
Lupino, Ida (77)—August 3, 1995
Lynn, Jeffrey (89)—November 24, 1995
Lynn, Rita (74)—January 21, 1996
Madison, Guy (74)—February 6, 1996
Martin, Dean (78)—December 25, 1995
Mathews, Carmen (84)—August 31, 1995
Mathis, Lee (44)—May 1, 1996
Maxwell, Larry (43)—December 7, 1995
Maya, Frank (45)—August 7, 1995
Maynor, Dorothy (85)—February 19, 1996
McDaniel, Floyd (80)—July 22, 1995

McDermott, Tom (83)—March 6, 1996
McKinley, Andrew (92)—January 11, 1996
McLean, David (73)—October 12, 1995
McQueen, Butterfly (84)—December 22, 1995
Meadows, Audrey (71)—February 3, 1996
Megna, John (42)—September 4, 1995
Meredith-Jones, Betty (87)—May 12, 1996
Michaels, Raf (66)—July 27, 1995
Miller, Patsy Ruth (91)—July 16, 1995
Morin, Jean-Louis (42)—May 24, 1995
Muir, Esther (92?)—August 1, 1995
Myers, William (74)—November 22, 1995
Nevarez, Aramando (44)—July 21, 1995
Norris, Donald L. (60)—March 23, 1996
Ober, Ann Cooper (83)—May 2, 1996
Okada, Eiji (75)—September 14, 1995
Oliver, George (76)—January 14, 1996
Olle, Andrew (47)—December 12, 1995
Opatoshu, David (78)—April 30, 1996
Patten, Luana (57)—May 1, 1996
Patterson, Robert (70)—October 31, 1995
Payan, Ilka (53)—April 6, 1996
Pearl, Minnie (63)—March 5, 1996
Pendleton, Wyman (79)—June 1, 1995
Regan, Phil (89)—February 11, 1996
Rettig, Tommy (54)—February 15, 1996
Revueltas, Rosaura (80s)—April 30, 1996
Rich, Charlie (62)—July 25, 1995
Roarke, Adam (58)—April 27, 1996
Roberson, Lar (48)—June 21, 1995
Roerick, William (82)—November 30, 1995
Roker, Roxie (66)—December 2, 1995
Ross, Gordon (65)—August 19, 1995
Sartorio, Angiola (91)—May 26, 1995
Schneider, Jürgen (59)—August 15, 1995
Sinclair, Madge (57)—December 20, 1995
Sinden, Jeremy (45)—May 29, 1996
Smith, David Rae (65)—January 31, 1996
Smith, Doris Sharp (86)—July 27, 1995
Soler, Antonio Ruiz (74)—February 6, 1996
Stephens, Robert (64)—September 10, 1995
Stevenson, McLean (66)—February 15, 1996
Stoneburner, Sam (66)—November 29, 1995
Strozzi, Kay (96)—January 18, 1996
Sutton, Grady Harwell (89)—September 17, 1995
Talbot, Lyle (94)—March 3, 1996
Teitel, Martin (40)—October 15, 1995
Tobin, Genevieve (93)—July 31, 1995
Toumanova, Tamara (77)—May 29, 1996
Truitte, James (72)—August 21, 1995
Turner, Lana (75)—June 29, 1995
Varno, Roland (88)—May 24, 1996
Venuta, Benay (84)—September 1, 1995
Verchinina, Nina (85)—December 14, 1995
Versalle, Richard (63)—January 5, 1996
Vinay, Ramon (83)—January 4, 1996
Vogeler, Dallas Mossman (64)—February 28, 1996

Wallenda, Angel (28)—May 3, 1996
Wallenda, Helen (85)—May 9, 1996
Ward, Janet (70)—August 2, 1995
Warrilow, David (60)—August 17, 1995
Westez, Carlos (76)—January 8, 1996
Weston, Jack (71)—May 3, 1996
White, Slappy (74)—November 8, 1995
Wickes, Mary (85)—October 22, 1995
Wilder, Honeychile (76)—August 11, 1995
Williams, Brent (85)—April 18, 1996

PLAYWRIGHTS

Beich, Albert (77)—March 30, 1996
Campbell, Blaine (43)—September 21, 1995
Gehrecke, Frank (74)—February 11, 1996
Gordone, Charles (70)—November 17, 1995
Harris, Aurand (80)—May 6, 1996
Hlibok, Bruce (34)—June 23, 1995
Ingrassia, Anthony (51)—December 16, 1995
Koch, Howard (93)—August 17, 1995
Matthews, Michael (37)—January 17, 1996
Morris, Richard (72)—April 27, 1996
Mueller, Heiner (66)—December 30, 1995
Osterman, George (42)—October 10, 1995
Patrick, John (90)—November 7, 1995
Rapp, Philip (88)—January 23, 1996
Richards, E. Claude (72)—February 4, 1996
Silliphant, Stirling (78)—April 26, 1996
Southern, Terry (71)—October 29, 1995
Wallach, Ira (83)—December 2, 1995

COMPOSERS, LYRICISTS, SONGWRITERS

Baxter, Les (73)—January 15, 1996
Bazelon, Irwin (73)—August 2, 1995
Berk, Lawrence (87)—December 22, 1995
Blane, Ralph (81)—November 12, 1995
Bush, Alan (94)—October 31, 1995
Clingan, Alton (27)—May 28, 1996
de Leon, Camilla (80)—April 3, 1996
Druckman, Jacob (67)—May 25, 1996
Eisenstein, Judith (86)—February 14, 1996
Elton, John M. (73)—May 19, 1995
Farrell, Wes (56)—February 29, 1996
Fetter, Theodore (89)—March 13, 1996
Fuchs, Lillian (91)—October 6, 1995
Gilbert, Kevin (29)—May 18, 1996
Gould, Morton (82)—February 21, 1996
Larson, Jonathan (35)—January 25, 1996
Miller, J.D. (73)—March 23, 1996
Pugliese, Osvaldo (89)—July 25, 1995
Romeo, Tony (56)—June 23, 1995

Rozsa, Miklos (86)—July 27, 1995
Sosnik, Harry (89)—March 22, 1996
White, Ronnie (57)—August 26, 1995
Wise, Chubby (80)—January 7, 1996
Yun, Isang (78)—November 3, 1995

CONDUCTORS

Argiris, Spiros (47)—May 19, 1996
Corradetti, Golfredo (74)—October 13, 1995
De Rugeriis, Joseph (48)—January 23, 1996
Elgart, Les (77)—July 29, 1995
Fistoulari, Anatole (88)—August 21, 1995
Garcia, Francisco M. (49)—January 21, 1996
Greenberg, Chuck (45)—September 4, 1995
Jorda, Enrique (84)—March 22, 1996
Keene, Christopher (48)—October 8, 1995
Kurtz, Efrem (94)—June 27, 1995
Lewis, Henry (63)—January 26, 1996
Neumann, Vaclav (74)—September 2, 1995
Paich, Martin Louis (70)—August 12, 1995
Rossy, Mercedes (34)—November 23, 1995
Slonimsky, Nicolas (101)—December 25, 1995
Vogt, Richard (65)—June 2, 1995
Waldman, Frederic (92)—December 1, 1995
Wyeth, Howard Pyle (51)—March 20, 1996

MUSICIANS

Aller, Eleanor (78)—October 12, 1995
Almeida, Laurindo (77)—July 26, 1995
Braggiotti, Mario (90)—May 18, 1996
Braunstein, Joseph (104)—July 9, 1995
Brown, Albert (79)—May 27, 1996
Cherkassky, Shura (84)—December 27, 1995
Cherry, Don (58)—October 19, 1995
Corb, Morty (78)—January 14, 1996
Davis, William Stratton (77)—August 17, 1995
Ellington, Mercer (76)—February 8, 1996
Fizdale, Robert (75)—December 6, 1995
Garcia, Jerry (53)—August 9, 1995
Geber, Gretchen (81)—December 16, 1995
Gilmore, John (63)—August 20, 1995
Goettel, Dwayne (31)—August 23, 1995
Goodman, Saul (89)—January 26, 1996
Gordon, Edward (65)—April 19, 1996
Hermanns, Heida (89)—December 27, 1995
Humphrey, Percy (90)—July 22, 1995
Johnson, Thruston (81)—January 25, 1996
LaBrecque, Rebecca (45)—January 28, 1996
Marks, Alan D. (46)—July 12, 1995
Michelangeli, Arturo Benedetti (75)—June 12, 1995
Morini, Erica (91)—November 1, 1995

Morrison, Sterling (53)—August 30, 1995
Mulligan, Gerry (68)—January 20, 1996
Ortenberg, Edgar (96)—May 9, 1996
Parker, Glenn (40)—February 15, 1995
Romero, Caledonio (83)—May 9, 1996
Rowles, Jimmy (77)—May 28, 1996
Rudge, Olga (101)—March 15, 1996
Stevens, Chuck (64)—March 2, 1996
Stroman, C. Scoby (64)—March 28, 1996
Walker, Junior (64)—November 23, 1995
Watson, Johnny (61)—May 17, 1996
Wilen, Barney (59)—May 25, 1996

PRODUCERS, DIRECTORS, CHOREOGRAPHERS

Aiello, Salvatore (51)—October 14, 1995
Allentuck, Max (84)—October 22, 1995
Barker, Word (72)—October 31, 1995
Berghaus, Ruth (68)—January 25, 1996
Cammell, Donald (62)—April 24, 1996
Douglas, Scott (70)—March 26, 1996
Douglas, William (42)—March 10, 1996
Platt, Ernest O. (76)—June 10, 1995
Gladke, Peter (74)—May 5, 1996
Greenberg, Edward M.—November 21, 1995
Harris, Albert (51)—March 1, 1996
Horak, Elaine Limpert (68)—December 20, 1995
Hover, Herman (88)—April 24, 1996
Hunter, Ross (75)—March 10, 1996
Kaufman, Martin R. (35)—April 11, 1996
Kaye, Toni (49)—December 29, 1995
Lentsch, William J. (53)—September 9, 1995
Lyon, Milton (72)—December 2, 1995
Malle, Louis (63)—November 23, 1995
Parrish, Robert (79)—December 4, 1995
Perry, Frank (65)—August 29, 1995
Rene, Norman (45)—May 25, 1996
Richardson, Don (77)—January 10, 1996
Rosati, Gregory Joseph (43)—March 31, 1996
Schulman, Edward L. (79)—December 16, 1995
Wisher, Peter (84)—October 8, 1995
Woodman, William (63)—December 19, 1995

CRITICS

Coe, Richard Livingston (81)—November 12, 1995
Harris, Dale (67)—March 14, 1996
Hemming, Roy (70)—September 11, 1995
Hirsch, Samuel (79)—February 15, 1996
Loew, Arthur Jr. (69)—November 10, 1995
Loynd, Ray (64)—October 9, 1995
Mazo, Joseph (56)—July 28, 1995

Powell, Dilys (93)—June 3, 1995
Saal, Hubert (72)—May 3, 1996
Shelton, Robert (69)—December 11, 1995
Sonbert, Warren (46)—May 31, 1995
Taubman, Howard (88)—January 8, 1996
Toeplitz, Jerzy (85)—July 24, 1995

OTHERS

Abreu, Danny William (39)—December 5, 1995
  NYC Opera
Allen, Jay (79)—May 22, 1996
  Publicist
Amis, Kingsley (73)—October 22, 1995
  Novelist
Bombeck, Erma (69)—April 22, 1996
  Columnist
Bowen, Roger (63)—February 16, 1996
  Second City
Braun, Susan (79)—October 3, 1995
  Dance archivist
Bruce, Mary (95)—December 12, 1995
  Dance instructor
Buchman, Herman (75)—January 27, 1996
  NYC Opera
Clurman, Richard M. (72)—May 15, 1996
  Editor
Cohn, Joseph Judson (100)—January 12, 1996
  Motion Picture Academy
Cole, Frances (94)—October 10, 1995
  Dance instructor
Crowley, Joan Howard (68)—July 6, 1995
  Variety
Daniel, Minna Lederman (99)—November 1, 1995
  Modern Music
Davis, Sheldon (68)—June 17, 1995
  Publicist
Day, Katharine (94)—August 25, 1995
  Clarence Day's widow
Dearing, Judy (55)—September 30, 1995
  Costume designer
Delany, Bessie (104)—September 25, 1995
  Subject of Broadway play
Egan, Eddie (65)—November 5, 1995
  NYC police officer
Everson, William K. (67)—April 14, 1996
  Publicist
Fehl, Fred (89)—October 4, 1995
  Photographer
Fini, Leonor (87)—January 18, 1996
  Set designer
Flint, Peter B. (67)—November 9, 1995
  Reporter
Foreman, Jack P. (71)—January 13, 1996
  Samuel Goldwyn Studios
Grimsby, Roger (66)—June 23, 1995
  Newscaster

Hill, Martha (94)—November 19, 1995
  Dance educator
Hodges, Gil (80)—December 29, 1995
  TV Guide
Kahn, Louise Wolff (85)—November 27, 1995
  Dallas Symphony
Kirstein, Lincoln (88)—January 5, 1996
  NYC Ballet
Leen, Dexter (85)—January 6, 1996
  Broadway show backer
Levy, Lou (84)—October 31, 1995
  Music publisher
Livingston, Bernice (79)—September 10, 1995
  Publicist
Mayer, Seymour R. (86)—June 27, 1995
  MGM International
Miceli, Grace (81)—November 14, 1995
  Costumer
Miller, Terry (47)—August 15, 1995
  Photographer
Moody, Richard A. (84)—March 29, 1996
  Theater historian
Morgan, Thomas Newbold (67)—October 20, 1995
  Clarion Music Society
Morris, Edwin H. (89)—April 1, 1996
  Music publisher
Naumberg, Edward S. (92)—June 28, 1995
  Music patron
Pettit, Tom—December 22, 1995
  Newscaster
Pfeiffer, Jack (75)—February 8, 1996
  RCA Records
Pollen, Michael (82)—January 9, 1996
  Westchester Conservatory
Polley, Victor (79)—July 12, 1995
  Stratford, Ont. Shakespeare
Powers, Dennis (59)—December 13, 1995
  American Conservatory Theater
Ratner, Anne (90)—June 10, 1995
  Music patron
Samrock, Victor (88)—September 30, 1995
  Theatrical manager
Schiff, Harold L. (76)—December 9, 1995
  Attorney
Semark, Philip (49)—August 17, 1995
  Joffrey Ballet
Semon, Florence (70)—January 7, 1996
  Publicist
Shull, Leo (90)—March 30, 1996
  Show Business
Siegal, Jerry (81)—January 28, 1996
  Superman
Smith, Albert F. Jr. (67)—August 3, 1995
  Attorney
Steinfeld, Larry (56)—August 27, 1995
  Publicist
Stokes, Geoffrey (55)—September 12, 1995
  Journalist

Swayze, John Cameron (89)—August 22, 1995
  Newscaster
Van Nostrand, M. Abbott (83)—September 27, 1995
  Samuel French Inc.
Welding, Pete (60)—November 17, 1995
  Downbeat
Wilson, Carl (48)—December 12, 1995
  Costume designer

Wolff, Payson (74)—September 14, 1995
  Attorney
Wolfman Jack (57)—July 1, 1995
  Radio show host
Yount, Kenneth M. (46)—February 24, 1996
  Costume designer
Zachary, George (63)—July 13, 1995
  Attorney
Zhito, Lee (77)—December 8, 1995
  Billboard

THE BEST PLAYS, 1894–1995

Listed in alphabetical order below are all those works selected as Best Plays in previous volumes of the *Best Plays* series. Opposite each title is given the volume in which the play appears, its opening date and its total number of performances. Two separate opening-date and performance-number entries signify two separate engagements off Broadway and on Broadway when the original production was transferred from one area to the other, usually in an off-to-on direction. Those plays marked with an asterisk (*) were still playing on June 1, 1996 and their number of performances was figured through May 31, 1996. Adaptors and translators are indicated by (ad) and (tr), the symbols (b), (m) and (l) stand for the author of the book, music and lyrics in the case of musicals and (c) signifies the credit for the show's conception, (i) for its inspiration.

PLAY	VOLUME	OPENED	PERFS
ABE LINCOLN IN ILLINOIS—Robert E. Sherwood	38–39	Oct. 15, 1938	472
ABRAHAM LINCOLN—John Drinkwater	19–20	Dec. 15, 1919	193
ACCENT ON YOUTH—Samson Raphaelson	34–35	Dec. 25, 1934	229
ADAM AND EVA—Guy Bolton, George Middleton	19–20	Sept. 13, 1919	312
ADAPTATION—Elaine May; and NEXT—Terrence McNally	68–69	Feb. 10, 1969	707
AFFAIRS OF STATE—Louis Verneuil	50–51	Sept. 25, 1950	610
AFTER THE FALL—Arthur Miller	63–64	Jan. 23, 1964	208
AFTER THE RAIN—John Bowen	67–68	Oct. 9, 1967	64
AFTER-PLAY—Anne Meara	94–95	Jan. 31, 1995	400
AGNES OF GOD—John Pielmeier	81–82	Mar. 30, 1982	599
AH, WILDERNESS!—Eugene O'Neill	33–34	Oct. 2, 1933	289
AIN'T SUPPOSED TO DIE A NATURAL DEATH—(b, m, l) Melvin Van Peebles	71–72	Oct. 20, 1971	325
ALIEN CORN—Sidney Howard	32–33	Feb. 20, 1933	98
ALISON'S HOUSE—Susan Glaspell	30–31	Dec. 1, 1930	41
ALL MY SONS—Arthur Miller	46–47	Jan. 29, 1947	328
ALL IN THE TIMING—David Ives	93–94	Feb. 17, 1994	526
ALL OVER TOWN—Murray Schisgal	74–75	Dec. 29, 1974	233
ALL THE WAY HOME—Tad Mosel, based on James Agee's novel *A Death in the Family*	60–61	Nov. 30, 1960	333
ALLEGRO—(b, l) Oscar Hammerstein II, (m) Richard Rodgers	47–48	Oct. 10, 1947	315
AMADEUS—Peter Shaffer	80–81	Dec. 17, 1980	1,181
AMBUSH—Arthur Richman	21–22	Oct. 10, 1921	98
AMERICA HURRAH—Jean-Claude van Itallie	66–67	Nov. 6, 1966	634
AMERICAN BUFFALO—David Mamet	76–77	Feb. 16, 1977	135
AMERICAN ENTERPRISE—Jeffrey Sweet (special citation)	93–94	Apr. 13, 1994	15
AMERICAN PLAN, THE—Richard Greenberg	90–91	Dec. 16, 1990	37
AMERICAN WAY, THE—George S. Kaufman, Moss Hart	38–39	Jan. 21, 1939	164
AMPHITRYON 38—Jean Giraudoux, (ad) S.N. Behrman	37–38	Nov. 1, 1937	153
AND A NIGHTINGALE SANG—C.P. Taylor	83–84	Nov. 27, 1983	177
ANDERSONVILLE TRIAL, THE—Saul Levitt	59–60	Dec. 29, 1959	179
ANDORRA—Max Frisch, (ad) George Tabori	62–63	Feb. 9, 1963	9

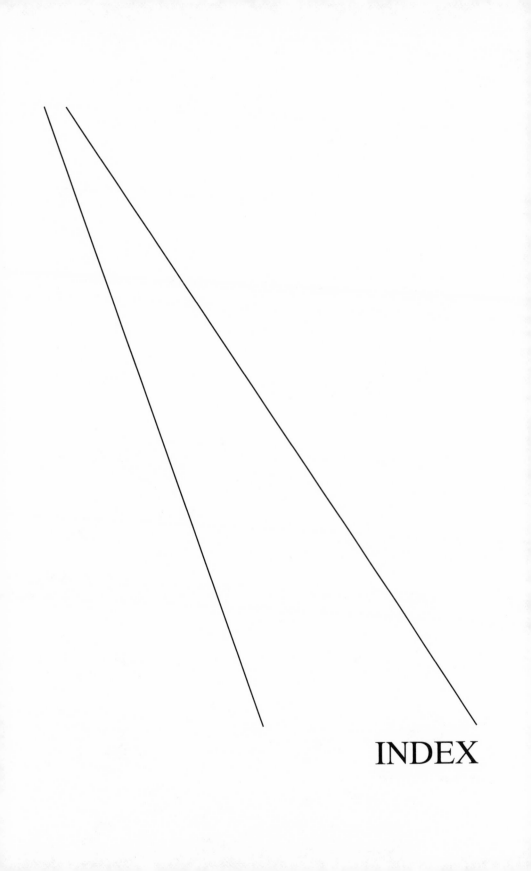

INDEX

INDEX

Play titles appear in **bold face.** *Bold face italic* page numbers refer to those pages where cast and credit listings may be found.

517